A Garland Series

The Modern Chinese Economy

Edited by
Ramon H. Myers
HOOVER INSTITUTION

Economic Facts
September 1936– April 1946

in four volumes

Vol. I
Nos. 1– 9
September 1936–April 1938

Department of Agricultural Economics
University of Nanking

Garland Publishing, Inc., New York & London
1980

Bibliographical note:
these facsimiles have been made from copies in
the Library of Congress and
the National Agricultural Library.

Library of Congress Cataloging in Publication Data

Chin-ling ta hsüeh, Nanking. Nung hsüeh yüan.
Nung yeh ching chi hsi.
Economic facts, September 1936–April 1946.

(The Modern Chinese economy)
English or Chinese.
CONTENTS: v. 1. Nos. 1–9, September 1936–April 1938.
v. 2. Nos. 10–17, June 1938–February 1943.
v. 3. Nos. 18–33, March 1943–June 1944.
v. 4. Nos. 34–55, July 1944–April 1946.
1. Agriculture—Economic aspects—China—History.
2. China—Economic conditions—1912–1949.
I. Title.   II. Series: Modern Chinese economy.
HD2097.C455   1980   338.1'0951   78-74325
ISBN 0-8240-4260-3

For a complete list of the titles in this series,
see the final pages of Volume IV.

250-year-life paper.

Printed in the United States of America

經 濟 統 計
ECONOMIC FACTS
南京金陵大學農學院農業經濟系出版
Department of Agricultural Economics
COLLEGE OF AGRICULTURE AND FORESTRY
UNIVERSITY OF NANKING
NANKING, CHINA

第一期 No. 1 　　　　　一九三六年九月 September 1936

中國貨幣及物價之變遷

研究之目的

根據本系從前之研究[1]，一九三一年前，中國物價之上漲，由於世界白銀價值之跌落，而一九三一年後中國物價之跌落，則由於世界白銀價值之上漲。一九三一年後物價之跌落，顯爲中國經濟大恐慌之主要原因。

(1)路易士與張履鸞合著之〔白銀與中國物價水準〕金陵大學叢刊十一號(新號)一九三三年十二月出版；路易士〔中國經濟恐慌〕刊登於上海銀行週報第三十七期，三十九期，四十期，四十一期，四十二期，四十三期，四十四期，四十五期及四十七期，一九三五年九月至十二月出版；兼參閱實業部白銀價物價討論委員會報告〔中國銀價物價問題〕

CHANGES IN CURRENCY AND PRICES IN CHINA

PURPOSE OF THESE STUDIES

Previous studies[1] made by this Department have shown that the rising trend in Chinese commodity prices before 1931 was due to a world-wide fall in the value of silver, and that the fall in commodity prices after 1931 was due to a world-wide rise in the value of silver. The fall in commodity prices after 1931 was apparently the chief cause of the severe economic depression in China.

(1) Lewis, A. B. and Chang, L. L., Silver and the Chinese Price Level, University of Nanking. Bul. No. 11 (New Series) Dec. 1933.
Lewis, A.B., Economic Depression in China, Shanghai Bankers' Weekly, Nos. 37,39,40,41,42,43,44,45, and 47. Sept. to Dec. 1935.
See also, Silver and Prices in China. Report of the Committee for the Study of Silver Values and Commodity Prices, Ministry of Industries, Nanking, China.

本研究係繼續本系從前之工作，其目的為探求各種與物價有關之原素，及物價動向與其他經濟情況變遷之關係，尤以農業為最所注意。

研究之一部份結果，將在本刊發表，藉以明變遷之經過。

一· 世界白銀價格與中國貨幣價格

在一九三四年十月十五日以前，中國係銀本位國家。其主要貨幣為白銀及照票面價值兌換白銀之紙幣，故中國貨幣之外匯價格，係按照銀價而定。

自一九三一年起，以物品計算之白銀價值上漲，遂使中國以白銀計算之物價下跌，而造成中國之經濟大恐慌。至一九三四年春已極尖銳化，其時美

The present studies are a continuation of previous research work of this Department and are undertaken in order to follow the relation of various factors to commodity prices in China and the relation between price movements and other economic changes, especially in agriculture.

Some of the results of these studies will be published in this bulletin, in order to show the changes that have taken place.

1. THE WORLD PRICE OF SILVER AND THE PRICE OF CHINESE CURRENCY.

For many years prior to October 15, 1934, the Chinese currency was on the silver standard. The principal currency was silver, and paper notes were redeemable in silver according to their face value. The foreign exchange price of the Chinese currency therefore depended upon the price of silver.

Beginning in 1931 the value of silver in terms of commodities rose, causing Chinese commodity prices, which were expressed in silver to decline. This decline in Chinese commodity prices brought about a severe economic depression, which had become well-deve-

國購銀條例尚未實行也。

一九三四年六月，美國實行購銀條例。此後各月，以物品計算之白銀價值上漲極烈。中國物價重復下跌，商業情形益趨惡化。中國貨幣之外匯價格上漲，但上漲之速率不足以遏止大量白銀之外流。為補救中國物價水準及貨幣制度感受白銀購買力及價格上漲之惡劣影響起見，中國政府遂漸使其貨幣脫離銀本位，至一九三五年十一月三日始實行最後之步驟。在一九三四年八月一日至一九三六年五月三十一日之間，中國貨幣之管理，可分為五個重要時期。茲附以第一圖及第一表說明之。

第一期，自一九三四年八月一日至十月十四日：在此時期，中國貨幣在外匯市場，仍為銀本位。

loped in the spring of 1934, before the United States Silver Purchase Act was made effective.

The American Silver Purchase Act became effective in June, 1934. During the following months, the value of silver, as measured in terms of goods, rose considerably. Commodity prices in China resumed falling, making business conditions worse. The foreign exchange price of the Yuan rose, but not fast enough to prevent the shipment of large amounts of silver out of China. In order to free the Chinese commodity price level and monetary system from the bad effects of the rising purchasing power and price of silver, the Chinese government gradually removed the currency from the silver standard. The final steps in this direction were taken on November 3, 1935. Between August 1, 1934, and May 31, 1936, there were five principal phases in the management of Chinese currency. These phases will be explained with the aid of Figure 1 and Table 1.

PHASE, 1, AUGUST 1-OCTOBER 14, 1934: During this period, the Chinese currency was still on the silver standard in foreign exchange. Since there are

— 3 —

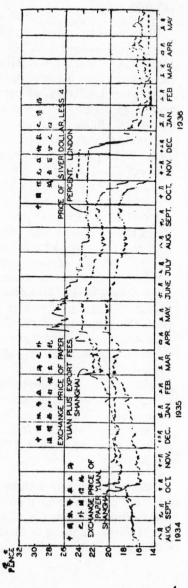

FIGURE 1. PRICE OF SILVER YUAN IN LONDON, LESS 4 PERCENT COST OF TRANSPORTATION FROM SHANGHAI, EXCHANGE MARKET PRICE OF THE PAPER YUAN IN SHANGHAI (T. T. ON LONDON), AND EXCHANGE MARKET PRICE OF THE YUAN IN SHANGHAI PLUS SILVER EXPORT FEES (Based on Table 1, Columns A, B and C).

第一圖。　中國銀元在倫敦之價格，減去百分之四之運費；中國紙幣在上海之外匯市價（倫敦電匯）反中國紙幣在上海之外匯市價，加白銀出口稅。（根據第一表A．B．C．三欄）

— 4 —

From August 1, 1934 to May 31, 1936, Chinese currency passed through five phases. Until October 14, 1934, it was on the silver standard. From October 15, 1934, to about March 31, 1935, the silver export duties were enforced, reducing the silver value of the Chinese paper Yuan in London. From about April 1, 1935 to about October 14, 1935, this discrepancy was maintained by a gentlemen's agreement against the exportation of silver and the silver export fees were only nominally in force. During this period, there was some effort to prevent the foreign exchange price of the Yuan from falling. From about October 14 to November 2, 1935, the foreign exchange price of the Yuan was allowed to fall. Beginning on November 3, 1935, the foreign exchange value of the Yuan was stabilized regardless of fluctuations in the price of silver.

自一九三四年八月一日至一九三六年五月三十一日，中國貨幣經過五個時期。在一九三四年十月十五日前，中國為銀本位國家。自一九三四年十月十五日，約至一九三五年三月三十一日　中國實行白銀出口徵稅,減低中國紙幣所含白銀在倫敦之價值。約自一九三五年四月一日至一九三五年十月十四日，此項差數以禁銀出口之紳士協定維持之。而白銀出口稅僅僅表面實行。在此時期有阻止中國貨幣外匯價格下墜之實施。但自一九三五年十月十四日至十一月二日,中國貨幣外匯價格則任其下跌。自一九三五年十一月三日起，中國貨幣之外匯價格安定，再不受銀價上漲之影響。

— 5 —

第一表: 白銀及中國紙幣之世界市價
TABLE 1. WORLD MARKET PRICE OF SILVER AND OF THE CHINESE PAPER YUAN

日期 Date	A 中國銀元一元在白銀市場之價格減去百分之四 Price of one silver Yuan in the silver market, less 4 per cent transport charges		B 上海白銀出口稅及平衡稅之總百分數 Total per cent tax and equalization fee on silver exports, Shanghai	C 中國紙幣在上海之外匯價格(3) Foreign exchange market price of the paper Yuan in Shanghai (5)		D 中國紙幣在上海之外匯價格加白銀出口稅(4) Foreign exchange market price of the paper Yuan in Shanghai plus silver export fees (4)		E 中國紙幣含銀價值之虛價與實價相差之百分數(5) Percent difference between nominal and actual market silver value of the paper Yuan (5)	
	在倫敦(1) in London (1)	在紐約(2) in New York (2)		倫敦電匯 T.T. on London	紐約電匯 T.T. on New York	倫敦 London	紐約 New York	在倫敦 in London	在紐約 in New York
一九三四1934	便士 Pence	分 Cents		便士 Pence	分 Cents	便士 Pence	分 Cents		
八月 August									
1	15.7760	55.1755	—	16.2500	54.1250	—	—	1	1
2	16.0209	55.6265	—	16.5125	54.2500	—	—	2	2
3	16.0209	55.6265	—	16.5750	54.5000	—	—	2	2
4	16.0209	55.6265	—	16.4575	54.5000	—	—	2	2
5	—	—	—	—	—	—	—	—	—
6	—	—	—	—	—	—	—	—	—
7	16.2169	54.0794	—	16.5750	54.4575	—	—	5	5
8	—	—	—	—	—	—	—	—	—
9	16.4129	54.8048	—	16.6875	55.1875	—	—	2	5
10	16.4129	54.8048	—	16.8125	55.1875	—	—	2	5
11	16.8048	56.0757	—	16.7500	55.1875	—	—	4	6
12	—	—	—	—	—	—	—	—	—
13	16.9028	56.0757	—	16.7500	55.6250	—	—	5	5
14	16.9028	56.0757	—	16.7500	55.6250	—	—	5	5
15	16.9028	56.0757	—	16.7500	55.6250	—	—	5	5
16	—	—	—	—	—	—	—	—	—
17	16.9028	56.0757	—	16.7500	55.5000	—	—	5	6
18	16.9028	56.0757	—	16.6250	55.5125	—	—	6	6
19	—	—	—	—	—	—	—	—	—
20	16.9518	56.0757	—	16.6250	55.1875	—	—	6	6
21	16.9518	56.0757	—	16.6250	55.5750	—	—	6	6
22	16.9518	56.0757	—	16.8125	55.0625	—	—	5	7
23	16.9028	56.0757	—	16.8125	55.6250	—	—	5	5
24	16.9028	56.0757	—	16.8125	55.6250	—	—	5	5
25	16.9028	55.9850	—	16.7500	55.5125	—	—	5	6
26	—	—	—	—	—	—	—	—	—
27	16.9028	55.9850	—	16.8125	55.5000	—	—	5	5
28	16.9028	55.9850	—	16.8125	55.5000	—	—	5	5
29	16.9028	55.9850	—	16.6875	55.5125	—	—	5	6
30	16.9028	55.9850	—	16.7500	55.2500	—	—	5	6
31	17.0008	55.9850	—	16.8750	55.5125	—	—	5	6
九月 September									
1	17.1478	55.9850	—	17.1875	55.7500	—	—	4	5
2	—	—	—	—	—	—	—	—	—
3	17.1478	55.9850	—	17.0625	55.5000	—	—	4	5
4	17.0988		—	17.0625	-	—	—	4	
5	17.0988	55.9850	—	17.0000	55.5625	—	—	5	5
6	16.5918	55.8960	—	17.0000	55.5000	—	—	4	5
7	17.0988	55.8960	—	17.1250	55.6875	—	—	4	5
8	17.0988	55.8960	—	17.1250	55.7500	—	—	4	4
9	—	—	—	—	—	—	—	—	—
10	17.1478	55.8960	—	16.8750	55.0000	—	—	6	6
11	17.0988	55.8960	—	16.9575	55.5125	—	—	5	6

(1)(2)(3)(4)及(5)見十六頁　　　　(1)(2)(3)(4) and (5) see page 16

日期 Date	A 倫敦 London	A 紐約 New York	B	C 倫敦 London	C 紐約 New York	D 倫敦 London	D 紐約 New York	E 倫敦 London	E 紐約 New York
一九三四 1934									
九月 September									
12	17.0498	55.7112	—	16.9575	55.4375	—	—	5	5
15	17.0008	55.7112	—	16.9575	55.5750	—	—	4	5
14	17.0008	55.7112	—	16.9575	55.5125	—	—	4	5
15	17.0008	55.7112	—	16.9575	55.4575	...	—	4	5
16	—	—	—	—	—	—	—	—	—
17	17.0988	55.8018	—	16.9375	55.4575	—	—	5	5
18	17.0498	55.8018	—	17.0000	55.5000	—	—	4	5
19	17.0498	55.8018	—	17.0625	55.6250	—	—	4	4
20	17.0498	55.8018	—	17.1250	55.7500	...	—	4	4
21	17.0498	55.8018	—	17.1875	55.8125	—	—	5	4
22	16.4619	55.8018	—	17.1875	55.7500	—	—	0	4
25	—	—	—	—	—	—	—	—	—
24	17.1967	55.8018	—	17.2500	55.8750	—	—	4	4
25	17.1967	55.8018	—	17.5750	56.0625	—	—	5	5
26	17.1967	25.8018	—	17.4575	56.1875	—	—	5	5
27	17.5598	55.9850	—	17.5625	56.5750	—	—	4	5
28	17.5598	55.9850	—	17.6875	56.6250	—	—	5	2
29									
十月 October									
1	17.4908	56.1644	—	17.5000	56.1875	—	—	4	4
2	17.5888	56.2550	—	17.6875	56.2500	—	—	4	4
5	17.7557	56.5456	—	17.6250	56.2500	...	—	5	2
4	17.7557	56.5456	—	17.5750	55.7500	—	—	6	6
5	17.6578	56.2550	—	17.5000	55.9575	—	—	5	5
6	17.7557	56.5456	—	17.5000	55.8750	—	—	5	5
7	—	—	—	—	—	—	—	—	—
8	17.7557	56.2550	—	17.5000	55.9575	—	—	5	5
9	17.9517	56.5269	—	17.7500	56.5125	—	—	5	5
10	—	—	—	—	—	—	—	—	—
11	18.5257	57.0707	—	18.1250	57.0000	—	—	5	4
12	19.2056	58.8855	—	18.4575	57.8125	—	—	8	7
15	19.1566	—	—	18.1875	57.5125	—	—	9	—
14	—	—	—	—	—	—	—	—	—
15	19.1076	58.8855	12.50	17.7500	56.5750	19.9688	40.9219	11	10
16	19.4995	40.0618	15.75	17.8750	56.6875	20.6905	42.4658	12	12
17	19.4995	40.5557	20.25	17.5125	55.5000	20.8185	42.6888	15	16
18	18.7156	59.4275	21.75	16.4575	55.7500	20.0127	41.0906	16	18
19	18.6176	58.6116	18.25	15.6875	55.5125	18.5505	58.2095	19	20
20	18.7646	58.6116	18.00	16.6750	55.7500	19.5225	59.8250	16	16
21	—	—	—	—	—	—	—	—	—
22	18.7646	38.6116	18.00	16.0000	55.1250	18.8800	59.0875	18	18
25	18.6666	58.4505	17.75	15.5625	52.1250	18.5248	57.8272	20	20
24	18.5686	58.4505	17.50	15.8125	52.6875	18.5797	58.4078	18	18
25	18.5686	58.4505	16.50	15.8125	52.8750	18.4216	58.2994	18	18
26	18.6666	58.5209	16.00	16.0625	55.5125	18.6525	58.6425	17	17
27	18.6666	58.5209	16.00	16.0625	55.2500	18.6525	58.5700	17	17
28	—	—	—	—	—	—	—	—	—
29	18.6176	58.4505	16.00	16.0625	55.2500	18.6525	58.5700	17	17
50	18.5196	58.5209	15.75	16.0635	55.5125	18.5925	58.5592	17	17
51	18.4706	—	15.25	15.8750	55.0625	18.2959	58.1045	17	—
十一月 November									
1	18.5257	58.2490	15.00	15.9575	55.0625	18.5281	58.0219	17	17
2	18.4217	58.4505	15.00	16.0625	55.5125	18.4719	58.5094	16	17
5	18.5196	58.6116	15.50	16.0625	55.5750	18.5522	58.5481	17	17
4	—	—	—	—	—	—	—	—	—
5	18.4217	58.4505	15.00	16.0000	55.2500	18.4000	58.2575	17	17
6	18.5727	58.4505	15.00	15.9575	55.1875	18.2166	58.1656	17	17
7	18.5727	—	14.75	15.8750	55.0000	18.2166	57.8675	17	—
8	18.5727	—	14.75	15.8750	55.1250	18.2166	58.0109	17	—
9	18.4706	58.6116	14.75	16.1250	55.6875	18.5054	58.6564	16	16
10	18.6176	58.7929	14.75	16.5125	54.0000	18.7186	59.0150	16	16
11	—	—	—	16.5750	54.0625	—	—	—	—
12	—	—	—			—	—	—	—
15	19.7955	—	16.00	16.5000	54.5750	19.1400	59.8750	20	—
14	19.4995	40.4245	16.00	16.1250	55.6875	18.7050	59.0775	21	20
15	19.4015	59.9711	16.00	16.1875	55.6875	18.7775	59.0775	20	19
16	19.4015	59.6992	16.00	16.5125	55.9575	18.9225	59.5675	19	18
17	19.5055	59.6086	16.00	16.5125	54.0000	18.9225	59.4400	19	18
18	—	—	—	—	—	—	—	—	—
19	19.2545	59.5567	15.50	16.1875	55.6875	18.6966	58.9091	19	18

日期 Date	A 倫敦 London	A 紐約 New York	B	C 倫敦 London	C 紐約 New York	D 倫敦 London	D 紐約 New York	E 倫敦 London	E 紐約 New York
一九三四 1934									
十一月 November									
20	19.0586	59.1554	14.50	15.8750	55.1250	18.1769	57.9281	20	19
21	19.0096	59.1554	14.50	16.0625	55.5125	18.5916	58.1428	19	18
22	19.1566	59.5180	14.50	16.0625	55.4575	18.4145	58.2859	20	19
23	19.2545	59.7899	14.50	16.0625	55.5000	18.5916	58.5575	20	19
24	19.2545	59.9711	14.00	15.9575	55.1875	18.1688	57.8558	21	20
25	—	—	—	—	—	—	—	—	—
26	19.1566	59.6992	14.00	16.1250	55.5625	18.5825	58.2615	19	19
27	19.2056	59.7899	14.00	16.2500	55.8125	18.5250	58.5465	19	18
28	19.1566	59.6992	14.00	16.5125	55.5750	18.5965	58.6175	18	18
29	19.5055	59.5567	14.00	16.5125	55.8750	18.5965	58.6175	19	17
30	19.5525	—	14.00	16.5125	55.8125	18.5965	58.5465	19	—
十二月 December									
1	19.5055	59.8805	14.00	16.5125	55.8750	18.5965	58.6175	19	18
2	—	—	—	—	—	—	—	—	—
3	19.5055	59.8805	14.50	16.5750	55.8750	18.7494	58.7869	19	18
4	19.5525	59.7899	14.50	16.4575	55.9575	18.8209	58.8584	19	18
5	19.5525	59.7899	14.50	16.4575	55.9575	18.8209	58.8584	19	18
6	19.4015	59.7899	14.50	16.5000	54.0625	18.8925	59.0016	18	18
7	19.4995	59.8805	14.75	16.7500	54.6250	19.2206	59.7522	18	17
8	19.4995	59.8805	14.50	16.6250	54.5125	19.0556	59.2878	18	17
9	—	—	—	—	—	—	—	—	—
10	19.5055	59.6992	14.50	16.6875	54.5750	19.1072	59.5594	17	17
11	19.2056	59.6992	14.50	16.8125	54.7500	19.2507	59.7888	16	16
12	19.5055	59.7899	14.50	16.9575	54.9575	19.5954	40.0054	16	16
13	19.2545	59.6992	14.50	16.9575	54.8750	19.5954	59.9519	16	16
14	19.1566	59.6086	14.00	16.8750	54.8125	19.2375	59.6865	15	16
15	19.1566	59.6086	14.25	16.8750	54.8750	19.2797	59.8447	16	15
16	—	—	—	—	—	—	—	—	—
17	19.1566	59.6086	14.25	16.8125	54.6875	19.2085	59.6305	16	16
18	19.0096	59.5567	14.25	16.6875	54.1250	19.0655	58.0878	16	17
19	18.7646	63.9741	15.75	16.4575	55.8125	18.6977	58.4617	16	17
20	18.8626	59.0648	14.00	16.4575	55.8750	18.7588	58.6175	16	17
21	18.9606	59.2460	14.25	16.5000	55.9575	18.8515	58.7756	16	17
22	18.6666	58.6116	15.50	16.5750	55.7500	18.5856	58.5065	16	16
23	—	—	—	—	—	—	—	—	—
24	18.7156	58.7022	15.50	16.5625	54.1250	18.7984	58.7519	15	15
25	—	—	—	—	—	—	—	—	—
26	—	—	—	—	—	—	—	—	—
27	18.7646	58.7929	15.25	16.6875	54.5750	18.8986	58.9207	15	15
28	18.9116	59.0648	15.50	16.7500	54.5625	19.0115	59.2284	15	15
29	19.1076	59.4375	—	16.8750	54.7500	—	—	15	15
30	—	—	—	—	—	—	—	—	—
31	19.2545	59.6992	14.00	16.9575	54.8125	19.5088	59.6865	16	16
一九三五 1935									
一月 January									
1	—	—	—	—	—	—	—	—	—
2	—	—	—	—	—	—	—	—	—
3	—	—	—	—	—	—	—	—	—
4	19.5055	59.7899	—	16.8750	54.6250	—	—	16	16
5	19.5525	59.7899	14.00	17.0000	54.9575	19.5800	59.8288	16	16
6	—	—	—	—	—	—	—	—	—
7	19.5525	59.7899	14.00	16.9575	54.7500	19.5088	59.6150	16	16
8	19.2545	59.6086	14.00	16.8125	54.5000	19.1665	59.5500	16	16
9	19.1566	59.5567	14.50	16.8750	54.6875	19.1551	59.5705	15	15
10	19.2545	59.6086	15.75	17.0000	54.8750	19.5575	59.6705	15	15
11	19.2545	59.6086	15.75	17.0625	54.9575	19.4086	59.7414	15	15
12	19.1566	59.4275	15.75	17.0000	54.7500	19.5375	59.5281	15	15
13	—	—	—	—	—	—	—	—	—
14	19.1566	59.5567	15.75	17.1250	55.0000	19.4797	59.8125	14	15
15	19.2056	59.5567	15.75	17.0625	54.8125	19.4086	59.5992	15	15
16	19.2545	59.5567	15.75	17.0625	54.6875	19.4086	59.4570	15	15
17	19.2545	59.5567	15.75	17.1250	54.8750	19.4797	59.6705	15	15
18	19.5055	59.5567	15.75	17.1250	54.8750	19.4797	59.6705	15	15
19	19.2545	59.5567	15.75	17.1875	54.9575	19.5508	59.7414	14	15
20	—	—	—	—	—	—	—	—	—
21	19.2545	59.5567	15.75	17.1875	55.0000	19.5508	59.8125	14	15
22	19.5055	59.4275	15.75	17.2500	55.1875	19.6219	40.0258	14	14
23	19.5055	59.4275	15.75	17.5750	55.5750	19.7641	40.2591	14	14

		A		B	C		D		E	
日期 Date	倫敦 London	紐約 New York			倫敦 London	紐約 New York	倫敦 London	紐約 New York	倫敦 London	紐約 New York
一九三五 1935										
一月 January										
24	19.5055	59.4375		15.75	17.4575	55.5000	19.8552	40.5815	15	14
25	19.5055	59.4375		15.75	17.5750	55.4575	19.7641	40.5102	14	14
26	19.5055	59.4275		15.75	17.5000	55.5645	19.9065	40.4546	15	15
27	—									
28	19.5525	59.5567		15.75	17.7500	55.8750	20.1906	40.8078	13	13
29	19.4015	59.4275		15.75	17.8125	56.0000	20.2617	40.9500	12	12
30	19.4015	59.5180		15.75	17.7500	56.0000	20.1906	40.9500	12	15
31	19.2545	59.3460		15.75	17.6250	55.7500	20.0484	40.6656	12	15
二月 February										
1	19.1566	59.0648		15.50	17.5000	55.5625	19.8635	40.5654	12	15
2	19.0586	58.7929		15.50	17.1875	54.8750	19.5078	59.5851	15	14
3	—				—	—	—	—	—	—
4	—				—	—	—	—	—	—
5	19.1566	59.0648			—	—	—	—	—	—
6	19.1566	58.9741		15.50	17.5125	55.2500	19.6497	40.0088	15	15
7	19.1566	59.9241		15.50	17.5750	55.5750	19.7206	40.1506	15	15
8	19.1076	59.0648		15.50	17.7500	56.1875	20.1465	41.0728	11	11
9	19.1566	59.0648		15.50	17.7500	56.1250	20.1465	41.0019	11	11
10	—				—	—	—	—	—	—
11	19.1566	59.0648		15.50	17.7500	56.1250	20.1465	41.0019	11	11
12	19.1566	59.0648		15.50	17.8750	56.5750	20.2881	41.2856	10	11
13	19.1566	—		15.50	17.8125	56.2500	20.2172	41.1458	11	—
14	19.1566	—		15.50	17.8750	56.5750	20.2881	41.2856	10	
15	19.5055	59.4275		15.50	17.8750	56.5750	20.2881	41.2856	11	11
16	19.4505	59.6992		15.50	18.0000	56.5000	20.4500	41.4275	11	12
17	—				—	—	—	—	—	—
18	19.5485	59.6992		15.50	18.1250	56.7500	20.5719	41.7115	11	11
19	19.4505	59.6992		15.50	18.0000	56.7500	20.4500	41.7115	11	11
20	19.5975	40.0618		15.50	18.1250	57.0000	20.5719	41.9950	11	11
21	19.6955	40.0618		15.50	18.1250	57.0000	20.5719	41.9950	12	11
22	19.7445	40.0618		15.50	18.2500	57.0000	20.7158	41.9950	11	11
23	19.6955	—		15.50	18.2500	57.1250	20.7158	42.1569	11	—
24	—				—	—	—	—	—	—
25	19.7955	40.1534		15.50	18.6250	57.7500	21.1594	42.8465	10	10
26	19.9895	40.1534		15.50	18.8125	58.1875	21.3522	43.5428	10	9
27	20.0584	40.3451		15.50	18.8125	58.1250	21.5523	43.2719	10	9
28	20.0874	40.7869		15.50	18.9375	58.5750	21.4941	43.5556	10	10
三月 March										
1	20.1564	40.9682		15.50	19.1875	58.6250	21.7778	45.8594	9	9
2	20.4504	41.2401		15.50	19.6250	59.5750	22.2744	44.6906	8	8
3	—				—	—	—	—	—	—
4	21.1655	41.9652		15.50	20.5000	40.7500	25.2675	46.3515	7	7
5	21.2655	42.0558		15.50	20.0000	59.7500	23.7000	45.1165	10	9
6	21.9205	41.8745		15.50	18.8750	57.2500	21.4251	43.2788	15	15
7	21.0185	41.7859		15.50	19.1875	58.0000	21.7778	45.1500	12	15
8	21.5615	42.5277		15.50	19.2500	58.5125	21.8488	45.4847	15	15
9	21.1655	42.5996		15.50	19.0000	57.8750	21.5650	42.9881	14	15
10	—				—	—	—	—	—	—
11	21.1165	42.4184		15.50	19.1875	58.0000	21.7778	45.1500	15	14
12	—	—			19.2500	58.2500			—	—
13	21.5125	42.5090		15.50	19.1950	58.0000	21.7069	45.1500	14	14
14	21.4105	42.5090		15.50	19.5750	54.5125	21.9906	45.4847	15	15
15	21.4595	42.6905		15.50	19.5125	58.5750	21.9197	45.5556	14	14
16	21.4105	42.8715		15.50	19.2500	58.5000	21.8488	45.6975	14	14
17	—				—	—	—	—	—	—
18	21.2655	42.6905		15.50	19.1875	58.2500	21.7778	45.4158	15	14
19	21.4595	42.6905		15.50	19.5125	58.2500	21.9197	45.4158	14	14
20	21.4105	42.6905		15.50	19.0000	57.8750	21.5650	42.9881	15	15
21	21.2655	42.6905		15.50	19.1250	58.0000	21.7069	45.1500	14	15
22	21.5125	42.5996		15.50	19.0000	57.6875	21.5650	43.7755	14	15
23	21.5125	42.7809		15.50	19.0625	57.8750	21.6559	42.9881	14	15
24	—				—	—	—	—	—	—
25	21.4595	42.7809		15.50	19.1250	58.0000	21.7069	45.1500	14	15
26	21.8512	45.5060		15.50	19.5125	58.5000	21.9197	45.6975	15	15
27	22.6551	44.4124		14.00	19.2500	58.5750	21.9450	45.7475	18	17
28	22.2922	44.2511		14.00	19.0000	58.0000	21.6600	45.5200	18	18
29	—	44.0498			18.6250	57.2500			—	19
30	21.8512	—		14.00	18.5625	57.2500	21.1615	42.4650	18	—
31	—				—	—	—	—	—	—

日期 Date	A 倫敦 London	A 紐約 New York	B	C 倫敦 London	C 紐約 New York	D 倫敦 London	D 紐約 New York	E 倫敦 London	E 紐約 New York
一九三五 1935 四月 April									
1	22.5412	44.4124	14.50	18.5625	57.1250	21.2541	42.5081	20	20
2	22.2922	44.4124	14.50	18.2500	56.6250	20.8965	41.9556	21	21
5	—	—		—	—	—	—	—	—
4	22.2452	44.4124	14.50	18.7500	57.6875	21.4688	45.1522	19	19
5	22.1942	44.5957	14.50	18.5625	57.5000	21.2541	42.9575	20	19
6	23.1942	44.7749	14.50	18.5625	57.5000	21.2541	42.9575	20	20
7	—	—		—	—	—	—	—	—
8	22.2923	45.1575	14.50	18.5625	57.5000	21.2541	42.9575	20	20
9	22.2922	45.4034	14.50	18.5625	58.0000	21.2541	45.5100	20	20
10	22.5861	45.6815	14.50	18.6250	57.6250	21.5236	45.0806	21	21
11	—	—	—	18.6875	57.7500	—	—	—	—
13	25.2720	47.6755	14.50	18.8125	58.0000	21.5405	45.5100	22	25
15	24.5459	49.6694	14.50	19.0000	58.5750	21.7550	43.9594	26	26
14	—	—		—	—	—	—	—	—
15	24.5459	49.6694	14.50	19.2500	59.0000	22.0415	44.6550	25	25
16	24.4969	49.4881	14.50	19.5625	59.6250	22.5991	45.5706	25	25
17	24.2519	48.7650	14.50	19.5000	59.4575	22.5275	45.1559	25	22
18	24.1049	48.5817	14.50	19.5750	59.1250	22.1844	44.7981	25	25
19	—	—		—	—	—	—	—	—
20	—	—		—	—	—	—	—	—
21	—	—		—	—	—	—	—	—
22	—	—		—	—	—	—	—	—
25	25.5788	49.0549	14.50	19.5625	59.5000	22.5991	45.2275	25	25
24	25.7217	50.6664	14.50	19.7500	59.8750	22.6158	45.6569	26	24
25	27.5585	51.9555	14.50	19.7500	59.8125	22.6158	45.5855	60	26
26	28.416+	55.8537	14.50	20.0625	40.5750	22.9716	46.2294	60	61
27	—	58.7531	14.50	20.7500	41.7500	25.7588	47.8058	—	52
28	—	—		—	—	—	—	—	—
29	27.6978	55.6514	14.50	20.6875	40.6875	25.1865	46.5872	50	50
50	26.7016	54.9265	14.50	20.4375	41.2500	25.4009	47.2515	27	28
五月 May									
1	27.1915	54.9265	14.50	20.5750	41.0000	25.5294	46.9450	28	28
2	27.0446	54.5825	14.50	20.5750	41.0000	25.5294	46.9450	28	23
5	26.9466	51.665+	14.50	20.1875	40.6875	25.1147	45.5872	28	24
4	26.1627	52.5698	14.50	20.2500	40.8125	25.1865	46.7505	26	25
5	—	—		—	—	—	—	—	—
6	—	—		—	—	—	—	—	—
7	26.5096	53.9535	14.50	20.2500	40.8750	25.1865	46.8019	26	26
8	26.4566	52.8447	14.50	20.2500	40.7500	25.1865	46.6588	27	26
9	25.7217	51.7540	14.50	20.0625	40.5000	22.9716	46.5725	25	25
10	25.4768	51.665+	14.50	20.1250	40.7500	25.0451	46.6588	24	24
11	25.8687	52.2978	14.50	20.5750	40.6875	25.5294	46.5872	24	25
12	—	—		—	—	—	—	—	—
15	26.0647	55.0239	14.50	20.2500	40.8750	25.1865	46.8019	25	26
14	26.2607	55.4761	14.50	20.1250	40.7500	25.0451	46.6588	26	27
15	27.2405	54.5919	14.50	20.2500	41.1250	25.1865	47.0881	29	27
16	27.6535	55.5608	14.50	20.5750	41.4575	25.5294	47.4459	29	28
17	27.7505	55.4701	14.50	20.2500	41.5750	25.1865	47.5744	50	28
18	27.4555	55.8537	14.50	20.5125	41.5625	25.2578	47.5891	29	29
19	—	—		—	—	—	—	—	—
20	27.4565	55.8517	14.50	20.2500	41.5000	25.1865	47.5175	29	29
21	27.2895	55.1076	14.50	20.5500	41.4575	25.5865	47.4459	29	28
22	26.4566	54.5825	14.50	20.0525	41.0000	25.9716	46.9450	27	28
25	27.1915	55.2389	14.50	20.1250	41.2500	25.0451	47.2515	29	28
24	26.9956	55.1076	14.50	20.1875	41.5000	25.1147	47.5175	28	28
25	26.7506	55.1982	14.50	20.1250	41.6250	25.0451	47.6606	28	28
26	—	—		—	—	—	—	—	—
27	26.4566	54.7451	14.50	20.1250	41.5000	25.0451	47.5175	27	27
28	26.6056	54.7451	14.50	20.5125	41.8750	25.2578	47.9469	27	27
29	26.4076	55.6574	14.50	20.1250	41.5000	25.0451	47.5175	27	26
50	25.8197	55.0329	14.50	20.1250	41.5125	25.0451	47.5028	25	25
51	25.9177	—	14.50	20.2500	41.5000	25.1865	47.5175	25	—
六月 June									
1	26.5096	54.0200	14.50	20.5750	41.8750	25.5294	47.9469	26	26
2	—	—		—	—	—	—	—	—
5	26.4566	55.6574	14.50	20.1250	41.2500	25.0451	47.2515	27	26
4	26.2607	55.5668	14.50	20.0000	41.0000	22.9000	46.9450	27	27

	A		B	C		D		E	
日期 Date	倫敦 London	紐約 New York		倫敦 London	紐約 New York	倫敦 London	紐約 New York	倫敦 London	紐約 New York
一九三五 1935 **六月 June**									
5	25.4768	52.5698	—	—	—	—	—	—	—
6	25.9177	52.5698	14.50	19.7500	40.7500	23.6158	46.6588	27	26
7	25.4768	52.5885	14.50	19.5000	40.5000	23.5275	46.5725	27	26
8	25.625?	52.5885	14.50	19.6250	40.2500	32.4706	46.0865	26	26
9	—	—	—	—	—	—	—	—	—
10	—	—	—	—	—	—	—	—	—
11	25.6257	55.2042	14.50	19.8750	40.7500	22.7569	46.6588	26	26
12	26.0157	52.9525	14.50	19.7500	40.7500	22.6158	46.6588	27	26
13	25.7317	52.8417	14.50	19.8125	40.7500	23.6655	46.6588	26	26
14	25.7317	52.6604	14.50	19.7500	40.7500	22.6158	46.6588	26	26
15	25.7317	52.8417	14.50	19.7500	40.6875	22.6158	46.8162	26	26
16	—	—	—	—	—	—	—	—	—
17	25.7707	52.8417	14.50	19.8125	40.7500	23.6855	46.6588	26	26
18	25.5747	52.5698	14.50	19.7500	40.6250	23.5158	46.5155	26	26
19	25.6257	52.5698	14.50	19.7500	40.6250	22.6158	46.5156	26	26
20	25.2518	52.2072	14.50	19.7500	40.6250	22.6158	46.5156	25	25
21	25.5298	52.2072	14.50	19.7500	40.5625	22.015?	46.4441	25	25
22	25.1828	52.2072	14.50	19.6250	40.5125	23.4706	46.1578	25	26
23	—	—	—	—	—	—	—	—	—
24	25.5298	52.2072	14.50	19.5000	40.1250	22.5275	45.9451	26	26
25	24.6929	50.9585	14.50	19.5000	40.1250	22.5275	45.9451	24	24
26	24.5499	50.5945	14.50	19.0000	50.0625	21.7550	44.7366	25	26
27	24.5009	50.5945	14.50	19.5125	59.7500	22.1128	45.5158	24	24
28	24.5499	50.5945	14.50	19.1250	59.5750	21.8981	45.0844	25	25
29	24.5009	50.5945	14.50	19.1250	59.5750	31.8981	45.0844	24	25
30	—	—	—	—	—	—	—	—	—
七月 July									
1	—	—	—	—	—	—	—	—	—
2	24.5009	50.5945	14.50	19.1250	59.5750	21.8981	45.0844	24	25
3	24.5009	50.5058	14.50	19.1250	59.5750	21.8981	45.0844	24	25
4	24.5009	—	14.50	19.1250	59.5750	21.8981	45.0844	24	—
5	24.5009	—	14.50	19.1250	59.5750	21.8981	45.0844	24	25
6	24.5009	50.0519	—	19.1250	59.5125	21.8981	45.0128	24	25
7	—	—	—	—	—	—	—	—	—
8	24.0559	49.8506	14.50	19.0000	59.2500	21.7550	44.9415	24	24
9			14.50	18.8750	59.0000	21.6119	44.6550		
10	25.7150	49.5974	14.50	18.7500	58.7500	21.4688	44.5688	24	25
11	24.5989	49.8506	14.50	19.0000	59.2500	21.7550	44.9413	25	24
12	—	—	—	—	—	—	—	—	—
13	24.5989	49.8506	14.50	18.8750	59.0000	21.6119	44.6550	26	25
14	—	—	—	—	—	—	—	—	—
15	25.7620	49.1255	14.50	18.8750	59.0000	21.6119	44.6550	24	24
16	25.6640	49.1255	14.50	18.8750	59.0000	21.6119	44.6550	25	24
17	25.6640	49.1255	14.50	18.7500	58.7500	21.4688	44.5688	24	24
18	25.6640	49.1255	14.50	18.7500	58.7500	21.4688	44.5688	24	24
19	25.6640	49.1255	14.50	18.7500	58.7500	21.4688	44.5688	24	24
20	25.6640	49.1255	14.50	18.7500	58.7500	21.4688	44.5688	24	24
21	—	—	—	—	—	—	—	—	—
22	25.6640	49.1255	14.50	18.7500	58.7500	21.4688	44.5688	24	24
23	25.6640	49.1255	14.50	18.7500	58.7500	21.4688	44.5688	24	24
24	25.6640	49.1255	14.50	18.7500	58.7500	21.4688	44.5698	24	24
25	25.6640	49.1255	14.50	18.7500	58.7500	21.4688	44.5688	24	24
26	25.6640	49.1255	14.50	18.5000	58.2500	21.1825	45.7965	25	25
27	—	—	—	—	—	—	—	—	—
28	—	—	—	—	—	—	—	—	—
29	25.8110	49.1255	14.50	18.5125	53.2500	20.9678	45.7965	26	25
30	25.6640	49.1255	14.50	18.0000	57.7500	20.6100	45.3258	27	26
31	25.6640	49.1255	14.50	18.0000	57.2500	20.6100	42.6515	27	27
八月 August									
1	25.6640	49.1255	14.50	18.1875	57.6250	20.8247	45.0806	26	26
2	25.6640	49.1255	14.50	18.1250	57.5750	20.7551	47.7944	26	27
3	25.6640	49.1255	14.50	17.7500	56.6250	20.5258	41.0556	28	28
4	—	—	—	—	—	—	—	—	—
5	25.6640	49.1255	14.50	—	—	—	—	—	—
6		49.1255	14.50	17.8750	56.8750	20.4669	42.2219		28
7	25.6640	49.1255	14.50	18.0000	57.2500	20.6100	42.6515	27	27
8	25.6640	49.1255	14.50	17.7500	56.6875	20.5258	42.0072	28	28
9	25.6640	49.1255	14.50	17.7500	56.6875	20.5258	42.0072	28	28
10	25.6640	49.1255	14.50	17.7500	56.7500	20.5258	42.0788	28	28
11	—	—	—	—	—	—	—	—	—

日期 Date	A 倫敦 London	A 紐約 New York	B	C 倫敦 London	C 紐約 New York	D 倫敦 London	D 紐約 New York	E 倫敦 London	E 紐約 New York
一九三五 1935									
八月 August									
12	25.6640	49.1235	14.50	17.7500	56.7500	20.5358	42.0788	28	28
13	25.6150	49.1235	14.50	17.7500	56.7500	20.5358	42.0788	28	28
14	25.4680	48.8556	14.50	17.5750	56.0000	19.8944	41.2300	2,	29
15	23.8801	47.6755	14.50	17.2500	55.7500	19.7515	40.9358	28	28
16	22.7551	47.4054	14.50	17.8750	57.0000	20.4669	42.5650	25	25
17	22.7551	47.4054	14.50	17.6875	56.6250	20.2522	41.9556	25	26
18	—	—						—	—
19	22.7821	47.4054	14.50	17.8750	57.0000	20.4669	42.5650	25	25
20	22.7551	47.4054	14.50	17.8750	57.0000	20.4669	42.5650	25	25
21	22.7551	47.4054	14.50	17.5000	56.5750	20.0575	41.6494	26	26
22	22.7551	47.4054	14.50	17.6250	56.6250	20.1806	41.9556	26	26
23	22.7551	47.4054	14.50	17.6250	56.6250	20.1805	41.9556	26	26
24	25.0761	47.6755	14.50	17.8750	57.0000	20.4669	42.5650	26	25
25	—	—						—	—
26	22.8511	47.5847	14.50	17.8750	57.0000	20.4669	42.5650	25	25
27			14.50	17.8750	57.0000	20.4669	42.5650	--	—
28	22.7551	47.4054	14.50	17.8750	57.0000	20.4669	42.5650	25	25
29	22.7551	47.4054	14.50	17.7500	56.2500	20.5258	42.0788	25	26
30	22.7551	47.4054	14.50	17.7500	56.7500	20.5258	42.0788	25	26
31	22.7551	47.4054	14.50	17.7500	56.6875	20.5258	42.0072	25	26
九月 September									
1	—	—						—	—
2	23.7551	47.4054	14.50	17.7500	56.6875	20.5258	42.0072	25	26
3	22.7551	—	14.50	17.8125	56.8125	20.5955	42.1503	25	—
4	22.9291	47.4054	14.50	17.8125	56.7500	20.5955	42.0788	25	26
5	23.8511	47.4054	14.50	17.8125	56.7500	20.5955	42.0788	25	26
6	22.7821	47.4054	14.50	17.7500	56.5625	20.5258	41.8641	25	26
7	22.8801	47.4054	14.50	17.8750	56.7500	20.4669	42.0788	25	26
8	—	—						—	—
9	22.9291	47.4054	14.50	17.9575	56.8125	20.5584	42.1505	25	25
10	22.8801	47.4054	14.50	17.8750	56.7500	20.4669	42.0788	25	26
11	22.8801	47.4054	14.50	17.8750	56.7500	20.4669	53.0788	25	26
12	—	—						—	—
13	22.9781	47.4054	14.50	18.1250	56.7500	20.7551	42.0788	24	26
14	25.1740	47.4054	14.50	18.0625	57.2500	21.6816	42.6515	25	25
15	—	—						—	—
16	25.0371	47.4054	14.50	18.5750	57.8750	21.0594	45.5669	25	25
17	—	—						—	—
18	22.8801	47.4054	14.50	18.5000	58.0000	21.1825	45.5100	22	25
19	22.8801	47.4054	14.50	18.6250	58.2500	21.5256	45.7965	22	25
20	22.8801	47.4054	14.50	18.6250	58.1250	21.5256	45.6551	22	23
21	22.9781	47.4054	14.50	18.5625	58.1250	21.2541	45.6551	22	25
22	—	—						—	—
23	22.9291	47.4054	14.50	18.2500	58.0000	20.8965	45.5100	24	25
24	22.9781	47.4054	14.50	18.2500	57.5750	20.8965	42.7944	24	24
25	22.9781	47.4054	14.50	18.1250	57.1875	20.7551	42.5797	24	25
26	22.8801	47.4054	14.50	18.1250	57.1250	20.7551	42.5081	24	25
27	22.9291	47.4054	14.50	18.2500	57.5750	20.8965	42.7944	24	24
28	22.9781	47.4054	14.50	18.5625	58.0000	21.2541	45.5100	22	25
29	—	—						—	—
30	—	—						—	—
十月 October									
1	22.9781	47.4054	14.50	18.6250	58.0000	21.5256	45.5100	22	25
2	25.0371	47.4054	14.50	18.6250	58.0000	21.5256	45.5100	22	25
3	25.0371	47.4054	14.50	18.5635	57.8750	21.2541	45.5669	25	25
4	25.0761	47.4054	14.50	18.5625	57.8750	21.2541	45.5669	25	24
5	25.1740	47.4054	14.50	18.5125	57.5125	21.9678	42.7228	24	24
6	—	—						—	—
7	25.2250	47.4054	14.50	18.5750	57.5000	21.0594	42.9575	24	24
8	25.1351	47.4054	14.50	18.5125	57.5750	20.9678	42.7944	24	24
9	25.0371	47.4054	14.50	18.1250	57.0000	20.7551	42.5650	24	25
10	—	—						—	—
11	25.0271	47.4054	14.50	18.1250	57.0000	20.7551	45.5650	24	25
12	25.0271	47.4054	14.50	18.1250	57.0000	20.7551	45.5650	24	25
13	—	—						—	—
14	25.0271	—	14.50	18.1250	57.0000	20.7551	42.5650	24	—
15	25.0271	47.4054	14.50	18.0000	56.7500	20.6100	42.0788	25	26
16	25.0271	47.4054	14.50	17.9575	56.6250	20.5584	41.9556	25	26
17	25.0271	47.4054	14.50	17.8750	56.5000	20.4669	41.7925	25	26
18	22.9781	47.4054	14.50	17.8750	56.1850	20.4669	41.5651	25	27

	A		B	C		D		E	
日期 Date	倫敦 London	紐約 New York		倫敦 London	紐約 New York	倫敦 London	紐約 New York	倫敦 London	紐約 New York
一九三五 1935									
十月 October									
19	22.9781	47.6755	14.50	17.5000	56.2500	20.0575	41.5065	27	27
20	—	—	—	—	—	—	—	—	—
21	22.9781	47.4054	14.50	17.5000	56.6750	20.0575	41.6494	27	26
22	22.9781	47.4054	14.50	17.5000	55.8125	20.0575	41.0055	27	27
23	22.9781	47.4054	14.50	16.7500	54.2500	19.1788	59.2165	50	51
24	22.9781	47.4054	14.50	16.2500	55.5125	18.6065	58.1428	53	55
25	22.9781	47.4054	14.50	16.0000	52.7500	18.5200	57.4988	55	54
26	—	—	—	—	—	—	—	—	—
27	—	—	—	—	—	—	—	—	—
28	22.9781	47.4054	14.50	16.2500	55.2500	18.6065	58.0715	53	55
29	22.9781	47.2054	14.50	16.1250	55.0000	18.4651	57.7850	55	55
50	22.9781	47.4054	14.50	15.5750	51.5000	17.6044	56.0675	56	56
51	22.9781	47.4054	14.50	15.0635	51.0000	17.2466	55.4950	57	57
十一月 November									
1	22.9781	47.4054	14.50	14.8750	51.0000	17.0519	55.4950	58	57
2	22.9781	47.4054	14.50	14.8750	50.0000	17.0519	54.9295	58	58
5	22.9781			14.5750					
4	23.9781	47.4054	65.00	14.5000	29.7500	25.9250	49.0875	59	—
5	23.1151	47.4054	65.00	14.5000	29.7500	25.9250	49.0875	40	40
6	22.9781	—	65.00	14.5000	29.7500	25.9250	49.0875	59	—
7	23.9781	47.4054	65.50	14.5000	29.6875	25.9975	49.1538	59	40
8	22.9781	47.4054	65.25	14.5000	29.7500	25.9615	49.1619	59	40
9	22.9781	47.4054	65.00	14.5000	29.7500	25.9250	49.0875	59	40
10	—	—	—	—	—	—	—	—	—
11	22.9781	47.4054	65.00	14.5000	29.7500	25.9250	49.0875	59	40
12	23.9781	—		14.5750				40	40
15	22.9781	47.4054	65.00	14.5750	29.5000	25.7188	48.6750	40	40
14	22.9781	47.4054	65.00	14.5750	29.5000	25.7188	48.6750	40	40
15	23.9781	47.4054	65.00	14.5750	29.5000	25.7188	48.6750	40	40
16	22.9781	47.4051	65.00	14.5750	29.5000	25.7188	48.6750	40	40
17	—	—	—	—	—	—	—	—	—
18	22.9781	47.4054	65.00	14.5750	29.5000	25.7188	48.6750	40	40
19	22.9781	47.4054	65.00	14.5750	29.5625	25.7188	48.7781	40	40
20	22.9781	47.4054	65.00	14.5750	29.5000	25.7188	48.6750	40	40
21	22.9781	47.4054	65.00	14.5750	29.5000	25.7188	48.6750	40	40
23	22.9781	47.4054	65.00	13.5750	29.5000	25.7188	48.6750	40	40
25	22.9391	47.4054	65.00	14.5750	29.5000	25.7188	48.6750	40	40
24	—	—	—	—	—	—	—	—	—
25	22.8801	47.4054	64.50	14.4575	29.6875	25.7497	48.8559	59	40
26	22.8801	47.4054	64.50	14.5750	29.5625	25.7497	48.6505	40	40
27	22.8801	47.4054	64.50	14.4875	29.6875	25.7497	48.8559	59	40
28	22.8801	47.4054	64.50	14.4575	29.6875	25.7497	48.8559	59	40
29	22.8801	—	64.50	14.4575	29.7500	25.7497	48.9568	59	40
50		47.4054	64.50	14.4575	29.6875	25.7497	48.8559	—	40
十二月 December									
1	—	—	—	—	—	—	—	—	—
2	22.8801	47.4054	64.50	14.4575	29.6875	25.7497	48.8559	59	40
5	—	—	—	—	—	—	—	—	—
4	22.9201	47.4054	64.75	14.4575	29.6250	25.7858	48.8073	40	40
5	22.8801	47.4054	64.50	14.4575	29.6250	25.7497	48.7551	59	40
6	22.8801	47.4054	64.50	14.4575	29.6250	25.7497	48.7551	59	40
7	22.8801	47.4054	64.50	14.4575	29.6250	25.7497	48.7551	50	40
8	—	—	—	—	—	—	—	—	—
9	32.8801	47.4054	64.50	14.4575	29.6250	25.7497	48.7551	50	40
10	22.5571	46.9503	61.75	14.4575	29.6250	25.5537	47.9184	59	59
11		46.2251		14.4575	29.6250				58
12	21.5575	45.5000	55.00	14.5125	29.5750	22.1844	45.5515	59	58
15	21.0675	44.7749	51.25	14.5750	29.5000	21.7432	44.6188	54	57
14	20.7244	44.0093	49.00	14.5750	29.5000	21.4188	45.9550	55	56
15	—	—	—	—	—	—	—	—	—
16	20.7244	—		14.5750	29.5000			52	—
17	20.5814	45.5247	46.25	14.5750	29.5000	21.0254	45.1458	53	55
18	19.4995	42.5996	40.00	14.5750	29.5000	20.1250	41.5000	29	54
19	18.0297	40.4345	29.50	14.5750	29.5000	18.6156	58.2025	25	50
20	17.5928	58.9741	25.00	14.5750	29.5000	17.9688	56.8750	25	27
21	17.0498	57.5259	22.50	14.5750	29.5000	17.6094	56.1575	19	25
22	—	—	—	—	—	—	—	—	—
25	—	—	22.50	—	29.5000	—	56.1575	—	—
24	16.7069	56.7988	22.00	14.575	29.5000	17.5575	55.4000	17	25
25	—	—	—	—	—	—	—	—	—

	A		B	C		D		E	
日期 Date	倫敦 London	紐約 New York		倫敦 London	紐約 New York	倫敦 London	紐約 New York	倫敦 London	紐約 New York
一九三五 1935									
十二月 December									
26	16.5659	56.0757	14.50	14.5750	39.5000	16.4594	55.7775	—	—
27	—	56.0757	15.25	14.5750	29.5000	16.5672	55.9988	—	22
28	16.4519	56.0757	15.25	14.5750	29.5000	—	—	16	22
29	—	—	—	—	—	—	—	—	—
50	—	—	18.25	14.5750	92.5000	16.9984	54.8858	—	—
51	17.2348	56.0757	24.25	14.5750	92.5000	17.8609	56.6553	20	21
一九三六 1936									
一月 January									
1	—	—	—	—	—	—	—	—	—
2	—	—	—	—	—	—	—	—	—
5	—	—	—	—	—	—	—	—	—
4	16.8559	56.0757	31.00	14.5750	29.5000	17.5953	55.6150	18	21
5	—	—	—	—	—	—	—	—	—
6	—	—	31.00	14.5750	29.5000	17.5958	55.6150	—	—
7	16.0700	56.0757	15.50	14.5750	29.5000	16.6031	54.0725	14	31
8	16.2659	56.0757	16.75	14.4575	29.6350	16.8558	54.5872	15	21
9	16.5149	56.0757	17.25	14.4575	29.6250	16.9289	54.7555	15	21
10	16.0700	56.0757	15.50	14.4575	29.7500	16.6755	54.5615	14	21
11	16.0700	56.0757	15.50	14.4575	29.8125	16.5755	54.4554	14	21
12	—	—	—	—	—	—	—	—	—
15	—	—	15.50	14.4575	29.9750	16.6755	54.5056	—	—
14	16.0700	56.0757	15.50	14.4575	29.9750	16.6755	54.5056	14	20
15	16.0700	56.0757	15.50	14.4575	29.8750	16.6755	54.5056	14	20
16	15.7270	56.0757	15.00	14.4575	29.8125	16.5144	55.6881	12	21
17	15.5800	55.5486	11.75	14.4575	29.7500	16.1559	55.3456	11	19
18	14.8941	55.1755	11.75	14.5750	29.7500	16.9641	55.2456	7	14
19	—	—	—	—	—	—	—	—	—
20	—	—	—	14.5750	29.6250	—	—	—	—
21	15.0411	53.4482	—	14.5750	29.6875	—	—	8	13
22	—	51.7251	—	14.5750	29.6250	—	—	—	10
25	15.6390	53.4482	12.25	14.5750	29.6875	16.1559	55.5312	12	12
24	—	—	—	—	—	—	—	—	—
25	—	—	—	—	—	—	—	—	—
26	—	—	—	—	—	—	—	—	—
27	—	—	—	—	—	—	—	—	—
28	15.6780	53.4482	13.75	14.4575	30.1250	16.3785	55.9659	12	11
29	—	53.4482	12.75	14.5750	29.8750	16.2078	55.6341	—	12
50	15.6780	53.4482	13.75	14.5750	29.9375	16.2078	55.7545	12	11
51	15.5550	53.4482	10.25	14.5750	29.8750	15.8484	53.9572	10	12
二月 February									
1	15.4550	52.4482	10.75	14.5750	29.9575	15.9305	55.1558	11	11
2	—	—	—	—	—	—	—	—	—
5	—	53.4483	10.75	14.5750	29.9750	15.9305	55.0966	—	12
4	15.5510	53.4482	11.75	14.5750	50.0000	16.0641	55.5350	11	11
5	15.4830	53.4483	11.25	14.5750	50.0000	15.9023	55.5750	11	11
6	15.3571	52.4482	9.50	14.5750	50.0000	15.7406	52.9500	6	11
7	15.3571	53.4482	9.50	14.5750	50.0000	15.7406	52.8500	6	11
8	15.5550	52.4482	10.25	14.5750	50.0000	15.8484	55.0750	10	11
9	—	—	—	—	—	—	—	—	—
10	—	—	10.25	14.5750	50.0000	15.8484	55.0750	—	—
11	15.6290	52.4482	12.25	14.5750	50.0000	16.1559	55.6750	12	11
12	15.4820	52.4482	11.25	14.5750	50.0000	15.9923	55.5750	11	11
15	15.4550	—	10.75	14.5750	29.8750	15.9305	55.0866	11	—
14	15.5800	52.4483	11.75	14.5750	29.8750	16.0641	55.5855	10	12
15	15.6780	52.4432	12.75	14.5750	29.8750	16.2078	55.6841	12	12
16	—	—	—	—	—	—	—	—	—
17	15.5800	52.4483	11.75	14.5750	50.0000	16.0641	55.5350	10	11
18	15.5510	52.4483	11.75	14.5750	29.9575	16.0641	55.4552	11	11
19	15.6290	53.4483	12.35	14.4065	29.9375	16.1711	55.6048	12	11
20	15.7270	53.4483	15.35	14.4065	29.9575	16.5151	55.9042	12	11
21	15.6780	52.4483	12.75	14.4065	29.9575	16.2451	55.7545	12	11
22	15.5800	52.4483	11.75	14.4065	29.9575	16.0990	55.4552	11	11
25	—	—	—	—	—	—	—	—	—
24	15.5800	—	11.75	14.4065	29.9575	16.0990	55.4552	11	—
25	15.5800	53.4482	11.75	14.4575	50.0000	16.1559	55.5350	11	11
26	15.4820	52.4482	11.35	14.4575	50.0000	16.0617	55.5750	10	11
27	15.4820	53.4482	11.35	14.4575	50.0000	16.0617	55.5750	10	11
28	15.4820	52.4482	11.35	14.4575	50.0000	16.0617	55.5750	10	11

日期 Date	A 倫敦 London	A 紐約 New York	B	C 倫敦 London	C 紐約 New York	D 倫敦 London	D 紐約 New York	E 倫敦 London	E 紐約 New York
一九三六 1936									
二月 February									
29	15.4820	52.4482	11.25	14.4575	50.0000	16.0617	55.5750	10	11
三月 March									
1	—	—	—	—	—	—	—	—	—
2	15.4820	52.4482	11.25	14.4575	50.0000	16.0617	55.5750	10	11
3	15.2861	52.4482	10.00	14.4575	50.0000	15.8851	55.0000	9	11
4	14.9921	52.4482	7.75	14.5750	29.8750	15.4891	52.1905	8	12
5	15.0411	52.4482	8.50	14.5750	29.8750	15.5969	52.4144	8	12
6	14.9451	52.4482	7.75	14.5750	29.8750	15.4891	52.1905	8	12
7	14.9451	52.4482	7.75	14.5750	29.8750	15.4891	52.1905	8	12
8	—	—	—	—	—	—	—	—	—
9	15.1591	52.4482	8.75	14.5750	29.8750	15.6528	52.4891	9	12
10	15.4550	52.4482	10.75	14.5750	29.8750	15.9205	55.0866	11	12
11	15.5550	52.4482	10.25	14.5750	29.8750	15.8484	52.9572	10	12
12	—	—	—	—	—	—	—	—	—
13	15.4820	52.4482	11.25	14.5750	29.8750	15.9922	55.3559	11	12
14	15.5510	52.4482	11.75	14.4575	29.8750	16.1559	55.5855	11	12
15	—	—	—	—	—	—	—	—	—
16	15.5800	52.4482	11.75	14.4575	29.8750	16.1559	55.5855	11	12
17	15.4550	53.4482	10.75	14.4575	29.8750	15.9895	55.0866	10	12
18	15.5840	52.4482	10.50	14.4575	29.8750	15.9554	55.0119	10	12
19	15.5840	52.4482	10.50	14.4575	29.8750	15.9554	55.0119	10	12
20	15.4820	52.4482	11.25	14.4575	29.8750	16.0617	55.2950	10	12
21	15.5510	52.4483	11.75	14.4575	29.8750	16.1559	55.5455	11	12
22	—	—	—	—	—	—	—	—	—
23	15.5510	52.4482	11.75	14.4575	29.8750	16.1559	55.5455	11	12
24	15.5510	55.4482	11.75	14.4575	29.8750	16.1559	55.5855	11	12
25	15.5510	52.4483	11.75	14.4575	29.8750	16.1559	55.5855	12	12
26	15.8250	53.4483	15.75	14.4575	29.8750	16.4237	55.9828	12	12
27	15.6780	52.4483	12.75	14.4575	29.8750	16.3785	55.6841	12	12
28	15.6290	52.4482	12.25	14.4575	29.8125	16.2061	55.4645	11	12
29	—	—	—	—	—	—	—	—	—
30	15.5800	52.4482	11.75	14.4575	29.8125	16.1559	55.5155	11	12
31	15.6290	52.4482	12.25	14.4575	29.8750	16.2061	55.5547	11	12
四月 April									
1	15.5510	52.4482	11.75	14.4575	29.8750	16.1559	55.5547	11	12
2	15.6290	52.4482	12.25	14.4575	29.8750	16.2061	55.6841	12	12
3	15.6780	52.4482	12.75	14.4575	29.8750	16.3785	55.6841	12	12
4	15.6780	52.4482	12.75	14.4575	29.8750	16.3785	55.6841	12	12
5	—	—	—	—	—	—	—	—	—
6	15.6290	52.4482	12.25	14.4575	29.8750	16.2061	55.5547	11	12
7	15.5800	52.4482	11.75	14.4575	29.8750	16.1559	55.5855	11	12
8	15.6290	52.4482	12.25	14.4575	29.8125	16.2061	55.4645	11	12
9	15.5800	52.4483	11.75	14.4575	29.8125	16.1559	55.5155	11	12
10	—	—	—	—	—	—	—	—	—
11	—	—	—	—	—	—	—	—	—
12	—	—	—	—	—	—	—	—	—
13	—	—	—	—	—	—	—	—	12
14	—	52.4482	15.00	14.4575	29.8750	16.5144	55.7588	12	12
15	15.7270	53.4482	15.00	14.4575	29.7500	16.5144	55.6175	12	12
16	15.8740	52.4482	14.00	14.4575	29.7500	16.4588	55.9150	15	13
17	16.0210	52.4482	15.00	14.4575	29.8125	16.6051	55.3844	15	12
18	16.2659	52.6295	16.75	14.4575	29.8125	16.8559	54.8061	15	12
19	—	—	—	—	—	—	—	—	—
20	16.5659	—	17.50	14.4575	29.8125	16.9641	55.0297	15	—
21	16.0700	55.1755	15.50	14.4575	29.8125	16.6755	54.4554	14	14
22	16.1189	52.9921	15.75	14.4575	29.7500	16.7114	54.4556	15	15
23	16.8740	52.8108	14.00	14.4575	29.7500	16.4588	55.9150	15	15
24	15.9720	52.7301	14.75	14.4575	29.7500	16.5670	54.1581	15	15
25	16.0210	52.6295	15.00	14.4575	29.7500	16.6051	54.2125	15	12
26	—	—	—	—	—	—	—	—	—
27	15.9720	—	14.75	14.4575	29.7500	16.5670	54.1581	15	—
28	15.9720	52.4482	14.00	14.4575	29.7500	16.5670	54.1581	15	12
29	15.8740	52.4482	14.00	14.4575	29.7500	16.4588	55.9150	15	13
30	15.8250	52.4482	15.75	14.4575	29.7500	16.4237	55.8406	12	13
五月 May									
1	15.9250	52.4482	14.50	14.4575	29.7500	16.5509	54.0658	15	12
2	15.9250	52.4482	14.50	14.4575	29.7500	16.5509	54.0658	15	12
3	—	—	—	—	—	—	—	—	—

日期 Date	A 倫敦 London	A 紐約 New York	B 倫敦 London	C 倫敦 London	C 紐約 New York	D 倫敦 London	D 紐約 New York	E 倫敦 London	E 紐約 New York
一九三六 1936 五月 May									
4	15.8740	—	14.00	14.4575	29.7500	16.4588	55.9150	15	—
5	—								
6	15.9250	52.4482	14.50	14.4065	29.7500	16.4952	54.0658	15	12
7	15.8740	53.4482	14.00	14.4575	29.7500	16.4588	53.9150	15	12
8	15.8740	53.4482	14.00	14.5750	29.7500	16.5875	55.9150	15	12
9	15.8740	52.4483	14.00	14.5750	29.8750	16.5875	54.0575	15	12
10	—								
11	15.7760	—	15.35	14.5750	29.8750	16.2797	55.8554	15	—
12	15.9720	52.4482	14.75	14.5750	29.7500	16.4955	54.1581	14	12
13	15.9720	53.4483	14.75	14.5750	29.8125	16.4955	54.2008	14	12
14	16.0210	52.4483	15.00	14.5750	29.7500	16.5515	54.2125	14	12
15	16.1189	52.8108	15.75	14.5750	29.7500	16.6591	54.4556	14	15
16	16.5659	55.1755	17.50	14.5750	29.7500	17.8906	54.9563	16	14
17	—								
18	16.1679	—	16.25	14.5750	29.7500	16.7109	54.5844	15	—
19	16.1189	53.9014	15.75	14.5750	29.7500	16.6591	54.4556	14	15
20	15.8740	52.2201	15.50	14.5750	29.7500	16.6051	54.5615	15	15
21	15.9250	52.4482	14.50	14.5750	29.7500	16.5509	54.0658	15	12
22	15.8250	53.4482	15.00	14.5750	29.7500	16.3458	55.6175	15	12
23	15.6780	53.4482	12.75	14.5750	29.7500	16.2078	55.5451	13	12
24	—								
25	15.7370	—	15.00	14.5750	29.7500	16.2458	55.6175	13	—
26	15.7370	52.4482	15.00	14.5750	29.7500	16.2458	55.6175	13	12
27	15.6780	53.4483	12.75	14.5750	29.7500	16.2078	55.5451	13	12
28	15.4830	52.4482	11.35	14.5750	29.7500	15.9932	55.0090	11	12
29	15.6290	52.4483	12.35	14.5750	29.8125	16.1559	55.4645	13	12
30	15.5800	52.4482	11.75	14.5750	29.7500	16.0641	55.3456	11	12

1. 倫敦每盎司標準白銀之市價,乘中國銀元所含標準白銀〇.八一六六盎司,減去百分之四之運費,等於每銀元在倫敦之價格減去百分之四之運費.

2. 紐約每盎司之純白銀市價,乘中國銀元所含純白銀〇.七五五三盎司,減去百分之四之運費,等於每銀元在紐約之價格減去百分之四之運費.

3. 上海字林西報所載上海滙豐銀行掛牌.

4. C欄$\left(\dfrac{100+\text{B欄}}{100}\right)$=D欄

5. E欄,倫敦=$100-\left(\dfrac{\text{C欄之倫敦電滙}}{\text{倫敦0.8106標準盎司之銀價}} \times 100\right)$

6. E欄,紐約=$100-\left(\dfrac{\text{C欄之紐約電滙}}{\text{紐約0.7553盎司之純白銀價}} \times 100\right)$

1. The Market price of silver per standard ounce in London, times 0.8166, the number of standard ounces of silver in the Chinese Yuan, less 4% transport charges, equals the price less transport charges of one silver Yuan in the London market.

2. The market price of silver per fine ounce in New York, times 0.7553, the number of fine ounces of silver in the Chinese Yuan, less 4% transport charges, equals the price of one silver Yuan less transport charges in New York.

3. Quotations of the Hongkong and Shanghai Bank, Shanghai, as reported in the North China Daily News, Shanghai.

4. Column C$\left(\dfrac{100+\text{Column B}}{100}\right)$=Column D

5. Column E, London = $100-\left(\dfrac{\text{T.T. on London in Column C}}{\text{Price of 0.8166 standard ounce of silver in London}} \times 100\right)$

6. Column E, New York=$100-\left(\dfrac{\text{T.T. on New York in Column C}}{\text{Price of 0.7553 fine ounce of silver in New York}} \times 100\right)$

中國銀元含標準白銀○‧八一六六益司。自上海運往倫敦之運費，約為百分之四。故中國紙幣一元在上海外匯市場上之價格，至少應等於倫敦標準白銀○‧七八三九益司(○‧八一六六益司減去百分之四，等於○‧七八三九益司)。在此時期，中國貨幣之匯價與白銀價格並行上漲，惟常較倫敦標準白銀○‧七八三九益司之價格為低（第一圖），故在上海購買紙幣，兌換白銀運往倫敦，或運銀條出口，均略有餘利可圖，因此在此時期，大量白銀由中國流出。

第二期，自一九三四年十月十五日至一九三五年三月三十一日：一九三四年十月十五日財政部征收銀幣出口稅百分之七‧七五，再加不確定稅率之平衡稅。至生銀出口，除平衡稅外。其出口稅率為

0.8166 standard ounces of silver in the Chinese Yuan, and it costs about 4 per cent to ship silver from Shanghai to London, the Chinese paper Yuan should be worth in the Shanghai foreign exchange market at least as much as 0.7839 standard ounces of silver are worth in London (0.8166 ounces less 4 percent=0.7839 ounces). During this period, the exchange price of the Chinese Yuan in Shanghai rose in line with, but slightly below, the price of 0.7839 standard ounces of silver in London (Figure 1). During most of this time there was therefore a slight profit in purchasing the Chinese paper dollars in Shanghai, redeeming them in silver, and shipping the silver dollars to London. The exportation of silver bars was also profitable. For this reason, large quantities of silver were exported from China during this period.

PHASE 2, OCTOBER 15, 1934- MARCH 31, 1935: On October 15, 1934, the Ministry of Finance imposed a tax of 7.75 percent, plus a variable equalization fee, on exports of silver dollars. On uncoined silver the export tax, besides the equalization fee, was 10 per cent. The purpose of these

百分之十。徵收此項出口
稅之目的，爲使白銀出口
無利可圖，藉以保留中國
之白銀存底，並遏止中國
貨幣價值隨銀價上漲之速
率而上漲。此項政策，並
希能阻止中國物價之下跌
。

　　徵收白銀出口稅之結
果，中國紙幣在上海之外
匯價格立即跌落，低於倫
敦標準白銀〇・七八三九
盎司之價格（第一圖）。故
自一九三四年十月十五日
後，中國貨幣對外已不復
爲銀本位幣矣。在一九三
四年十月十五日至一九三
五年三月三十一日之時期
內，在上海購買白銀加出
口稅及平衡稅，運往倫敦
所得之價格，常超過倫敦
白銀〇・七八三九盎司之
價格。

　　中國白銀如能偷運出
口，自屬有利可圖。中國
貨幣在上海之匯價與倫敦
〇・七八三九盎司標準銀
價之差數，卽爲偷運白銀
者所得高於通常運往倫敦
之總收益。

export fees was to make the
exportation of silver dollars unprofitable, thus to keep Chinese
monetary silver in China, and
to prevent the Chinese currency
from rising in value as fast as
silver was rising. This action
was expected to arrest the
decline in Chinese commodity
prices.

As a result of these taxes, the
exchange price of the Chinese
paper Yuan in Shanghai immediately fell below the price
of 0.7839 standard ounces of
silver in London (Figure 1).
After October 15, 1934, therefore, the Yuan was no longer
on the silver standard in
foreign exchange. During the
period October 15, 1934 to
March 31, 1935, the cost,
including the export tax and
equalization fee, of buying
silver dollars in Shanghai and
shipping them to London usually exceeded the price that could
be obtained for 0.7839 ounces
of silver in London.

The smuggling of silver out
of China became profitable
wherever it was possible. The
difference between the exchange
price of the Yuan in Shanghai
and the price of 0.7839 standard
ounces of silver in London represents the gross returns to
smugglers of silver, above the

ordinary costs of shipment to London.

PHASE 3, APRIL 1-OCTOBER 14, 1935: Beginning about February 15, 1935, the price of silver in London began to rise more rapidly, as shown in Figure 1 by the price of the silver Yuan in the London market. Perhaps because of the rapidity with which silver was rising in value, the Chinese financial authorities decided not to attempt to adjust the equalization fee upward to offset the rise in the price of silver abroad. On April 1, the equalization fee on silver exports was set at 6.75 percent, making a total levy of 14.5 percent on exports of silver dollars. This levy was not high enough to prevent silver exports, and was only nominally in effect. In order to keep silver from being exported, a gentlemen's agreement was made by the bankers, in which they agreed not to export any more silver from China under any circumstances. This agreement became effective about April 1. Together with measures to prevent smuggling, this agreement constituted a practical embargo on silver exports.

As a result of the practical embargo on silver exports, and

第三期，一九三五年四月一日至十月十四日：約自一九三五年二月十五日起，倫敦銀價之上漲更速，如第一圖所示中國銀元在倫敦市場之價格。中國財政當局或以白銀價格上漲之速率過甚，遂決定不再運用白銀出口稅及平衡稅之制度，以抵制國外白銀價格之上漲。四月一日之平衡稅爲百分之六‧七五，合計銀元出口稅總數爲百分之一四‧五。此項稅率之高度，不足以遏止白銀之出口，僅爲表面之實施。爲阻止白銀之外流，有各銀行之紳士協定，規定無論在任何環境下，不再運銀出口。此項協定約自四月一日起實行，連同其他禁止偸運白銀之實施，實無異爲對白銀出口之封鎖。

此項實際封鎖白銀出口及銀價上漲之結果，使

— 19 —

一九三四年四月一日後，倫敦〇‧七八三九盎司標準白銀之價格與中國貨幣外匯之價格相差較前益巨，因此白銀偷運出口之利潤亦增。於是促成中國有許多地方之銀元價格高出於紙幣之面值。

銀價與國外匯價，雖無固定之關係，但當局仍設法抬高匯價。凡貨幣貶值之謠言均加否認。故貨幣之價值亦被逼相當上漲，但不及銀價上漲之速耳。

第四期，一九三五年十月十五日至十一月二日：約在一九三五年十月十五日，企圖維持中國貨幣外匯價格愈高愈佳之政策，顯然放棄。對于中國貶低貨幣價值之投機者，亦不復加以阻止。故在一九三五年十月十五日至十一月二日之時期內，中國幣價下跌極速。

the rising price of silver, the discrepancy between the price of 0.7839 standard ounces of silver in London and the price of Chinese currency in the exchange market became much wider after April 1, 1935, than it had been previously. Profits in smuggling silver out of China increased correspondingly. In many places in China, silver dollars came to be worth more than their face value in terms of paper dollars.

Although there was no definite connection between the price of silver and the foreign exchange price of the paper Yuan, nevertheless an effort was made to hold up the exchange price of the Yuan. Any rumors of depreciation of the currency were vigorously denied, and to some degree the currency was forced to rise in value, although not nearly so rapidly as silver rose.

PHASE 4, OCTOBER 15-NOVEMBER 2, 1935: About the 15th of October, 1935, the policy of attempting to hold the Chinese Yuan as high as possible in foreign exchange was apparently abandoned. No resistance was offered to the speculative forces which operated to cause the Chinese dollar to fall in value, and it declined rapidly during the period October 15 to November 2, 1935.

第五期，一九三五年十一月三日至現在：一九三五年十一月三日(星期日)財政部宣佈中國紙幣之價格，將照該時之外匯價格穩定之。財政部並未聲言，將與何國貨幣發生穩定。但自一九三五年十一月三日至一九三五年五月三十一日，據上海中央銀行對倫敦之掛牌匯價，始終為一四‧五便士。至對其他重要各國之匯價，包括美，日在內，至少有二次之變動。

在此時期內，〇‧七八三九盎司標準之白銀價格，自十二月九日至二十一日，由二二‧九便士跌至一七‧〇便士。十二月二十一日後，銀價跌勢漸緩。惟銀價雖跌，中國紙幣之外匯價格，仍不受其影響。

一九三五年十一月三日之新貨幣政策並規定此後中央，中國，交通三銀行所發行之紙幣為法幣，

PHASE 5, NOVEMBER 3, 1935 TO DATE: On November 3, 1935, which was a Sunday, the Ministry of Finance announced that the paper Yuan would be stabilized in foreign exchange at the level prevailing at that time. The Ministry of Finance did not specify the currency with which the Yuan was to be kept stable, but during the period November 3, 1935 to May 31, 1936, the official exchange on London in Shanghai, as quoted by the Central Bank of China, remained at 14.5 pence, although the official rates for all other important currencies, including the yen and the United States dollar, changed at least twice.

During this period, the price of 0.7839 standard ounces of silver in London underwent a decline from 22.9 pence on December 9 to 17 pence on December 21. After December 21, the price of silver declined gradually. This decline in the price of silver had no effect on the price of the paper Yuan in foreign exchange.

The announcement of November 3, 1935, also specified that the paper Yuan notes issued by the Central Bank of China, the Bank of China, and the Bank of Communications would hence-

以代銀元爲支付債務，捐
稅等用。

一九三五年十一月三
日所宣佈之各項改革，爲
使中國脫離僅表面上維持
之銀本位，而代以外匯本
位。在此本位之下，紙幣
之價值，以其能在匯兌市
塲購得固定之外匯數量定
之。至此項外匯之安定，
由中央銀行運用其在國外
之外匯存欵及庫存現金現
銀以維持之。

二·白銀出口稅及中國紙
　幣在國際匯兌市場之貶
　值

當中國爲銀本位時，每
元紙幣可在上海兌換銀幣
，計含標準銀〇·八一六
六益司或純銀〇·七五五
三益司。在此情況之下，
中國貨幣在紐約或倫敦匯
兌市塲之價格，最少爲標

forth be legal tender, instead
of silver dollars, in paying all
debts, taxes, and other obliga-
tions.

The combined effect of the
various changes announced on
November 3, 1935, was to
remove the Chinese currency
from a silver standard which
was being maintained only
nominally, and to place it upon
a foreign exchange standard.
Under this standard, the value
of the paper currency is derived
from the fact that it will buy
a standard amount of foreign
money in the exchange market.
This foreign exchange stability,
in turn, is guaranteed by deposits of foreign currencies held
by the Central Bank in foreign
countries, and by silver and
gold possessed by the Central
Bank in China.

2. SILVER EXPORT FEES, AND
THE DEVALUATION OF THE
PAPER YUAN IN FOREIGN
EXCHANGE.

When the Yuan was on the
silver standard, each paper
Yuan could be redeemed in
Shanghai in terms of a silver
Yuan containing 0.8166 standard ounces or 0.7553 fine ounces
of silver. Under these conditions, Yuan credits, as purchased
on the exchange market in New
York or London, were worth at

準銀·八一六六益司或純銀〇·七五五三益司，減去運往倫敦或紐約之運貨。此項運費普通為百分之四。易言之，平時中國費幣在倫敦或紐約之貶值，最多不得超過百分之四。倘貶值超過百分之四，則倫敦購買中國匯兌者，將運白銀入口，藉以圖利。

自一九三四年八月一日至十月十四日，中國紙幣之外匯價格，未能隨銀價上漲之速率而上漲，故中國紙幣在倫敦及紐約之貶值，常在百分之四以上（第二圖及第一表）。大量白銀遂由中國流出。

自一九三四年十月十五日財政部征收白銀出口稅及平衡稅後，中國紙幣在倫敦之貶值遂漲。此項出口稅之徵收，實際上約實行至一九三五年四月一

least as much as the price of 0.8166 standard ounces or 0.7553 fine ounces of silver, less the cost of transporting such silver from Shanghai to New York or London. This cost was usually about 4 per cent. In other words, under normal conditions, the paper Yuan in London or New York was devaluated by not more than about 4 per cent. In case the devaluation was more than 4 per cent, purchasers of Chinese Yuan exchange in London would import the actual silver from China, thus making a profit.

During the period August 1 to October 14, 1934, the foreign exchange price of the paper Yuan failed to rise as fast as the price of silver rose, and the paper Yuan was frequently devalued in London and New York by more than 4 per cent (Figure 2 and Table 1). Large amounts of silver were shipped out of China.

On October 15, 1934, when the Ministry of Finance imposed the export tax and equalization fee on silver exports, the devaluation of the paper Yuan in London rose accordingly. These export levies had the practical effect of increasing the cost of ship-

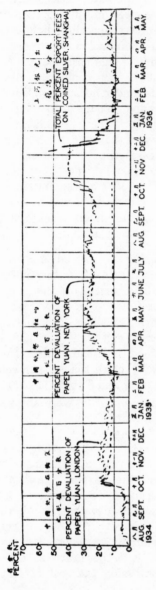

第二圖，白銀出口稅及中國紙幣之外匯價格貶值百分數，一九三四年八月一日至一九三六年五月三十一日（根據第一表B欄及E欄）

當中國貨幣在紐約及倫敦之匯價，低於銀元所含白銀之價格時，中國紙幣之外匯價格即行跌低。自一九三四年十月十五日起中國紙幣之外匯價格常被跌低，最高時為自一九三五年十一月三日至十二月九日期間約達百分之四十。

FIGURE 2. SILVER EXPORT FEES AND PERCENTAGE DEVALUATION OF THE PAPER YUAN IN FOREIGN EXCHANGE, AUGUST 1, 1934-MAY 31, 1936. (Based on Table 1, Columns B and E).

When Yuan credits can be purchased in the foreign exchange markets of New York and London for less than the price of the silver contained in a silver Yuan, then the paper Yuan is devaluated in foreign exchange. Since October 15, 1934, the Yuan has constantly been devaluated in foreign exchange. The maximum, about 40 percent devaluation, occurred between November 3 and December 9, 1935.

日。事實上無異增加白銀運赴倫敦或紐約之運費。當實行之時，中國紙幣在倫敦或紐約之貶值，應等於白銀出口稅加百分之四之運費。倘貶值百分數超過此水準時，則在倫敦及紐約匯兌市塲購中匯者，仍能自上海運銀入口，而獲利潤。自一九三四年十月十五日至一九三五年四月一日，中國紙幣之貶值倘不足吸引白銀之出口也。

自一九三五年四月一日至十月十五日，實際上白銀出口稅已不復實行，而代以其他禁銀出口之切實辦法，以防中國白銀之外流。當白銀價格上漲時，中國幣價亦隨之上漲，惟不若白銀之速。中國幣價上漲後，其貶值百分數之變動，在百分之二〇至三〇之間，此足顯示中國

ping silver from Shanghai to London or New York, and were actually in force until about April 1, 1935. While they were in force, the devaluation of the paper Yuan in London or New York would be expected to be about as much as the export fees plus 4 per cent. Whenever the percent devaluation rose above this level, buyers of paper Yuan on the London and New York foreign exchange markets could import the silver from Shanghai, pay the export taxes, and still have a profit. During most of the period October 15, 1934, to April 1, 1935, the devaluation of the paper Yuan was not sufficient to encourage silver exports from China.

During the period April 1 to October 15, 1935, the silver export fees ceased to be in force in actual practice. Other measures, constituting a practical embargo on silver exports, were substituted as means of keeping silver in China. As silver rose in price, the paper Yuan also rose, but not nearly so rapidly, and the percentage devaluation of the Yuan, after rising, fluctuated between 20 and 30 per cent. There was apparently some effort to prevent the foreign exchange

是時尚有防止中國紙幣匯價跌落過甚之實施也。

自一九三五年十月十五日至十一月二日，紙幣價格任其迅速跌落，其貶值亦漲至百分之四十。至十一月三日，紙幣之外匯價格，始告穩定。

因銀價尚屬穩定，故紙幣貶值在十二月九日前，始終約為百分之四十左右。在此時期內，白銀出口稅增至百分之六十五。但以新法幣不能兌現，故此項出口稅與外匯價格毫無關係。

銀行收入銀元，而以面值之法幣付出之。然以法幣在世界市場上僅值銀元六角，故銀元一元值法幣一‧六七元。因此白銀國有之實行，約可獲利百分之六十七。

自十二月九日後，世界白銀價格陡跌，但中國貨幣匯價則仍與十一月三

devaluation of the Yuan from becoming greater.

During the period October 15 to November 2, 1935, the Yuan was allowed to depreciate rapidly, and the devaluation of the Yuan rose to 40 per cent. On November 3, the Yuan was stabilized in foreign exchange.

Since the price of silver was about stable, the percentage devaluation remained at about 40 per cent until December 9. During this period, the silver export fees were raised to about 65 per cent, but since the new legal tender was not redeemable in silver, such fees had no connection with the foreign exchange price of the currency.

The banks were receiving silver dollars and paying out their face value in legal tender notes. Since the legal tender notes were worth in the world market just 60 cents in silver, the silver dollars were worth $1.67 in legal tender. The nationalization of silver was thus being executed at a profit of about 67 percent.

After December 9 the world price of silver fell precipitously, while the Yuan remained stable at the price set on November 3.

日者相同。至一九三六年一月二十二日，法幣之價格僅較銀元低百分之一○。自一月二十二日至五月三十一日，法幣價格亦僅常較銀元低百分之一○至一五。

當十二月間白銀跌價時，白銀出口稅亦隨之下降，約等於中國貨幣貶值之百分數。因法幣不能兌現，此項白銀出口稅遂與幣價無關，在事實上已無何作用。

白銀由上海運往倫敦之運費，與運往紐約者，大約相同，故中國紙幣之貶值在兩處常屬相同。惟一九三五年十二月及一九三六年一月之銀價下跌，爲一例外。其時銀價在倫敦之跌落較紐約爲速。故在此時期，中國紙幣在紐約之貶值亦較倫敦爲甚。美國不復在倫敦市場購銀及倫敦對于美國財政部之政策捉摸不定，或爲倫敦

By January 22, 1936, the legal tender currency was worth only 10 per cent less than the silver Yuan. During most of the time between January 22 and May 31, the legal tender Yuan was worth only 10 to 15 per cent less than the silver Yuan.

When silver fell in price in December, 1935, the silver export fees were reduced to a point about equal to the percent devaluation of the Yuan. Since the legal tender currency is not redeemable in silver, these fees have no effect upon its value, and may be disregarded in practice.

Since the cost of transportation of silver from Shanghai to London is about the same as the cost of shipment to New York, the percentage devaluation of the paper Yuan was usually the same in both markets. An exception occurred during the fall in the price of silver in December, 1935, and January 1936, when the price of silver fell more rapidly in London than in New York. For a time, the Yuan was thus devaluated more in New York than in London. The withdrawal of American silver purchases from the London market, and uncertainty in London regarding the future

銀價跌落較紐約為速之原
因也。

三. 中國貨幣價值及上海
　　批發物價之變遷

　　據斯答的斯脫週報之
指數，在一九三四年八月
至一九三六年四月之時期
內，英國之批發物價幾無
變動(第二表)。因英國物
價，以英磅計算，故一般
物價之穩定，即表示英國
貨幣價值在此時期之穩定
也。

　　英國貨幣價值，係由
供需之情況而決定。但斯
答的斯脫指數包括若干物
品之價格並不隨時受貨幣
供需變動之影響。若有一
指數僅包括許多交易於自
由市場之大量物品，則當
供需情形造成貨幣價值跌
落之時，此項指數，將立
即上漲。倘貨幣價值繼續
跌落,則斯答的斯脫指數，

policy of the United States Treasury, probably explain why the price of silver fell more rapidly in London than in New York.

3. CHANGES IN THE VALUE OF CHINESE CURRENCY, AND CHANGES IN WHOLESALE COMMODITY PRICES IN SHANGHAI.

During the period August 1934 to April 1936, wholesale prices in England, as reported by the Sauerbeck-Statist index, remained practically stable (Table 2). Since prices in England are paid in terms of the pound sterling, stability of average prices indicates stability in the real value of the British currency during this period.

The real value of the British currency is that which is determined by supply of and demand for it. Some of the commodity prices included in the Sauerbeck-Statist index are not immediately sensitive to changes in the supply of and demand for money. If there were available an index composed only of commodities that are traded in large volume on an unrestricted market, such an index would rise whenever the net result of supply and demand forces brought about a

亦將繼之上漲。倘貨幣價值上漲，則物價將反應下跌。故斯答的斯脫批發物價指數之穩定，表示在此時期內，英國貨幣價值無較大或較久之變遷，足影響一般物價，僅有微小或暫時上落，只能牽及較為靈敏之指數。所以本文採用英國貨幣為度量自一九三四年八月至一九三六年五月中國貨幣價值變遷之標準。

外匯市場對於供需之感覺，最為靈敏。兩國貨幣實在比值，在匯兌市場之變遷常較物價為早。

因英國貨幣之價值，事實上穩定不變，則自一

decrease in the value of money, provided that the index included a sufficient number of commodities. If this decrease in the value of money persisted, then the Sauerbeck - Statist index would later respond by rising. Corresponding reasoning would apply in the case of a rise in the value of money. Thus the stability of the Sauerbeck-Statist index of wholesale prices indicates that during the period in question there was no change in the value of British currency sufficiently great or lasting to affect this average of prices. There could have been only small or temporary fluctuations that would have affected a more sensitive average. The British currency has therefore been used as a measure in showing changes in the value of Chinese currency during the period August 1934 to May 1936.

The foreign exchange market is very sensitive to forces of supply and demand. Changes in the real comparative value of two currencies are usually registered sooner in the exchange market than in terms of average commodity prices.

The British currency remaining practically stable in real value, changes in its foreign

九三四年八月至一九三六
年五月上海對英匯價之變
更，必泰半由於中國貨幣
自身價值之變遷。其變遷
如第三圖所示。

　　第三圖並載有上海小
麥，麵粉，米，美棉，中
棉，棉紗，及豆油批發價
格每日平均之指數。此項
物品，在交易所自由買賣
，不受物價之統制，其平
均數堪爲測驗貨幣價值變
遷較靈敏之標準。但所包
括之物品僅有七種，且其
中有五種爲農產品。其平
均指數難免有時不受某種
物品暫時供需之影響，例
如旱災足減少此項全部或
大部物品之供給。平均物
價勢將因此上漲，與貨幣
價值固無關係也。

　　國定稅則委員會之上
海每月批發物價指數亦載
於第三圖。此指數係根據

exchange market price in
Shanghai during the period
August 1934 to May 1936 must
therefore be due mostly to
changes in the value of the
Chinese currency itself. These
changes are shown in figure 3.

In figure 3 is also shown an
average daily index of the
wholesale prices of wheat,
wheat flour, rice, American
cotton, Chinese cotton, cotton
yarn, and soybean oil in Shanghai. These commodities are
traded on the exchanges, where
they are not subject to price
control, and their average is
a fairly sensitive measure of
changes in the value of money.
However, since there are only
seven of them, and five of them
are agricultural commodities,
there may occasionally be times
when the supply and demand
forces operating on the individual commodities will not
average out completely. For
instance, in a severe drought,
that reduced the supply of all
or most of these commodities,
their average price might rise
for this reason, independent of
changes in the value of money.

In figure 3, the National
Tariff Commission's monthly
index of wholesale prices in
Shanghai is also shown. This

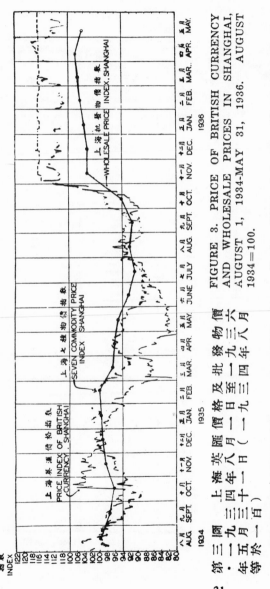

第三圖 上海英匯價格及批發物價
一九三四年八月一日至一九三六
年五月三十一日（一九三四年八月
等於一百）

中國物價指數在此貨幣劇變時期，追隨上海英匯價格之
趨勢而漲落。當中國貨幣匯值在匯兌市場跌落峙，中國物價亦上
漲反之則下跌。一九三五年九月至十月間，中國物價在中國貨
幣匯值價格跌落之前即行上漲，爲僅有之例外。七種物價指數均
爲交易所買賣實物品。較易於批發物價指數爲敏銳。
故較易與貨幣價值之變遷相調正。當發生變遷峙，批發物價指
數之反應，常較七種物價指數爲遲緩。

FIGURE 3. PRICE OF BRITISH CURRENCY
AND WHOLESALE PRICES IN SHANGHAI,
AUGUST 1, 1934-MAY 31, 1936. AUGUST
1934=100.

During this period of rapid currency change,
the Chinese commodity price indexes followed the
trend of the price of British currency in Shanghai
in rising and falling. When the value of the
Chinese currency fell in the exchange market, the
Chinese commodity prices rose and vice versa.
The only exception occurred during the period
September to October, 1935, when commodity
prices rose before the Chinese currency depreciated
in foreign exchange. The seven commodity price
index, composed of commodities traded on the
exchange, is more sensitive and is quicker to come
into adjustment with the value of the currency
than the National Tariff Commission wholesale
price index. When changes occurred, the wholesale price index therefore lagged behind the seven
commodity price index.

第二表: 英國物價，上海英匯價格及上海物價

TABLE 2.　COMMODITY PRICES IN ENGLAND, PRICE
OF BRITISH CURRENCY IN SHANGHAI AND
COMMODITY PRICES IN SHANGHAI

日　期 Date	A 英國斯答的斯脫批發物價指數(1) 一九三四年八月等於一百 Sauerbeck-Statist index of wholesale prices in England (1) August 1954=100	B 上海英匯指數(上海對倫敦電匯)(2) 一九三四年八月等於一百 Index of the price of British currency in Shanghai (T. T. on London in Shanghai) (2) August 1954=100	C 上海七種物價指數(3) 一九三四年八月等於一百 Index of seven commodity prices in Shanghai (5) August 1954=100	D 國定稅則委員會上海批發物價指數(1) 一九三四年八月等於一百 National Tariff Commission index of wholesale prices in Shanghai (1) August 1954=100
一九三四 1934 八月 August				
1	—	102.6	97.4	—
2	—	102.2	98.5	—
5	—	101.8	98.8	—
4	—	101.4	99.6	—
5	—	—	—	—
6	—	—	104.5	—
7	—	101.8	105.4	—
8	—	100.9	105.1	—
9	—	99.9	105.8	—
10	—	99.2	105.6	—
11	—	99.5	102.6	—
12	—	—	101.2	—
15	—	99.5	—	—
14	—	99.5	99.7	—
13	100.0	99.5	98.7	100.0
16	—	—	98.1	—
17	—	99.5	98.4	—
18	—	100.2	98.5	—
19	—	—	99.8	—
20	—	100.2	99.1	—
21	—	100.2	—	—
22	—	97.2	100.0	—
25	—	99.2	97.9	—
24	—	99.2	98.7	—
25	—	99.5	98.6	—
26	—	—	98.5	—
27	—	99.2	98.5	—
28	—	99.2	97.8	—
29	—	99.9	—	—
50	—	99.5	98.7	—
51	—	98.7	96.5	—
九月 September				
1	—	97.0	95.7	—
2	—	—	—	—
5	—	97.7	95.8	—
4	—	97.7	94.2	—
5	—	98.0	94.0	—
6	—	98.0	94.2	—
7	—	97.5	94.5	—
8	—	97.5	94.0	—
9	—	—	—	—
10	—	98.7	95.8	—
11	—	98.4	95.5	—
12	—	98.4	95.7	—
15	—	98.4	95.8	—
14	—	98.4	95.7	—

(1) (2) 及 (3) 見四十一頁　　　　　　(1) (2) and (3) see page 41

	A	B	C	D
一九三四 1934				
九月 September				
15	98.4	98.4	95.5	97.5
16	—	98.4	—	—
17	—	98.4	95.5	—
18	—	98.0	95.1	—
19	—	97.7	92.1	—
20	—	97.5	91.1	—
21	—	97.0	91.8	—
22	—	97.0	92.2	—
23	—	—	—	—
24	—	—	92.1	—
25	—	96.6	92.2	—
26	—	95.9	91.9	—
27	—	95.6	92.1	—
28	—	94.9	91.4	—
29	—	94.2	90.5	—
30	—	—	—	—
十月 October				
1	—	95.2	89.7	—
2	—	94.2	89.0	—
3	—	94.5	89.0	—
4	—	95.9	89.0	—
5	—	95.2	88.9	—
6	—	95.2	88.8	—
7	—	—	—	—
8	—	95.2	88.9	—
9	—	95.9	88.5	—
10	—	—	—	—
11	—	91.9	88.4	—
12	—	90.4	88.5	—
13	—	91.6	89.0	—
14	—	—	—	96.5
15	97.9	95.9	90.7	—
16	—	95.2	90.5	—
17	—	96.5	92.1	—
18	—	101.4	96.1	—
19	—	106.2	94.5	—
20	—	101.8	95.1	—
21	—	—	—	—
22	—	104.1	95.7	—
23	—	107.1	95.2	—
24	—	105.4	92.7	—
25	—	105.4	92.9	—
26	—	105.8	95.5	—
27	—	105.8	95.6	—
28	—	—	—	—
29	—	105.8	94.1	—
30	—	105.8	94.0	—
31	—	105.0	95.9	—
十一月 November				
1	—	104.6	95.6	—
2	—	105.8	95.6	—
3	—	105.8	95.6	—
4	—	—	—	—
5	—	104.2	95.2	—
6	—	104.6	96.2	—
7	—	104.9	96.6	—
8	—	104.9	96.2	—
9	—	105.5	95.7	—
10	—	102.2	96.2	—
11	—	—	—	—
12	—	101.8	96.5	—
13	—	101.0	96.0	—
14	—	105.5	96.2	—
15	99.1	105.0	96.5	98.5
16	—	102.2	96.5	—
17	—	102.2	95.7	—
18	—	—	—	—
19	—	105.0	97.1	—
20	—	105.0	96.0	—
21	—	105.8	96.8	—
22	—	105.8	96.4	—
23	—	105.8	97.6	—
24	—	104.6	98.7	—
25	—	—	—	—
26	—	105.5	99.5	—

	A	B	C	D
一九三四 1934				
十一月 November				
27	—	102.6	98.9	—
28	—	102.2	99.0	—
29	—	102.2	99.4	—
50	—	102.2	100.0	—
十二月 December				
1	—	102.2	100.5	—
2	—	—	—	—
5	—	101.8	100.2	—
4	—	101.4	99.9	—
5	—	101.4	100.1	—
6	—	101.0	101.4	—
7	—	99.5	100.4	—
8	—	100.5	100.7	—
9	—	—	—	—
10	—	99.9	101.5	—
11	—	99.1	101.1	—
12	—	98.4	100.2	—
15	—	98.4	99.7	—
14	—	98.7	99.5	—
15	99.5	98.7	99.8	99.2
16	—	99.1	—	—
17	—	99.9	100.0	—
18	—	101.4	100.0	—
19	—	101.4	100.1	—
20	—	101.0	99.7	—
21	—	101.8	100.4	—
22	—	—	100.2	—
25	—	—	—	—
24	—	100.6	101.1	—
25	—	—	101.0	—
26	—	—	101.2	—
27	—	101.4	101.2	—
28	—	99.5	101.0	—
29	—	98.7	101.2	—
50	—	—	—	—
51	—	98.4	—	—
一九三五 1935				
一月 January				
1	—	—	—	—
2	—	—	—	—
5	—	—	—	—
4	—	98.7	102.5	—
5	—	98.0	101.7	—
6	—	—	—	—
7	—	98.4	102.5	—
8	—	99.1	102.7	—
9	—	98.7	101.9	—
10	—	98.0	102.0	—
11	—	97.7	101.4	—
12	—	98.0	101.5	—
15	—	—	—	—
14	—	97.5	100.6	—
15	100.2	97.7	100.8	99.6
16	—	97.7	100.4	—
17	—	97.5	100.4	—
18	—	97.5	100.0	—
19	—	97.0	100.9	—
20	—	—	—	—
21	—	97.0	102.5	—
22	—	96.6	102.5	—
25	—	95.9	102.5	—
24	—	95.6	102.7	—
25	—	95.9	105.2	—
26	—	95.2	105.5	—
27	—	—	—	—
28	—	95.9	—	—
29	—	95.6	—	—
50	—	95.9	—	—
51	—	94.6	—	—
二月 February				
1	—	95.2	—	—
2	—	97.0	—	—

	A	B	C	D
一九三五 1935				
二月 February				
5	—	—	—	—
4	—	—	—	—
5	—	—	—	—
6	—	96.5	—	—
7	—	95.9	—	—
8	—	95.9	101.4	—
9	—	95.9	101.5	—
10	—	—	—	—
11	—	95.9	102.2	—
12	—	95.2	101.8	—
15	—	95.6	101.5	—
14	—	95.2	101.7	—
15	100.0	95.2	101.9	100.1
16	—	92.6	101.6	—
17	—	—	—	—
18	—	92.0	100.6	—
19	—	92.6	100.5	—
20	—	92.0	99.9	—
21	—	92.0	100.1	—
22	—	91.5	99.5	—
25	—	91.5	99.0	—
24	—	—	—	—
25	—	89.5	99.4	—
26	—	88.6	98.5	—
27	—	88.6	98.6	—
28	—	88.0	98.4	—
三月 March				
1	—	86.9	97.7	—
2	—	84.9	95.6	—
5	—	—	—	—
4	—	81.5	94.5	—
5	—	85.5	95.6	—
6	—	88.5	96.5	—
7	—	86.9	96.0	—
8	—	86.6	96.2	—
9	—	87.7	96.5	—
10	—	—	—	—
11	—	86.9	94.6	—
12	—	86.6	94.5	—
15	—	87.2	94.5	—
14	—	86.0	95.9	—
15	99.4	86.5	95.7	96.6
16	—	86.6	95.8	—
17	—	—	—	—
18	—	86.9	95.1	—
19	—	86.5	92.1	—
20	—	87.7	92.6	—
21	—	87.2	92.7	—
22	—	87.7	92.1	—
25	—	87.4	95.1	—
24	—	—	—	—
25	—	87.2	92.9	—
26	—	86.5	95.0	—
27	—	86.6	91.7	—
28	—	87.7	95.8	—
29	—	89.5	94.0	—
50	—	89.8	95.7	—
四月 April				
1	—	89.8	95.1	—
2	—	91.5	95.7	—
5	—	90.1	95.5	—
4	—	88.9	95.5	—
5	—	89.3	95.2	—
6	—	89.8	95.5	—
7	—	—	—	—
8	—	89.8	95.6	—
9	—	89.8	96.9	—
10	—	89.5	97.1	—
11	—	89.2	97.1	—
12	—	88.6	97.4	—
15	—	87.7	97.2	—
14	—	—	—	—
15	100.8	86.6	96.5	1.69
16	—	85.2	95.7	—
17	—	85.5	95.9	—

	A	B	C	D
一九三五 1935				
四月 April				
18	—	86.0	96.4	—
19	—	--	97.5	—
20	—	--	97.0	—
21	—	—	—	—
22	—		97.0	—
23	—	85.3	96.6	—
24	—	84.4	96.1	—
25	—	84.4	95.4	—
26	—	85.1	95.2	—
27	—	80.5	94.9	—
28	—	—	—	—
29	—	82.5	95.9	—
50	—	81.6	94.6	—
五月 May				
1	—	81.8	94.4	—
2	—	81.8	94.2	—
5	—	82.6	94.2	—
4	—	82.5	94.1	—
5	—	—	—	—
6	—	—	94.5	—
7	—	82.5	94.6	—
8	—	82.5	94.5	—
9	—	85.1	94.7	—
10	—	82.8	94.8	—
11	—	81.8	95.5	—
12	—	—	—	—
13	—	82.5	94.6	—
14	—	82.8	94.7	—
15	103.2	82.5	94.6	95.2
16	—	81.8	94.4	—
17	—	82.5	95.9	—
18	—	82.0	95.6	—
19	—	—	—	—
20	—	82.5	95.2	—
21	—	82.5	95.2	—
22	—	85.1	95.2	—
25	—	82.8	95.6	—
24	—	82.6	95.4	—
25	—	82.8	95.2	—
26	—	—	—	—
27	—	82.8	95.1	—
28	—	82.1	92.7	—
29	—	82.8	52.5	—
50	—	82.8	91.8	—
51	—	82.5	91.0	—
六月 June				
1	—	81.8	90.5	—
2	—	—	—	—
5	—	82.8	90.0	—
4	—	85.5	89.5	—
5	—	85.0	89.0	—
6	—	84.4	89.2	—
7	—	85.5	89.0	—
8	—	84.9	88.0	—
9	—	—	—	—
10	—	—	88.7	—
11	—	85.8	89.5	—
12	—	84.4	89.4	—
15	—	84.1	88.6	—
14	—	84.4	89.0	—
15	100.4	84.4	89.5	92.8
16	—	—	—	—
17	—	84.1	87.5	—
18	—	84.4	88.9	—
19	—	84.4	88.1	—
20	—	84.4	88.2	—
21	—	84.4	89.1	—
22	—	84.9	89.5	—
25	—	—	—	—
24	—	85.5	89.1	—
25	—	85.5	88.5	—
26	—	87.7	89.1	—
27	—	86.5	89.5	—
28	—	87.1	89.1	—
29	—	87.1	89.4	—

	A	B	C	D
一九三五 1935				
七月 July				
1	—	—	89.5	—
2	—	—	89.5	—
3	—	87.1	88.7	—
4	—	87.1	89.5	—
5	—	87.1	89.1	—
6	—	87.1	89.1	—
7	—	—	—	—
8	—	87.7	89.1	—
9	—	88.5	88.9	—
10	—	88.9	89.6	—
11	—	87.7	89.0	—
12	—	—	88.7	—
13	—	88.5	88.5	—
14	—	—	—	—
15	101.1	88.5	88.4	90.1
16	—	88.5	89.4	—
17	—	88.9	89.4	—
18	—	88.9	89.8	—
19	—	88.9	89.8	—
20	—	88.9	90.4	—
21	—	—	—	—
22	—	88.9	90.4	—
23	—	88.9	90.4	—
24	—	88.9	91.0	—
25	—	88.9	91.5	—
26	—	88.9	91.1	—
27	—	90.1	91.8	—
28	—	—	—	—
29	—	91.0	94.5	—
30	—	92.6	95.0	—
31	—	92.6	94.6	—
八月 August				
1	—	91.6	95.0	—
2	—	91.9	95.9	—
3	—	95.9	94.0	—
4	—	—	—	—
5	—	—	95.9	—
6	—	95.2	94.2	—
7	—	92.6	95.2	—
8	—	95.9	95.4	—
9	—	95.9	95.6	—
10	—	95.9	95.4	—
11	—	—	—	—
12	—	95.9	95.6	—
13	—	95.9	95.4	—
14	—	95.9	95.5	—
15	100.8	96.6	94.2	92.1
16	—	95.2	95.8	—
17	—	94.2	94.0	—
18	—	—	—	—
19	—	95.2	94.1	—
20	—	95.2	95.6	—
21	—	95.2	95.6	—
22	—	94.5	95.1	—
23	—	94.5	92.2	—
24	—	95.2	91.5	—
25	—	—	—	—
26	—	95.2	91.4	—
27	—	95.2	90.9	—
28	—	95.2	90.4	—
29	—	95.9	90.5	—
30	—	—	89.9	—
31	—	—	89.8	—
九月 September				
1	—	—	—	—
2	—	95.9	89.9	—
3	—	95.5	89.0	—
4	—	95.5	89.4	—
5	—	95.5	90.0	—
6	—	95.9	90.4	—
7	—	95.2	89.9	—
8	—	—	—	—
9	—	9.29	90.1	—

一九三五 1935	A	B	C	D
九月 September				
10	—	95.2	89.5	—
11	—	95.2	89.8	—
12	—	—	—	—
13	—	91.9	90.4	—
14	—	92.5	90.6	—
15	102.0	—	—	91.5
16	—	90.7	90.2	—
17	—	—	90.1	—
18	—	90.1	90.9	—
19	—	89.5	92.7	—
20	—	89.5	95.1	—
21	—	89.8	95.5	—
22	—	—	—	—
23	—	91.5	95.4	—
24	—	91.5	95.8	—
25	—	91.9	94.4	—
26	—	91.9	94.7	—
27	—	91.5	95.1	—
28	—	89.8	95.9	—
29	—	—	—	—
30	—	—	94.2	—
十月 October				
1	—	89.5	94.6	—
2	—	89.5	95.4	—
3	—	89.8	96.7	—
4	—	89.8	98.0	—
5	—	91.0	98.8	—
6	—	—	—	—
7	—	90.7	99.7	—
8	—	91.0	99.4	—
9	—	91.9	98.7	—
10	—	—	99.2	—
11	—	91.9	99.6	—
12	—	91.9	100.1	—
13	—	—	—	—
14	—	91.9	99.5	—
15	102.9	92.6	99.8	94.5
16	—	92.9	100.0	—
17	—	95.2	99.0	—
18	—	95.2	99.5	—
19	—	95.2	100.5	—
20	—	—	—	—
21	—	95.2	99.9	—
22	—	95.2	99.9	—
23	—	99.5	101.4	—
24	—	102.6	101.6	—
25	—	104.2	102.9	—
26	—	—	105.5	—
27	—	—	—	—
28	—	102.6	107.0	—
29	—	105.5	106.6	—
30	—	108.4	109.5	—
31	—	110.7	110.6	—
十一月 November				
1	—	112.0	111.0	—
2	—	112.0	115.5	—
3	—	—	—	—
4	—	115.0	116.5	—
5	—	115.0	115.5	—
6	—	115.0	112.1	—
7	—	115.0	111.6	—
8	—	115.0	111.6	—
9	—	115.0	111.7	—
10	—	—	—	—
11	—	115.0	112.5	—
12	—	115.9	112.0	—
13	—	115.9	111.9	—
14	—	115.9	111.6	—
15	105.5	115.9	111.8	—
16	—	115.9	112.4	105.5
17	—	—	—	—
18	—	115.9	112.7	—
19	—	115.9	115.2	—
20	—	115.9	115.7	—
21	—	115.9	114.5	—

	A	B	C	D
一九三五 1935				
十一月 November				
22	—	115.9	115.6	—
23	—	115.9	114.9	—
24	—	—	—	—
25	—	115.4	114.6	—
26	—	115.9	115.8	—
27	—	115.4	115.8	—
28	—	115.4	115.8	—
29	—	115.4	114.0	—
30	—	115.4	115.8	—
十二月 December				
1	—	115.4	115.4	—
2	—	—	115.8	—
3	—	115.4	114.4	—
4	—	115.4	115.6	—
5	—	115.4	115.2	—
6	—	115.4	115.1	—
7	—	—	—	—
8	—	115.4	112.7	—
9	—	115.4	112.8	—
10	—	115.4	112.8	—
11	—	116.5	111.9	—
12	—	115.9	111.5	—
13	—	115.9	115.7	—
14	—	—	—	—
15	104.0	115.9	115.0	105.5
16	—	115.9	112.2	—
17	—	115.9	112.4	—
18	—	115.9	112.1	—
19	—	115.9	112.0	—
20	—	115.9	111.9	—
21	—	—	—	—
22	—	115.9	112.2	—
23	—	115.9	112.9	—
24	—	—	—	—
25	—	—	—	—
26	—	115.9	—	—
27	—	115.9	—	—
28	—	—	—	—
29	—	115.9	—	—
30	—	115.9	—	—
31	—	—	—	—
一九三六 1936				
一月 January				
1	—	—	—	—
2	—	—	—	—
3	—	—	—	—
4	—	115.9	—	—
5	—	—	—	—
6	—	115.9	115.2	—
7	—	115.9	115.2	—
8	—	115.4	115.4	—
9	—	115.4	115.6	—
10	—	115.4	111.7	—
11	—	115.4	111.8	—
12	—	—	—	—
13	—	115.4	112.1	—
14	—	115.4	112.2	—
15	104.0	115.4	112.2	104.5
16	—	115.4	—	—
17	—	115.4	—	—
18	—	115.9	—	—
19	—	—	—	—
20	—	115.9	—	—
21	—	115.9	—	—
22	—	115.9	—	—
23	—	115.9	—	—
24	—	—	—	—
25	—	—	—	—
26	—	—	—	—
27	—	—	—	—
28	—	115.4	—	—
29	—	115.9	—	—
30	—	115.9	—	—
31	—	115.9	—	—

	A	B	C	D
一九三六 1936				
二月 February				
1	—	115.9	—	—
2	—	—	115.0	—
3	—	115.9	—	—
4	—	115.9	115.5	—
5	—	115.9	115.2	—
6	—	115.9	111.8	—
7	—	115.9	111.7	—
8	—	115.9	111.7	—
9	—	—	111.5	—
10	—	115.9	—	—
11	—	115.9	111.9	—
12	—	115.9	111.5	—
13	—	115.9	110.9	—
14	—	115.9	111.4	—
15	104.0	115.9	111.8	105.6
16	—	—	111.5	—
17	—	115.9	—	—
18	—	115.9	111.0	—
19	—	115.7	111.4	—
20	—	115.7	111.5	—
21	—	115.7	111.5	—
22	—	115.7	112.1	—
23	—	—	112.5	—
24	—	115.7	—	—
25	—	115.4	112.6	—
26	—	115.4	—	—
27	—	115.4	—	—
28	—	115.4	—	—
29	—	115.4	—	—
三月 March				
1	—	—	115.8	—
2	—	115.4	114.5	—
3	—	115.4	114.1	—
4	—	115.9	111.8	—
5	—	115.9	112.0	—
6	—	115.9	115.5	—
7	—	115.9	—	—
8	—	—	116.5	—
9	—	115.9	117.1	—
10	—	115.9	117.5	—
11	—	115.9	116.6	—
12	—	—	115.5	—
13	—	115.9	118.7	—
14	—	115.4	—	—
15	—	—	119.8	—
16	105.6	—	—	160.6
17	—	115.4	—	—
18	—	115.4	—	—
19	—	115.4	—	—
20	—	115.4	—	—
21	—	115.4	—	—
22	—	—	—	—
23	—	115.4	118.2	—
24	—	115.4	—	—
25	—	115.4	—	—
26	—	115.4	—	—
27	—	115.4	—	—
28	—	115.4	—	—
29	—	—	—	—
30	—	115.4	—	—
31	—	115.4	—	—
四月 April				
1	—	115.4	—	—
2	—	115.4	116.5	—
3	—	115.4	116.0	—
4	—	115.4	—	—
5	—	—	—	—
6	—	115.4	—	—
7	—	115.4	116.7	—
8	—	115.4	—	—
9	—	115.4	—	—
10	—	—	—	—

	A	B	C	D
一九三六 1936				
四月 April				
11	—	—	—	—
12	—	—	—	—
13	—	—	—	—
14	—	115.4	118.8	—
15	105.0	115.4	118.0	107.5
16	—	115.4	118.5	—
17	—	115.4	118.7	—
18	—	115.4	119.5	—
19	—	—	—	—
20	—	115.4	118.5	—
21	—	115.4	118.8	—
22	—	115.4	119.0	—
23	—	115.4	118.7	—
24	—	115.4	119.4	—
25	—	115.4	119.7	—
26	—	—	—	—
27	—	115.4	119.6	—
28	—	115.4	119.4	—
29	—	115.4	120.4	—
30	—	115.4	—	—
五月 May				
1	—	115.4	—	—
2	—	115.4	117.2	—
3	—	—	—	—
4	—	115.4	118.0	—
5	—	—	116.2	—
6	—	115.7	115.5	—
7	—	115.4	115.1	—
8	—	116.0	115.4	—
9	—	116.0	114.4	—
10	—	—	—	—
11	—	116.0	114.5	—
12	—	116.0	115.9	—
13	—	116.0	115.5	—
14	—	116.0	114.9	—
15	—	116.0	115.2	106.0
16	—	116.0	114.5	—
17	—	—	—	—
18	—	116.0	115.1	—
19	—	116.0	114.1	—
20	—	116.0	115.5	—
21	—	116.0	112.9	—
22	—	116.0	111.6	—
23	—	116.0	111.0	—
24	—	—	—	—
25	—	116.0	112.1	—
26	—	116.0	111.8	—
27	—	116.0	112.1	—
28	—	116.0	112.2	—
29	—	116.0	112.8	—
30	—	116.0	115.1	—
31	—	116.0	114.2	—

一. 逐月指數

(1) Monthly Index

二. 根據上海字林西報所載上海匯豐銀行掛牌

(2) This index is based on Quotations of the Hongkong and Shanghai Bank, Shanghai, as published in the North China Daily News.

三. 下列七種物品之簡單平均幾何指數： 一九三四年八月 = 100

密�‍脫林姜棉 （上海字林西報）
近期小麥 （申報）
近期中棉 （申報）
近期標紗 （申報）
近期豆油 （申報）
近期麵粉 （申報）
南市常州白粳米（申報）

(3) Simple geometric average of price indexes for following seven commodities, daily average for August, 1934 = 100.
Cotton, mid-American (from North China Daily News); wheat, nearest future (From Shun Pao); Chinese Cotton, nearest future (from Shun Pao); cotton yarn, nearest future (from Shun Pao); soybean oil, nearest future (from Shun Pao); wheat flour, nearest future (from Shun Pao); rice, Changchow, South Market (from Shun Pao).

每月十五日之價格編成。
因其中包括若干製造品及
完全或一部份受市場統制
之物品，故此指數對於貨
幣價值變遷之反應，不若
七種物價指數為靈敏。

　　自一九三四年八月一
日至十月十四日，英匯價
格之趨勢下降，表示中國
貨幣價值之上漲（第三圖）
。同時七種物價指數之下
跌更甚。國定稅則委員會
物價指數之下跌，果如所
料，較七種物價指數為緩
。

　　自一九三四年十月十
五日征收白銀出口稅後，
中國貨幣價值驟跌，可以
上海英匯價格猛漲證之。
七種物價指數之上漲亦速
，至十二月一日，已與貨
幣價值相調正。此項調正
之迅速，一部份由於其時
中國貨幣價值已復回漲，

index is computed for prices
recorded on the fifteenth of
each month. Since it contains
the prices of some manu-
factured commodities, and of
some commodities with re-
stricted or partially controlled
markets, this index cannot be
expected to be as sensitive as
the seven commodity index to
changes in the value of money.

. From August 1 to October
14, 1934, the trend in the price
of British currency was downward, indicating a rise in the
value of Chinese currency
(Figure 3). This rise was also
registered by an even greater
fall in the seven commodity
price index. The Tariff Commission index, as would be
expected, declined less rapidly
than did the seven commodity
index.

When the silver export fees
were applied on October 15,
1934, the value of the Yuan
suddenly fell, as shown by the
sharp rise in the price of
British currency in the Shanghai exchange market. The
seven-commodity price index
also rose rapidly, and by
December first was in adjustment with the value of the
Yuan. This adjustment came
quickly, partly because the

而使英匯跌落。自八月至十月，一般批發物價，無如此劇烈之跌落，故至十二月十五日僅須稍漲已與貨幣價值相調正矣。

至一九三五年四月底，中國貨幣之價值繼續上漲，促成英匯之跌落。七種物價指數亦繼續上漲至二月，始漸隨下降，但不若英匯下降之甚。一般批發物價，有相同之趨勢，但波動極少。自一九三五年二月一日至六月一日，七種物價水準較英匯為高之原因，或由於一九三四年之旱災，農產收穫減少，而冬季新農產，須至六七月間，方大量上市也。

中國貨幣價值之上漲，約至四月三十日始告停止。自此以後，英匯上漲，即表示中國幣值之逐漸

value of the Yuan had risen again meanwhile, bringing down the price of British currency. General wholesale prices had not fallen so much, during the period August to October, and so had to rise little to be in line with the value of money about December 15.

The value of the Yuan continued to rise, causing a fall in the price of British currency, until the last of April, 1935. The seven-commodity index continued to rise until February, and then fell in line with but considerably behind the price of British currency. General commodity prices followed a similar trend, with fewer fluctuations. The high level of the seven-commodity index compared to the price of British currency from February 1 to June 1, 1935, may be attributed to the scarcity of crop supples in China caused by the disastrous drought of 1934. New winter crop supplies do not come on the market in much volume until June and July.

The rise in the value of the Chinese Yuan was checked about April 30, and henceforth there was a gradual decline, as shown by the rise in the price

下跌。當七月十五日，英
匯上漲至七種物價尚未跌
落之水準時，七種物價始
開始上漲。一般物價，雖
亦上漲，但較迂緩。

至一九三五年九月，
七種物價指數之上漲，較
英匯之上漲為先，蓋英匯
約至十月一日始上漲也，
此或由於希冀中國貨幣貶
值之投機。當十月間英匯
猛漲，即中國貨幣價值跌
落之時，七種物價指數幾
並行上漲。及外匯穩定，
亦即停止上漲。此項變化
之來勢，既驟且烈，故非
國定稅則委員會較不靈敏
之物價指數所能完全並立
即隨從變化者。該指數自
十一月起停止猛烈上漲，
還低於英匯及七種物價指
數。

自一九三五年十一月
後，七種物價指數，仍低
於英匯價格。自一九三六

of British currency. When the
rise in British currency had
reached the level from which
the seven-commodity index had
not yet fallen, about July 15, the
seven-commodity index began
to rise. General commodity
prices also responded slightly.

In September 1935, the
seven-commodity price index
began to rise even before the
rise in the price of British
currency, which began about
October first. This relationship
was probably due to speculation
based on the expectation of the
devaluation of the Yuan. While
this devaluation was going on,
as shown by the rapid rise in
the price of British currency in
October, the seven-commodity
index rose almost in line, and
ceased to rise as soon as the
currency was stabilized in
foreign exchange. This fluctuation was too sudden and violent
to be followed completely and
immediately by the less sensitive Tariff Commission index,
which stopped rising rapidly in
November, while still considerably below the price of British
currency and the seven-commodity index.

After November 1935, the
seven-commodity index remained below the price of British
currency until early in March

年三月初至五月初始較英匯稍高。嗣後乃逐漸下降，與英匯之關係，恢復原狀。將來如英匯穩定，而中國幣值亦始終為十四·五便士，則七種物價指數與英匯指數相差之百分數當極微也。

至一九三六年四月十五日，國定稅則委員會之批發物價指數，逐漸上漲，有漸漸與英匯上漲，即中幣貶值之程度相調正之趨勢。如中國幣值不變，則國定稅則委員會之指數，或將繼續上漲，迄於達到高出一九三四年八月指數百分之十五，其指數約為一一五，如以一九二六年物價為一〇〇。此物價較一九三二年稍高，約與一九三〇年相同，但較一九三一年之高價為低。

下數期當繼續登載上海物價與內地物價之密切

1936. From early in March until early in May 1936, it was a little higher, and then returned to a normal relationship to the price of British currency. In future, if the value of the British currency remains stable, and if the Yuan continues at 14.5 pence, the seven-commodity index can be expected to fluctuate within a few percent above and below the index of the price of British currency.

Until April 15, 1936, the Tariff Commission's general wholesale price index gradually rose, slowly approaching an adjustment with the decline in the value of money as registered in the rise of the price of British money. If the Yuan does not again change in value, the National Tariff Commission index will probably continue to rise until it reaches a level about 15 percent above that of August 1934, which is also about 115 when 1926 prices are considered 100. This is a little higher than the prices that prevailed in 1932, about equal to those of 1930, but less than the high prices of 1931.

In later publications, evidence of the close connection between commodity prices in Shanghai

關係。據現所有之材料，一九三四年十月十五日之貨幣政策，乃救濟中國物價之跌落。而一九三五年十一月之政策，促成物價之上漲，及以後之穩定。物價穩定，自屬農商業發達之必要條件也。

四·廣東毫洋之變遷

廣東幣制與中國其他各處不同。毫洋一元計爲二角銀幣五枚，含純銀一八·八一公分[1]。而上海銀元含純銀二三·四九三四四八公分，兩相比較，理論上之平價應爲上海銀元八〇一元換毫洋一，〇〇〇元。如再將運輸及鎔銀費用算入，上海對廣州之匯價變動，平時當在八〇一元上下。廣州對上海之匯價，亦應與在上海匯價之倒數，大約相同。即毫

(1) 廣東統計局;金融物價月刊第一期十九頁，一九三六年一月出版

and in interior China will be given. Available facts indicate that the currency measures of October 15, 1934 provided for temporary relief from the fall of commodity prices in China, while the measures of October and November 1935 provided for their rise and subsequent stabilization. Stable prices are necessary for prosperity in agriculture and industry.

4. CURRENCY CHANGES IN CANTON.

Canton currency is different from currencies in other parts of China. A Canton dollar consists of five twenty-cent coins, and contains 18.81 grams of fine silver[1]. Compared with the Shanghai dollar, containing 23.493448 grams of fine silver, the theoretical parity is 801 Shanghai dollars against 1,000 Canton dollars. With due regard to the transport charges and cost of melting silver the exchange rate in Shanghai for 1000 Canton dollars should normally fluctuate somewhat above or below 801 Shanghai dollars. In Canton, the exchange rate on Shanghai should be about the same as the reciprocal of the rate in Shang-

(1) Kwangtung Provincial Statistical Bureau Money and Price. No. 1 January 1936 Page 19.

洋一，二四九元左右，換上海銀元一，〇〇〇元。

但一九三四年八月後，以上海貨幣計算之毫洋價值上漲。至一九三五年五月二日，其匯價漲至上海幣一，〇三五元換毫洋一，〇〇〇元（第四圖）。在此時間，世界銀價之上漲極烈。爲防止現銀之外流，中國於一九三四年十月十五日開始徵收白銀出口稅。但廣東未曾嚴格執行此項辦法，故白銀偷運出口，廣州較上海爲易，致造成廣州白銀之價值高於上海。上海紙幣於事實上不能在廣州依照票面兌換白銀，因自上海運銀至廣州有限制也。上述各端，顯爲此時期廣東毫洋以滬幣計算價格上漲之原因。

自一九三四年五月後，上海對廣州之匯率逐漸下降，至十月二日達九一

hai, or somewhat below or above 1249 Canton dollars per 1000 Shanghai dollars.

After August 1934, however, Canton currency increased in value in terms of the Shanghai dollar, and in Shanghai on May 2, 1935, the exchange rate on Canton reached 1035 Shanghai dollars per 1000 Canton dollars (Figure 4). During this period the world silver price increased rapidly. In order to check the exportation of silver from China, silver export fees were levied beginning on October 15, 1934. This measure was not strictly enforced in Canton, and silver could be more easily smuggled out than in Shanghai, causing the value of silver in Canton to become higher than in Shanghai. The Shanghai paper currency was not, in practice, redeemable in silver at face value in Canton, since there were restrictions on the shipment of silver from Shanghai to Canton. These were apparently the chief reasons for the increasing price of Canton currency in terms of Shanghai paper money during this period.

After May, 1935, the exchange rate of Shanghai on Canton fell gradually, until it

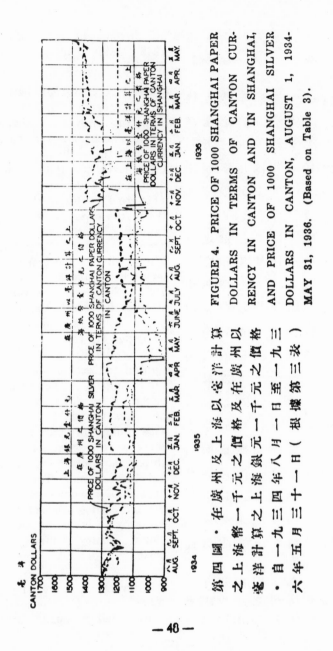

FIGURE 4. PRICE OF 1000 SHANGHAI PAPER DOLLARS IN TERMS OF CANTON CURRENCY IN CANTON AND IN SHANGHAI, AND PRICE OF 1000 SHANGHAI SILVER DOLLARS IN CANTON, AUGUST 1, 1934-MAY 31, 1936. (Based on Table 3).

第四圖・在廣州以毫洋計算之上海幣一千元之價格及在廣州以毫洋計算之上海銀元一千元之價格・自一九三四年八月一日至一九三六年五月三十一日（根據第三表）

Before October 15, 1934 the price of 1000 Shanghai paper dollars in terms of Canton currency in Canton and in Shanghai, and of 1000 Shanghai silver dollars were about the same. After the introduction of the silver export fees, there was no longer much relationship between the price of Shanghai silver dollars in Canton, and the price of Shanghai paper dollars in terms of Canton currency in Canton and in Shanghai. The value of Shanghai paper currency depreciated in terms of Canton currency. After the new monetary reform in November, 1935, the value of Canton currency fell suddenly and then continued to fall less rapidly. After February 12, 1936, the exchange rate on Canton in Shanghai had no relation to the price of Shanghai currency in Canton, and was apparently only a nominal rate. After February the Canton currency maintained a fixed relation to silver in Canton, according to Canton newspaper reports.

在一九三四年十月十五日以前在廣州及上海以毫洋計算之上海紙幣一千元之價格，及上海銀元一千元之價格大約相同。自徵收白銀出口稅後，在廣州之上海銀元價格與在上海及廣州所計算之上海紙幣價格已無關係。以毫洋計算之上海紙幣，價值跌落。一九三五年十一月實行新貨幣改政策後，毫洋價格驟跌。嗣後繼續下跌，惟速率漸緩。一九三六年二月十二日，照報載廣州對於上海匯率與上海在廣州之價格毫無關係，此照毫洋幣值低之表示。照廣州報紙所載，則二月後，毫洋在廣州與銀元維持一定之比例。

二·五〇在十月間，上海幣價任其下降，因此對廣州之匯率乃上漲。至十一月一日，達上海幣九七六元換毫洋一，〇〇〇元。

十一月六日，廣東亦放棄銀本位，廣東財政廳宣佈廣東省銀行之紙幣爲法幣[1]。白銀均須售於政府，調換法幣。惟中央政府在白銀收歸國有時，不予貼水，廣東則不然，給加二之貼水，故廣東毫洋一元可換廣東法幣一元二角，而上海銀元可換廣東法幣一·四四元。在行使大洋區域者，每銀元亦照付加二之大洋法幣。照此規定，則上海法幣將值廣東法幣一元二角。自以上海法幣一元二角，加加二之貼水將等於上海銀元一元之價格，計合毫洋一·四四元。

reached 912.5 on October 2. During October, the Shanghai dollar was allowed to depreciate, and the exchange on Canton consequently rose, reaching 976 Shanghai dollars per 1000 Canton dollars on November 1.

On November 6, the Canton currency was itself removed from the silver standard, with an announcement by the Canton Bureau of Finance that Provincial Bank notes were henceforth to be legal tender in Canton[1]. All silver was required to be sold to the provincial government in exchange for notes. Contrary to the policy of the National Government in offering no premium for silver purchased during nationalization, the Canton authorities offered a premium of 20 per cent for silver. Thus five twenty-cent Canton coins were to be worth $1.20 in legal tender, while the Shanghai silver dollar was to be purchased at $1.44. In areas where big money notes, such as Shanghai dollar notes, were in circulation, a 20 per cent premium was to be paid for silver dollars in terms of such notes. By the terms of this provision, Shang-

1) 廣州統計局；金融物價月刊第一期十一頁至十二頁，一九三六年一月出版

(1) Kwangtung Provincial Statistical Bureau Money and Price. No. 1 January, 1936 Pages 11-12.

第三表　上海與廣州間之匯價
TABLE 3.　EXCHANGE RATES BETWEEN SHANGHAI AND CANTON CURRENCIES

日期 Date	A 上海對廣州匯價 (1) Domestic Exchange Rate, Shanghai on Canton (1) (匯幣數)(Shanghai dollars)	B 上海紙幣一,000元換毫洋數(A欄之倒數) Number of Canton dollars per 1,000 Shanghai paper dollars (Reciprocal of Column A) (毫洋數)(Canton dollars)	C 上海紙幣一,000元在廣州之價格(2) Price of 1000 Shanghai dollar notes in Canton (2) (毫洋數)(Canton dollars)	D 上海銀元一,000元在廣州之價格(3) Price of 1000 Shanghai silver dollars in Canton (5) (毫洋數)(Canton dollars)	E 上海紙幣一,000元換毫洋數目指數一九三四年八月=100(B欄) Index of the number of Canton dollars per 1,000 Shanghai dollars. August 1954=100 (Column B)	F 上海紙幣在廣州之價格指數,一九三四年八月=100(C欄) Index of the price of Shanghai notes in Canton. Auugst 1954=100 (Column C)
一九三四 1934						
八月 August						
1	—	—	1,285	1,290	—	101.5
2	785.0	1.274	1,285	1,292	101.6	101.5
3	785.0	1.274	1,280	1,285	101.6	101.2
4	—	—	1,280	1,285	—	101.2
5	—	—	—	—	—	—
6	—	—	—	...	—	—
7	—	—	1,380	1,285	—	101.2
8	785.0	1.274	1,370	1,285	101.6	100.4
9	—	—	1,360	1,270	—	99.6
10	790.0	1 266	1,268	1,372	101.0	100.3
11	—	—	1,275	1,285	—	100.8
12	—	—	—	—	—	—
13	790.0	1.266	1,270	1,280	101.0	100.4
14	795.0	1.258	1,272	1,281	100.5	100.5
15	795.0	1.258	1,375	1,285	100.5	100.8
16	795.0	1.258	1,377	1,285	100.5	100.9
17	—	—	1,275	1,285	—	100.8
18	795.0	1.258	1,270	1,282	100.5	100.4
19	—	—	—	—	—	—
20	795.0	1.258	1,270	1,280	100.5	100.4
21	795.0	1.258	1,265	1,275	100.5	100.0
22	805.0	1.342	1,255	1,270	99.0	99.2
23	805.0	1.342	1,255	1,270	99.0	99.2
24	805.0	1.242	1,255	1,270	99.0	99.2
25	—	—	1,250	1,270	—	98.8
26	—	—	—	—	—	—
27	805.0	1.242	—	—	99.0	—
28	—	—	—	—	—	—
29	815.0	1.227	1,255	1,255	97.8	97.6
30	—	—	1,228	1,242	—	97.0
31	830.0	1.220	1,255	1,252	97.5	97.6
九月 September						
1	—	—	1,235	1,240	—	96.8
2	—	—	—	—	—	—
3	830.0	1.220	1,225	1,240	97.5	96.8
4	822.5	1.216	1,215	1,225	97.0	96.0
5	855.0	1.170	1,204	1,220	95.5	95.1
6	862.5	1.159	1,182	1,195	92.4	95.4
7	842.5	1.187	1,190	1,215	94.7	94.0
8	842.5	1.187	1,185	1,205	94.7	95.6
9	—	—	—	—	—	—

(1)(2)及(3)見六十頁　　　　　　　　(1)(2) and (3) see page 60

	A	B	C	D	E	F
一九三四 1934						
九月 Sept.						
10	845.0	1,185	1,187	1,205	94.5	95.8
11	845.0	1,185	1,210	1,225	94.5	95.6
12	842.5	1,187	1,195	1,220	94.7	94.4
13	840.0	1,190	1,208	1,225	94.9	95.5
14	852.5	1,201	1,215	1,240	95.8	96.0
15	822.5	1,216	1,227	1,245	97.0	97.0
16	—	—	—	—	—	—
17	820.0	1,220	1,225	1,245	97.5	96.8
18	812.5	1,251	—	—	98.2	—
19	812.5	1,251	1,240	1,250	98.2	98.0
20	805.0	1,242	1,260	1,270	99.0	99.6
21	800.5	1,249	1,255	1,250	99.6	97.6
22	—	—	1,245	1,250	—	98.4
23	—	—	—	—	—	—
24	—	—	1,245	1,255	—	98.2
25	810.4	1,254	1,260	1,270	98.4	99.6
26	800.5	1,249	1,255	1,265	99.6	99.2
27	—	—	1,250	1,260	—	98.8
28	800.5	1,249	—	—	99.6	—
29	800.5	1,249	—	—	99.6	—
30	—	—	—	—	—	—
十月 October						
1	805.0	1,242	1,247	1,255	99.0	98.5
2	812.5	1,251	1,240	1,250	98.2	98.0
3	812.5	1,251	1,255	1,250	98.2	97.6
4	812.5	1,251	1,245	1,255	98.2	98.4
5	—	—	—	—	—	—
6	810.0	1,255	1248	1,257	98.5	98.6
7	—	—	—	—	—	—
8	810.0	1,255	1,245	1,255	98.5	98.4
9	—	—	1,245	1,255	—	98.4
10	—	—	—	—	—	—
11	812.5	1,251	1,248	1,258	98.2	98.6
12	812.5	1,251	1,255	1,245	98.2	97.6
13	817.5	1,225	1,240	1,250	97.5	98.0
14	—	—	—	—	—	—
15	842.5	1,187	1,240	1,250	94.7	98.0
16	—	—	1,232	1,250	—	96.6
17	850.0	1,205	1,195	1,255	96.1	94.4
18	850.0	1,205	1,195	1,265	96.1	94.4
19	—	—	—	—	—	—
20	880.0	1,156	1,160	1,265	90.6	91.7
21	—	—	—	—	—	—
22	1002.5	998	1,180	1,260	79.6	95.2
23	—	—	1,165	1,265	—	92.1
24	1002.5	998	1,170	1,270	79.6	92.5
25	—	—	1,165	1,250	—	92.1
26	—	—	1,165	1,255	—	92.1
27	—	—	1,155	1,240	—	91.5
28	—	—	—	—	—	—
29	890.0	1,124	1,160	1,240	89.6	91.7
30	—	—	1,160	1,240	—	91.7
31	—	—	1,155	1,255	—	91.5
十一月 Nov.						
1	890.5	1,125	—	1,240	89.6	—
2	890.5	1,125	—	1,225	89.6	—
3	890.0	1,124	—	1,210	89.6	—
4	—	—	—	—	—	—
5	—	—	1,142	1,195	—	90.2
6	—	—	1,145	1,195	—	90.5
7	—	—	1,142	1,185	—	90.2
8	890.5	1,125	1,140	1,175	89.6	90.1
9	890.5	1,125	1,150	1,175	89.6	89.5
10	—	—	1,145	1,182	—	90.5
11	—	—	—	—	—	—
12	890.5	1,125	—	—	89.6	—
13	880.0	1,156	1,158	1,205	90.6	89.7
14	880.0	1,156	1,140	1,190	90.6	90.1
15	—	—	1,140	1,185	—	90.1
16	880.5	1,156	1,140	1,175	90.6	90.1
17	—	—	1,145	1,175	—	90.5
18	—	—	—	—	—	—
19	—	—	1,142	1,170	—	90.2
20	890.0	1,124	1,155	1,195	89.6	89.7
21	—	—	1,158	1,225	—	89.9

	A	B	C	D	E	F
一九三四1934						
十一月Nov.						
22	890.5	1,125	1,175	1,215	89.6	92.9
23	890.5	1,125	1,165	1,215	89.6	92.1
24	895.0	1,117	1,165	1,200	89.1	92.1
25	—	—	—	—	—	—
26	—	—	1,180	1,195	—	95.2
27	895.0	1,117	1,170	1,190	89.1	92.5
28	890.5	1,125	1,165	1,192	89.6	92.1
29	890.0	1,124	1,150	1,205	89.6	89.5
30	890.0	1,124	—	—	89.6	—
十二月 Dec.						
1	—	—	1,127	1,220	—	89.1
2	—	—	—	—	—	—
3	890.0	1,124	1,131	1,230	89.6	89.4
4	890.0	1,124	1,127	1,220	89.6	89.1
5	890.0	1,124	1,119	1,218	89.6	88.4
6	—	—	1,120	1,220	—	88.5
7	890.0	1,124	1,124	1,206	89.6	88.8
8	—	—	1,118	1,200	—	88.4
9	—	—	—	—	—	—
10	890.5	1,125	1,119	1,207	89.6	88.4
11	890.8	1,125	1,124	1,207	89.6	88.8
12	900.0	1,111	1,124	1,205	88.6	88.8
13	900.0	1,111	1,124	1,200	88.6	88.8
14	900.0	1,111	1,120	1,200	88.6	88.5
15	—	—	1,116	1,210	—	88.2
16	—	—	—	—	—	—
17	—	—	1,118	1,200	—	88.4
18	900.0	1,111	1,111	1,188	88.6	87.8
19	917.5	1,090	1,100	1,180	86.9	86.9
20	920.0	1,087	1,094	1,162	86.7	86.5
21	920.0	1,087	1,099	1,177	86.7	86.8
22	920.0	1,087	1,097	1,180	86.7	86.7
23	—	—	—	—	—	—
24	920.0	1,087	1,095	1,175	86.7	86.5
25	—	—	—	—	—	—
26	—	—	—	1,170	—	—
27	910.5	1,099	1,097	1,180	87.6	86.7
28	—	—	1,104	1,188	—	87.2
29	910.0	1,099	1,104	1,190	87.6	87.2
30	—	—	—	—	—	—
31	—	—	1,112	1,205	—	87.9
一九三五1935						
一月January						
1	—	—	—	—	—	—
2	—	—	—	—	—	—
3	—	—	—	—	—	—
4	905.0	1,105	1,115	—	88.1	88.0
5	905.0	1,105	1,114	1,215	88.1	88.0
6	—	—	—	—	—	—
7	—	—	1,115	1,222	—	88.1
8	—	—	1,112	1,225	—	87.9
9	905.0	1,105	1,111	1,238	88.1	87.8
10	—	—	1,108	1,230	—	87.6
11	902.5	1,108	1,110	1,235	88.4	87.7
12	902.5	1,108	1,108	1,240	88.4	87.6
13	—	—	—	—	—	—
14	902.5	1,108	1,107	1,242	88.4	87.5
15	905.0	1,105	1,108	1,248	88.1	87.6
16	905.0	1,105	1,107	1,252	88.1	87.5
17	912.5	1,096	1,108	1,252	87.4	87.6
18	—	—	1,106	1,245	—	87.4
19	912.5	1,096	1,104	1,242	87.4	87.2
20	—	—	—	—	—	—
21	912.5	1,096	1,105	1,242	87.4	87.5
22	—	—	1,108	1,243	—	87.6
23	912.5	1,096	1,116	1,245	87.4	88.2
24	912.5	1,096	1,117	1,245	87.4	88.5
25	912.5	1,096	1,117	1,240	87.4	88.5
26	—	—	1,125	1,240	—	88.9
27	—	—	—	—	—	—
28	912.5	1,096	1,128	1,232	87.4	89.1
29	910.0	1,099	1,135	1,235	87.6	89.5
30	—	—	1,145	1,250	—	90.5
31	—	—	1,144	1,228	—	90.4

	A	B	C	D	E	F
一九三五 1935						
二月 February						
1	—	—	1,127	1,227	—	89·1
2	—	—	1,127	1,240	—	89·1
3	—	—	—	—	—	—
4	—	—	—	1,255	—	—
5	—	—	—	—	—	—
6	—	—	—	—	—	—
7	—	—	—	—	—	—
8	895.0	1·117	1,127	1,255	891	89·1
9	891.0	1·122	1,140	1,255	895	90·1
10	—	—	—	—	—	—
11	—	—	1,145	1,240	—	90·5
12	895.0	1,117	1,144	1,242	891	90·4
13	895·0	1,117	1,144	1,245	891	90·4
14	895·0	1,117	1,140	1,240	891	90·1
15	895.0	1,117	1,147	1,240	891	90·6
16	895.0	1,117	1,145	1,258	891	90·5
17	—	—	—	—	—	—
18	895.0	1,117	1,142	1 240	891	90·2
19	895.0	1,117	1,144	1,240	891	90·4
20	895.0	1,117	1,144	1,257	891	90·4
21	—	—	1,145	1,257	—	90·5
22	895·0	1,117	1,146	1·258	891	90·6
23	—	—	1,144	1,240	—	90·4
24	—	—	—	—	—	—
25	895·0	1,117	1,149	1,240	891	90·8
26	890·0	1·124	1,150	1,258	896	90·9
27	—	—	1,152	1,255	—	91·0
28	890·0	1·124	1,149	1,255	896	90·8
三月 March						
1	—	—	1,155	1,255	—	91·1
2	885.0	1,150	1,148	1,250	90.1	90·7
3	—	—	—	—	—	—
4	885.0	1,150	1,145	1,235	90.1	90·5
5	—	—	1,148	1,230	—	90·7
6	880.0	1,156	1,147	1,255	90.6	90·6
7	—	—	1,159	1,255	—	90·0
8	885.0	1,150	1,125	1,215	90.1	88·9
9	—	—	1,121	1,205	—	88·6
10	—	—	—	—	—	—
11	895.5	1,119	1,125	1,205	89.2	88·7
12	895.8	1,119	—	—	89.2	—
13	895.8	1,119	1,125	1,205	89.2	88·9
14	—	—	1,120	1,205	—	88·5
15	895.0	1,117	1,121	1,205	89.1	88·6
16	—	—	1,119	1,205	—	88·4
17	—	—	—	—	—	—
18	895.0	1,117	1,121	1,200	89.1	88·6
19	895.0	1,117	1,120	1,200	89.1	88·5
20	—	—	1,121	1,200	—	88·6
21	892.8	1,120	1,119	1,200	89.5	88·4
22	892.5	1,120	1,119	1,200	89.5	88·4
23	—	—	1,122	1,200	—	88·7
24	—	—	—	—	—	—
25	902.5	1,108	1,122	1,200	88.4	88·7
26	902.5	1,108	1,111	1,195	88.4	87·8
27	902.5	1,108	1,114	1,205	88.4	88·0
28	—	—	1,109	1,220	—	87·6
29	910.0	1,099	—	—	87.6	—
30	—	—	1,095	1,255	—	86·5
31	—	—	—	—	—	—
四月 April						
1	—	—	1,084	1,255	—	85·7
2	—	—	1,049	1,258	—	82·5
3	950.0	1,055	1,075	1,240	84.0	84·6
4	—	—	1,081	1,248	—	85·4
5	—	—	1,079	1,247	—	85·5
6	—	—	—	1,247	—	—
7	—	—	—	—	—	—
8	—	—	1,068	1,247	—	84·4
9	945.0	1,058	1,062	1,248	84.4	85·7
10	945.0	1,058	1,065	1,255	84.4	84·2
11	945.0	1,058	1,055	1,255	84.4	85·2

— 54 —

	A	B	C	D	E	F
一九三五1935 四月April						
12	945.0	1.038	1,017	1,255	84.4	80.4
15	—	—	1.008	1,255	--	79.6
14	—	—	—.	—	—	—
15	945.0	1.058	1.042	1,270	84.4	82.5
16	—	—	1,050	1,255	—	81.4
17	—	—	1,056	1,265	—	81'9
18	995.0	1.005	1,050	1,260	80.1	81.4
19	—	—	—	—	—	--
20	--	—	—	1,260	—	—
21	--	—	—	—	—	--
22	--	—	—.	—	—	—
25	—	--	1,054	1,268	—	81.7
24	995.0	1.005	1,050	1,260	80.1	81.4
25	995.0	1.005	1,005	1,262	80.1	77.4
26	995.0	1.005	965	1,255	80.1	76.5
27	1100.0	909	965	1,228	72.5	76.5
28	—	—	—	—	—	—
29	1100.0	909	980	1,235	72.5	77.4
50	1080.0	926	990	1,255	75.8	78.2
五月May						
1	—	—	960	1,240	—	75.9
2	1100.0	909	955	1,240	73.5	75.5
5	—	—	985	1,245	—	77.8
4	1080.0	936	960	1,225	75.8	75.9
5	—	—	—	—	—	—
6	—	—	975	1.255	--	77.0
7	—	—	975	1,227	—	77.0
8	1080.0	926	980	1,250	75.8	77.4
9	1060.0	945	965	1,227	75.2	77.7
10	1060.0	945	988	1,227	75.2	78.1
11	—	—	985	1,215	—	77.8
12	—	—	—	—	—	—
15	--	—	992	1,220	--	78.4
14	1080.0	926	980	1,215	75.8	77.4
15	—	—	980	1,205	—	77.4
16	1070.0	955	972	1,207	74.6	76.8
17	—	—	957	1,225	—	75.6
18	1070.0	955	957	1,222	74.6	75.6
19	—	—	—	—	—	—
20	1070.0	955	955	1,222	74.6	75.5
21	—	—	955	1,225	—	75.5
22	1060.0	945	977	1,235	75.2	77.2
25	1060.0	945	975	1,225	75.2	77.0
24	—	—	972	1,210	--	76.8
25	1050.5	952	970	1,205	75.9	76.7
26	—	—	—	—	—	—
27	1070.0	955	970	1,220	74.6	76.7
28	—	—	980	1,215	—	77.4
29	1055.0	94.8	977	1,205	75.6	77.3
50	1055.0	96.6	980	1,207	77.0	77.4
51	--	—	982	1,212	—	77.6
六月June						
1	1055.0	966	985	1,215	77.0	77.8
2	—	—	—	—	—	—
5	—	—	985	1,217	—	77.8
4	1050.0	952	986	1,215	75.9	77.9
5	—	--	—	—	—	—
6	--	--	982	1,212	—	77.6
7	1045.0	957	980	1,205	76.5	77.4
8	—	—	985	1,200	—	77.8
9	—	—	—	--	—	—
10	--	—	—	—	—	—
11	—	—	1,000	1,207	—	79.0
12	—	—	1.012	1,205	—	80.0
15	1020.0	980	1,007	1,187	78.1	79.6
14	1055.0	966	1,012	1,180	77.0	80.0
15	1020.0	980	1,020	1,180	78.1	80.6
16	—	—	—	—	—	--
17	1020.0	980	1,020	1,180	78.1	80.6
18	—	—	1,020	1,170	—	80.6
19	1000.0	1000	1,027	1,190	79.7	81.2
20	1000.0	1000	1,025	1,185	79.7	81.0
21	990.0	1010	1,045	1,187	80.5	82.6
22	—	—	1,042	1,172	—	82.5
25	—	—	—	—	—	—

	A	B	C	D	E	F
一九三五 1935						
六月 June						
24	980.0	1020	1,055	1,165	81.5	81.8
25	980.0	1020	1,045	1,180	81.5	82.6
26	970.0	1051	1,070	1,175	82.2	84.6
27	970.0	1051	1,050	1,170	82.2	85.0
28	—	—	1,045	1,170	—	82.6
29	970.0	1051	1,060	1,168	82.2	85.8
50	—	—	—	—	—	—
七月 July						
1	—	—	—	—	—	—
2	—	—	—	—	—	—
5	970.0	1,051	1,058	1,162	82.2	85.6
4	970.0	1,051	1,070	1,155	82.2	84.6
5	960.0	1,042	1,070	1,152	85.1	84.6
6	—	—	1,067	1,142	—	84.5
7	—	—	—	—	—	—
8	—	—	1,075	1,155	—	85.0
9	940.0	1 064	1,108	1,140	84.8	87.6
10	940 0	1,064	1,125	1,158	84.8	88.9
11	940.0	1,064	1,090	1,158	84.8	86.1
12	—	—	1,095	1,157	—	86.4
15	940.0	1.064	1,088	1,140	84.8	86.0
14	—	—	—	—	—	—
15	—	—	1,090	1,140	—	86.1
16	940.0	1,064	1,100	1,145	84.8	86.9
17	—	—	1,095	1,140	—	86.5
18	940.0	1.064	1,090	1,140	84.8	86.1
19	940.0	1,064	1,092	1,140	84.8	86.5
20	—	—	1,095	1,140	—	86.5
21	—	—	—	—	—	—
22	940.0	1,064	1,090	1,145	84.8	86.1
25	940.0	1,064	1,085	1,140	84.8	85.7
24	940.0	1.064	1,087	1,142	84.8	85.9
25	940.0	1.064	1,082	1,140	84.8	85.5
26	940.0	1.064	1,082	1,140	84.8	85.5
27	940.0	1.064	1,082	1,140	84.8	85.5
28	—	—	—	—	—	—
29	940.0	1.064	1,082	1,140	84.8	85.5
50	940.0	1.064	1,070	1,140	84.8	84.6
51	—	—	1,070	1,145	—	84.6
八月 August						
1	950.0	1,055	1,084	1,160	84.0	85.7
2	950.0	1,055	1,080	1,162	84.0	85.5
5	960.0	1,042	1,081	1,165	85.1	85.4
4	—	—	—	—	—	—
5	960.0	1,042	1,072	1,157	85.1	84.7
6	960.0	1,042	1,074	1,161	85.1	84.9
7	950.0	1,055	1,079	1,165	84.0	85.6
8	940.0	1,064	1,072	1,160	84.8	84.7
9	940.0	1,064	1,069	1,167	84.8	84.5
10	950.0	1,055	1,065	1,169	84.0	84.2
11	—	—	—	—	—	—
12	950.0	1,055	1,065	1,188	84.0	84.0
15	950.0	1,055	1,064	1,195	84.0	84.1
14	950.0	1,055	1,076	1,204	84.0	85.0
15	—	—	1,086	1,190	—	85.8
16	945.0	1,058	1,087	1,186	84.4	85.9
17	—	—	1,095	1,182	—	86.4
18	—	—	—	—	—	—
19	950.0	1.075	1,100	1,185	85.7	86.9
20	950.0	1,075	1,099	1,179	85.7	86.8
21	920.0	1,087	1 160	1,172	86.7	91.7
22	970.0	1,051	1,121	1,174	82.2	88.6
25	—	—	1,110	1,170	—	87.7
24	940.0	1,064	1,096	1,180	84.8	86.6
25	—	—	—	—	—	—
26	940.0	1,064	1,086	1,177	84.8	85.8
27	—	—	—	—	—	—
28	955.0	1,070	1,086	1,177	85.5	85.8
29	955.0	1,070	1,098	1,187	85.5	86.8
50	950.0	1,075	1,099	1,186	85.7	86.8
51	—	—	1,099	1,184	—	86.8
九月 Sept.						
1	—	—	—	—	—	—
2	—	—	10,89	1,175	—	86.1

Date	A	B	C	D	E	F
一九三五1935 九月Sept.						
5	950.0	1.075	1,087	1.170	85.7	85.9
4	—	—	1,084	1,166	—	85.7
5	—	—	1,090	1,175		86.1
6	—	—	1,094	1,174		86.5
7	925.0	10.81	1,082	1,159	86.2	85.5
8	—	—	—			—
9	950.0	1.055	1,082	1.175	84.0	85.5
10	—	—	1,085	1,176		85.6
11	935.0	1.070	1,080	1,177	85.5	85.5
12	—	—	1,075	1,175		85.0
15	955.0	1.070	1,078	1,176	85.5	85.2
14	935.0	1.070	1,085	1,177	85.5	85.6
15	—	—	—		—	
16	—	—	1,082	1,176	—	85.5
17	—	—	1,085	1,165		85.7
18	922.5	1.084	1,091	1,175	86.4	86.3
19	—	—	1,097	1,181		86.7
20	920.0	1.087	1,099	1,181	86.7	86.8
21	915.0	1.095	1,094	1,175	87.2	86.5
52	—	—	—			—
25	920.0	1.087	1,096	1,181	86.7	86.6
24	—	—				—
25	917.5	1.090	1,097	1,181	86.9	86.7
26	—	—	1,095	1,174		86.5
27	920.0	1.087	1,095	1,172	86.7	86.5
28	—	—	1,098	1,175		86.8
29	—	—	—			
50	917.5	1.090	1,098	1,172	86.9	86.8
十月October						
1	—	—	1,112	1,185	—	87.9
2	912.5	1.096	1,110	1,185	87.4	87.7
5	—	—	1,108	1,182	—	87.6
4	914.0	1.094	1,075	1,170	87.2	85.6
5	938.0	1.078	1,075	1,175	86.0	84.8
6	—	—	—			—
7	950.0	1.055	1,068	1,175	84.0	84.4
8	—	—	1,080	1,177		85.5
9	956.0	1.068	1,085	1,180	85.2	85.7
10	—	—	—			—
11	955.0	1.070	—	—	85.5	—
13						
15						
14	955.0	1.070	1,080	1,185	85.5	85.5
15	955.0	1.070	1,085	1,185	85.5	85.7
16	—	—	1,085	1,185	—	85.7
17	939.0	1.076	1,080	1,185	85.8	85.5
18	—	—	1,075	1,185		84.8
19	942.0	1.062	1,067	1,185	84.7	84.5
20	—	—	—		—	—
21	—	—	1,080	1,188		85.5
25	942.0	1.062	1,077	1,188	84.7	85.1
25	942.0	1.062	1,070	1,188	84.7	84.6
24	960.0	1.042	1,067	1,190	85.1	84.5
25	969.0	1.052	1,055	1,195	82.5	85.2
26	976.0	1.025	1,040	1,192	81.7	82.2
27	—	—	—			—
29	975.0	1.028	1,047	1,202	82.0	82.7
29	989.0	1.011	1,045	1,215	80.6	82.6
50	975.0	1.026	1,058	1,207	81.8	82.0
51	975.0	1.026	1,025	1,215	81.8	81.0
十一月 Nov.						
1	976.0	1.025	1,050	1,208	81.7	85.0
2	—	—	1,058	1,215		85.6
5	—	—	—			—
4	966.0	1.055	1,085	1,200	82.5	85.6
5	—	—	1,110	1,200		87.7
6	869.0	1,151	1,155	1,210	91.8	91.5
7	869.0	1,151	—	—	91.8	—
8	970.0	1.051	—	—	82.2	—
9	970.0	1.051	—	—	82.2	—
10	—	—	—	—		—
11	970.0	1.051	—	—	82.2	—
12	—	—	—	—	—	—
15	—	—	1,400	1,450	—	110.6
14	—	—	1,570	1,420	—	108.5

	A	B	C	D	E	F
一九三五1935						
十一月Nov.						
15	—	—	1,520	1,420	—	104·5
16	—	—	1,270	1,400	—	100·4
17	—	—	—	—	—	—
18	—	—	1,265	1,400	—	100·0
19	—	—	1,290	—	—	101·9
20	1001·0	999	1,510	1,400	79·7	105·5
21	—	—	1,510	1,400	—	105·5
22	—	—	1,510	1,400	—	105·5
25	—	—	1,285	1,400	—	101·5
24	—	—	—	—	—	—
25	825·0	1,212	1,260	1,400	96·7	99·6
26	850·0	1,205	1,270	1,420	96·1	100·4
27	805·0	1,243	1,290	1,410	99·0	101·9
28	790·0	1,266	1,290	1,400	101·0	101·9
29	—	—	1,285	1,400	—	101·5
50	790·0	1,266	1,280	1,400	101·0	101·2
十二月 Dec.						
1	—	—	—	—	—	—
2	789·0	1,267	1,280	1,410	101·0	101·2
5	—	—	1,285	1,400	—	101·4
4	890·0	1,124	1,290	1,410	89·6	101·9
5	—	—	1,150	1,410	—	105·5
6	757·0	1,521	1,550	1,410	105·5	105·1
7	762·0	1,512	1,550	1,410	104·6	105·1
8	—	—	—	—	—	—
9	—	—	—	—	—	—
10	761·0	1,514	1,510	1,400	104·8	105·5
11	772·0	1,295	1,295	1,400	105·5	102·5
12	776·0	1,289	1,275	1,590	102·8	100·8
15	794·0	1,259	1,270	1,590	100·4	100·4
14	794·0	1,259	1,500	1,590	100·4	102·7
15	—	—	1,290	1,570	—	101·9
16	771·0	1,297	—	—	105·4	—
17	—	—	1,295	1,560	—	102·2
18	772·0	1,295	1,287	1,560	105·5	101·7
19	785·0	1,277	1,280	1,560	101·8	101·2
20	—	—	1,247	1,560	—	98·5
21	—	—	1,267	1,560	—	100·1
22	—	—	1,265	1,560	—	100·0
25	789·0	1,267	—	—	101·0	—
24	—	—	1,268	1,570	—	100·2
25	—	—	1,268	1,560	—	100·2
26	805·0	1,242	—	—	99·0	—
27	—	—	—	—	—	—
28	—	—	1265	1,560	—	99·8
29	—	—	1258	1,560	—	99·4
50	815·0	1,227	1252	1,555	97·8	98·9
51	—	—	1220	1,555	—	96·4
一九三六1936						
一月January						
1	—	—	—	—	—	—
2	—	—	—	—	—	—
5	—	—	—	—	—	—
4	—	—	1,215	1,545	—	96·0
5	—	—	1,220	1,550	—	96·4
6	—	—	1,215	1,550	—	96·4
7	826·0	1,211	1,315	1,550	96·6	96·0
8	846·0	1,182	1,255	1,555	94·5	97·4
9	—	—	1,315	1,550	—	96·0
10	827·0	1,209	1,217	1,510	96·4	96·2
11	850·0	1,205	1,250	1,550	96·1	97·2
12	—	—	—	—	—	—
15	850·0	1,205	1,275	1,560	96·1	100·8
14	—	—	1,515	1,570	—	105·9
15	778·0	1,285	1,278	1,570	102·5	101·0
16	785·0	1,277	1,265	1,560	101·8	100·0
17	802·0	1,247	1,280	1,580	99·4	101·2
18	801·0	1,248	1,275	1,570	99·5	100·8
19	—	—	—	—	—	—
20	801·0	1,248	1,278	1,580	99·5	101·0
21	—	—	1,280	1,560	—	101·2
22	—	—	1,282	1,560	—	101·5
25	—	—	1,280	1,560	—	101·2

	A	B	C	D	E	F
一九三六 1936						
一月 January						
24	—	—	—	—	—	—
25	—	—	—	—	—	—
26	—	—	—	—	—	—
27	—	—	—	—	—	—
28	—	—	1,282	1,580	—	101.5
29	—	--	1,278	1,410	—	101.0
30	—	—	1,287	1,410	—	101.7
31	802.0	1,247	1,287	1,410	99.4	101.7
二月 February						
1	794.0	1,259	—	—	100.4	—
2	—	—	—	—	—	—
3	—	—	—	—	—	—
4	—	—	—	—	—	—
5	810.0	1,255	—	—	98.5	—
6	—	—	—	—	—	—
7	800.0	1,250	—	—	99.7	—
8	—	—	1,502	1,400	—	102.9
9	—	—	—	—	—	—
10	800.0	1,250	1,295	1,590	99.7	102.5
11	—	—	1,298	1,400	—	103.6
12	850.0	1,205	1,297	1,400	96.1	102.5
13	850.0	1,205	1,292	1,590	96.1	102.1
14	850.0	1,205	1,292	1,595	96.1	102.1
15	850.0	1,205	1,289	1,585	96.1	101.9
16	—	—	—	—	—	—
17	850.0	1,205	1,291	1,585	96.1	102.0
18	850.0	1,205	1,501	1,400	96.1	102.8
19	850.0	1,205	1,502	1,405	96.1	102.9
20	850.0	1,205	1,522	1,410	96.1	104.5
21	850.0	1,205	1,540	1,425	96.1	105.9
22	850.0	1,205	1,558	1,410	96.1	105.7
23	—	—	—	—	—	—
24	850.0	1,205	1,544	1,425	96.1	106.2
25	850.0	1,205	1,548	1,420	96.1	106.5
26	850.0	1,205	1,541	1,415	96.1	106.0
27	850.0	1,205	1,547	1,415	96.1	106.4
28	850.0	1,205	1,555	1,425	96.1	106.9
29	850.0	1,205	1,557	1,425	96.1	107.2
三月 March						
1	—	—	—	—	—	—
2	850.0	1,205	1,571	1,450	96.1	108.5
3	850.0	1,205	1,596	1,455	96.1	110.5
4	850.0	1,205	—	1,455	96.1	—
5	850.0	1,205	1,554	1,425	96.1	107.5
6	850.0	1,205	1,574	1,425	96.1	108.6
7	850.0	1,205	1,586	1,450	96.1	109.5
8	—	—	—	—	—	—
9	850.0	1,205	1,565	1,425	96.1	107.7
10	850.0	1,205	1,565	1,425	96.1	107.9
11	850.0	1,205	1,570	1,455	96.1	108.5
12	850.0	1,205	—	—	96.1	—
13	850.0	1,205	1,580	1,458	96.1	109.4
14	850.0	1,205	—	—	96.1	—
15	—	—	1,580	1,455	—	109.1
16	850.0	1,205	1,580	1,455	96.1	109.1
17	850.0	1,205	1,588	1,458	96.1	109.7
18	850.0	1,205	1,589	1,455	96.1	109.8
19	850.0	1,205	1,588	1,458	96.1	109.7
20	850.0	1,205	1,585	1,455	96.1	109.4
21	850.0	1,205	1,582	1,455	96.1	109.2
22	—	—	—	—	—	—
23	850.0	1,205	1,585	1,457	96.1	109.5
24	850.0	1,205	1,581	1,455	96.1	109.1
25	850.0	1,205	1,582	1,455	96.1	109.2
26	850.0	1,205	1,582	1,455	96.1	109.2
27	850.0	1,205	1,582	1,458	96.1	109.2
28	850.0	1,205	1,584	1,440	96.1	109.4
29	—	—	—	—	—	—
30	850.0	1,205	1,585	1,458	96.1	109.5
31	850.0	1,205	1,585	1,458	96.1	109.4
四月 April						
1	850.0	1,205	1,587	1,459	96.1	109.6
2	850.0	1,205	1,591	1,440	96.1	109.8
3	850.0	1,205	1,591	1,440	96.1	109.8

	A	B	C	D	E	F
一九三六 1936						
四月 April						
4	850·0	1,205	1,590	1,440	96·1	109·8
5	—	—	—	—	—	—
6	850·0	1,205	—	—	96·1	—
7	850·0	1,205	—	—	96·1	—
8	850·0	1,205	1,594	1,440	96·1	110·3
9	850·0	1,205	1,595	1,440	96·1	110·3
10	—	—	1,595	1,440	—	110·1
11	—	—	1,596	1,440	—	110·5
12	—	—	—	—	—	—
15	—	—	1,401	1,458	—	110·7
14	850·0	1,205	1,597	1,440	96·1	110·4
15	850·0	1,205	1,596	1,440	96·1	110·5
16	850·0	1,205	1,401	1,440	96·1	110·7
17	850·0	1,205	1,402	1,440	96·1	110·8
18	850·0	1,205	1,402	1,440	96·1	110·8
19	—	—	—	—	—	—
20	850·0	1,205	1,402	1,440	96·1	110·8
21	850·0	1,205	1,402	1,440	96·1	110·8
22	850·0	1,205	1,402	1,440	96·1	110·8
25	850·0	1,205	1,401	1,440	96·1	110·7
24	850·0	1,205	—	—	96·1	—
25	850·0	1,205	1,400	1,440	96·1	110·6
26	—	—	—	—	—	—
27	850·0	1,205	1,405	1,444	96·1	110·9
28	850·0	1,205	1,405	1,444	96·1	111·0
29	850·0	1,205	—	—	96·1	—
50	850·0	1,205	1,409	1,442	96·1	111·5
五月 May						
1	850·0	1,205	1,408	1,443	96·1	111·5
2	850·0	1,205	1,404	1,441	96·1	111·0
5	—	—	—	—	—	—
4	850·0	1,205	1,405	1,459	96·1	111·0
5	850·0	1,205	—	—	96·1	—
6	850·0	1,205	1,402	1,440	96·1	110·8
7	850·0	1,205	1,405	1,440	96·1	111·0
8	850·0	1,205	1,408	1,440	96·1	111·5
9	850·0	1,205	1,407	1,440	96·1	111·3
10	—	—	—	—	—	—
11	850·0	1,205	1,408	1,445	96·1	111·5
12	850·0	1,205	1,415	1,442	96·1	111·8
15	850·0	1,205	1 414	1,443	96·1	111·7
14	850·0	1,205	1,416	1,443	96·1	111·9
15	850·0	1,205	1,416	1,440	96·1	111·9
16	850·0	1,205	1,418	1,440	96·1	112·1
17	—	—	—	—	—	—
18	850·0	1,205	1,458	—	96·1	115·6
19	850·0	1,205	1,455	1,440	96·1	114·8
20	850·0	1,205	1,445	1,440	96·1	114·2
21	850·0	1,205	1,445	1,440	96·1	114·2
22	850·0	1,205	1,448	1,440	96·1	114·4
25	850·0	1,205	1,442	1,440	96·1	114·0
24	—	—	—	—	—	—
25	850·0	1,205	1,457	1,440	96·1	115·1
26	850·0	1,205	1,459	1,440	96·1	115·5
27	850·0	1,205	1,454	1,440	96·1	114·9
28	850·0	1,205	1,459	1,440	96·1	115·5
29	850·0	1,205	1,478	1,440	96·1	116·8
50	850·0	1,205	1,500	1,440	96·1	118·5
51	—	—	—	—	—	—

(1) 字林四報

(2) 中國銀行(一九三四年八月至一九三五年八月)廣東統計月報(一九三五年九月)，國華報(一九三六年二月至五月)

(3) 中國銀行(一九三四年八月至一九三五年八月及一九三五年十月至一九三六年一月)廣東統計月報(一九三五年九月)，國華報(一九三六年二月至五月)

(1) From North China Daily News

(2) From Bank of China (August 1934-August 1935), Kwangtung Statistical Monthly (September 1935) and Kwoh Wa Pao (February 1936-May 1936).

(3) From Bank of China (August 1934-August 1935 and October 1935-January 1936), Kwangtung Statistical Monthly (September 1935) and Kwoh Wa Pao (February 1936-May 1936)

hai dollar notes would be worth $1.20 in Canton legal tender, since the price of the Shanghai legal tender at $1.20 plus 20 per cent would equal the price of the Shanghai silver dollar, $1.44 Canton dollars.

As a result of the announcement of November 6, the exchange rate of Shanghai on Canton immediately fell. Considerable fluctuations occurred. On November 30, the rate was 790. It averaged about 789 in December, and about 811 in January, as reported in the North China Daily News financial columns.

On February 12, 1936, the exchange rate on Canton, as quoted in the financial columns of the North China Daily News, began to be stable at 830, and was still being published at that rate on May 31. However, this is apparently only a nominal rate, and not one at which business is actually done. This conclusion is reached by examining prices of Shanghai money as they are quoted in Cantonese papers in Canton. Examination of exchange rates published in bank reports also supports this conclusion[1].

十一月六日宣布新政策之結果，上海對廣州之匯率立即下落，且波動極巨。照字林西報金融欄所載，十一月三十日之匯率為七九〇，十二月之平均匯率為七八九，翌年一月為八一一。

在一九三六年二月十二日，據上海字林西報金融欄所載，上海對廣州之匯價開始平穩為八三〇，延至五月三十一日，仍為此數。但考查廣州報紙所載之上海幣價，則此顯為虛價，而無實際交易者也。查銀行之報告亦得同樣之結論[1]。

(1) 中國銀行:[中外商業金融彙報]第三卷第三期第三十三頁，一九三六年三月出版

(1) Bank of China, Financial and Commercial Monthly Bulletin, Vol. 3. No. 3 March 1936, page 33.

在一九三四年八月一日至一九三六年正月十七日，上海紙幣一，〇〇〇元在廣州之價格，通常約為上海對廣州匯率之倒數。例如一九三五年九月三日，上海對廣州之匯率為九三〇，應等於在廣州毫洋一，〇七五元換上海幣一，〇〇〇元。在廣州實際價格為上海幣一，〇〇〇元換毫洋一，〇八七元。

至一九三六年二月一日，雙方相互之關係，顯然不同，雖上海紙幣一，〇〇〇元在廣州換毫洋一，三〇二元。但上海報紙所載，上海對廣州之匯率則為七九四，僅等於在廣州毫洋一，二五九元換上海紙幣一，〇〇〇元。自二月十二日照上海報紙所載上海對廣州之匯率表面穩定後，上海紙幣在廣州之實價，仍逐漸上漲。至五月三十日達一，五〇〇。在此時期，以上海對外匯價毫無漲落，故上海紙幣在廣州價格之上漲，完全由於毫洋之貶值。

During the period August 1, 1934 to January 17, 1936, the price of 1000 Shanghai notes in Canton was usually about the same as the reciprocal of the Shanghai exchange on Canton. For instance, on September 3, 1935, in Shanghai, the exchange on Canton was 930, justifying a price in Canton of 1075 Canton dollars per 1000 Shanghai dollars. In Canton, 1000 Shanghai dollars were actually worth 1087 Canton dollars.

By February 1, 1936, a quite different relationship was evident. Although 1000 Shanghai dollars. In Canton, 1000 Canton dollars in Canton, the Shanghai exchange on Canton, as quoted in the Shanghai newspapers, was 794, justifying a rate in Canton of only 1259 Cantonese per 1000 Shanghai dollars. After the nominal stabilization of Canton currency in Shanghai on February 12, as indicated in Shanghai newspapers, the actual price of Shanghai currency in Canton rose gradually, reaching 1500 on May 30. Since there was no rise or fall in the world exchange value of Shanghai currency during this period, this rise in the price of Shanghai currency in Canton was due to a depreciation of the Canton currency.

毫洋與白銀關係之變遷，為毫洋貶值原因之一。十一月六日，廣東省政府宣佈毫洋紙幣一・四四元換上海銀元一元。該時在世界市場上海銀元一元值上海法幣一・六七元。十二月初，銀價猛跌，以上海法幣計算之白銀價格亦自動跌落。銀價之下跌，至一九三六年二月二十三日始約告停止，計銀元一元僅值上海法幣一・一四元。五月十五日，上海銀元一元值上海法幣一・一六元。在此變動時期內。廣東當局，不採用毫洋與上海法幣一定之比價，而採用與銀元一定之比價。以上海法幣計算之毫洋價值，自如白銀價值相同跌落。

雖廣州報紙所載上海銀元一，〇〇〇元之價格仍為毫洋一，四四〇元，但上海法幣價格則繼續上

One reason for the depreciation of the Canton currency may be seen in its relation to silver. On November 6, the Canton government announced that it would pay 1.44 Canton legal tender dollars for a Shanghai silver dollar. At that time, the Shanghai silver dollar was worth $1.67 in terms of the Shanghai legal tender in the world market. In early December, the price of silver began a precipitous drop, automatically lowering the price of silver in terms of Shanghai legal tender. This drop was mostly completed by January 23, 1936, at which time the silver dollar had become worth only $1.14 in legal tender. On May 15, it was worth $1.16. During this period of change, the Canton authorities chose to pay a nearly fixed price for the si'ver dollar, instead of a fixed price for Shanghai legal tender. Naturally, Canton currency fell in value in terms of Shanghai legal currency, just as silver itself fell.

However, although the price of 1000 Shanghai silver dollars in Canton, as reported in financial news, has continued to remain stable at about 1440 Cantonese dollars, the price of

漲，故在廣州以上海法幣計算之白銀價格低於在倫敦或紐約之價格。例如一九三六年五月一日上海法幣一，〇〇〇元在廣州值毫洋一，四〇八元，而上海銀元一，〇〇〇元爲一，四四二元。照此比例，則上海銀元一元在廣州值上海法幣一‧〇二五元。但同日在倫敦上海銀元一元值上海法幣一‧一五元。此項差價，或半由於偷運白銀赴倫敦之危險及運費較大故也。

惟所奇者，當上海法幣價格在廣州之上漲，遠高出其與白銀價格關係之上時，而銀價在廣州仍如此之穩定。同時廣州物價，亦顯示上漲之趨勢。在此情況之下，明示毫洋之貶值，銀價在廣州理應上漲。故廣州現在之銀價，是否實價，即白銀是否確

Shanghai legal tender has continued to rise, so that silver is worth less in terms of the Shanghai legal tender in Canton than in London or New York. For instance, on May 1, 1936, 1000 Shanghai legal tender dollars were worth 1408 Canton dollars in Canton, while 1000 Shanghai silver dollars were worth 1442. At this rate, the Shanghai silver dollar was worth $1.025 in Shanghai legal tender in Canton. In London, the silver dollar was worth $1.15 in Shanghai legal currency on that day. The difference may have been due partly to the costs and risks of smuggling the silver out of Canton and to the costs of shipping it to London.

It seems strange, however, that the price of silver should have remained so very stable in Canton, while the price of Shanghai notes in Canton rose far above its world market relation to the price of silver. Commodity prices have also shown a rising trend in Canton. These factors indicate a depreciation of Canton money, and the price of silver in Canton would therefore be expected to rise. There are grounds for doubt as to whether the silver

照此價格買賣，極為可疑也。

如毫洋價格現將穩定為上海法幣八三〇元等於毫洋一，〇〇〇元。換言之，即毫洋一，二〇五元等於上海幣一，〇〇〇元，則上海法幣價格將自毫洋一，五〇〇元[1]左右，跌至此水準，計為百分之二十。如此則在廣州較易變之批發物價，亦將跌落百分之二十，恐有害於廣州之農工商業也。

price now quoted in Canton is the real market price, that is, the price at which silver could be bought and sold.

If the Canton currency were now to be actually stabilized at a rate of 830 Shanghai dollars per 1000 Canton dollars, or, in other words, at a rate of 1205 Canton dollars per 1000 Shanghai dollars, then the price of Shanghai dollars in Canton would have to decline to this level from about 1500[1]. This decline would be about 20 per cent, and would bring about a fall of about 20 percent in the more flexible wholesale prices of commodities in Canton. Such a fall in prices would be a hardship to Canton industry and agriculture.

路易士
王 廉
一九三六年六月

A. B. LEWIS
LIEN WANG
June, 1936.

(1) 一九三六年五月三十日　　(1) May 30, 1936

江陰人事登記區之生育與死亡率[1]

本登記區範圍僅限於江陰縣峭岐鎮附近之二一鄉村，按照一九三二年本區之戶口普查，共有四，五七九戶，計二一，八六四人。本登記始於一九三一年九月一日至一九三四年八月三十一日，爲期凡三年。本區登記材料，由遴選二〇二誠信而經訓練之登記員蒐集之。

此三年中，每千人之生育率爲四八·三，四四·一，及四〇·〇，而死亡率爲四二·八，三六·一及五二·〇(第四表)。三年之總平均生育率爲四四·二，死亡率爲四三·六，可見生育率逐年減低，而第一年至第二年之死亡率亦減低，惟第二年至第三年則增高。

生育率遞降之原因，大概由於農產價格之跌落，結婚率之減低，及虎疫

(1) 本文材料採用金陵大學農業經濟系江陰人事登記區一九三一至三四年登記之生死紀錄.

BIRTH AND DEATH RATES IN KIANGYIN REGISTRATION AREA[1]

The present study is confined to a small definite rural area in Kiangyin county, including 4,579 familes with a resident population of 21,864 according to the census released for 1932. This study includes a period of three years, from September 1, 1931 to August 31, 1934. The data were collected through the cooperation of 202 faithful reporters who had been carefully selected and trained for several months.

During the three years, the birth rates were 48.3, 44.1, and 40.0, while the death rates were 42.8, 36.1 and 52.0 per 1000, respectively (Table 4). The average birth rate for three years was 44.2 and the average death rate was 43.6. The birth rate declined from year to year, and the death rate declined from the first year to the second year, but increased from the second year to the third year.

The steady decline in the birth rate was probably due to the decline in farm prices, the decline in the marriage

(1) The data presented in this article are from the birth and death registration records of Kiangyin Registration Area, 1931-34. Department of Agricultural Economics, University of Nanking.

第四表　　江蘇江陰四，五七九依經濟狀況而分之農戶
之生育與死亡率
（一九三一年九月至一九三四年八月）
TABLE 4. Birth and Death Rate by Economic Status,
4,579 Rural Families, Kiangyin, Kiangsu, China
(September 1931-August 1934)

經濟狀況 Economic status	每 千 人 之 生 育 率 Births per 1,000 Population				每 千 人 之 死 亡 率 Deaths per 1,000 Population			
	第一年 1st year 1951-52	第二年 2nd year 1952-55	第三年 5rd year 1955-54	總平均 Total 1951-54	第一年 1st year 1951-52	第二年 2nd year 1952-55	第三年 5rd year 1955-54	總平均 Total 1951-54
富 Rich	37.3	34.7	34.6	35.5	26.5	32.3	33.9	30.9
小康 Well-to-do	50.6	46.3	44.9	47.2	39.6	31.0	49.3	40.0
貧 Poor	48.5	44.1	37.9	43.6	46.6	39.6	56.0	47.3
總平均 Total	48.3	44.1	40.0	44.2	42.8	36.1	52.0	43.6

與瘧疾之流行。農產價格之跌落，即農民收入之減少，所以許多已婚農民，尤為青年，離棄家室，出外謀生。結果，婦女之生殖力減低。且際茲經濟恐慌時期，農民因無力舉行婚禮，而遲延婚期者，為數甚多。結果結婚率降低，而生育率因此更為降低。一九三二年發生之虎疫及一九三三年發生之瘧疾

rate, and epidemics of cholera and malaria. Declining farm prices meant decreasing farm incomes, causing many married people, especially the young people, to go out, without their families, to hunt for jobs. As a result, the productivity of women became lower. During the depression, many people could not find or spare any money for holding weddings, and postponed their marriages. As a result, the marriage rate declined and the birth rate was further decreased. A cholera epidemic occurred in 1932 and

，皆影響生育率，尤以瘧疾爲甚，例如當一九三三年秋季流行瘧疾時，孕婦因患瘧疾而流產者，不在少數。流產自不免減低生育率也。

死亡率年有差異，且其差異，更較生育率爲大。江陰登記區係一缺乏現代衛生設備及生活程度極低之農村社會，其每年死亡率之懸殊自屬常事，無論何地，若不能防患於未然，則一旦發生灾患，其死亡率遂不免於大增。第三年(一九三三至三四年)死亡率極高之原因，由於該年發生瘧疾，痢疾，腦膜炎，及痲疹等流行病。第一年(一九三一至三二年)死亡率高之原因，由於虎疫，該年之虎疫爲三年中之最烈者，且流行全國。

a malaria epidemic in 1933. These two epidemics, especially the malaria epidemic, affected the birth rate to some extent. During the time when malaria was spreading in the autumn months of 1933, for instance, many women miscarried when attacked by the fever. These miscarriages naturally tended to lower the birth rate.

The death rate varied from year to year and its variation was much greater than that of the birth rate. Probably this great variation in the death rate from one year to another is the usual thing in a community like Kiangyin registration area, where modern sanitation is entirely lacking and the standard of living is exceedingly low. Wherever the margin of safety is small, a bad year cannot fail to result in a greatly increased death rate. The very high death rate in the third year, 1933-34, was due to the presence, throughout the year, of epidemic diseases such as malaria, diphtheria, meningitis and measles. The high death rate in the first year, 1931-32, was due to a cholera epidemic. This year's cholera outbreak was one of the worst on record. Cholera was prevalent throughout China in that year.

在此一九三一至三四
之三年中，每年人口之自
然增加為百分之〇·〇六
，若與通常年之百分之一
·〇九相較[1]，則江陰登記
區之百分率極低。中國人
口或已達至最高之數量，
高生育率時為高死亡率所
抵銷，勢所難免。生而不
存，徒傷生命而已。

如按農民之經濟狀況
而分生育率與死亡率，則
知此三年中之生育率平均
以小康之家為最高，富家
為最低，而死亡率平均以
貧家為最高，富家為最低
。歐西各國之生育率與死
亡率，均以經濟程度最低
者為最高，經濟程度最高
者為最低。由此觀之，按
經濟狀況而言之死亡率，
江陰與歐西各國相同。然
江陰貧民之生育率較小康

In the three years' period,
1931-34, the annual increase of
population was about 0.06 per
cent. In comparison with the
annual increase of 1.09 per cent,
which was found in a normal
year[1], the annual increase
of 0.06 per cent in Kiangyin
registration area is exceedingly
low. It is probably true that
China's population has already
reached the maximum number
and that the high birth rate be
frequently compensated by a
high death rate is inevitable.
This is a waste of life.

The average birth rate for
the three years was highest in
the well-to-do families and
lowest in the rich families, and
the average death rate was
highest in the poor families and
lowest in the rich families. In
western countries, both the
birth rate and the death rate
are highest among the class
lowest in the economic scale,
and lowest among the class
highest in the economic scale.
Apparently, the death rate
according to eocnomic status
was the same in Kiangyin as
in western countries; but the
birth rate in Kiangyin was
lower among poor people than

(1)喬啓明:中國農村人口之結構及其消長，又
中國農村人口六十年來增減之趨勢.

(1) See "A Study of the Chinese Population," by C. M. Chiao, and "China's
Rural Population Trend during the Last
60 Years", by the same author.

之人爲低，而歐西各國則反是。江陰小康之家之生育率所以較高於貧民者，由於近年貧民之遷移。蓋富有及小康農民無遷移之趨勢，但貧苦農民因經濟之拮据，不得不抛棄妻室，時往他鄉或錫滬一帶工作。

江陰富民之生育與死亡率，雖較其他各階級之人民爲低，然與多數歐西各國相較，則覺甚高。現時多數歐西各國之生育率，大約爲一六，死亡率大約爲一二。例如在一九三二年[1]，大不列顛及愛爾蘭之生育率爲一五‧八，德意志爲一五‧一，澳大利亞爲一七‧〇，法蘭西爲一七‧三，美利堅爲一七

among well-to-do people, while in western countries the figures would be opposite. The higher birth rate among well-to-do people than among poor people may be explained by the large movement of poor people in recent years. The rich and the well-to-do people do not tend to move; but among the poor, because of economic insufficiency, husbands are bound to leave their wives frequently, and go to other villages as farm laborers or go to Shanghai and Wusih as coolie and factory laborers.

The birth and death rates found among the rich people in Kiangyin, although low compared to those of other classes in Kiangyin, are very high rates when compared with those of most western countries. At the present time, the birth rate in most western countries is around 16 and the death rate is around 12. For instance, the birth rate in Great Britain and Ireland in 1932 was 15.8, in Germany 15.1, in Australia 17.0, in France 17.3, and in the United States 17.4; while the death rates were 12.3, 10.8, 8.7, 15.8 and 10.8 respectively.[1]

(1)澳大利亞共和國年鑑

(1) Official Year Book of Commonwealth of Australia, 1933.

Evidently, the comparatively high birth rate found in the United States is only one-half of the rate found among rich people in Kiangyin; and the comparatively high death rate found in France is about one-half of the death rate of rich people in Kiangyin. There was almost no increase in Kiangyin, while in these western countries the annual increase was from 1.5 to 8.3 per thousand. The very high birth rate compensated by the very high death rate in this country is probably the result of the great density of population compared to available resources. At present it seems that the population is subject to the constant menace of famine and disease.

・四，而各國之死亡率為一二・三，一〇・八，八・七，一五・八，及一〇・八¹。由是可知美國較高之生育率僅及江陰富民生育率之二分之一，法國較高之死亡率約及江陰富民死亡率之二分之一。江陰人口幾無自然增加，而上述歐西各國每年每千人之增加，則自一・五至八・三，中國極高之生育率為極高之死亡率所低銷，乃人口密度過大之結果。今日中國之人口似獨特乎災荒及疫病之限制也。

陳彩章
喬啓明

Tsai-Djang Chen
Chi-Ming Chiao

經 濟 統 計
ECONOMIC FACTS

南京金陵大學農學院農業經濟系出版
Department of Agricultural Economics
COLLEGE OF AGRICULTURE AND FORESTRY
UNIVERSITY OF NANKING
NANKING, CHINA

第二期 No. 2　　　　一九三六年十月 October 1936

江蘇武進之農村物價

FARM PRICES IN WUCHIN, KIANGSU

江蘇武進之農村物價曾經張君履鸞研究並撰成[江蘇武進物價之研究]一書，列登金陵大學叢刊第八號（新號），一九三三年出版，至於搜集材料及計算指數之法，均詳載於該叢刊之中文本及較早之英文本

Previous studies of farm prices in Wuchin, Kiangsu, were made by Lu-Luan Chang and results were published in "Farm Prices in Wuchin, Kiangsu," University of Nanking Bulletin Number 8 (New series), in 1933. For details as to the methods used in collecting data and constructing the index numbers, this bulletin in Chinese, or an earlier edition in English, should be consulted.

自一九一〇年至一九三一年，如以一九一〇年至一九一四年之物價爲一〇〇，則江蘇武進農民所得物價指數自一〇〇漲至一七三（第一圖七十五頁）

During the period 1910 to 1931, prices received by farmers in Wuchin, Kiangsu rose from an index number of 100 to an index number of 173, when prices in the period 1910-1914 are taken as 100 (figure 1, page

。以農民售出之物品，泰半均爲糧食，其供給隨收獲之豐歉而不同，故農民所得之物價之變動亦巨。例如一九二九年及一九三〇年之高價則由於旱災，使中國北部及西北部之糧食收獲，大爲減少。[1] 除每年之物價變動外，農民所得物價有上漲之趨勢，則由於白銀購買力之跌落，蓋白銀爲計算該項物價之基本貨幣也。[2]

當農民所得物價上漲之時，農民購入之生產品及消費品價格亦隨之上漲，但變動較爲和緩。以農民購買之生產品及銷費品價格指數，包括多量物品

75). Since most of the products sold by farmers were cereal crops and the total supply fluctuated with changes in weather conditions, year-to-year changes in average prices received were considerable. The high prices prevailing in 1929 and 1930 were due to a severe drought which greatly reduced the supplies of cereal crops in North and Northwest China.[1] Aside from the yearly fluctuations, the general rising trend in prices received by farmers was due to the gradual fall in the purchasing power of silver, which formed the basis of the currency in which these prices were expressed.[2]

During the period when prices received by farmers were rising, average retail prices paid by farmers for commodities used in living and production also rose, but fluctuated much less violently than did the prices

1. 根據已付印之金陵大學農業經濟系卜凱著 [中國土地利用]物價章.

2. 實業部銀價物價討論委員會: [中國銀價及物價問題]一九三五年出版.

1. This statement is based on a chapter on Prices in J. Lossing Buck's China Land Utilization Study, Department of Agricultural Economics, University of Nanking, now in process of publication.

2. Committee for the Study of Silver Values and Commodity Prices, Ministry of Industries, "Silver and Prices in China." 1935.

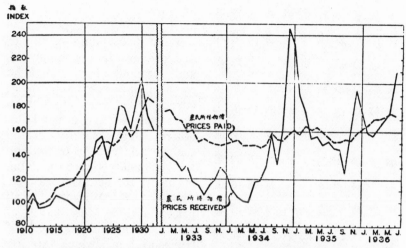

第一圖：江蘇武進農民售
出農產品所得價格及購買
生產品及消費品所付零售
價格指數，一九一〇年至
一九三六年

一九一〇年至一九一
四年＝一〇〇

FIGURE 1. INDEX NUMBERS OF PRICES RECEIVED BY FARMERS FOR COMMODITIES SOLD AND OF PRICES PAID BY FARMERS FOR COMMODITIES USED IN LIVING AND PRODUCTION, WUCHIN, KIANGSU, 1910-1936.

1910-1914＝100

農民所得物價較所付零售物價之波動爲
巨。自一九三二年至一九三五年八月，除
一九三四年以旱災物價有暫時上漲之情形外
，農民所得物價比較低落。自一九三五年中
國貨幣貶值後，農民所得物價漸與所付零售
物價相調正。

Prices received by farmers fluctuated more violently than did retail prices paid by farmers. Prices received by farmers were relatively low from 1932 to August 1935, except temporarily because of the great drought of 1934. After the reduction in the value of Chinese currency in October 1935, prices received by farmers approached nearer the level of prices paid.

，故各個物價供求之變動，似常為他項物品供求相反之變動所抵消。所以農民購買價格指數，似亦以此較為穩定。再則零售物價，包括製造工資，及運輸費等在內，均為較固定而不易變者，故當物價上漲之時，農民所得物價之上漲較農人購買之生產品及消費品價格為速。

一九三一年後，白銀價值上漲，物價乃因此下跌。一九三二年武進農民所得物價指數為一六一，但農民購買之生產品及消費品零售價格較之一九三一年跌落極微，其指數為一八四。

一九三二年後，各種物價均有每月指數之編製（第一二表及第一圖）。

of farm crops. Commodities used in living and production were of many different kinds, and changes in the supply of, and demand for, individual commodities were likely to be offset by contrary changes in the supply of, and demand for, others. Partly for this reason the average trend in prices paid for commodities used in living is likely to be comparatively smooth. Furthermore, retail prices include the labor of manufacture and the cost of transportation, which are relatively inflexible items. As a result of these various factors, when prices were rising, prices received by farmers tended to rise faster than retail prices of commodities used by them in living and production.

After 1931, the value of silver rose, and commodity prices consequently fell. In Wuchin, the average index number of prices received by farmers was 161 in 1932; but retail prices of commodities used in living and production declined very little below the 1931 level, the average index number remaining at 184.

After 1932, monthly index numbers are available (tables 1, and 2, and figure 1). By

一九三四年四月農民所得物價指數跌至一〇〇，而農民購買之生產品及消費品價格數僅跌至一四九。此項農民所得與購買物價之不平衡，為一九三一年中國農村經濟恐慌原因之一。以零售物價，固定不變，故物價跌落之時，其相互之關係，常有不平衡之現象發生。

一九三四年夏之旱災，中國中部及南部之農產數量大減。據中央農業試驗所之估計，江蘇米之產量減少百分之四十八。[1]夏季及春季之農產亦受其影響。數處且有荒災之現象。農產之供給大減，農民所得物價指數乃大漲，至一九三四年秋達最高峯，嗣後始漸降。但此時期物價之上漲，並不足說明農

April, 1934, the index number of farm prices had declined to 100, while the index number of retail prices of commodities used in living and production had declined only to about 149. This great discrepancy between the prices received by farmers and those paid by them is part of the reason for the severe agricultural depression which prevailed in China after 1931. Because of the inflexibility of retail prices, this discrepancy always appears if commodity prices are allowed to fall.

In the summer of 1934 a severe drought greatly reduced the crop supplies in Central and South China. The National Agricultural Research Bureau estimated that the supply of rice in Kiangsu was reduced by 48 per cent.[1] Other summer and spring crops were also affected. Famine conditions occurred in some localities. As a consequence of this unusual scarcity of food crops, the prices received by farmers rose to a very high peak in the autumn of 1934, and then declined rapidly again. This rise in farm prices did not

1. 中央農業試驗所；農情報告第二卷第九期，一九三四年九月一日出版

1. The National Agricultural Research Bureau, Crop Reports. Vol. 2, No. 9, Sept. 1, 1934.

Table 1. Prices Received by Farmers for Commodities Sold in

物品名稱 Commodities		衡量單位 Unit of Measurement	正月 Jan.	二月 Feb.	三月 Mar.	四月 Apr.	五月 May	六月 June
								1933
白米	White Rice	升 Shen	.076	.079	.077	.067	.072	.070
糯米	Glutinous Rice	升 Shen	.084	.083	.075	.076	.075	.075
小麥	Wheat	升 Shen	.063	.065	.060	.060	.042	.041
元麥	Barley (Hulless)	升 Shen	.057	.058	056	.054	.050	.041
黃豆	Soy bean, Yellow	升 Shen	.068	.072	.073	.076	.068	.066
蠶豆	Broad Beans	升 Shen	.042	.056	.052	.035	.045	.042
毛油	Cotton Seed-Soy bean oil	斤 Catty	.148	.144	.142	.140	.135	.135
粳稻	Rice (unhulled late)	斤 Catty	.036	.034	.034	.033	.032	.032
								1934
白米	White Rice	升 Shen	.060	.060	.063	.061	.077	.076
糯米	Glutinous Rice	升 Shen	.067	.068	.067	.068	.092	.093
小麥	Wheat	升 Shen	.050	.049	.048	.048	.048	.040
元麥	Barley (Hulless)	升 Shen	.037	.039	.038	.039	.041	.042
黃豆	Soy bean, Yellow	升 Shen	.048	.050	.046	.046	.045	.055
蠶豆	Broad Beans	升 Shen	.042	.043	.037	.040	.043	.038
毛油	Cotton Seed-Soy bean oil	斤 Catty	.092	.100	.090	.082	.083	.100
粳稻	Rice (unhulled late)	斤 Catty	.030	.029	.029	.030	.035	.037
								1935
白米	White Rice	升 Shen	.115	.113	.108	.113	.117	.117
糯米	Glutinous Rice	升 Shen	.120	.117	.112	.116	.121	.118
小麥	Wheat	升 Shen	.065	.063	.060	.062	.058	.053
元麥	Barley (Hulless)	升 Shen	.065	.065	.051	.042	.045	.047
黃豆	Soy bean, Yellow	升 Shen	.063	.064	.060	.056	.047	.055
蠶豆	Broad Beans	升 Shen	.058	.058	.058	.059	.059	.041
毛油	Cotton Seed-Soy bean oil	斤 Catty	.136	.130	.134	.115	.135	.110
粳稻	Rice (unhulled late)	斤 Catty	.051	.050	.047	.050	.053	.053
								1936
白米	White Rice	升 Shen	.093	.095	.101	.103	.101	.102
糯米	Glutinous Rice	升 Shen	.091	.092	.096	.098	.098	.101
小麥	Wheat	升 Shen	.077	.083	.086	.090	.085	.085
元麥	Barley (Hulless)	升 Shen	.057	.058	.064	.067	.065	.053
黃豆	Soy bean, Yellow	升 Shen	.066	.067	.076	.088	.085	.090
蠶豆	Broad Beans	升 Shen	.045	.047	.050	.050	.055	.055
毛油	Cotton Seed-Soy bean oil	斤 Catty	.160	.156	.177	.220	.204	.185
粳稻	Rice (unhulled late)	斤 Catty	.039	.040	.045	.047	.046	.046

七月 July	八月 Aug.	九月 Sept.	十月 Oct.	十一月 Nov.	十二月 Dec.		物品名稱 Commodities

1933

.068	.067	.068	.065	.064	.065	白 米	White Rice
.075	.075	.073	.071	.070	.072	糯 米	Glutinous Rice
.042	.040	.045	.050	.048	.048	小 麥	Wheat
.031	.034	.039	.036	.038	.038	元 麥	Barley (Hulless)
.055	.063	.052	.053	.046	.049	黃 豆	Soy bean, Yellow
.038	.036	.041	.035	.035	.032	蠶 豆	Broad Beans
.120	.115	.123	.120	.120	.113	毛 油	Cotton Seed-Soy bean oil
.031	.030	.031	.028	.029	.029	粳 稻	Rice (unhulled late)

1934

.107	.117	.107	.103	.128	.125	白 米	White Rice
.110	.128	.117	.098	.133	.128	糯 米	Glutinous Rice
.045	.060	.057	.058	.065	.064	小 麥	Wheat
.045	.050	.053	.055	.050	.060	元 麥	Barley (Hulless)
.055	.056	.058	.060	.055	.065	黃 豆	Soy bean, Yellow
.040	.050	.050	.060	.061	.057	蠶 豆	Broad Beans
.100	.100	.105	.110	.105	.115	毛 油	Cotton Seed-Soy bean oil
.049	.055	.050	.047	.058	.056	粳 稻	Rice (unhulled late)

1935

.108	.106	.103	.105	.104	.098	白 米	White Rice
.106	.098	.093	.096	.098	.094	糯 米	Glutinous Rice
.051	.055	.057	.066	.072	.076	小 麥	Wheat
.050	.050	.050	.055	.061	.055	元 麥	Barley (Hulless)
.060	.051	.055	.062	.072	.065	黃 豆	Soy bean, Yellow
.040	.038	.038	.041	.043	.044	蠶 豆	Broad Beans
.110	.110	.118	.148	.160	.170	毛 油	Cotton Seed-Soy bean oil
.047	.046	.048	.044	.043	.041	粳 稻	Rice (unhulled late)

第二表：江蘇武進農民傳出農產品所得之價格指數（一九三三年一月

Table 2. Index Numbers of Prices Received by Farmers for January 1933—June 1936

物品名稱 Commodities		正月 Jan.	二月 Feb.	三月 Mar.	四月 Apr.	五月 May	六月 June
							1933
白 米	White Rice	133	134	131	114	120	109
小 米	Glutinous Rice	135	130	119	121	115	110
罔 麥	Wheat	154	155	140	143	111	117
元 麥	Barley (Hulless)	143	145	133	135	147	117
黃 豆	Soy bean, Yellow	139	144	143	141	124	125
毛 豆	Broad Beans	131	175	158	109	150	140
油	Cotton Seed-Soy bean oil	151	148	146	147	145	141
粳 稻	Rice (unhulled late)	164	148	155	127	128	133
每月楒 量指數	Aggregative Index Numbers	142	138	135	127	132	118
							1934
白 米	White Rice	105	102	107	103	128	119
糯 米	Glutinous Rice	108	106	106	108	142	137
小 麥	Wheat	122	117	112	114	126	114
元 麥	Barley (Hulless)	93	98	90	98	121	120
黃 豆	Soy bean, Yellow	98	100	90	85	82	104
毛 豆	Broad Beans	131	134	112	125	143	127
油	Cotton Seed-Soy bean oil	94	103	93	86	89	104
粳 稻	Rice (unhulled late)	136	126	132	115	140	154
每月楒 量指數	Aggregative Index Numbers	111	104	101	100	118	119
							1935
白 米	White Rice	202	192	183	192	195	183
糯 米	Glutinous Rice	194	183	178	184	186	174
小 麥	Wheat	159	150	140	148	153	151
元 麥	Barley (Hulless)	163	163	121	105	132	134
黃 豆	Soy bean, Yellow	129	128	118	104	85	104
毛 豆	Broad Beans	181	181	176	184	197	137
油	Cotton Seed-Soy bean oil	139	134	138	121	145	115
粳 稻	Rice (unhulled late)	232	217	214	192	212	221
每月楒 量指數	Aggregative Index Numbers	190	176	154	156	149	152
							1936
白 米	White Rice	163	161	171	175	158	159
糯 米	Glutinous Rice	147	144	152	156	151	149
小 麥	Wheat	188	198	200	214	224	243
元 麥	Barley (Hulless)	143	145	152	168	191	151
黃 豆	Soy bean, Yellow	135	134	149	163	155	170
毛 豆	Broad Beans	141	147	152	156	183	183
油	Cotton Seed-Soy bean oil	163	161	182	232	219	193
粳 稻	Rice (unhulled late)	177	174	204	181	184	192
每月楒 量指數	Aggregative Index Numbers	159	156	163	170	176	210

至一九三六年六月）一九二〇年至一九一四年＝一〇〇

Commodities Sold in Wuchin, Kiangsu, 1910-1914＝100

七月 July	八月 Aug.	九月 Sept.	十月 Oct.	十一月 Nov.	十二月 Dec.	全年權數平均指數 Annual weighted aggregative Index	物品名稱 Commodities
1933							
108	105	108	112	116	116	—	白　米 White Rice
110	110	107	109	115	118	—	糯米 Glutinous Rice
120	108	113	125	117	117	—	小麥 Wheat
89	92	100	90	95	95	—	元麥 Barley (Hulless)
106	131	116	110	105	107	—	黃豆 Soy bean, Yellow
115	106	121	97	100	91	—	蠶豆 Broad Beans
120	116	121	121	126	119	—	毛豆油 Cotton Seed-Soy bean oil
111	130	155	140	138	132	—	粳稻 Rice (unhulled late)
115	106	115	120	130	125	123	每月權數指數 Aggregative Index Numbers
1934							
170	183	170	178	233	223	—	白　米 White Rice
162	188	172	151	218	210	—	糯米 Glutinous Rice
129	162	143	145	159	156	—	小麥 Wheat
129	135	136	138	125	150	—	元麥 Barley (Hulless)
106	117	129	125	125	141	—	黃豆 Soy bean, Yellow
121	147	147	167	174	163	—	蠶豆 Broad Beans
100	101	103	111	111	121	—	毛豆油 Cotton Seed-Soy bean oil
175	239	250	235	276	255	—	粳稻 Rice (unhulled late)
131	157	132	165	247	232	137	每月權數指數 Aggregative Index Numbers
1935							
171	166	163	181	189	175	—	白　米 White Rice
156	144	137	148	161	154	—	糯米 Glutinous Rice
146	149	143	165	176	185	—	小麥 Wheat
143	135	128	138	153	138	—	元麥 Barley (Hulless)
115	106	122	129	164	141	—	黃豆 Soy bean, Yellow
121	112	112	114	123	126	—	蠶豆 Broad Beans
110	111	116	144	168	179	—	毛豆油 Cotton Seed-Soy bean oil
168	200	215	220	205	186	—	粳稻 Rice (unhulled late)
146	145	125	162	195	178	158	每月權數指數 Aggregative Index Numbers

民收入之增加，以農民受旱災之影響，固無大量農產售出之可能也。俟一九三五年之新穀上場，該年九月之農民所得物價指數跌至一二五。但農民購買之生產品及消費品之指數為一五三，並未大受旱災之影響。

一九三四年至一九三五年秋多物價之上漲，如高山之在平原。若無旱災，則物價水準或將仍如平原。雖物價不漲，但農民情況或反稍佳，蓋有較多糧食以供生活之需，故減低產量，決不足以解決此次以銀價上漲而發生之經濟恐慌。

一九三五年十月，中國幣價跌落，至十一月三

indicate an increase in farm incomes, because the farmers had very little to sell at the high prices, because of the drought. After the new crop supplies began to be available in 1935, the index number of prices received by farmers declined to a level of 125 in September, 1935, while the index number of retail prices of commodities used in living and production remained at 153. This index number was not much affected by the drought.

The high farm prices prevailing in the autumn and winter of 1934-1935 were like a mountain rising in a great valley. If the drought had not occurred, farm prices would probably have remained at about the level of the foot of this mountain. Farmers would have been better off, in spite of the low prices, because they would have had more to eat. A reduction in the supplies of all crops does not help to cure a depression that is due to a recent rise in the value of money.

In October, 1935, the Chinese currency was allowed to fall in

日，其外匯價格，始告穩
定。[1]武進農民所得物價指
數自九月之一二五漲至十
一月之一九五，約上漲百
分之三十。但農民購買之
物品價格指數則仍約為一
五三。嗣後數月農民所得
之物價指數漲落極巨，至
一九三六年六月達二一〇
，而農民購買物品指數亦
漸漲至一七四。以貨幣之
貶值，農民所得及購買物
品之價格，事實上已恢復
其平衡。

如中國貨幣之購買力
維持現在水準，不再使其
價值上漲，則如一九三二
年至一九三五年之農村經
濟大恐慌將不致再行發生
。農民所得之物價當仍將
較農民購買之物價變動為
巨，蓋每年收獲之豐稔不
同，及零售物價之固定性
使然也。

當一九三二年前物價
上漲之時，武進農民所得

value, and on November 3 it
was stabilized in foreign
exchange.[1] In Wuchin, farm
prices rose from an index
number of 125 in September to
162 in October, or about 30 per
cent. Retail prices paid by
farmers remained at about 153.
In succeeding months, farm
prices fluctuated considerably
but had reached a level of 210
in June, 1936, while retail prices
of commodities used in living
and production had gradually
risen to about 174. By reducing
the value of the currency the
discrepancy between prices
received and prices paid by
farmers was practically overcome.

As long as the currency is
held to its present purchasing
power level, and is not allowed
to rise in value, there will be no
reason to expect an agricultural
depression as severe as that of
1932 to 1935. Farm prices will
continue to fluctuate more
violently than retail prices,
because of the yearly variations
in the harvest, and the inflexibility of retail prices.

During the period of rising
prices ending in 1931, prices

1. 路易士三廉1中國貨幣與物價之變遷1載於
本刊第一期一九三六年九月出版.

1. A. B. Lewis and Lien Wang,
Economic Facts, No. 1, Sept.,
1936.

之物價較農民所付之長工
工資及地稅爲速（第三四
表及第二圖）。在此情況
之下，農民自能支付工資
及地稅。地稅與工資上漲
之速率相同，但地稅之波
動極巨。

　自一九三一年後，物
價下跌，地稅亦略有下跌
之趨勢，但工資則不跌。
與前數年相較，農民支付
工資及地租已感覺困難。
此常發現於物價跌落之時
，亦爲中國一九三二年至
一九三五年農村經濟恐慌
原因之一。

　當一九三二年前物價
上漲之時，武進地價之上
漲且較農人所得之物價爲
速（第三圖及第三四表）
。但查金陵大學業已付印
之卜凱中國土地利用之物
價章，據其搜集較爲豐富
之材料，則此項價格關係
，並非爲中國此時期普遍

received by farmers for
commodities sold rose more
rapidly than the wages of farm
year labor and farm land taxes
in Wuchin (tables 3 and 4
and figure 2). Under these
conditions farmers could afford
to pay taxes and employ labor.
Taxes and wages rose at about
the same rate, but there were
wide fluctuations in taxes.

During the period of low
farm prices after 1931, farm
taxes fluctuated around a
slightly declining trend, and
farm wages failed to decline.
In comparison with previous
years, taxes and wages were
difficult to pay. This relationship always occurs when prices
fall, and partly explains the
Chinese agricultural depression
of 1932 to 1935.

During the period of rising
prices ending in 1931, farm
land values in Wuchin rose
even faster than the prices
received by farmers for farm
products (figure 3 and tables 3
and 4). According to more
comprehensive data presented
in a chapter on Prices in J.
Lossing Buck's China Land
Utilization Study, now in
process of publication by the
University of Nanking, this
relationship was not typical of

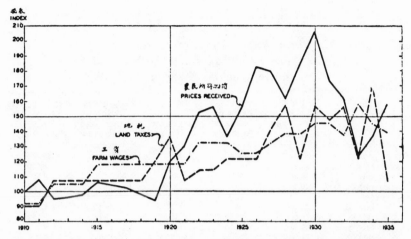

第二圖：江蘇武進農民售
出農產品所得價格指數，
長工工資指數，及地稅指
數，一九一〇年至一九三
五年。

　　一九一〇年至一九
一四年＝一〇〇

　　當一九一〇年至一九三一年物價上漲之
時，農民所得物價較地稅及工資上漲為速。
至一九三一年物價跌落以來，工資及地稅所
受之影響極微。

FIGURE 2. INDEX NUMBERS OF
PRICES RECEIVED BY FARMERS
FOR COMMODITIES SOLD, OF
WAGES OF FARM YEAR LABOR,
AND OF FARM LAND TAXES,
WUCHIN, KIANGSU, 1910-1935.

1910-1914=100.

From 1910 to 1931, when the
general trend in farm prices was
upward, prices received by farmers
rose more rapidly than farm taxes
and the wages of farm year labor.
When prices declined after 1931, the
general trends in wages and taxes
were little affected.

第五表： 江蘇武進農民所付之長工工資，水牛及黃牛價格，每畝
農田地稅與農地價格(一九一〇年至一九三五年)

Table 3. Farm Wages, Price of Water Buffalos, Price of Yellow Cows, Land Taxes and the Value of Farm Land in Wuchin, Kiangsu, 1910-1935

年 數 Year	長工工資 Wages of Farm Year Labor	水牛價格 Price of Water Buffalos	黃牛價格 Price of Yellow Cows	農田價格 Value of Farm Land Per Mow	每畝農田之地稅 Taxes Per Mow of Farm Land
1910	$35.00	$50.00	$20.00	$ ───	$0.630
1911	35.00	60.00	30.00	───	0.630
1912	40.00	60.00	30.00	41.78	0.750
1913	40.00	60.00	30.00	41.67	0.750
1914	40.00	60.00	30.00	28.57	0.750
1915	45.00	65.00	35.00	53.13	0.750
1916	45.00	65.00	35.00	55.56	0.750
1917	45.00	65.00	35.00	57.14	0.750
1918	45.00	70.00	40.00	42.05	0.750
1919	45.00	70.00	40.00	61.29	0.850
1920	45.00	70.00	40.00	62.50	0.950
1921	45.00	70.00	40.00	57.78	0.750
1922	50.00	70.00	40.00	72.34	0.800
1923	50.00	70.00	40.00	66.67	0.800
1924	50.00	80.00	50.00	85.29	0.850
1925	47.50	63.00	45.00	97.73	0.850
1926	47.50	70.00	47.50	108.33	0.850
1927	50.00	70.00	47.50	127.27	0.990
1928	52.50	75.00	52.50	139.34	1.100
1929	52.50	85.00	62.50	149.00	0.850
1930	55.00	85.00	62.50	153.25	1.090
1931	55.00	87.50	62.50	139.50	1.030
1932	52.00	85.00	60.00	122.50	1.090
1935	60.00	75.00	50.00	80.00	0.850
1934	55.00	76.50	57.10	83.33	1.200
1935	53.00	64.20	42.50	92.50	0.750

第六表： 江蘇武進農民所付之長工工資指數，役畜價格指數，地稅指
數，農地價格指數，農民所付生產品與消費品零售價格指數
與農民出售農產品所得價格指數(一九一〇年至一九三五年)
一九一〇年至一九一四年 = 一〇〇

Table 4. Index Numbers of Farm Wages, Prices of Labor Animals,
Land Taxes, the Value of farm land, Retail Prices Paid by
farmers for Commodities used in living and production
and Prices Received by farmers for Commodities
sold in Wuchin, Kiangsu 1910—1935
1910-1914=100

年數 Years	長工工資 Wages of Farm labor	役畜價格 Prices of labor Animals	農地價格 Value of Farm land	地 稅 Taxes on Farm land	農民所付零 售價格 Retail Prices paid by farmers	農民所得價格 Prices Received by farmers
1910	92	79	—	90	93	100
1911	92	105	—	90	104	108
1912	105	105	112	107	98	95
1913	105	105	112	107	100	96
1914	105	105	77	107	103	98
1915	118	119	142	107	113	106
1916	118	119	149	107	115	104
1917	118	119	153	107	117	102
1918	118	132	113	107	119	98
1919	118	132	164	121	126	94
1920	118	132	167	136	136	120
1921	118	132	155	107	139	130
1922	132	132	194	114	143	152
1923	132	132	179	114	151	156
1924	132	159	228	121	151	136
1925	125	135	262	121	148	156
1926	125	146	290	121	153	182
1927	132	146	341	141	164	179
1928	138	159	373	157	155	161
1929	138	185	399	121	161	185
1930	145	185	410	156	177	206
1931	145	187	374	157	188	173
1932	137	181	328	156	184	161
1933	158	154	214	121	162	123
1934	145	168	223	171	155	137
1935	139	132	248	107	158	158

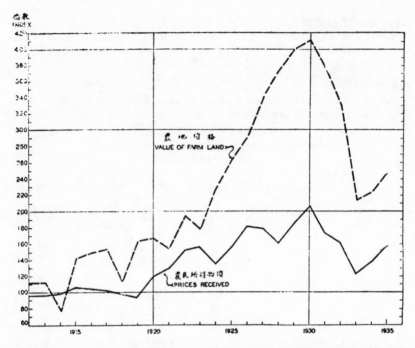

第 三 圖：江 蘇 武 進 農 民 傳
出 農 產 品 所 得 價 格 及 農 地
價 格 指 數，一 九 一 二 年 至
一 九 三 五 年。

　　一 九 一 〇 年 至 一 九 一
五 年 ＝ 一 〇 〇

　　當農民所得物價上漲之時，農地價格上
漲更速，物價下跌時農地價格下跌亦更速。

FIGURE 3. INDEX NUMBERS OF
PRICES RECEIVED BY FARMERS
FOR COMMODITIES SOLD AND
THE VALUE OF FARM LAND,
WUCHIN, KIANGSU, 1912-1935.

1910-1914＝100.

When prices received by farmers
were rising, the value of farm land
in Wuchin rose much more rapidly.
When farm prices fell, land values
fell more precipitously.

之現象。中國地價較農人所得物價上漲為遲滯。一九二五年後，則趨勢穩定。

Chinese price relationships during this period. According to the more comprehensive study, farm land values in China rose somewhat more slowly than farm prices, and remained about stable after 1925.

地價指數自一九三一年之三七四跌至一九三五年之二四八。惟一九三三年至一九三五地價略見上漲。總計自一九三一年以來，地價跌落百分之四十四○同時農民收入物價指數，自一九三一之一七三跌至一九三三年之一二三，但至一九三五年上漲至一五八，共計跌落百分之九○但此據前述卜凱之研究，亦並非為中國普遍之現象。地價之跌落常較農民收入之物價為遲滯。

Farm land values in Wuchin declined from an index number of 374 in 1931 to 248 in 1935, including a slight rise from 1933 to 1935. This decline was 44 per cent. of the 1931 level. During the same period, farm prices fell from 173 in 1931 to 123 in 1933 a decline of only 9 per cent. This is not a typical relationship between farm prices and farm land values, according to the more comprehensive study previously mentioned. The decline in land values is usually less rapid than the decline in farm prices.

地價之跌落，顯示中國農村經濟恐慌之嚴重。

The decline in land values reflects the severity of the agricultural depression.

地價跌落亦為促進經濟恐慌尖銳化原素之一，蓋此無異減低農民之財產，致農民還債及借債之能，亦隨之減退。

It is itself also a factor in intensifying the depression, because it represents a reduction in the value of the farmer's assets and in their security for borrowing.

已如上述，武進農民售出之物品，泰半為糧食

As previously mentioned, most of the commodities sold

第四圖：江蘇武進農民售
出農產品所得價格及上海
糧食批發物價指數，一九
二一年至一九三五年

一九二六年＝一〇〇

武進農民售出之農產泰半為糧食品。農
民所得物價之波動僅較上海糧食批發價格稍
大耳。

FIGURE 4. INDEX NUMBERS OF
PRICES RECEIVED BY FARMERS
FOR COMMODITIES SOLD IN WU-
CHIN, KIANGSU, AND THE
WHOLESALE PRICES OF CEREALS
IN SHANGHAI, 1921-1935.

1926＝100.

Most of the commodities sold by
Wuchin farmers are cereals. The
prices received by the farmers,
fluctuated only slightly more than
wholesale prices of cereals in Shanghai.

第五表： 江蘇武進農民售出農產品所得價格指數及上海糧食批
發價格指數（一九二一年至一九三五年）

Table 5. Index Numbers of Prices Received by Farmers for
Commodities sold in Wuchin, Kiangsu and Wholesale
Prices of Cereals in Shanghai, 1921—1935.

日期 Date	江蘇武進農民售出農產品所得 價格指數，一九二六年=一〇〇 Index Numbers of Prices Received by Farmers for Commodities sold in Wuchin, Kiangsu 1926=100	國定稅則委員會之糧食批發價 格指數，一九二六年=一〇〇 National Tariff Commission, Index Numbers of Wholesale Prices of Cereals, 1926=100
1921	71.4	72.2
1922	83.5	82.6
1923	85.7	86.3
1924	74.7	83.3
1925	85.7	91.1
1926	100.0	100.0
1927	98.4	100.6
1928	88.5	89.6
1929	101.6	97.2
1930	113.2	110.3
1931	95.1	94.4
1932	88.5	81.7
1933	67.6	69.6
1934	75.3	69.1
1935	86.8	80.0

品（第一圖）。自一九二
一年至一九三五年武進農
民所得物價指數與上海稅
則委員會之糧食批發物價
指數有相同之趨勢（第五
表及第四圖）。鄉鎮物價
較城市者波動較大。

by farmers in Wuchin are
cereal products (table 1). From
1921 to 1935, the average
index number of their prices
fluctuated very closely in line
with the average index number
of wholesale cereal prices in
Shanghai as compiled by the
National Tariff Commission
(table 5 and figure 4). Prices
in the country town fluctuated
only slightly more than city
prices.

路易士

王 廉

A. B. LEWIS

LIEN WANG

一九三〇年至一九三六年 中國各地及香港之 批發物價

批發物價平均數之趨勢幾全隨計算價格之貨幣價值而變遷。當一九三〇年時中國銀元含純銀二三·九〇二五公分，爲華北（天津），青島，及南京各地之主要貨幣。至一九三三年每元改爲含純銀二三·四九三四四八公分。廣東毫洋，計爲雙角五枚，含純銀一八·八一公分。至香港貨幣則每元含純銀二四·二六公分。

以上述各項貨幣均爲白銀，故其價值之變遷，常屬相同。香港廣州及其他通用中國銀元之地，其批發物價似應有相同之趨勢。但貨幣含銀量之變更，與兌換及流通之限制，均足使各地物價，失去平時之關係。至各地之災禍

The trends of averages of wholesale prices depend primarily upon changes in the value of the currency in which the prices are expressed. In 1930, the Chinese silver dollar, containing 23.9025 grams of fine silver, was the principal currency in North China (Tientsin), Shanghai, Tsingtao, and Nanking. In 1933 the fine silver content of this dollar was changed to 23.493448 grams. In Canton, the Cantonese silver dollar, consisting of five 20-cent coins containing 18.81 grams of fine silver was in use. The Hongkong dollar, with 24.26 grams of fine silver, was the currency of Hongkong.

Since silver was the basis of all these currencies, changes in their value would ordinarily be similar. Wholesale prices would therefore be expected to follow a similar course in Canton, in Hongkong, and in cities using the Chinese dollar. Changes in the silver content of the currencies, and restrictions on their redemption and movement, would disturb the usual relationship between commodity prices

，如水災，旱災及戰事等，僅有暫時之影響。

一九三〇年廣東與香港之物價無可靠之統計。中國其他各地以銀幣計算之物價，有同漲之趨勢。（第一表及第一圖）

因白銀價值之跌落，一九三一年各地之物價依舊上漲。四月及五月間青島及華北之物價已達最高峯。

一九三一年八月及以後各月，漢口，南京及上海之物價上漲，蓋因揚子江及淮河流域水災之故。此水災自漢口以至海邊，泛濫區域約計八七，〇〇〇，〇〇〇畝。其中以漢口物價所受之影響最巨，故上漲最高，為期亦最久。南京物價八九月間上漲最甚，以迄于冬。至上海則以粮食之供給較易，其物價僅於八月一度上漲後即低跌。

in different places. Severe local calamities such as floods, droughts, and wars would have a similar effect temporarily.

In 1930, no reliable wholesale prices data were available for Canton and Hongkong. In other Chinese cities, prices expressed in terms of the silver dollar followed a very similar rising trend (table 1 and figure 1).

Because of the declining value of silver, the rise in commodity prices continued in 1931. In Tsingtao and North China the highest level of prices was reached in April and May.

In Hankow, Nanking, and Shanghai, prices were raised in August, 1931, and later months because of the great flood in the Yangtze and Hwai river valleys. The flood covered an area of about 87,000,000 mow between Hankow and the sea, and its effects on prices were naturally especially acute in Hankow, where prices were raised the most and remained high the longest. In Nanking, prices rose in August and September and remained high through the following winter. In Shanghai, which is nearer to outside sources of food and other supplies, prices were high in August and declined thereafter.

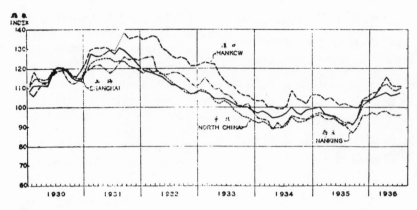

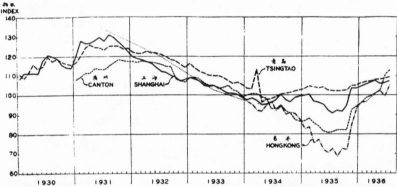

第 一 圖 : 中 國 各 地 及 香 港
批 發 物 價 指 數 , 一 九 三 〇
年 一 月 至 一 九 三 六 年 七 月
一 九 二 六 年 = 一 〇 〇

中國各地及香港之批發物價有相同之趨
勢。一九三二年前白銀價值下跌，物價乃上
漲。一九三一年後，銀價上漲，而物價乃又
應下跌。各地物價相互之關係，僅受一九三
一年水災及一九三四年旱災之影響，暫時的
失去其共同性。當中國實行白銀出口稅時，
中國法幣價值較廣州及香港貨幣爲低。自一
九三五年十一月實行新貨幣政策後，毫洋與
港洋之貶值高於法幣，因此廣州及香港物價
之上升，亦較中國各處爲烈。

FIGURE 1. INDICES OF WHOLE-
SALE PRICES, IN DIFFERENT
CITIES IN CHINA AND IN HONG-
KONG, JANUARY 1930-JULY 1936.

1926 = 100.

Wholesale prices in different cities
in China and in Hongkong, had
nearly the same trend. Prices rose
until 1931 and fell after 1931. The
similar price movements in different
cities were only temporarily dis-
turbed by the flood in 1931 and the
drought in 1934. During the period
of the enforcement of silver export
fees in China, the Chinese national
legal currency was lower in value
than the Canton and Hongkong
currencies. After the currency reform in November 1935, Canton and
Hongkong currencies depreciated
more than the Chinese national currency. Consequently prices in Canton
and Hongkong rose more rapidly than
in other cities.

第一表：中國各地及香港之批發物價指數，自一九三〇年一月
至一九三六年七月．

Table I. Index numbers of wholesale prices in different cities in
China and in Hongkong, Jan. 1930 to July 1936

	上海[1] Shang- hai[1]	華北[2] North China[2]	廣州[3] Canton[3]	南京[4] Nan- king[4]	漢口[1] Han- kow[4]	青島[4] Tsing- tao[4]	香港[5] Hong- kong[5]
Number of commodities	154	106	190	106	111	121	85
1930	114.8	115.9	——	100.0	100.0	100.0	——
1931	126.7	122.6	112.6	106.1	114.5	107.6	134.7
1932	112.4	112.9	113.8	100.8	112.4	103.6	120.7
1933	103.8	100.6	104.5	92.2	98.9	94.9	102.1
1934	97.1	91.8	94.8	80.6	89.0	86.9	92.3
1935	96.4	95.4	84.6	80.4	89.3	89.4	76.8
1930							
一 月 Jan.	108.3	111.3	——	111.4	107.8	110.7	——
二 月 Feb.	111.3	114.5	——	118.4	105.8	108.8	——
三 月 Mar.	111.3	114.9	——	113.7	109.8	111.8	——
四 月 Apr.	111.2	114.1	——	112.8	112.9	115.7	——
五 月 May	111.0	114.8	——	111.3	112.8	113.6	——
六 月 June	117.5	118.6	——	116.6	118.0	114.7	——
七 月 July	120.4	120.5	——	118.3	118.4	119.7	——
八 月 Aug.	119.6	120.2	——	119.1	119.1	117.2	——
九 月 Sept.	118.4	118.3	——	114.5	119.5	118.3	——
十 月 Oct.	115.4	116.0	——	112.3	116.6	116.8	——
十一月 Nov.	114.1	115.0	——	112.8	115.8	115.7	——
十二月 Dec.	113.6	114.5	——	115.7	119.1	115.2	——
1931							
一 月 Jan.	119.7	118.2	107.8	118.4	123.1	116.4	——
二 月 Feb.	127.4	122.2	109.1	119.9	129.2	119.7	——
三 月 Mar.	126.1	124.0	111.0	121.7	130.4	123.9	——
四 月 Apr.	126.2	124.5	111.2	121.8	130.4	125.4	——
五 月 May	127.5	125.0	113.6	119.7	130.7	124.4	——
六 月 June	129.2	124.8	113.1	117.5	129.9	124.0	——
七 月 July	127.4	123.3	113.0	119.4	129.0	123.1	——
八 月 Aug.	130.3	128.8	114.7	122.7	——	124.6	——
九 月 Sept.	129.2	123.5	116.2	125.6	138.3	124.8	——
十 月 Oct.	126.9	121.3	118.1	124.4	135.4	124.6	——
十一月 Nov.	124.8	120.5	117.5	124.9	135.6	123.4	——
十二月 Dec.	121.8	119.4	117.2	124.1	136.4	123.7	——
1932							
一 月 Jan.	119.3	117.7	117.2	125.0	134.8	121.8	——
二 月 Feb.	118.4	119.9	116.7	125.6	135.6	121.2	——
三 月 Mar.	117.6	118.0	117.1	125.9	136.5	121.2	——
四 月 Apr.	116.7	118.8	116.8	117.5	135.5	122.0	——
五 月 May	115.7	117.0	116.6	117.1	130.5	121.3	——
六 月 June	113.6	115.0	116.1	116.9	128.8	121.2	——

1, 2, 3, 4, 5 見九十七頁附註

1, 2, 3, 4, 5. For footnotes see page 97.

			上海[1] Shang-hai[1]	華北[2] North China[2]	廣州[5] Canton[3]	南京[4] Nan-king[4]	漢口[4] Han-kow[4]	青島[4] Tsing-tao[4]	香港[5] Hong-kong[5]
1932									
七	月	July	111.8	112.4	115.3	117.6	126.6	120.5	—
八	月	Aug.	111.3	111.3	114.5	117.7	125.2	119.2	—
九	月	Sept.	109.8	109.5	114.4	116.9	125.7	117.7	—
十	月	Oct.	108.7	107.5	108.3	115.1	124.9	117.1	—
十一月		Nov.	106.9	106.9	107.1	112.6	121.3	115.4	—
十二月		Dec.	107.5	107.1	106.3	110.8	121.4	113.8	—
1933									
一	月	Jan.	108.6	109.1	108.8	112.1	122.4	115.7	—
二	月	Feb.	107.6	108.5	108.8	115.2	123.2	113.5	—
三	月	Mar.	106.7	106.7	108.2	112.4	122.6	112.0	—
四	月	Apr.	104.5	103.0	106.0	109.4	122.2	111.1	—
五	月	May	104.2	101.8	104.9	109.7	117.4	109.9	—
六	月	June	104.5	103.1	104.6	106.9	114.1	109.7	—
七	月	July	103.4	101.9	103.0	106.0	112.0	109.6	—
八	月	Aug.	101.7	98.5	103.6	103.6	110.7	108.6	—
九	月	Sept.	100.4	97.2	104.7	100.8	107.6	107.0	—
十	月	Oct.	100.3	95.2	102.3	100.6	106.4	105.5	—
十一月		Nov.	99.9	94.5	101.4	101.8	106.0	106.0	—
十二月		Dec.	98.4	93.1	98.8	97.6	103.8	104.8	—
1934									
一	月	Jan.	97.2	92.0	99.8	94.5	103.3	103.2	96.4
二	月	Feb.	98.0	92.5	100.4	93.9	103.6	102.8	94.8
三	月	Mar.	96.6	91.1	100.1	93.2	100.2	112.9	91.6
四	月	Apr.	94.6	89.2	98.6	88.2	100.2	95.8	91.3
五	月	May	94.9	89.4	98.0	92.1	99.3	97.3	94.3
六	月	June	95.7	89.5	92.5	89.6	99.2	97.6	96.0
七	月	July	97.1	90.9	92.5	92.1	100.9	98.7	91.7
八	月	Aug.	99.8	94.8	94.6	95.4	108.9	100.0	94.0
九	月	Sept.	97.3	92.5	91.6	94.6	104.6	100.4	89.9
十	月	Oct.	96.1	92.3	90.4	94.0	103.3	100.7	90.7
十一月		Nov.	98.3	93.0	87.0	93.6	101.9	101.7	90.0
十二月		Dec.	99.0	95.0	86.2	94.0	105.6	102.3	87.0
1935									
一	月	Jan.	99.4	96.1	86.4	95.3	106.2	103.0	82.2
二	月	Feb.	99.9	96.9	87.6	95.8	105.9	104.1	83.1
三	月	Mar.	96.4	95.8	85.5	94.0	103.6	103.7	75.0
四	月	Apr.	95.9	95.3	83.8	93.6	104.9	103.3	76.8
五	月	May	95.0	95.1	81.1	94.0	103.0	103.6	72.1
六	月	June	92.1	93.5	80.2	92.1	100.8	102.2	70.1
七	月	July	90.5	91.8	80.8	91.1	101.6	101.8	72.4
八	月	Aug.	91.0	92.2	81.7	88.7	100.7	101.7	68.4
九	月	Sept.	91.1	90.7	82.0	86.5	99.8	101.8	72.3
十	月	Oct.	94.1	94.2	81.9	90.1	99.6	102.3	71.6
十一月		Nov.	103.8	100.9	92.3	95.5	104.0	104.4	84.3
十二月		Dec.	103.3	102.5	94.0	95.6	105.2	104.9	93.0

1, 2, 3, 4, 5 見九十七頁附註
1, 2, 3, 4, 5. For footnotes see page 97.

第一表一續
Table 1—*Continued*

			上海[1] Shang-hai[1]	華北[2] North China[2]	廣州[5] Canton[3]	南京[4] Nan-king[4]	漢口[4] Han-kow[4]	青島[4] Tsing-tao[4]	香港[5] Hong-kong[5]
	1936								
一	月	Jan.	104.3	104.1	95.6	97.1	107.3	105.8	96.0
二	月	Feb.	105.4	107.1	98.3	96.1	107.7	106.6	96.3
三	月	Mar.	106.4	110.5	99.4	97.5	111.8	107.0	—
四	月	Apr.	107.3	111.5	100.9	97.7	115.3	107.6	100.8
五	月	May	105.8	109.1	102.3	96.1	111.3	107.8	101.9
六	月	June	106.1	108.1	110.5	95.6	110.6	108.3	99.5
七	月	July	107.2	109.6	112.9	96.0	110.7	109.2	

1. 國定稅則委員會之上海物價月報，一九二六年＝一〇〇

2. 南開經濟研究所編製，抄自上海物價月報，一九二六年＝一〇〇

3. 廣東統計局編製，抄自該局寄送金陵大學農業經濟系之報告。

4. 實業部編製之物價統計月報。 此指數僅於一九三〇年以後始行編製，因欲使與上海華北之指數能互相比較，將其基數換算爲一九三〇年＝一一五·三二五，因上海華北指數一九三〇年之平均爲一一五·三二五。

5. 香港政府進出口部之統計室編製。 此指數乃以一九二二年爲一〇〇。一九二三，一九二五，一九二六，一九二七，一九二八，一九二九，及一九三〇諸年均無指數可求。每月指數始於一九三四年，因欲使此指數與上海指數能互相比較，特將其基數換算爲一九二二年＝九八·六，因一九二二年上海指數之平均爲九八·六。

1. National Tariff Commission, Prices and Price Indexes in Shanghai, 1926 = 100.

2. Compiled by Nankai Economic Institute, and taken from Prices and Price Indexes in Shanghai, 1926 = 100.

3. Compiled by Kwangtung Statistical Bureau, and taken from the reports of the said bureau send to the Department of Agricultural Economics, University of Nanking, 1926 = 100.

4. Compiled by Ministry of Industries, Monthly Price Statistics. These indexes have been compiled only since 1930. In order to make them comparable with the Shanghai and North China Indexes, they were converted to a base of 1930 = 115.325, since the average of the Shanghai and North China index numbers for 1930 was 115.325.

5. Compiled by the Statistical Office of the Imports and Exports Department of the Hongkong government. The index is based on 1922 as 100, no indexes are obtainable for the years 1923, 1925, 1926, 1927, 1928, 1929 and 1930. The monthly figures have been compiled only since 1934. In order to make these index numbers comparable with the Shanghai index numbers, they were converted to a base of 1922 = 98.6, since the average of the Shanghai index numbers for 1922 was 98.6.

如以一九二六年為一〇〇，則廣州一九三一年之批發物價較中國其他各處為低。其差異之原因，著者尚未完全明瞭，但一九三一年廣州曾一度缺乏現銀，五月一日省政府命令廣州中國銀行分行停止行鈔兌現[1]。一九三二年之毫洋價格，如以滬幣計算之，計較一九三一年者低百分之八[2]。廣州批發物價遂上漲與國內其他各處相齊。

香港方面，一九三一年僅有該年之批發物價指數，可資參考較。此指數與上海每年批發物價指數相近似。

一九三二年，一九三三年及一九三四年之上半年，香港，廣州及中國其他各地之物價，均逐漸下跌。至于各地物價趨勢之差異，如就指數所含物品之不同種類及數量而論，

1. 實業部；[中國銀價及物價問題] 一六五頁，一九三五年出版。

2. 主計處統計局；[統計季刊] 第五期，一四三頁，一九三六年出版。

When 1926 is considered 100, Canton wholesale prices in 1931 were lower than in other Chinese cities. The reasons for this discrepancy are not yet fully known to the authors, but there was a scarcity of silver in Canton in 1931, and on May 8 the government ordered the Canton branch of the Bank of China to stop redeeming its notes in silver.[1] In 1932 the Canton currency was worth 8 per cent. less than in 1931 in terms of Shanghai money,[2] and wholesale prices in Canton came into line with those in other Chinese cities.

For Hongkong, only an annual index number of wholesale prices was available for 1931, and this was approximately in line with that for Shanghai.

During the years 1932, 1933, and the first six months of 1934, wholesale commodity prices in Hongkong, Canton, and the other Chinese cities gradually fell. Differences between the various cities with respect to price trends were not

1. Ministry of Industries, Nanking, China "Silver and Prices in China," page 165, 1935.

2. The Directorate of Statistics, Nanking, China, "The Quarterly Journal of Statistics." No. 5, 1936. Page 143.

則似不甚顯著。

物價之跌落，造成全中國之經濟恐慌。工資，租稅，債務等固定開支之償付，逐日趨困難。白銀出口遠過其進口之量。以收藏白銀之故，銀幣幾至絕跡。自一九三四年下半年起，紙幣兌換白銀須找給貼水。自此以後，紙幣與現銀之關係因各地而不同。職此之故，各批發物價之指數，遂呈顯著之分岐。

一九三四年夏，華中奇旱歉收，漢口，南京，上海，廣州，及華北各地之批發物價，因而上漲。旱災之後，物價開始回跌。除廣州及香港外，此跌勢因政府徵收白銀出口稅及平衡稅而中止。此稅則乃於一三九四年十月十五日開始課徵。

remarkable considering that different commodities and different numbers of commodities are included in the indexes. The general decline in commodity prices produced an economic depression in all parts of China. Wages, taxes, debts and other fixed charges became difficult to pay. Silver exports were greatly in excess of silver imports, and other silver disappeared from circulation because of hoarding. After the first half of 1934, premiums for silver over banknotes began to appear, and from this time forward the relation between paper money and silver varied in different cities and at different times. Consequently, a marked spreading of the various indexes of wholesale prices took place. In the summer of 1934, wholesale prices in Hankow, Nanking, Shanghai, Canton and North China were raised by the scarcity caused by the drought, which was especially severe in Central China. After this calamity, prices began to fall again. Except in Canton and Hongkong, this decline was arrested by the export taxes and equalization fees which were levied by the Government on all exports of silver. These fees were imposed on October 15, 1934.

香港政府當局緊守銀本位政策，不容紙幣之貶值，故既不禁止白銀出口，亦不加徵白銀出口稅，使港幣之價值在世界市場上與白銀同時升漲，而物價之跌落較中國各地為速。

當一九三五年之際，各地物價水準大相懸殊，其差別因當地貨幣與白銀之相關之程度而異。香港因堅欲維持其銀本位制，其八月間之物價水準為六十五，如以一九二六年為一百。廣州因白銀走私較易，價值較他地為貴，其物價指數為八十四。上海南京及天津（即華北）之白銀出口稅費足以阻幣值與廣州香港作等速之升漲。二月以後物價跌落，但至八月仍在九十左近，如以一九二六年物價為一百。漢口及青島之物價於一九三五年二月以後跌落甚微。八月間之物價指數維持

The Hongkong government followed the policy of adhering strictly to the silver standard, and did not permit its notes to fall in value in terms of silver. Neither a silver embargo nor an export tax was imposed. Consequently, the value of the Hongkong dollar rose as fast as silver rose in the world market, and commodity prices fell faster than in any of the cities of China.

During 1935, there were great differences between price levels in different cities, depending on the degree to which the currency was attached to silver. In Hongkong, the silver standard was strictly maintained, and prices were at a level of 65 in August, when 1926 is considered 100. In Canton, silver smuggling was comparatively easy, and silver was worth more than in other places. The index number of prices was 84. In Shanghai, Nanking, and Tientsin (North China), the silver export fees were effective in preventing the currency from rising in value as fast as it rose in Canton and Hongkong. After February, prices declined, but were still about 90 in August, when 1926 prices are taken as 100. In Hankow and Tsingtao, prices declined very little after February, 1935. In

於一〇三左右，如以一九二六年為一〇〇。其所以未能跌落之原因，顯係貨幣不能盡量兌換現銀，致不能與銀價並駕齊驅。其他內地各都市均有同樣現象，以物價市情從此係根據於紙幣而非復白銀矣。

一九三五年十月中旬中國中央政府放棄維持國幣之外匯價格，國幣價值乃驟然猛跌。上海及華北批發物價上升，較漢口及青島反為猛速，致一九三五年十一月，四指數實際上竟升至同一水準。南京之批發物價亦漲，然不能與其他流通同樣貨幣之各地相齊。

十一月三日中國『元』在外匯上業已穩定，而置銀白於不問矣。此後數月間，上海，華北，漢口，

.1. 見一九三六年四月五日字林西報之『一九三五年中國銀行報告.』

August they stood at an index of about 103, compared to 1926 as 100. The reason for this failure to decline was apparently that the currency was not redeemable in silver in any appreciable amount, and so failed to rise in value in line with silver. Similar conditions prevailed in other interior points.[1] Price quotations were based upon paper rather than upon silver.

In the middle of October, 1935, the Chinese Central Government abandoned the policy of supporting the Chinese dollar in foreign exchange, and its value rapidly fell. Wholesale prices in Shanghai and North China rose more rapidly than those in Hankow and Tsingtao, causing the four indexes to reach practically a common level by November, 1935. Wholesale prices in Nanking also rose, but not enough to come into line with those in cities with similar currency.

On November 3, the Chinese Yuan was stabilized in foreign exchange, regardless of silver. During the following months, prices in Shanghai, North China, Hankow, and Tsingtao

1. "Report of the Bank of China for the year 1935" published in the North China Daily News, April 5, 1936.

青島物價乃繼續上升，漸至與穩定貨幣之水準相調整。

一九三五年十一月四日後數日，廣東省政府乃佈告與中央採取同樣法幣政策。廣東省當局之目的顯然在使廣東幣制與中央幣制保持原有之關係。此目的果於一九三六年四月暫時達到。廣州批發物價已回至與華中及華北批發物價相似之水準。一九三六年春及初夏廣東貨幣貶價，物價挺漲。

一九三五年十月及十一月香港貨幣以白銀計算之價值任其下落，至十二月始穩定之，約略恢復其當初與上海貨幣同為銀本位時之關係。香港幣漲值既高於中幣，則其所需之貶價亦須較大，同時物價

continued to rise gradually, approaching an adjustment to the level at which the currency had been stabilized.

In Canton, measures similar to those adopted by the Central Government were announced by the Kwangtung Provincial Government, only a few days after November 4, 1935. The intention of the Canton government was apparently to bring the Canton currency into its former relationship with that of the Central government. By April, 1936, this result had been temporarily accomplished, and wholesale prices in Canton had returned to a level comparable with that of prices in central and northern China. In the spring and early summer of 1936, the Canton currency depreciated, and commodity prices rose further.

In Hongkong the currency was permitted to depreciate in terms of silver in October and November, 1935, and was stabilized in December at approximately the relationship to the Shanghai currency that previously existed when both were on the silver standard. Since the Hongkong currency had risen in value much more than the Shanghai currency, a much greater devaluation was

於一九三五年八月低落以後，復見一度猛漲。

目前除西南諸省外，國內各地之幣制根據同一標準，大都穩定。如貨幣穩定能維持長久，則各地之平均批發物價，可重循一極相似之趨勢。香港貨幣在外匯上亦經穩定，平均物價亦將循一與中國各地（除西南諸省市）相同之趨勢。

<u>相對幣值與批發物價</u>：自一九三四年八月始，當貨幣激烈變化之際，廣州，香港，及上海批發物價之相對水準與該三地貨幣之相對價值成反比之趨勢。當上海物價以廣州貨幣計算時其趨勢與廣州物價相似（第二表及第二圖）。同樣以香港貨幣計算所得之上海物價亦與香港物

necessary; and a much greater rise in commodity prices occurred after the low point of August, 1935.

At present, Chinese currency in most places outside the Southwest Provinces is stabilized on a common basis. It is to be expected that average wholesale prices in the various cities will follow a very similar trend as long as this stabilization is maintained. The Hongkong currency has also been stabilized in foreign exchange, and average commodity prices in Hongkong will probably follow a trend similar to that of prices in Chinese cities, except those of the Southwest Provinces.

Relative Currency Values and Wholesale Prices—During the period of rapid currency changes, beginning in August 1934, the relative levels of wholesale commodity prices in Canton, Hongkong, and Shanghai have tended to correspond inversely with the relative values of the three currencies. When commodity prices in Shanghai are expressed in terms of Canton currency they are similar in trend to commodity prices in Canton (table 2 and figure 2). Likewise, when commodity prices in Shanghai

第二表：以毫洋計算之上海及廣州批發物價，一九三四年八月至一九三六年七月·

Table 2. Wholesale Commodity Prices Expressed in Canton Currency, in Shanghai and in Canton, August 1934 to July 1936

日 期 Date	以毫洋計算之遞幣價格指數（1），一九三四年八月等於一〇〇 Index numbers of the price of Shanghai currency in terms of Canton currency(1) August 1934＝100	上海批發物價指數 (2) 一九二六年等於一〇〇 Index numbers of wholesale commodity prices in Shanghai(2) 1926＝100	以毫洋計算之上海批發物價指數，一九二六年等於一〇〇 Index numbers of wholesale commodity prices in Shanghai in terms of Canton currency 1926＝100	廣州批發物價指數 (5)，一九二六年等於一〇〇 Index numbers of wholesale commodity prices in Canton(3) 1926＝100
1934				
八 月 Aug·	100.0	99.8	99.8	94.6
九 月 Sept·	96.6	97.3	94.0	91.6
十 月 Oct·	95.2	96.1	91.5	90.4
十一月 Nov·	90.7	98.3	89.2	87.0
十二月 Dec·	88.0	99.0	87.1	86.2
1935				
一 月 Jan·	88.2	99.4	8.77	86.4
二 月 Feb·	90.3	99.9	90.2	87.6
三 月 Mar··	88.9	96.4	85.7	85.5
四 月 Apr·	81.6	95.9	78.3	83.8
五 月 May·	76.9	95.0	73.1	81.1
六 月 June·	80.5	92.1	74.1	80.2
七 月 July·	85.8	90.5	77.6	80.8
八 月 Aug·	86.0	91.9	79.0	81.7
九 月 Sept·	86.1	91.1	78.4	82.0
十 月 Oct·	84.7	94.1	79.7	81.9
十一月 Nov·	98.8	103.3	102.1	92 3
十二月 Dec·	101.5	103.8	104.8	94.0
1936				
一 月 Jan·	94.9	104.8	99.0	95.6
二 月 Feb·	104.2	105.4	109.8	98.3
三 月 Mar·	109.0	106.4	116.0	99.4
四 月 Apr·	110.5	107.3	118.6	100.9
五 月 May·	113.6	105.8	120.2	102.3
六 月 June·	129.9	106.1	137.8	110.5
七 月 July·	126.1	107.2	135.2	112.9

1. 根據每上海紙幣一，〇〇〇元換毫洋數（自一九三四年八月一日至一九三五年八月二日及自一九三五年十月一日至一九三六年一月三十一日之材料，得自中國銀行；自一九三五年八月三日至一九三五年九月三日，得自廣東統計月報；自一九三六年二月一日起得自廣州國華報）一九三四年八月之平均價等於一〇〇

2. 國定稅則委員會：上海物價月報

3. 廣東統計局供給

1. Based upon number of Canton dollars per $1,000 in Shanghai notes (Aug. 1, 1934-Aug. 2, 1935 and Oct. 1, 1935-Jan. 31, 1936 from Bank of China; Aug. 3, 1935-Sept. 3, 1935 from Kwangtung Statistical Monthly; Since Feb. 1, 1936 from Kwoh Wah Pao) The average price of Aug. 1934＝100.

2. National Tariff Ccmmission: Prices and Prices Indexes in Shanghai.

3. Supplied by Kwangtung Statistical Bureau.

第三表: 以港洋計算之上海及香港批發物價指數，一九三四年
八月至一九三六年七月。

Table 3. Wholesale Commodity Prices Expressed in Hongkong
Currency, in Shanghai and in Hongkong,
August 1934 to July 1936

日 期 Date		以港洋計算之滬幣價格指數(1)，一九三四年八月等於一〇〇 Index number of the price of Shanghai currency in terms of Hongkong currency (1) Aug. 1934 = 100	上海批發物價指數(3)，一九二六年等於一〇〇 Index numbers of Wholesale commodity prices in Shanghai, (2) 1926 = 100	以港洋計算之上海批發物價指數，一九二六年等於一〇〇， Index numbers of wholesale commodity prices in Shanghai in terms of Hongkong currency 1926 = 100	香港批發物價指數(3)，一九二二年等於九八・六 Index numbers wholesale commodity prices in Hongkong(5) 1922 = 98.6
1934					
八 月	Aug·	100.0	99.8	99.8	94.0
九 月	Sept·	100.0	97.3	97.3	89.9
十 月	Oct·	94.6	96.1	90.9	90.7
十一月	Nov·	89.8	98.3	88.3	90.0
十二月	Dec·	89.2	99.0	88.3	87.0
1935					
一 月	Jan·	88.6	99.4	88.1	82.2
二 月	Feb·	90.3	99.9	90.2	83.1
三 月	Mar·	88.1	96.4	84.9	75.0
四 月	Apr·	82.0	95.9	78.6	76.8
五 月	May·	75.3	95.0	71.5	72.1
六 月	June·	76.5	92.1	70.5	70.1
七 月	July·	80.9	90.5	73.2	72.4
八 月	Aug·	79.8	91.9	73.3	68.4
九 月	Sept·	81.7	91.1	74.4	72.3
十 月	Oct·	81.4	94.1	76.6	71.6
十一月	Nov·	88.6	103.3	91.5	84.3
十二月	Dec·	9C.7	103.3	103.0	93.0
1936					
一 月	Jan·	101.4	104.3	105.8	96.0
二 月	Feb·	100.3	105.4	105.7	96.3
三 月	Mar·	101.1	106.4	107.6	
四 月	Apr·	101.1	107.3	108.5	100.8
五 月	May·	100.8	105.8	106.6	101.9
六 月	June·	102.5	106.1	108.8	99.5
七 月	July·	102.5	107.2	109.9	105.3

1. 根據上海之香港電匯（國定稅則委員會:
上海物價月報）一九三四年八月之平均匯
率等於一〇〇。

2. 國定稅則委員會:上海物價月報。

3. 香港出入口貿易處統計室編。參看第九
十七頁註五。

1. Based upon T. T. on Hongkong
in Shanghai (National Tariff
Commission, Prices and Price
Indexes in Shanghai), average
rate of August 1934 = 100.

2. National Tariff Commission,
Prices and Price Indexes in
Shanghai.

3. Compiled by the statistical office
of the imports and exports
department of the Hongkong
government. See also note 5
page 97

價有相似之趨勢（第三表及第三圖）。此種關係並不十分準確，半由於各指數並非由同樣之物品編組而成，半由於貨幣價值激烈變化時，物價並不立刻隨之完全調整。

are expressed in Hongkong currency, they are similar in trend to prices in Hongkong (table 3 and figure 3). These relationships are not exact, partly because the indexes are not composed of the same commodities, and partly because prices do not immediately become completely adjusted to rapid changes in the value of money.

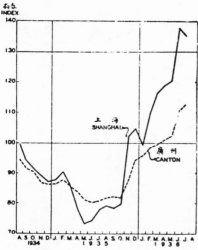

第二圖：以毫洋計算之上海批發物價指數，及廣州批發物價指數，一九三四年八月至一九三六年七月　一九二六年＝100

倘幣制相同，則上海批發物價之趨勢，當與廣州類似。

FIGURE 2. INDEX NUMBERS OF WHOLESALE COMMODITY PRICES EXPRESSED IN CANTON CURRENCY, SHANGHAI AND IN CANTON, AUGUST 1934 TO JULY 1936.
1926 = 100.
Wholesale commodity prices in Shanghai would have followed a trend similar to that of prices in Canton, if the currency had been the same.

路　易　士
王　　　廉

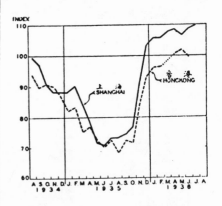

第三圖：以港洋計算之上海批發物價指數及香港之批發物價指數，一九三四年八月至一九三六年六月　一九二六年＝一〇〇

如上海通用港洋，則上海批發物價之趨勢當與香港同。

FIGURE 3. INDEX NUMBERS OF WHOLESALE COMMODITY PRICES EXPRESSED IN HONGKONG CURRENCY, IN SHANGHAI AND IN HONGKONG, AUGUST 1934 TO JULY 1936.
1926 = 100.
If Hongkong currency had been used in Shanghai, wholesale commodity prices in Shanghai would have followed a trend similar to that of prices in Hongkong.
A. B. LEWIS
LIEN WANG

花行與棉花販運商營業成功與失敗之關鍵

SOME PRINCIPLES GOVERNING
THE SUCCESS AND FAILURE
OF MERCHANTS AND COT-
TON WHOLESALERS

During the two-year period, 1933 to 1935, 154 cotton commission merchants' shops in 11 localities, and 201 cotton wholesalers' shops in 12 localities, in the provinces of Hupeh and Honan, were studied. Relationships between the amount of capital, the efficiency of capital, the volume of business, the number of employees, labor efficiency, fixed expenditures, running expenses, and net profits were tabulated, and as a result several principles determining the success or failure of these cotton merchants were illustrated. Knowledge of these principles may be very useful to business men and co-operatives engaged in the cotton trade.

民國二十二至二十四年之兩年間，曾在豫鄂兩省十一地區，調查一五四家花行，十二地區，調查二○一家棉花販運商。關於資本數額，資本效能，營業數額，職工人數，職工效能，固定開支，營業費用，及純利數額等等之相互關係，曾一一加以統計分析，結果吾人得到幾種似乎極能決定此等棉商營業成功和失敗之原則。此種原則之認識，對於棉商與棉運合作社或亦不無相當裨益也。

1. 資本數額與純利之關係

資本數額對於花行與棉花販運商之純利，關係並不密切，蓋因資本數額並非決定營業數額之重要因素（第一與第二表）。在多數時期，花行自身並不從事買賣，而棉花販運商

1. *Amount of Capital in Relation to Net Profit.*

The amount of capital showed no close relationship to the net profit of cotton commission merchants and wholesalers, because the amount of capital was not an essential factor in determining volume of business (tables 1 and 2). In most cases, the commission merchants

則又多從銀行抵押放款方面，獲取資金。

are not engaged in buying and selling on their own account, while the wholesalers obtain most of their funds from security loans from banks.

花行方面，資本數額最高之一組，純利最多，但中級組不但毫無純益，而反有純損，較之低資本組不及遠甚（第一表）。

In the case of commission merchants, the highest net profit occurred in the group with the highest capital, but the middle group showed a net loss instead of a gain and compared exceedingly unfavorably with the lowest capital group (table 1).

第一表： 花行資本數額與純利之關係

Table 1. Amount of Capital in Relation to Net Profit of Cotton Commission Merchants.

	資本數額 Amount of capital		
	$0-225	$226-624	$625 and more
家　　數 Number of shops	52	51	51
平均純利 Average net profit	$1,677	$ -1	$6,400

棉花販運商方面，僅有一四〇家有資本數額之準確數字。有七十家資本數額在一萬元以下者純利較多。其餘七十家，在一萬元以上者者純利則較少（第二表）。

In the case of wholesalers, there were 140 shops with reliable records with respect to the amount of capital. Profits were greater for the 70 shops with $10,000 capital or less than for the 70 shops with more than $10,000 capital (table 2).

Table 2.   Amount of Capital in Relation to Net
Profits of Cotton Wholesalers.

	資 本 數 額 Amount of capital	
	$100-10,000	$10,001 and more
家　　　數 Number of shops	70	70
平 均 純 利 Average net proft	$2,768	$1.549

2. 營業數額與純利之關係

　　營業數額爲決定成敗最重要因素之一。花行與販運商之營業數額最高者，純利亦最巨（第三與第四表）。其原因則由於固定開支雖與營業數額同時並進，但營業數額較大者資本與工作之效能亦較巨。因此營業數額愈大時，則經手之棉花每担所攤之固定開支，即愈見減少。

2.   *Volume of Business in Re-lation to Net Profit.*

Volume of business is one of the most important factors in determining success.   For commission merchants and wholesalers, the highest net return was obtained by the group with the largest volume of business (tables 3 and 4).   The reason for this relationship is that, although fixed expenditures increase as the volume of business increases, nevertheless the efficiency of capital and labor is much greater in businesses with the greater volume.   Therefore, the fixed expenditure per picul of cotton handled is greatly reduced as the volume of business increases.

第三表： 花行營業數額與純利之關係
Table 3.   Volume of Business in Relation to Net
Profits of Cotton Commission Merchants.

	經 手 棉 花 之 担 數 Number of piculs of cotton handled		
	140-940	941-2.800	2.801 and more
家　　　數 Number of shops	52	51	51
平 均 純 利 Average net profit	$134	$256	$8,988

第四表： 棉花販運商營業數額與純利之關係

Table 4. Volume of Business in Relation to Net Profits of Cotton Wholesalers.

	銷 售 棉 花 之 担 數 Number of piculs of cotton sold		
	74-1,399	1,400-4,000	4,001 and more
家 數 Number of shops	71	70	70
不 均 純 利 Average net profit	$-1,292	$-201	$10,747

3. 營 業 數 額 與 每 担 棉 花 所 攤 之 固 定 開 支

營業數額愈巨，則每担棉花所攤之固定開支，即愈見低減（第五與第六表）。吾人前已言之，營業數額較大，則人工與資本之效能亦愈巨，因此營業數額增多時，固定開支通常並不增多至同等程度。

3. *Volume of Business in Relation to Fixed Expenditures Per Picul of Cotton.*

Fixed expenditures per picul of cotton decreased as the volume of business increased (tables 5 and 6). As explained before, labor and capital are more efficiently used by the large sized businesses, and therefore the fixed expenditure usually does not rise to the same degree as the volume of business increases.

第五表： 花行營業數額與每担棉花所攤固定開支之關係

Table 5. Volume of Business of Commission Merchants in Relation to Fixed Expenditures per Picul of Cotton.

	經 手 棉 花 之 担 數 Numbers of piculs of cotton handled		
	140-940	941-2,800	2,801 and more
家 數 Number of shops	52	51	51
棉花每担所攤之固定開支 Fixed expenditure per picul of cotton	$1.247	$0.615	$0.256
佔最低數額組之百分數 Per cent of lowest volume group	100	49	21

第六表：　棉花販運商營業數額與每担銷售棉花所攤之固定開支
Table 6.　Volume of Business of Wholesalers in Relation
to Fixed Expenditures per Picul of Cotton Sold.

	銷售之担數 Number of piculs sold		
	74-1,399	1,400-4,000	4,001 and more
家　數 Number of shops	71	70	70
每担棉花所攤之固定開支 Fixed expenditure per picul of cotton	$3.775	$1.910	$0.728
佔最低數額組之百分數 Per cent of lowest volume group	100	51	19

4. 營業數額與每担棉花之營業費用

棉花販運商之營業數額與每担棉花之營業費用多寡，並無密切關係。原因則由於每担營業費用如捐稅，運費包裝費等皆有一定例規，並不因營業數額而變更。營業數額較高之兩組，每担營業費用且略巨（第七表），此或係由於距離市場較遠故也。

對於花行營業數額與每担營業費用之關係，未加以統計，因花行每担營

4. *Volume of Business in Relation to Running Expense per Picul of Cotton.*

There was no close relation between volume of business and running expense per picul of cotton sold by wholesalers. The reason is that running expenses per picul, such as taxes, freight rates, and packing expenses, are traditionally fixed and do not change with volume of business. Running expenses per picul were even slightly greater in the higher volume groups (table 7). This relationship might be due to the longer distance to market for these groups.

No attempt was made to study the relation of volume of business to running expenses per picul of cotton handled by commission merchants, because run-

— 111 —

業費用差別極大。而此種
差別則又多由於慣例與花
行所盡之職責多寡，而未
必由於營業數額也。

ning expenses per picul vary
greatly in different markets,
and these differences are largely
due to different customs and
different degrees of service
rendered by the commission
merchants rather than to the
volume of business.

第七表： 棉花販運商營業數額與每担棉花之營業費用
Table 7. Volume of Business of Wholesalers in Relation
to Running Expenses per Picul of Cotton.

	銷售棉花之担數 Number of piculs of cotton sold		
	74-1,399	1,400-4,000	4,001 and more
家 數 Number of shops	71	70	70
每担之營業費用 Running expense per picul	$5.092	$5.496	$5.504
佔最低數額組之百分數 Per cent of lowest volume group	100	108	108

5. 資本效能與純利之關係

5. *Efficiency of Capital in Relation to Net Profit.*

資本效能與純利關係
之密切，遠甚於資本數額
。資本效能係按每百元資
本之營業數額計算。花行
資本效能與純利之關係，
各組高低不一，惟最高效
能組之純利較最低效能組
約高四倍（第八表）。棉
花販運商資本效能極關重

Efficiency of capital, rather
than the amount of capital, is
very closely related to net
profits. Efficiency of capital is
measured by the volume of
business per 100 dollars of
capital. For commission merchants, the relation between
capital efficiency and net profits
was irregular, but, in the group
with the highest capital
efficiency, the net profit was
about four times that of the

要，最高效能組之純利平均爲 4,592 元，而最低效能組則反損失二七五元（第九表）。

group with the lowest capital efficiency (table 8). For wholesalers, capital efficiency was very important. The most efficient group had an average net profit of $4,592, compared with a net loss of $275 for the least efficient users of capital (table 9).

第八表： 花行資本效能與純利之關係

Table 8. Efficiency of Capital in Relation to Net Profits of Cotton Commission Merchants.

	每百元資本經手棉花之担數 Number of piculs of cotton handled per $100 capital		
	0-75	76-240	241 and more
家　　數 Number of shops	52	51	51
平　均　純　利 Average net profit	$1,683	$308	$7,085
佔最低效能之百分數 Per cent of least efficient group	100	18	421

第九表： 棉花販運商資本效能與純利之關係

Table 9. Efficiency of Capital in Relation to Net Profits of Cotton Wholesales.

	每百元資本銷售棉花之担數 Number of piculs sold per 100 dollars capital	
	2-16.9	17.0 and more
家　　數 Number of shops	70	70
佔最低效能之百分數 Average net profit	$-275	$4,592

6. 職工人數與純利之關係

花行與棉花販運商之純利與職工人數成正比例（第十與第十一表）。其理由則由於職工人數之多，為營業較巨之明證，營業數額較巨，則管理效能較高，因此而能多得純利也。

6. Number of Employees in Relation to Net Profit.

Net profit was directly proportional to the number of employees, for both commission merchants and wholesalers (tables 10 and 11). The reason is that a large number of employees is an indication of a large sized business, which is usually more efficient to manage and, therefore, yields more profit.

第十表： 花行職工人數與純利之關係

Table 10. Number of Employees in Relation to Net Profits of Cotton Commission Merchants.

	職 工 人 數 Number of employees		
	0.9-4.9	5-10.9	11 and more
家 數 Number of shops	52	51	51
平 均 純 利 Average net profit	$367	$616	$8,118
佔人數最少組之百分數 Per cent of lowest size group	100	168	2,212

第十一表： 棉花販運商職工人數與純利之關係

Table 11. Number of Employees in Relation to Net Profits of Cotton Wholesalers.

	職 工 人 數 Number of employees		
	1-8	9-12	13 and more
家 數 Number of shops	71	70	70
平 均 純 利 Average net profit	$2,256	$1,477	$5,470
佔人數最少組之百分數 Per cent of lowest size group	100	65	242

7. 職工人數與工作效能之關係

花行職工人數最多之一組，每一職工之營業數額最高。惟中級組則較之人數最少組略低（第十二表）。職工人數最多之一組，其工作支配方面與他組比較，顯然較佔優勢也。

棉花販運商方面情形則與此相反。工作效能與職工人數，恰成反比例。（第十三表）其原因則由於規模較大之棉花販運商多在終點市場或較大之轉載市場營業，只聘用待遇高經驗富之職員數人，以經營鉅額買賣；規模較小之販運商則多在鄰近產地之較小轉載市場營業，而派遣夥友分赴原始市場收購貨物，故需要待遇較低而人數較多之職工也。

7. *Number of Employees in Relation to Efficiency of Labor.*

For commission merchants, the volume of business per employee was greater in the group with the most employees, but the medium sized group was slightly inferior to the small group (table 12). Apparently there was better labor efficiency in the group with most employees than in other groups.

In the case of wholesalers, the situation was reversed. Efficiency of labor was inversely proportional to the number of employees (table 13). The reason is that in the cotton trade the large wholesalers usually run their businesses in terminal or big transhipping markets, where they buy and sell in huge amounts and keep only very few intelligent, highly paid employees in their offices. The smaller wholesalers usually run their businesses in smaller transhipping markets near the production area, and send their agents to different primary markets to purchase cotton, so they need to keep a bigger staff with lower salaries.

第十二表：　　花行職工人數與每一職工營業數額之關係
Table 12.　Number of Employees of Commission Merchants in Relation to Volume of Business per Employee.

	職 工 人 數 Number of employees		
	0.9-4.9	5-10.9	11 and more
家　　數 Number of shops	52	51	51
每一職工之營業數額(担) Number of piculs of cotton handled per employee	366	265	938
佔人數最少組之百分數 Per cent of smallest sized group	100	72	256

第十三表：　　棉花販運商職工人數與每一職工營業數額之關係
Table 13.　Number of Employees of Cotton Wholesalers in Relation to the Volume of Business per Employee.

	職 工 人 數 Number of employees		
	1-8	9-12	13 and more
家　　數 Number of shops	71	70	70
每一職工銷售之担數 Number of Piculs Sold per employee	1,187	655	436
佔人數最少組之百分數 Per cent of smallest sized group	100	55	37

8. 工作效能與純利之關係

工作效能愈高，則純利愈見增進（第十四與第十五表）。花行與棉花販運商，在工作最低之一組，不但毫無所獲，而皆有純損。在棉花販運商方面

8. Labor Efficiency in Relation to Net Profit.

Net profit increased as labor efficiency rose (tables 14 and 15). For both commission merchants and wholesalers in the low efficiency group, there was a net loss instead of a gain. For wholesalers, net returns

，純利最低為負 2,006 元，最高為 11,228 元。高低相差所以如此之大者，因薪資佔固定開支之主要部份；若工作效能高，則每單位所攤之固定開支即見低減，因此純利為之增加。

ranged from a net loss of $2,006 to a net gain of $11,228. The reason for this wide difference in net profit is that salaries and wages constitute a very important part in fixed expenditure; and if labor efficiency is high, the fixed expenditure per unit of measure is low. Therefore, the net profit is increased.

第十四表：花行人工效能與純利之關係

Table 14. Efficiency of Labor in Relation to Net Profits of Cotton Commission Merchants.

	每一職工經手棉花之擔數 Number of piculs of cotton handled per employee		
	20-166.6	166.7-444.3	444.4 and more
家　　數 Number of shops	52	51	51
平　均　純　利 Average net profit	$-173	$464	$8,822

第十五表： 棉花販運商人工效能與純利之關係

Table 15. Efficiency of Labor in Relation to Net Profits of Cotton Wholesalers.

	每一職工銷售棉花之擔數 Number of piculs of cotton sold per employee		
	4-168	169-493	494 and more
家　　數 Number of shops	71	70	70
平　均　純　利 Average net proft	$-2,006	$42	$11,228

9. 工作效能與每擔棉花所攤之固定開支

花行與販運商，每擔棉花所攤之固定開支，皆與工作效能成反比例。換言之，即工作效能愈高，則每單位所攤之固定開支亦愈見低減。若效能低，即愈見高昂（第十六與第十七表）。每擔棉花，因工作效能之高，固定開支所低減之百分數，花行與販運商二者大致相同。每擔固定開支之低減，釋明高純利與高工作效能所以密切聯繫之原因。

9. Efficiency of Labor in Relation to Fixed Expenditures per Picul of Cotton.

In both cases, fixed expenditures per picul of cotton were inversely proportional to labor efficiency; that is, if labor efficiency was high, fixed expenses per unit of measures were low, and vice versa (tables 16 and 17). The rate by which fixed expenditures per picul of cotton were reduced by high labor efficiency was nearly the same for commission merchants and wholesalers. The reduction of fixed expenditures per picul explains why high profits are associated with high labor efficiency.

第十六表： 花行工作效能與每擔棉花所攤固定開支之關係

Table 16. Efficiency of Labor in Relation to Commission Merchants' Fixed Expenditures per Picul of Cotton.

	每 一 職 工 經 手 之 擔 數 Number of piculs handled per employee		
	20-166.6	166.7-444.3	444.4 and more
家 數 Number of shops	52	51	51
每擔棉花所攤之固定開支 Fixed expenditure per picul of cotton	$1.333	$0.575	$0.208
佔最低效能組之百分數 Per cent of lowest efficiency group	100	43	16

第十七表 ： 棉花販運商人工效能與銷售每担棉花所攤固定開支之關係
Table 17.   Efficiency of Labor in Relation to Fixed Expenditures
per Picul of Cotton Sold by Cotton Wholesalers.

	每一職工銷得棉花之担數 Number of piculs of cotton sold per employee		
	4-168	169-493	494 and more
家數 Number of shops	71	70	70
每担棉花所攤之固定開支 Fixed expenditure per picul of cotton	$4.172	$1.686	$0.564
佔最低效能組之百分數 Per cent of lowest efficiency group	100	40	14

10. 每担棉花所攤固定開支與純利之關係

每担棉花所攤固定開支幾何，爲決定純利平均數額多寡最重要因素之一。花行最低固定開支組，純利平均數額爲 8,023 元，中級開支組，純利平均數額爲 841 元，最高開支組僅得 88 元，其比例恰爲 100:10:1。

棉花販運商銷售每担棉花所攤之固定開支與所得之純利，各組差別之大尤甚於花行。在低開支組，純利平均數額爲 11,631

10.   *Fixed Expenditures per Picul of Cotton in Relation to Net Profit.*

Fixed expenditures per picul of cotton was one of the most important factors in determining the average amount of net profit. In the low expenditure group of commission merchants, the average amount of net profit was $8,023, while in the medium expenditure group the average amount of net profit was $841, and, in the high expenditure group, only $88. The ratio was just 100:10:1.

For wholesalers, the variation, both in the amount of fixed expenditures per picul of cotton sold and the amount of net profit in different groups, was very much greater than for commission merchants. In the

— 119 —

元，而高開支組不但無利可圖，反虧3,809元（第十八與第十九表）。

low expenditure group, the average amount of net profit was $11,631, while in the high expenditure group there was a net loss of $3,809 instead of a profit (tables 18 and 19).

第十八表：　花行每担棉花所攤固定開支與純利之關係

Table 18. Fixed Expenditure per Picul of Cotton in Relation to Net Profits of Cotton Commission Merchants.

	經手每担棉花所攤固定開支 Fixed expenditure per picul of cotton handled		
	$.038-.333	$.334-.664	.665 and more
家數 Number of shops	52	51	51
平均純利 Average net profit	$8,023	$841	$88
佔最低開支組之百分數 Per cent of lowest expenditure group	100	10	1

第十九表：　棉花販運商每担棉花所攤固定開支與純利之關係

Table. 19. Fixed Expenditure per Picul of Cotton in Relation to Net Profits of Cotton Wholesalers.

	銷售每担棉花所攤之固定開支 Fixed expenditure per picul of cotton sold		
	$.027-.700	$.701-2.138	$2.139 and more
家數 Number of shops	71	70	70
平均純利 Average net profits	$11,631	$1,247	$-3,809

11. 工作效能與每担棉花所攤固定開支之關係

11. *Efficiency of Labor in Relation to Net Profit per Picul of Cotton.*

工作效能不但與每家純利多寡關係密切，即與每担棉花所攤之固定開支

Labor efficiency was very closely related not only to net profit for each shop, but also

亦極有關係。因此在吾人之意像中，工作效能當亦與每擔棉花之純利有關。實際上亦確與吾人意像相同，每擔純利與每一職工之營業數額成正比例。換言之，卽工作效能愈高每擔棉花之純利亦愈巨（第二十與第二十一表）。

to fixed expenditures per picul of cotton. Therefore, labor efficiency would be expected to be related to net profit per picul of cotton. Actually, as expected, net profit per picul of cotton handled was directly proportional to the volume of business per employee; that is, higher labor efficiency yielded higher net profits per picul of cotton (tables 20 and 21).

第二十表： 花行工作效能與每擔棉花純利之關係

Table 20. Efficiency of Labor of Cotton Commission Merchants in Relation to Net Profits per Picul of Cotton.

| | 每一職工經手棉花之擔數
Number of piculs of cotton handled per employee | | |
	20-166	167-444.3	444.4 and more
家　數 Number of shops	52	51	51
每擔棉花之平均純利 Average net profit per picul of cotton	$-0.032	$0.031	$0.147

第二十一表： 棉花販運商工作效能與每擔棉花純利之關係

Table 21. Efficiency of Labor in Relation to Net Profits per Picul of Cotton Sold by Cotton Wholesalers.

| | 每一職工銷售棉花之擔數
Number of piculs of cotton sold per employee | | |
	4-168	169-493	494 and more
家　數 Number of shops	71	70	70
每擔棉花之平均純利數 Net profit per picul of cotton	−$0.30	$0.002	$0.094

張 履 鸞   LU-LUAN CHANG

地主投資田產之報酬

金陵大學農學院農業經濟系於民國二三至二四年間作豫鄂皖贛四省租佃制度之調查，並包括地主投資耕地之研究。

綜計四省一四地區內被調查之地主凡三三○戶。地主田場面積平均為一○一·八市畝[1]（第一表），而每一地主之平均投資總額計國幣二，二○七·二七元，或每市畝二一·一三元。地主投資中之主要項目為耕地，佔資本總額百分之九四·四。農舍次之，佔百分之四·六。他如農具，種籽，肥料，牲畜等則均屬甚微（第二與第三表）。

RETURNS ON LANDLORD'S CAPITAL INVESTMENT IN FARMS

During the years 1934-1935, the Department of Agricultural Economics, College of Agriculture, University of Nanking, studied the farm tenancy problem in the provinces of Honan, Hupeh, Anhwei and Kiangsi, and a study of the landlords' capital investment in farm land was included in this project.

In this study, 330 landlords' holdings in fourteen localities in the four provinces were studied. The average landlord's holding consisted of 101.8 shih mow[1] of land (table 1), and the average capital investment per landlord amounted to $2,207.27, or $21.13 per shih mow. The landlords' capital was chiefly invested in land, which constituted 94.4 per cent of the total investment. Buildings were next in importance and constituted 4.6 per cent of the total. Investment in farm tools, seeds, fertilizers, livestock, and other supplies was comparatively small (tables 2 and 3).

---

1. 市畝一畝＝0.1644英畝

1. 1 shih mow＝0.1644 acres.

For all localities expenses per landlord averaged $51.65 or $0.53 per shih mow (tables 4 and 5). The outstanding expenses were taxes, which constituted 78.4 per cent of the

各用費一·五)，
地支六三元，佔總
區出，五元之支出
內五元（第
每均或四出
一為每與厥
地國市第
主賦五地
之五〇表稅·

第一表： 地 主 田 場 之 平 均 面 積
（自行耕種之田地未計算在內）

Table 1. Average Size of Landlords' Holdings Excluding
the Land farmed by themselves

省別及地區 Provinces and localities	地主田場調查數目 Number of landlords' holdings	灌溉田 Irrigated land	旱地 Dry land	其他 Other land	總計 Total
河南 Honan			(市畝)	shih mow	
南陽 Nanyang	20	—	78.0	—	78.0
淮陽 Hwaiyang	20	—	200.3	—	200.3
信陽 Sinyang	25	27.2	40.3	—	67.5
總計或平均 Total or average	65	9.0	106.2		115.2
湖北 Hupeh					
襄陽 Siangyang	28	43.1	18.3	0.8	62.2
江陵 Kiangling	26	23.0	—	—	23.0
黃梅 Hwangmei	11	14.3	—	—	14.3
總計或平均 Total or average	65	26.8	6.1	0.3	33.2
安徽 Anhwei					
貴池 Kweichih	27	14.9	34.2	—	49.1
蕪湖 Wuhu	16	247.1	27.5	—	274.6
桐城 Tungchen	8	175.7	12.7	—	188.4
合肥 Hofei	20	119.6	45.3	—	164.9
滁 Chu	12	152.6	68.9	—	221.5
總計或平均 Total or average	83	142.0	37.7		179.7
江西 Kiangsi					
南昌 Nanchang	59	25.3	—	—	25.3
浮梁 Fowliang	35	43.6	0.9	—	44.5
吉安 Kian	23	11.6	—	—	11.6
總計或平均 Total or average	117	26.8	0.3		27.1
四省總計或平均 Total or average for the four provinces	330	64.1	37.6	0.1	101.8

省別及地區 Provinces and localities	出地 Land	庄舍 Buildings	農具 Farm tools	種籽 Seeds	肥料 Fertilizer	牲畜 Live Stock	貸給農產品 Crops loaned	現款借出 Cash loaned	總值 Total value
河南 **Honan**									
南陽 Nanyang	$1314.19	$96.10	$ 1.37	$9.64	$4.37	$3.85	$ —	$ —	$1429.52
淮陽 Hwaiyang	2324.10	71.00	19.05	16.43	9.85	45.90	2.65	—	2488.98
信陽 Sinyang	1783.44	105.56	11.91	—	—	—	1.79	—	1902.70
平均 Average	$1807.24	$90.89	$10.78	$8.69	$4.74	$16.58	$1.48	—	$1940.40
湖北 **Hupeh**									
襄陽 Siangyang	$ 796.63	$38.72	$ 5.36	—	—	—	$0.16	$0.37	$ 841.24
江陵 Kiangling	116.53	2.50	—	—	—	—	—	—	119.03
黃梅 Hwangmei	298.16	1.42	—	—	—	—	—	—	299.58
平均 Average	$ 403.77	$14.21	$ 1.79	—	—	—	$0.06	$0.12	$ 419.95
安徽 **Anhwei**									
貴池 Kweichih	$1204.10	$43.69	$ 0.15	—	—	—	—	$0.35	$1248.29
蕪湖 Wuhu	5445.14	59.25	5.00	—	—	—	$7.81	0.31	5517.51
桐城 Tungcheng	3973.69	72.50	6.75	0.31	—	4.69	2.17	16.25	4076.36
合肥 Hofei	5549.62	822.60	68.60	—	1.20	12.00	—	0.18	6454.20
滁 Chu	4421.67	103.00	16.29	9.77	—	15.00	2.67	9.50	4577.90
平均 Average	$4118.84	$220.21	$19.36	$2.01	$0.24	$6.34	$2.53	$5.32	$4374.85
江西 **Kiangsi**									
南昌 Nanchang	$ 701.90	—	—	—	—	—	—	—	$ 701.90
浮梁 Fowliang	999.67	1.14	—	—	—	—	—	—	1000.81
吉安 Kian	243.78	—	—	—	—	—	—	—	243.78
平均 Average	$ 648.45	$ 0.38	—	—	—	—	—	—	$ 648.83
四省平均 Average for the four provinces	$2083.76	$101.25	$ 9.60	$2.58	$1.10	$5.82	$1.23	$1.93	$2,207.27
百分率 Per cent of total	94.4	4.6	0.4	0.1	—	0.3	0.1	0.1	100.0

第三表：每市畝敝地主供給佃農之資本

Table 3. Landlords' Capital Furnished to Tenants, per shih mow.

省別及地區 Provinces and localities	田地 Land	農舍 Buildings	農具 Farm tools	種籽 Seeds	肥料 Fertilizer	牲畜 Livestock	穀類借出 Crops loaned	現款借出 Cash loaned	總值 Total value
	$	$	$	$	$	$	$	$	$
河南 Honan									
南陽 Nanyang	16.85	1.24	0.02	0.12	0.06	0.04	—	—	18.33
淮陽 Hwaiyang	11.61	0.36	0.10	0.08	0.05	0.22	0.01	—	12.43
信陽 Sinyang	26.43	1.56	0.18	—	—	—	0.02	—	28.19
平均 Average	18.29	1.05	0.10	0.07	0.04	0.09	0.01	—	19.65
湖北 Hupeh									
襄陽 Siangyang	11.63	0.57	0.08	—	—	—	—	—	12.28
江陵 Kiangling	5.06	0.11	—	—	—	—	—	—	5.17
黃梅 Hwangmei	20.88	0.10	—	—	—	—	—	—	20.98
平均 Average	12.52	0.26	0.03	—	—	—	—	—	12.81
安徽 Anhwei									
貴池 Kweichih	24.82	0.90	—	—	—	—	—	0.01	25.73
蕪湖 Wuhu	19.84	0.21	0.02	—	—	—	0.03	—	20.10
桐城 Tungcheng	21.09	0.38	0.04	—	—	0.03	0.01	0.08	21.63
合肥 Hofei	33.66	4.98	0.41	—	0.01	0.07	0.01	—	39.13
滁 Chu	19.96	0.47	0.08	0.04	—	0.07	0.01	0.04	20.67
平均 Average	23.87	1.39	0.11	0.01	—	0.03	0.01	0.03	25.45
江西 Kiangsi									
南昌 Nanchang	27.71	—	—	—	—	—	—	—	27.71
浮梁 Fowliang	22.46	0.03	—	—	—	—	—	—	22.49
吉安 Kian	21.01	—	—	—	—	—	—	—	21.01
平均 Average	23.73	0.01	—	—	—	—	—	—	23.74
四省平均 Average for the four provinces	20.21	0.78	0.06	0.02	0.01	0.03	0.01	0.01	21.13

第四表：每一地主用欵之支出
Table 4. Landlords' Farm Expenses, per Landlord.

省別及地區 Provinces and localities	地稅 Taxes	修理食舍 Repairing buildings	修理農具 Repairing farm tools	收租用欵 Cost of rent collection	修理堤坪 Repairing dikes	掘井 Digging wells	其他用欵 Other expenses	總計 Total
	$	$	$	$	$	$	$	$
河南 Honan								
南陽 Nanyang	10.50	19.50	—	—	—	—	—	30.00
淮陽 Hwaiyang	90.10	2.02	4.25	—	—	—	—	96.37
信陽 Sinyang	10.42	0.32	—	0.80	2.03	—	—	13.57
平均 Average	37.00	7.28	1.42	0.27	0.68	—	—	46.65
湖北 Hupeh								
襄陽 Siangyang	5.80	5.74	—	—	0.63	0.80	—	12.97
江陵 Kiangling	8.01	—	—	0.07	0.07	—	—	8.08
黃梅 Hwangmei	11.35	—	—	0.45	0.07	—	—	11.87
平均 Average	8.39	1.91	—	0.17	0.23	0.27	—	10.97
安徽 Anhwei								
貴池 Kweichih	9.50	—	—	—	13.88	0.96	0.59	24.93
蕪湖 Wuhu	169.12	—	0.19	32.21	0.48	—	—	202.00
桐城 Tungcheng	45.92	—	0.13	1.34	11.25	0.37	0.50	59.51
合肥 Hofei	39.70	4.75	—	31.73	—	—	10.30	86.48
滁 Chu	96.38	3.18	—	3.64	—	—	—	103.20
平均 Average	72.12	1.59	0.06	13.78	5.12	0.27	2.28	95.22
江西 Kiangsi								
南昌 Nanchang	15.31	—	—	0.02	—	—	—	15.33
浮梁 Fowliang	48.48	—	—	0.22	3.51	—	—	52.21
吉安 Kian	6.52	—	—	0.11	—	—	—	6.63
平均 Average	23.43	—	—	0.12	1.17	—	—	24.72
四省不均 Average for four provinces	40.51	2.54	0.33	5.04	2.27	0.15	0.81	51.65
百分率 Per cent of total	78.4	4.9	0.6	9.8	4.4	0.3	1.6	100.0

第五表： 每市畝租出田地之地主用費
Table 5. Landlords' Expenses per shih mow of Rented Land.

省別及地區 Provinces and localities	地稅 Taxes	修理廠舍 Repairing buildings	修理農具 Repairing farm tools	收租用費 Cost of rent collection	修理堤坪 Repairing dikes	測井 Digging wells	其他用費 Other expenses	總計 Total
	$	$	$	$	$	$	$	$
河南 Honan								
南陽 Nanyang	0.13	0.25	—	—	—	—	—	0.38
淮陽 Hwaiyang	0.45	0.01	0.02	—	—	—	—	0.48
信陽 Sinyang	0.15	—	—	0.02	0.04	—	—	0.21
平均 Average	**0.24**	**0.09**	**0.01**	**0.01**	**0.01**	—	—	**0.36**
湖北 Hupeh								
襄陽 Siangyang	0.09	0.08	—	—	—	—	—	0.19
江陵 Kiangling	0.39	—	—	—	0.01	0.01	—	0.39
黃梅 Hwangmei	0.79	—	—	0.04	0.01	—	—	0.84
平均 Average	**0.42**	**0.03**	—	**0.01**	**0.01**	—	—	**0.47**
安徽 Anhwei								
貴池 Kweichih	0.21	—	—	—	0.29	0.02	0.01	0.53
蕪湖 Wuhu	0.62	—	—	0.12	—	—	—	0.74
桐城 Tungcheng	0.25	—	—	0.01	0.05	—	—	0.31
合肥 Hofei	0.24	0.03	—	0.19	—	—	0.06	0.52
滁 Chu	0.40	0.01	—	0.01	—	—	—	0.42
平均 Average	**0.34**	**0.01**	—	**0.07**	**0.07**	—	**0.01**	**0.50**
江西 Kiangsi								
南昌 Nanchang	0.61	—	—	—	—	—	—	0.61
浮梁 Fowliang	1.08	—	—	0.01	0.08	—	—	1.17
吉安 Kian	0.58	—	—	0.01	—	—	—	0.59
平均 Average	**0.75**	—	—	**0.01**	**0.03**	—	—	**0.79**
四省平均 Average for the four provinces	0.43	0.03	—	0.03	0.03	—	0.01	0.53

第六表： 每一地主之收入
Table 6. Landlords' Receipts from Tenants, per Landlord.

省別及地區 Provinces and localities	主產物 Crops	現款 Cash	其他產物 Other products	使用佃農用畜操作之收入 Receipts of farm work rendered by the tenants and their labor animals		家庭工役 Household work	總計 Total
				人工 Man Labor	畜工 Anaimal Labor		
河南 Honan							
南陽縣 Nanyang	$95.06	$—	$6.48	$0.06	$0.07	$6.69	$108.36
淮陽縣 Hwaiyang	302.06	—	12.14	—	—	4.70	318.90
信陽縣 Sinyang	134.80	30.61	1.31	0.21	0.38	2.43	169.74
平均 Average	177.31	10.20	6.64	0.09	0.15	4.61	199.00
湖北 Hupeh							
襄陽縣 Siangyang	118.57		—	—	—	0.10	118.67
江陵縣 Kiangling	37.39	0.33	—	—	—	—	37.72
黃梅縣 Hwangmei	48.58	—	—	—	—	—	48.58
平均 Average	68.18	0.11	—	—	—	0.03	68.32
安徽 Anhwei							
貴池縣 Kweichih	122.47	19.46	0.05	—	—	—	141.98
蕪湖縣 Wuhu	519.52	—	—	—	—	—	519.52
桐城縣 Tungcheng	265.43	—	4.23	—	—	—	269.66
合肥縣 Hofei	523.77	—	0.08	—	—	—	523.85
滁縣 Chu	597.05	—	—	—	—	—	597.05
平均 Average	405.65	3.89	0.87	—	—	—	410.41
江西 Kiangsi							
南昌縣 Nanchang	99.40	—	1.58	—	—	0.03	101.01
浮粱縣 Fowliang	163.79	3.09	—	—	—	0.01	166.89
吉安縣 Kian	24.07	—	—	—	—	—	24.07
平均 Average	95.75	1.03	0.53	—	—	0.01	97.32
四省平均 Average for the four provinces	217.99	3.82	1.85	0.02	0.03	1.00	224.71
百分率 Per cent of total	97.0	1.7	0.8	—	—	0.5	100.0

第七表：每市畝畝租出田地之地主收入
Table 7. Landlords' Receipts per shih mow of the Rented Land.

省別及地區 Provinces and localities	主產物 Crops	現款 Cash	其他產物 Other products	使用農田器操作之收入 Receipts of farm work rendered by tenants and their labor animals		家庭工作 House-hold work	總計 Total
				人工 Man Labor	畜工 Animal Labor		
河南 Honan							
南陽 Nanyang	$1.22	$—	$0.08	$—	$—	$0.09	$1.39
淮陽 Hwaiyang	1.51	—	0.06	—	—	0.02	1.59
信陽 Sinyang	2.00	0.45	0.02	0.01	—	0.04	2.52
平均 Average	1.58	0.15	0.05	—	—	0.05	1.83
湖北 Hupeh							
襄陽 Siangyang	1.75	—	—	—	—	—	1.75
江陵 Kiangling	1.69	0.01	—	—	—	—	1.70
黃梅 Hwangmei	3.40	—	—	—	—	—	3.40
平均 Average	2.28	---	—	—	—	—	2.28
安徽 Anhwei							
貴池 Kweichih	2.49	0.40	—	—	—	—	2.89
蕪湖 Wuhu	1.89	—	—	—	—	—	1.89
桐城 Tungcheng	1.41	—	0.02	—	—	—	1.43
合肥 Hofei	3.18	—	—	—	—	—	3.18
滁 Chu	2.86	—	—	—	—	—	2.86
平均 Average	2.37	0.08	—	—	—	—	2.45
江西 Kiangsi							
南昌 Nanchang	3.93	—	0.06	—	—	—	3.99
浮梁 Fowliang	3.68	0.07	0.02	—	—	—	3.75
吉安 Kian	2.07	—	—	—	—	—	2.07
平均 Average	3.23	0.02	—	—	—	—	3.27
四省平均 Average for the four provinces	2.36	0.07	0.02	—	—	0.01	2.46

第八表： 各種收租法地主所佔之百分比 (1)

Table 8. Per cent of Landlords Renting Land Under Different Systems[1]

省別及地區 Provinces and localities		分租法[2] Share rent[2]	錢租法[5] Cash rent[3]	穀租法[4] Crop rent[4]	幫工分租法[5] Cropper[5]
河 南	Honan				
南 陽	Nanyang	100.0	—	—	—
淮 陽	Hwaiyang	50.0	—	15.0	40.0
信 陽	Sinyang	92.0	16.0	4.0	—
平 均	Average	80.7	5.3	6.3	13.3
湖 北	Hupeh				
襄 陽	Siangyang	—	—	100.0	—
江 陵	Kiangling	—	—	100.0	—
黃 梅	Hwangmei	—	—	100.0	—
平 均	Average	—	—	100.0	—
安 徽	Anhwei				
貴 池	Kweichih	50.0	15.4	34.6	—
蕪 湖	Wuhu	87.5	—	18.8	—
桐 城	Tungcheng	100.0	—	—	—
合 肥	Hofei	100.0	—	—	—
滁	Chu	100.0	—	—	—
平 均	Average	87.5	3.1	10.7	—
江 西	Kiangsi				
南 昌	Nanchang	—	—	100.0	—
浮 梁	Fowliang	2.9	8.6	97.1	—
吉 安	Kian	—	—	100.0	—
平 均	Average	1.0	2.9	99.0	—
四省平均	Average for the four provinces	48.7	2.9	47.8	2.9

(1) 有數處百分率之和高過一百者，乃因地主採用二種或三種收租法。

(1) In some cases the total percentage is more than 100, because one landlord may have two or three types of renting systems on his land.

(2) 農產物由地主與佃農按份攤分。

(2) Crops are divided between the landlord and the tenant.

(3) 佃農每年繳納定額之租金。

(3) A definite amount of cash is given as rent each year.

(4) 佃農每年繳納定額之租穀，有時繳納農產物，有時將農產物折價換繳現金。

(4) A definite amount of crop by measure is given as rent each year, sometimes the crop itself being taken as rent and sometimes the money value of the crop.

(5) 除勞力外，地主供給一切用品，惟在分種時，地主取農產物之大部分耳。

(5) The landlord furnishes everything except the labor and takes a higher percentage of the produce.

Table 9. Net Profit per Landlord and per shih mow
of Rented Land.

省別及地區 Provinces and localities	每一地主之純利 (以國幣元計) Net profit per landlord	每市畝地主之純利 (以國幣元計) Landlord's net profit per shih mow	地主投資所獲之利率 Net profit on landlord's investment
河南　Honan	dollars	dollars	per cent.
南陽　Nanyang	78.36	1.01	5.5
淮陽　Hwaiyang	222.53	1.11	8.9
信陽　Sinyang	156.18	2.31	8.2
平均　Average	152.36	1.48	7.5
湖北　Hupeh			
襄陽　Siangyang	105.69	1.56	12.7
江陵　Kiangling	29.64	1.31	25.3
黃梅　Hwangmei	36.71	2.56	12.2
平均　Average	57.35	1.81	16.7
安徽　Anhwei			
貴池　Kweichih	117.04	2.36	9.2
蕪湖　Wuhu	317.53	1.15	5.7
桐城　Tungcheng	210.15	1.12	5.2
合肥　Hofei	437.37	2.66	6.8
滁　Chu	483.85	2.44	11.8
平均　Average	315.19	1.95	7.7
江西　Kiangsi			
南昌　Nanchang	85.68	3.38	12.2
浮梁　Fowliang	114.68	2.58	11.5
吉安　Kian	17.43	1.48	7.0
平均　Average	72.60	2.48	10.2
四省平均 Average for the four provinces	173.06	1.93	10.2

四〇六爲收租用費，佔百分之九‧八〇他如修理農舍，農具等用費皆較微細。

各地區內每一地主之收入，平均爲國幣二二四‧七一元，或每市畝二‧四六元（第六與第七表）。其中穀類之收入佔百分之九七。此乃因農藝方式

total. The cost of rent collection was the next item in importance and constituted 9.8 per cent of all expenses. Various other expenses, such as building repairs and farm tool repairs were small.

For all localities, average receipts amounted to $224.71 per landlord or $2.46 per shih mow (tables 6 and 7). Of the total receipts, 97.0 per cent were from grain crops. This percentage is high because of

與納租制之不同而使然。地主收租時，採用分租法者，佔百分之四八‧七。而採用穀租法者佔百分之四七‧八（第八表）。分租法盛行於豫皖二省，而穀租法則於鄂贛二省較為普遍。

由地主田場收入減去支出即可核計地主所獲之利潤，投資田產之利率亦可由是而決算。每一地主所獲之純利平均為國幣一七三‧○六元，或每市畝一‧九三元（第九表）。此利潤即為地主資本總值之百分之一○‧二。鄂省江陵之週年利率特高，乃因該處水田易遭浸淹，地稅繁重，地價因之低跌。

地主投資田產之報酬與銀行定期貸欵收入之利率近似。

the type of farming and the renting systems. Of the land 48.7 per cent was share rented, while 47.8 per cent was "crop rented" (table 8). Share renting was more prevalent in Honan and Anhwei, and "crop renting" was more important in Hupeh and Kiangsi.

By subtracting the landlords' expenses from their receipts, the profits gained by the landlords were measured, and the interest rate on the capital investment was then determined. The net profit per landlords was $173.06, or $1.93 per shih mow (table 9). These profits were 10.2 per cent of the total investment in land and other capital rented to tenants. In the locality of Kiangling, the annual interest rate was unusually high, because the farm lands are frequently flooded, are burdened with heavy taxes, and are, therefore, for sale at low prices.

The landlords' return upon their investment was about the same as the interest rate on time credit generally received by the banks.

LIEN-KEN YIN

經 濟 統 計
ECONOMIC FACTS

南 京 金 陵 大 學 農 學 院 農 業 經 濟 系 出 版
Department of Agricultural Economics
COLLEGE OF AGRICULTURE AND FORESTRY
UNIVERSITY OF NANKING
NANKING, CHINA

第三期 No. 3　　　　一九三六年十一月 November 1936

第一圖： 英美白銀及中國與香港貨幣之購買力，一九二一年至一九三六年，一九二六年等於一〇〇

　　一九三四年十月前，中國貨幣之價值與白銀在英美之價值有相同之趨勢，僅波動較少耳。一九三四年十月後，中國白銀不能自由出口，在世界市塲上，其價值與其所含白銀之價值不同。但港幣於未放棄銀本位前，其價值仍與世界白銀價值有相同之趨勢。

FIGURE 1. PURCHASING POWER OF SILVER IN ENGLAND AND THE UNITED STATES AND OF CHINESE DOLLARS AND HONGKONG DOLLARS IN CHINA AND HONGKONG, 1921-1936, 1926=100.

　　Until October, 1934, the value of the Chinese dollar fluctuated with the value of silver in England and the United States; but the fluctuations were less erratic. After October, 1934, the Chinese dollar was not equivalent to a fixed quantity of silver in the world's markets, but the value of the Hongkong dollar continued to fluctuate with the world value of silver until, in October, 1935, Hongkong also left the silver standard.

中國與香港貨幣及白銀之購買力

白銀價值，即白銀以物品計算之購買力，其漲落在各國有相同之趨勢。故在銀本位國家，其貨幣之價值將隨世界白銀之價值而上落。

自一九二一年一月至一九三五年九月，中國貨幣可兌換固定數量之白銀，故其購買力應與英美白銀購買力相類似。（第一圖第一三三頁及第一表第一三六頁）英美二國之白銀購買力於一九二一年及一九二二年上漲。自一九二三年至一九二六年夏趨勢穩定。嗣乃稍降。自一九二七年至一九二八年復漸上漲。但一九二九年至一九三一年夏又急劇下跌。自此至一九三五年五月又轉而猛漲。既乃重行猛跌，至一九三六年二月止。一九三四年十月前中國貨幣購買力有相同之趨勢，惟波動較少耳。

一九三四年十月前，英美白銀之購買力（第一圖第一三三頁）波動較中國貨幣購買力為巨，蓋以物價上落較巨故也。當物價上漲之時，基本物品之價格上漲較速。以白銀為基本物品之一，故其購買力上漲亦速。例如英國物價於一九三一年秋及美國物價於一九三三年春之上漲是也。再當物價下跌之時，基本物價下跌亦較速，故白銀之購買力亦隨之下跌。例如一九二九至一九三一年秋英國之情形。至在美國則自一九二九年至一九三三年春物價上漲之時，其白銀之購買力乃比較下降。

是以當一九二一年物價猛跌之時，白銀在英美之購買力亦低；當一九二二年英國之物價驟然停止下跌而美國物價上漲之時，白銀購買力亦隨之迅速猛漲。

白銀為中國之貨幣，而非若歐美各國為基本物品，故以各種物品計算之中國貨幣購買力之波動亦較少。雖中國物價之漲落較國外白銀購買力為穩定，惟受世界白銀供求之影響則一也。

自一九三一年秋以來，世界白銀價值上漲，促成中國之經濟大恐慌[1]。因白銀價值之上漲，以銀幣計算之物價遂亦上漲。生產原料品者之支付租稅，債務，工資銷售費用，及其他固定開支之能力，漸形薄弱，乃無力再購製造品。

---

1. 實業部銀價物價討論委員會[中國銀價及物價問題]一九三五年出版。路易士著：[中國經濟恐慌]一九三五年金陵大學農業經濟系油印出版。中文譯稿登一九三五年九月至十二月之銀行週報。

PURCHASING POWER OF CHINESE AND HONGKONG CURRENCIES, AND SILVER.

The value of silver, its purchasing power in terms of other commodities, tends to fluctuate in the same way in different countries. Therefore, in countries where the currency is exchangeable for a fixed amount of silver, the value of the currency, its purchasing power in terms of commodities, tends to follow fluctuations in the value of silver in the world as a whole.

From January, 1921, to September, 1935, the Chinese dollar was exchangeable for a fixed amount of silver. Consequently, it had a purchasing power which fluctuated with the purchasing power of silver in England and the United States (figure 1, page 133 and table 1, page 136). In these countries the purchasing power of silver rose during 1921 and 1922; fluctuated about the same level from 1923 until summer, 1926; fell slightly; rose slowly during 1927 and 1928; fell rapidly from 1929 until summer, 1931; rose rapidly until May, 1935; and then fell rapidly until February, 1936. In China, the purchasing power of the Chinese dollar followed a similar, but slightly less erratic course up to October, 1934.

Prior to October, 1934, fluctuations in the purchasing power of silver in England and in the United States, as shown in figure 1, page 133, were more erratic than fluctuations in the purchasing power of the Chinese dollar because, in these countries, prices of all commodities fluctuated erratically. When the prices of all commodities rose, the prices of basic commodities rose faster. Silver is a basic commodity and therefore its purchasing power in terms of all commodities rose. This happened when prices of all commodities rose in England in autumn, 1931, and in the United States in spring, 1933. When prices of all commodities fell, the prices of basic commodities fell more rapidly. The purchasing power of silver in terms of all commodities, therefore, fell. This happened in England from 1929 until autumn, 1931. In the United States after 1929, the purchasing power of silver in terms of all commodities remained relatively low until the prices of all commodities began to rise in spring, 1933.

The purchasing power of silver was likewise low in England and the United States during the rapid fall of prices in 1921, but rose rapidly in 1922 when commodity prices suddenly stopped fall-

第一表： 英美白銀及中國與香港貨幣之購買力，一九二一年至一九
三五年。一九二六年等於一〇〇。

TABLE 1. PURCHASING POWER OF SILVER IN ENGLAND AND THE
UNITED STATES AND PURCHASING POWER OF CHINESE
AND HONGKONG CURRENCIES, 1921-1935, 1926=100.

年數 Year	白銀在美國 之購買力 指數(1) Index of purchasing power of silver in United States (a)	白銀在英國 之購買力 指數(2) Index of purchasing power of silver in England (b)	中國貨幣 之購買力 指數(3) Index of purchasing power of Chinese currency (c)	香港貨幣 之購買力 指數(4) Index of purchasing power of Hongkong currency (d)
1921	104	98	96	—
1922	113	112	101	101
1923	103	104	98	—
1924	110	106	102	95
1925	108	104	101	—
1926	100	100	100	—
1927	95	95	96	—
1928	97	99	98	—
1929	90	93	96	—
1930	71	76	87	—
1931	63	72	79	74
1932	69	91	89	83
1933	85	93	96	98
1934	103	106	103	108
1935	129	141	104	130

(1) 白銀在美之購買力指數 $= \dfrac{100\,(紐約之白銀價格指數)}{美國勞工局之美國批發物價指數}$

(2) 白銀在英之購買力指數 $= \dfrac{100\,(倫敦之白銀價格指數)}{英國商務處之英國批發物價指數}$

(3) 國定稅則委員會上海批發物價指數之倒數

(4) 香港貿易處統計室香港批發物價指數之倒數

(a) Index of purchasing power of silver in the United States $= \dfrac{100\ (\text{Index of the price of silver in New York}).}{\text{Bureau of labor index of wholesale prices in U.S.A.}}$

(b) Index of purchasing power of silver in England $= \dfrac{100\ (\text{Index of the price of silver in London}).}{\text{Board of trade index of wholesale prices in England.}}$

(c) Reciprocal of the National Tariff Commission's index of wholesale prices in Shanghai.

(d) Reciprocal of index of wholesale prices in Hongkong calculated by the Statistical Office of the Imports and Exports Department of Hongkong.

ing in England and rose in the United States.

In China, silver was not a basic commodity, but money. The purchasing power of the Chinese dollar in terms of all commodities did not fluctuate as much as the purchasing power of silver in countries where silver is a basic commodity. But, although changes in the level of prices in China were less erratic than changes in the purchasing power of silver abroad, prices in China were also influenced by changes in the supply of, and demand for, silver in the world as a whole.

The rise in the world value of silver that began in autumn, 1931, caused prices expressed in silver dollars to fall. A severe economic depression in China was the result.[1] It became more and more impossible for producers of primary products to pay debts, taxes, distribution costs, wages and other inflexible items. They could not buy manufactured goods.

The world value of silver was forced up even higher by the Silver Purchase policy of the United States which became effective in summer, 1934. This policy was apparently changed in 1935, and the world value of silver fell rapidly thereafter.

In China, however, economic conditions had become so depressed and so much silver had been exported that on October 15, 1934, the Ministry of Finance imposed export taxes and equalization fees which made the legal exportation of silver unprofitable. These fees and taxes remained in force until the beginning of April, 1935, when an agreement with the banks and other restrictions made the exportation of silver practically impossible.

The Chinese dollar was, therefore, not equivalent to a fixed quantity of silver on the world's markets after October 15, 1934. Its purchasing power did not follow the purchasing power of silver in the world's markets after that date. None the less, an attempt was made to keep the Chinese dollar worth as much as possible in terms of foreign currencies. Rumors of devaluation were emphatically denied. As a consequence, the purchasing

[1]. Committee for the Study of Silver Values and Commodity Prices, Ministry of Industries; "Silver and Prices in China", 1935.
Lewis, A. B., Economic Depression in China, 1935. Mimeographed by Department of Agricultural Economics, University of Nanking. Published in Chinese in Shanghai Bankers' Weekly, September—December, 1935.

第二表： 美國白銀購買力指數，(1)一九三〇年至一九三六年。
一九二六年等於一〇〇。
TABLE 2. INDEX OF PURCHASING POWER OF SILVER IN THE
UNITED STATES(a) 1930-1936, 1926=100.

年數 Year	一月 Jan.	二月 Feb.	三月 Mar.	四月 Apr.	五月 May	六月 Jun.	七月 Jul.	八月 Aug.	九月 Sep.	十月 Oct.	十一月 Nov.	十二月 Dec.
1930	78	77	75	76	74	63	66	67	69	69	71	68
1931	61	56	62	61	62	60	63	61	63	68	71	71
1932	71	73	73	70	69	70	67	69	68	69	68	65
1933	68	71	75	82	89	90	89	83	88	87	97	99
1934	99	99	100	100	97	97	100	105	103	112	115	114
1935	111	110	119	136	149	145	138	133	130	131	131	118
1936	93	89	91	91	92	91	—	—	—	—	—	—

第三表： 英國白銀購買力指數，(2)一九三〇年至一九三六年。
一九二六年等於一〇〇。
TABLE 3. INDEX OF PURCHASING POWER OF SILVER IN
ENGLAND(b) 1930-1936, 1926=100.

年數 Year	一月 Jan.	二月 Feb.	三月 Mar.	四月 Apr.	五月 May	六月 Jun.	七月 Jul.	八月 Aug.	九月 Sep.	十月 Oct.	十一月 Nov.	十二月 Dec.
1930	82	81	80	82	80	68	69	71	75	76	77	72
1931	67	61	66	65	64	62	66	66	68	86	92	97
1932	96	97	89	85	86	89	89	93	91	91	92	87
1933	87	88	93	97	100	97	93	90	92	91	92	93
1934	96	99	101	100	98	99	103	106	107	118	122	121
1935	111	110	119	153	166	159	149	145	141	139	139	121
1936	95	93	93	95	95	92	—	—	—	—	—	—

　　美國於一九三四年夏實行購銀政策後，世界白銀價值益形上漲。但至一九三五年，美國方顯然改變其政策，白銀價值乃行猛跌。

　　但在中國，經濟恐慌益甚，大量白銀源源出口。爲遏止白銀之外流起見，中國政府於一九三四年十月十五日起開始徵收白銀出口稅。至一九三五年四月初，乃代以銀行之紳士協定，無異禁止白銀之出口。

　　自一九三四年十月十五日起，中國銀元價值，在世界市場已不爲固定白銀數量之價值，其購買力不復追隨世界白銀之購買力。惟當時中國尚極力維持其貨幣之外匯價格，否認一切貶值之謠言，故其購買力乃逐漸上漲，至一九三五年夏較同年一月高百分之十。物價乃反暦下跌。但物價下跌將更甚，倘貨幣仍維持其從前所含白銀數量之價值。

　　至一九三五年十月，中國貨幣之外匯價格，任其下跌，其國內購買力亦隨之下降。迨一九三五年十一月三日，其外匯價格始告穩定。

(1) 見一三六頁第一表附註
(2) 見一三六頁第一表附註
(a) See footnote (a), table 1, page 136.
(b) See footnote (b), table 1, page 136.

第四表： 中國貨幣之購買力指數，(3) 一九三〇年至一九三六年。一九二六年等於一〇〇。

TABLE 4. INDEX OF PURCHASING POWER OF CHINESE CURRENCY (c) 1930-1936, 1926=100.

年數 Year	一月 Jan.	二月 Feb.	三月 Mar.	四月 Apr.	五月 May	六月 Jun.	七月 Jul.	八月 Aug.	九月 Sep.	十月 Oct.	十一月 Nov.	十二月 Dec.
1930	92	90	90	90	90	85	83	84	85	87	88	88
1931	84	79	79	79	78	77	79	77	77	79	80	82
1932	84	85	85	86	86	88	89	90	91	92	94	93
1933	92	93	94	96	96	96	97	98	100	100	100	102
1934	103	102	104	106	105	105	103	100	103	104	102	101
1935	101	100	104	104	105	109	111	109	110	106	97	97
1936	96	95	94	93	95	94	93	—	—	—	—	—

power of the currency gradually rose until, in the summer of 1935, it was 10 per cent higher than in January, 1935. Prices fell; but they would have fallen more had the currency continued to be equivalent to the same amount of silver as formerly.

In October, 1935, the Chinese dollar was allowed to fall in value in terms of foreign exchange, and a decline in its domestic purchasing power consequently occurred. It was stabilized in terms of foreign exchange on November 3, 1935, and thereafter its domestic purchasing power continued to decline only gradually. This gradual decline is expected to cease as soon as an adjustment with the reduced exchange value of the currency has been reached.

Since the Chinese dollar is no longer exchangeable for a fixed amount of silver, future fluctuations in the purchasing power of silver in the world's markets cannot be expected to disturb the level of commodity prices in China.

Conditions in Hongkong.—In Hongkong, the Hongkong dollar was redeemable in silver, and the export of silver was not restricted in October, 1934, as in China. Consequently, the purchasing power of Hongkong dollars rose almost as rapidly as did the value of silver in England and the United States during 1934 and 1935 (figure 1, page 133). Commodity prices declined and economic conditions grew correspondingly worse. If the Shanghai currency had been kept on the silver standard from October, 1934, until October, 1935, its purchasing power would probably have risen as much as that of Hongkong currency, and commodity prices in Shanghai would have fallen as much as they did in Hongkong.

(3) 見第一三六頁第一表附註　(c) See footnote (c), table 1, page 136.

國內購買力僅逐漸下跌。物價下跌至與外匯價格落貶程度相調正時，似將即行停止。

以中國貨幣不復能兌換白銀，將來世界白銀購買力之變遷，將不再牽動中國之物價。

香港情形：港元為銀本位貨幣。一九三四年十月後，亦未若中國之禁止現銀出口，故自一九三四年至一九三五年(第一圖第一三三頁)港元購買力上漲之速率幾與英美相同。物價乃下跌。經濟情形日趨衰落。如自一九三四年十月至一九三五年十月中國仍維持銀本位，則其貨幣之購買力將亦如港元之上漲，物價亦應同樣下跌也。

一九三五年十月及十一月間，以白銀計算之港元價格任其下跌，故其購買力之跌落遠高出於英美白銀之購買力，迨一九三五年十二月，港元價格約恢復與中國貨幣從前之比例。

將來港滬間之匯價，大約將頗穩定。其購買力將有同樣之趨勢，但不再受世界銀價之影響，以港滬貨幣均不再為固定數量之白銀，而為相當數量之外匯也。

路易士
王　廉

豫鄂皖贛四省三十四縣土地分類之研究*

投資農村，以圖農村經濟之發展，為最近國家之急務。本研究對於豫鄂皖贛四省各區合理之經濟發展，供獻較為適宜性之資料。

土地分類之定義：

四省土地係根據其最適合之精密利用而分類。其經營之現狀，及將來利用之可能，如土壤種類，地勢與氣候，農藝方式，作物收獲量，作物災歉，灌溉與排水及地價等，均考慮及之。

土地共分甲，乙，丙，丁，戊，己，庚七區，庚區土地多屬山石，河灘，沙丘。己區土地低窪潮濕，僅生蘆葦。戊區土地之利用，不甚集約，大部荒蕪，雜生林草，最宜造林。丁區土地之利用，較戊區為集約。該區土地雖有一部分業已耕種，然大部分仍為荒地或林地，

---

* 四省土地分類圖，尚未能製就付印，但欲閱縣單位之土地分類圖及詳情者，請與著者函詢，極為歡迎。

第五表： 香港貨幣購買力指數，(4)一九三四年至一九三六年。
一九二二年等於一〇一・四。

TABLE 5. INDEX OF PURCHASING POWER OF HONGKONG
CURRENCY (d) 1934-1936. 1922=101.4.

年數 Year	一月 Jan.	二月 Feb.	三月 Mar.	四月 Apr.	五月 May	六月 Jun.	七月 Jul.	八月 Aug.	九月 Sep.	十月 Oct.	十一月 Nov.	十二月 Dec.
1934	104	106	109	110	106	104	109	106	111	110	111	115
1935	122	120	133	130	189	143	138	146	138	140	119	108
1936	104	104	—	99	98	101	95	—	—	—	—	—

In October and November, 1935, the Hongkong currency
was allowed to fall in value in terms of silver. Its purchasing
power fell more rapidly than the purchasing power of silver in
the United States and England. By December, 1935, the foreign
exchange value of the Hongkong dollar was at a level which made
it equivalent to the same amount of Chinese currency as formerly.

In the future, the exchange rate between Hongkong and
Chinese currencies will probably be stable. The purchasing powers
of the two currencies will fluctuate together but will not be
determined by the world value of silver because both currencies
are now equivalent, not to a fixed amount of silver, but to a relatively fixed amount of foreign exchange.

A. B. LEWIS
LIEN WANG

LAND CLASSIFICATION OF 34 HSIEN IN ANHWEI, HONAN, HUPEH AND KIANGSI

At the present time, capital is available for the development
of rural areas. This study furnishes information on the comparative suitability for sound economic development of different
areas in Anhwei, Honan, Hupeh and Kiangsi.

Definition of land classes

The land in these provinces was classified on the basis of the
intensity of use to which it was apparently best adapted. Both
present and probable future uses were considered, taking into
account type of soil, topography, climate, type of farming, crop
yields, crop failures, irrigation, drainage, and land values.

---

(4)：見第一三六頁第一表附註　　(d)　See footnote (d), table 1, page 136.

其地用于農作，不如用于造林之爲宜也。丙乙甲三區土地，宜于農業，尤以甲區之耕種最爲集約。

各類土地之特徵：

淮河以北，麥爲主要作物，稱麥農作區。調查之各縣位于淮北者屬之。淮河以南，冬季雖亦有麥，然春季夏季之稻，實爲最主要之農作物，稱稻農作區。各縣位于淮南者屬之。麥農作區及稻農作區各類土地之面積及百分比，詳見第一表。

第一表：　　豫鄂皖贛四省麥稻兩農作區各類土地之面積*及其百分比

TABLE 1.　AREA AND PROPORTION OF LAND IN EACH LAND CLASS IN THE WHEAT AND RICE REGIONS OF ANHWEI, HONAN, HUPEH AND KIANGSI,* 1933-1934.

土地分類區域 Land class	麥農作區 Wheat region	稻農作區 Rice region	麥農作區 Wheat region	稻作農區 Rice region	麥稻兩農 作區總計 Total
	方市里 square shih li	方市里 square shih li	百分比 per cent	百分比 per cent	百分比 per cent
甲　V	3,644	35,796	4.2	22.9	16.2
乙　IV	16,618	38,975	19.1	24.9	22.9
丙　III	51,200	26,737	58.9	17.1	32.0
丁　II	9,104	19,500	10.5	12.5	11.8
戊　I	5,441	34,074	6.2	21.8	16.2
已　X	303	599	0.3	0.4	0.4
庚　O	670	588	0.8	0.4	0.5
總計 Total	86,980	156,269	100.0	100.0	100.0

甲乙兩區面積在麥農作區佔百分之二三‧三，而在稻農作區佔百分之四七‧八。此爲稻農作區優沃土地耕種極爲集約之明證。

未墾土地——地區等級愈高，其未墾土地面積之成分愈低（見第三表）。在稻農作區，丙區未墾土地面積之成分，較乙甲兩區爲低。蓋以稻農作區之丙區土地，多接近麥農作區，且地勢平坦，墾地之百分比較大。

農作——在麥農作區，甲區多夏二季作物面積，佔該區已墾土地面積之百分數，較戊區爲大（見第四表）。土地分類等級之低者，因土壤氣候等因素之不適於農作，故每歲兩穫之作物面積甚少。

---

*水面面積除外　　　　　　　　　　　　* Water area excluded.

Seven classes of land were designated O, X, I, II, III, IV and V. Land in class O is rocks, river wash and sand dunes. Land in class X is low and marshy, growing only rushes. Land in class I is the least intensively used land, a large proportion of it

第二表：　　　　豫鄂皖贛四省三十四縣各類土地面積之百分比

TABLE 2. PROPORTION OF LAND IN EACH LAND CLASS, 34 HSIEN IN ANHWEI, HONAN, HUPEH AND KIANGSI, 1933-1934.

縣 名 Hsien		面 積 Area (a)	土地分類區域 Land Class							總計 Total
			甲 V	乙 IV	丙 III	丁 II	戊 I	己 X	庚 O	
		(方市里) Square shih li	百分比 per cent	百分比 per cent	百分比 per cent	百分比 per cent	百分比 per cent	百分比 per cent	百分比 per cent	百分比 per cent
參 晨 作 區 Wheat region										
靈寶	Ling Pao	8,036	0	6	21	56	13	0	4	100
洛陽	Lo Yang	4,094	0	18	64	13	5	0	0	100
鄭縣	Cheng	3,309	0	0	72	24	3	1	0	100
開封	Kaifeng	6,557	0	14	45	37	0	4	0	100
許昌	Hsuchang	4,328	31	63	0	5	0	1	0	100
襄城	Hsiangcheng	4,803	0	11	84	0	5	0	0	100
郾城	Yencheng	3,552	0	83	11	6	0	0	0	100
南陽	Nanyang	11,963	0	0	78	0	20	0	2	100
淮陽	Hwai Yang	12,123	0	44	56	0	0	0	0	100
宿縣	Su	16,682	0	0	92	3	5	0	0	100
懷遠	Hwai Yuan	11,533	20	26	49	0	5	0	0	100
稻晨作區 Rice region										
鳳陽	Fengyang	9,224	0	35	52	0	13	0	0	100
全椒	Chuan Chiao	4,800	82	0	0	9	9	0	0	100
繁昌	Fanchang	2,983	48	42	0	0	0	10	0	100
光化	Kuang Hwa	3,054	0	39	61	0	0	0	0	100
嘉山	Ka Shan	5,907	15	67	0	0	18	0	0	100
和縣	Ho	5,824	48	23	0	25	0	4	0	100
銅陵	Tung Ling	1,920	35	11	10	0	44	0	0	100
孝感	Hsiao Kan	9,516	10	36	34	0	18	0	2	100
穀城	Ku Cheng	8,666	18	26	0	0	55	0	1	100
滁縣	Chu	5,656	52	0	0	48	0	0	0	100
蕪湖	Wuhu	2,272	87	0	0	11	2	0	0	100
東流	Tung Liu	2,839	26	0	0	41	30	3	0	100
襄陽	Hsiang Yang	13,571	0	12	74	14	0	0	0	100
信陽	Hsin Yang	12,997	3	15	22	0	57	0	3	100
南陵	Nan Ling	3,305	78	0	0	0	22	0	0	100
祁門	Chi Men	11,630	10	0	0	60	30	0	0	100
咸寧	Hsien Ning	5,643	16	38	0	0	46	0	0	100
歙縣	Hsi	7,940	0	84	0	0	16	0	0	100
青陽	Ching Yang	4,492	4	30	0	0	66	0	0	100
至德	Chih Teh	7,712	13	1	0	53	33	0	0	100
南昌	Nanchang	5,718	84	0	12	0	4	0	0	100
新建	Hsin Chien	10,800	64	0	29	0	7	0	0	100
宣城	Hsuancheng	9,800	0	84	0	6	10	0	0	100

(a) 水面面積除外　　　　　　　　　(a) Water area excluded.

第三表： 豫鄂皖贛四省麥稻兩農作區各類土地未墾面積之百分比

TABLE 3. PROPORTION OF UNCULTIVATED LAND IN EACH LAND CLASS IN THE WHEAT AND RICE REGIONS OF ANHWEI, HONAN, HUPEH AND KIANGSI, 1933-1934.

土地分類區域 Land class		麥農作區 Wheat region	稻農作區 Rice region
		百分比 per cent	百分比 per cent
甲	V	0.3	36.0
乙	IV	0.9	40.6
丙	III	3.2	18.1
丁	II	22.9	50.0
戊	I	79.8	85.7
已	X	100.0	100.0
庚	O	100.0	100.0
總計 Total		11.6	45.3

在稻農作區，丙丁兩地區內，一歲兩種之作物面積，與甲乙兩地區，不相上下，惟戊區則相差甚遠（見第五表）。平均言之；稻農作區內已墾土地利用之程度，較麥農作區為大。

作物收穫量：——在麥農作區高地區，各種重要作物，如小麥，大麥，高粱，棉花，菸草，玉蜀黍，及黃豆之收穫量，皆較低地區為高（見第六表）。甲區小麥每市畝之平均收穫量，為二八七市斤，戊區者僅為八九市斤。

在稻農作區，甲區春季水稻每市畝之收穫量，為六五八市斤，而戊區則僅三〇一市斤。甲區夏季水稻每市畝收穫六三八市斤，而戊區則僅三一六市斤。其他作物之收穫量，亦皆以高地區較低地區為高。

甲乙兩地區，各種重要作物之收穫量，皆較他區為優。所以其地能集約利用之，且供養多數人民也。

灌溉：——在麥稻二農作區，各土地分類區域與已墾土地之灌溉面積，皆有密切之關係（見第八表）。麥農作區內甲區僅有小部分灌溉者。蓋以甲乙兩區之劃分大多以生產菸草地價之高低而定，而不甚注意其灌溉面積之多寡也。稻農作區內，丁戊兩區已墾土地灌溉面積之百分數較高，蓋以其中可墾之土地甚多，農民能選可行灌溉之土地，而墾種之；因此墾地灌溉者面積之成分遂高。

being idle or in woods and grass. It is best adapted to forests. Land in class II is more intensively used than land in class I. A considerable proportion is farmed but a large proportion is idle or in woods. It is better adapted to forests than to agriculture. Land in classes III, IV and V is adapted to agriculture, land in class V being the most intensively used.

General characteristics of the different classes of land

For purposes of study, land north of the Hwai river on which wheat is the principal crop was considered separately from land in the rice growing region south of the Hwai river. The area and proportion of land in each class in the wheat region and the rice region are shown in table 1 (page 142).

In the wheat region, 23.3 per cent of the land is in classes V and IV but in the rice region, 47.8 per cent is in these classes.

第四表： 豫鄂皖贛四省麥農作區各類土地各季作物面積之百分比

TABLE 4. PROPORTION OF CULTIVATED LAND GROWING CROPS IN DIFFERENT SEASONS, 5 CLASSES OF LAND IN THE WHEAT REGION OF ANHWEI, HONAN AND HUPEH, 1933-1934.

季別 Season		土地分類區域 Land Class					平均 Average
		甲 V	乙 IV	丙 III	丁 II	戊 I	
		百分比 per cent	百分比 per cent	百分比 per cent	百分比 per cent	百分比 per cent	百分比 per cent
冬季	Winter	80.7	66.1	63.3	51.7	63.1	62.8
春季	Spring	18.9	32.9	36.4	39.1	34.7	34.3
夏季	Summer	74.2	56.9	49.1	31.1	38.4	48.4
秋季	Fall	—	0.6	0.1	—	—	0.1
長年	Perennial	0.4	1.0	0.3	9.2	2.2	2.9
總計	Total	174.2	157.5	149.2	131.1	138.4	148.5

Uncultivated land.—The higher the land class, the lower is the proportion of uncultivated land (table 3 page 144). In the rice region, the proportion of uncultivated land in class III is lower than that in classes IV and V, because much of the class III land in the rice region is on the border of the wheat region, and has a level topography.

Cropping.—In the wheat region, the proportion of the cultivated land growing a crop was larger for class V land than for class I land both in winter and in summer (table 4, page 145).

— 145 —

第五表： 豫鄂皖贛四省稻農作區各類土地各季作物面積之百分比

TABLE 5. PROPORTION OF CULTIVATED LAND GROWING CROPS IN DIFFERENT SEASONS, 5 CLASSES OF LAND IN THE RICE REGION OF ANHWEI, HONAN, HUPEH AND KIANGSI, 1933-1934.

季別 Season		土地分類區域 Land Class					平均 Average
		甲 V	乙 IV	丙 III	丁 II	戊 I	
		百分比 per cent	百分比 per cent	百分比 per cent	百分比 per cent	百分比 per cent	百分比 per cent
冬季	Winter	52.1	62.3	56.7	64.0	53.9	58.2
春季	Spring	43.4	34.2	38.8	30.4	39.4	37.7
夏季	Summer	52.1	60.7	56.7	62.2	24.2	57.2
秋季	Fall	5.1	8.7	4.9	1.5	2.5	5.7
長年	Perennial	4.5	3.5	4.5	5.6	6.7	4.1
總計	Total	157.2	169.4	161.6	163.7	126.7	162.9

第六表： 豫鄂皖贛四省麥農作區各類土地各種作物每市畝之通常收穫量。

TABLE 6. AVERAGE (MODAL) YIELDS PER SHIH MOW OF VARIOUS CROPS ON 5 CLASSES OF LAND IN THE WHEAT REGION OF ANHWEI, HONAN, AND HUPEH, 1933-1934.

土地分類區域 Land class		冬季作物 Winter crops		春季作物 Spring crops			夏季作物 Summer crops	
		小麥 Wheat	大麥 Barley	高粱 Kaoliang	籽棉 Seed cotton	菸草 Tobacco	玉蜀黍 Corn	黃豆 ∞ Soy beans
		市斤 shih chin	市斤 shih chin	市斤 shih chin	市斤 shih chin	市斤 shih chin	市斤 shih chin	市斤 shih chin
甲	V	287	356	310	119	286	—	288
乙	IV	172	215	210	87	212	230	186
丙	III	137	168	192	57	187	119	153
丁	II	115	134	99	57	—	113	87
戊	I	89	—	78		23	69	—
平均	Average	149	172	185	88	183	129	160

　　地價：——民國二十年，麥農作區之農田價格，由甲區每市畝之八〇·三元，至戊區之一〇·六元不等(見第九表)。稻農作區之甲區為五九·二元，戊區為二八·六元。在農業恐慌時期，高地區內之農田價格，仍較低地區為高。

　　農舍及農具之總值：——作區農民之房屋及農具總值，由麥農作區甲區之五〇〇元，至戊區之三二六元不等(見第十表)。稻農作區之甲區為五一四元，丁區為三三八元。

There was less double cropping on low class land where soil conditions were unfavorable.

In the rice region, double cropping was as common on land in classes II and III as on land in classes IV and V, but land in class I was not double cropped as much (table 5, page 146). On the average, cultivated land was more fully used in the rice region than in the wheat region.

Yields.—In the wheat region, the yields of important crops such as wheat, barley, kaoliang, cotton, tobacco, corn, and soy beans were all greater on high class than on low class land (table 6, page 146). The yield of wheat was 287 shih chin per shih mow on land in class V and only 89 on land in class I.

In the rice region the yield of spring rice was 658 shih chin per shih mow on land in class V and only 301 on land in class I (table 7, page 148). Summer rice yielded 638 shih chin per shih mow on land in class V and only 316 on land in class I. Other crops also yielded more on high class than on low class land.

The comparatively good yields of all important crops on land in classes V and IV explain why this land can be used more intensively and support more people.

Irrigation.—In both the wheat region and the rice region there was a close relationship between land class and the proportion of cultivated land which was irrigated (table 8, page 148). Only a small proportion of the cultivated land in class V in the wheat region was irrigated because the division between classes V and IV was determined chiefly by high land values due to the growing of tobacco rather than by the proportion of irrigated land. A large proportion of the cultivated land in classes I and II in the rice region was irrigated because arable land in these classes was abundant and farmers could select for cultivation that portion which could be irrigated.

Land values.—In 1931, the value of farm land in the wheat region ranged from an average of 10.6 yuan per shih mow for land in class I to 80.3 yuan per shih mow for land in class V (table 9, page 149). In the rice region, class I land was worth 28.6 yuan per shih mow and class V land, 59.2 yuan. High class land was still worth much more than low class land during the agricultural depression.

第七表： 豫鄂皖贛四省稻農作區各類土地各種作物每市畝之通常收
穫量

TABLE 7. AVERAGE (MODAL) YIELDS PER SHIH MOW OF VARIOUS CROPS ON 5 CLASSES OF LAND IN THE RICE REGION OF ANHWEI, HONAN, HUPEH AND KIANGSI, 1933-1934.

土地分類區域 Land class	冬季作物 Winter crops		春季作物 Spring crops				夏季作物 Summer crops			
	小麥 Wheat	大麥 Barley	紅花草 Red clover	玉蜀黍 Corn	水稻 Rice	籽棉 Seed cotton	水稻 Rice	黃豆 Soy beans	芝蔴 Sesame	籽棉 Seed cotton
	市斤 shih chin	市斤 shih chin	市斤 shih chin	市斤 shih chin	市斤 shih chin	市斤 shih chin	市斤 shih chin	市斤 shih chth	市斤 shih chih	市斤 shih chin
甲 V	223	280	2670	395	658	98	638	210	150	141
乙 IV	179	188	1161	296	425	78	429	180	149	113
丙 III	152	152	—	—	382	72	314	175	107	92
丁 II	152	168	730	250	422	72	330	147	101	78
戊 I	151	189	—	—	301	64	316	149	93	54
平均 Average	190	227	2302	307	569	80	463	185	142	109

第八表： 豫鄂皖贛四省麥稻兩農作區五類土地已墾土地灌溉面積之
百分比

TABLE 8. PROPORTION OF CULTIVATED LAND IRRIGATED, 5 CLASSES OF LAND IN THE WHEAT AND RICE REGIONS OF ANHWEI, HONAN, HUPEH AND KIANGSI, 1933-1934.

土地分類區域 Land class	麥農作區 Wheat region	稻農作區 Rice region	麥稻兩農作區總計 Whole area
	per cent	per cent	per cent
甲 V	0.3	69.8	62.8
乙 IV	13.8	64.1	48.9
丙 III	4.0	42.7	21.2
丁 II	2.6	54.1	31.6
戊 I	0.1	45.6	34.3
平均 Average	4.4	58.7	41.1

各土地分類區域內經濟之展望：

　　甲等地區因土壤，氣候及地勢之適宜，故作物收穫量，及農作之精密，皆優於乙區，又灌溉面積，亦多於乙區。因此地價亦較乙區爲高。於是甲區農舍及農具之價值，較乙區爲高。而其所能供養之農家，亦較多。乙區之與丙區，及丙區之與丁區，其關係亦莫不皆然。

　　土地分類之不同，大多由于土壤，氣候及地勢，故極難使之改變。此土地分類之研究，所以在計劃農村事業發展，佔重要之地位也。

Value of buildings and equipment.—The value of farmers' buildings and equipment in the wheat region ranged from 326 yuan per farm in land class I to 500 yuan in land class V. (table 10). In the rice region, the range was from 338 yuan per farm in land class II to 514 yuan in land class V.

第九表： 豫鄂皖贛四省麥稻兩農作區五類之農田價格(民國二十年及民國二十三年至二十四年)

TABLE 9.   VALUE OF CULTIVATED LAND, 5 CLASSES OF LAND IN THE WHEAT AND RICE REGIONS OF ANHWEI, HONAN, HUPEH AND KIANGSI, 1931 AND 1934-1935.

土地分類區域 Land class		麥農作區 Wheat region		稻農作區 Rice region	
		1931	1934-35	1931	1934-35
		每市畝價格(元) *yuan per shih mow*	每市畝價格(元) *yuan per shih mow*	每市畝價格(元) *yuan per shih mow*	每市畝價格(元) *yuan per shih mow*
甲	V	80.3	45.3	59.2	37.9
乙	IV	35.7	29.2	41.4	28.9
丙	III	21.8	18.5	31.4	22.4
丁	II	11.5	10.4	29.6	21.2
戊	I	10.6	8.4	28.6	20.6
平均	Average	26.2	21.4	48.3	32.4

第十表： 民國二十年，豫鄂皖贛四省麥稻兩農作區五類土地每一農家農舍及農具之總值(元)。

TABLE 10.   VALUE OF FARMERS' BUILDINGS AND EQUIPMENT, 5 CLASSES OF LAND IN THE WHEAT AND RICE REGIONS OF ANHWEI, HONAN, HUPEH AND KIANGSI, 1931.

土地分類區域 Land class		麥農作區 Wheat region	稻農作區 Rice region	麥稻兩農作區總計 Whole area
		yuan per farm	*yuan per farm*	*yuan per farm*
甲	V	500	514	512
乙	IV	485	496	493
丙	III	371	378	374
丁	II	327	338	334
戊	I	326	486*	408
平均	Average	397	504	470

* 戊區每一農家財富之總價為四八六元為較高。以計算該區農民財富之區域，不僅為戊區，實仍包括若干小塊甲等區域之田地也。因無較為準確數字，故誌之。

* The high value of 486 yuan per farm in land class I is due to the fact that these data were reported for rather large areas, which included some patches of land later classified as class V.

銀行或其他團體之以長期貸款於農民者，當知甲區農民償還借款本利之能力，必較其他各區之農民爲易。因借款用於優良田地改良所得之進款，較低地區爲高也。

合作倉庫或運銷合作社設立於高等地區，其成功之機會，必較低地區爲大。因生產之集約，倉庫或合作社之營業數量較大。

根據以上理由，對於引種優良之作物品種，及耕種與施肥方法，所得之利益，在適合農業之地區必較不適合農作之地區爲大。

凡于因土壤氣候及地勢不適宜於農作之區，投以相當之金錢或努力，以作農村建設之舉，未有不失敗者。

高等土地分類每方市里之兒童數目，必較劣等爲多。因此每一兒童之教育用費較低。且用于教育之經費甚低，而所收之功效較大。丁戊兩區之農村教育費則必極大。

興築或改良道路，皆有鉅益。但道路建設費如用於甲乙兩區則收益更大。

本研究昭示增加地價之因子，如道路建設，改良學校，改良作物及牲畜生產，治安及自衛，其各類土地地價增加之百分數，與原地價成正比例。若土地每畝價值四〇元，改良後增加百分之一〇，即增加地價四元。若土地每畝價值一〇元，則同等改良僅增加地價一元耳。此所以豫鄂皖贛四省土地經濟分類研究之在計劃農村建設過程中，極爲重要者也。

崔毓俊

Economic Development of different land classes.

Because of favorable soil, climate and topography, class V land has higher crop yields and can profitably be cropped more and irrigated more than class IV land. It is therefore valued higher than class IV land. It pays to have better buildings and more implements on class V land; and more families can be supported. Class IV land has similar advantages over class III, and class III, over class II.

The differences between the land classes are primarily due to soil, climate and topography and are therefore not easily subject to change. It is therefore important in planning rural developments to study the classification of the land.

Banks or associations that make long term loans to farmers can be more sure of the payment of interest and principal by farmers of class V land than by farmers of lower classes of land. The better land gives a better and surer return than poor land on the improvements made possible by loans.

Co-operative warehouse or marketing associations have better chances of success on high class than on low class land. There is a larger volume of business for them where production is more intensive.

For the same reason the introduction of improved varieties of crops and better methods of cultivation and manuring will yield better returns where the land is well adapted to agriculture than where experience shows it to be poorly adapted.

No amount of money or effort spent in rural reconstruction in areas where the soil, climate and topography are not favorable to agriculture will succeed in making agricultural areas out of such districts.

In areas where most of the land is high class, there are more children per square shih' li than in the less fertile areas. The cost of education per pupil is therefore considerably lower and money spent on education will yield a higher return in these areas. Rural education in land classes I and II will always be exceedingly costly.

Great benefits can result from the making or re-making of roads. The greatest benefits will result from money spent for roads in land classes V and IV.

中國農具經濟之初步研究[1]

農具使用研究之材料，係於民國二四年夏蒐集一，四二六田場，浙江二一八，江蘇八四一，安徽二〇〇，江西一〇九及湖北五八之調查而成。

水稻與小麥爲本研究區域之主要作物。水稻佔夏季耕地百分之五二，小麥佔冬季耕地百分之二六。次要作物爲棉花，玉米，芝蔴，粟米，高粱，豆類，油荣子，大麥，瓜類及蔬菜等。多數耕地，均用以栽種夏冬二季作物，惟南昌每年收穫稻作兩次，而不栽種冬季作物。

每縣平均家庭大小，田場大小，耕地價值，及農具價值等均在第一表內示明。

第一表： 民國二十四年，中國中部迤東，一一縣，一，四二六田場之家庭大小，田場大小，及耕地價值。

TABLE 1. SIZE OF HOUSEHOLD, SIZE OF FARM, AND VALUE OF LAND ON 1,426 FARMS IN 11 HSIEN IN EAST CENTRAL CHINA, 1935.

縣 Hsien	農家數目 Number of farms	家庭大小 Size of house- hold	田塲工作 人數 Number of farm workers	田塲總 面佰 Total area per farm	每年田塲 作物面積 Crops per farm per year	耕種地 價值 Value of culti- vated land per farm	所有農具 價值 Value of imple- ments per farm
	數目 number	人數 persons	人數 persons	畝 mow	畝 mow	元 yuan	元 yuan
浙江 *Chekiang*							
杭州 Hangchow	218	5.4	2.3	14.6	25.1	518	35
江蘇 *Kiangsu*							
宜興 I-shing	100	5.5	1.6	16.2	31.0	800	50
崑山 Kunshan	105	5.1	3.3	23.8	38.4	760	111
蘇州 Soochow	98	5.2	2.1	6.3	12.5	251	10
鎮江 Chinkiang	60	4.9	2.2	29.0	58.7	2,166	58
揚州 Yangchow	359	5.3	3.4	19.9	38.1	1,282	59
南京 Nanking	119	5.5	2.0	12.0	24.1	1,327	21
安徽 *Anhwei*							
來安 Laian	100	7.9	3.9	27.4	46.4	603	43
桐城 Tungcheng	100	4.9	1.6	8.1	14.7	504	41
江西 *Kiangsi*							
南昌 Nanchang	109	5.6	1.8	10.4	26.0	394	33
湖北 *Hupeh*							
孝感 Siaokan	58	6.3	2.2	14.3	27.8	235	78
平均 Average		5.5	2.6	16.7	31.2	804	48

(1) 本研究結果之詳細報告不久將行出版。

Studies have shown that factors which tend to increase the value of land, such as road construction, improvement of schools, improvement in crop and livestock production, and security and protection, increase the value of different grades of land by a uniform percentage of the original value. If land is worth $40.00 per mow, a 10% improvement results in a $4.00 increase in value. If land is worth only $10.00 per mow, the same improvement results in an increase of only $1.00 per mow. It is therefore exceedingly important that plans for rural reconstruction should be based on an economic classification of land such as is here summarized for the four provinces of Anhwei, Honan, Hupeh and Kiangsi.

RUH-TSUIN TSUI

PRELIMINARY NOTE ON AN ECONOMIC STUDY OF FARM IMPLEMENTS[1]

Data on the use of farm implements were collected on 1,426 farms, 218 in Chekiang, 841 in Kiangsu, 200 in Anhwei, 109 in Kiangsi, and 58 in Hupeh, in the summer of 1935.

Rice and wheat are the major crops in the localities studied and occupy 52 per cent of the cultivated land in summer and 26 per cent in winter. Minor crops are cotton, corn, sesame, millet, kaoliang, beans, rapeseed, barley, melons, and vegetables. Most of the land is used for a summer and winter crop, except in Nanchang where there is double cropping with rice but no winter crop.

The average size of family, size of farm, value of land and value of implements are shown for each hsien in table 1, page 152.

Efficiency of Labor and of Implements.—In the region as a whole, 31.2 mow of crop land worth 804 yuan were cultivated by 2.6 workers with implements worth only 48 yuan (table 1, page 152). On a mow of rice, 86.0 hours of man labor, but only 7.6 hours of animal labor, were spent (table 2, page 154). On a mow of wheat, 54.5 hours of man labor, but only 5.3 hours of animal labor, were spent. The labor required to grow rice and wheat varied greatly between individual hsien but nowhere was animal labor employed more than human labor.

---

1. A full report of the results of this study will be published in the near future.

田場人工及農具之效率：

以全地區而言，價值八〇四元之三一‧二畝作物面積，由二‧六農民以僅值四八元之農具耕種之(見第一五二頁第一表)。每畝水稻需要人工八六‧〇小時，但僅耗用畜工七‧六小時（見第一五四頁第二表）。每畝小麥需要人工五四‧五小時，但僅耗用畜工五‧三小時。水稻與小麥生長所需之人工，雖各縣差別甚大，然無一縣所用之畜工較人工為多。

田場面積之狹小，限制畜工及大件農具之使用。平均每畝大小僅有二‧八畝(見第一五四頁第二表)。如有一〇畝之畦，則每日用犁可耕四‧七畝，但僅有〇‧九畝之畦，每日僅可耕二‧九畝。小畦田地使用手用農具之效率雖與大畦田地相同，但其效率甚低。

畜工及大件農具之使用，亦常為作物地內之墳墓所限制，墳墓約有百之六〇葬於耕地內。

第二表：　民國二十四年，中國中部迄東，一一縣，一，四二六田場之人工效率及田畦大小。

TABLE 2.　EFFICIENCY OF LABOR AND SIZE OF FIELDS ON 1,426 FARMS IN 11 HSIEN IN EAST CENTRAL CHINA, 1935.

縣 Hsien	水稻每畝 人工 Man labor per mow of rice	水稻每畝 畜工 Animal labor per mow of rice	小麥每畝 人工 Man labor per mow of wheat	小麥每畝 畜工 Animal labor per mow of wheat	田畦 大小 Size of fields
	小時 hours	小時 hours	小時 hours	小時 hours	畝 mow
浙江　Chekiang					
杭州　Hangchow	134.5	17.1	91.7	5.3	2.0
江蘇　Kiangsu					
宜興　I-shing	135.3	7.4	78.5	5.3	1.7
崑山　Kunshan	81.0	8.6	32.3	3.4	3.2
蘇州　Soochow	118.6	3.5	91.3	2.1	1.1
鎮江　Chinkiang	96.9	4.5	87.4	3.6	—
揚州　Yangchow	43.7	7.2	25.3	8.3	7.6
南京　Nanking	73.0	4.3	49.7	2.6	4.9
安徽　Anhwei					
來安　Laian	41.6	6.5	30.0	7.1	4.2
桐城　Tungcheng	85.8	4.6	27.3	5.2	1.5
江西　Kiangsi					
南昌　Nanchang	56.7	7.5	0	0	2.2
湖北　Hupeh					
孝感　Siaokan	79.0	12.6	31.2	10.4	2.0
平均　Average	86.0	7.6	54.5	5.3	2.8

The smallness of the fields limited the use of animal labor and large implements. The average size of field was only 2.8 mow (table 2, page 154). In a field of 10 mow it is possible to plow at the rate of 4.7 mow per day, but in a field of only 0.9 mow, the rate is only 2.9 mow per day. Hand implements can be used as efficiently in small as in large fields; but their efficiency is low.

The use of animals and large implements is also often limited by graves in the crop land. Of all the graves, 60 per cent were located in cultivated fields.

The efficiency of each implement is shown in table 3, page 156. On the average, a plow covered 3.1 mow in a day but only 0.7 mow were dug with a digging hook. More than four times as much work was done by the larger implement. But, those farmers who had plows plowed 26.0 mow with each plow and those who had digging hooks dug a *total* of only 22.1 mow. With an animal, wooden chain pump, 5.1 mow were irrigated each day; with a hand, wooden chain pump, only 2.2 mow. Those who had animal, wooden chain pumps used each for 15.4 mow. Those who had hand, wooden chain pumps used them for a *total* of only 9.2 mow. It may not have been profitable for some farmers with digging hooks and hand, wooden chain pumps to have bought plows and animal, wooden chain pumps because they had too little land to use these economically. The use of work animals and larger implements is limited by size of farm as well as by inconveniently small fields.

Both these limitations might be overcome if farmers would co-operate in using work animals and larger implements, in re-arranging the layout and size of their fields, and in levelling graves. Some groups of farmers already co-operate in the use of threshing boxes, rice hullers and fan-mills. Only if this co-operation increases can the efficiency of the farmers increase and their standard of living rise.

Even where the farmers are not willing to consolidate their holdings so as to make possible the use of efficient implements, it may still be possible to remove the balks between the fields, keeping only the cornerstones. It would then be possible at least to plow bigger areas together at one time.

每種農具之工作效率，述明於第一五六頁第三表。平均每犁每日耕地三・一畝，但用釘耙每日祇能掘地〇・七畝。可見大件農具之工作較小件農具多出四倍餘。惟備犁之農民，每犁耕地二六・〇畝，備釘耙之農民僅共掘地二二・一畝。用牛車灌溉，每日可灌溉五・一畝，如用手車，每日僅能灌溉二・二畝。備牛車之農民，每具共灌溉一五・四畝，備手車之農民，僅共灌溉九・二畝。使用釘耙及手車之小田場農民，如購置耕犁及牛車，未必有利，因農民之田場過小，不能經濟使用之。使用役畜及較大之農具，又為田場大小所限制，且小坵田地，亦不便使用。

第三表：　民國二十四年中國中部遊東，一一縣，一，四二六田場各種農具工作之效率及數量。

TABLE 3.　RATE AND AMOUNT OF WORK DONE BY VARIOUS IMPLE-MENTS ON 1,426 FARMS IN 11 HSIEN, IN EAST CENTRAL CHINA, 1935.

農具 Implement	每十小時 工作效率 Rate of work per 10 hours	每件農具使 用之時間 Time each imple- ment in use	每件農具使 用之面積 Area covered by each imple- ment	每田場每件農 具使用之面積 Area covered by such imple- ments per farm
	畝 mow	小時 hours	畝 mow	畝 mow
耕植　Cultivating				
犁　　Plow	3.1	85	26.0	35.2
釘耙　Digging hook	0.7	131	9.2	22.1
鍬　　Sppd	0.9	144	12.8	26.9
耙　　Harrow	8.4	76	63.9	63.9
大鋤　Large hoe	1.0	97	9.6	26.0
小鋤　Small Hoe	1.2	45	5.6	14.0
禾耙　Scuffle hoe	1.0	141	14.2	37.3
灌溉　Irrigating				
牛車　Animal, wooden chain pump	5.1	30	15.4	20.6
脚車　Foot.　　"　　"　　"	3.9	32	12.4	14.8
手車　Hand,　　"　　"　　"	2.2	40	8.8	9.2
打落　Threshing				
石滾　Stone roller	2.0	188	38.0	43.0
禾斛　Threshing box	1.6	88	14.4	11.9
打落床 Threshing rack	1.6	135	21.2	24.5
鏈枷　Flail	1.4	34	4.8	11.4
其他　Other				
米礱　Rice huller	1.9	159	30.1	28.8
風車　Fan-mill	3.8	90	34.4	32.4
籮　　Open baskets for grains	8.2	12	9.9	24.2
竹蓆　Drying baskets	8.9	25	22.3	43.5
糞桶　Night soil bucket	2.0	71	14.3	26.9
鐮刀　Sickle	1.4	77	10.7	33.6
叮担　Carrving pole	2.6	85	21.9	34.5

Improvement of implements.—It would pay to improve the design of some of the implements. That many implements could be improved is shown by their present low efficiencies (table 3, page 156). Plows, wooden chain pumps, harvesting and threshing machines should be improved first because they are used in the rush seasons. At present, crops are often damaged by the weather because they can be harvested only slowly.

第四表： 民國二十四年, 中國中部迤東, 一一縣. 一, 四二六田場農民
置備各種農具之百分率及其原價, 使用年限及每年之折舊費

TABLE 4.   PROPORTION OF FARMERS OWNING VARIOUS IMPLEMENTS
AND INITIAL COST, LENGTH OF LIFE AND COST PER YEAR
OF IMPLEMENTS ON 1,426 FARMS IN 11 HSIEN IN EAST
CENTRAL CHINA, 1935.

農具 Implement	農民所有之 百分率 Per cent of farmers owning	原價 Inital cost	使用 年限 Lenth of life	每年之(1) 折舊費 Deprecia- tion per year (a)
	百分率 per cent	元 yuan	年數 years	元 yuan
耕植 *Cultivation*				
犂 Plow	50.9	5.00	20	0.17
釘耙 Digging hook	65.3	0.71	10	0.08
鍬 Spud	79.1	0.65	10	0.09
耙 Harrow	55.5	3.89	21	0.22
大鋤 Large hoe	73.3	0.60	11	0.07
小鋤 Small hoe	45.1	0.45	11	0.04
禾耙 Scuffle hoe	76.7	0.39	7	0.06
灌溉 *Irrigation*				
牛車 Animal, wooden chain pump	18.3	33.30	29	1.01
脚車 Foot, ,, ,, ,,	52.0	18.70	27	0.40
手車 Hand, ,, ,, ,,	19.9	10.50	27	0.38
打落 *Threshing*				
石滾 Stone roller	69.6	4.07	110	0.50
禾斛 Threshing box	62.0	5.85	24	0.19
打落床 Threshing rack	53.0	1.82	23	0.08
鏈耞 Flail	42.6	0.21	8	0.03
其他 *Other*				
米礱 Rice huller	29.8	5.51	13	0.43
風車 Fan-mill	26.0	8.50	29	0.32
籮 Open baskets for grains	50.9	1.10	11	0.10
竹簍 Drying baskets	67.3	1.05	13	0.08
糞桶 Night-soil bucket	69.5	1.04	16	0.08
鐮刀 Sickle.	85.1	0.22	6	0.05
扁担 Carrying pole	58.7	0.40	12	0.04

(1) 每年之折舊費，係以原價減去目前價值，除以使用之年數而得。

(a) Depreciation per year was calculated by substracting the present value from the initial cost and dividing by the number of years used.

上述兩種限制，如農民合用役畜及較大農具，足能解除，同時重整農場佈置，重劃塊坵大小，及平墓工作。有少數農民已有合用禾斛，米礱及風車。僅此種合作如能增廣，農民工作之效率卽能增加，而其生活程度亦可提高。

卽農民不願合併其小塊田地，俾以使用較高效率之農具者，仍能除去田間田塍，而僅存留石界，則一時至少亦可耕植較大之面積。

農具之改進：

改良一部分農具之設計，必有所獲。現有許多農具已證明效力之低，能加以改良（第一五六頁第三表）。耕犂，水車，收割及打落等用具應先加以改良，因此種農具，均在農忙季節時使用。目前作物常遭氣候之損害，因僅能遲緩收穫故也。

多數人以爲輸入外國農具可以解決中國之農具問題，實則不然，因外國農具不適合小田場及小塊坵之中國貧苦農民也。在目今狀況下，中國農民惟有共同購買及使用較適合其本地情形之改良農具。

在開始任何工作前，中國應先成立一中央組織，研究各地情形，製造適合各地實際情形之改良農具，此種組織，應先指示農民，使用改良農具之方法，並使彼等明瞭其利益。

農具費用及資金需要

在設計改良農具或推廣其使用時，目前價值應考慮及之。各種農具之新購價值及每年之折舊費均在第一五七頁第四表中示明。比較農具原價及第一五六頁第三表之工作效率，同時亦知飼養役畜之費用，則農民卽可決定購置何種農具。每具耕犂雖值五‧〇〇元，而每具釘鈀僅值〇‧七一元，但耕犂每年之折舊費僅〇‧一七元，而釘鈀則爲〇‧〇八元，然耕犂每日耕地面積較釘鈀多四倍有餘。

購置牛車之費用較購置任何農具爲高，但其每年之折舊費爲一‧〇一元。禾斛每年之折舊費爲〇‧一九元，米礱僅爲〇‧四三元。農民如能借得支付此種原價低利貸欵，則置備此種農具之農民，將日益增多。

潘鴻聲
金克敦

— 158 —

Many people think that the importation of foreign implements will help China to solve her implement problem, but actually foreign implements are not suitable for poor farmers with small farms, and small fields. Under the circumstances, it would be wiser for them to buy and use co-operatively improved implements better suited to their local conditions.

Before anything else is done, China should establish a central organization to study conditions in the country and to manufacture improved implements suited to the actual conditions. The organization should demonstrate to the farmers the use of the improved implements and make their advantages clear.

Cost of implements and need for credit.—In planning the improvement of implements or their wider use, present costs should be considered. The initial cost and actual yearly depreciation of various implements are shown in table 4, page 157. By comparing these costs and, at the same time, the rates of work shown in table 3, page 156, a farmer may decide which implements to buy if he knows also the cost of a keeping a work animal. Although a plow cost 5.00 yuan and a digging hook only 0.71 yuan, the yearly depreciation was only 0.17 yuan on the plow as compared to 0.08 yuan on the digging hook and in a day the plow covered more than four times as much land as the digging hook.

Animal, wooden chain pumps cost more to buy than any other implements but the yearly depreciation on them was only 1.01 yuan. The yearly depreciation on a threshing box was only 0.19 yuan and on a rice huller only 0.43 yuan. More farmers could profitably own these implements if they could cheaply borrow money with which to pay the initial costs.

PAN HONG-SHENG

O. KING

經濟統計
ECONOMIC FACTS

南 京 金 陵 大 學 農 學 院 農 業 經 濟 系 出 版
Department of Agricultural Economics
COLLEGE OF AGRICULTURE AND FORESTRY
UNIVERSITY OF NANKING
NANKING, CHINA

第四期 No. 4 　　　　一九三七年二月 February 1937

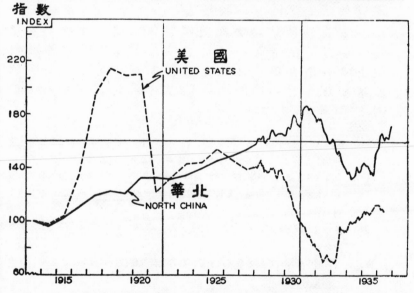

第一圖：華北及美國之批發物價指數，一九一三年至
一九三六年，一九一三年＝一〇〇。

自一九三一年至一九三四年華北物價猛跌。在美國則物價跌落，計有二次，始於一九二
〇年及一九二九年。

FIGURE 1.—INDEX NUMBERS OF WHOLESALE PRICES IN NORTH CHINA
AND THE UNITED STATES, 1913-1936, 1913 = 100.

In North China, prices fell rapidly between 1931 and 1934. The United States
suffered two major price declines, one beginning in 1920 and the other in 1929.

華北・東三省・香港及美國之批發物價[1]

自一九一三年至一九三一年九月，華北之批發物價指數，自一〇〇漲至一八四（第一圖第一六一頁）。雖政治紛擾，災旱頻仍，度支困難，貿易入超，現銀進出無常，世界經濟恐慌及其他之變動，但物價上漲之趨勢，極為穩定。

自一九三一年九月至一九三四年四月，物價自一八四跌至一三三（一九一三＝一〇〇），計三十一月內共跌百分之二十八。此低落之物價水準，迄至一九三五年十月而不變。嗣後物價上漲極速，迄今已達一九三〇年之水準。

華北物價之趨勢與美國完全不同。（第一圖第一六一頁）在一九一三年至一九一九年間，美國物價上漲一倍有餘。自一九二〇年至一九二一年，物價指數乃自二一〇跌至一二二（一九一三年＝一〇

(1) 各項統計數字係根據下列各書:—

物價指數

華北：南開大學經濟學院一九三四及一九三五年之"南開指數年刊"一九三五年四月及一九三六年一月出版。其指數基期原為一九二六年，現改為一九一三年，以一‧四八五乘之。南開經濟學院"南開社會經濟季刊"第九卷第三期第七三六頁，一九三六年十月出版；及國定稅則委員會"上海物價月報"一九三六年十一月期。

香港：香港進出口部統計處，一九三四年及一九三五年之"香港貿易統計"及未公佈之材料。

東三省：偽滿中央銀行所編之奉天六十種物品之批發價格載於其所出版之月刊"經濟金融概況"。

美國：華倫及皮而生："英國之司答的斯脫物價指數及美國相同之物價指數"，載於農業經濟第八十五期，第二〇四九頁至二〇五二頁，一九三四年五月出版及未公佈之材料。

英國：華倫及皮而生："農業經濟"第八十五期，第二〇四九頁至二〇五二頁，一九三四年五月出版。

國定稅則委員會上海物價月報所登之"英國司答的斯脫批發物價指數"（一九二九年＝一〇〇），其指數基期換算為一九一三年，以一‧三五二九乘之。

WHOLESALE PRICES IN NORTH CHINA, HONGKONG, MANCHURIA AND THE UNITED STATES[1]

Between 1913 and September 1931, the index of wholesale prices in North China rose from 100 to 184 (figure 1, page 161). In spite of political disturbances, balanced and unbalanced budgets, floods, droughts, erratic changes in a continuously 'unfavorable' balance of trade, fluctuating imports and exports of silver, economic depressions abroad, and many other major changes, the rise of prices was remarkably regular.

Between September 1931, and April 1934, prices fell from 184 to 133 (1913 = 100), a fall of 28 per cent within thirty-one months. The low level was maintained until October 1935, after which prices rose rapidly. The index is now as high as in 1930.

Prices in North China have followed a course entirely different from that of prices in the United States (figure 1, page 161). Between 1913 and 1919, prices in the United States were more than doubled. Between 1920 and 1921, they fell from 210 to 122 (1913 = 100). They rose to 154 in 1925, fell to 139 in September 1929, and thereafter fell precipitously to 70 in March 1933. Prices

---

[1] The following sources have been used:

Index numbers of wholesale prices

North China.—Nankai Institute of Economics, *Nankai Index Numbers* 1934 and 1935, published April 1935, and January 1936. The general index was converted from a 1926 to a 1913 base by multiplying by 1.4885.

Nankai Institute of Economics, *Nankai Social and Economic Quarterly*, Vol, IX No. 3, page 736, October 1936, and reports by National Tariff Commission, *Prices and Price Indexes in Shanghai*, November 1936.

Hongkong.—Statistical Office of the Imports and Exports Department, *Hongkong Trade and Shipping Returns*, 1934 and 1935, and unpublished monthly data.

Manchuria.—Central Bank of Manchou, "Index Numbers of Prices of 63 Commodities in Mukden", *Economics and Currency*, monthly issues.

United States.—Warren, G. F. and Pearson, F. A., "Sauerbeck-Statist index for the United Kingdom and a comparable index number for the United States", *Farm Economics*, No. 85, pp. 2049-2052, May 1934, and unpublished data.

United Kingdom.—Warren, G. F. and Pearson, F. A., *Farm Economics*, No. 85, pp. 2049-2052, May 1934.
National Tariff Commission, "Statist index of wholesale prices in the United Kingdom (1929 = 100)" *Prices and Price Indexes in Shanghai*, monthly issues, The index was converted from a 1929 to a 1913 base by multiplying by 1.3529.

Footnote continued on page 165.

〇）。一九二五年復漲至一五四，一九二九年九月跌至一三九，自此繼續迅速跌落，至一九三三年三月竟達七〇。但自一九三三年四月至一九三四年三月美國物價迅速上漲，不過同時中國物價反迅速下跌。自一九一三年起，中國物價之趨勢較美國波動為少，蓋中國僅有一次之物價跌落也。

以白銀計算之華北及美國物價

自一九一〇年五月二十四日至一九三三年三月十日，中國銀元名義上含純銀〇‧七七〇九盎司（〇‧八三三四標準盎司），其在世界市場之價格，亦以此為標準。自一九三三年三月十日起至一九三五年十一月中國銀元之含銀改為純銀〇‧七五五三（〇‧八一六六標準盎司）。但在此期間內其外匯價格常低於所含之白銀，蓋初則一般預測銀價有跌落之趨勢，繼則中國自一九三四年十月十四日起實行徵收白銀出口稅也。自一九三五年十一月四日新貨幣政策實行後，中國貨幣價格低於其所含之白銀，其百分數上落不定。為計算一九三三年三月十日

國際匯兌：

上海匯倫敦及紐約：國定稅則委員會之"上海貨價季刊"及"上海物價月報"自一九二〇年至一九三四年四月規元照該季刊所登之折合率，折算為國幣。一九二〇年前則照官價〇‧七一五折合。

香港匯倫敦：喬治‧陪而汲及克藍敦合著："中國之經濟及貿易情況"第九十七頁。一九三五年國外貿易部在倫敦出版。香港進出口部統計處"香港貿易統計"第六頁，一九三五年出版。上海字林西報所載之路透匯價。

長春匯倫敦：偽滿中央銀行"經濟金融概況"第四十六期及四十七期。

銀價

倫敦：國定稅則委員會"上海貨價季刊"及"上海物價月報"。

紐約：華倫及皮而生："黃金及物價"第二五七頁，一九三五年紐約出版。上海字林西報所載中央銀行匯價。

— 164 —

rose rapidly in the United States between April 1933, and March 1934, at a time when, in China, prices were falling rapidly. Since 1913, prices in China have followed a less erratic course than that of prices in the United States. China has suffered only one period of rapidly falling prices.

Prices in terms of Silver in North China and the United States

From May 24, 1910, until March 10, 1933, the Chinese national yuan was officially 0.7709 ounces of fine silver (0.8334 ounces standard silver) and was exchanged on this basis on the world's markets. From March 10, 1933, until November 1935, the yuan was officially 0.7553 ounces of fine silver (0.8166 ounces standard silver) but during almost all this period had a lower foreign exchange value than this amount of silver. This was the result of a lack of confidence in the future silver value of the yuan and the actual restriction of silver exports after October 14, 1934. Since the currency reform of November 4, 1935, the yuan has also been at a varying discount below its former silver value. In order to calculate prices after March 10, 1933, in terms of the

---

Footnote continuted from page 163:

Foreign exchange rates

Shanghai on London and New York.—National Tariff Commission, *Shanghai Marke Prices Report,* quarterly issues, and *Prices and Price Indexes in Shanghai* monthly issues.

From 1920 until April 1934, taels were converted to yuan according to the rates quoted in the *Shanghai Market Prices Report.* Prior to 1920, yuan were take as equivalent to 0.715 taels.

Hongkong on London.—George, A. H., and Pelham, G. Clinton, *Trade and Economic Conditions in China,* p. 97. Department of Overseas Trade, London, 1935.
Statistical Office, Imports and Exports Department, Hongkong, *Hongkong Trade and Shipping Returns,* page VI, 1935.
Reuter's report *North China Daily News,* Shanghai.

Changchun, Manchuria, on London.—Central Bank of Manchou, *Currency and Economics,* Nos. 46 and 47.

Silver Prices

London.—National Tariff Commission, *Shanghai Market Prices Report,* quarterly issues, *Prices and Price Indexes in Shanghai,* monthly issues.

New York.—Warren, G. F., and Pearson, F. A., *Gold and Prices,* p. 257. John Wiley and Sons, New York, 1935.
Central Bank of China's quotations, *North China Daily News,* Shanghai.

後，以從前標準銀元計算之價格，用下列公式：

$$\frac{\text{以銀元（純銀〇·7709盎司）計算之物價指數，一九一三年}=\text{一〇〇}}{}=\text{以國幣計算之物價指數，一九一三年}=\text{一〇〇}\times\frac{\text{以美金計算之國幣價格（上海電匯紐約）}}{\text{在紐約以美金計算之純銀0.7709盎司價格}}$$

　　自一九一三年至一九三三年三月三日，美國倘維持金本位，美金二〇·六七元等於純金一盎司。一九三三年三月後，金元之價格低於其所含之純金。至一九三四年一月三十一日始定爲美金三十五元等於純金一盎司。美國物價之趨勢完全與中國不同，蓋以不同之貨幣計算也。以美金計算之物價，可用下列公式折合爲以白銀計算之物價。

$$\frac{\text{以白銀計算之物價，一九一三年}=\text{一〇〇}}{}=\frac{100[\text{（以美金計算之物價），一九一三年}=\text{一〇〇})]}{\text{紐約銀價指數，一九一三年}=\text{一〇〇}}$$

　　自一九一三年以來，華北及美國以白銀計算之物價，有相同之趨勢（第二圖第一六八頁）。美國指數自一九一三年之一〇〇，漲至一九三一年之一八七，跌至一九三五年之一〇二，復漲至一九三六年五月之一四五。至華北指數，則自一九一三年之一〇〇，漲至一九三一年之一八二，跌至一九三五年之一〇四，至一九三六年五月漲至一四〇。惟在歐戰期內，美國白銀之需要，不若其他物品爲切，故以白銀計算之物價遂上漲極速。自一九二九年至一九三一年，美國以白銀計算之物價上漲較中國爲烈，蓋銀價在此時跌落過速也。

　　自一九三一年九月至十二月，美國以白銀計算之物價自一八〇跌至一六一（一九一三年＝一〇〇）。其最大原因爲各國放棄金本位，白銀之需要急增，造成世界白銀價值之猛漲。以白銀計算之物價，自然下降。中國自銀價上漲後，倘繼續維持銀本位，物價慘跌所形成之經濟恐慌，乃不能避免矣。

silver standard currency used prior to that time, the following equation was used:—

$$\begin{array}{l}\text{Index of prices in terms}\\\text{of yuan of 0.7709 ounces}\\\text{of fine silver (1913=100)}\end{array} = \begin{array}{l}\text{Index of prices in}\\\text{terms of}\\\text{National yuan}\\\text{(1913 = 100)}\end{array} \times \begin{array}{l}\text{T. T. exchange value of yuan}\\\text{in terms of U. S. dollars}\\\text{(Shanghai on New York)}\\\hline\text{Dollar price of 0.7709 ounces}\\\text{of fine silver in New York.}\end{array}$$

From 1913 until March 3, 1933, the United States maintained the gold standard, U. S.$20.67 being equivalent to one ounce of fine gold. After March 1933, the gold value of the dollar fell until January 31, 1934, when it was fixed, U.S.$35.00 then being made equivalent to one ounce of fine gold. Prices in the United States have followed a course different from that of prices in China because they were in terms of a different money. Prices in terms of dollars can be converted into prices in terms of silver as follows:—

$$\begin{array}{l}\text{Index of prices in}\\\text{terms of silver}\\\text{(1913 = 100)}\end{array} = \frac{100\ [\text{Index of prices in terms of U. S. dollars, (1913 = 100)}]}{\text{Index of price of silver in New York, (1913 = 100)}}$$

Since 1913, prices in terms of silver have fluctuated in much the same way in North China as in the United States (figure 2, page 168). The index number for the United States rose from 100 in 1913 to 187 in 1931, fell to 102 in 1935, and was 145 in May, 1936. The index for North China rose from 100 in 1913 to 182 in 1931, fell to 104 in 1935, and was 140 in May, 1936. During the World War, prices in terms of silver rose rapidly in the United States where the demand for silver increased by less than the demand for other commodities. Between 1929 and 1931, prices in terms of silver in the United States rose more rapidly than prices in China. The world value of silver was falling very rapidly during this period.

Between September and December 1931, prices in terms of silver in the United States fell from 180 to 161 (1913 = 100). This rapid drop was chiefly the result of an increased world demand for silver following abandonment of the gold standard by Great Britain and twenty other nations. The commodity value of silver rose rapidly in the world as a whole. Prices in terms of silver therefore fell rapidly. China maintained the silver standard for many months after this world-wide change began

當一九三三年七月倫敦白銀協定簽訂時，美國以白銀計算之物價已跌落至一五一（一九一三年＝一〇〇）。及一九三四年六月美國購銀案通過，其指數跌至一三三。一九三五年五月再下降至八七。嗣後乃猛漲。一九三五年十一月爲一〇四，一九三六年五月爲一四五。美國購銀政策之變更，當爲白銀忽跌之最大原因。

　　華北以白銀計算之物價與美國以白銀計算之物價有相同之趨勢，足證中國白銀之出口，美國白銀之進口，及政府財政與貨幣政策之變更，均不足影響物價一般之關係。

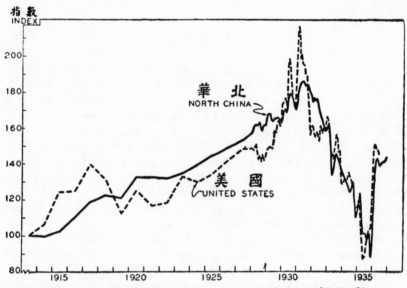

第二圖：華北與美國以白銀計算之批發物價指數，一九一三年至一九三六年，一九一三年＝一〇〇。

除歐戰期內及一九三四年十月後，華北及美國以白銀計算之物價有相同之趨勢。

FIGURE 2.—INDEX NUMBERS OF WHOLESALE PRICES EXPRESSED IN TERMS OF SILVER FOR THE UNITED STATES AND IN TERMS OF SILVER YUAN FOR NORTH CHINA, 1913-1936, 1913＝100

In North China, prices in terms of silver yuan followed much the same course as prices in terms of silver in the United States except during the World War.

and was thus unable to avoid a rapid fall of prices and the general distress which it entailed.

By July 1933, when the London Silver Agreement was signed, prices in terms of silver in the United States had already fallen to 151 (1913 = 100). By June 1934, when the United States Silver Purchase Act was passed by Congress, the index was 133. By May 1935, it was 87. Thereafter, the index rose rapidly. In November 1935, it was 104 and in May 1936, 145. A change in the silver purchasing policies of the United States Treasury was the major reason for the sudden reversal.

In North China, prices in terms of silver followed a course very similar to that of prices in terms of silver in the United States. The increasing exportation of silver from China, the importation of silver by the United States and changes in currency policies and government finance did not affect the general relationship.

Prices in terms of Silver in North China, Manchuria and Hongkong

Prices expressed in terms of silver followed the same course in Hongkong and Manchuria as in the United States and North China. Between 1931 and 1935, prices in terms of silver were halved (figure 4 page 170). The world-wide rise of the value of silver caused prices expressed in terms of silver to fall by a like amount in all four countries irrespective of differences in trade balances, silver movements, bank management, currency policies, taxation systems, and foreign debts. During December 1935, and early in 1936, prices in terms of silver rose rapidly to approximately their level in 1933.

Since the early part of 1934, the world demand for silver has been largely based on the Silver Purchase Act of the United States, but it alone was not responsible for economic depression in the Far East. Between September 1931 and January 1934, prices in terms of silver had already fallen from 125 to 93 in North China (1933 = 100).

Prices in terms of Currency in North China, Manchuria
and Hongkong

The movements of prices actually experienced by North China, Manchuria and Hongkong differed from movements of the general level of prices in terms of silver as soon as the yuan, Manchurian

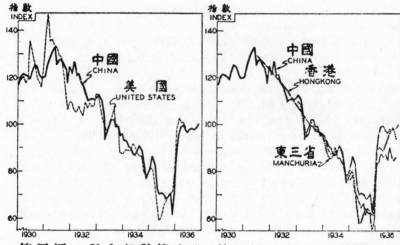

第三圖：以美國一九三〇年，六〇〇白銀計算之華北及美國之批發年物價至一九三三年之指數一九三一

以白銀計算之華北及美國之批發物價有相同之趨勢。一九三一年來猛烈跌落，至一九三五年怨轉而上漲。

FIGURE 3.—INDEX NUMBERS OF WHOLESALE PRICES EXPRESS-ED IN TERMS OF SILVER FOR NORTH CHINA AND THE UNITED STATES, 1930-1936, 1933 = 100

The general movements of prices expressed in terms of silver have been the same in North China as in the United States. The rapid downward movement after 1931 was suddenly reversed in 1935

第四圖：以東三省及香港一九三〇年，六〇〇白銀計算之華北，東三省及香港之物價至一九三三年之指數一九三一

以白銀計算之華北，東三省及香港之物價，有相同之趨勢。一九三一年來猛烈跌落，至一九三五年怨轉而上漲。

FIGURE 4.—INDEX NUMBERS OF WHOLESALE PRICES EXPRESS-ED IN TERMS OF SILVER FOR NORTH CHINA, MANCHURIA AND HONGKONG, 1930-1936, 1933 = 100

The general movements of prices expressed in terms of silver have been the same in Manchuria and Hongkong as in North China. The rapid downward movement after 1931 was suddenly reversed in 1935.

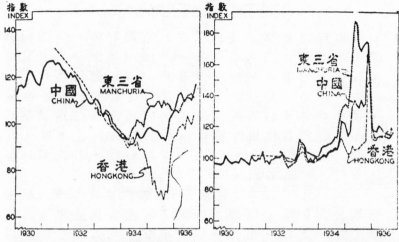

第五圖：以華北一九三○年物價至一九三六年計算之各省批發物價指數，通東三省物價處，北發用三省一三○指一九三○白銀幣及數六以貨價至一○○

在一九三四年前，各地貨幣尚未貶值，華北、東三省及香港之物價有同樣下跌之趨勢。嗣後東三省貨幣貶值，促其物價上漲。一九三五年十一月前中國貨幣之貶值，較低於東三省，故俾能維持物價之不跌。至香港則幾完全受銀價之影響，受物價跌落之害。

FIGURE 5.—INDEX NUMBERS OF WHOLESALE PRICES IN TERMS OF YUAN FOR NORTH CHINA, MANCHURIAN YUAN FOR MANCHURIA AND HONGKONG DOLLARS FOR HONGKONG, 1930-1936

(Prices in terms of silver in 1933 = 100)

In Manchuria and North China, prices followed the downward course of prices expressed in terms of silver until the silver value of the yuan and Manchurian yuan began to fall in 1934. At first, the Manchurian yuan was devalued sufficiently to raise prices in Manchuria. The devaluation of the yuan was only sufficient to keep prices in North China level until November 1935, when the yuan was devalued as much as the Manchurian yuan. Hongkong suffered almost the full amount of the general deflation of prices expressed in terms of silver.

第六圖：以中國一九三○年至一九三六年計算之世界銀價，及香港市場香港指數，在偽白銀年價＝一○○上幣，以貨數三六白

自一九三四年十月起，以偽幣計算之銀價猛漲。同時以國幣計算之銀價亦上漲，但在一九三五年十一月前，不若偽國之烈。至港幣則在一九三五年十一月前，以白銀計算之價格並未下跌。

FIGURE 6.—INDEX NUMBERS OF THE PRICE OF SILVER IN TERMS OF CHINESE YUAN, MANCHURIAN YUAN AND HONGKONG DOLLARS ON WORLD MARKETS, 1930-1936 (Par = 100)

The Manchurian yuan price of silver began to rise rapidly in October 1934. The yuan price of silver also rose at this time but was not as high as the yen price until November 1935. The Hongkong dollar did not fall much in value in terms of silver until November 1935.

— 171 —

以白銀計算之華北，東三省及香港之物價

以白銀計算之香港及東三省之物價，與美國及華北者有相同之趨勢。自一九三一年至一九三五年，以白銀計算之物價，跌落及半。雖貿易之情形，白銀之移動，銀行之管理，貨幣政策，賦稅之制度，及外債之多寡等情完全不同，而世界白銀價值之跌落，促成以白銀計算之物價在四處同樣下跌，自一九三五年十二月至一九三六年初期，以白銀計算之物價，約上漲至一九三三年之水準。

自一九三四年之初期起，世界白銀之需要，幾大部根據美國購銀條例。但此不爲遠東經濟恐慌之唯一原因，蓋自一九三一年九月至一九三四年一月以白銀計算之華北物價已自一二五跌至九三也（一九三三年＝一〇〇）。

以各該地貨幣計算之華北，東三省及香港之物價

自華北，東三省及香港放棄銀本位以來，其貨幣之價值，低於其所含之白銀，故各該地物價之趨勢，亦顯然與以白銀計算者不同。（第四五六圖第一七〇及一七一頁）中國貨幣之貶值程度，最好將中國貨幣法定所含白銀在世界市場之價格，以電匯率，算出其以中國貨幣計算之價格度量之。用下列公式可求出以中國貨幣計算之白銀價格指數[2]，以平價等於一〇〇。

$$\text{以中國貨幣計算之白銀價格指數，平價＝一〇〇} = \frac{\text{在紐約以美金計算之純銀 0.7553 盎司之價格}}{\text{中國貨幣以美金計算之電匯價格（上海電匯紐約）}} \times 100$$

用同樣方法，可求以東三省及香港貨幣計算之世界白銀價格指數[3]。

(2) 平價爲純銀〇．七五五三盎司，即一九三三年三月十日宣布之法定含銀量。

(3) 東三省銀元之含銀量作爲純銀〇．七六八七盎司。港元一九三三在倫敦之價值，爲純銀〇．八三一二盎司，即以此爲平價。

— 172 —

yuan, and Hongkong dollar were exchanged on the world's markets for less than their original silver equivalents (figures 4, 5 and 6, pages 170, 171). The most satisfactory measure of the devaluation of the yuan is obtained by converting into yuan the price, on a free silver market, of the official silver equivalent of the yuan, using current T. T. rates of exchange. The yuan price can then be expressed as a per cent of par.[2] Thus:—

$$
\begin{array}{c}
\text{ndex of yuan} \\
\text{price of silver} \\
(\text{par} = 100)
\end{array}
=
\frac{
\begin{array}{c}
\text{U. S. dollar price of 0.7553 ounces of fine silver} \\
\text{in New York}
\end{array}
}{
\begin{array}{c}
\text{T. T. exchange value of yuan in terms of U.S. dollars} \\
\text{(Shanghai on New York)}
\end{array}
} \times 100
$$

In a similar manner, the price of silver on the world's markets in terms of Manchurian yuan and Hongkong dollars can be expressed as a per cent of par.[3]

The Manchurian yuan was at first devalued more than the yuan and the yuan more than the Hongkong dollar (figure 6, page 171). In Manchuria, prices in terms of Manchurian yuan rose above the general level of prices in terms of silver by as much as the Manchurian yuan was devalued. Between December 1933, and May 1935, prices in Manchurian yuan rose from 97 to 109, while the general level of prices in terms of silver fell from 96 to about 65 (prices in terms of silver in 1933 = 100). Manchuria avoided a disastrous fall of prices because her money was devalued. In spite of the rapid fall and rise of prices expressed in terms of silver in the world as a whole, there has been a comparatively regular rise of prices in Manchuria since April 1934.

The yuan began to depreciate at the same time as the Manchurian yuan but depreciated more slowly. In September 1934, the yuan price of silver in New York was only 106 per cent of par. In November 1934, after the legal export of silver was restricted, it was 124 per cent of par; in October 1935, before the currency reform, 135 per cent. This amount of devaluation was not sufficient to raise prices as in Manchuria (the Manchurian yuan price of silver was 174 per cent of par in October 1935), but did prevent a drastic fall. The general level of prices in

---

2 The par value used here is that of 0.7553 ounces of fine silver, the official silver value of the yuan as announced on March 10, 1933.

3 The par value of the Manchurian yuan was taken as 0.7687 ounces of fine silver. The silver value of the Hongkong dollar in London in 1933 was 0.8322 fine ounces, and this has been taken as its par.

最初東三省貨幣之貶值較中國本部爲甚，而中國本部貨幣之貶值又較香港爲烈（第六圖一七一頁）。東三省物價上漲之程度，與其貶值相同。自一九三三年十二月至一九三五年五月，以僞圓計算之物價自九七漲至一〇九，而以白銀計算之物價，則自九六跌至六五左右（一九三三年以白銀計算之物價＝一〇〇）。東三省以貨幣貶值之關係，遂得免去物價慘跌之痛苦。自一九三四年四月以來，世界以白銀計算之物價，漲落雖極互，但東三省物價上漲之趨勢比較極爲穩定。

當東三省貨幣貶值時，中國貨幣亦已開始貶值，惟趨勢較緩。一九三四年九月在紐約以中國貨幣計算之白銀價格指數，僅爲一〇六（平價＝一〇〇）。當一九三四年十一月，白銀出口稅業已實行時，其指數爲一二四：一九三五年十月——新貨幣政策未實行前——爲一三五：故其貶值程度，雖不足將物價抬高與東三省相同（一九三五年十月以僞圓計算之白銀價格指數爲一七四），但確阻止物價之慘跌也。一般以白銀計算之物價，自一九三四年九月之八八，跌至一九三五年十月之六八左右（一九三三年＝一〇〇）。但以中國貨幣計算之華北物價，一九三四年九月爲九四，一九三五年十月爲九六（一九三三年以白銀計算之物價＝一〇〇）。

二九三五年十月來，華北物價之上漲，係受銀價之影響[4]。一九三五年中國貨幣以白銀計算之價格跌落（第六圖第一七一頁），以中國貨幣計算之物

（4）爲解釋中國實行新貨幣政策後物價之變動，似以國外物價及國幣之外匯價作爲比較研究之根據，較爲合理。自一九三五年十月至一九三六年四月，美國物價跌落百分之二，而以國幣計算之美匯價格上漲百分之二十三，華北物價亦上漲百分之十九。故下叙述，所以仍根據國幣白銀價值者，僅求前後一致耳。

terms of silver fell from 88 in September 1934, to about 68 in October 1935 (1933 = 100). Prices in yuan in North China were 94 in September 1934, and 96 in October 1935 (prices in terms of silver in 1933 = 100).

The rise of prices in North China since October 1935, can be considered in relation to silver values.[4] During November 1935, the yuan fell in value in terms of silver (figure 6, page 171). Prices in terms of yuan rose from 96 to 102 (prices in terms of silver in 1933 = 100). During December 1935, and January 1936, the yuan rose rapidly in terms of silver but the world value of silver fell rapidly. The general level of prices in terms of silver rose so rapidly that, in spite of the increased silver value of the yuan, prices in terms of yuan rose (figures 4 and 5, pages 170, 171). On the free silver markets, the yuan is now worth more silver than in October 1935 (figure 6, page 171). Prices in North China are no higher than would be expected on the basis of the general level of prices in terms of silver (figures 3 and 4, page 170) and the silver value of the yuan.

The silver value of the Hongkong dollar was maintained much longer than that of the yuan or Manchurian yuan. Between 1933 and October 1935, the price of silver in terms of Hongkong dollars rose only 11 per cent. As an unavoidable result, prices in Hongkong fell almost as fast and as far as the general level of prices in terms of silver (figure 5, page 171). The spectacular rise of prices in Hongkong after October 1935, can be considered as a result, at first, of a fall in the silver value of the Hongkong dollar and, after December 1935, of the general rise of prices in terms of silver. At present, the index number of prices in Hongkong is 10 per cent below what would be expected on the basis of the general level of prices in terms of silver and the silver value of the Hongkong dollar. This is chiefly because the prices of textiles have remained relatively low and, in compiling the index number, these prices are given a greater weight in Hongkong than elsewhere.

---

4 It is more logical to explain the movements of prices after the adoption of a foreign exchange standard on the basis of movements of prices abroad and the value of the domestic currency in terms of foreign exchange. Between October 1935, and April 1936, prices in the United States fell 2 per cent and the yuan price of U. S. dollars rose 23 per cent. Prices in North China rose 19 per cent. The discussion is continued on the basis of silver values only for the sake of completeness.

價乃由九六漲至一〇二（一九三三年以白銀計算之物價＝一〇〇）。自一九三五年十二月至一九三六年一月以白銀計算之中國貨幣價格飛漲，但世界白銀價值反行猛跌。以白銀計算之物價亦上漲，雖國幣之含銀量增加，而以國幣計算之物價仍行上漲（第四及第五圖第一七〇及一七一頁）。在世界白銀

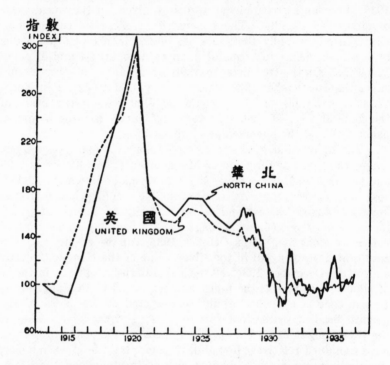

第七圖：以英磅計算之華北及英國批發物價指數，一九一三年至一九三六年，一九一三年＝一〇〇。

以英磅計算之華北及英國之物價，有同樣之趨勢。

FIGURE 7.—INDEX NUMBERS OF WHOLESALE PRICES FOR NORTH CHINA AND THE UNITED KINGDOM, 1913-1936
Prices in terms of sterling. 1913=100

Prices expressed in terms of sterling have followed much the same course in North China as in the United Kingdom.

— 176 —

Prices in North China in terms of Foreign Currencies

If, in 1913, China had adopted and maintained as her currency sterling or a money with a constant exchange value in terms of sterling, prices in North China would have followed a course comparable to that shown in figure 7 (page 176).

| Index of prices in North China in terms of sterling (1913 = 100) | = | Index of prices in North China in terms of yuan (1913 — 100) | × | Index of the T.T. exchange value of the yuan in terms of sterling (1913 — 100) |

Prices in terms of sterling fluctuated in North China in the same way as in the United Kingdom except during the World War

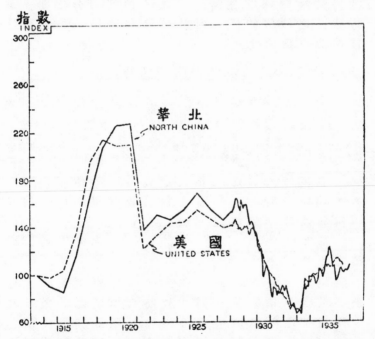

第八圖：以美金計算之華北及美國批發物價指數，一九一三年至一九三六年，一九一三年＝一〇〇。
以美金計算之華北及美國批發物價有相同之趨勢。

FIGURE 8.—INDEX NUMBERS OF WHOLESALE PRICES FOR NORTH CHINA AND THE UNITED STATES, 1913-1936

Prices in terms of United States dollars. 1913 = 100

Prices expressed in terms of United States dollars have followed much the same course in North China as in the United States.

市場，國幣可購之白銀較一九三五年十月爲多。（第六圖，第一七一頁）現華北之物價較以白銀計算之物價，相差有限。

香港銀本位之放棄較遲於華北及東三省。自一九三三年至一九三五年十月，以港幣計算之銀價，僅漲百分之十一，故香港物價之跌落，幾與以白銀計算者相同。（第五圖第一七一頁）自一九三五年十一月起香港物價飛漲，蓋港幣亦開始貶值也。現香港物價指數較以白銀計算之物價低百分之十，則以紡織品之價格較低，而紡織品在香港物價指數之權量較他處爲重也。

以外幣計算之華北物價

倘一九一三年，中國維持與英匯固定之關係，則華北之物價將如第七圖（第一七六頁）：

以英匯計算之華北物價指數，一九一三年＝一〇〇 ＝ 以中國貨幣計算之華北物價指數，一九一三年＝一〇〇 × 以華匯計算之中國貨幣價格指數，一九一三年＝一〇〇

以英匯計算之華北物價與英國物價有相同之趨勢，僅歐戰時，歐洲需要物品較白銀爲切，促成英國白銀及華匯價格之下跌（第八圖，第一七七頁）。

如華北物價，以美金計算，其趨勢亦若美國物價之不穩定。

現在中國之物價水準，如以英匯或美匯計算，幾與英美物價完全相同。故將來中國之物價，將隨中國貨幣之外匯價格及外國以外匯計算之物價之變動而轉移。此爲極可能者，中國貨幣將與英匯或美匯維持相當固定之比價，而物價亦將與英美有同樣之趨勢。至現則物價有上漲之趨勢（第七八圖第一七六及一七七頁）。

雷伯恩
王 廉

— 178 —

when the demand for commodities was high in Europe and the price of silver—and therefore of the yuan—was held artificially low in the United Kingdom.

Similarly, prices in North China calculated in terms of United States dollars have followed the same unsteady course as prices in the United States (figure 8, page 177).

At the present time, prices in China are at almost exactly the level to be expected on the basis of the sterling and dollar value of the yuan and prices in the United Kingdom and the United States.

While there will be irregular variations from time to time, the future course of prices in China will depend on changes in the foreign exchange value of the yuan and on the course of prices in terms of foreign currencies abroad. If relatively fixed rates of exchange are maintained between the yuan and sterling and United States dollars, prices in China will follow the trend of prices in the United Kingdom and the United States. At present, this is upward (figures 7 and 8, pages. 176, 177).

JOHN R. RAEBURN
WANG LIEN

中國生育率之成因 *

一國之隆替，大都繫於其人口數量之多寡，與其天然資源之利用。人口數量之多寡，又繫於生育率，而生育率則決於已婚婦女之生育率及其人數。

中外已婚女子之生育率

中國江蘇省江陰縣在一九三一至一九三四年間，已婚婦女，年達一五至四四歲者，每千人每年生育之嬰兒數為二六〇。中國全國，在一九二九至一九三一年之調查，足與此數相比較者為二〇二。此與保加利亞，日本，西班牙，意大利，或瑞典諸國相較，相差不遠（第一表）。英格蘭及威爾斯之平均生育率，較中國全國，僅少千分之二三。

自一五至一九歲，中國已婚女子，每千人每年僅產嬰兒一三六人，而江蘇江陰為二一一人，美利堅，保加利亞，法蘭西及瑞典諸國則又較多（第二表）。

青年已婚女子，產兒數量，較老年者為多。大體言之，自一五至一九歲女子之生育率最高。自二〇至二四歲之生育率次之，但自此以後，年齡愈高，生育愈少。江陰及中國全國已婚女子之生育率，一五至一九歲者，較二十至二四歲者為低（第二表）。蓋中國女子於一八或一九歲結婚者居多，故至二〇歲始能生育。至於一五至一九歲已婚女子生育率較低之原因，由於中國俗例，新婚女子在婚後一年，時常歸寧，與其父母同居。此外則因青年男子常離鄉背井，出外謀生，而農村經濟恐慌，更為減低青年女子生育率之原因。

＊本文根據江蘇江陰之原始資料。江陰之每通死亡率，載於本刊第一期六六至七一頁，一九三六年九月。

FACTORS AFFECTING THE BIRTH RATE IN CHINA*

The prosperity of a nation depends largely on the size of its population relative to the natural resources it uses. The size of the population depends largely on the birth rate. This is determined by the fertility of married women and the proportion of women married.

Fertility rate of married women in China and abroad

In Kiangyin, Kiangsu, China, the number of babies born each year per 1000 married women aged 15 to 44 was 260 in the years from 1931 to 1934. A comparable figure for China as a whole for the period from 1929 to 1931 was 202. These fertility rates are not high as compared to those for Bulgaria, Japan, Spain, Italy or Sweden (table 1, page 182). The average fertility rate for England and Wales was only 23 per thousand less than the rate in China as a whole.

In China, only 136 babies were born each year per 1000 married women aged 15-19 (table 2, page 183). In Kiangyin, Kiangsu, there were 211 such births but in the United States, Bulgaria, France and Sweden, many more.

Young married women give birth to proportionately more babies than older women. In general, women aged 15 to 19 have the highest fertility rate. The rate is also high for the ages from 20 to 24 but thereafter declines as age increases. In Kiangyin and in China as a whole, the fertility rate for married women was much lower for ages from 15 to 19 than for ages from 20 to 24 (table 2, page 183). Most Chinese women are married at the age of eighteen or nineteen so many do not give birth until they are 20. The lower fertility rate of married women aged 15 to 19 may also be due to the fact that, because of the customarily required obedience of daughters-in-law, newly married women frequently stay in their parents' homes during the first year after marriage. Another reason may be that young men have frequently to leave home to hunt for work. The rural depression may therefore have further reduced the fertility rate of young women.

---

* This article presents original data for Kiangyin, Kiangsu, China. The crude birth rate in Kiangyin was discussed in *Economic Facts*, Number 1, pages 66 to 71, September, 1936.

中國已婚女子一五至一九歲時，生育之嬰兒數，較美國爲少（第二表）。中國女子自二〇至二四歲之生育率，亦較其他各國爲低，而江陰較美國北卡羅來納，及馬薩諸塞，歐州保加利亞或瑞典爲低。自二五至二九歲女子之生育率，中國低於美國北卡羅來納，歐州保加利亞或瑞典，而江陰亦低於保加利亞。至三〇歲以上女子之生育率，中國與北卡羅來納或瑞典，無甚差異，而較保加利亞爲低，但江陰則足與保加利亞相頡頏。

第一表：　中外生育率，初次結婚平均年齡及已婚女子之比較

TABLE 1.—COMPARISON OF THE BIRTH RATE, AVERAGE AGE AT FIRST MARRIAGE AND PROPORTION OF WOMEN MARRIED, CHINA AND ABROAD

區 域 Region	研究時期 Period of study	每千人之生育數目 Births per 1000 people	自一五至四四歲每千已婚女子之生育數 Births per 1000 married women aged 15 to 44	女子初次結婚年齡 Average age of women at first marriage	自一五至四四歲已婚女子 Women aged 15 to 44, married
		數目 number	數目 number	年齡 years	百分比 per cent
中國* China*	1929-31	37	202	18.8	84
江蘇 Kiangyin, 江陰 Kiangsu	1931-34	44	260	18.7	82
日本† Japan†	1921	34	246	—	67
歐洲† Europe†					
保加利亞 Bulgaria	1921	35	256	—	64
西班牙 Spain	1921	30	232	—	52
意大利 Italy	1921	26	252	24.3	48
德意志 Germany	1921	22	162	—	48
瑞典 Sweden	1921	21	197	26.6	41
英格蘭及威爾斯 England and Wales	1921	21	179	25.5	48
法蘭西 France	1921	17	149	23.7	52

* 喬啓明：中國人口之研究，米爾班紀念基金季刊第一一卷第四期，一九三三年十月，及第一二卷第一至第三期，一九三四年一，四，七月。

* Chiao, C. M., A Study of the Chinese Population, The Milbank Memorial Fund Quarterly Bulletin, Vol. XI, No. 4, October, 1933, and Vol. XII, Nos. 1-3, January, April and July, 1934.

† 湯柏孫：人口問題，一九三〇年。
† Thompson, W. S., Population Problems, McGraw-Hill, New York, 1930.

In China, married women aged 15 to 19 had fewer babies than women of similar ages in the United States, Bulgaria, France and Sweden (table 2, page 183). The fertility rate of women aged 20 to 24 was also lower in China than in these countries and lower in Kiangyin than in North Carolina and Massachusetts, United States, or in Bulgaria or Sweden. For women aged 25 to 29, the rate was lower in China than in North Carolina, United States or in Bulgaria or Sweden, and lower in Kiangyin than in Bulgaria. For women over 30, the rate in China was not greatly different from that in North Carolina or Sweden and was less than in Bulgaria, while the rate in Kiangyin was comparable to that in Bulgaria.

第二表： 中國，美國與歐洲數國各年齡組已婚女子生育率之比較
TABLE 2.—COMPARISON OF THE FERTILITY RATES OF MARRIED WOMEN, VARIOUS AGE GROUPS, CHINA, UNITED STATES AND EUROPE

區　域 Region	研究時期 Period of study	已婚女子年齡 Age of married women 每千已婚女子出生兒童數 births per 1000 mairred women						
		15-19	20-24	25-29	30-34	35-39	40-44	45-49
中國* China*	1929-34	136	267	257	220	168	88	22
江蘇 Kiangyin,								
江陰 Kiangsu	1931-34	211	333	328	264	231	91	7
美國† United States†								
堪薩斯 Kansas	1920	383	286	195	134	91	38	—
北卡羅								
來納 North Carolina	1920	397	342	264	214	172	75	—
馬薩諸塞 Massachusetts	1920	523	352	250	179	104	37	—
歐洲† Europe†								
保加利亞 Bulgaria	1920-21	275	405	337	262	197	107	—
法蘭西 France	1911-13	282	269	193	127	84	32	—
瑞典 Sweden	1916-20	596	392	277	209	154	80	10

* 卜凱: 中國土地利用，正在印刷中。
* Euck, J. L., Land Utilization in China, in course of publication.
† 湯柏森: 人口問題，一九三〇年。
† Thompson, W. S., Population Problems, McGraw-Hill, New York, 1930.

While the fertility rate of married women was lower in China than in other countries for ages from 15 to 19, it was not greatly different for ages from 20 to 29. For ages over 30, it was considerably higher than in some countries (table 2, page 183).

自一五至一九歲已婚女子之生育率，中國雖較其他各國爲低，但自二〇至二九歲，則無甚差異。自三〇歲以上，中國女子之生育率，較數國爲高（第二表）。

已婚女子比例

中外女子婚姻狀況之差異，較其生育率之差異爲大。自一五至四四歲女子結婚者，中國佔百分之八一，江陰佔百分之八二，而保加利亞僅佔百分之六四，美利堅僅佔百分之六〇（第三表），瑞典僅佔百分之四一。自一五至一九歲女子結婚者，中國佔百分之五〇，江陰佔百分之三八，但美利堅僅佔百分之一二，保加利亞僅佔百分之一〇，瑞典僅佔百分之一。甚至自二〇至二九歲已婚女子之比例，中國（百分之九一）亦較其他各國爲大。瑞典自二〇至二九歲女子已婚者，僅佔百分之三四。江陰女子婚姻狀況，與中國全國之狀況，無甚差異。

江陰登記區域以及中國其他區域生育率極高之主要原因，實由於女子在三〇歲以下結婚者爲多，且此時之生育率甚高，雖較諸其他各國，中國未見更高。瑞典之普通生育率較江陰少二分之一強，而較中國全國少二分之一有奇。此非因女子生育率之異殊，乃因中國女子在三〇歲以前結婚者，超過百分之九〇，而瑞典在三〇歲以下結婚者，僅百分之三四，且三〇歲以下女子之生育率較三〇歲以上者爲高。若江陰婚姻習慣與瑞典相同，則其普通生育率或可自每千人每年之四四減至二〇·六，平均女子結婚年齡或可減至二六·六歲。

江陰一九三一至一九三四年間，結婚年齡平均

— 184 —

The proportion of women married

The difference between the marital state of Chinese and of foreign women is much greater than the difference in their respective fertility rates. In China, 81 per cent of the women aged 15 to 44 were married; in Kiangyin, 82 per cent; but in Bulgaria, only 64 per cent and in the United States only 60 per cent were married (table 3, page 185). In Sweden, only 41 per cent were married. In China, 50 per cent of the women aged 15 to 19 were married, in Kiangyin, 38 per cent, but in the United States only 12 per cent, in Bulgaria only 10 per cent, and in Sweden only 1 per cent. Even the proportion of the women aged 20 to 29 who were married was much greater in China (91 per cent) than in many other countries. In Sweden only 34 per cent of the women aged 20 to 29 were married. The marital state of women in Kiangyin did not differ considerably from that of Chinese women in general.

第三表：　中國，美國與歐洲數國各年齡組已婚女子比例之比較

TABLE 3.—COMPARISON OF THE PROPORTION OF WOMEN MARRIED, VARIOUS AGE GROUPS, CHINA, UNITED STATES AND EUROPE

區　域 Region		研究時期 Period of study	女子年齡 Age of women					
			15-19	20-24	20-29	30-39	40-44	15-44
			已婚女子百分率 per cent of women married					
中國*	China* Kiangyin,	1929-34	50	89	91	89	82	81
江蘇 江陰	Kiangsu	1931-34	38	93	94	93	87	82
美國†	United States	1920	12	51	62	81	80	60
歐洲†	Europe†							
保加利亞	Bulgaria	1920	10	63	74	88	84	64
英格蘭 與威爾斯	England and Wales	1920	2	27	42	72	75	48
法蘭西	France	1920	6	—	50	72	74	52
德意志	Germany	1920	1	24	42	76	78	48
意大利	Italy	1920	4	32	44	73	77	48
西班牙	Spain	1920	4	40	51	72	78	52
瑞典	Sweden	1920	1	20	34	65	70	41

* 卜凱：中國土地利用，正在印刷中。
* Buck, J. L., Land Utilization in China, in course of publication.

† 湯柏森：人口問題，一九三〇年。
† Thompson, W. S., Population Problems, McGraw-Hill, New York, 1930.

數，男子爲二一‧八，女子爲一八‧七，此與中國全國之數字，無甚差異，但在歐西各國，女子平均結婚年齡，約爲二五歲。

欲減低生育率，勢必提高中國現行之結婚年齡。江陰近四十年來，結婚年齡，無甚變遷，男子結婚仍約爲二二歲，女子二〇歲（第四表）。江陰接近工業發達之無錫上海，尚屬如此，其他內地之無甚變遷，概可想見。從知移風易俗，殊非易易也。

第四表：　江蘇江陰八五五男子及八七五女子初次結婚平均之年齡
TABLE 4.—AVERAGE AGE AT FIRST MARRIAGE, 855 MEN AND
875 WOMEN LIVING IN KIANGYIN, KIANGSU, 1932

結婚年度 Year of marriage	男子 Men	女子 Women	男子年齡 Age of men	女子年齡 Age of women
	數目 *number*	數目 *number*	年 *years*	年 *years*
1875-1887	4	6	22.3	21.8
1887-1891	17	21	21.8	18.5
1892-1896	22	27	21.8	19.5
1897-1901	45	45	22.2	20.2
1902-1906	53	54	22.9	19.7
1907-1911	72	71	22.8	19.4
1912-1916	108	106	22.0	19.3
1917-1921	115	121	22.4	19.9
1922-1926	182	184	21.7	19.4
1927-1931	237	240	22.1	19.8
1875-1911	213	224	22.5	19.6
1912-1931	642	651	22.0	19.6

節制生育

衆信各農村，若敎以節育方法，生育率或可減低，而普通生活程度亦因以提高。但美國通行受胎防止法對於生育率之減低，尚無極大效果。故節育之意念與方法，欲使中國人民明瞭而實行之，決非一朝一夕之功也＊。

＊ 阮耳：家庭限制研究第三次報告，米爾班紀念基金季刊，第一九卷第三期第二八四頁，一九三六年七月。

The very high birth rate in Kiangyin registration district as well as in other areas of China was chiefly due to the fact that a very high proportion of the women under 30 were married and the fertility of such women was high, although not considerably higher in China than elsewhere. The crude birth rate in Sweden was less than half that in Kiangyin and little more than half that in China as a whole, not because of great differences in fertility, but because, while over 90 per cent of the Chinese women were married before they are 30, only 34 per cent of the Swedish women under 30 were married, and women under 30 were more fertile than women over 30. If marriage customs were the same in Kiangyin as in Sweden the crude birth rate would be reduced from 44 to 20.6 births per year per 1,000 people. The average age of women at marriage would be reduced to 26.6 years.

The average age at marriage in Kiangyin between 1931 and 1934 was 21.8 years for men and 18.7 years for women. These figures do not differ greatly from those for China as a whole. In Western countries the average age of women at marriage is about 25.

In order to reduce the high birth rate, the customary age at marriage must be raised. In Kiangyin, the age at marriage has not changed considerably in the last forty years, the men continuing to marry at about 22 years and the women at 19 (table 4, page 186). It is improbable that there has been any greater change in interior districts, further than Kiangyin from the industrial cities of Wusih and Shanghai. It is exceedingly difficult to change old customs.

Birth control

Many people believe that if birth control methods were taught in every village, the birth rate would decline and the general standard of living be thereby raised. Contraceptive methods as generally adopted in the United States have not resulted in any very large reduction in the birth rate.[1]

The general acceptance of the ideals as well as the methods of

---

Pearl, R., Third progress report on a study of family limitation, The Milbank Memorial Fund Quarterly, Vol. XIV, No. 3, page 284, July, 1936.

結 論

　　如政府能限制結婚年齡，使二四或二五歲以下者不能結婚，則數年之內，生育率或可降低，而死亡率亦可降低。少生少死或可促成國富民強。

　　中國急需確定人口政策。朝野應一致努力如何改進並保持較高之生活程度。

喬啟明
陳彩章

農業貸款與佃權

　　民國二十三年與二十四年，曾在豫鄂皖贛四省作一縝密之農家經濟研究。本研究之一部份關涉十四地區八百五十二農家之借貸。當調查時，每地區先作一初步農家清查，而後再另行選查此類農家以代表當地一般狀況。上述農家數目中，約有三分之一為自耕農，三分之一為半自耕農，三分之一為佃農。處茲致力改善農業貸款之際，關於借貸現況，必有準確報告，此所重要者也。

調查週年內農家獲有之貸款 *

　　調查週年內獲有貸款之農家佔百分之四十六（第一表，第一九〇頁）。此類農家所佔比率之差異，自豫省百分之三十四至鄂省百分之五十六。就各類農家言，平均自耕農佔百分之四十一，半自耕農佔百分之四十六，佃農佔百分之五十一，然豫省佃農獲有貸款者較自耕農為少；鄂省各類農家獲有貸款者所佔之比率，大致相同。

　　＊豫省各地區與皖省五地區之四地區，係在民國二十三年調查；其餘地區均在民國二十四年調查。

birth control could not be brought about in China for many years.

Conclusion

If the Government could regulate marriage customs so that marriages of women under 24 or 25 were impossible, the birth rate would fall within a few years. The death rate would also decline. Fewer births and fewer deaths would lead to greater prosperity.

There is an urgent need for a definite population policy. Both the Government and the people should face the question of how to improve and maintain a higher standard of living.

Chiao Chi-ming

Chen Tsai-chang

FARM CREDIT AND FARM OWNERSHIP

In 1934 and 1935 an intensive economic study was made of agriculture in Honan, Hupeh, Anhwei and Kiangsi provinces. A part of this study concerned the credit used on 852 farms located in 14 areas. After a preliminary census study in each area, these farms were chosen as representing the most usual type of farming. Approximately one-third of the farms studied in each area were operated by owners, one-third by part-owners, and one-third by tenants. When much effort is being made to improve agricultural credit it is important to have accurate information on existing conditions.

Credit obtained during the year[1].—During the year studied, 46 per cent of the operators obtained credit (table 1, page 190). The portion that obtained credit varied from 34 per cent in Honan to 56 per cent in Hupeh. On the average, 41 per cent of the owners, 46 per cent of the part-owners and 51 per cent of the tenants obtained credit. However, in Honan, fewer tenants than owners obtained credit; in Hupeh, approximately the same portion of owners, part-owners and tenants obtained credit.

The average amount of credit obtained per farm was 19.37 yuan (table 2, page 191). It varied from 6.71 yuan in Honan to 28.56 yuan in Anhwei. The average credit obtained in Anhwei was

---

All localities in Honan, and four of the five localities in Anhwei were studied in 1934; other localities, in 1935.

每一農家之平均貸額，計國幣一九‧三七元（第二表，第一九一頁）。其差別自豫省六‧七一元至皖省二八‧五六元。皖省平均貸額較豫省多四倍。佃農舉借之貸額平均計一六‧六七元；半自耕農，二〇‧六四元；自耕農，二一‧〇九元。

第一表： 豫鄂皖贛四省農家獲有貸款者之比率
（民國廿三年或廿四年）

TABLE 1.—PROPORTION OF OPERATORS OBTAINING CREDIT IN 1934 OR 1935, HONAN, HUPEH, ANHWEI, KIANGSI

各類農家 Tenure		河南 Honan	湖北 Hupeh	安徽 Anhwei	江西 Kiangsi	平均 Average
		百分率 per cent	百分率 per cent	百分率 per cent	百分率 per cent	百分率 per cent
自 耕 農	Owners	39	55	42	28	41
半自耕農	Part-owners	31	57	52	39	46
佃　　農	Tenants	34	55	57	54	51
各農家平均	All operators	34	56	50	41	46

農家負債總額

調查週年內農家獲有貸款者雖佔百分之四十六，然迄調查年年終時，負債之農家佔百分之七十一，此乃以往債額積欠所致（第三表，第一九〇頁）。負債農家所佔比率差別自豫省百分之六十六至皖省百分之八十。四省自耕農負債者，平均佔百分之六十三，半自耕農佔百分之七十二，佃農佔百分之七十八。除皖省佃農與半自耕農負債者相等外，自耕農負債者較半自耕農或佃農為少。

第三表： 豫鄂皖贛四省農家負債者之比率
（民國廿三年終或廿四年終）

TABLE 3.—PROPORTION OF OPERATORS IN DEBT AT THE END OF 1934 OR 1935, HONAN, HUPEH, ANHWEI, KIANGSI

各類農家 Tenure		河南 Honan	湖北 Hupeh	安徽 Anhwei	江西 Kiangsi	平均 Average
		百分率 per cent	百分率 per cent	百分率 per cent	百分率 per cent	百分率 per cent
自 耕 農	Owners	62	65	76	42	63
半自耕農	Part-owners	66	77	82	58	72
佃　　農	Tenants	71	82	82	72	78
各農家平均	All operators	66	74	80	57	71

four times that in Honan. The tenants borrowed an average of
16.67 yuan; part-owners, 20.64 yuan; and owners, 21.09 yuan.

第二表：　　豫鄂皖贛四省農家之告貸者之貸款總額
(民國廿三年或廿四年)

TABLE 2.—TOTAL CREDIT OBTAINED DURING 1934 OR 1935 BY
OPERATORS WHO BORROWED, HONAN,
HUPEH, ANHWEI, KIANGSI

各類農家 Tenure		河 南 Honan	湖 北 Hupeh	安 徽 Anhwei	江 西 Kiangsi	平 均 Average
		元 yuan	元 yuan	元 yuan	元 yuan	元 yuan
自 耕 農	Owners	9.61	17.06	28.12	24.88	21.09
半自耕農	Part-owners	5.05	14.75	36.87	15.06	20.64
佃 農	Tenants	5.50	8.91	21.53	27.49	16.67
各農家平均	All operators	6.71	13.58	28.56	22.48	19.37

Total indebtedness of farm operators.—Although only 46 per
cent of the operators obtained credit during the year studied, 71
per cent of the operators were in debt at the end of the year due
to previous borrowing (table 3, page 190). The proportion of the
operators in debt varied from 66 per cent in Honan to 80 per cent
in Anhwei. On the average, 63 per cent of the owners in the four
provinces were in debt, 72 per cent of the part-owners, and 78 per
cent of the tenants. Fewer owners than part-owners or tenants
were in debt except in Anhwei where an equal portion of tenants
and part-owners were in debt.

At the end of the year the average total indebtedness per
farm was 66.66 yuan (table 4, page 191). The average debts per
farm varied from 24.43 yuan in Honan to 120.88 yuan in Anhwei.
In Anhwei, the indebtedness per farm was more than twice as
high as in Kiangsi, about four times as high as in Hupeh, and
five times as high as in Honan. In the four provinces, the

第四表：　　豫鄂皖贛四省每一農家之負債總額
(民國廿三年終或廿四年終)

TABLE 4.—INDEBTEDNESS PER FARM AT THE END OF 1934 OR
1935, HONAN, HUPEH, ANHWEI, KIANGSI

各類農家 Tenure		河 南 Honan	湖 北 Hupeh	安 徽 Anhwei	江 西 Kiangsi	平 均 Average
		元 yuan	元 yuan	元 yuan	元 yuan	元 yuan
自 耕 農	Owners	19.47	39.63	127.28	62.97	71.61
半自耕農	Part-owners	20.12	30.37	164.35	38.62	77.79
佃 農	Tenants	34.09	23.56	75.92	60.10	52.35
各農家平均	All operators	24.43	31.19	120.88	54.01	66.66

迄調查週年終了時，每一農家之平均負債總額計國幣六六‧六六元（第四表，第一九一頁）。其差別自豫省二四‧四三元至皖省一二〇‧八八元。皖省每一農家之負債額較贛省高二倍有奇，較鄂省約高四倍，而較豫省則高五倍。就四省言，每一佃農之負債額平均計五二‧三五元，自耕農計七一‧六一元，半自耕農計七七‧七九元。然豫省佃農之平均負債額則較自耕農或半自耕農為高。上述數字顯示佃農負債者佔大部份，然其平均債額則較自耕農或半自耕農為少。

貸款用途

調查週年內，四省貸款之目的為生產者平均佔百分之八‧四，為非生產者佔百分之九一‧六（第五表，第一九三頁）。其為生產目的而告貸之資金大多用以雇用勞工，修理農舍，與購買牲畜。購買食糧尤為貸款最重之用途。就四省言，此類目的之貸款平均佔百分之四二‧一。自耕農之貸款用以購買食糧者佔百分之二五‧六；半自耕農，百分之四三‧九，佃農，百分之六〇‧三。婚喪亦為借貸之重要目的。平均言之，用於此兩類目的之貸款均較用於生產目的者為高。

貸款來源

農業貸款最主要之兩大來源，厥為親友。就四省言，朋友供給之款佔百分之四五‧五，親戚佔百分之三七‧七（第六表，第一九四頁）。然殊難單確判明親友與放債人之別異，蓋農民不願表示其向放債人告貸故也。

半自耕農獲有之貸款，由地主供給者僅佔百分

average indebtedness per tenant was 52.35 yuan as compared to 71.61 yuan for the owners and 77.79 yuan for the part-owners. However, average debts of the tenants in Honan exceeded the debts of owners or part-owners. These data show that a larger portion of the tenants were in debt but their average indebtedness was less than that of owners or part-owners.

Uses of credit.—In the four provinces, an average of 8.4 per cent of the credit borrowed during the year studied was used for productive purposes and 91.6 per cent for unproductive purposes (table 5, page 193). The funds borrowed for productive purposes

第五表： 豫鄂皖贛四省農家貸款目的所佔之比率
(民國廿三年或廿四年)

TABLE 5.—PROPORTION OF CREDIT BORROWED IN 1934 OR 1935 USED FOR DIFFERENT PURPOSES, HONAN, HUPEH, ANHWEI, KIANGSI

目 的 Purposes		自 耕 農 Owners	半自耕農 Part-owners	佃 農 Tenants	平 均 Average
生產者	*Productive:*	百分率 *per cent*	百分率 *per cent*	百分率 *per cent*	百分率 *per cent*
僱 工	Hiring labor	1.0	5.2	2.5	2.8
修理農舍	Repairing farm buildings	4.7	0.9	0.2	2.2
購買牲畜	Purchasing livestock	0.7	4.1	1.3	2.1
購買農具	Purchasing farm tools	0.4	0.8	0.5	0.5
掘 溝	Digging ditches	0.3	0.0	0.0	0.1
其 他	Other purposes	0.3	0.6	1.3	0.7
共 計	Total	7.4	11.6	5.8	8.4
非生產者	*Unproductive:*				
伏 食	Human food	25.6	43.9	60.3	42.1
喪 葬	Funerals	12.3	8.1	7.6	9.5
婚 娶	Weddings	9.2	4.6	12.7	8.6
訴 訟	Law suits	2.2	1.4	1.1	1.6
捐 稅	Taxes	0.7	0.1	0.0	0.3
其 他	Other purposes	42.6	30.3	12.5	29.5
共 計	Total	92.6	88.4	94.2	91.6
總 計	*Total*	100.0	100.0	100.0	100.0

were used largely in hiring labor, repairing buildings and purchasing livestock. The purchase of human food was by far the most important use made of borrowed funds. In the four areas, 42.1 per cent of the entire credit was used for this purpose. The owners used 25.6 per cent of their credit to purchase human food; the part-owners, 43.9 per cent; and the tenants, 60.3 per

之二・九，佃農獲有之貸欵由地主供給者佔百分之四・四。鄂省某地區，地主為貸欵之主要來源。

第六表：　豫鄂皖贛四省農家貸款各種來源所佔之比率
（民國廿三年或廿四年）

TABLE 6.—PROPORTION OF LOANS OBTAINED IN 1934 OR 1935
FROM VARIOUS SOURCES, HONAN, HUPEH, ANHWEI, KIANGSI

來源 Source		自耕農 Owners 百分率 per cent	半自耕農 Part-owners 百分率 per cent	佃農 Tenants 百分率 per cent	平均 Average 百分率 per cent
商人	Merchants	7.3	6.1	4.7	6.6
地主	Landlords	0.8	2.9	4.4	2.8
朋友	Friends	40.6	52.6	47.5	45.5
親戚	Relatives	44.6	34.5	33.3	37.7
族人	Clan	4.2	3.3	9.6	6.1
其他	Others	2.5	0.6	0.5	1.3
各來源總計	All sources	100.0	100.0	100.0	100.0

利率

調查週年內之貸款利率平均為月利二分八厘（第七表，第一九四頁）。其平均利率自贛省一分九厘至豫省平均三分三厘不等。除豫省佃農所付之利率較高外，各類農家所付之利率，大約相同。豫省農民之貸額較低，然所付之利率則較他處為高。

貸欵平均月利自向商人告借之二分一厘至族人之四分二厘不等（第八表，第一九五頁）。親友為貸款

第七表：　豫鄂皖贛四省各類農家與平均貸款月利之關係
（民國廿三年或廿四年）

TABLE 7.—RELATION OF TYPE OF TENURE TO AVERAGE
MONTHLY INTEREST RATES PAID ON FARM CREDIT,
HONAN, HUPEH, ANHWEI, KIANGSI 1934, 1935

各類農家 Tenure		河南 Honan 百分率 per cent	湖北 Hupeh 百分率 per cent	安徽 Anhwei 百分率 per cent	江西 Kiangsi 百分率 per cent	平均 Average 百分率 per cent
自耕農	Owners	2.4	2.2	3.2	2.0	2.6
半自耕農	Part-owners	3.6	2.9	3.2	1.9	2.9
佃農	Tenants	4.0	2.4	2.7	2.0	2.8
各農家平均	All operators	3.3	2.6	3.0	1.9	2.8

cent. Funerals and weddings were also important purposes for which credit was borrowed. On the average, more credit was used for each of these two purposes than for all productive purposes.

第八表： 豫鄂皖贛四省貸款來源與貸款月利之關係
（民國廿三年或廿四年）

TABLE 8.—RELATION OF SOURCE OF CREDIT TO AVERAGE MONTHLY INTEREST RATES PAID ON FARM CREDIT, HONAN, HUPEH, ANHWEI, KIANGSI, 1934, 1935

來源 Source	自耕農 Owners	半自耕農 Part-owners	佃農 Tenants	平均 Average
	百分率 per cent	百分率 per cent	百分率 per cent	百分率 per cent
商 人 Merchants	2.6	3.6	2.1	2.1
地 主 Landlords	2.5	3.7	2.9	3.0
朋 友 Friends	2.5	3.0	2.8	2.8
親 戚 Relatives	2.4	2.7	2.7	2.5
族 人 Clan	2.3	7.6	3.0	4.2
其 他 Others	4.7	2.5	3.1	3.7
各來源平均 All sources	2.6	2.9	2.8	2.8

Sources of credit.—Friends and relatives were the two most important sources of farm credit. In the four provinces, 45.5 per cent of the loans were supplied by friends and 37.7 per cent by relatives (table 6, page 194). But it was impossible accurately to distinguish money lenders from friends and relatives, because farmers did not wish to reveal that they borrowed from money lenders.

Landlords supplied only 2.9 per cent of the loans obtained by part-owners and 4.4 per cent of the loans obtained by tenants. In one area in Hupeh, landlords were an important source of credit.

Interest rates.—The average monthly interest rate paid on the credit obtained during the year was 2.8 per cent (table 7, page 194). The average rate varied from 1.9 per cent in Kiangsi to 3.3 per cent in Honan. Owners, part-owners and tenants paid about the same rates of interest except in Honan, where the tenants paid higher rates. In Honan, farmers used much less credit but paid higher interest rates than in other areas.

The average monthly interest rate varied from 2.1 per cent on credit obtained from merchants to 4.2 per cent on credit obtained from clans (table 8, page 195). Friends and relatives, who were the most important sources of credit, received interest

最主要之來源，所取之利率，前者平均爲月利二分五厘，後者爲二分八厘。由此可知利率高低之決定，地區較貸款來源，尤爲重要。

喬　啓　明
應　廉　排

averaging 2.8 and 2.5 per cent per month respectively.　Evidently the locality was more important in determining the interest rate than was the source of the credit.

CHIAO CHI-MING
YIN LIEN-KEN

經 濟 統 計
ECONOMIC FACTS

南 京 金 陵 大 學 農 學 院 農 業 經 濟 系 出 版
Department of Agricultural Economics
COLLEGE OF AGRICULTURE AND FORESTRY
UNIVERSITY OF NANKING
NANKING, CHINA

第五期 No. 5　　　　　　　一九三七年五月 May 1937

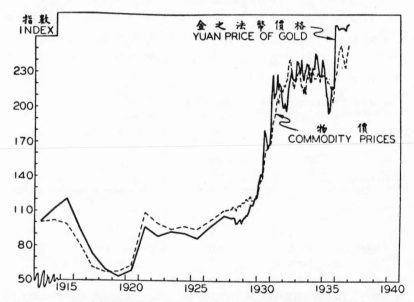

第一圖　金之國幣價格指數與華北物價算爲美國以金計算之物價之百分數
，一九一三年至一九三六年(一九一三年 = 一〇〇)

一九一三年後，大部華北物價與美國以金計算之物價兩者關係之變動，可以金之國幣價格之
變動解釋之，自一九二九年至一九三一年間金之國幣價格已倍之，而今已爲一九一三年之百分之
二七二。

FIGURE 1.—INDEX NUMBERS OF THE YUAN PRICE OF GOLD AND COMMODITY PRICES IN
NORTH CHINA IN PER CENT OF COMMODITY PRICES IN TERMS OF GOLD IN THE
UNITED STATES, 1913-1936

1913=100

Since 1913, changes in the yuan price of gold have explained the major changes in the relationship
between prices in North China and prices in terms of gold in the United States. The yuan price of gold was
doubled between 1929 and 1931 and is now 272 per cent of 1913.

中國將來之物價水準 *

自國幣之外匯價值始終能維持於十四便士又四分之一至十四便士又四分之三，與美金二角九分五厘至三角另五厘之間以來，國際外匯貿易及買賣之投機數量，已大形減少，外幣借款亦便於處理，然吾人所亟宜注意而不可忽視者，厥爲其影響國幣在國內之購買物品價值。目前美金元恆等於每兩純金三十五分之一，英鎊之金值自一九三五年六月以後，亦無多變化，故吾國如能繼續維持現狀，則國幣勢必等於一定重量之黃金。

以金計算之物價

以前採用金本位各國之物價水準，近年來各相歧異，蓋因各國貨幣貶價時期與數量之不同。特將以貶值貨幣計算之物價指數，變爲以戰前金本位貨幣計算之物價指數，以資比較。卽如：

$$\frac{以金計算之物價指數}{(一九一三年=一〇〇)} = \frac{以貨幣計算之物價指數（一九一三年=一〇〇）}{以貨幣計算之金價格指數（戰前平價=一〇〇）}$$

英，法，瑞典，美，及加拿大五國[1] 基本物品，以金計算之價格指數，均以此法計算之，而以此五者之平均，爲全世界以金計算之物價水準指數，殊爲可靠。此指數以一九一

---

*本文引據美國康乃而大學，華爾倫及皮而生兩教授所著之「黃金與物價」一書甚多，特此誌謝

1. 本文所採用之物價指數如下：

   英國：以一八六七年至一八七七年作基期之司答的斯脫指數，乘以一·一七六四七一，而以得一九一三年作基期之指數。

   法國：法蘭西統計局之二十五種工業原料品指數，一九一三年=一〇〇。

   瑞士：斯文斯克漢德斯班肯之原料品指數（一九一三年=一〇〇）。此指數分以貨幣計算及以金計算兩者登載。

   美國：司答的斯脫指數（一九一三年=一〇〇）乃華倫及皮而生二氏所計算，載于一九三五年出版之『金與物價』第一百八十二頁。

   加拿大：商業貿易部之原料品及半製造品指數（一九二六年=一〇〇），其指數以一·五六七乘之，使一九一三年爲基期。

   計算金之價格佔歐戰前平價之百分數之法見下頁附註

CHINA'S FUTURE PRICE LEVEL*

The foreign exchange value of the National yuan is being successfully maintained within the limits of 14¼—14¾ pence and U.S. $0.29½—0.30½. This reduces the amount of speculation, or foreign exchange trading, necessary in transacting foreign business and will facilitate the service of debts contracted in foreign currencies but a very important consideration is the effect on the commodity value of the yuan within China. If present relationships are maintained, the yuan will be equal to an almost constant weight of gold because the U.S. dollar is equivalent to one-thirty fifth of an ounce of fine gold and the gold value of sterling has been kept relatively constant since June, 1935.

Prices in terms of gold

The price levels experienced by many countries previously on the gold standard have differed during recent years because currencies have been devalued at different times and by different amounts. A common basis for comparison can be obtained by converting the index numbers of prices in terms of devalued currencies into index numbers of prices in terms of the corresponding pre-war gold currencies. Thus:—

$$\text{Index of prices in terms of gold } (1913=100) = \frac{\text{Index of prices in terms of currency } (1913=100)}{\text{Index of price of gold in terms of currency } (\text{pre-war par}=100)}$$

Such index numbers of prices in terms of gold have been calculated for basic commodities in the United Kingdom, France, Sweden, the United States and Canada.[1] The average of these provides a reliable index of the world level of prices in terms of gold

* Acknowledgement is due to Drs. G. F. Warren and F. A. Pearson of Cornell University upon whose book (*Gold and Prices*, John Wiley and Sons, New York, 1935) much of this study is based.

1 The index numbers of prices used were as follows:-

United Kingdom: Sauerbeck-Statist index converted from the 1867-77 base to a 1913 base by multiplying by 1.176471.

France: Statistique Generale de la France index for 25 industrial raw materials, 1913=100.

Sweden: Svenska Handelsbanken index for raw materials, 1913=100. This index is quoted both in terms of currency and in terms of gold.

United States: Sauerbeck Statist index, 1913=100, calculated by G. F. Warren and F. A. Pearson; Gold and Prices, p. 182, 1935.

Canada: Department of Trade and Commerce index for raw materials and semi-manufactured goods converted from the 1926 base to a 1913 base by multiplying by 1.567.

The prices of gold in per cent of pre-war were calculated as follows:-

United Kingdom: The London price of gold as a per cent of 84s. 9 3/4d. per fine ounce.

France: Prior to September 1936, 492 per cent of pre-war par as fixed in 1928, thereafter, by multiplying 492 by 6.63⁴⁶ (the par U.S. cents value of the yuan established when the dollar was fixed at $35 per fine ounce of gold) and dividing by the foreign exchange value of the franc in U.S. cents.

United States: From April 1933 to January 1934, on the basis of the price of gold in London and the closing sterling exchange rate, New York on London; thereafter, the fixed price of U.S.$35.00 per fine ounce was expressed in per cent of U.S.$20.67.

— 199 —

三年爲一〇〇，則一九二九年九月爲一三八，一九三三年跌
至六十一。四年之內，以金計算之基本物價格跌落一半。

此迅速跌落之原因，可以世界幣用金貯存量，與世界基
本物生產量之比率解釋之[2]。

第一表． 世界幣用金之貯存量，世界生產量，與以金計算之批發物價*

TABLE 1. RELATION BETWEEN WORLD'S MONETARY STOCKS OF GOLD, PHYSICAL
VOLUME OF PRODUCTION, AND WHOLESALE PRICES IN TERMS OF GOLD*

年 Year	年底之金存量 指數 一八八〇年至一 九一四年 ＝一〇〇 Index of gold stocks at end of the year, 1880-1914＝100	世界生產量 指數 一八八〇年至一 九一四年 ＝一〇〇 Index of world physical volume of production, 1880-1914＝100	金存量與物品 生產量之比 一八八〇年 至一九一四年 ＝一〇〇 Ratio of gold stocks to production, 1880-1914＝100	英國以金計之 鉄斯鉄指數 一八八〇年 至一九一四年 ＝一〇〇 Statist index of prices in gold in England 1880-1914＝100
1870	57	42	136	131
1880	65	60	108	120
1890	73	74	99	98
1900	101	106	95	102
1910	147	140	105	106
1929	238	208	114	156
1930	246	198	125	132
1936	301†	208‡	145‡	73

* 一八七〇至一九三〇年材料乃取自：一九三五年在紐約出版之華而倫及皮而生所著之 "金
與物價" 第九十二至九十三頁.

† 根據一九三六年二月二十一號星期日出版之紐約時報所載之材料.

‡ 假定與一九二九年之世界物之生產量相等.

* Data for the years 1870-1930 are taken from: Warren, G F. and Pearson, F.A., *Gold and Prices* pp.
92-93, New York, 1935.

† Based on data published in *The New York Times* p. 6E. Sunday, February 21, 1936.

‡ Assuming a physical volume of production equal to that of 1929.

當世界幣用金之貯存量比較上高於物品生產量時，物價
漸趨上漲，（第二〇〇頁第一表）。根據世界大戰以前兩者
之關係，一九二九年黃金足以維持以金計算之物價水準指數

英國：倫敦金價等于平價每兩純金值八十四先令九又四分之三便士之百分數。

法國：一九三六年九月以前，一九二八年規定金價等于戰前平價百分之四百九十二；因此
，四百九十二乘以六．六三四六（當美金三十五元等于純金一兩之價格時之元對美
國之平價）再除以法郎之美頭價格卽得之。

美國：自一九三三年四月至一九三四年一月，根據倫敦金價及紐約之倫敦英幣之收盤匯價
；此使美金三十五元等于純金一兩之固定價格卽用美金二十元六角七分之百分數表
示之。

2. 華爾倫及皮而生：『金與物價』第八十九頁至百〇三頁，紐約約翰威利書局一九三五年出
版。

(figure 2, page 201). In September 1929, this index was 137 (1913= 100). By September 1933, it had fallen to 61. Within four years, the prices of basic commodities in terms of gold fell 55 per cent.

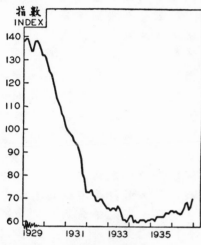

指數
INDEX

第二圖　五國本基物物價指數一九二九年至一九三六年。

以金計算之物價

一九一三年＝一〇〇

始於一九二九年之基本物價格之暴跌於一九三四年告止，一九三四年後物價上升。

FIGURE 2.—INDEX NUMBERS OF PRICES OF BASIC COMMODITIONES IN FIVE COUNTRIES. 1929—1936

Prices in terms of gold: 1913＝100

The rapid decline of prices of basic commodities which began in 1929 was completed by 1934. Since 1934, prices have been rising.

This rapid decline has been explained on the basis of the ratio of the world's stocks of monetary gold to the world's production of basic commodities.[2] When stocks of monetary gold are large relative to the production of commodities, the price level tends to be high (table 1, page 200). On the basis of the relationships existing prior to the World War, there was enough gold in 1929 to support a general level of prices in terms of gold at an index of 114 (1880 —1914＝100). The 'Statist' index for England was then 156 (1880—1914＝100). At that time, the demand for gold by central banks was increasing and, when the price level began rapidly to adjust itself in accordance with pre-war relationships, the resulting distress further increased the need for reserves. Hoarding by individuals developed on a world-wide basis because it was profitable as a result both of the increasing value of gold and of prospects of currency devaluation caused thereby. The demand for gold became so abnormally large that prices declined more than was to be expected on the basis of the ratio of gold stocks to the production of basic commodities.

The index of prices in terms of gold was at its lowest level in 1934. In December 1936, the index was 70 having risen from 61 (1913＝100) within two years. During 1935 and the first half of 1936, the world demand for gold, although still high, lessened appreciably. During the latter part of 1936, the index of prices in gold rose rapidly.

2   Warren. G. F. and Pearson. F. A. *Gold and Prices*, pp. 89—103. John Wiley and Sons, New York. 1935.

於一一四（一八八〇年——一九一四年＝一〇〇）。當時各國中央銀行需金日多，同時物價復循大戰前兩者之關係亟謀調整，結果愈形困難，所需準備金額遂益增加，當時私人窖金有利可牟，相襲成風，遍於世界，卒致金值飛漲，貨幣貶值。金之需求激增逾恆，遂令物價跌落，遠甚於根據幣用金貯存量與基本物生產量之比率所能逆料者。

一九三四年以金計算之物價指數低落達於最低點，其後兩年指數自六十一漸升，至一九三六年十二月其指數爲七十（一九一三年＝一〇〇）。一九三五年及一九三六年上半年內，世界金之需求雖仍甚高，特較曩日已爲退減・九三六下半年以金計算之物價指數則又猛猛增。

目前金之價值似仍將下跌，以金計算之物價亦有相當上漲之勢，窖金牟利者，未必如願以償，蓋目前不致再有大量之貨幣貶值，因金之價值已日見跌落。各國中央銀行對金不致續有反常之需求。金之高值不特激勵其生產，亦且減少其工業上之使用。雖然目前世界幣用金之貯存量仍足以維持以金計算之物價總水準於一四五（一八八〇年——一九一四年＝一〇〇），假定（甲）世界基本物品之生產量與一九二九年相同（乙）金之供給及物品之生產量兩者之關係對物價水準之影響亦與戰前相同。此將致英國用以金計算之物價所編之司答的斯脫指數爲一二五（一九一三年＝一〇〇），較一九三六年十二月高百分之八十一。

一九二九年金之數量過少，致不能維持當時之物價水準，而金之價值仍失之稍低。目前金之數量似覺過多，致不能保其高值，而使以金計算之物價日趨上漲。物價之開始上漲實在爭購戰用品之前。

以貶值貨幣計算之物價

已往各國實際上之物價水準，原係根據以金計算之一般物價水準，以後仍保留在此水準以上與各該國貨幣貶值之多寡相當高度。

一九三一年九月英鎊即以金計算開始貶跌，時適金值飛

At the present time, it seems probable that the value of gold will continue to fall and prices in terms of gold rise correspondingly. Profits from hoarding are now unlikely because large currency devaluations are improbable and because the value of gold is already falling. The abnormally high demands of central banks will probably not continue indefinitely. The high value of gold has both stimulated production and curtailed industrial use of gold; but, even now, the world's stocks of monetary gold are large enough to maintain the general level of prices in terms of gold at 145 (1880—1914=100) provided (i) the world's production of basic commodities were the same as in 1929 and (ii) the relationship between the supply of gold and the production of commodities affected the price level in the same manner as prior to the World War. This would make the 'Statist' index for England, when calculated for prices in terms of gold, 125 (1913=100), 81 per cent higher than in December, 1936.

In 1929 there was too little gold to support the prevailing price level. Gold was undervalued. Now there appears to be too much gold to allow its value to remain so high and prices in terms of gold are rising. The rise began before the general rush for war materials.

Prices in terms of devalued currencies

The price levels actually experienced by different countries have been based on the general level of prices in terms of gold and have remained above this level by amounts proportionate to the devaluation of the respective currencies.

Sterling began to depreciate in terms of gold in September 1931 at a time when the commodity value of gold was rapidly increasing, prices in terms of gold declining. The depreciation was sufficient to allow prices to remain comparatively level in the United Kingdom and in 'Sterlingarea' as a whole, while severe deflation continued elsewhere (figure 3, page 204). Prices of basic commodities in the United Kingdom have tended upwards since spring 1933, chiefly because of further advances in the sterling price of gold.

A clear picture of the relation of prices of basic commodities in the United Kingdom to the level of such prices in terms of gold in the United States, Canada, France and Sweden is obtained by expressing the index for the United Kingdom in per cent of the average index for these four countries. The results can be compared with the sterling price of gold expressed in per cent of par (figure 4, page 204). Prices in terms of sterling fluctuated around the general level of prices in terms of gold until the sterling price of gold rose in September 1931. Thereafter prices in sterling rose above the general

第三圖：英國與其他四國之基本物價格指數，一九二九年至一九三六年

一九一三年＝一〇〇

以金鎊計算之英國物價及以金計算之其他國物價

自一九三一年九月至一九三三年春英鎊貶跌，足以維持其物價平衡，其後英鎊更跌，而足使以鎊計之物價上漲。

FIGURE 3.—INDEX NUMBERS OF PRICES OF BASIC COMMODITIES IN THE UNITED KINGDOM AND IN FOUR OTHER COUNTRIES. 1929-1936

1913＝100

United Kingdom's prices, in sterling; Other countries' prices, in gold.

From September 1931, to spring 1933, sterling was devalued sufficiently to keep sterling prices level. Thereafter, sterling was devalued sufficiently to raise sterling prices.

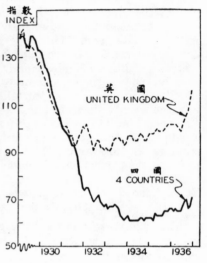

第四圖：金之英鎊價格爲平價之百分數與英國之基本物價指數爲其他各國以金計算之基本物價指數之百分數，一九二九年至一九三六年

一九一三年＝一〇〇

以英鎊計算之物價升至以金計算之物價以上與金之英鎊價格所增之數相當之高度

FIGURE 4.—STERLING PRICE OF GOLD IN PER CENT OF PAR AND INDEX OF *STERLING* PRICES OF BASIC COMMODITIES IN THE UNITED KINGDOM IN PER CENT OF INDEX OF *GOLD* PRICES OF BASIC COMMODITIES IN OTHER COUNTRIES 1929-1936
1913＝100

Prices in sterling have risen above the level of prices in gold by an amount proportionate to the increase in the sterling price of gold

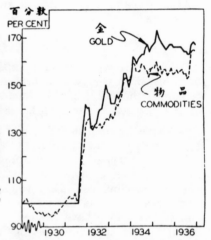

漲，而以金計算之物價慘跌之際，其貶價足使英國物價較爲平衡，而其他各國則通貨緊縮方與未艾（第二〇四頁，第三圖）。一九三三年春後，英國基本物價格已有欣欣向榮之勢，要由於金之英鎊價格一再增進之故也。

欲求英國之基本物品價格，對以金計算之美，加拿大，法，及瑞典各國之物價水準之關係。可將英國之指數，算爲

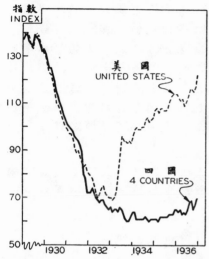

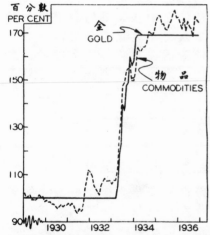

level of prices in gold in proportion to the increase in the sterling
price of gold. In December 1936, the index was 164 per cent of
the average index for the other four countries. The sterling price
of gold was then 167 per cent of par.

The devaluation of the United States dollar began in April 1933,
at a time when the commodity value of gold was increasing only
slowly. The devaluation was sufficient to raise prices rapidly (figure
5, page 205).

後四國平均指數之百分數，卽得一明析之印象。其結果可與以平價百分數計算之金之英鎊價格相比較（第二〇四頁，第四圖）。以英鎊計算之物價，隨以金計算之一般物價水準而變動，直至一九三三年九月金之英鎊價格乃上漲，其後以英鎊計算之物價上升於一般物價水準以上與金之英鎊價格增加數額相當之高度。一九三六年十二月其指數爲其他四國平均指數之百分之一六四，金之英鎊價格則爲其平價之百分之一六七。

美國金元貶值，始於一九三三年四月，其時金價值之增加，已趨和緩，故貶價足使物價提高甚速（第二〇五頁第五圖）。

美國以美金計之基本物品價格指數，亦經換算爲英，法，瑞及加拿大四國以金計算之物價平均指數之百分數，可以所得數字持較金之美元價格（第二〇五頁第六圖）。一九三三年四月以前，以美元計算之物價從未嘗與其他各國以金計之物價有所不符，自一九三三年四月十九日黃金出口禁令實施以後，金之美元價格挺漲，始則爲經濟勢力所造成之自然反應，但一九三三年十月二十二日以後，美國政府故意將金價自平價之百分之一〇四‧三提高至百分之一六九‧三（每兩純金等於二九‧〇一元至三十五元）。物價在所逆料之高水準上繼續變動（第二〇五頁第六圖）。

華北物價與以金計算之一般物價水準

第二〇八頁第七圖爲以國幣計算之華北物價指數與以金計算之一般物價水準之比較。華北物價在一九二九年爲一六五，一九三一年爲一八二，一九三四年爲一三七（一九一三年＝一〇〇）[3]。而以金計算之基本物價指數在一九二九年爲一三六，一九三一年爲九十一，一九三四年爲六十一（一九一三年＝一〇〇）。自一九二九年至一九三一年，以金計算之一般物價水準猛跌，以國幣計算之物價上漲。一九三二，

---

3. 以國幣計算之物華北物價指數係天津南開大學經濟研究所所編製，請參閱『南開社會經濟季刊』指數均以一‧四八八五乘之使基期由一九二六年換爲一九一三年。

The index of prices of basic commodities in the United States in terms of dollars has been expressed in per cent of the average index of prices in terms of gold in the United Kingdom, France, Sweden and Canada and the resulting figures are compared with the dollar price of gold in figure 6, page 205. Prior to April 1933, prices in dollars were never far out of line with prices in gold in other countries. Following the embargo on gold exports enforced on April 19, 1933, the dollar price of gold advanced as a result of the free play of economic forces but, after October 22, 1933, the price was purposefully raised by the government from 140.3 per cent to 169.3 per cent of par (from $29.01 to $35.00 per fine ounce). Prices have continued to fluctuate at the level expected on the basis of the higher figure (figure 6, page 205).

Prices in North China and the general level of prices in terms of gold

The general index of prices in terms of yuan for North China is compared with the world level of prices in gold in figure 7, page 208. The index for North China was 165 in 1929, 182 in 1931, and 137 in 1934 (1913=100).[3] The index of prices of basic commodities in terms of gold was 136 in 1929, 91 in 1931, 61 in 1934 (1913=100). From 1929 to 1931, prices in yuan rose while the general level of prices in gold fell rapidly. During 1932, 1933 and 1934, the index for China declined at approximately the same rate as the index of prices in gold but at a higher level. After October 1935, prices in China rose rapidly but prices expressed in terms of gold, only slowly. The index for North China was 183 in December 1936. The highest figure recorded prior to that time was 186 in May 1931 (1913=100).

The level of prices in China can be explained on the basis of the world level of prices in gold and changes in the yuan price of gold (figures 1, 8; pages 197, 209)[4]. From 1929 to 1931 the yuan price of gold was more than doubled as a result of the world wide depreciation of silver in terms of gold. Prices in yuan rose above the world level of prices in gold by an amount proportionate to the rise in the yuan price of gold (figure 8). From 1932 to 1935, the yuan price of gold fluctuated at a high level and prices in North China were correspondingly high relative to prices in gold. The increase in the yuan price of gold caused by the currency reform again raised the index relative to the level of prices in gold, but by

---

3   The index for North China is that calculated by the Nankai Institute of Economics, Tientsin; see *Nankai Social and Economic Quarterly.* The index was converted from the 1926 to a 1913 base by multiplying by 1.4885.

4   The yuan price of gold has been calculated on the basis of Shanghai on New York exchange rates and the price of gold in the United States.

一九三三，及一九三四年中國物價指數跌落約與以金計算之指數等速，惟其水準較高而已，一九三五年十月以後中國物價上漲甚速，而其以金計算之物價則上漲甚緩，一九三六年十二月華北指數為一八三，該時以前之最高點為一九三一年五月之一八六（一九一三年＝一〇〇）。

中國物價水準，可根據以金計算之一般物價水準，及金之國幣價格之變動解釋之（第一九七及二〇九頁第一，八圖）。自一九二九年至一九三一年，因世界以金計算之銀價貶值之故，金之國幣價格上漲至一倍以上。以元計之物價乃上升於以金計算之一般物價水準以上與金之國幣價格所增之數相等比之高度（第八圖）。自一九三二年至一九三五年，金之國幣價格依一高水準而波動，華北物價亦隨之較以金計算之物價為高。

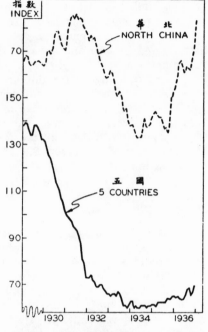

第七圖　華北之總物價指數與其他五國之基本物物價指數，一九二九年至一九三六年

一九一三年＝一〇〇

以國幣計之物價循一與以金計之物價不同相之路線既以國幣計之物價較一九二九年者高，而以金計者則低，大部之歧異乃由於金之國幣價格之變動之故也。

FIGURE 7.—INDEX NUMBERS OF PRICES OF 'ALL' COMMODITIES IN NORTH CHINA AND OF BASIC COMMODITIES IN FIVE OTHER COUNTRIES, 1929-1936
1910＝100
North China's prices, in yuan;
Other countries' prices, in gold.
Prices in yuan have followed a course different from that of prices in gold. Prices in yuan are now higher than in 1929; prices in gold, much lower. Changes in the yuan price of gold explain most of the divergencies.

因幣制改革而增加之金之國幣價格，使與以金計算之一般物價作比較之中國物價指數提高，但至一九三六年十二月未提至漲勢之最高限度，此種失調大部由於華北指數內所包括之製造品價格不易變動之故，而其他各國之指數，乃由基

4. 金之國幣價格，乃根據上海紐約間之匯價及美國之金價計算之，並以一九一三年為一〇〇換算為指數。

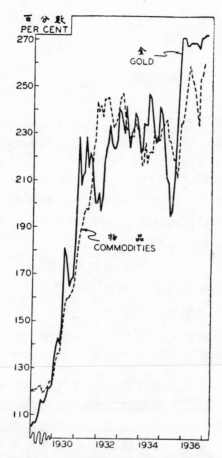

第八圖　金之國幣價格與華北以國幣
計之總物價指數為其他以金計之基
本物價指數之百分數，一九二九年
至一九三六年。

一九一三年 ＝ 一〇〇

　　至一九二九年至一九三一年，金之國幣價格
上漲一倍有餘。以國幣計之物價上漲於以金計之
物價以上約相當之數量。

FIGURE 8.—YUAN PRICE OF GOLD AND INDEX
OF *YUAN* PRICES OF 'ALL' COMMODITIES
IN NORTH CHINA IN PER CENT OF INDEX
OF *GOLD* PRICES OF BASIC COMMODITIES
IN OTHER COUNTRIES 1929-1936
1913 = 100

From 1929 to 1931, the yuan price of gold was more
than doubled. Prices in yuan rose above the level of
prices in gold by a corresponding amount.

本物品價格編成者也，華北指數自一九三六年十二月至一九三七年三月間由一八三升至一九二(一九一三年＝一〇〇)。

結　論

任何國之以貨幣計算之金價能維持於一定之限度內，則該國之物價水準，將與世界以金計算之世界物價水準相平行，如金價上漲，則物價亦將根據以金計算之一般物價而隨之上升，至與金所漲之數相當。反之如金價下跌，物價亦隨之根據以金計算之一般物價而作等比之下跌，故根據以金計算之一般物價水準以提高，或抑低物價之惟一有效方法，厥爲提高或抑低金之貨幣價格。

中國將來之物價水準基於兩要素，即以金計算之世界物價水準，與金之國幣價格是也。

以金計算之世界物價水準將有上漲之可能。

目前金之國幣價格較爲穩定，因國幣之外匯價值乃規定與一定或幾乎一定金價之外國貨幣相等。

此後數年內此規定之金價或將大有變動亦未可知。貶值固非吾人所願，而目前物價已上漲，足以糾正緊縮時期之物價機構諸重要弊病，貶值亦大可避免。金之英鎊價格及其美元價格不致再有跌落，蓋美國及金鎊國所受物價徐漲之利益，遠甚於膨脹之恐怖，如以金計算之一般物價水準增加甚速，則抑低金價之實施，或將應用，但比較上目前基本物品價格，仍較低於賦稅，運銷費，都市工資以及一九二九年以前所增加之長期債務之水準。大致國幣之英鎊價格及其美元價格亦不致有上漲之勢。

根據許多因素均預證中國物價之趨勢，行將向上，且不日將達到一空前之高峯也。

雷　伯　恩

胡　國　華

December 1936, the full extent of the probable rise had not·been brought about. The greater part of this apparent maladjustment is due to the inflexibility of the prices of manufactured goods included in the general index for North China. The index for other countries is calculated from prices of basic commodities. The index for North China rose from 183 to 193 between December 1936 and March 1937 (1913=100).

Conclusions

The level of basic commodity prices experienced by any country will parallel the world level of such prices in gold, provided the price of gold in terms of that country's currency is maintained within narrow limits. If the currency price of gold is raised, prices in currency will rise by a corresponding amount relative to the general level of prices in gold. Conversely, if the currency price of gold is lowered, prices will fall by a corresponding amount relative to the general level of prices in gold. The only effective method of raising, or lowering, prices in currency relative to prices in gold is to raise, or lower, the currency price of gold.

Future changes in the level of commodity prices in China depend on two factors—the world level of prices in gold and the yuan price of gold.

It is probable that the world level of prices in gold will rise.

The yuan price of gold is now relatively constant, the foreign exchange value of the yuan being fixed in terms of currencies with constant or almost constant gold values. It is not probable that these gold values will be greatly changed within the next few years. Devaluation is not generally desired and can be avoided because prices have already risen sufficiently to correct the major anomalies in the price structure caused by deflation. The sterling and U.S. dollar prices of gold will probably not be lowered because the benefits of gradually rising commodity prices are more important for the United States and for 'Sterlingarea' as a whole than are fears of inflation. If the general level of prices in gold rises very rapidly, it is possible that the power to change the currency prices of gold will be used, but prices of basic commodities are still low relative to taxes, distribution costs, city wages and the level at which many long-term debts were incurred prior to 1929. It is also not probable that the sterling and U.S. dollar values of the yuan will be raised.

Many factors indicate that the trend of prices in China will be upward and may reach a level much higher than any yet recorded.

JOHN R. RAEBURN
HU KWOH-HWA

— 211 —

農民所得之小麥價格

小麥價格變遷甚大。江蘇省武進縣農民所得小麥每石[1]價格在一九〇〇年為二元五角，一九一〇年為四元，一九二〇年為五元，一九三〇年為七元六角，一九三五年為六元二角。至一九三七年一月間竟漲至每石拾元六角，為歷來所未有（見第214頁第一圖）。按小麥價格之劇變為該作物供求變遷之結果，此為一般人所洞悉。氣候，野草，病虫害，國內外小麥產量，進出口，以及其他因素均可影響其價格。小麥買賣所用貨幣價值之變動亦足以左右其價格。據一般人之推測，最近小麥價格之激漲，乃因一般農民不願輕易接受紙幣之故。

一八九四年至一九三〇年間，以元計算之小麥價格呈一顯著之上升趨勢，其主要原因為以物品計算之銀元價值之跌落，並與該期間內一般物價之上升相符。其超越普通趨勢之變動，則由於小麥本身供求之變遷。一九三一年至一九三四年間，小麥價格依下降趨勢而波動，該年六月間，每石小麥僅值四元，但此後則猛漲而不定，一九三七年三月間，小麥價格達每石拾元二角。近年來價格不規則之漲落為小麥本身供求以及元價之變遷所致。

貨幣價值之變動對於購買小麥一石所需米之石數無影響（見第215頁第二圖）。一八九四年至一九三〇年間，小麥以米計算之價格漲落懸殊，乃小麥與米兩者之供求變遷所致。但此種以米計算之麥價非但無上升之趨勢，而反稍有下跌之趨勢（見第215頁第二圖）。自一九三一年直至最近小麥價格漲落亦劇，但此種種均不足以解釋一九三一年至一九三四年以元計算之小麥價格之跌落，以及此後之上漲。自一九三一年以來，以元計算之小麥價格之主要變動，乃由貨幣物品價值之變遷所致。一九三六，一九三四，一九三三諸年一月份以米計算之小麥價格無多差別，但此三時期以元計算之小麥價格則大不相同。一九三六年一月每石小麥價格值七元七角

---

1. 小麥一石重 85.9 基羅格蘭姆或 189 磅

PRICES PAID TO FARMERS FOR WHEAT

The price of wheat is very variable. In Wuchin, Kiangsu, the price paid to farmers per shih[1] was 2.50 yuan in 1900, 4.00 in 1910, 5.00 in 1920, 7.60 in 1930, 6.20 in 1935 and, in January 1937, was the highest ever recorded, 10.60 yuan per shih (figure 1, page 214). It is commonly understood that these wide fluctuations are the results of changes in the supply of wheat and, to a lesser extent, in the demand for wheat. The weather, weeds, insects, diseases, crops in other parts of China, crops abroad, exports, imports and many other factors affect the price. Changes in the value of the money for which the wheat is sold also determine price. A reason commonly given for the recent spectacular rise in the price of wheat is that farmers do not readily accept the new paper currency.

In terms of yuan, the price of wheat showed a definite upward trend from 1894 to 1930. This rising trend was chiefly caused by the falling commodity value of the yuan and corresponded to the gradual upward tendency of the general level of commodity prices during this period. Fluctuations above and below this trend were due to changes in the supply of, and demand for, wheat itself. From 1931 to 1934, the price fluctuated above and below a falling trend and, in June 1934, reached a low point of 4.00 yuan per shih. Since that time the rise has been rapid, although irregular. In March 1937, the price was 10.20 yuan per shih. The erratic changes in recent years are the results both of changes in the supply of, and demand for, wheat and of changes in the value of the yuan itself.

Changes in the value of money have no effect on the number of shih of rice required to buy one shih of wheat (figure 2, page 215). From 1894 to 1930, there were wide fluctuations in the relative value of wheat due to changes in the supply of, and demand for, wheat and in the supply of, and demand for, rice; but there was no gradual upward trend in the ratio of wheat to rice (figure 2, page 215). In fact, there was a slight tendency for wheat to decline. From 1931 to the present time, there have also been wide fluctuations, but these do not explain the downward tendency of the yuan price of wheat from 1931 to 1934 and the upward tendency thereafter. The major movements of the yuan prices of wheat since 1931, have been due to changes in the commodity value of the yuan. The relative value of wheat in terms of rice was the same in January 1936 as in January 1934, and January 1933, but the yuan price of wheat was 7.70 per shih in January 1936; 5.00, in January 1934; 6.30, in January 1933.

At the present time, wheat is valuable relative to rice chiefly because of a poor wheat crop in China and a low world supply of

---

[1] 1 shih of wheat=85.9 kilograms, 189 lbs.

，一九三四年一月值五元，一九三三年一月值六月三角。

今則小麥較米爲貴，蓋因中國小麥之歉收及世界小麥供給之缺乏。此均足以促成以元計算之小麥價格較高於以其他物品計算之小麥價格也。

如中國採取一種貨幣其外匯價值與英鎊成一固定之比例，則武進小麥價格之變動情形可如第217頁第三圖所示。除歐戰時期外，武進小麥價格之主要變動情形與英國小麥價格相似。自一九二一年至一九二九年間，以英鎊計算之小麥價格較諸戰前水準約高一倍半。一九二九年至一九三一年間，則跌落至戰前水準以下。一九三六年以來上漲甚速，又復超出戰前水準。最近武進以英鎊計算之小麥價格如此之高，乃因去冬中國小麥歉收之故。自一九二一年以來，武進與英國以

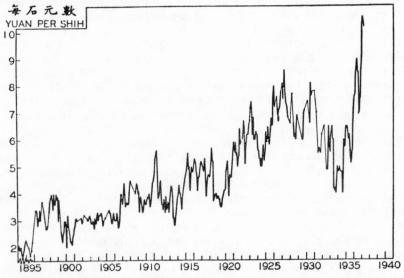

第一圖　江蘇武進農民所得之小麥價格，一八九四年至一九三七年。

一八九四年至一九三〇年小麥元價之上升趨勢以及一九三一年至一九三四年之下降趨勢爲元之物品價值之變遷所促成，最近小麥價格異常高，因元之物品價值又復低如一九三〇年，同時由於小麥之缺乏。

FIRURE 1.—PRICES PAID TO FARMERS FOR WHEAT IN WUCHIN, KIANGSU, 1894-1937

Changes in the commodity value of the yuan caused the upward trend in the yuan price of wheat from 1894 to 1930 and the downward trend from 1931 to 1934. The price is now exceedingly high because the commodity value of the yuan is as low as in 1930 and wheat is scarce.

wheat. These have caused the yuan price of wheat to rise above the level of yuan prices of other commodities.

If China had adopted a money with a constant foreign exchange value in terms of sterling, the price of wheat in Wuchin would have followed a course comparable to that shown in figure 3, page 217. Except during the World War period, the major movements of the Wuchin price have been similar to those of wheat prices in England. From 1921 to 1929, the sterling price of wheat fluctuated at about one and one-half times the pre-war level. From 1929 to 1931, the price declined to below the pre-war level. During 1936, it rose rapidly and is now again above this level. At the present time the sterling price in Wuchin is high chiefly because this winter's wheat crop in China is poor. The margin between the Wuchin and the English prices has been as wide as at present on several occasions since 1921. Because of the scarcity of food caused by the drought of 1934 and the small wheat crop harvested in 1935, the Wuchin price was high during 1934 and 1935. In September and October, 1936, before drought had reduced the present crop, the Wuchin price was at par with the English price.

Conclusions

The price paid to farmers for wheat in Wuchin, Kiangsu, is determined by changes in the commodity value of the yuan as well

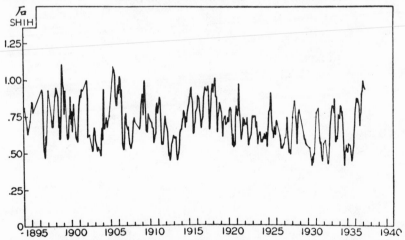

第二圖　江蘇武進購買小麥一石所需米之石數，一八九四年至一九三七年。

以米計算之小麥價值呈一微降之趨勢。近來因小麥之缺乏以及米之豐饒，故小麥對米之相對價值則較為。

FIGURE 2.—NUMBER OF SHIH OF RICE REQUIRED TO BUY ONE SHIH OF WHEAT
IN WUCHIN, KIANGSU, 1894-1937

There has been a very slightly downward trend in the value of wheat in terms of rice. At the present time, wheat is high relative to rice because wheat is scarce.

英鎊計算之小麥價格嘗有幾度相差如今之大。一九三四年武進發生旱災，翌年收成大減，糧食缺乏，因之一九三四，三五兩年武進以英鎊計算之小麥價格較高。一九三六年九，十月間，小麥供給在未因旱災而減少之前，武進小麥價格則與英國小麥價格相同。

結　論

江蘇武進農民所得之小麥價格，決之於貨幣之物品價值及小麥本身之供求變遷。四十二年來以米計算之小麥價值並無上升之趨勢。但以貨幣計算之價格則不然。一八九四年至一九〇〇年間平均每石約三元，一九三〇年每石七元六角，而一九三七年三月石每則爲拾元二角。如武進與英國小麥價格均以英鎊計算則可互相比較。

一九三五年以來小麥價格劇漲，可以下列之各事實解釋之。（ⅰ）世界以英鎊計算之小麥價格上漲（ⅱ）以英鎊計算之元之貶值（ⅲ）中國小麥產量之減少。

雷　伯　恩
徐　壯　懷

as by the supply of, and demand for, wheat itself.   In terms of rice
the value of wheat has shown no significant trend during the last
42 years.   The currency price fluctuated at about 3.00 yuan per shih

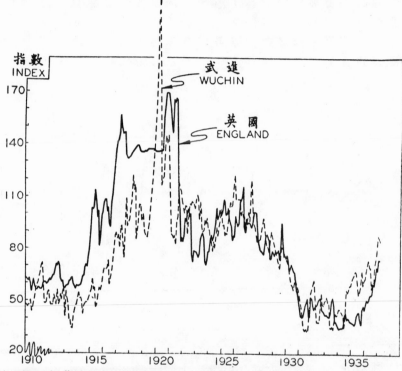

第三圖　江蘇武進及英國以英鎊計算之小麥價格指數，一九一〇年至一九
三七年。　一九二六年 ＝ 一〇〇

除歐戰時期外，武進及英國小麥價格之主要變動相似。近來中國有旱因災故武進小麥價格較高。

FIGURE 3.—INDEX NUMBERS OF PRICES OF WHEAT IN WUCHIN, KIANGSU, AND ENGLAND,
1910-1937

Prices in sterling
1926=100

Except during the World War period, the major movements have been the same in Wuchin as in
England.   At present the Wuchin price is high as a result of drought in China.

for 6 years prior to 1900, in 1930 it was 7.60 yuan and in March
1937, 10.20 yuan.   The course of wheat prices in Wuchin is comparable to that of wheat prices in England when both are expressed
in terms of sterling.

The spectacular rise in the price of wheat since 1935 can be
explained on the basis of (i) a rise in the sterling, world price of
wheat, (ii) devaluation of the yuan in terms of sterling, (iii) a pro-
spective scarcity of wheat in China.　　JOHN R. RAEBURN.

TSU CHWAN HWAI.

以米計算之豆油，棉布與火油之價值

米為江蘇武進農家最重要之銷售品，豆油粗棉布及火油為農民最重要之購買品，而此三種消費物各定量所值白米之數量日新月異無時或同。

每擔豆油所值之白米升數乃以每升白米之農民所得價格除每擔豆油之農民所付價格而得之（第二一八頁第一圖）。

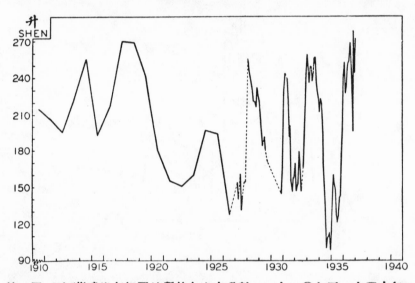

第一圖 在江蘇武進每擔豆油所值白米之升數，一九一〇年至一九三六年。

以米計算之豆油價值變動甚激，自一九一〇年以後，了無一定之趨勢可尋。一九三六年豆油較之白米為高。

FIGURE 1.—NUMBER OF SHEN OF WHITE RICE REQUIRED TO BUY ONE PICUL OF SOYBEAN OIL IN WUCHIN, KIANGSU, 1910 1936

The value of soybean oil in terms of rice has fluctuated widely but has shown no definite trend since 1910. In 1936, oil was high relative to rice.

一九一〇年每擔豆油值白米二一五升，一九一八年值二七〇升，一九一六年值一二七升，一九三三年十二月值二一二升，一九三四年十二月值一一八升，一九三六年十二月值二七二升，此種激烈之變動大都由於各年米與大豆之歲收豐歉不一之故，而可食用脂肪類（豆油亦其一也）之供給亦足以影

1. 一升＝一・一九三六公升

2. 一擔＝五九・六八瓩

THE VALUES OF SOYBEAN OIL, COTTON CLOTH
AND KEROSENE IN TERMS OF RICE

The most important product sold by farmers in Wuchin, Kiangsu, is rice. Three of their most important purchases are soybean oil, coarse cotton cloth and kerosene. The amount of rice that has to be sold in order to buy a uniform quantity of these varies from year to year and from day to day.

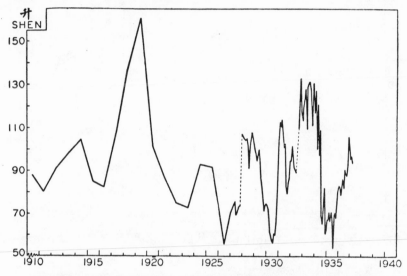

第二圖　在江蘇武進每疋十六磅土產粗棉布所值白米之升數
一九一〇年至一九三七年

以米計算之布價變動甚激，於一九一八，一九一九及自一九三二，以至一九三四年之旱災爲止其價值甚高，目前布之價值，無甚高低。

FIGURE 2 —NUMBER OF SHEN OF WHITE RICE REQUIRED TO BUY ONE 16 LB. PIECE OF NATIVE
COARSE. COTTON CLOTH IN WUCHIN, KIANGSU. 1910-1937

The value of cotton cloth in terms of rice has fluctuated widely. It was high in 1918 and 1919 and from 1932 until the drought of 1934. At the present time, it is neither high nor low.

The number of shen[1] of white rice required to buy one picul[2] of soybean oil was calculated by dividing the prices farmers paid for this amount of oil by the prices they received for one shen of white rice (figure 1, page 218). In 1910, one picul of soybean oil was worth 215 shen of rice; in 1918, 270; in 1926, 127; in December 1933, 212; in December 1934, 118; in December 1936, 272. These wide

---

1　1 shen = 1.1936 litres

2　1 picul = 59.68 kilograms

響其比率。

　　近二十八年內，米與豆油之比較價值並無顯著之趨勢，但最近豆油之以米計之價值激增逾恆，此隱證目前世界脂肪供給之缺乏與夫我國去歲米谷之豐收，世界可食脂肪之供給

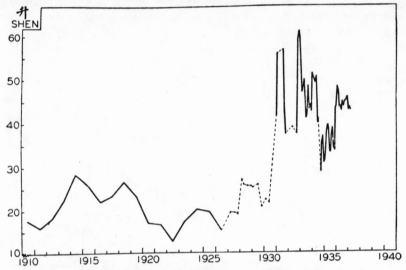

第三圖　每五美加倫火油在江蘇武進所值白米之升數　一九一〇年至一九三七年。

　　一九三〇年以後火油所值之米量已倍之

已在增加。

　　一九一〇年每疋十六磅土產粗棉布值米八十八升，一九一八年值一三四升，一九二六年值五十六升，一九三三年十二月值一三一升，一九三五年十二月值八十一升，一九三六年十二月值一〇一升（第二一九頁，第二圖），以米計算之粗布價值變動亦廣，特不若豆油者之甚，一九一八年及一九一九年布之價值極高，要由於世界棉價高昂之故，而國內米價之特低亦不無影響。

　　一九三〇年米季豐收之後，每疋布所值白米之數量，亦隨之激增甚速，一九三一年之水災雖暫使此數量減低但自一九三二年後半年截至一九三四年旱災時為止，米之價值比之

fluctuations were chiefly the results of year to year changes in the size of the rice crop and the soybean crop. The world's supply of edible fats, of which soybean oil is only one, may also have affected the ratio.

During the last 28 years there has been no definite trend in the relative values of rice and soybean oil but, at the present time, oil is worth an unusually large amount of rice. This reflects the present comparatively low world supply of fats and China's unusually large rice crop of last year. The world's supply of fats is increasing.

In 1910, one 16-lb. piece of native, coarse, cotton cloth was worth 88 shen of white rice; in 1918, 137; in 1926, 55; in December 1933, 131; in December 1935, 81; in December 1936, 101 (figure 2, page 219). In terms of rice, the value of cloth has varied widely but not as widely as the value of soybean oil. The value of cloth in terms of rice was very high in 1918 and 1919 chiefly because the world value of cotton was high but partly because, in China, rice was abnormally cheap.

Following the harvest of a good crop of rice in 1930 the amount of rice required for one piece of cloth increased rapidly. The flood in 1931 reduced the amount temporarily but from the latter part of 1932 until the drought of 1934, rice was low relative to cloth. The drought raised the value of rice but farmers had less to sell. From 1932 to 1935 farmers bought little cloth. At the present time, the value of native cloth in terms of rice is neither high nor low.

From 1910 to 1929, the number of shen of white rice required to buy 5 U.S.-gallons of kerosene fluctuated between 12.5 and 28.4 (figure 3, page 220). The size of the rice crop, the price of kerosene abroad and the foreign exchange value of the yuan were the major determining factors. From 1930 to the present time, the fluctuations have continued but kerosene has been worth more than twice as much rice as previously. This permanent change resulted when the import duty on kerosene was greatly increased in 1930 in order to obtain security for a new domestic loan. The extra duty has been paid more by the farmers than by the importing companies.

JOHN R. RAEBURN
HU KWOH-HWA.

土布價值爲低，旱荒雖使米價高漲，奈農民已幾無米可售，自一九三二年至一九三五年農民買布甚微，目前以米計之土布價值無甚軒輊。

自一九一〇年至一九二九年每五美加侖之火油所值白米之升數，波動於一二•五升至二七升之間，（第二二〇頁第三圖）。米之收穫量，國外火油之價格以及國幣之外匯價值均爲其變動之主要因素。自一九三〇年迄今火油之價值繼續變動，但其對米而言，價值已倍於前，此永久之變動，乃因於一九三〇年爲保證一新國債而增加火油之入口稅之故。此額外增加之稅額實際上進口商行所付者甚微，大部仍加於農民之身。

雷 伯 恩

胡 國 華

第二二四頁材料之來源：

（一） 上海物價

   米與小麥

     一九一〇至一九三〇——上海市社會局一九三一年六月出版之"上海民食問題"．

     一九三一至一九三二——中國銀行一九三三年出版之"中國及近物價統計圖表"．

     一九三三至現　　在——國定稅則委員會出版之"上海物價月報"．

   黃豆

     一九二三至一九三二——"中國及近物價統計圖表"．

     一九三三至現　　在——"上海物價月報"．

（二） 其他材料乃金陵大學農業經濟系調查所得．

Sources of data on page 22{:

    (1) Prices in Shanghai :

      Rice and wheat

          1910—1930——Bureau of Social Affairs: *Food Problems in Shanghai,* June 1931.
          1931—1932——Bank of China : *An Analysis of Shanghai Commodity Prices,* 1933.
          1933 to date—National Tariff Commission, *Price and Prices Indexes in Shanghai,* monthly.

      Soybeans

          1923—1932——*An Analysis of Shanghai Commodity Prices.*
          1933 to date—*Prices and Price indexes in Shanghai.*

    (2) Other data were reported privately to the Department of Agricultural Economics, University
        of Nanking.

主要農作物之批發物價
WHOLESALE PRICES OF IMPORTANT FARM CROPS

年 Year	米 Rice			小麥 Wheat					黃豆 Yellow Soybeans			
	上海 Shanghai. 私米 early white	上海 Shanghai 粳米 late white	江蘇武進 Wuchin, Kiangsu. 粳米 late white	上海 Shanghai.	江蘇進武 Wuchin, Kiangsu.	南京 Nanking	安徽宿縣 Suhsien Anhwei	山西靜樂 Tsingloh Shansi	上海 Shanghai.	江蘇武進 Wuchin, Kiangsu.	安徽宿縣 Suhsien Anhwei	河北正定 Chenting. Hopeh
	每市石價格(元)* yuan per shih tan*			每市担價格(元)† yuan per shih picul†					每市担價格(元)† yuan per shih picul†			
1910	6.47	6.89	5.60	4.00	2.33	—	—	3.45	—	3.11	—	2.36
1911	6.72	7.71	6.08	4.52	2.62	—	—	2.88	—	3.17	—	2.78
1912	7.12	7.67	6.08	3.62	2.09	—	—	2.24	—	2.69	—	2.25
1913	6.57	6.96	5.99	3.80	2.09	—	—	3.27	—	2.75	—	2.34
1914	5.89	6.20	5.21	4.18	2.38	—	—	3.13	—	3.11	—	2.34
1915	6.83	7.15	5.89	4.59	2.85	—	—	3.15	—	2.87	—	2.18
1916	6.10	6.88	5.70	3.46	2.85	—	—	2.55	—	2.93	—	2.86
1917	5.53	6.30	5.21	3.88	2.73	—	—	1.57	—	3.11	—	2.54
1918	5.35	6.39	5.02	3.84	2.56	—	—	2.00	—	2.99	—	2.31
1919	6.14	6.70	5.12	3.19	2.27	—	—	3.02	3.43	2.87	—	2.43
1920	8.18	9.28	6.95	3.50	2.91	—	—	3.58	3.78	3.41	—	4.16
1921	9.10	9.35	7.44	3.98	3.32	—	—	3.16	3.83	3.41	—	4.01
1922	9.51	10.87	8.88	4.24	3.61	—	—	3.44	4.75	3.95	—	3.50
1923	9.44	10.82	9.27	4.37	3.72	—	—	3.58	4.36	3.89	—	3.19
1924	9.72	10.90	8.40	3.90	3.14	—	—	3.78	4.35	4.31	—	3.44
1925	9.96	10.57	8.88	4.77	3.78	4.19	—	4.24	4.94	4.31	—	2.96
1926	13.49	15.23	11.88	5.11	4.25	4.58	—	4.45	4.98	4.37	—	4.48
1927	13.05	14.26	11.68	5.04	4.36	4.20	—	3.95	5.76	4.55	—	4.24
1928	8.90	10.79	8.69	4.69	3.84	4.00	—	4.75	4.23	5.45	—	4.30
1929	12.12	13.05	10.72	4.85	3.78	4.76	—	7.31	5.70	5.45	—	4.97
1930	14.73	16.44	13.91	5.53	4.42	4.93	3.77	7.47	6.01	5.51	3.86	4.65
1931	10.81	12.11	9.75	4.47	3.43	4.00	4.95	5.74	5.31	5.57	4.48	5.78
1932	10.30	11.71	9.46	4.13	3.32	3.65	4.32	5.12	3.88	4.31	4.81	3.92
1933	7.36	8.38	6.76	3.54	2.91	2.92	2.87	3.28	4.10	3.71	2.59	2.79
1934	9.23	10.27	8.69	3.18	3.08	2.87	2.56	2.68	2.96	3.17	1.99	2.16
1935	10.52	12.27	10.53	3.83	3.61	3.28	3.31	2.88	3.85	3.53	2.83	3.30
1936	9.71	10.42	9.56	4.79	4.89	4.00	4.51	4.59	5.61	4.91	4.52	4.60
1936												
一月 Jan.	8.75	9.80	8.98	4.85	4.48	3.70	4.10	3.28	4.70	3.95	3.75	3.92
二月 Feb.	9.35	9.90	9.17	5.00	4.83	3.72	4.40	3.91	4.65	4.01	4.00	4.00
三月 Mar.	10.30	11.10	9.75	5.05	5.00	4.06	4.63	3.91	5.40	4.54	4.82	4.20
四月 Apr.	10.30	11.10	9.95	5.08	5.23	4.26	4.67	3.84	5.95	5.27	5.14	4.40
五月 May.	9.80	10.50	9.75	4.50	4.94	4.25	4.21	3.84	5.60	5.09	4.57	4.60
六月 June	10.00	10.70	9.85	4.05	4.94	3.67	3.50	3.91	5.90	5.39	4.82	5.00
七月 July	10.20	10.60	9.75	4.35	4.07	3.57	3.87	3.84	6.20	6.01	4.61	4.80
八月 Aug.	10.20	10.60	9.46	4.77	4.36	3.50	4.23	3.84	5.85	4.25	4.60	4.56
九月 Sept.	9.55	10.50	9.27	4.80	4.36	3.15	4.27	4.54	5.90	4.97	4.29	3.80
十月 Oct.	9.30	9.90	9.17	5.40	5.00	4.00	4.79	6.42	5.80	4.85	4.40	5.32
十一月 Nov.	9.20	9.80	9.27	5.80	5.23	4.61	5.40	7.19	5.45	4.91	4.49	5.40
十二月 Dec.	9.60	10.30	9.95	6.55	5.99	5.50	6.00	6.49	5.90	5.33	4.80	5.16
1937												
一月 Jan.	10.65	11.60	10.43	6.30	6.17	4.77	5.76	7.68	6.15	5.33	4.95	5.40
二月 Feb.	11.00	12.00	10.62	6.50	6.05	4.83	5.73	7.12	6.00	5.33	4.96	5.48
三月 Mar.	10.20	11.00	10.43	6.25	5.93	4.80	5.73	7.33	6.20	5.45	4.96	5.60
四月 Apr.	—	—	9.75	5.99	4.65	—	—	6.07	—	5.58	—	5.40

* 一市石＝一公石
† 一市担＝五十公斤
來源： 見第二二二頁

* 1 shih tan＝1 hectolitre
† shih picul＝50 kgs.
Sources: See page 223

戈福鼎
KO FUH-TING

— 224 —

經 濟 統 計
ECONOMIC FACTS

南 京 金 陵 大 學 農 學 院 農 業 經 濟 系 出 版
Department of Agricultural Economics
COLLEGE OF AGRICULTURE AND FORESTRY
UNIVERSITY OF NANKING
NANKING, CHINA

第六期 No. 6   一九三七年七月 July 1937

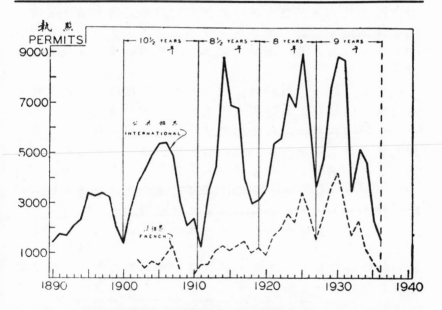

第一圖　　上海公共租界及法租界所發之營造執照之數目一八九〇年至一九
三六年。

建築活動形成劇烈之變遷，至一九三六年降至低點。

FIGURE 1.—NUMBER OF BUILDING PERMITS ISSUED IN THE INTERNATIONAL SETTLEMENT
AND THE FRENCH CONCESSION, SHANGHAI, 1890-1936

There have been violent, cyclical changes in building activity. A 'low' was reached in 1936.

上海建築之營造*

欧西各國建築營造及其有關之工商業乃整個經濟活動之一主要部分。建築數量之變動，對於繁榮影響甚鉅，美國此種變動每呈環形轉變，盛衰更替，差有規律，兩峯相間，可十六年至十九年，下屆之高峯，當在一九四一年至一九四四年之間。英國此種環變之週期約爲二十年至三十年[1]。

一旦房屋缺乏，一般估計過於實況，乃致營造立時激增，遠超當時之需要，由此造成房屋過剩之現象人復估計過高，未幾又蹈缺乏之覆轍。若紡織業之活動則不受長期激烈變動之影響，蓋生產苟有剩餘，可以立時用罄，稍有缺乏，亦可立時補足，調劑之方易而且速。食糧業亦復如是，蓋其普通生產期限。祇需一年。故實業活動之主要成分中，當以營造業之變化爲最烈，而所遭之環變，實爲一般景氣榮枯之主因。

建築營造在中國經濟機構中，所佔之地位遠不若其在欧西之重要，然在上海等各大工業都市中亦頗重要。

總營造執照——由上海公共租界及法租界每年所發之執照之總數可見以上地界內建築活動之變動甚烈（第二二五頁第一圖）[2]。其繁盛期高峯在一八九四年至一八九七年，一九〇五年至一九〇六年，一九一四年，及一九二五年，彼此相距約爲十年，八·五年與十一年。沉靜期在一九〇〇年，一九一〇年至一九一一年，一九一九年與一九二七年，彼此相距約一〇·五年，八·五年與八年。一九二七年以前各高峯相距時間平均爲九·八年，各沉靜期間相距九年。一九二七年沉靜期以後一度猛增，迄於一九三〇年。一九三一年雖有

* 本文資料多由上海公共租界工部局及法租界工部局供給特此鳴謝。

1 凱爾克勞斯：—「一八七〇年至一九一四年英國葛拿斯哥營造事業」經濟研究叢刊第二卷第一期第十五頁一九三四年十月。

馬佛立克：「蕭金山地產活動之環變」土地與公用經濟期刊卷八，第二期第一九九頁一九三二年五月。

斯潘斯萊：「都市居住問題」皇家統計學會會刊卷一三一第二部第二一〇頁一九一八年三月。

華爾倫及皮而生：「金與物價」第三九二至四〇〇頁一九三五年。

文才立克：米索里州聖路易士地產分析雜誌一九三四年。

2 法租界之材料僅包括居房營造之執照數目。

— 226 —

AGENTS AUTHORISED TO SELL "ECONOMIC FACTS":-

SHANGHAI: Kelly & Walsh, P.O. Box 613.
            Chinese American Publishing Co., P.O. Box 256.
            Commercial Press, Ltd., 211 Honan Road.

TIENTSIN: The Oriental Bookstore, 69-71 Rue de France.

PEIPING: The French Bookstore, Grand Hotel de Pekin.

TOKYO: Maruzen Company, Ltd., 6 Nihonbashi, Tori-Nichome.

LONDON: Arthur Probsthain, 41 Great Russell Street, W.C.2.

NEW YORK: G. E. Stechert & Co., 31 East 10th Street.

— O R D E R F O R M —

ECONOMIC FACTS,

Department of Agricultural Economics,
University of Nanking,
Nanking, China.

I enclose .... as subscription for 12 issues of

ECONOMIC FACTS to start from Number ......

REVISED RATES

	Twelve issues	One issue
CHINA & JAPAN	C$10.00	C$1.00
U.S.A & CANADA	US$ 5.00	US$0.50
GREAT BRITAIN & OTHER COUNTRIES	£1	2/-

Name ....

Address ....

....

....

....

BUILDING CONSTRUCTION IN SHANGHAI*

In Western countries, building construction and the numerous industries and trades connected with it make up an important part of economic activity as a whole. Changes in the amount of building have significant effects on general prosperity. In the United States, these changes are cyclical, periods of active building and periods of relative idleness following each other more or less regularly. Between one peak of activity and the next, 16 to 19 years elapse. The next peak is expected to occur between 1941 and 1944. In the United Kingdom, cycles 20 to 30 years in length have occurred.[1]

When a shortage of buildings exists, it is overestimated and construction soon proceeds at a rate too active for current needs. A surplus is created which, being also overstimated, leads, in time, to shortage. Clothing industries are not subject to long violent changes in activity because any surplus they create can normally be used up quickly and any shortage of their products, quickly corrected. The same is true for food industries concerned with crops produced on a yearly basis. Of the major components of industrial activity, construction industries are the most variable and the cycles to which they are subject cause up-and down-swings in general prosperity.

In China's economic system building construction is much less important than in the West. In such large industrial towns as Shanghai, however, its significance is considerable.

Total permits.—The total number of building permits issued yearly in the International Settement and the French Concession indicates that building activity in these areas has varied widely (figure 1, page 225).[2] Peaks in activity occurred in 1894-1897, 1905-1906, 1914, and 1925, being 10, 8½. and 11 years apart. Lows in activity occurred in 1900, 1910-1911, 1919, and 1927, being 10½, 8½ and 8 years apart. Before 1927, the average time between peaks was 9 8 years; between lows, 9.0. After the low of 1927, there was a rapid upswing of activity until 1930. In 1931, the number of permits fell only slightly in spite of the hostilities which began in

* Acknowledgment is due to the Department of Public Works, Shanghai Municipal Council, and the Municipal Administration Department of the French Concession for their kindness in making available the data necessary for this study.

1 Cairncross, A K , The Glasgow Building Industry, 1870-1914, *Review of Economic Studies*, Vol. II. No. 1, page 15, October 1934.

Maverick, L.A., Cycles in Real Estate Activity (San Francisco), *Journal of Land and Public Utility Economics*, Vol. VIII, No 2, p. 199, May 1932.

Spensley, J. C., Urban Housing Problems, *Journal of Royal Statistical Society*, Vol. LXXXI, part II. p. 210, March 1918.

Warren, G.F. and Pearson, F. A , *Gold and Prices*, pp. 392-401, John Wiley and Sons, New York, 1935

Wenzelick, R., *The Real Estate Analyst*, St. Louis, Missouri, 1934.

2 The data for the French Concession include only permits for houses.

九一八之變，然全年營造執照數目減少甚微，一九三二年建築數目大見減削，一半由滬戰之直接影響，一半實由於整個工商業之不景氣。設一九三一年及一九三二年之情形較爲正常，則最近之環變高峯，應稍後於一九三〇及一九三一年。根據以前之變動，下旋當始於一九三一年至一九三二年間。低點宜在一九三六年至一九三七年之間。實際上一九三六年之低點較低於吾人所逆料者。一九三六年所發執照數目之少，與一九一〇年至一九一一年之低點相同而遜於一九一九年及一九二七年。

　　每口執照數目 —— 在資料足徵之期限內，公共租界及法租界內，以中西人口總數計，每口執照數目呈下降之勢（本頁第二圖）。新建築之數目不能與人口之激增並駕齊驅。當建築環變上旋之時，新建築之增加遠速於人口之增加，當其

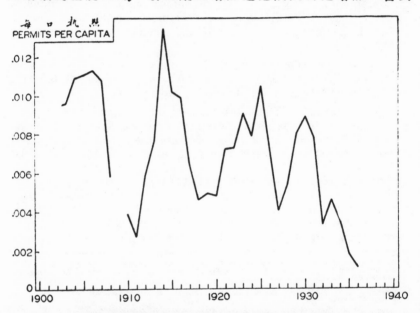

第二圖　　上海公共租界與法租界所發每口之營造執照數目，一九〇二年至一九三六年。

一九三六年所發者特少。

FIGURE 2.—NUMBER OF BUILDING PERMITS ISSUED PER CAPITA IN THE INTERNATIONAL SETTLEMENT AND THE FRENCH CONCESSION, SHANGHAI, 1902-1936

An unusually small number of permits was issued in 1936.

September 1931. In 1932, building was greatly curtailed partly because of these hostilities but partly also because of a very rapid drop in trade and industry as a whole. Had conditions in 1931 and 1932 been more normal, the most recent 'cycle' might have reached a peak a little later than 1930-1931. A down-swing starting about 1931-1932 would have been in accordance with previous movements. A low would have been expected about 1936-1937. The low level of 1936 was actually lower than might have been judged. As few permits were issued in 1936 as during the low of 1910-1911 and fewer than in 1919 and 1927.

Permits per capita.—During the period for which data are available, the number of permits issued per head of total population in the International Settlement and French Concession has tended downward (figure 2, page 228). The number of new buildings has not, on the whole, kept pace with the rapid growth of population. During up-swings of the building cycle, the number of buildings has increased much more rapidly than the population; during down-swings, much more slowly. In 1936, the number of permits issued per capita was the lowest ever recorded. The downward trend in the number of new buildings has, however, been partly counter-balanced by an upward trend in their size (figure 3).

Value per permit.—Data on the value of new buildings in the

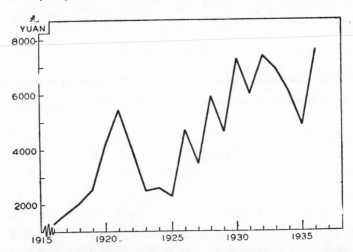

第三圖　上海公共租界每建築執照之價值，一九一六年至一九三六年。

以上行傾向而論，一九三〇年至一九三一年與一九三六年每一執照之價值並不反常。

FIGURE 3.—VALUE PER PERMIT FOR NEW BUILDING, INTERNATIONAL SETTLEMENT, SHANGHAI, 1916-1936

Considering the upward tendency, the value per permit was not abnormal either in 1930-1931 or in 1936.

下旋之時，則又較人口之增加遲緩特甚。一九三六年每口之
執照數目為有紀錄以來之最低者，一部份新建築數目之下行
趨勢，適足為新建築體積增大之上行趨勢所平衡（第二二九
頁第三圖）。

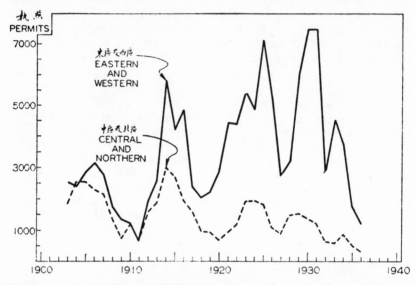

第四圖　　上海公共租界各段所發執照之數目，一九○三年至一九三六年。
東段及西段建築活動之變化較鉅且日益劇烈。

FIGURE 4.—NUMBER OF PERMITS ISSUED IN DISTRICTS OF THE INTERNATIONAL SETTLE-
MENT, SHANGHAI 1903-1936

Cyclical changes in building activity have had greater and increasing violence in the Eastern and
Western districts.

　　每執照之平均價值——一九一六年以後公共租界內新建
築之價值數字明示每執照價值有扶搖直上之趨勢，此固表明
建築體積增大，以及市場財產價值加增，而物價上漲與之不
無關係。

　　一般見解以為一九三○年及一九三一年之新建築之總值
高於尋常，實則是年之執照數目比之以前環變之諸高峯不得
謂之特高，以長期趨勢論，每執照之平均價值，亦不曾有異
常態。目前建築活動不為特低，實際上每執照之價值雖屬如
常，然執照數目較以前環變之諸低點亦遠不逮矣。

　　按區發給之執照——近二十五年來，公共租界內，東西

— 230 —

International Settlement since 1916 indicate a rapidly upward trend in the value per permit (figure 3, page 229). This reflects the increasing size of buildings and the increasing value of town property as a whole. To a small extent, it is due to rising prices.

The total value of new buildings constructed in 1930 and 1931 has often been considered exceptionally high. Actually, the number of permits granted in those years was not abnormal relative to previous peaks in the building cycle. The average value per permit was not abnormal, considering the long term tendency. At the present time, building activity is not considered exceptionally low. Actually, although the value per permit is not abnormal, the number of permits is very low even in comparison with previous lows in the building cycle.

Permits issued for various districts.—For the last twenty-five years, building has been more active in the Eastern and Western districts of the International Settlement than in the older Central and

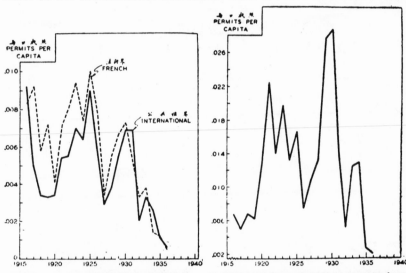

第五圖　上海公共租界及法租界每中國人中房營造執照之數目，一九一六年至一九三六年。

兩界述築活動頗相近似，一九三六年中房營造者頗少。

FIGURE 5.—NUMBER OF PERMITS FOR CHINESE HOUSES ISSUED PER HEAD OF CHINESE POPULATION. FRENCH AND INTERNATIONAL CONCESSIONS. SHANGHAI. 1916-1936.

Changes in building activity have been the same in both districts. Very few Chinese houses were built in 1936.

第六圖　上海公共租界及法租界每西人洋房營造之數目，一九一六年至一九三六年。

一九一六年以後，曾有兩次述築繁榮期，一九三六年之述築甚少。

FIGURE 6—NUMBER OF PERMITS ISSUED FOR FOREIGN HOUSES PER HEAD OF FOREIGN POPULATION. FRENCH AND INTERNATIONAL CONCESSIONS. SHANGHAI, 1916-1936

Since 1916, there have been two periods of active building. Very few houses were built in 1936.

兩區之建築活動，遠甚於中區及北區（第二三〇頁第四圖）。東西兩區環變之升降較大且日益劇烈，中段及北段之環變升降較小，且日漸緩和。一九三六年東西兩段之建築並不較中北兩段特多，大概以後營造之大部增加，將在東西兩地段內。

建築種類——一九一六年以後，公共租界內所發執照百分之七六為中房營造，而在法租界內者百分之八三為中房營造，各種建築之營造似均受劇烈環形變動之影響（第二三一頁第五，六圖）。

一九三六年所發之中房營造執照之數目奇少，然其建築環變之上下在公共租界及法租界頗形一致（第二三一頁第五圖）。

建築活動與國際貿易及物價變動之關係——一九三一年以前，上海國際貿易數量之變動，對建築活動之環變並無猛

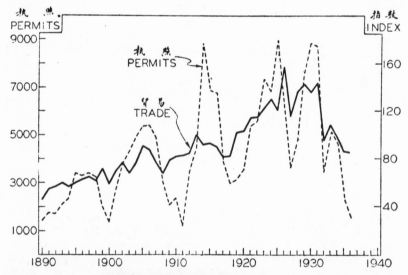

第七圖　上海公共租界營造執照之總數與上海國際貿易之總額指數，一八九〇年至一九三六年（一九一三年＝一〇〇）。

貿易數量之變動不足以解釋建築活動之高低變變。

FIGURE 7.—TOTAL NUMBER OF BUILDING PERMITS, INTERNATIONAL SETTLEMENT, SHANG-HAI, AND INDEX OF THE VOLUME OF SHANGHAI'S TOTAL FOREIGN TRADE, 1890-1936 (1913＝100).

Changes in the quantity of trade have not explained the recurring peaks and lows in building activity.

Northern (figure 4, page 230). Up- and down- swings in activity have had greater and increasing violence in the newer Eastern and Western districts but less and decreasing violence in the Central and Northern. In 1936, building was not much greater in the Eastern and Western districts than in the Central and Northern. Any general increase in construction will probably take place mostly in the Eastern and Western districts.

Types of building.—Since 1916, 76 per cent of the permits granted in the International Settlement have been for Chinese houses. In the French Concession since 1916, 83 per cent of the houses built have been Chinese. Foreign houses were much less numerous than Chinese houses. The construction of both types seems to have been subject to violent cyclical changes (figures 5, 6; page 231).

The number of permits issued for new Chinese houses was exceptionally low in 1936. Up- and down- swings in the building of these houses occur at the same time in the International Settlement as in the French Concession (figure 5, page 231).

Relation of building activity to foreign trade and changes in the price level.—Prior to 1931, changes in the quantity of Shanghai's

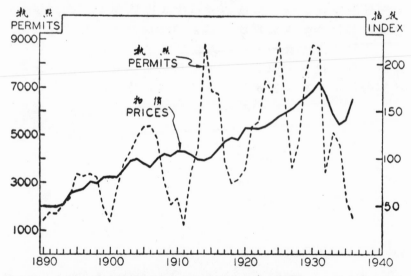

第八圖　上海公共租界營造執照之總數與上海物價指數，一八九〇年至一九三六年（一九一三＝一〇〇）。

物價水準之變動不足以解釋建築活動之變遷。

FIGURE 8.—TOTAL NUMBER OF BUILDING PERMITS, INTERNATIONAL SETTLEMENT, SHANGHAI, AND INDEX OF COMMODITY PRICES 1890-1936 (1913=100).

Changes in the price level have not explained the recurring peaks and lows in building activity.

烈之影響（第二三二頁第七圖）。可見此種變化實係對於建築需求估計過高或過低所形成，與國際貿易之變化，實無多大關係。而建築活動之變化其本身反足影響建築材料之貿易。

中國物價水準之變動亦不足以解釋建築活動之變化（第二三三頁第八圖）。

一九三一年之末及一九三二年建築多因戰事而中輟，其後雖時局平定，但建築不見增加，蓋其時正值國內物價慘跌，國際貿易銳減遂爾形成上海不景氣之現象。雖然，即如前述各點均維持常態，則根據以前之變動，一九三三年建築活動，亦應趨下流，而一九三六年至一九三七年為環變之低點。

物價慘落所造成種種嚴重之失調，現已因回漲而復元第二三八頁。且以各國貨幣計算之原料品價格日見上升，整個世界貿易蒸蒸日上，國際貿易數量，不致長似今日之低落。故在近數年內，建築活動基於以往變動或將上旋之際，不至有使建築低落於根據以前之環變而預測之水準以下之趨勢。

凡如目前之情勢，一般對新建築供給之需求增加，不甚顯然可察，建築似無利可牟，此期之前必曾一度缺乏建築而增加營造，此期後亦將缺乏建築復繼以營造激增之象也。

total foreign trade did not cause the violent cyclical changes in building activity (figure 7, page 232). These were the result of recurring over- and under-estimation of building requirements rather than of year to year changes in foreign trade. Changes in building activity may themselves have affected trade in building materials.

Changes in China's price level also did not explain changes in building activity (figure 8 page 233).

During the latter part of 1931 and in 1932, building was curtailed by military disturbances and even when these were removed, did not increase greatly because of the general depression in Shanghai brought about by a rapidly falling price level and diminishing foreign trade. But, even if general conditions had been more normal, a down-swing in building activity about 1933 and a low about 1936-1937 might have been expected on the basis of previous movements.

The serious maladjustments caused by rapidly falling prices have now been corrected (page 238). The quantity of foreign trade cannot be expected to remain for long as low as at present because raw material prices in terms of international currencies and world trade as a whole are increasing. The major factors which reduced building to a level even lower than that expected on the basis of cyclical changes may therefore not operate during the cyclical up-swing in building activity which, on the basis of previous movements, is to be expected within the next few years.

In periods such as the present, effective demand for new accomodation is not apparent. Building seems unprofitable. Such periods have occured before and have been followed by a scarcity of accomodation and rapid construction.

JOHN R. RAEBURN
HU KWOH HWA

上海物價之沙爾白克司答的斯脫指數[*]

本文旨在以上海物價編製一種指數，使其組織適與英國及美國之沙爾白克司答的斯脫指數相同[1]。所含之物品就現有資料，俾與沙爾白克氏所引用者相同，並各加以權量，庶各組重要性，亦與沙氏所擬者相等。所包含之三十一種物品中，中國土產品佔權量總數之百分之七十[2]。

以貨幣計算之物價

此新編之指數圖載於第二三八頁第一圖。物價自一九一三年二月上漲，至一九三一年六月計漲百分之九二。自一九三一年六月至一九三四年十月，指數跌落百分之二五。此低水平繼續延至一九三五年，隨後物價乃猛烈反漲，一九三七年五月指數較一九三五年十月高百分之四二，較一九三一年六月則高百分之七。

上海指數之一般變動，與華北指數之變動頗相符合[3]。華北指數包含一百另六種物品價格，而其中六十五爲製造品價格。

---

[*] 本文物價材料多係抄自國定稅則委員會特此鳴謝

1 司答的斯脫主筆一九一七年之批發物價皇家統計學會會刊第一百三十一卷第二篇第三三四至三四九頁一九一八年三月出版。

華而倫及皮而生：農家經濟第八十五期第二〇四九至二〇五三頁，一九三四年五月出版。

2 該指數包含下列物品之價格，刮弧內之數字即其權量：

素食類(八)；漢口小麥(三)；河南車黃豆(一)；浦口白豌豆(一)；牛莊高粱(一)；蘇同機粳米(一)；常熟河下機粳(一)。

肉食類(七)；上海鮮牛肉(二)；上海鮮羊肉(二)；上海鮮猪肉(二)；十四兩老牌飛鷹煉乳(一)。

糖及飲品類(四)；十號荷蘭赤糖(二)；爪哇咖啡(一)；屯溪珍眉綠茶(一)。

礦產類(七)；河南六河炭生鐵 二‧三三)；美，老 T.C.葉銅錠(一‧一七)；加拿大大鉛條(一‧一七)；日，杆島塊煤(二‧三三)。

纖維類(八)；通州棉(二‧二八六)；湖北白苧蔴(二‧二八六)；四川羊毛(二‧二八六)；滬白廠經(一‧一四三)。

雜項類(十一)；漢口生牛皮(二)；平祇荆油(一)；大連豆油(一)；上海生油(一)；上海鳥牌漆油(一)；美孚煤油(一)；純鹼(一)；湖南洪江製桐(一)；德國二成鹼油(一)；美國花族松(一)。

所採物價多爲每月十五號之市價，因材料缺乏之故，惟有採用一九一三年二月爲基期——即以一九一三年二月爲一〇〇，其權法則沿用沙氏所用之相對價格之平均法計算之。

3 何廉著：南開中國批發物價指數，中國經濟期刊第二卷第五期第四一一至四一七頁一九二八年四月出版，此指數現仍由南開經濟研究所賡續編製。

'SAUERBECK-STATIST' INDEX OF PRICES IN SHANGHAI*

An index of prices has been calculated for Shanghai which is similar in composition to the 'Sauerbeck-Statist' indices for England and the United States.[1] The commodities included are as nearly identical with those originally used by Sauerbeck as available data permit and they have been weighted so that the various groups have the same importance as in the original index. Quotations for 31 commodities are included. Of the total weight, 70 per cent is for commodities produced in China.[2]

Prices in terms of currency.

The index is shown in figure 1, page 238. Prices advanced from February 1913 to June 1931, by 92 per cent. From June 1931, to October 1934, they fell 25 per cent. The low level continued until October 1935 after which there was rapid reflation. The index for May 1937 was 42 per cent higher than for October 1935 and 7 per cent higher than for June 1931.

The general movements of the index for Shanghai have corresponded closely to those of the index for North China.[3] This index includes 106 quotations of which 65 are for manufactured goods.

The general movements of the index for Shanghai have not corresponded to those of the indices for England and the United States. In these countries, prices began to decline rapidly in 1929 while, in China, such a decline did not occur until the latter part of 1931. In May 1937, the index for England was lower than in

*Acknowledgment is due to the National Tariff Commission for their kindness in making available the data from which this index was calculated.

1   Editor of the *Statist*. Wholesale prices of commodities in 1917. *Journal of the Royal Statistical Society*, Volume LXXXI. Part II. pp. 334-349, March 1918.

Warren. G F. and Pearson. F.A., *Farm Economics*, No. 85. pp. 2049-2053, May 1934.

2   The following quotations were included. The weights are given in parenthesis.

Vegetable foods (8): Wheat, Hankow (3); soybeans, yellow, Honan (1); peas. Pukow (1); kaoliang. Newchang (1); rice, long Soochow (1); rice. long Changsu (1);

Animal food (7): Beef. fresh. Shanghai (2); mutton. fresh, Shanghai (2); pork. fresh. Shanghai (2); milk, condensed, "Eagle", 14 oz.-tin. 4 doz.-case, U.S.A. (1):

Sugar, coffee and tea (4); Sugar, brown. Dutch standard No. 10. Netherlands (2); coffee, second quality, Java (1); tea, green. Tungki (1):

Minerals (7); Pig iron. first quality, Liu Ho Kou, Honan, (2.33); copper, ingots. T.C., U.S.A. (1.17) lead bars, Canada (1.17); coal. lump. Japan. (2.33):

Textiles (8); Cotton, raw, Tungchow (2,286); ramie. Hupeh (2,286); wool, sheep's, Szechuan (2,286); silk, first and second choice, 13/15 dens Double Extra. Shanghai (1.143):

Sundry materials (11): Hides. cow. dried, Hankow (2); tallow, vegetable, Hupeh (1); soybean oil. Dairen (1); groundnut oil. Shanghai (1); paint oil "Bird". Shanghai (1); kerosene. "Brilliant", U.S.A. (1); soda ash. U.K. (1); wood oil, Huangk'ing, Hunan (1); indigo paste, 20 per cent. Germany (1); timber, Oregon pine, U.S.A. (1).

The quotations were gathered for one day about the 15th of each month. Lack of data made it necessary to use the quotations for only one month. February 1913 as a base—February 1913=100.

As for the original Sauerbeck index, the mean of relatives method of calculation was used.

3   Ho. Franklin L., The Nankai weekly index number of commodity prices at wholesale in China, *Chinese Economic Journal*, Vol. II. No. 5, pp. 411-417, May. 1928. This index is calculated currently by the Nankai Institute of Economics. Tientsin, China

上海物價指數之一般變動，並不與英國與美國者相治合。英美兩國物價於一九二九年開始猛跌，而我國物價至一九三一年之末始行猛跌。一九三七年五月英國指數較一九二九年者低百分之八。我國指數在一九三七年五月較一九二九年者高百分之三〇。較一九三一年者高百分之一二。

以金計算之物價

上海物價指數向與英國指數分道背馳，因上海所流通之國幣，與英鎊完全不同，故如將兩地物價以同一貨幣表示，

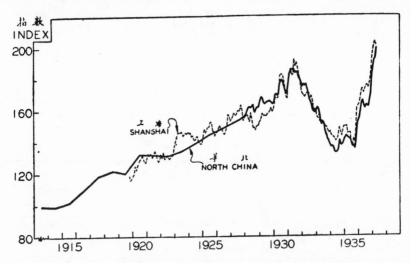

第一圖： 中國批發物價—上海之沙爾白克司答的司脫指數
與華北之南開指數，一九一三年，至一九三七年。

以貨幣計算之物價

上海，一九一三年二月＝一〇〇。華北，一九一三年＝一〇〇

自一九一三年至一九三一年上海物價上漲百分之九二，自一九三一年至一九三五年十月跌落百分之二五，自一九三五年十月至一九三七年五月物價復升百分之四二，華北物價之變動與之頗形一致．

FIGURE 1.—WHOLESALE PRICES IN CHINA—'SAUERBECK STATIST' INDEX FOR SHANGHAI AND NANKAI INDEX FOR NORTH CHINA, 1913-1937

Prices in currency

Shanghai, February 1913=100: North China, 1913=100

From 1913 to June 1931 prices in Shanghai rose 92 per cent; from June 1931 to October 1935, fell 25 per cent; from October 1935 to May 1937 rose 42 per cent. Movements in North China have been similar.

1929 by 8 per cent. In China, the index was 30 per cent higher than in 1929 and 12 per cent higher than in 1931.

Prices in terms of gold

The index for Shanghai followed a course entirely different from that of the index for England because Shanghai's money was entirely different from sterling. If prices are expressed in terms of the same money in both places, the similarity of movement is obvious. The indices of prices expressed in terms of gold are shown in figure 2, page 239.[4] In spite of differences in the type of currency used,

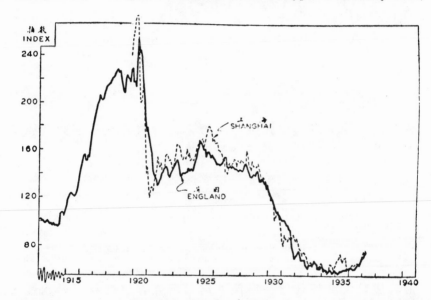

第二圖： 上海與英國批發物價之沙爾白克，司答的斯脫指 ，數一九一三年至一九三七年。

以金元計算之物價

上海，一九一三年二月＝一〇〇。英國，一九一三年＝一〇〇

上海與英國以金計算之物價均循一相似之路線而變動

FIGURE 2.—'SAUERBECK STATIST' INDEX OF WHOLESALE PRICES FOR SHANGHAI AND ENGLAND, 1913-1937

Prices in gold

Shanghai. February 1913=100: England. 1913=100

Prices expressed in terms of gold have followed a similar course in Shanghai and England.

---

4   Index of prices in terms   =   Index of prices in terms of currency (1913=100)
    of gold (1913=100)   Index of the price of gold in terms of currency (1913=100)

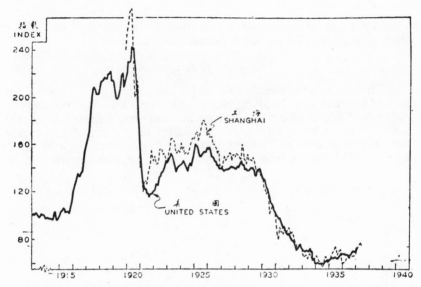

第三圖： 上海與美國批發物價之沙爾白克，司答的斯脫指
數，一九一三年至一九三七年。

以金計算之物價

上海，一九一三年二月＝一○○○ 美國，一九一三年＝一○○

上海與美國以金計算之物價循一相似之路線而變動

FIGURE 3.–'SAUERBECK-STATIST' INDEX OF WHOLESALE PRICES FOR SHANGHAI AND
THE UNITED STATES. 1913 1937

Prices in gold

Shanghai, February 1913=100 United States, 1913=100

Prices expressed in ter ns of gold have followed a similar course in Shanghai and the United States

則其變動之共同性常甚明顯。第二三九頁第二圖 [4] 乃兩國之
以金計算之物價指數，雖兩國之貨幣種類，關稅政策，國際
平衡，正金移動，利率高低，銀行管理，稅賦制度以及外國
公債均不相同，然以金計算之兩指數仍循同一途徑。一九三
七年五月上海指數爲七七，英國指數爲七五，雖兩者之基期
均遠在一九一三年，但兩者極少差別之處。

4
以 金 計 算 之 物 價 指 ＝ 以 貨 幣 計 算 之 物 價 指 數
數（一九一三年＝一○○）　　（一九一三年＝一○○）
　　　　　　　　　　　　　以 貨 幣 計 算 之 金 價 指 數
　　　　　　　　　　　　　（一九一三年＝一○○）

in tariff policies, trade balances, bullion movements, interest rates, bank management, taxation systems and foreign debts the indices of prices in terms of gold followed much the same course in Shanghai as in England. In May 1937, the index for Shanghai was 77, that for England, 75. Although the base periods for both were as far away as 1913, there was little difference between the indices.

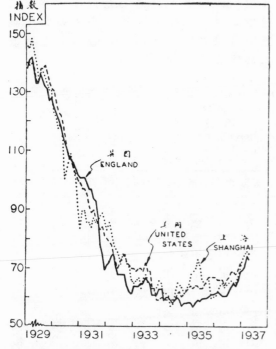

第四圖：上海，英
國，及美國批發
物價之沙爾白克
，司答的斯脫指
數，一九二九年
至一九三七年。

以金計算之物價

上海, 一九一三年二月
＝一○○
英國及美國, 一九一三年
＝一○○

自一九二九年直至一九三四
年以金計算之物價慘跌甚速
，一九三四年後物價趨勢始
向上行．

FIGURE 4.—'SAUERBECK-STATIST' INDEX OF WHOLESALE PRICES FOR SHANGHAI, ENGLAND AND THE UNITED STATES, 1929-1937

Prices in gold

Shanghai, February 1913=100: England and the United States, 1913=100

Prices expressed in terms of gold declined rapidly from 1929 until 1934. Since then, the trend has been upward.

The course of prices in terms of gold has been much the same in the United States as in England and China. The amount of gold which it would have been necessary to exchange for the group of commodities included in Sauerbeck's index has varied in the same way in all three countries. Divergencies in the movements of prices in terms of yuan, sterling and U.S. dollars have been due to changes in the prices of gold in terms of these currencies—their gold contents.

美國以金計算之物價，亦與英國，中國者循同一途徑。沙氏指數包含之物品所值金量之變動，在三國可稱一致。以國幣，英鎊及美金計算之物價變動彼此間形成之分歧，咸因以各自貨幣計算之金價之變異與夫各貨幣之法定含金量之變動不等之故也。

一九三五年十一月以後，以國幣計算之金價已較為固定，因國幣對含有一定金價之貨幣之換價保持不變，如此類關係能永久維持，則以國幣計算之物價，將循以金計算之物價趨勢而變，目前此項趨勢係屬上行。

第一表：一　上海批發物價之沙爾白克司答的司脫指數
一九一三年二月＝一〇〇
以貨幣計算之物價

TABLE 1.— 'SAUERBECK–STATIST' INDEX NUMBERS OF WHOLESALE PRICES IN
SHANGHAI, FEBRUARY 1913=100
Prices in currency

	一月 Jan.	二月 Feb.	三月 Mar.	四月 Apr.	五月 May	六月 June	七月 July	八月 Aug.	九月 Sept.	十月 Oct.	士月 Nov.	兰月 Dec.	年平均 Year
1919	—	—	—	—	—	—	—	—	—	119	116	117	—
1920	118	120	125	122	125	127	129	129	132	129	128	127	126
1921	130	133	132	133	131	130	132	134	133	130	127	128	131
1922	132	130	134	129	130	130	132	129	130	131	131	136	131
1923	140	143	145	146	146	146	146	144	144	146	145	146	145
1924	145	146	143	144	141	141	143	144	140	139	138	139	142
1925	144	148	146	148	149	149	153	152	146	147	144	146	148
1926	146	149	150	149	148	146	144	146	150	158	156	153	150
1927	154	156	158	156	157	159	160	159	163	160	153	155	158
1928	156	157	154	152	158	153	148	149	147	150	150	152	152
1929	153	155	158	156	157	156	158	158	159	162	159	160	158
1930	163	168	168	167	170	182	183	182	179	174	169	167	173
1931	176	182	186	182	182	192	188	190	187	182	178	172	183
1932	170	169	168	170	171	170	166	169	166	160	160	159	166
1933	156	155	153	152	153	152	150	149	149	147	145	146	151
1934	144	143	143	142	140	141	144	119	146	143	147	150	144
1935	149	150	145	145	146	141	136	142	140	144	161	162	147
1936	164	166	171	173	170	172	175	176	174	176	181	190	174
1937	197	200	203	201	205								

雷伯恩
胡國華

Since November 1935, the price gold in terms of yuan has been relatively fixed because the yuan has been kept almost constant in value in terms of currencies with constant or almost constant gold values. If these relationships are maintained prices in yuan will follow the trend of prices in gold. At present, this is upward.

第二表，一　上海批發物價之沙爾白克司答的司脫指數

一九一三年二月＝一〇〇

以金計算之物價

TABLE 2.— 'SAUERBECK—STATIST' INDEX NUMBERS OF WHOLESALE PRICES IN SHANGHAI, FEBRUARY 1913=100

Prices in gold

	一月 Jan.	二月 Feb.	三月 Mar.	四月 Apr.	五月 May	六月 June	七月 July	八月 Aug.	九月 Sept.	十月 Oct.	士月 Nov.	士月 Dec.	年平均 Year
1919	—	—	—	—	—	—	—	—	—	—	—	—	—
1920	270	272	273	245	220	197	202	214	211	240	254	259	—
1921	146	128	119	128	129	126	132	137	143	187	169	139	217
1922	149	143	143	145	155	156	156	151	152	154	147	146	136
1923	152	156	165	164	163	160	155	152	154	149	144	148	149
1924	154	158	151	152	152	151	154	158	162	165	152	161	157
												165	157
1925	168	170	162	166	171	174	180	180	177	175	167	168	
1926	165	165	166	159	159	158	156	152	154	142	142	139	172
1927	145	149	145	149	149	152	152	146	151	150	149	151	155
1928	151	150	148	147	159	154	147	146	142	150	146	146	149
1929	146	145	149	144	140	134	137	137	135	133	131	130	149
													138
1930	122	121	117	119	115	100	103	106	109	104	101	91	109
1931	84	80	90	86	86	84	87	86	85	88	89	86	86
1932	83	86	82	79	76	75	71	75	74	72	70	66	76
1933	65	66	67	63	67	68	65	64	62	62	63	66	65
1934	65	61	61	61	57	58	61	65	64	63	61	63	62
1935	64	68	69	70	73	71	66	65	65	66	59	60	66
1936	60	62	64	65	63	64	65	66	65	65	65	70	65
1937	73	74	76	75	77						67		

JOHN R. RAEBURN

HU KWOH-HWA

金之價格與價值

　　<u>金之價值</u>（後簡稱金值）乃根據其交換其他物品或應有其他物品之量而計算者，其價值恆在變動，雖逐月之變動量較小於一般原料品者，而其逐年之變動至爲可觀。英國根據沙爾白克，司答的司脫指數所含之三十五種原料品而計算之金之價值自一八四九年至一八七三年跌落百分之三四，自一八七三年至一八九六年漲百分之八三，自一八九六年至一九二〇年又跌百分之六八，自一九二〇年至一九二一年漲百分之五三，自一九二一年至一九二五年跌百分之九，自一九二五年至一九二九年漲百分之一七，自一九二九年至一九三四年漲百分之一二六，自一九三四年至一九三六年跌百分之五第二四四頁第一圖。

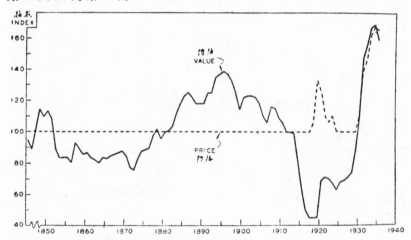

　　第一圖　英國以基本物品計算之金價格及金價之指數一八四五年————一九三六年，一九一三＝一〇〇

　　　　政府雖能使金之價格於相常時期內保持鑑定，但金之價值仍繼續大爲變動，金之價值於一九三四年曾達其最高水準

FIGURE 1.–INDEX NUMBERS OF THE PRICE OF GOLD AND OF THE VALUE OF GOLD IN TERMS OF BASIC COMMODITIES, ENGLAND, 1845-1936, 1913=100

　　Although the government was able to keep the price of gold fixed during certain periods, the value of gold continued to vary widely. The value of gold was at its highest level in 1934.

　　全世界以基本物計算之金值之改變，幾一例相同，中國之金值向與英美者循同一途徑（第二四五頁第三圖）。

　　<u>金之價格</u>（後簡稱金價）乃根據各國不同之貨幣而計算

THE PRICES AND VALUE OF GOLD

The value of gold is measured by exchanging gold, or the title to gold, for other commodities. The value of gold is continually changing and, although month to month changes are small as compared to those of most raw materials, year to year changes are considerable. In England, the value of gold measured in terms of the 35 raw materials included in the 'Sauerbeck-Statist' index fell 34 per cent from 1849 to 1873, rose 83 per cent from 1873 to 1896, fell 68 per cent from 1896 to 1920, rose 53 per cent from 1920 to 1921, fell 9 per cent from 1921 to 1925, rose 17 per cent from 1925 to 1929, rose 126 per cent from 1929 to 1934, and fell 5 per cent from 1934 to 1936 (figure 1, page 244).

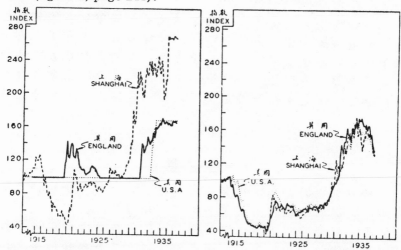

第二圖　上海英國及美國之金之價格指數

一九一三年——一九三七年
一九一三年＝一〇〇

FIGURE 2.—INDEX NUMBERS OF THE PRICES OF GOLD. SHANGHAI. ENGLAND AND THE UNITED STATES. 1913-1937
1913=100

第三圖　上海英國及美國以基本物品計算之金之價值指數一九一三年——一九三七年

上海一九一三年二月＝一〇〇
英國及美國一九一三年＝一〇〇

FIGURE 3.—INDEX NUMBERS OF THE VALUE OF GOLD IN TERMS OF BASIC COMMODITIES. SHANGHAI. ENGLAND AND THE UNITED STATES. 1913-1937
Shanghai, February 1913=100
England and U.S.A., 1913-1937

金之價格曾循各種不同途徑而變動，但上列三處金價值之變動殆一致金值自一九二九年至一九三四年約漲一二六，自一九三七年五月約跌二〇。

The prices of gold have followed different courses but the value of gold has changed in much the same way in all three places. The value of gold rose by about 126 per cent from 1929 to 1934 and fell by about 20 per cent from 1934 to May 1937.

Changes in the value of gold in terms of basic commodities as a group are always much the same the world over. The value of

者，凡金本位國家，其政府必使金價保持不變。英國自一八一六年六月至一九一四年八月，及自一九二五年五月至一九三一年九月每兩純金之價格爲八十四先令九又四分之三便士，自一九三五年六月以後金價恆等於一四一先令。美國自一八七八年至一九三三年每兩純金之價格固定爲二〇・六七美元，一九三四年二月後重定爲三十五美元，而金之價值則罕有能保持兩年而不變者。中國金價於一九三五年十一月以後始稍能保持不變，以前中國所保持不變者，乃銀價而非金價，故金之國幣價格隨以金計算之白銀價格而變。

　　一般人士對於金價與金值常相混亂，近年以各國貨幣計算之金價均屬上漲，金值亦特高。惟當一九二九年至一九三四年間各國金值猛漲之際，金價上漲之時期與數量各國不同。英國金價之上漲始於一九三一年九月至一九三七年五月計漲百分之六十七，特當時之金值已較一九二九年高百分之八〇。

固定金之價格

　　於可能之時期內，固定以各貨幣計算之金價大可減少國際匯率之波動，債務亦以黃金決定，但以物品計算之金值繼續變動，故債務之償還，雖爲昔日所借之金量之償還而不得謂係原來債項之物品價值之償還矣。一九二九年後因金之價值暴漲，以金訂立之債務之清償殊爲困難，而常有不能清償者。反之，目前金值將跌，債務清償便利，借債者實首蒙其利，且清償旣易，償還者亦自較多而速也，故此時誠爲中國借債之良機也。

　　如各國政府根據其貨幣以固定金價，則其貨幣之價值將隨金值而上下，當國際匯價較爲穩定時，則借貸雙方之關係，以及其他國內外重要經濟關係因金值之變異而時呈翻覆之現象。

　　故凡貨幣改革必須籌貨幣物品價值之統制，蓋若僅以某一種物品如金爲貨幣本位時，其貨幣之物品價值勢難固定不

gold in China has followed the same course as the value of gold in England and the United States (figure 3, page 245).

The prices of gold are measured in terms of different national currencies. When a country is on the gold standard, the government keeps the price of gold constant. In England, the price of gold was 84s. 9¾d. per fine ounce from May 1821 until August 1914, and from May 1925 until September 1931. It has been fairly constant at about 141s. since June 1935. In the United States, the price of gold was fixed at $20.67 per fine ounce from 1878 until March 1933, and at U.S.$35 since February 1934. The value of gold has hardly ever been constant from one year to the next. In China, the price of gold has been kept comparatively constant only since November 1935. Before that date, it was the price of silver that China kept constant, so the yuan price of gold varied with the gold price of silver.

The price of gold is often confused with the value of gold. In recent years, the prices of gold in terms of most currencies have risen and the value of gold has also been abnormally high. But, while the value of gold rose rapidly in all countries from 1929 until 1934, the price of gold advanced at different times and by different amounts in various countries. In England the price of gold began to rise in September 1931. By May 1937, it had advanced by 67 per cent, but the value of gold was then 80 per cent higher than in 1929.

Fixing the price of gold

During such periods as it was feasible, fixing the price of gold in terms of different currencies greatly reduced fluctuations in exchange rates between countries. Debts were fixed in terms of gold. But the value of gold in terms of commodities continued to vary. The repayment of debts meant the repayment of the amount of gold originally borrowed but it scarcely ever meant the repayment of the commodity value of the original loan. After 1929 it was hard, indeed often impossible, to repay debts contracted in gold because the value of gold was rising. On the other hand, the present time appears to be favourable to borrowers as the value of gold will probably fall, making debts easier to repay. The easier their repayment, the more likely will they be repaid. This is a good time for China to borrow.

If governments fix and keep fixed the prices of gold in terms of their respective currencies, the values of these currencies will fluctuate up and down with the value of gold. While exchange rates between countries will be more constant, the relationships between debtors and creditors and many other important economic relationships, both domestic and international, will be upset from decade to decade, because of these fluctuations of the value of gold.

變。設各國以貨幣計算之金價能同時作近乎等量之漲落時，則貨幣之價值可以不變，國際匯價亦得穩定。如此庶可避免一九二九年以後金本位國及一九三一年後中國所受之重要經濟紊亂。惟欲實施此方案非各國共同密切合作不爲功，目前似方力倡不息，實施國際管理之前，各國首宜使國內物價機構調整完善。現英美兩國之物價關係已趨調整，中國之調整已臻完善。實行之際任何加入此國際管理之國家必須能繼續控制其金價，此舉雖稍難於固定金價於金值下落之際，然較固定金價於金值上漲之際則甚易矣。同時應力求節省政府支出，限制紙幣之發行，與採用金本位或銀本位時初無二致。

金值下落之時期，固定金價較爲易行，因此而物價高漲，生產與貿易受其卵翼而勃興。雖然，吾人慎勿忘金值必將再漲，且卽使仍有長期之下落，其每年下落之程度亦逐年不同也。

雷伯恩
胡國華

Plans for monetary reform should provide for control of the commodity values of currencies. These will never be constant if a single commodity, gold, is made the standard. Currencies could be constant in value and, in addition, exchange rates between currencies stabilized, provided the prices of gold in terms of these currencies were raised and lowered by proportionately equal amounts and always at the same time. This would make it possible to avoid most of the major disturbances experienced since 1929 in gold standard countries and since 1931 in China. Close international cooperation would be necessary but already this seems to be developing at key points. Within each country it would be necessary to have a well adjusted price structure before such a plan was put in operation. In England and the United States, the price structure is approaching adjustment. In China, the adjustment is already good. Any country entering into the international plan would also have continually to be able to control its currency price for gold. This would be slightly more difficult than keeping the price of gold fixed when the value of gold is falling, but much more easy than trying to keep the price fixed when the value is rising. It would be essential to limit government expenditures and note issues just as under a fixed gold or silver standard.

During periods such as the present when the value of gold is falling, it is easier to fix the price of gold, thereby allowing commodity prices to rise and permitting the rapid expansion of production and trade which rising prices foster. It is well, however, to bear in mind that, in the future, the value of gold may rise again and that, even should it continue for a long time to fall, the rate of fall will vary from year to year.

JOHN R. RAEBURN
HU KWOH-HWA

江蘇武進農民所付及所得之物價 *

作物產量之估計常因氣候變動發生必有之修正，農產品價格亦因而時時改變，縱使吾人於任何一地區中將農民售出各種農產品所得之物價平均之而編成一物價指數，該指數之變動仍巨。當作物歉收時，物價恆上漲，但農民所能出售者甚少，當作物豐穫時，價格恆下跌，但農民所售出者甚多。

農民購進之物品，種類繁多。由此等購進物品之價格，平均之而編為一指數，其變動較由售出物品所得物價指數為小。布類，火油，火柴及其他高貴食品之價格受氣候之影響遠不若米，麥，及其他作物類之甚。決定製造品及運銷品價格之成本，其變動遠不著作物生產成本之甚。

農民所付出之現金工資，其變動亦不若農民所得物價變動之巨。捐稅之征收乃用以酬付公務員工之薪金與工資者，故其變動亦稍遲於作物價格。

倘作物產量之變動為造成物價變動之唯一主要因子，則農民所得物價與工資，捐稅，及所付物價之差數，逐年常不致差別特大。歉收之影響恆為高價所平衡，而豐收之效果亦為低價所抵制。捨吾人所不能控制之氣候影響外，實尚有其他因子足以引起物價變動過程中之騷動者在，國幣價值之改變是也。一九三一年前數年中世界白銀之價值漸次跌落。白銀為中國貨幣本位，其與他種物品之交換價值日漸跌落，以白銀計算之物價自必日漸上漲矣。[2] 一九一三年至一九三一年，江蘇武進農民售出穀類及蠶繭所得之價格，上漲百分之七十四。農民所付物價上漲百分之七十五（第二五二頁第一圖）。因上漲之勢漸而不猛，故並未形成武進物價關係之騷動。作物荒歉時，農民所得物價恆高於所付物價，而作物豐

---

* 武進農民所得及所付物價原係張履鸞氏所搜集，並曾著有"江蘇武進物價之研究"一文，一九三二年六月由實業部國際貿易局刊為該局小冊第十九號，一九三三年復編為金陵大學叢刊第八號 新號）。此後仍由特約商號於每月十五日繼續報告物價，茲根據卜克氏所著之"中國土地利用"（尚在印行中）及熟諳該處情形者之意見，得將原編物價指數重新加權編製，俾使每物品依其實際之重要性，使物價趨勢更為顯著。

2 關於中國及國外白銀價值之關係，詳情請參閱"經濟統計"第四期第一六一頁至一七五頁，一九三七年二月。

PRICES PAID AND RECEIVED BY FARMERS IN WUCHIN, KIANGSU[1]

Changes in the weather make necessary continual revision of estimates of crop production thereby causing continual changes in the prices of farm products. Even when the prices received for the various products sold by farmers in any district are averaged together to make an index of prices, this index fluctuates widely. When crops are poor, prices usually rise, but farmers have less to sell. When crops are good, prices usually fall, but farmers have more to sell.

Purchases by farmers are of numerous kinds. The prices paid for them when averaged together make an index which is less varible than that of prices received for sales. The weather does not determine the price of cloth, kerosene, matches and some of the luxury foods as much as it determines the prices of rice, wheat and other grains. The prices of manufactured goods and of goods brought from elsewhere are determined by costs which are much less variable than crop production costs.

Cash wages paid by farmers are also less variable than prices received by farmers. Taxes are levied chiefly to pay wages and salaries and are less variable than crop prices.

If changes in crop production were the only major factors causing prices to change, the balance between prices received and wages, taxes and prices paid might not differ very greatly from year to year. The effects of small crops would be to some extent counterbalanced by higher prices: large crops, by lower prices. There are, however, certain disturbances of major significance which arise, not because of such an uncontrollable thing as the weather, but because of changes in the value of the national currency. For many years prior to 1931, there was a world-wide, gradual decline in the value of silver. Silver, China's currency, was becoming less valuable in exchange for other commodities: prices in terms of silver were rising.[2] From 1913 to 1931, prices received by farmers for cereals and silk coccoons in Wuchin, Kiangsu, rose 74 per cent and prices paid by farmers, 75 per cent (figure 1, page 252). Because the advance was gradual, it caused no major disturbances to price relationships in Wuchin.

---

1   Prices paid and received by farmers in Wuchin were originally collected by Chang Lu-luan and published in "Farm Prices in Wuchin." Kiangsu, Booklet Series No. 19 Bureau of Foreign Trade. Ministry of Industry, June 1932, and "Farm Prices in Wuchin", University of Nanking Bulletin No. 8 (New Series), 1933   The price series have been kept up to date by reports from merchants on prices for the 15th of each month. On the basis of data collected for J. Lossing Buck's 'Land Utilization in China' now in process of publication and the opinion of men familiar with the district it has been possible to reconstruct the original index numbers of prices so as to make month to month changes more comparable and give to individual commodities weights more nearly corresponding with their actual importance.

2   For a fuller discussion of the connection between the value of silver in China and abroad, see Economic Facts, No. 4, pp. 161-175, February 1937.

收時，結果適得其反。雇工所得之現金工資漲進緩於物價，故工資之支付日漸便易，反之，物價漲進勝於工資，則雇工之購買力減低。捐稅變動甚於工資，但長期之結果，其增加之數額幾等於工資矣。概言之，物價水準上漲對於農民不無裨益。

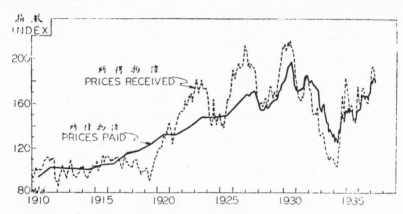

第一圖　江蘇武進農民所得之穀類及蠶繭價格與所付物價之指數，一九一〇至一九三七年，一九一〇至一九一四年＝一〇〇。

作物歉收之年，農民所得物價恒高於所付物價，但作物豐收之年則反是。惟自一九三一年至一九三四年因物價水準普遍下跌，作物收成雖不特殊良好，而農民所得物價跌落較所付物價為速。

FIGURE 1.—INDEX NUMBERS OF PRICES RECEIVED BY FARMERS FOR CEREALS AND SILK COCCOONS AND PRICES PAID BY FARMERS FOR THEIR PURCHASES. WUCHIN, KIANGSU. 1910-1937, 1910-14 = 100

In years of poor crops, prices received by farmers have usually been higher than prices paid and, in years of good crops, lower. But, from 1931 to 1934, when the general price level fell, prices received fell more rapidly than prices paid, although crops were not especially good.

　　一九三一年九月以後世界白銀價值猛漲，中國貨幣之交換價值遂日益增高，但因其上漲過速以致形成物價關係上之重大騷動也。

　　自一九三一年九月至一九三四年四月，上海基本物品之價格跌落百分之二十四，農民所付物價跌百分之三十二，而所得物價却慘跌百分之四十三。一九三三年夏季作物及一九三三年至翌年之冬季作物，收成並不特豐，大豆之收成雖較良好，但在武進實無足輕重耳。農民所得物價結果仍趨於極低之水準，較之農民所付物價誠低落多多矣。同時捐稅工資跌落不若農民所得物價之甚，故其支付日益艱難，較之昔日易於支付不啻霄壞（第二五九頁第四圖）。此等種種現象乃

Prices received were higher than prices paid when crops were poor, lower when crops were good. Cash wages paid to hired men advanced more slowly than prices so that wages became more and more easy to pay. On the other hand, they bought less for those who earned them. Taxes varied more than wages, but, in the long run, increased only by about the same amount. The rising price level was not unfavorable for farmers.

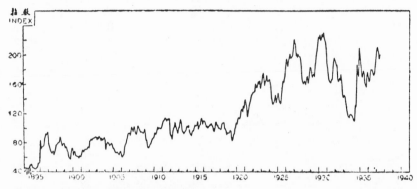

第二圖　江蘇武進農民所得穀類價格之指數，一八九四至一九三七年，一九一〇至一九一四年＝一〇〇。

國幣之物品價值改變，使穀類價格上漲直至一九三一年為止，一九三一至一九三四年復行下跌，一九三四年後又行上漲突，至此等趨勢上下不規則之變動主由於物作情形不同耳。

FIGURE 2.—INDEX NUMBERS OF PRICES RECEIVED BY FARMERS FOR CEREALS, WUCHIN, KIANGSU 1894-1937, 1910-14 = 100

Changes in the commodity value of the yuan caused cereal prices to rise until 1931, fall from 1931 to 1934 and rise again thereafter. Changes in crop conditions caused irregular fluctuations above and below these trends.

After September 1931 there was a rapid, world-wide advance in the value of silver. China's money became more and more valuable in exchange for commodities. The advance was so rapid that it caused major disturbances to price relationships.

From September 1931 to April 1934, prices of basic commodities in Shanghai fell 24 per cent. Prices paid by farmers fell 32 per cent but prices received by them fell 43 per cent. The summer crops of 1933 and the winter crops of 1933-34 were not abnormally large, except for soybeans which are relatively unimportant in Wuchin. Yet, prices received by farmers fell to a very low level. As compared to prices paid, prices received by farmers became very low. Taxes and cash wages did not decline as much as prices received by farmers so that their payment became more and more difficult instead of more and more easy as formerly (figure 4, page

第一表 江蘇武進農民所得穀類及蠶繭價格之加權總合指數
一九一〇年至一九一四年(相當月)＝一〇〇

TABLE 1.—WEIGHTED AGGREGATIVE INDEX NUMBERS OF PRICES RECEIVED BY FARMERS FOR CEREALS AND SILK COCOONS, WUCHIN, KIANGSU.[3]

1910-14 (corresponding months) = 100

	一月 Jan.	二月 Feb.	三月 Mar.	四月 Apr.	五月 May	六月 June	七月 July	八月 Aug.	九月 Sept.	十月 Oct.	十一月 Nov.	十二月 Dec.	年平均 Year
1910	95	93	95	98	102	100	101	101	100	100	102	105	99
1911	109	109	111	112	111	108	110	109	111	110	92	90	107
1912	90	86	94	98	99	104	100	98	95	92	99	99	96
1913	104	109	104	98	95	96	93	94	97	98	102	103	99
1914	101	104	97	95	93	93	96	98	98	101	104	103	98
1915	103	103	108	99	102	103	104	111	113	107	112	112	106
1916	113	111	110	108	110	108	110	110	111	110	112	109	110
1917	107	103	101	105	111	111	106	108	104	104	104	102	106
1918	102	108	109	109	109	102	102	100	96	99	98	99	103
1919	99	102	101	94	90	92	99	100	106	108	113	112	101
1920	118	119	120	119	122	130	131	128	135	133	140	143	128
1921	137	134	123	128	133	139	141	145	150	150	152	152	140
1922	153	154	162	159	158	162	167	164	169	161	167	170	162
1923	177	181	175	168	174	176	181	173	173	172	174	170	174
1924	163	150	145	140	141	164	146	149	140	145	147	151	148
1925	143	140	141	138	148	155	164	162	165	170	181	190	158
1926	185	182	189	191	196	191	192	193	194	201	211	207	194
1927	206	193	196	191	195	193	192	191	188	178	165	161	187
1928	158	160	161	147	158	163	165	157	160	168	176	175	163
1929	170	164	171	167	166	176	182	191	195	204	210	205	184
1930	213	207	209	214	210	216	210	208	206	198	184	179	204
1931	172	166	165	163	163	167	165	176	182	185	182	177	172
1932	172	172	158	151	150	152	150	157	148	136	131	132	151
1933	135	133	127	122	116	114	110	110	112	112	111	110	118
1934	108	105	104	104	121	121	147	167	156	151	183	179	137
1935	170	161	154	157	159	156	145	146	143	155	176	165	158
1936	160	162	170	175	173	167	162	161	160	167	174	190	168
1937	194	192	187	179	186	176							

物品種類及其編製物價指數時所用之權數:

白 米	1000 升	大 麥	400 升
粳 稻	1000 升	黃 豆	500 升
糯 稻	1500 升	蠶 豆	300 升
小 麥	2000 升	乾 繭	60 斤

3 The commodities included and their respective weights were as follows:-

Rice, white	1000 shen	Barley, hulless	400 shen
Rice, unhulled late	4000 shen	Soybeans	500 shen
Rice, glutinous	1500 shen	Broad beans	300 shen
Wheat	2000 shen	Silk cocoons, dried	60 catties

第二表　江蘇武進農民所得穀類價格之加權總合指數
一九一〇年至一九一四年(相當月)=一〇〇[4]

TABLE 2.—WEIGHTED AGGREGATIVE INDEX NUMBERS OF PRICES RECEIVED BY FARMERS FOR CEREALS, WUCHIN, KIANGSU.[4]
1910-14 (corresponding months)=100

	一月 Jan.	二月 Feb.	三月 Mar.	四月 Apr.	五月 May.	六月 June	七月 July	八月 Aug.	九月 Sept.	十月 Oct.	十一月 Nov.	十二月 Dec.	年平均 Year
1894	46	45	45	45	45	44	44	45	46	49	50	51	46
1895	47	46	46	45	45	44	46	47	48	52	52	53	48
1896	84	72	75	75	75	77	86	89	93	91	94	95	84
1897	78	75	72	69	68	65	69	69	63	68	71	77	70
1898	78	79	81	80	82	88	83	79	76	78	79	80	80
1899	73	76	74	70	68	62	58	58	58	68	73	72	68
1900	63	68	68	62	63	62	61	61	59	63	61	61	63
1901	66	70	70	67	70	71	71	71	71	73	74	73	71
1902	82	83	85	84	85	86	87	87	87	88	88	84	86
1903	87	85	89	88	87	83	87	83	85	85	87	84	86
1904	70	77	80	81	80	79	76	78	79	80	76	73	77
1905	72	70	67	66	67	67	66	65	64	68	69	65	67
1906	60	60	64	64	74	78	79	84	89	93	94	94	78
1907	90	96	102	100	95	101	103	95	93	92	99	103	98
1908	102	98	94	94	96	94	93	93	95	99	91	83	95
1909	84	76	72	73	74	78	78	81	85	86	86	86	80
1910	93	90	92	96	102	98	100	100	99	99	101	106	98
1911	110	110	113	114	112	109	112	111	113	112	92	89	108
1912	90	84	94	100	101	108	102	100	96	92	101	100	97
1913	107	112	106	98	94	95	92	93	96	96	102	102	99
1914	101	103	95	92	91	89	94	97	96	100	104	103	97
1915	104	103	109	99	102	104	104	112	114	105	110	110	106
1916	110	107	105	101	103	100	102	102	105	104	106	103	104
1917	102	97	95	100	108	108	103	104	100	100	99	98	101
1918	98	106	107	107	108	99	99	96	91	94	93	93	99
1919	93	97	95	86	82	94	91	92	99	101	107	106	94
1920	112	114	114	113	116	125	126	122	131	128	136	139	123
1921	132	129	115	121	126	134	136	141	146	146	149	149	135
1922	149	151	161	156	155	160	165	161	166	155	161	163	159
1923	171	176	167	159	164	166	173	164	165	165	167	164	167
1924	157	142	138	132	134	137	142	146	135	141	143	148	141
1925	139	135	137	133	146	154	165	163	166	172	185	196	158
1926	190	185	194	196	202	197	197	199	200	209	222	217	201
1927	215	199	203	197	202	200	199	198	195	183	168	164	194
1928	161	164	165	160	163	169	172	162	165	174	184	183	168
1929	176	170	177	173	171	183	191	202	206	218	225	223	193
1930	228	220	223	229	224	231	224	220	217	209	191	184	217
1931	176	167	166	163	163	167	167	182	190	197	194	190	177
1932	186	187	170	164	165	169	166	174	163	149	142	143	165
1933	146	144	136	129	121	119	115	115	118	119	119	118	125
1934	116	113	111	110	131	139	161	188	176	171	209	202	152
1935	190	182	170	173	179	175	162	159	156	170	177	169	172
1936	164	166	176	180	180	180	176	172	173	183	191	206	179
1937	211	208	204	194	201	188							

4　江蘇武進農民售出之農產品(包括乾繭)物價指數與不包括乾繭之農產品物價指數計算時，二者所用之農產品種類及其權數相同

4　The commodities included and their respective weights were the same as those for the index of prices received for cereals and silk, except that silk coccons, dried, were excluded.

第三表　江蘇武進農民所付物價之加權總合指數[5]
一九一〇年至一九一四年＝一〇〇

TABLE 3.—WEIGHTED AGGREGATIVE INDEX NUMBERS OF PRICES PAID BY FARMERS,
WUCHIN, KIANGSU, 1910-14＝100

年份 Year	指數 Index	年份 Year	指數 Index	年份 Year	指數 Index
1910	94	1920	132	1930	186
1911	102	1921	132	1931	177
1912	102	1922	139	1932	170
1913	101	1923	148	1933	142
1914	100	1924	147	1934	140
1915	105	1925	149	1935	151
1916	106	1926	161	1936	166
1917	115	1927	167		
1918	118	1928	156		
1919	124	1929	168		

5. 物品種類及其編製物價指數時所用之權數

農產品:一

白米	85	升
白元米	18	,,
元秈米	58	,,
元大麥	33	,,
大糠	20	,,
黃豆	39	,,
綠豆	17	,,
蠶豆	7	,,
棉子	9	,,
	8	斤

其他食品:一

豆油	14	斤
菜油	13	,,
蔴油	3	,,
鹽	27	,,
茶葉	3.5	,,
白糖	3	,,
冰糖	0.5	,,
鮮松片	0.5	,,
雪梨	0.5	,,
市桃	2	,,
鮮桃乾	0.5	,,
湖筍	0.6	,,
木耳	3.5	,,
新花桃	1.5	,,
酒	0.7	,,
	5	,,

衣着:一

粗布	0.23	疋
細布	0.13	疋
傯布子	0.13	疋
花標布	2	碼
竹布	0.08	疋
紗(16支)	1	包
紗(14支)	1	包
斜紋布	0.08	疋
杭泰西紡緞	0.07	兩
洋緞	3	碼
毛線	1	兩
白絨花	8	兩
棉	0.05	疋
	7	斤

燃料:一

美孚洋油	1	聽
紅市火柴	2	包
洋燭	2	斤
洋燭	1	半打

雜項:一

肥皂	0.2	箱
西洋釘	0.2	斤
白磁油扣	1	板
桐油	0.1	桶柄
粗竹	2	
蔴線	1	斤

第四表 江蘇武進農民所付物價之加權總合指數
一九一〇年至一九一四年＝一〇〇

TABLE 4.—WEIGHTED AGGREGATIVE INDEX NUMBERS OF PRICES PAID BY
FARMERS. WUCHIN, KIANGSU, 1910-14＝100[5]

	一月 Jan.	二月 Feb.	三月 Mar.	四月 Apr.	五月 May	六月 June	七月 July	八月 Aug.	九月 Sept.	十月 Oct.	十一月 Nov.	十二月 Dec.	年平均 Year
1927	168	168	166	167	169	170	170	171	170	166	164	162	167
1928	156	155	154	154	154	155	159	156	156	156	160	160	156
1929	161	162	163	163	163	164	169	171	172	177	177	179	168
1930	182	184	188	193	193	195	197	191	187	177	175	172	186
1931	172	171	172	172	173	173	175	183	185	184	182	180	177
1932	179	181	179	177	176	175	174	173	169	158	154	152	170
1933	157	150	151	148	143	142	134	137	135	132	130	133	142
1934	126	130	127	125	137	136	146	152	146	144	155	154	140
1935	152	156	152	155	154	151	146	116	141	150	155	154	151
1936	154	156	165	168	167	164	167	167	164	169	169	181	166
1937	178	184	182	180	183	172							

5 The commodities included and their respective weights were as follows:-

Grains:

Rice, white	85 shen
Rice, glutinous	18 shen
Rice, early	58 shen
Barley, hulless	33 shen
Barley	20 shen
Bran	39 shen
Soybeans, yellow	17 shen
Soybeans, green	7 shen
Broad beans	9 shen
Cotton seeds	8 catties

Other food:

Soybean oil	14 catties
Rapeseed oil	13 catties
Sesame oil	3 catties
Salt	27 catties
Tea	3.5 catties
Sugar, white	3 catties
Rock candy	0.5 catties
Sweets (鮮松北)	0.5 catties
Sweets (鮮油苏)	0.5 catties
Sweets (雪片糕)	2 catties
Sweets (市蜜宁)	0.5 catties
Sweets (鮮桃絲)	0.5 catties
Dried jelly fish	0.6 catties
Dried bamboo shoots	3.5 catties
Judas' ear	1.5 catties
Walnuts	0.7 catties
Liquor, barley	5 catties

Clothing materials:

Coarse cotton cloth	0.23 piece of 16 lbs.
Fine cotton cloth	0.13 piece of 16 lbs.
Striped cloth	0.13 piece of 40 yards
T cloth	2 yards
Glazed cotton cloth	0.08 piece of 16 lbs.
Cotton yarn (counts 16)	1 pao
Cotton yarn (counts 14)	1 pao
Twill	0.08 piece of 40 yards
Cotton venetians	0.07 yards
Hangchow silk	3 liang
Sateen	1 yards
Knitting yarn	8 liang
Cotton flannel, white	0.05 piece
Raw cotton	7 catties

Fuel and lighting:

Kerosene oil	1 tin
Safety match	2 pao (10 boxes)
Candle, native	2 catties
Candle, imported	1 1/2 dozen

Miscellaneous:

Soap	0.2 case
Wire nails	0.2 catty
White buttons	1 card
Wood oil	0.1 barrel
Umbrellas	2
Hemp thread	1 catty

— 257 —

中國物價水準慘跌之自然結果也。

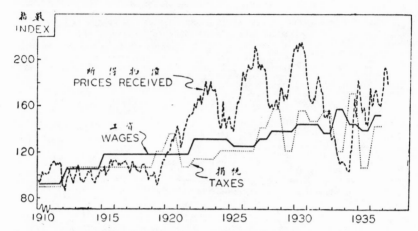

第三圖　江蘇武進農民所得物價及所付工資捐稅之指數，一九一〇至一九三六年，一九一〇至一九一四年＝一〇〇。

　　當一九三一年前物價上漲之期間，工資捐稅上漲不若農民所得物價之速，故工資及捐稅支付較易，自一九三一年至一九三四年物價下跌期間，工資及捐稅跌落亦不若所得物價之速，故其支付較爲困難矣。

FIGURE 3.–INDEX NUMBERS OF PRICES RECEIVED AND OF WAGES AND TAXES PAID BY FARMERS IN WUCHIN, KIANGSU, 1910-1936, 1910-14＝100

During the period of rising prices before 1931, wages and taxes did not advance as rapidly as prices received and, therefore, were easier to pay. During the period of falling prices from 1931 to 1934, they did not decline as rapidly and, therefore, were more difficult to pay.

第五表　民國二十年至民國二十五年各年農作物產量之最後估計

TABLE 5.–FINAL ESTIMATES OF CROP PRODUCTION, CHINA, 1930–1936

	冬季作物 Winter Crops			夏季作物 Summer Crops		
	小麥 Wheat	大麥 Barley		稻 Rice	糯稻† Glutinous rice†	大豆 Soybeans
	各年產量佔六年平均數之百分率 Per cent of six-year average			各年產量佔六年平均數之百分率 Per cent of six-year average		
1930-31	97	100	1931	97	—	96
1931-32	102	102	1932	111	—	109
1932-33	101	94	1933	104	98	121
1933-34	101	101	1934	82	98	94
1934-35	96	100	1935	103	102	83
1935-36	104	103	1936	103	101	98

來源：　中央農業實驗所，農情報告，第四卷第九及第十二期，廿五年九月及十二月。

Source: National Agricultural Research Bureau, Crop reports, Vol. IV Nos. 9 and 12, September and December, 1936.

†　各年產量佔四年平均數之百分率

† Per cent of four-year average

259). Such conditions were the natural outcome of the rapid decline
of the general price level in China.

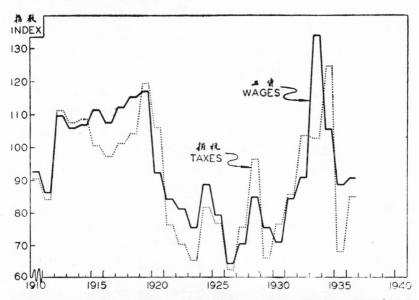

第四圖　江蘇武進以農民售出之穀類及蠶繭計算之工資及捐稅價值之指數
　，一九一〇至一九三六年，一九一〇至一九一四年＝一〇〇。

工資及捐稅在一九三一年物價未跌前，支付日易一日，自一九三一年至一九三四年，農民
因償付工資捐稅必須售出多量之穀類及蠶繭，此乃造成農村不景氣之主因也，幸此種紊亂情
形已因物價回漲而校正矣。

FIGURE 4.—INDEX NUMBERS OF THE VALUE OF FARM WAGES AND TAXES IN TERMS OF
CEREALS AND SILK COCCOONS SOLD BY FARMERS, WUCHIN, KIANGSU, 1910-1936, 1910-14
=100.

Wages and taxes were becoming easier to pay until, in 1931, prices began to decline. From 1931 to
1934, much more cereals and silk had to be sold in order to pay taxes and wages, and this was a major
cause of the agricultural depression. Reflation has corrected the maladjustment.

When the price level declines, wages and debt service charges
are lowered only slowly. The costs of government, manufacturing
and handicraft work, transportation, marketing and other items
which consist largely of charges for labor and credit decline slowly,
while prices of farm crops are much more flexible and decline rapidly.
Crops become cheaper and cheaper relative to wages, taxes, interest
rates and prices paid for goods bought. A falling price level is
therefore very unfavorable for farmers. It results in their being
unable to pay taxes and buy manufactured goods.

From April 1934 to November 1934, prices received by farmers
in Wuchin advanced by 76 per cent. This was the result of a severe
drought and not of a rise in the general price level. China's 1934

物價水準慘跌時，工資及債務費用下落恆緩，政府公費，機器工業及手工業，運輸，銷售，以及其他事項，凡包含大部勞工及資金者，跌落甚緩，而農作物價格較易變動，故跌落愈速。因而農作物之價格較之工資，捐稅，利率及購買物價日漸低落，所以物價水準低落對於農民極為不利，結果甚至使農民無力納稅及購買製造品。

自一九三四年四月至同年十一月，武進農民所得之物價竟上漲百分之七十六，此乃是年奇旱之結果，非物價水準普遍上漲也。一九三四年中國稻作產量較六年來平均數低百分之十八，一九三四年春季以後農民所得物價與工資，捐稅，及農民所付物價似已較為調和，惟以當時荒歉情形而論，農民所得物價似仍嫌過低。一九三五年十月以後因幣制改革物價水準漸次上升，上述關係始漸得調整。一九三五至一九三六年之冬季作物及一九三六年之夏季作物，收成均超過平均收成，但一九三六年之農民所得物價指數較一九三一年以後任何年為高，且較一九三三年高百分之四十二。

一九三七年五月上海物價指數較一九三一年高百分之十二。武進農民所得物價及所付物價已極調整。捐稅與工資比之農民所得物價已恢復一九三一年低落之狀態。此等關係對於農村復興之進展，社會幸福之增進，及貿易之繁榮，至為重要也。

雷伯恩
戈福鼎

---

6 ''經濟統計''，第四期第一七二至一七五頁，一九三七年二月。

rice crop was 18 per cent below the average of the six years for which data are available. Thus, while the adjustment between prices received and wages, taxes and prices paid, appeared to be better after the spring of 1934, prices received were still low considering the small crops available for sale. Proper adjustment came only after October 1935 when the general price level began to rise as a result of currency reform.[6] The winter crops of 1935-36 and summer crops of 1936 were above average but, for 1936, the index of prices received was higher than for any year since 1931 and 42 per cent higher than for 1933.

In May 1937, the index of prices in Shanghai was 12 per cent higher than in 1931. In Wuchin, the prices received by farmers were in good adjustment with the prices paid. Relative to prices received, taxes and wages were again as low as in 1931. Such relationships are fundamental to the continued progress of rural reconstruction and to further improvement in general welfare and trade.

JOHN R. RAEBURN
KO FUH-TING

---

6 *Economic Facts*, No. 4 pp. 175. February 1937.

農作物之價格

繼續可靠之農產物價報告之價值良非淺鮮。蓋各種農作物之價格，因地而別，因時而異，以及彼此間之比價對於判斷生產之趨勢與運輸貿易之發展極關重要。農商界之經濟活動亦莫不受物價之支配。物價更足以斷定各合作社及政府農業推進及運銷事業之成敗。籌劃幣制改革時農產物價尤須與以深切之注意。凡此諸端，早為識者所公認。

中國目前欲得滿意之物價報告實屬匪易，因各地物品之品質等級既漫無標準，度量衡單位及貨幣單位復龐雜無章，且報告恆不能按時彙集。此種工作固感困難，但其需要尤為迫切，故此種物價報告誠有努力改善與推進之必要。

近年以來，金陵大學農業經濟系曾搜集國內各地（見第二六三頁，第一圖）之作物價格。茲擇其尤要者，根據各地之兌換率及度量衡制度，將各種作物之價格均化為每市石或每市擔之法幣價格。各地價格之差異，由於品質之不同固為明顯，但供求影響更為重要，糧食不足之地其一部分或全部供應須以高昂運費自過剩之地移運而來，故其價格恆高也。

米——陝西華縣，河北正定，安徽宿縣均為缺乏稻米之區，故報價最高，江西泰和產米極豐，但運銷不便，報價最低。一九三七年五月份，泰和米價每市石較華縣低八‧四四元較正定低八‧〇九元。

江蘇武進米價高於南京米價，主要原因乃品質之不同也。

華縣米價，因大軍屯集，供不應求，上漲特甚。

廣西幣制頗不穩定，一九三六年七月以後物品之法幣價格常多意外之變動，最近十八閱月中，廣西物價上漲之速遠勝其他各地，可證該省幣制尚未臻於完善。

小麥——各地麥價自一九三四年即開始上漲，至一九三六年，元之價值減低，海外麥價報漲，最後數月更發生旱災，故各地麥價均突飛孟晉。[1]一九三七年一月起，各地麥價已經下跌，但價格仍高。

---

[1] 一九三七年五月"經濟統計"第五期第二一三頁至二一七頁曾刊載一關於小麥價格猛漲之論文

CROP PRICES

Continuous, reliable reports on prices of farm products can be of great value. Geographical differences in price, changes with time, and changes in the relative values of different crops determine trends in production and are of fundamental importance in the development of transportation and trade. Prices control the economic activities of farmers and merchants. They likewise determine the success or failure of cooperative and government efforts in agriculture and marketing. In planning monetary reforms, prices of farm products must be given careful consideration.

第一圖　報告物價各鎮市之位置

FIGURE 1.—LOCATION OF TOWNS SENDING PRICE REPORTS

In China, satisfactory reports on prices are difficult to obtain because of undescribed differences in quality, differences in weights, measures and monetary units, and tardy reporting. None the less, the need for reports is greater than the difficulty of obtaining them and concerted efforts should be made greatly to improve and extend price reporting work.

In recent years, crop prices have been reported to this Department from several towns scattered throughout the country (figure 1, page 263). The more important of the series have been calculated in terms of National yuan per shih picul, or shih tan, on the basis of the best available data on domestic exchange rates and units of weight and measure (table 1-7, page 264-268). Differences between

華北小麥種植密度不若華南水稻種植之密，故各地小麥價格之變動較爲一致，但各地間仍有相當差額存在，河北正定之麥價恆高，乃因該地小麥品質較佳故也。

陝西華縣自一九三六年十月後，小麥價格飛漲，亦因西安事變前後，大軍屯集，供不應求耳。

大麥——大麥價格之變動大致與小麥價格變動情形相似。

江蘇武進大麥價格特高，乃因該地大麥報價係裸大麥之價格也。

第一表　鄉鎮市場的白米批發價格

TABLE 1.—WHOLESALE PRICES OF WHITE RICE IN RURAL
MARKET TOWNS

年 Year	廣西富川羊岩 Kwangsi Fu-chwan Yangai	江西泰和沿溪渡 Kiangsi Taiho Yenkitu	浙江桐廬橫村 Chekiang Tunglu Hwengchwen	江蘇武進禮家橋 Kiangsu Wuchin Li Chai	南京中華門 Kiangsu Nanking Chung Hwa Men	湖北黃陂張家店 Hupeh Hwang-pe Changcha'ten	安徽宿縣 Anhwei Suhsien	河北正定傅家村 Hopeh Cheng-ting Fuchai-chwen	陝西華縣赤水 Shensi Hwa hsien Chishui
				每市石元敷 *yuan per shih tan*					
1930	—	—	—	13.91	—	—	15.50	13.24	—
1931	—	—	—	9.75	—	—	10.79	12.91	—
1932	—	—	—	9.46	—	—	11.76	11.78	—
1933	—	—	—	6.76	—	—	9.07	10.36	—
1934	—	—	—	8.69	—	—	8.10	8.56	—
1935	—	—	—	10.53	—	—	10.26	10.36	—
1936	7.05	5.18	—	9.56	—	7.90	10.52	10.90	—
Oct. 1935	—	5.41	—	10.14	—	—	8.65	9.51	--
Jan. 1936	6.38	5.50	—	8.98	—	8.33	9.70	10.06	—
Feb.	6.72	5.79	—	9.17	—	8.64	9.20	10.24	—
Mar.	6.89	6.37	—	9.75	—	8.64	9.40	10.37	—
Apr.	7.13	6.37	—	9.95	—	8.95	10.20	10.49	—
May	7.20	5.79	10.26	9.75	—	9.26	10.88	10.98	—
June	7.80	5.60	11.16	9.85	8.80	8.95	10.90	12.20	13.46
July	7.69	3.67	9.54	9.75	8.70	6.48	11.20	12.20	12.93
Aug.	9.49	3.57	9.00	9.46	8.60	5.19	11.04	10.98	14.00
Sept.	5.66	4.15	9.00	9.27	6.75	5.56	10.40	9.70	16.16
Oct.	5.99	4.64	8.82	9.17	7.70	9.07	10.96	10.06	15.08
Nov.	6.12	5.12	9:00	9.27	8.10	8.33	11.15	12.20	17.23
Dec.	7.51	5.60	9.54	9.95	9.20	7.41	11.25	11.28	15.08
Jan. 1937	8.09	5.60	10.26	10.43	9.50	7.87	11.28	12.07	15.08
Feb.	8.09	5.60	10.26	10.62	9.40	7.59	11.20	12.62	16.14
Mar.	8.20	5.70	9.36	10.43	8.75	7.59	11.15	12.80	18.62
Apr.	11.25	5.79	9.36	9.75	8.40	7.59	11.20	13.41	15.08
May	11.76	5.02	9.36	10.24	8.40	7.69	—	13.11	13.46
June	—	4.44	8.64	9.27	8.30	7.87	—	—	12.93
July									

districts due to quality are evident in the price series but supply conditions explain the major differences between districts. High prices prevail in deficit areas which depend for some or all of their supply on grain brought from surplus areas by costly transportation.

Rice.—The highest prices for rice were reported from Hwa hsien, Shensi; Chenting, Hopeh; and Su hsien, Anhwei. These are deficit areas. The lowest prices were reported from Taiho, Kiangsi, a surplus area with poor marketing facilities. For May 1937, Taiho reported a price per shih tan 8.44 yuan lower than Hwa hsien, 8.09 yuan lower than Chenting.

In Wuchin, Kiangsu, prices are higher than in Nanking chiefly

第二表　鄉鎮市場之小麥批發價格
TABLE 2.–WHOLESALE PRICES OF WHEAT IN RURAL MARKET TOWNS

年 Year	江西泰和沿溪渡 Kiangsi Taiho Yenkitu	江蘇武進禮家橋 Kiangsu Wuchin Li Chai Chiao	南京中華門 Nanking Chung Hwa Men	湖北黃陂張家店 Hupeh Hwangpe Changchaiten	湖北遠安南關 Hupeh Yuanan South gate	安徽宿縣 Anhwei Suhien	河北正定傅家村 Hopeh Chengting Fuchaichwen	陝西華縣赤水 Shensi Hwahsien Chishui	山西靜樂 Shansi Tsingloh
				每市担元數 *yuan per shih picul*					
1930	—	4.42	4.96	—	—	3.77	5.32	—	7.48
1931	—	3.43	4.28	—	—	4.95	5.20	—	5.74
1932	—	3.32	3.54	—	—	4.32	5.00	—	5.12
1933	—	2.91	2.61	—	—	2.87	3.60	—	3.28
1934	—	3.08	2.80	—	—	2.56	3.34	—	2.68
1935	-	3.61	3.42	—	—	3.31	3.64	—	2.88
1936	4.03	4.87	4.38	5.09	4.15	4.51	5.40	—	4.58
Oct. 1935	2.58	3.84	3.24	3.68	3.24	3.77	4.15	—	2.65
Jan. 1936	2.58	4.48	3.80	5.96	3.58	4.10	4.39	—	3.28
Feb.	3.44	4.83	4.00	6.34	3.69	4.40	4.51	—	3.91
Mar.	2.75	5.00	4.14	6.34	3.81	4.63	4.79	—	3.91
Apr	2.58	5.23	4.69	6.98	4.34	4.67	5.11	--	3.84
May	3.01	4.95	5.14	2.85	5.03	4.21	4.59	—	3.84
June	3.61	4.95	3.35	3.30	3.62	3.50	4.71	3.49	3.91
July	4.12	4.07	3.73	3.49	3.43	3.87	4.79	4.36	3.84
Aug.	4.30	4.36	4.17	3.81	3.43	4.23	5.19	5.24	3.84
Sept.	3.95	4.36	4.07	4.06	3.43	4.27	5.27	5.24	4.54
Oct.	6.87	5.00	4.66	6.15	4.19	4.79	6.54	8.73	6.42
Nov.	6.01	5.23	5.18	6.02	5.14	5.40	7.18	10.82	7.19
Dec.	5.15	5.99	5.62	5.83	6.09	6.00	7.78	10.47	6.49
Jan. 1936	7.22	6.17	5.83	6.15	6.09	5.76	7.98	9.43	7.68
Feb.	5.84	6.05	5.68	5.83	5.71	5.73	8.18	9.77	7.12
Mar.	6.70	5.93	5.87	5.83	5.33	5.73	8.06	9.77	7.35
Apr.	4.04	5.99	5.20	3.81	4.19	5.60	7.90	9.77	6.07
May	6.87	5.70	4.97	3.93	3.81		7.38	8.03	6.84
June	5.15	4.89	4.62	4.12	2.89			6.98	6.98
July									

高梁——高梁價格自一九三四年上漲後，至一九三六年春末夏初時忽形停滯，但自八月後至一九三七年年初數月又復繼續上漲。山西靜樂，及河北正定二地現在報價較一九三一年報價猶高。

靜樂高梁處於生產過剩之地位，而運輸又極不便，故報價恆較正定爲低。

陝西華縣自西安事變後，物價至今仍呈非常高昂之象。

黃豆——各地黃豆報價自一九三五年十月後，均呈猛漲之勢，一九三六年九月因收成良好，曾一度下落，但爲時極暫，一九三七年五月各地報價均較一九三一年爲高。

第三表　鄉鎮市場之大麥批發價格
TABLE 3.—WHOLESALE PRICES OF BARLEY IN RURAL MARKET TOWNS

年 Year	江蘇武進禮家橋 Kiangsu Wuchin Li-chai	南京中華門 Kiangsu Nanking Chung Hwa Men	湖北黃陂張家店 Hupeh Hwangpo Changchai-ten	湖北遠安南關 Hupeh Yuanan south gate	安徽宿縣 Anhwei Suhsien	陝西華縣赤水 Shensi Hwa hsien Chishui	山西靜樂 Shansi Tsingloh
			每市擔元數 yuan per shih picul				
1930	6.03	3.48	—	—	2.2?	—	4.22
1931	5.09	3.32	—	—	3.34	—	2.99
1932	4.74	2.63	—	—	2.96	—	2.90
1933	3.79	2.00	—	—	1.54	—	1.30
1934	3.97	1.75	—	—	1.37	—	1.05
1935	4.57	2.19	—	—	2.25	—	1.83
1936	5.42	3.10	3.12	3.03	2.99	—	3.58
Oct. 1935	4.74	2.14	3.42	2.51	2.68	—	1.68
一月 Jan. 1936	4.91	2.14	4.11	2.93	2.92	—	2.98
二月 Feb.	5.00	2.14	4.11	2.93	3.11	—	3.35
三月 Mar.	5.52	3.29	4.11	2.93	3.50	—	3.26
四月 Apr.	5.78	3.39	4.20	3.04	3.73	—	3.17
五月 May	5.60	2.93	1.97	3.25	2.77	—	3.07
六月 June	4.57	2.61	1.80	2.62	1.92	2.93	2.79
七月 July	4.66	2.89	2.40	2.62	2.42	3.77	2.98
八月 Aug.	4.91	3.04	2.40	2.88	2.49	3.77	3.54
九月 Sept.	5.34	3.11	2.14	2.62	2.69	3.35	3.44
十月 Oct.	5.78	3.43	3.25	3.56	3.12	6.29	4.65
十一月 Nov.	6.47	4.00	3.42	3.67	3.40	9.22	4.65
十二月 Dec.	6.47	4.21	3.51	3.25	3.83	10.06	5.03
一月 Jan. 1937	5.43	4.29	3.25	3.93	3.71	5.87	4.65
二月 Feb.	5.52	4.43	3.25	3.67	3.67	6.29	4.84
三月 Mar.	5.78	5.36	3.42	4.50	3.60	6.29	4.84
四月 Apr.	5.00	4.05	2.65	3.40	3.31	7.54	4.19
五月 May	4.48	3.61	2.23	1.83		7.54	4.28
六月 June	4.66	3.82	2.40	2.20		5.87	4.47
七月 July							

because of a difference in quality.

Military operations near Hwa hsien have raised prices there considerably.

In Kwangsi, sudden changes in the currency situation resulted in erratic price movements after July 1936. During the last eighteen months prices have advanced much more than in other districts indicating that confidence in the provincial currency is not yet fully restored.

Wheat.—Prices began to rise in all districts in 1934 and, during 1936, rose rapidly as a result of devaluation of the yuan, rising prices for wheat abroad and, during the last months of 1936, drought.[1] Since January 1937, prices have declined in all districts but are

第四表　鄉鎮市場之高粱批發價格
TABLE 4.—WHOLESALE PRICES OF RED KAOLIANG IN RURAL MARKET TOWNS

年 Year	湖北遠安 南　關 Hupeh Yuanan South gate	安徽宿縣 Anhwei Suhsien	河北正定 傅家村 Hopeh Chengting Fuchaichwen	陝西華縣 赤　水 Shensi Hwahsien Chishui	山西靜樂 Shansi Tsingloh
		每市担元数 *yuan per shih picul*			
1930	—	2.13	3.59	—	4.06
1931	—	3.63	3.52	—	2.51
1932	—	3.41	3.56	—	1.95
1933	—	1.61	2.52	—	0.83
1934	—	1.31	2.09	—	0.72
1935	—	2.24	3.09	—	1.20
1936	2.32	3.00	4.69	—	2.30
Oct. 1935	2.51	2.41	3.49	—	1.31
一 月 Jan. 1936	1.84	2.68	3.84	—	1.97
二 月 Feb.	2.01	2.89	3.92	—	2.18
三 月 Mar.	2.26	3.32	4.14	—	2.18
四 月 Apr.	2.60	3.54	4.58	—	2.18
五 月 May	2.60	2.86	4.45	—	2.18
六 月 June	2.51	2.89	5.23	—	2.18
七 月 July	2.51	3.07	4.79	—	2.18
八 月 Aug.	2.51	2.51	4.58	—	2.33
九 月 Sept	2.09	2.57	4.32	2.79	2.18
十 月 Oct.	2.09	2.84	5.45	4.19	2.99
十一月 Nov.	2.35	3.18	5.54	4.65	2.77
十二月 Dec.	2.51	3.61	5.45	5.58	2.33
一 月 Jan. 1937	3.18	3.41	5.62	5.12	2.33
二 月 Feb.	2.93	3.36	5.54	5.12	2.77
三 月 Mar.	3.43	3.29	5.75	5.12	3.42
四 月 Apr.	2.09	3.16	5.19	6.98	3.06
五 月 May	—		4.97	9.30	2.99
六 月 June	—			5.12	3.13
七 月 July					

1　A discussion of the spectacular advance of wheat prices is presented in *Economic Facts*, Number 5, pp. 213-217, May 1937.

山西靜樂報價恆爲最低者。

豌豆——價格變動與黃豆無甚出入。

南京市報價較華北各地報價之變動爲小，因南京豌豆供給情形較爲穩定也。

河北正定豌豆價格之變動與山西靜樂極爲一致，但正定報價恆較靜樂爲高。

芝蔴——自一九三五年十月至一九三六年四月，芝蔴價格上漲極速，但此後變動極無規律，然尚未達一九三一年之高度，惟陝西華縣已或屬例外。

安徽宿縣爲產芝蔴之區，故報價恆較南京爲低。

第五表　鄉鎮市場之黃豆批發價格

TABLE 5.—WHOLESALE PRICES OF YELLOW SOYBEANS IN RURAL MARKET TOWNS

年 Year	江西 泰和 沿溪渡 Kiangsi Tsiho Yenkitu	江蘇 武進 禮家橋 Kiangsu Wuchin Li Chai	南　京 中華門 Nanking Chung Hwa Men	湖北 黃陂 張家店 Hupeh Hwang- pe Chang- chaiten	湖北 遠安 南關 Hupeh Yuanan South gate	安徽 宿縣 Anhwei Suhsien	河北 正定 傅家村 Hopeh Cheng- ting Fuchai- chwen	陝西 華縣 赤水 Shensi Hwa- hsien Chishui	山西 靜樂 Shansi Tsingloh
				每市担元數 *yuan per shih picul*					
1930	—	5.51	5.51	—	—	3.86	4.65	—	5.00
1931	—	5.57	6.20	—	—	4.48	4.78	—	3.13
1932	—	4.31	5.43	—	—	4.81	3.92	—	2.54
1933	—	3.71	3.80	—	—	2.57	2.79	—	1.69
1934	—	3.17	3.16	—	—	1.99	2.16	—	1.19
1935		3.53	3.69			2.83	3.30		1.63
1936	5.56	4.91	5.16	5.02	3.58	4.52	4.60	—	3.19
Oct. 1935	3.44	3.71	3.83	4.57	3.16	3.02	3.68	—	1.74
Jan. 1936	6.01	3.95	4.14	5.14	2.59	3.75	3.92	—	2.61
Feb.	6.36	4.01	3.97	5.20	2.63	4.00	4.00	—	3.08
Mar.	5.58	4.54	4.83	5.07	2.74	4.82	4.20	—	3.02
Apr.	6.01	5.27	5.07	5.14	3.12	5.14	4.40	—	3.08
May	6.44	5.09	5.18	5.14	3.16	4.57	4.60	—	3.15
June	6.01	5.39	5.59	5.20	3.05	4.82	5.00	2.58	3.08
July	5.58	6.04	6.69	5.39	4.57	4.61	4.80	2.90	3.02
Aug.	5.02	4.25	5.52	5.07	5.71	4.60	4.56	3.54	3.08
Sept.	4.64	4.97	4.97	3.42	3.05	4.29	3.80	3.22	2.81
Oct.	5.50	4.85	4.93	5.14	4.19	4.40	5.32	4.83	3.69
Nov.	4.81	4.91	5.00	5.14	3.81	4.48	5.40	4.83	3.82
Dec.	4.47	5.33	6.04	5.14	4.38	4.80	5.16	5.16	3.82
Jan. 1937	6.01	5.33	6.59	4.57	4.57	4.96	5.40	5.80	3.89
Feb.	6.70	5.33	6.45	5.20	5.71	4.97	5.48	6.12	3.62
Mar.	5.41	5.45	6.69	5.58	5.52	4.88	5.60	5.80	4.56
Apr.	5.33	5.57	6.51	5.33	5.71	5.00	5.40	5.16	3.89
May	5.41	5.27	6.52	5.33	4.57		5.52	6.44	3.69
June	4.47	5.15	6.73	5.26	3.88			5.48	3.89
July									

（年份左側直行標注：一月、二月、三月、四月、五月、六月、七月、八月、九月、十月、十一月、十二月；一月、二月、三月、四月、五月、六月、七月）

still high.

Wheat growing is less concentrated in North China than rice growing is in South China. Prices for wheat are therefore more uniform between districts; but even so, considerable margins do exist. In Chenting, Hopeh, there is usually a premium because of high quality.

In Hwa hsien, Shensi, prices have been high since October 1936 as a result of military operations.

Barley.—The general movements of prices for barley have been similar to those for wheat.

A large premium is paid for the high quality, hulless barley sold in Wuchin, Kiangsu.

Kaoliang.—The advance of prices which began in 1934 was checked in the late spring and early summer of 1936 but continued from August 1936 until the first months of 1937. In Tsingloh, Shansi, and Chenting, Hopeh, prices are now higher than in 1931.

Tsingloh is situated in a surplus area for kaoliang and lacks marketing facilities. Prices there are usually lower than in Chenting.

Prices are still abnormally high in Hwa hsien, Shensi.

Soybeans.—In all reporting districts, prices advanced rapidly after October 1935. The good crops of 1936 lowered prices in September, but only temporarily. In May 1937, prices were everywhere higher than in 1931.

The lowest prices have usually been reported from Tsingloh, Shansi.

Field peas.—Price movements have corresponded closely to those for soybean prices.

In Nanking, prices have been less variable than in North China because of more uniform supply conditions.

Prices in Chenting, Hopeh usually parallel prices in Tsingloh, Shansi but at a much higher level.

Sesame.—From October 1935, to April 1936, prices advanced rapidly but have since been very irregular. The 1931 level has not yet been reached except, perhaps, in Hwa hsien, Shensi.

Su hsien, Anhwei, is a surplus area for sesame and prices there are usually much lower than in Nanking.

第六表　鄉鎮市場之豌豆批發價格

TABLE 6.—WHOLESALE PRICES OF FIELD PEAS IN RURAL MARKET TOWMS

年 Year	南　京 中華門 Nanking Chung Hwa Men	湖北黃陂 張家店 Hupeh Hwangpe Changchaiten	河北正定 傅家村 Hopeh Chengting Fuchaichwen	陝西華縣 赤　水 Shensi Hwa Hsien Chishui	山西靜樂 Shansi Tsingloh
		每市担元數 *yuan per shih picul*			
1930	4.63	—	4.14	—	5.12
1931	4.77	—	4.31	—	3.08
1932	4.22	—	4.36	—	2.14
1933	3.25	—	2.98	—	1.14
1934	2.68	—	2.12	—	0.92
1935	3.15	—	3.23	—	1.81
1936	3 80	3.13	4.75	—	2.91
Oct. 1935	7.89	4.16	3.18	—	1.74
一　月　Jan. 1936	5.42	3.69	3.61	—	2.61
二　月　Feb.	3.66	3.69	3.72	—	2.98
三　月　Mar.	3.63	3.69	4.82	—	2.86
四　月　Apr.	3.88	3.69	4.23	—	2.80
五　月　May	4.19	2.08	4.00	—	2.80
六　月　June	3.42	2.50	5.45	—	2.92
七　月　July	3.73	2.08	4.82	—	2.73
八　月　Aug.	3.73	2.08	4.51	—	2.61
九　月　Sept.	3.73	2.85	4.59	4.80	2.42
十　月　Oct.	3.85	3.63	5.57	5.40	3.42
十一月　Nov.	4.35	3.74	5.88	7.50	3.35
十二月　Dec.	4.04	3.86	5.80	6.90	3.42
一　月　Jan. 1937	3.73	3.69	5.96	8.40	3.60
二　月　Feb.	3.66	3.75	6.08	8.40	3.98
三　月　Mar.	4.04	3.57	6.23	8.40	4.13
四　月　Apr.	4.35	3.63	6.59	7.50	3.85
五　月　May	4.35	3.69	6.23	6.60	3,23
六　月　June	4.97	3.63		6.00	3.79
七　月　July					

　　物價因地而異須視下列情形爲定，（ⅰ）將此地之產物市諸彼地所需運輸上及管理上之費用，（ⅱ）貿易上之便利。倘能減少運輸成本，增進貿易便利，使農作物之流動暢達，則目前各地間之巨大差額必形縮小，然後各種作物生長適宜之區必盡量從事種植該項作物，而產量亦可因之大增矣。

雷伯恩

戈福鼎

第七表　郷鎮市場之芝蔴批發價格

TABLE 7.—WHOLESALE PRICES OF SESAME IN RURAL MARKET TOWNS

年 Year	南　京 中華門 Nanking Chung Hwa Men	安　徽 宿　縣 Anhwei Suhsien	河北正定 傳家村 Hopeh Chengting Fuchaichwen	陝西華縣 亦　水 Shensi Hwahsien Chishui
	每市担元數 *yuan per shih picul*			
1930	8.22	4.86	6.97	—
1931	12.14	9.34	7.91	—
1932	12.31	10.28	7.63	—
1933	7.52	4.82	4.86	—
1934	5.24	3.40	4.49	—
1935	5.91	4.49	6.08	—
1936	9.01	6.96	7.76	—
Oct. 1935	5.28	4.33	6.44	—
一 月 Jan. 1936	6.34	5.66	6.96	—
二 月 Feb.	6.02	5.64	7.08	—
三 月 Mar.	6.50	6.56	7.30	—
四 月 Apr.	7.93	7.54	7.47	—
五 月 May	10.57	7.56	7.73	—
六 月 June	9.92	7.43	8.80	—
七 月 July	11.38	7.65	8.59	—
八 月 Aug.	10.77	7.59	7.94	—
九 月 Sept	9.35	6.49	7.08	11.63
十 月 Oct.	9.15	6.78	7.81	11.16
十一 月 Nov.	9.76	7.13	8.37	11.63
十二 月 Dec.	10.37	7.54	7.94	9.30
一 月 Jan. 1937	11.06	7.29	8.16	13.95
二 月 Feb.	11.38	7.20	9.02	13.95
三 月 Mar.	11.38	7.20	9.23	13.95
四 月 Apr.	10.38	7.13	9.23	11.63
五 月 May	10.08		9.02	13.95
六 月 June	10.57			7.91
七 月 July				

Geographical differences in price are determined by (i) handling and transportation costs involved in marketing products of one district in another and (ii) trading facilities. If costs were reduced and facilities improved a freer movement of crops would be possible and the wide margins at present existing would narrow. Efforts in the production of individual crops would then be automatically directed to those areas where they are naturally most fruitful.

JOHN R. RAEBURN

KO FUH-TING

Footnotes, to page 272.

Calculated on the basis of Shanghai on New York exchange rates and the price of gold in the United States

Economic Facts pp 242—243. Number 6, July, 1937

Warren, G.F. and Pearson, F.A.. *Gold and Prices*, P.181, John Wiley and Sons. New York, 1935

Economic Facts, pp. 254—257, Number 6, July, 1937

指　數
INDEX NUMBERS

	以國幣計算之金價1 Price of gold in terms of yuan 1 1913=100	上海物價之沙爾白克司答的司脫指數 'Sauerbeck-Statist' index of prices in Shanghai		英國物價之沙爾白克司答的司脫指數以金計3 'Sauerbeck Statist' index of prices in England in gold 3 1913=100	江蘇武進農民所得物價4 Prices received by farmers, Wuchin, Kiangsu 4 1910-14=100	江蘇武進農民所付物價4 Prices paid by farmers, Wuchin Kiangsu 4 1910-14=100
		以國幣計2 in yuan 2 Feb.（二月） 1913=100	以金計2 in gold 2 Feb.（二月） 1913=100			
1913	100	—	—	100	99	101
1914	109	—	—	101	98	100
1915	121	—	—	124	106	105
1916	95	—	—	156	110	106
1917	73	—	—	201	106	115
1918	60	—	—	221	103	118
1919	53	—	—	220	101	124
1920	61	126	217	222	128	132
1921	97	131	136	144	140	132
1922	88	131	149	140	162	139
1923	92	145	157	143	174	148
1924	91	142	157	149	148	147
1925	86	148	172	159	158	149
1926	97	150	155	148	194	161
1927	106	158	149	144	187	167
1928	102	152	149	141	163	156
1929	114	157	138	135	184	168
1930	160	173	109	114	204	186
1931	214	183	86	91	172	177
1932	220	166	76	68	151	170
1933	232	150	65	64	118	142
1934	235	144	62	59	137	140
1935	222	147	66	59	158	151
1936	269	174	65	63	168	166
十　月 Oct. 1935	219	144	66	60	155	150
一　月 Jan. 1936	271	164	60	61	160	154
二　月 Feb.	268	166	62	62	162	156
三　月 Mar.	268	171	64	61	170	165
四　月 Apr.	269	173	65	60	175	168
五　月 May.	269	170	63	60	173	167
六　月 June	269	172	64	60	167	164
七　月 July	269	175	65	62	162	167
八　月 Aug.	268	176	66	64	161	167
九　月 Sept.	266	174	65	65	160	164
十　月 Oct.	271	176	65	64	167	169
十一月 Nov.	271	181	67	66	174	169
十二月 Dec.	271	190	70	69	190	181
一　月 Jan. 1937	269	197	73	70	194	178
二　月 Feb.	269	206	74	71	192	184
三　月 Mar.	268	203	76	74	187	182
四　月 Apr.	268	201	75	73	179	180
五　月 May	268	205	77	75	186	183
六　月 June	269				176	172

1　根據上海之美滙及美金之金價計算之
2　經濟統計　六期第二四二至二四三頁一九三七年七月出版
3　華而倫及皮而生「金與物價」第一八一頁一九三五年出版
4　經濟統計第六期第二五四至二五七頁一九三七年七月出版

Footnotes, see page 271.

經 濟 統 計
ECONOMIC FACTS

南京金陵大學農學院農業經濟系出版
DEPARTMENT OF AGRICULTURAL ECONOMICS
COLLEGE OF AGRICULTURE AND FORESTRY
UNIVERSITY OF NANKING
NANKING, CHINA

第七期 No. 7.　　　　　一九三七年十月 October, 1937.

第一圖　以法幣計算之金價指數，一九二八年一月至一九三七年六月。

一九一三年＝一〇〇

一九二八年至一九三一年之間及一九三五年十一月貨幣改革期間以法幣計算之金價猛烈上漲，一九三五年十一月以後金之國幣價格，始經固定。

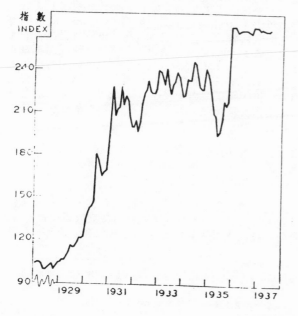

FIGURE 1.—INDEX NUM-
BERS OF THE PRICE
OF GOLD IN TERMS
OF NATIONAL YUAN,
JAN., 1928—June 1937
(1913＝100)

The price of gold in
terms of yuan rose rapidly
between 1928 and 1931 and
at the time of currency
reform in November, 1935.
After this reform the price
was practically fixed.

抗戰與中國物價

中國物價水準之變動，取決於二大因素：（一）世界以金計算之物價水準，（二）以法幣計算之金價[1]。在一九三七年六月，（爲本文可得蒐集充分材料之最後一月），中國物價幾處與此兩因素所期達之水準。（第三圖第二七六頁）近年世界物價日漲，中國物價因亦隨之趨漲。自一九三五年十一月四日，中國實行新貨幣政策以來，法幣與金鎊美元之滙價，迄無若何變動，而國內之金價亦無甚上下，蓋新政策之實施，實使法幣脫離銀本位，而與金發生極密切之關係。

中日戰爭雖不致使世界以金計算之物價發生重大變動，但我政府穩定外滙之困難，卻因此而增劇。就理論言，於自由滙兌市場，若任法幣之外滙價值跌落，即任金價升漲，結果可使中國物價漲越世界物價水準。

<u>物價不宜再漲</u>　以中國物價之現狀而論，一九三七年六月之平均物價，較一九三一年約高百分之十三，（第二圖第二七六頁）足徵當英美各國物價尚未完全恢復不景氣以前之水準時，我國似已完全恢復。凡一九三一年至一九三五年間，國內因物價慘跌而發生之各種失調現象，早已完全恢復常態，故在戰爭未爆發時，不復期物價之暴漲。

工業國家於戰爭時期，物價似須畧有增漲，俾平時工業之勞力，便於轉而致力於戰時工業。如能增加戰用工業之工資，則此項轉變最易達到。然若徒增工資，而不提高物價，必使戰時工業之勞力成本過高，政府固可減低普通工業之工資，然此不特收效遲緩，且困難叢生也。故提高物價，足以支付戰用工業之高大工資，同時使其他普通工業保持其較低之工資。且物價提高，即無形減低贍養金，利息等固定收入之價值，故平昔持以維持生活之婦女及休退人民，不得不群起而謀工作，戰時工業所吸收之普通勞力，遂可因此而填補[2]。惟中國工業尚未發達，抗戰以來，勞工離廠參戰者尚無所聞，國內戰用工業爲數既微，而普通生產工業之勞工，一時亦無缺乏之現象，故提高物價，尚非其時也。

工業國家提高物價，並能增加食物生產。中國以農立國，食糧之仰給於外者，僅爲少數，故農業生產一時不致因徵兵徵工而形減少。且提高物價每致發生囤積糧食之結果，此則應免除者也。

自另一方面言之，防止物價水準之劇烈升漲，亦爲有益，蓋以此種膨脹能減低儲金，公私償欵，以及其他一切固定或遲緩變動之收益價值。若戰後物價跌落，則政府與人民在物價高漲時舉借之債務，必難償還。在期價上非良也。

附註 1. 關於影響中國物價水準各因素之詳論可參看一九三七年五月出版之經濟統計第五期第一百九十七頁至二百一十一頁。

2. 華爾倫及皮爾生：「黃金與物價」第四百二十五頁至四百二十六頁。

紐約　約翰威利書局一九三五年出版。

WAR AND CHINA'S GENERAL PRICE LEVEL

The general level of prices in terms of National yuan is determined by two factors, *(a)* the world level of prices in terms of gold, and *(b)* the price of gold in terms of yuan.[1] In June, 1937, the last month for which adequate figures are available, prices in China were at almost exactly the level expected on the basis of these two factors (figure 3, page 276). The world level of prices in terms of gold was tending upward and prices in China were rising accordingly. The price of gold had been practically fixed since November 4, 1935, by fixing the exchange value of the yuan in terms of currencies with constant, or almost constant, gold values. Sterling and U. S. dollars could be freely bought and sold at approximately constant rates.

Sino-Japanese war will not greatly alter the world level of prices in gold but the difficulties of maintaining a fixed foreign exchange value for the National yuan will increase. If, on free exchange markets, the value of the yuan in terms of sterling and U. S. dollars is allowed to fall—that is, the yuan price of gold allowed to rise—the general level of prices in China will rise proportionately above the world level of prices in terms of gold.

Rising prices no longer desirable

In June, 1937, prices were at a high level in China, being 13 per cent above the average for 1931 (figure 2, page 276). While reflation to pre-depression price levels had not been completed in England or the United States, it was more than complete in China. A further rapid advance was no longer necessary to correct the maladjustments caused by severe deflation between 1931 and 1935.

In industrialized countries during war periods, some advance of prices is desirable in order to facilitate the transfer of labor from peace to war-time industries. This transfer can be brought about most easily by paying higher wages for war work, but, if no advance of prices occurs, this is costly and any reduction of wages for non-essential work is difficult and slow. Rising prices make it possible to pay high wages for war work while other wages are kept relatively low. An advance of prices also reduces the value of fixed incomes from pensions, interest, and the like, so many women and retired people are forced to undertake tasks normally undertaken by those drawn to war work.[2] In China it is not necessary to facilitate the transfer of workers because only a very small additional portion of the man-power has to be withdrawn for the army, war manufactures are few, and there is ample labor for ordinary productive work.

---

1 For a fuller discussion of these factors, see *Economic Facts*, No. 5, pp. 197-211, May, 1937.
2 Warren, G. F. and Pearson, F. A., GOLD AND PRICES, pp. 425-426, John Wiley and Sons, New York, 1935.

第二圖　中國以法幣計算之物價指數與英國及美國以金計算之物價指數，一九二八年一月至一九三七年六月。

一九一三年＝一〇〇

金之法幣價格之上漲使中國物價超越世界以金計算之物價水準，自金之法幣價格穩定後，中國物價上漲蓋因中國以金計算之物價水準激漲所致。

FIGURE 2.—INDEX NUMBER OF PRICES IN TERMS OF *YUAN* IN CHINA AND IN TERMS OF *GOLD* IN THE UNITED STATES AND ENGLAND, JAN., 1928—JUNE, 1937

1913 = 100

The rise in the yuan price of gold raised prices in China above the general level of prices expressed in terms of gold. After the yuan price of gold was fixed, prices in China rose because the level of prices expressed in terms of gold was rising.

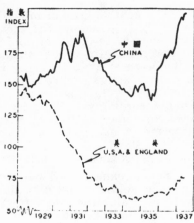

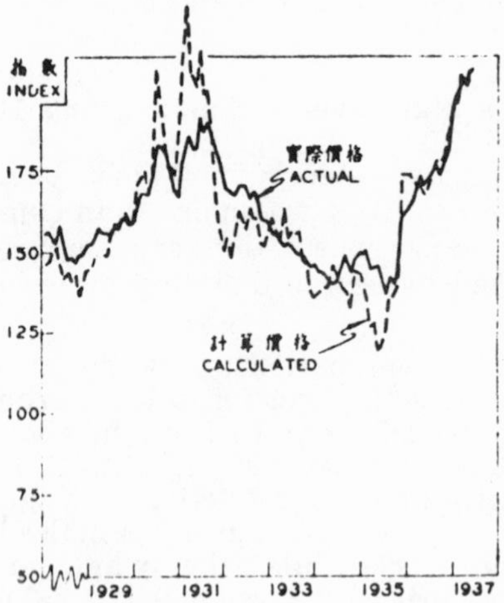

第三圖　中國以法幣計算之物價指數，一九二八年一月至一九三七年六月。

一九一三年＝一〇〇

自一九三六年三月以後中國物價水準與根據以法幣計算之金價及金計算之一般物價所計算之物價水準極為接近。

FIGURE 3.—INDEX NUMBERS OF PRICES IN TERMS OF YUAN IN CHINA, JAN., 1928—JUNE, 1937

1913 = 1C0

After March, 1936, China's price level was in very close adjustment with the level calculated from the general level of prices in terms of gold and the price of gold in terms of yuan.

　　抑制物價　金價現係根據自由交易市場，法幣之英美滙率而定。故欲維持法幣在一九三五年十一月規定之外滙價值，中國政府銀行務須無限止供給外滙。但法幣之準備，約有百分之四十為國債券。在此期內，無論此種債券所佔準備總額之百分比之增多，或其價值或還本付息能力之減少，均足減損政府銀行維持法幣價值，及降低物價之能力。

In industrial countries, rising prices also tend to increase the production of foodstuffs. This is not so important in China where only a small part of the food supply comes from abroad, and the need for soldiers and war workers does not curtail farm production. Rising prices also result in the hoarding of food, which is to be avoided.

On the other hand it would be advantageous to prevent the price level from rising greatly for such inflation would lower the value of savings, loans, and fixed or only slowly adjustable incomes. Should prices fall later, debts incurred at the high level by the Government and by individuals would be difficult to pay.

Keeping prices down

The yuan price of gold is now determined by the value of the yuan in terms of sterling and U. S. dollars on free exchange markets. To maintain this value at the level fixed in November, 1935, the Government banks must be in a position freely to sell foreign exchange in return for yuan notes. A little less than 40 per cent of the reserve backing for yuan notes is in the form of Government securities. Whatever increases the proportion of the total reserve made up by these securities or reduces their value or liquidity impairs the ability of the Government banks to maintain the value of the yuan and keep prices down.

Of the Government's total revenue as budgeted for 1937-38, a little more than one-third was to come from Customs revenue. Now only a small fraction of this third can be collected. Expenses for ordinary purposes may be reduced but total expenses will be increased due to war-time operations.

The Government can obtain additional funds by *(a)* increasing salt, consolidated and income tax rates, and imposing new taxes, *(b)* by encouraging and compelling the dishoarding of gold and silver and the repatriation of Chinese capital, thereby obtaining additional cash reserves for the issue of more yuan notes with the same cash reserve ratio, or *(c)* by going into debt with soldiers and suppliers of goods and services. These methods will not impair the Government's credit significantly but neither will they provide any large amount of money. The Government could also *(d)* borrow directly from individuals or *(e)* indirectly through banks after limiting the withdrawal of private deposits and compelling the liquidation of commercial loans. These methods would provide larger sums but they would reduce the Government's credit, and therefore, confidence in the security reserve behind the currency. Borrowing indirectly through banks *(e)* also invites rapid withdrawal by depositors and leaves ordinary business very seriously short of funds. This leads to new credit arrangements

據一九三七至一九三八年度預算之中國國庫收支總額，其中關稅約佔三分之一。現以抗戰，國際貿易頗感困難，國內運輸亦覺不易，故關稅收入銳減。普通行政費用雖可力求節省，但以戰費浩繁，支出終必增加。

當此之時，政府能藉下列各法，以裕收入：

(a) 增高鹽稅。統稅及所得稅之稅率，並加徵各項新稅，(b) 鼓勵並強制收兌民間窖藏之金銀，以充實現金準備，俾能以相同之現金準備比率增加法幣之發行額 (c) 暫停支發軍餉，並向軍用品供給商賒欠貨款，上述諸点雖不致減損政府之信用，然可能供給之資金，皆屬有限，(d) 政府並可直接向人民借款，即發行公債，或 (e) 間接向銀行借款，即限制私人提取存款，並強迫銀行收囘其商業貸款。以上二法可供政府鉅額資金，但能減低政府之信用，於是公債準備之信用亦跌。且直接向銀行借款，而限制私人提款，必使存款人急於提取，同時商業銀根必因而奇緊，結果銀行不得不拒絕付現，而以互相抵劃代之，貼現之運用亦將增加，而增發紙幣之議益力 (f)。除舉借外債外，增發法幣為另一增加資金之唯一要法，然如無相當之現金準備，則現金準備百分比率必致降低。當和平時，現金準備比率或可較低——僅經驗能以指明——但值公債準備之債價日跌未定時，現金準備比率之低減，足以影響外滙之價值。

若法幣未來滙價之信仰日減，則下兩種政策，可擇一而行。第一，各銀行根據法定滙率自由出賣外滙。此法之成效，端賴現金準備之比率及政府信用之穩定。第二，限制各銀行賣買外滙。此法實施之步驟，不一而足，如勸告買主停購，銀行非正式拒絕出賣，限定買主能獲購買外滙之目的，訂立「君子協定」，及明令禁止賣買外滙。依照限制之程度，法幣之自由滙值漸減，而其脫離外滙本位亦漸遠。於是中國物價自有相當之上升，而超越世界以金計算之物價水準。

一九三四年初，國幣未來銀值兌價之信仰，即開始減低，其時世界銀價暴漲，而國內物價遂慘跌。中國白銀源源外流，致政府深感不得不徵以白銀出口稅。稍後「君子協定」之訂立，遂完全停止當時合法之白銀出口。上述諸法，使國幣之實際銀值與法定銀值，相去懸殊，故中國物價得以相當上漲，而超越世界以銀計算之物價水準，(第四，五圖，第二八○，二八一頁)。可知目前若對法幣之自由滙兌加以限制，則其在世界市場之外滙價值必與其法定外滙價值，相離不等。

such as transfer money, which can be transferred from one bank to another but never cashed, a wider use of discounting, and suggestions for the issue of more paper yuan notes (f). Unless foreign funds are made available, issuing more notes is the only other important method by which funds can be provided, and, unless more cash reserves can be drawn in, it necessitates a proportional reduction in the cash reserves supporting the currency. A lower cash reserve ratio might have been practical during peace time— only experience could show—but a reduction of the ratio now, when the security reserve behind the currency is of probably declining and undeterminable value, would threaten the foreign exchange value of the yuan.

If lack of confidence in the future exchange value of the yuan were to arise, two policies might be adopted. Foreign currencies could be sold freely by banks for yuan at current official rates. The success of this method depends ultimately on the ratio of cash to total reserves behind the currency and the stability of the Government's credit. The other policy would be to restrict sales of foreign exchange by banks. This can be done in several ways and to varying degrees by advice to customers, unofficial refusals to sell, restrictions on the purposes for which foreign exchange may be obtained by customers, gentlemen's agreements, and official embargoes. According to the degree of restriction, the free exchange value of the yuan would be reduced and the currency divorced, by that amount, from the foreign exchange standard. Prices in China would rise proportionately above the world level of prices in terms of gold.

Early in 1934, lack of confidence in the future silver value of the yuan on world markets began to develop as a consequence of the world-wide rise in the commodity value of silver and the resulting deflation in China. Silver began to flow out of China so quickly that the Government felt compelled to impose export fees. Later a gentlemen's agreement practically stopped the legal export of silver. These measures divorced the free exchange value of the yuan from its official silver value, and prices in China rose proportionately above the declining world level of prices in silver (figure 4, 5, pages 280, 281). Should restrictions on the free exchange of foreign currencies for yuan now be imposed, the value of the yuan in terms of foreign exchange on world markets will be divorced from its official foreign exchange value.

If restrictions are necessary, they should be as slight as circumstances permit. Otherwise control of the price level will

第四圖　自由市場以法幣計算之白銀價格指數，一九三〇年一月至一九三
五年十月。

平價＝一〇〇

自由市場中銀之法幣價格高於其法定價格，首因一般對銀本位制之維持之信仰動搖。其次
即因政府限制白銀出口。

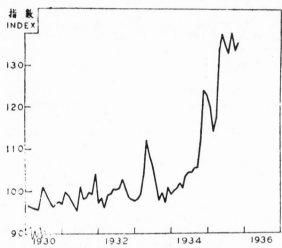

指數
INDEX

FIGURE 4.— INDEX NUM-
BERS OF THE FREE
MARKET PRICE OF
SILVER IN TERMS OF
NATIONAL YUAN,
JAN., 1930—OCT., 1935

(Par = 100)

The yuan price of sil-
ver on free markets rose
above the official price, firstly
because of a lack of con-
fidence in the maintenance
of the silver standard, and
more markedly later because
of restrictions on the export
of silver.

　　若限制外滙為必需時，其限制應力求輕微；否則，必致喪失物價統制
之效能。當一九三四及一九三五年法幣貶值之時，世界以銀計算之物價水
準，正在迅速低跌中，故中國物價並未上漲。現值世界物價狂漲之際，若
限制法幣外滙，迫令法幣脫離外滙本位，則中國物價勢將隨金價上漲，而
超越世界物價水準。

　　故欲避免物價之繼續膨脹，惟有減輕外滙買賣之限制，而外滙限制之
能否減輕，惟政府之信用及其財政之來源是賴。最近據『司答鉄司脫』經濟
週刊所稱『中國政府財政來源十分充足，現有之來源，最少可供抗戰至一
年以上』。該週刊在歐西極有地位，所言良可信也。

雷伯恩

第五圖　中國以法幣計算之物價指數與美國以銀計算之物價指數。一九三〇年一月至一九三五年十月。

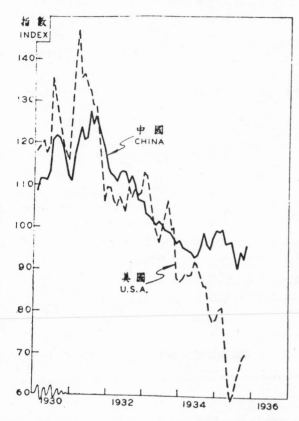

一九一三年＝一〇〇

白銀之法幣價格上漲使中國物價高越一般以銀計算之物價水準。自世界以銀計算之物價水準下跌以來中國物價水準於一九三四年至一九三五年實際上保持不變。

FIGURE 5.—INDEX NUMBERS OF PRICES IN TERMS OF *YUAN* IN CHINA AND IN TERMS OF *SILVER* IN THE UNITED STATES, JAN., 1930—OCT., 1935

(1933 = 100)

The rise in the yuan price of silver raised prices in China relative to the general level of prices expressed in terms of silver. Since this general level was declining, prices in China actually remained steady from 1934 to 1935.

be unnecessarily lost.　In 1934 and 1935 when the yuan was being divorced from silver, the world level of prices in terms of silver was declining rapidly so yuan prices did not rise.　Should restrictions now divorce the yuan from its foreign exchange standard, prices in yuan will rise relative to a level of prices in terms of gold which is itself rising (figure 2, page 276).

The extent to which it will be possible to minimize restrictions depends chiefly on the credit of the Government and the methods it adopts to obtain funds.

JOHN R. RAEBURN

一八七一年以來中國物價水準之變遷

中國長期之物價指數迄今尚付闕如，著者乃根據歷年海關十年報告冊擇取基本物品十五種，[1]編爲一八七一至一九二一年之長年指數。雖不敢自信其可靠程度，然因中國素乏大規模之長年物價指數，則本指數當足以代表中國物價之普通趨勢。上海之『沙氏』指數得視爲，此新指數延續迄今之指數。[2]

以白銀及法幣計算之物價

自一八七一至一八九一年物價甚爲穩定。自一八九二至一九三一年之指數自五十四漲至一八三（一九一三年或一九一三年二月爲一○○），三十九年之內，計漲百分之二三九。自一九三一至一九三四年，物價自一八三跌至一四四，三年之內，計跌百分之二十一。自一九三五年十月至一九三七年六月，因貨幣貶值，物價自一四四漲至二○六，二十個月內，計漲百分之四十三（第一，二圖，第二八四，二八五頁）。

中國物價之趨勢，僅能以中國貨幣本身價值之變遷解釋之。當貨幣價值跌落時，則用以交換物品之幣量增加，於是物價指數上漲。反之，當貨幣價值上漲時，則用以交換物品之幣量減少，於是物價指數下落。一九三四年十月十四日以前，中國以銀爲本位，即白銀可自由兌換，每國幣一元等于純銀○·七七○九兩。[3]故物價指數之升降，即可代表銀值之漲落，惟其結果適相反耳。自一八七一至一八九二年，白銀之物品價值確無變更；自一八九二至一九三一年，銀值跌百分之七十一；自一九三一至一九三五年七月，銀值漲百分之七十八；自一九三五年十月至一九三七年六月，

附註
附註　1.　物品種類如下　括弧內數字爲編製指數時所用之權數

　　　糧食類 (10)：　　稻 (4)　　小麥 (4)　　麵粉 (2)

　　　飲茶類 (4)：　　紅茶 (2)　　紅糖)2)

　　　金屬類 (8.5)：　　釘條鐵 (2.5)　　紫銅錠 (2)　　生鉛塊 (2)　　錫塊 (2)

　　　紡織原料 (10)：　　棉花 (4)　　生繭 (3)　　羊毛 (3)

　　　雜項類 (12.5)：　　牛皮 (4)　　桐油 (4.5)　　花生油 (4)

　　　權數採用時，係盡量使本指數與"司答的斯脫"指數之組織相同。總權數中本國土產品佔百分之七十七。

　　　本指數之編製，係採用算學加權平均法。

　　2.　上海物價之沙爾白克司答的斯脫"指數"見經濟統計第六期第二百三十六頁至二百四十三頁，一九三七年七月出版。

　　3.　自一九三三年三月十號至一九三四年十月十四號法幣一元等於純銀 0.7553 兩

CHANGES IN CHINA'S PRICE LEVEL SINCE 1871

An annual index of prices for the years 1871 to 1921 has been constructed from quotations for fifteen basic commodities reported in the Decennial Reports of the Maritime Customs Service.[1] This index shows approximately the general movements of prices experienced by China during a period for which more comprehensive index numbers are not available, (table 1, page 289). The new index is discussed here together with the "Sauerbeck-Statist" index for Shanghai which may be regarded as its continuation up to date.[2]

Prices in terms of silver and yuan

From 1871 to 1891, prices were approximately stable. From 1892 to 1931, they rose from 54 to 183 (1913, or Feb., 1913 = 100), 239 per cent in 39 years. From 1931 to 1934, they fell from 183 to 144, 21 per cent in 3 years. From October, 1935 to June, 1937, they rose from 144 to 206, 43 per cent in 20 months (figures 1, 2, pages 284, 285).

These general movements can be explained only on the basis of changes in the value of China's money itself. When the value of money is declining, more of it is given in exchange for commodities, index numbers of prices are rising. When the value of money is rising, less of it is given in exchange for commodities, index numbers of prices are falling. Before October 14, 1934, China's money was silver, or freely exchangeable for silver, one yuan being equivalent to 0.7709 ounces of fine silver.[3] From 1871 to 1892, the commodity value of silver did not change decidedly; from 1892 to 1931 it fell by 71 per cent; from 1931 to October, 1935, it rose by 78 per cent; from October, 1935, to June, 1937, it fell by 41 per cent. These changes were world-wide. In the United States prices expressed in terms of silver[4] reflected these

---

1 The commodities included were as follows: their respective weights are given in parentheses:
Vegetable foods (10) : Rice (4) ; Wheat (4) ; Wheat flour (2).
Sugar, tea (4) : Tea, black (2) ; Sugar, brown (2).
Metals (8.5) : Iron, nail rods (2.5) ; Copper, ingots (2).
                Lead, pigs (2) ; Tin, slabs (2).
Textiles (10) : Cotton, raw (4) ; Silk cocoons (3) ; Wool, sheeps (3).
Sundry (12.5) : Hides (4) ; Wood oil (4.5) ; Ground nut oil (4).
The 'weights' were chosen so as to make the composition of the index as similar to that of the "Statist" indices as possible. Of the total 'weight,' 77 per cent is for domestic goods. The mean of relatives method was used in compilation.

2 "Sauerbeck-Statist Indices of Prices in Shanghai"; *Economic Facts*, No. 6, pp. 236-243, July, 1937.

3 From March 10, 1933 until October 14, 1934, 0.7553 ounces of fine silver.

4 Index of prices in $= \dfrac{100 \text{ [Index of prices in terms of U.S. dollars } (1913=100)]}{\text{Index of price of silver in New York } (1913=100)}$
terms of silver
(1913 = 100)

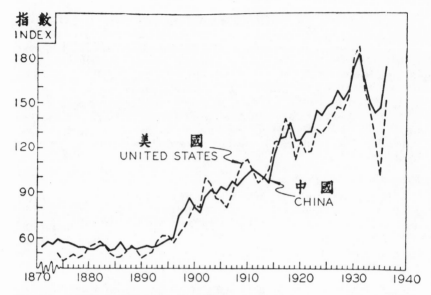

第一圖　中國與美國基本物品價格指數一八七一年至一九三六年。

一九一三年＝一〇〇

中國物價以法幣計算之

美國物價以白銀計算之

以銀計算之物價自一八九一年至一九三一年逐漸上升一九三一年至一九三五年轉而暴跌及一九三五年至一九三六年復猛烈回漲。中國於一九三四年以前始終保持其銀本位制，故其物價變動與世界以銀計算之物價水準甚相契合。

FIGURE 1.—INDEX NUMBERS OF PRICES OF BASIC COMMODITIES IN CHINA AND THE UNITED STATES, 1871-1936, (1913＝100)

Prices in terms of yuan in China

Prices in terms of silver in the United States

Prices in terms of silver rose from 1891 to 1931, fell rapidly from 1931 to 1935, and rose rapidly from 1935 to 1936. China maintained the silver standard until 1934 and thus incurred price movements similar to those of the world level of prices in terms of silver.

銀值跌百分之四十一。此種變動，舉世皆然，中國放棄銀本位以前，其以元計算之物價變動與美國以銀計算之物價變動 4，頗爲相同，中國向以銀爲本位，故其物價變動仍以世界銀值之變動爲轉移。

自一九三一年九月至一九三五年九月，銀價上漲甚速。在此四年之內，美國以銀計算之物價慘跌百分之四十四（第二圖第二八五頁）。銀價暴漲，致中國物價驟縮，並形成其他一切不良影響。物價經四十年和緩之上

4.　以白銀計算之物價
　　指數（一九一三年＝一〇〇） ＝ 100〔以美元計算之物價指數（一九一三年＝一〇〇）〕 / 紐約白銀價格指數（一九一三年＝一〇〇）

changes just as, in China, prices expressed in yuan did, until the yuan was divorced from silver. By using silver as her currency, China incurred price movements which were determined by world-wide changes in the value of silver.

The value of silver advanced rapidly from September, 1931, to September, 1935. Prices expressed in terms of silver declined by 44 per cent within 4 years in the United States (figure 2, page 285). In China this caused sudden deflation and all its serious consequences. After forty years of rising prices, prices began to decline rapidly. Debts, taxes, transportation costs, salaries, wages and other items that can be scaled down only slowly became so

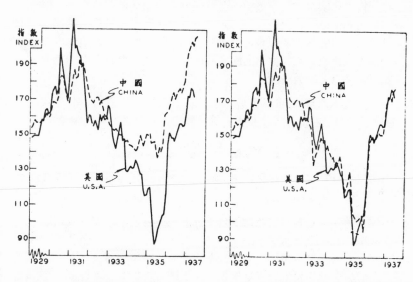

第二圖　中國以法幣計算之物價指數與美國以白銀計算之物價指數。

一九一三年＝一〇〇

法幣在世界市場之銀值貶落後，中國物價即中止隨世界以銀計算之物價水準而變動。

FIGURE 2.—INDEX NUMBERS OF PRICES IN TERMS OF *YUAN* IN CHINA AND IN TERMS OF *SILVER* IN THE UNITED STATES

1913 = 100

After the silver value of the yuan on world markets declined, prices in China ceased to follow the world level of prices expressed in terms of silver.

第三圖　中國及美國以銀計算之物價指數。

一九一三年＝一〇〇

中國與美國以白銀計算之物價幾循一相同之路線而變動，最近該兩指數已回復一九三〇年之高水準。

FIGURE 3.—INDEX NUMBERS OF PRICES IN TERMS OF *SILVER* IN CHINA AND THE UNITED STATES

1913 = 100

Prices expressed in terms of silver have continued to follow much the same course in China as in the United States. They are now as high as in 1930.

升，至此猛跌。債務，稅賦，運費，薪金，工資及其他一切降落較緩項目之物品價值相形過高，以致償付極感困難。 農民被迫減低其購買製造品之數量。銀價日漲，致窖銀牟利者日增。 於是國幣未來之兌現信用漸形搖動。迨一九三四年初，國幣之外滙價值低於其法定含銀之外幣價值。 一般奸商紛以紙幣兌現，將白銀運往國外市塲，換取外幣， 再向國內售得國幣，兌取白銀，反復圖利。政府對此不得不有限制白銀出口之擧， 遂於一九三四年十月十五日，課徵白銀出口稅。 因此世界市塲上國鈔之價值益形慘跌。一九三五年經官方否認國幣有再行貶值之說後， 國幣跌價曾一度中止。但迄一九三五年十月下旬國幣仍有貶值之現象， 財政部不得不於是年十一月三日宣佈此後國幣之外滙價值，而非國幣之銀值，將行穩定。 自國幣在世界市塲之銀價貶跌後，中國物價亦不復依附世界以銀計算之物價。 中國以元計算之物價依附世界以銀計算之物價水準而變動，但恒超此水準， 其超額以世界市塲銀之國幣價格之漲額爲準。惟以銀元計算之中國物價， 仍循世界以銀計算之物價猛跌。[5]（第二，三圖，第二八五頁）。

一九三七年六月，世界市塲白銀之國幣價格等于面值百分之一一六，[6]以國幣計算之物價較美國以銀計算之物價高百分之一一九。

以 金 計 算 之 物 價

中國以銀計算之物價變動依附美國， 故中國以金計算之物價變動亦依附美國（第四圖第二八八頁）。

中國與美國以金計算之物價，自一八七一至一八九六年一致跌落， 自一八九六至一九一三年相率上漲，一九一三至一九二〇年上漲益猛，其後自一九二〇至一九二一年，及一九二九至一九三四年跌落甚速。 可見以金計算之物價變動較以銀計算者更無規律。美國爲維持其金本位制， 迭遭幣值劇烈之變異。

以金計算之物價趨勢與以銀計者完全不同， 蓋以金銀價值之變動各異。中國以金計算之物價，自一八七一至一八九六年跌落百分之三十五； 自一九〇六至一九二一年上漲百分之四十七；自一九一三至一九二〇年上漲百分之一〇七；自一九二〇至一九二一年跌落百分之三十七； 以後續在此高水準波動，及至一九二九至一九三四年慘跌百分之五十五。 故以金計算

5　以含純銀 0.7700 兩之銀　　　　以法幣計算　　　　上海法幣對美元之電滙率
　　幣計算之物價指數　　＝　　之物價指數　　×　　紐約 0.7709 兩之純銀價格
　　（一九一三年＝一〇〇）　　（一九一三年＝一〇〇）

6.　一九一〇年五月二十四號規定每一銀幣含純銀 0.7709 兩

— 286 —

valuable in terms of commodities that their payment grew steadily more difficult. Farmers were forced to reduce their purchases of manufactured goods. Because its value was increasing, silver was hoarded. A lack of confidence in the future value of the yuan developed and early in 1934 the foreign exchange value of the yuan fell below the foreign currency prices of its official silver content. It became profitable to redeem paper yuan for silver, ship the silver abroad and obtain foreign exchange with which to acquire more paper yuan and silver. The Government was forced to attempt a restriction of silver exports and imposed variable export fees on October 15th 1934. Thereafter, the silver value of the paper yuan on world markets declined further. The decline was halted to some extent during the summer of 1935 by official denials of rumors of further depreciation. During the latter part of October, 1935, however, the decline continued, and on November 3, 1935, the Ministry of Finance announced that henceforth the foreign exchange value of the yuan, not its silver value, would be stabilized.

After the silver value of the yuan on world markets began to decline, prices in China ceased to follow the world level of prices expressed in silver. In China, prices expressed in yuan followed a course that was based on the world level of prices expressed in silver but remained above this level by amounts proportionate to the increase in the yuan price of silver on world markets. Prices expressed in terms of yuan of full silver value continued to follow the rapidly downward course of the general level of prices in silver[5] (figures 2, 3, page 285).

In June, 1937, the yuan price of silver on world markets was 116 per cent of par[6], prices in terms of yuan were 119 per cent higher than prices in terms of silver in the United States.

Prices in terms of gold

Just as prices expressed in terms of silver have followed the same course in the United States as in China, so prices expressed in terms of gold have followed the same course in China as in the United States (figure 4, page 288).

Both in China and the United States, prices in terms of gold fell from 1871 to 1896, rose from 1896 to 1913, rose rapidly from 1913 to 1920, and fell very rapidly from 1920 to 1921 and from 1929 to 1934. These fluctuations have been more erratic than those of the level of prices in terms of silver. By maintaining the gold standard during most of this period, the United States incurred serious changes in her measure of value.

---

[5]
$$\begin{matrix} \text{Index of prices} \\ \text{in terms of yuan} \\ \text{of 0.7709 ounces} \\ \text{of fine silver} \\ (1913 = 100) \end{matrix} = \begin{matrix} \text{Index of prices} \\ \text{in terms of} \\ \text{National yuan} \\ (1913 = 100) \end{matrix} \times \frac{\text{T. T. exchange value of yuan in terms of U.S. dollars (Shanghai on New York)}}{\text{Dollar price of 0.7709 ounces of fine silver in N.Y.}}$$

[6] The par announced on May 24, 1910, 1 yuan=0.7709 ounces of fine silver.

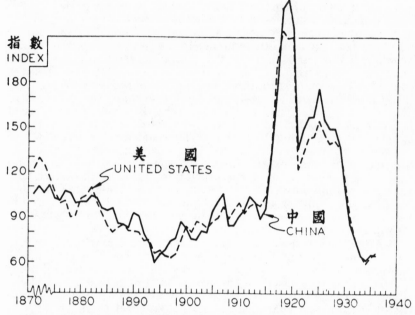

第四圖　中國及美國以金計算之基本物品價格指數一八七一年至一九三六年。

一九一三年＝一〇〇

FIGURE 4.—INDEX NUMBERS OF PRICES OF BASIC COMMODITIES IN TERMS OF GOLD IN CHINA AND THE UNITED STATES, 1871-1936. (1913＝100)

之物價較以銀計算者更無規律。中國向以銀爲貨幣本位，故僅有一時期慘遭物價緊縮。美國因採用金本位，故自一八七一以來，前後慘遭受物價緊縮三次，即一八七一至一八九六年，一九二〇至一九二一年，及一九二九至一九三四年是也。美國提高金價，超過以往所值百分之一六九以來，凡一九二九至一九三三年緊縮時期所造成之一切失調現象，現均漸次料正。

結　論

一九三四年十月十五日以前，中國採用銀本位制故其普通物價水準隨白銀價值之漲落而轉移。中國物價依附美國以銀計算之普通物價水準。惟自一九三一年九月世界銀價暴漲後，中國曾遭受嚴重之物價緊縮。

研究中國與美國已往物價之歷史，即可知金銀兩者之價值，無一能長入穩定也。

雷伯恩

The course of prices in gold has been entirely different from that of prices in silver because the values of gold and silver have not fluctuated together. In China, prices in gold fell 35 per cent from 1871 to 1896; rose 47 per cent from 1906 to 1913; rose 107 per cent from 1913 to 1920; fell 37 per cent from 1920 to 1921; fluctuated at a high level until 1929, and from 1929 to 1934 fell 55 per cent. Prices in terms of gold have changed more erratically than prices in terms of silver. China suffered only one major deflation period because she used silver as her measure of value. Since 1871 the United States has suffered three deflation periods, 1871-1896, 1920-1921, and 1929-1933, because she used gold as her measure. The United States has now corrected some of the maladjustment caused by the deflation from 1929 to 1933 by raising the U.S. dollar price of gold to 169 per cent of its previous par.

Conclusions

Until October 15, 1934, China's money was on the silver standard and she experienced changes in the general level of prices that reflected closely changes in the value of silver. Prices in China followed the general level of prices expressed in terms of silver in the United States. When silver rose rapidly in value after September, 1931, China suffered severe deflation.

If any lesson is to be learned from the past history of prices in China and the United States, it is that neither silver nor gold has proved to be a stable measure of value.

第一表 中國十五種物品之批發物價指數，一八七一年至一九二一年(註)
一九一三年＝一〇〇年

TABLE 1.—INDEX NUMBERS OF WHOLESALE PRICES OF 15
COMMODITIES, CHINA, 1871—1921 (a)
1913 = 100

年 Year	以銀計 算之物價 Prices in silver	以金計 算之物價 Prices in gold	年 Year	以銀計 算之物價 Prices in silver	以金計 算之物價 Prices in gold	年 Year	以銀計 算之物價 Prices in silver	以金計 算之物價 Prices in gold
1871	54	105	1891	55	91	1911	106	95
1872	57	110	1892	54	79	1912	103	104
1873	56	106	1893	55	73	1913	100	100
1874	59	111	1894	57	60	1914	97	88
1875	57	102	1895	59	65	1915	115	96
1876	57	101	1896	61	68	1916	126	132
1877	56	107	1897	75	74	1917	127	174
1878	54	106	1898	79	76	1918	136	229
1879	54	99	1899	86	86	1919	125	235
1880	53	100	1900	80	83	1920	126	207
1881	53	100	1901	77	76	1921	126	130
1882	55	104	1902	87	75			
1883	56	103	1903	92	81			
1884	52	96	1904	89	80			
1885	53	94	1905	94	94			
1886	57	96	1906	92	101			
1887	52	86	1907	98	106			
1888	54	85	1908	95	85			
1889	53	83	1909	99	85			
1890	54	93	1910	103	91			

(註)一九二一年以後資料請參看經濟統計第六期第二四二及二四三頁
(a) For data after 1921 refer to " Economic Facts " No. 6, pp. 242,243.

JOHN R. RAEBURN

安徽宿縣農民所付及所得之物價

物價變動，有一定之程序。當物價水準跌落之時，製成品及零售品價格之跌落不若原料品批發價格之迅速。蓋以製造及分配成本，大多爲工資及利息，不能遽予減低。勞動者絕不願工資驟減，而債權人亦不允削減債額。所以現存製成品之價格，不易驟然降低。因此當物價緊縮時，農民所得之物價猛跌，而其購買品之物價及工資利息等開支，則跌落較緩。

茲將安徽宿縣農民出售及購買之物價分別編爲指數，用以研究物價變動對於該地農民之影響。（第一，二圖，第二九〇，二九二頁）。當一九三一年九月以後，國內一般物價水準跌落之際，宿縣物價並未立即隨之下跌。因是年淮水爲患，農作收成大減，價格得以維持高度。但至一九三二年，新穀登場，物價開始猛跌。自一九三二年六月至一九三四年六月，農民所得物價計跌百分之五十八，而所付物價僅跌百分之四十二。農民在一九三四年出售之產物，較一九三〇年物價關係通常時，須多百分之三十八，始能購得與一九三〇年同量之衣食燃料等物品。

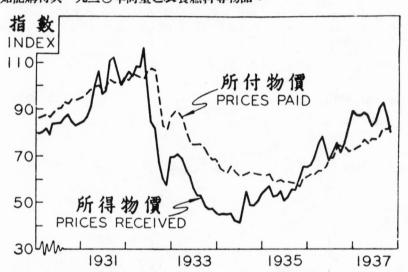

第一圖　安徽宿縣農民所得及所付物價之加權總合指數一九三〇年一月至一九三七年八月。

一九三一年＝一〇〇

當物價水準下降時，農產品價格之下跌較農民所購買之他種物品價格爲劇。由此而發生之失調現象已因近年之物價回漲而得矯正。

FIGURE 1.—WEIGHTED AGGREGATIVE INDEX NUMBERS OF PRICES RECEIVED AND PAID BY FARMERS IN SUHSIEN, ANHWEI, JAN., 1930—AUGUST, 1937

1931 = 100

When the general level of prices declined, prices of farm produce declined more rapidly than the prices of goods purchased by farmers. Reflation has corrected the maladjustment.

PRICES PAID AND RECEIVED BY FARMERS
IN SUHSIEN, ANHWEI

When the price level declines, prices of manufactured goods and retail prices do not decline as rapidly as wholesale prices of raw materials. Much of the cost of manufacture and of distribution is made up by wages and interest charges which cannot be reduced rapidly. Wage earners will not accept a rapid reduction of wage rates nor creditors a scaling down of debts. The prices of existing stocks of manufactured goods are not marked down rapidly. Thus, while prices of the commodities sold by farmers decline rapidly in a deflation period, the prices of their purchases and their expenses for wages and interest decline more slowly.

Index numbers of the prices of commodities sold and commodities bought by farmers in Suhsien, Anhwei, have been compiled (figures 1, 2; pages 290, 292). In Suhsien, the decline of the general price level after September, 1931, was not accompanied immediately by a decline of local prices. Prices were kept high by serious scarcities due to the flooding of the Wei River valley. But after 1932 crops began to enter the market, prices declined. From June 1932 to June 1934, prices received by farmers declined 58 per cent, prices paid by farmers only 42 per cent. In order to buy the same quantities of food, clothing, fuel, etc., farmers would have had to have sold 38 per cent more produce in June 1934 than in 1930 when price relationships were more normal.

After the flood of 1931, farm wages rose slightly as a result of the increased costs of food (figure 2, page 292). Later they did not decline as rapidly as prices received by farmers. In 1934, farm wages were lower than in 1930 by 11 per cent, prices received were lower by 44 per cent. Hired labor had become very expensive for farmers.

The scarcity of food caused by the flood of 1931 increased the need for loans and interest rates were raised (figure 3, page 293). During the rapid decline of prices, interest rates were held at 13 per cent above their 1930 level and, early in 1934, were raised to 50 per cent above this level. During the depression period many loans could not be repaid.

Farmers suffered in 1931-32 because their crops were seriously short and, since the general level of prices had fallen, prices were not correspondingly high. In addition, wages and interest rates advanced. Farmers suffered in 1932-33 and 1933-34 because,

自一九三一年發生水災後，因糧食價格飛漲，農業工資亦略有增加。（第二圖第二九二頁）其後物價跌落，工資跌落遠不及農民所得物價跌落之速。至一九三四年，工資較一九三〇年低百分之十一，而所得物價則低百分之四十四。農民僱工，需費甚鉅。

一九三一年水災後，糧食缺乏，農民借欵需要孔殷，於是利率增高（第三圖第二九三頁）。當物價猛落之際，利率較一九三〇年之水準高百分之十三，而至一九三四年竟較此水準高出百分之五十。當經濟恐慌時期，債欵多陷於不能償還之態。所以貸欵不得不愼重將事，於是借貸供求懸殊，高利由是產生。

一九三二至一九三三年水災之後，農作歉收，復以一般物價下降，農產品不能善價脫售，工資與利率有漲無已，農民受數重難關，困苦已極。一九三二至一九三三年間及一九三三至一九三四年間，收成較豐，方冀可

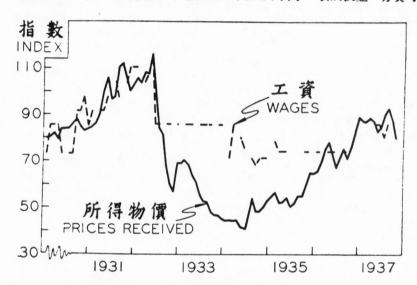

第二圖　安徽宿縣農民所得物價指數與農工工資指數一九三〇年一月至一九三七年八月。

一九三一年＝一〇〇

不景氣時期內農產物價格下跌甚速農場僱用偏工頗感昂貴。

FIGURE 2.—INDEX NUMBERS OF PRICES RECEIVED BY FARMERS AND OF FARM WAGES IN SUHSIEN, ANHWEI, JAN., 1930-AUG., 1937

1931 = 100

During the depression period hired labor was very costly in terms of farm produce.

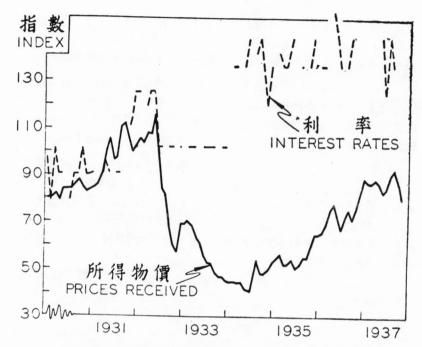

指數
INDEX

第三圖　安徽宿縣農民所得物價指數與借債利率指數一九三〇年一月至一九三七年八月

當不景氣時農民需欵孔殷，而償付困難。故利率高漲一九三五年物價囘漲以後，利率仍不見減落，盖不景氣期內債權人所受之損失尚未恢復也。

FIGURE 3.—INDEX NUMBERS OF PRICES RECEIVED BY FARMERS AND OF INTEREST RATES IN SUHSIEN, ANHWEI, JAN., 1930-AUG., 1937

1931 = 100

During the depression the need for loans increased and many loans could not be repaid. Interest rates were raised to a high level. After reflation began in 1935, interest rates were not lowered because the losses suffered during the depression had not been made up.

although crops were more normal, prices were very low relative to farm wages, interest rates and the prices of goods purchased. In the summer of 1934, prices of farm produce advanced again but this advance did not improve the farmers' position since it was due to drought and, as in 1931-32, less than the normal amount of produce was available for sale.

Effects of reflation

Better adjustment of price relationships was brought about only after the currency reform of November 1935, when the

以收之桑榆，而一般物價一瀉千里，農民所得物價慘落於工資利率及所付物價之下，農民得不償失，仍不能脫離困境。一九三四年夏，農產物價上漲，但是年旱魃為患，農產收獲自食尚虞不足，出售者當極微細。

自一九三五年十一月幣制改革後，原料品物價回漲迅速，各種物價關係得以逐漸調整。農民所得物價之回漲速於所付物價，故一九三七年八月農民可出售較一九三○年小百分之十九之產品，以得與一九三○年同量之購買品。農家工資與所得物價之關係，亦恢復一九三○年之常態。

然宿縣物價調整以來，借貸利率並未因之改變。自一九三四年二月以後，始終維持高於一九三○年百分之五十之水準。考其原因，由於經濟恐慌時期所放之大宗貸欵，尚未清償。放欵人因物價跌落，受累非淺，故今農村經濟雖已轉佳，苟非高利，仍不願增加其貸欵數額。在一九三七年八月，宿縣之短期借欵利率達年利七分二厘，故欲救濟農村，低利貸欵實有刻不容緩之勢也。

雷伯恩
胡國華

general level of prices of raw materials began to rise again. Prices received by farmers advanced more rapidly than prices paid so that in August 1937, farmers had actually to sell 19 per cent less produce than in 1930 in order to obtain the same amount of purchased goods. Farm wages were in approximately the same relation to prices received as in 1930.

Interest rates in Suhsien have not, however, been affected by the return of more normal price relationships. They have been maintained at a level 50 per cent above 1930 since February 1934. Large loans had to be made during the depression and apparently many have not yet been repaid. After having suffered losses when prices declined, money lenders are still unwilling to increase their outstanding loans except at high rates. There is a great need for cheaper credit. In August, 1937, the interest rate on short term loans was 72 per cent per year.

JOHN R. RAEBURN
HU KWOH-HWA

安徽宿縣六〇農家農具役畜所有權及成本之研究

人工效率爲影響田塲收入主要因子之一。惟此全視農具與役畜使用之適當與否。

安徽宿縣六〇農家所蒐集之材料乃中國北部農具與役畜所有權，使用效率及成本大規模調查之一部。本文爲該縣農具與役畜所有權及成本之初步研究。本縣之主要作物爲冬季之小麥與混種之豌豆及小麥，春季之高粱及小米，以及夏季之大豆及絲豆。每農家之作物面積平均爲六三・一畝（約合十二・三英畝）註一。其中有二二・九畝（約合四・五英畝）爲複種面積。

役 畜 之 所 有 權 及 使 用

宿縣最普通之役畜厥爲黃牛。六〇農家均使用黃牛，而使用驢者三三家，馬者三家（第一表第二九八頁）。其借用黃牛者一九家，驢者六家。役畜之借用時期平均各約一月。黃牛每頭價格爲五三元，較驢每頭二四元超出二倍有奇，幾及馬每頭三七元之一倍又半。其中無有役畜者計一〇家（第二表第二九八頁）。

耕耙工作之效率以用二頭黃牛爲最高，惟普通均合用黃牛與驢。播種工作則以用黃牛一頭之效率爲最高（第三表第二九八頁）。

黃 牛 及 驢 之 飼 養 成 本

週年內使用役畜工作之成本，黃牛爲四八元，驢爲三一元（第四表第二九九頁）。最大之成本項目厥爲飼料，黃牛飼料成本佔總費用百分之八〇，驢佔百分之七八。飼料成本昂貴之原因，一部由於該縣牧塲之缺乏。黃牛之人工成本佔總費用百分之七，驢佔百分之一〇。黃牛每頭年需人工五一天，驢四四天。週年內黃牛之糞便價值爲六・四八元，而驢爲三・七四元。

主 要 農 具 之 所 有 權 及 使 用

宿縣六〇農家中置備價廉之小農具，如鋤，鐮，木叉及木柵者，約有五〇餘家，其置備較大而價值較高之農具，如石滾，落石及耕犁者，約有四〇至五〇家（第五表第三〇〇頁）。置備播種器者，僅有三十二家，因其使用時間短少；置備撒刀者，僅有十三家，因其僅于穀類作物歉收時用之。置備價值極昂之大車者，僅有三十二家。一般未置備農具之農家，均向他人借用，至借用時間，平均犁爲一〇至一二天，耙爲八至一二天。

註一　當地一畝＝1.874 市畝，0.0790 公頃，0.19521 英畝

OWNERSHIP AND COSTS OF FARM IMPLEMENTS AND WORK ANIMALS IN SUHSIEN, ANHWEI

One of the major factors controlling farm income is the efficiency of labor. This depends largely on the proper use of farm implements and work animals.

As part of a comprehensive study of the ownership, efficiency and costs of farm implements and work animals in North China, data were obtained for 60 farms in Suhsien, Anhwei. The following is a preliminary note on ownership and costs in this locality. The important crops in this district are wheat, and wheat with field peas in winter, kaoliang and millet in spring, and soybeans and green beans in summer. The average crop area per farm is 63.1 mow (12.3 acres)[1], of which 22.9 mow (4.5 acres) are double cropped.

Ownership and use of work animals

Yellow oxen are the most common work animals in Suhsien. All 60 farms used them, while only 33 used donkeys and 3 used horses (table 1, page 298). Yellow oxen were borrowed by 19 of the farms and donkeys by 6. The periods borrowed averaged about one month for each type of animal. The value of the yellow oxen was 53 yuan per head, more than twice that of donkeys, 24 yuan, and almost one-and-a-half times that of horses, 37 yuan. Ten farms owned no work animals (table 2, page 298).

The most efficient working team for plowing and harrowing was two yellow oxen, but one ox and one donkey were as commonly used. Drilling was done efficiently with only one yellow ox (table 3, page 298).

Cost of keeping yellow oxen and donkeys

The cost of the year's work by work animals amounted to 48 yuan for yellow oxen as compared to 31 yuan for donkeys (table 4, page 299). The largest item was food which made up 80 per cent of the total expenses for yellow oxen and 78 per cent for donkeys. The high costs for food are partly due to the absence of pasture in this district. Labor costs made up 7 per cent of the total expenses for yellow oxen and 10 per cent for donkeys. An ox required 51 days of labor and a donkey 44. The manure was valued at 6.48 yuan for oxen as compared to 3.74 yuan for donkeys.

---

1   One local mow=1.874 shih mow, 0.0790 hectares, 0.19521 acres.

第一表　安徽宿縣六〇農家田塲役畜之所有權使用及價值

（民國二十四年至二十五年）

TABLE 1.—OWNERSHIP, USE AND VALUE OF FARM WORK ANIMALS

60 farms, Suhsien, Anhwei, 1935-1936

役　畜 Work animals	農家使 用數目 Number of farms using	每一農家 使用數目 Number used per farm using	飼養農 家數目 Number of farms owning	出借農 家數目 Number of farms lending	借用農 家數目 Number of farms borrowing	出借 日數 Days lent, if lent	借用 日數 Days borrowed, if borrowed	價格（元） 廿五年九月 Current value (Sept.1936)
黃牛Yellow oxen ...	60	1.5	45	6	19	29	31	yuan 53
驢Donkeys	33	1.0	27	1	6	30	29	24
馬Horses	3	1.0	3	0	0	0	0	37

第二表　安徽宿縣六〇農家飼養各種役畜之農家數目

（民國二十四年至二十五年）

TABLE 2.—NUMBER OF FARMS OWNING VARIOUS
TYPES OF WORK TEAM

60 farms, Suhsien, Anhwei, 1935-1936

		數目 Number			數目 Number
兩頭黃牛	2 oxen 11		一頭黃牛	Ox	10
兩頭黃牛,馬及驢	2 oxen, horse and donkey 1		黃牛及馬	Ox and horse	1
兩頭黃牛及馬	2 oxen and horse 1		黃牛及驢	Ox and donkey	18
兩頭黃牛及驢	2 oxen and donkey 3		一頭驢	Donkey	5
			無役畜	No team	10

第三表　安徽宿縣六〇農家之役畜工作種類及工作效率

（民國二十四年至二十五年）

TABLE 3.—TYPES OF WORK ANIMAL TEAM AND RATES OF WORK

60 farms, Suhsien, Anhwei, 1935-1936

役畜工作方式 Types of team	工作種類 Types of operation						
	耕地 Plowing	耙平 Harrowing	播種 Drilling	拉車 Carting	耕地 Plowing	耙平 Harrowing	播種 Drilling
	農家數目 Number of farms				每天工作畝數 Mow covered per day		
兩頭黃牛Two yellow oxen 29	29	2	26		3.7	19.9	16.0
一頭黃牛One yellow ox	—	—	55	—	—	—	16.2
黃牛及馬One yellow ox and one horse	1	1	—	1	3	20.0	—
黃牛及驢One yellow ox and one donkey	30	30	1	31	2.7	13.5	15.0

第四表　安徽宿縣六〇農家飼養黃牛及驢之成本

(民國二十四年至二十五年)

TABLE 4.—COST OF KEEPING YELLOW OXEN AND DONKEYS
60 farms, Suhsien, Anhwei, 1935-1936.

	黃牛 Yellow oxen		驢 Donkeys	
役畜數目 Number of animals	61		27	
	市担(註二) shih piculs [2]	元 yuan	市担 shih piculs [2]	元 yuan
每役畜每年之成本 Cost per animal per year				
飼料 Food — 大豆 Soybeans	4.80	21.33	2.65	11.52
大麥 Barley	1.64	5.11	1.26	3.93
酒渣 Wine residue	2.15	1.76	1.32	1.04
高粱殼 Kaoliang hulls	1.02	0.69	.60	0.40
小麥稈 Wheat straw	47.12	13.21	33.09	9.24
高粱葉 Kaoliang leaves	4.30	1.15	2.86	0.80
總計 Total....		43.25		26.93
	日數 days	元 yuan	日數 days	元 yuan
人工 Labor —飼喂 Feeding	46.4	3.48	39.4	3.05
其他 Other	4.9	0.53	4.4	0.43
總計 Total....	51.3	4.01	43.8	3.48
廐舍 (註三) Housing [3]	—	1.61	—	1.14
價值減少 Decrease in value	—	1.03	—	1.00
利息 (註四) Interest [4]	—	4.28	—	1.92
總計 Total....	—	6.92	—	4.06
合計 Grand Total....	—	54.18	—	34.47
每役畜每年之收入 Returns per animal per year				
出借 Lending out	—	0.0	—	0.0
糞便 Manure	—	6.48	—	3.74
生殖 Calves or foals	—	0.07	—	0.0
總計 Total....	—	6.55	—	3.74
每種役畜工作之成本 Cost of work done per animal	—	47.63	—	30.73

註二　每市担＝50公斤。
註三　廐舍費用乃根據每種役畜所佔成數百分之十二之廐舍價值計之。
註四　役畜利息乃根據每種役畜百分之八之年初及年終平均價值而計算之。

2　One shih picul=50 kilograms.
3　Calculated on the basis of 12 per cent of the average value of the proportion of the ‘stable’ chargeable to the animals concerned.
4　Calculated on the basis of 8 per cent of the average of the beginning and end inventories.

Ownership and use of important farm implements

More than 50 of the 60 farms owned the small, cheap implements—hoes, sickles, wooden forks and wooden spades; 40 to 50 of the 60 owned larger and more costly implements—stone rollers and stone drags for threshing and plows (table 5, page 300). Only 32 owned drills which are needed only for short periods, and only 13 owned swinging sickles which are useful only when cereal crops are poor. Only 32 owned carts which are very costly. Those farmers who did not own implements borrowed them in almost every case, the average time borrowed amounting to as much as 10 to 12 days for plows and 8 to 12 days for harrows.

第五表 安徽宿縣六〇農家主要農具之所有權使用及價值

(民國二十四年至二十五年)

TABLE 5.—OWNERSHIP, USE AND VALUE OF IMPORTANT FARM IMPLEMENTS

60 farms, Suhsien, Anhwei, 1935-1936

農 具 Implement	使用農家數目 Number of farms using	每一農家使用數目 Number used per farm using	倜備農家數目 Number of farms owing	出借農家數目 Number of farms lending	借用農家數目 Number of farms borrowing	出借日數 Days lent, if lent	借用日數 Days borrowed, if borrowed	價值(元)廿五年九月 Current value (Sept. 1936)
耕耡 Cultivating:								(yuan)
犁 Plow	60	1.02	40	29	20	12	10	1.61
耙 Harrow	60	1.07	42	31	18	12	8	1.60
耩 Drill	60	1.02	32	20	28	8	4	1.50
耡 Hoe, large ..	60	2.32	60	5	0	6	—	0.58
收穫及打落 Harvesting and threshing:								
鐮刀 Sickle	60	3.08	59	1	1	2	2	0.11
撒刀 Sickle, swinging	13	1.31	13	0	0	—	—	0.91
石滾 Roller, stone	60	1.13	47	0	13	—	3	0.34
落石 Drag, stone	59	1.12	44	0	15	—	3	1.01
木叉 Fork, wooden	60	2.67	53	0	7	—	2	0.31
木枚 Spade, wooden	60	1.82	54	1	6	10	2	0.21
其他 Other								
大車 Cart	60	1.00	32	21	28	18	8	27.31

主要農具之使用成本

農具使用之最大成本，厥爲折舊及利息兩項(第六表第三〇一頁)。耕犂配件及大車油漆等費用亦鉅。大車之週年使用成本最大，達六·一〇元。其利息以農具現值百分之八計算，數達二·一八元，而其全年折舊爲三·七七元(註五)。犂全年之使用成本爲五一分；耙爲二七分；播種器爲二四分，大鉏爲一一分。鐮，木枚及木叉等之成本各爲六，五及九分而已。石滾之成本爲五分，而落石爲一六分，以其石質較佳，故其成本較多。

根據蒐集之材料，各種農具之出借，既無現金之收入，又無農工之報酬。

雷伯恩

潘鴻聲

註五 農具折舊費之計算乃以已使用之年數除新舊價值之差。

第六表　安徽宿縣六〇農家主要農具之成本
（民國二十四年至二十五年）

TABLE 6.—COSTS OF IMPORTANT FARM IMPLEMENTS OWNED
60 farms, Suhsien, Anhwei, 1935-1936

農　具 Implement	購置農家數目 Number of farms owning	價　值 民國二十五年九月 Value (September 1936)		全年使用費用 Cost per year					
		新價（元）New	現值（元）Current	折舊（註五）（元）Depre-ciation	家工 At farm	請工 Out-side	配件 New parts	利息（元）Interest	總計（元）Total
耕耡 *Cultivating*									
		(yuan)	(yuan)	(yuan)	(yuan)	(yuan)	(yuan)	(yuan)	(yuan)
犁　Plow 40		3.82	1.61	0.13	0.03	—	0.22	0.13	0.51
耙　Harrow 42		3.37	1.60	0.14	—	—	—	0.13	0.27
搖種器 Drill 32		4.08	1.50	0.11	—	0.01	—	0.12	0.24
鋤　Hoe, large .. 60		1.35	0.58	0.06	—	—	—	0.05	0.11
收穫及打落 *Harvesting and threshing*									
鐮刀　Sickle 59		0.19	0.11	0.05	—	—	—	0.01	0.06
撒刀 Sickle, swinging 13		2.12	0.91	0.23	—	—	—	0.07	0.30
石滾　Roller, stone 47		1.01	0.34	0.02	—	—	—	0.03	0.05
落石　Drag, stone 44		3.30	1.01	0.08	—	—	—	0.08	0.16
木乂 Fork, wooden 53		0.50	0.31	0.07	—	—	—	0.02	0.09
木㳂 Spade, wooden 54		0.27	0.21	0.03	—	—	—	0.02	0.05
其他 *Other*									
大車　Cart 32		75.56	27.31	3.77	.02	—	—	2.18	6.10*

* 包括油漆費用壹角叁分　Including 0.13 yuan for oil and grease.

Costs of operation for important farm implements

The major costs of operation were depreciation and interest (table 6, page 301).New parts for plows and oil and grease for carts were also considerable. The annual operation costs for carts were by far the highest, 6.10 yuan. The interest charge at 8 per cent of the farm value amounted to 2.18 yuan and depreciation charges to 3.77 yuan.[5] Plows cost 0.51 yuan per year; harrows 0.27 yuan, drills, 0.24 yuan, large hoes, 0.11 yuan. Sickles, wooden spades and wooden forks cost 0.06, 0.05, and 0.09 yuan respectively. Stone rollers cost 0.05 yuan and stone drags 0.16 yuan—more because of the higher quality of stone used for the drag.

Data show that there were no cash returns from lending out implements, and labor returns were negligible.

JOHN R. RAEBURN
PAN HONG-SHENG

5　The depreciation was calculated by dividing the difference between the current farm value and the current value if new, by the number of years actually used.

江蘇省秣陵區五三三農家之初步研究

本研究所得材料，爲向秣陵區信用合作社聯合社借款之五三三農家之經濟狀況。調查年度，包括一九三四年二月十四日至一九三五年二月三日；一九三五年二月四日至一九三六年一月二三日，一九三六年一月二四日至一九三七年二月十日。後二週年之材料，較第一年度爲完善。茲將農塲大小及租佃制度與家庭工作効率及生活改善之關係，分別討論之如下。

名 詞 釋 義

作物面積，包括耕地總面積，然複種地之面積不以兩倍計數。

家庭賺欵，包括出售與自用農產之價值，副業淨收入及利息收入，減去農塲用費，此包括利息支出，而不包括塲主或地主之資本利息或折舊。

田地，房屋及農具之價值，僅包括塲主所有之田地，房屋及農具，如爲租入或半租入農塲，則不包括地主之資本。

工人等數，計算成年男人工作十二個月所得之工作等數，其計算標準如下：

男人年齡自一六至六十歲工作十二個月等於 1.0 工人等數
女人年齡自一六至六十歲工作十二個月等於 0.8 工人等數
男女兒童在一六歲以下及男女在六十歲以上工作十二個月
　　等於 0.5 工人等數

圩田農塲，　乃圩內低窪稻田農塲。此項農塲，直接以圩後塢水灌溉之。

山田農塲，　乃位於山地之農塲。此項農塲之稻田，多係梯田至其灌溉，則爲塘沼所畜之水。

農塲大小與家庭大小及家庭賺欵之關係

圩田農塲一九三五年度之平均作物面積爲二五·〇畝（四·二英畝）平均每家人口爲六·四人（第一表第三〇四頁），平均家庭賺欵爲二〇八元，（美金六一元）每人三三元（美金一〇元）；在一九三六年，平均家庭賺欵增至三〇九元（美金九一元），每人四八元（美金十四元）（第二表第三〇四頁）。一九三六年家庭賺欵較一九三五年增加之至要原因，爲物價增高之結果。

PRELIMINARY NOTE ON A STUDY OF 533 FARMS NEAR MOLINGKWAN, KIANGSU

Data were obtained on the farm business of 533 families borrowing through credit cooperatives within the Molingkwan cooperative union. The years February 14, 1934—February 3, 1935; February 4, 1935—January 23, 1936; January 24, 1936—February 10, 1937, were studied. The data for the last two years are more complete than those for the first year. The following is a discussion of the relation of size of farm and land tenure to the efficiency and welfare of the families.

Definition of terms

Crop area comprises the total area of cultivated land. Double cropped land is not counted twice.

Operator's family income includes the value of products sold or used by the family, net income from other business and interest income, less farm expenses including interest expenses but not including interest or depreciation charges on the operator's or landlord's capital.

Value of land, buildings and implements includes only the value of the land, buildings and important implements owned by the operator's family. It does not include the landlord's capital in the case of rented or part-rented farms.

Man equivalent measures the number of farm workers in terms of the equivalent of one man working for a period of twelve months. The standard of calculation is as follows:

Man, 16 to 60 years old working 12 months = 1 man equivalent.

Woman, 16 to 60 years old working 12 months = 0.8 man equivalent.

Boy or girl below 16 years old and man or woman above 60 years old working 12 months = 0.5 man equivalent.

Dyke-land farms are low lying farms with rice land within the dykes. They are irrigated from ditches immediately behind the dykes.

Up-land farms are the farms located on the hilly land. Their rice land is largely terraced but fields are almost as big as on the dykeland. Water drained off the hills into ponds is used for irrigation.

農家之經營大農場者較小農場為多，故其每人所有之田地較多，因此每人之家庭賺欵亦較大。經營圩田農場四〇畝之農家，一九三五年每人之家庭賺欵為三八元，在一九三六年為五六元，其經營一四至一五畝者，則在一九三五年僅二九元，在一九三六年僅三九元。

至於山地農場，在一九三五年平均作物面積為二五‧六畝（四‧三英畝），平均每家人口為六‧一人（第三表第三〇五頁）。平均家庭賺欵為一三八元，每人二三元，至一九三六年，則每家家庭賺欵增至三〇四元，每人為四九元（第三，四表，第三〇五頁）。

第一表　農場面積與家庭大小及家庭賺欵之關係

江蘇省秣陵區三四三圩田農場，一九三五年

TABLE 1.—RELATION OF SIZE OF FARM TO SIZE OF FAMILY AND INCOME

343 dyke-land farms, Molingkwan, Kiangsu, 1935

作物面積 Crop area		農家數目 Number of farms	每家人口 Number of persons per farm family	每人作物面積 Crop area per person	家庭賺欵 Operator's family income	每人家庭賺欵 Operator's family income per person
組距 Range	平均 Average					
畝 mow	畝 mow	數目 number	數目 number	畝 mow	元 yuan	元 yuan
少於 Less than 19.5	14.4	123	5.2	2.8	150	29
19.5–29.5	23.7	125	6.2	3.8	187	30
多於 More than 29.5	40.4	95	8.2	4.9	309	38
平均 Average	25.0	343	6.4	3.9	208	33

第二表　農場面積與家庭大小及家庭賺欵之關係

江蘇省秣陵區三四二圩田農場，一九三六年。

TABLE 2.—RELATION OF SIZE OF FARM TO SIZE OF FAMILY AND INCOME

342 dyke-land farms, Molingkwan, Kiangsu, 1936

作物面積 Crop area		農家數目 Number of farms	每家人口 Number of persons per farm family	每人作物面積 Crop area per person	家庭賺欵 Operator's family income	每人家庭賺欵 Operator's family income per person
組距 Range	平均 Average					
畝 mow	畝 mow	數目 number	數目 number	畝 mow	元 yuan	元 yuan
少於 Less than 19.5	14.9	119	5.4	2.8	209	39
19.5–29.5	23.5	116	6.1	3.9	274	45
多於 More than 29.5	40.0	107	8.2	4.5	459	56
平均 Average	25.7	342	6.5	4.0	309	48

Relation of size of farm to size of family and operator's family income

The average crop area on dyke-land farms studied in 1935 was 25.0 mow (4.2 acres) and this supported 6.4 persons (table 1, page 304). Operators' family incomes on these farms averaged 208 yuan (U.S.$61) being 33 yuan (U.S.$10) per person. In 1936, operators' family incomes were higher, 309 (U.S.$91) or 48 yuan (U.S.$14), per person (table 2, page 304). The increased income in 1936 as compared to 1935 was chiefly the result of rising prices.

第三表　農塲面積與家庭大小及家庭賺欵之關係

江蘇省秣陵區一八九山地農塲，一九三五年。

TABLE 3.—RELATION OF SIZE OF FARM TO SIZE OF FAMILY AND INCOME

189 up-land farms, Molingkwan, Kiangsu, 1935

作物面積 Crop area			農家數目 Number of farms	每家人口 Number of persons per farm family	每人作物面積 Crop area per person	家庭賺欵 Operator's family income	每人家庭賺欵 Operator's family income per person
組距 Range		平均 Average					
畝 mow		畝 mow	數目 number	數目 number	畝 mow	元 yuan	元 yuan
少於 Less than 19.5		14.6	56	5.2	2.9	98	19
19.5–29.5		23.7	84	6.3	3.8	134	21
多於 More than 29.5		41.6	49	6.8	6.1	191	28
平均 Average		25.6	189	6.1	4.2	138	23

第四表　農塲面積與家庭大小及家庭賺欵之關係

江蘇省秣陵區一九一山地農塲，一九三六年。

TABLE 4.—RELATION OF SIZE OF FARM TO SIZE OF FAMILY AND INCOME

191 up-land farms, Molingkwan, Kiangsu, 1936

作物面積 Crop area			農家數目 Number of farms	每家人口 Number of persons per farm family	每人作物面積 Crop area per person	家庭賺欵 Operator's family income	每人家庭賺欵 Operator's family income per person
組距 Range		平均 Average					
畝 mow		畝 mow	數目 number	數目 number	畝 mow	元 yuan	元 yuan
少於 Less than 19.5		14.5	53	4.9	3.0	181	37
19.5–29.5		24.0	80	6.4	3.8	178	28
多於 More than 29.5		41.5	58	7.3	5.8	453	62
平均 Average		26.7	191	6.2	4.3	304	49

山田農場大小與家庭大小及家庭賺欵之關係，大致與圩田農場同。在一九三六年其耕種 41.5 畝者，人口佔 7.3 人，而其家庭賺欵每人爲 62 元，其耕種 14.5 畝者，人口佔 4.9 人，而每人家庭賺欵僅 37 元。

農場大小與工作效率之關係

大農場進欵較高之一原因，乃爲其能盡量使用其人工。農場之僅有作物面積一一・五畝者，有二・五工人，每人僅耕五・二畝（0.9 英畝）可見其人工未能利用也，而農場作物面積爲四七・七畝，每人耕作一二・九畝（二・二英畝），其工作增大一倍（第五表第三〇六頁）。因其用之於耕耘，佈種，收穫與打落工作爲多，換言之即其値用之於眞正生產者爲少也，由此可知小農場人工閒暇較多，故其效率遞減也。

第五表 農場大小與工作效率之關係
汇蘇省林陵區五三二農家一九三四至一九三六年

TABLE 5.—RELATION OF SIZE OF FARM TO LABOR EFFICIENCY
532 farms, Molingkwan, Kiangsu, 1934-36

組距 Range	作物面積 Crop area 不均 Average	農家數目 Number of farms	農業工 人等數 Man equiva- lent in agriculture	每工人等數 之作物面積 Crop area per man equivalent
畝 mow	畝 mow	數目 number	數目 number	畝 mow
少於 Less than 14.6	11.5	88	2.3	5.2
14.6-24.5	19.6	225	2.6	7.5
24.6-39.4	29.9	152	3.2	9.3
多於 More than 39.4	47.7	67	3.8	12.9
不均 Average	25.0	532	2.9	8.7

農場大小與場主資本之關係

大農場之優於小農場之另一点，即每畝房金及農具所需之資本較小。蓋農場面積增大而所需之房屋及農具資本，尚無遞增之需要也（第六，七表第三〇八頁）。

Families operating large farms were larger than those on small farms but they had more land per person. They had a much larger family income and a larger income per person. Families operating 40 mow of dyke-land had a family income per person of 38 yuan in 1935 and 56 yuan in 1936, while those operating only 14 to 15 mow had only 29 yuan in 1935 and 39 yuan in 1936.

Up-land farms studied in 1935 had an average crop area of 25.6 mow (4.3 acres) and this supported 6.1 persons (table 3, page 305). Operators' family incomes averaged 138 yuan, 23 yuan per person in 1935, and 304 yuan, 49 yuan per person, in 1936 (tables 3, 4; pages 305).

The relation of size of farm to size of family and family income was much the same on the up-land as on the dyke-land farms. In 1936, families operating 41.5 mow comprised 7.3 persons with a family income of 62 yuan per person while those operating 14.5 mow comprised only 4.9 persons with only 37 yuan per person.

Relation of size of farm to labor efficiency

One reason for the higher incomes on the larger farms is that these farms can make more efficient and complete use of their labor supply. Farms with only 11.5 mow of crop land had 2.3 men working on them but these men were not efficiently employed. They looked after only 5.2 mow (0.9 acres) per man while men on farms with 47.7 mow of crop land looked after more than twice as much, 12.9 mow (2.2 acres) per man (table 5, page 306). So much time has to be spent on work other than the various operations of cultivation, sowing, harvesting and threshing, that on small farms a large proportion of the total time is taken up by this other work and less by actually productive work. Also men on small farms are more often completely idle.

Relation of size of farm to operator's capital

Another advantage of the large as opposed to the small family farm is that per mow, less capital is required for buildings and implements. As the size of farm increases the need for buildings and implements does not increase proportionately (tables 6, 7; page 308).

農塲大小與健康習慣及教育程度之關係

　　大農塲人民之衛生程度及有煙酒略嗜好者較少，而其識字者較多（第八表第三〇九頁）蓋因農塲較大進欵稍豐者教育醫藥設備均可有力辦理識字之機會自多，衛生自易講求而能提高社會道德；至其小農之進欵，多爲衣食所需，尚虞不足，自無餘資，可供教育之用，因之其僅耕11.5畝農田者，其年齡在八歲以上者，僅有百分之21能識字。

第六表　　農塲大小與塲主資本之關係

江蘇省秣陵區一〇五自耕農一九三四至一九三六年

TABLE 6.—RELATION OF SIZE OF FARM TO OPERATOR'S CAPITAL
105 owner operated farms, Molingkwan, Kiangsu, 1934-36

作物面積 Crop area			農家數目 Number of farms	田地價值 Value of land	房屋與農具價值 Value of buildings and implements	每畝作物面積田地價值 Value of land per mow of crop area	每畝作物面積之房屋及農具價值 Value of buildings and implements per mow of crop area
組距 Range	平均 Average						
	畝 mow	畝 mow	數目 number	元 yuan	元 yuan	元 yuan	元 yuan
少於 Less than 14.6		10.5	24	459	164	44	3.4
14.6—24.5		19.4	40	754	224	39	2.3
24.6—39.4		29.8	23	1152	296	39	2.1
多於 More than 39.4		51.2	18	1961	456	38	1.9
平均 Average		25.0	105	977	265	39	2.2

第七表　農塲大小與塲主資本之關係

江蘇省秣陵區四一九半自耕農一九三四至一九三六年

TABLE 7.—RELATION OF SIZE OF FARM TO OPERATOR'S CAPITAL
419 part-owner operated farms, Molingkwan, Kiangsu, 1934-36

作物面積 Crop area			農家數目 Number of farms	田地價值 Value of land	房屋與農具價值 Value of land, buildings and implements	每畝作物面積田地價值 Value of land per mow of crop area	每畝作物面積之房屋及農具價值 Value of buildings and implements per mow of crop area
組距 Range	平均 Average						
	畝 mow	畝 mow	數目 number	元 yuan	元 yuan	元 yuan	元 yuan
少於 Less than 14.5		11.9	63	219	120	18	2.4
14.6—24.5		19.7	180	352	163	18	2.2
24.6—39.4		29.9	127	550	228	18	1.9
多於 More than 39.4		49.2	49	967	344	20	1.6
平均 Average		25.1	419	464	197	19	2.0

Relation of size of farm to health, habits and literacy

Families operating large farms are healthier, smoke, drink and gamble less and are much more literate (table 8 page 309). It is easier to keep healthy, avoid bad habits and learn to read if your income is not reduced to a bare minimum as it is on small farms. The difference between families on large and on small farms was greatest with respect to literacy. Where no money is available above what is necessary for food and clothing, nothing can be spent for education. On farms with only 11.5 mow of crop land only 21 per cent of the persons above eight years could read.

Relation of land tenure to size of farm, operator's capital and labor efficiency

Tenants had smaller families (5.7 persons) than owners (6.1 persons) and they operated smaller farms (table 9, page 310). Part-owners had the largest families (6.4 persons) but they operated the same amount of land as the full-owners. The full-owners had the highest labor efficiency chiefly because they had larger farms and more incentive to work, none of their returns being required as rent.

第八表　農場大小與農家健康習慣及教育程度之關係

江蘇省秣陵區五三二農家一九三四年一九三六年

TABLE 8.—RELATION OF SIZE OF FARM TO HEALTH, HABITS AND LITERACY OF FARM FAMILIES

532 farms, Molingkwan, Kiangsu, 1934-36

作物面積 Crop area		農家數目 Number of farms	每百上等健康人數之下等健康人數 Number of persons of C grade health per 100 persons of A grade	農家人民有煙酒或賭嗜好之比 Proportion of family smoking, drinking or gambling	人民年齡在八歲以上識字之比 Proportion of persons over 8 years literate
組距 Range	平均 Average				
畝 mow	畝 mow	數目 number	數目 number	% per cent	% per cent
少於 Less than 14.6	11.5	88	4.4	12.1	21
14.6—24.5	19.6	225	4.6	12.6	24
24.6—39.4	29.9	152	4.0	11.4	26
多於 More than 39.4	49.7	67	3.5	11.7	35
平均 Average	25.0	532	4.2	12.0	28

第九表　租佃制度與農塲大小塲主資本及工作效率之關係

江蘇省秣陵區五三二農家一九三四至一九三六年

TABLE 9.—RELATION OF LAND TENURE TO SIZE OF FARM, OPERATOR'S CAPITAL AND LABOR EFFICIENCY

532 farms, Molingkwan, Kiangsu, 1934-36

租佃種類 Type of tenure	農家數目 Number of farms	人口數目 Number of persons	作物面積 Crop area	每工人等數 之作物面積 Crop area per man equivalent	塲主之田地 房屋及農具 資本共值 Operator's capital in land, buildings. & implements
	數目 number	數目 number	畝 mow	畝 mow	元 yuan
自耕農 Ownership	105	6.1	25.0	9.1	1242
半自耕農 Part ownership ...	419	6.4	25.1	8.6	661
佃　農 Tenancy	8	5.7	20.6	8.0	111
平均 Average	532	6.3	25.0	8.7	767

租佃制度與農塲之大小及塲主資本及工作效率之關係

佃農家庭人口(5.7人)較自耕農耕(6.1人)為少，而其經營之農田亦小，(第九表第三一〇頁)半自耕農家庭人口(6.4人)最大，其所耕種之農田與自耕農同，因其經營之田塲面積較大，工作較多，故其工作效率最高，同時不需繳租，故願努力工作也。

佃農之資本(111元)較之自耕農之資本(1242元)為小，半自耕農之耕地面積與自耕農相等，而其資本僅佔自耕農之半(661元)，故良農乃佃田以增加其農塲經營利益也。

租佃制度與健康習慣及敎育之關係

自耕農與半自耕農家庭人口，較佃農家庭人口具有煙酒或賭嗜好者為少，然其健康程度較劣(第十表第一一一頁)。其原因乃由于佃農自他處遷來，其年老者或不健全者，未能與之同來，而因經濟關係，自耕農與半自耕農家庭人口之認字者較佃農為多。

李　德　謙

第十表　租佃制度與健康習慣及敎育之關係

汇蘇省秣陵區五三二農家一九三四至一九三六年

TABLE 10.—RELATION OF LAND TENURE TO HEALTH, HABITS AND LITERACY

532 farms, Molingkwan, Kiangsu, 1934-36

佃租種類 Type of tenure	農家數目 Number of farms	每百上等健 康人數之下 等健康人數 Number of persons of C grade health per 100 persons of A grade	家庭人民有 煙酒或賭嗜 好者之比 Proportion of family smoking, drinking or gambling	人民年齡八 歲以上認字 人數之比 Proportion of persons over 8 years literate
	數目 number	數目 number	% per cent	% p.r cent
自 耕 農 Ownership	105	4.7	11.4	31.6
半自耕農 Part ownership	419	4.1	12.1	24.7
佃　　農 Tenancy	8	2.6	16.1	21.7
平均 Average	532	4.2	12.0	25.9

The tenants had much less capital (111 yuan) than the full-owners (1242 yuan). The part-owners had only a little more than half as much capital (661 yuan) as the full-owners although they operated as much land. Provided rents are not exhorbitant, renting land is one way in which a good farmer with small capital can gain the advantages of a larger farm business.

Relation of land tenure to health, habits and literacy

Although the families of full-owners and part-owners smoked, drank and gambled less than tenant families, they were not as healthy (table 10, page 311). This was partly due to the smaller proportion of old people in the tenant families. Tenants who moved in from other districts did not bring their older relatives with them. The full-owners were much more literate than the tenants and part-owners.

LI HWEI-CHIEN

農 作 物 價 格

各地物價報告因中日戰爭發生多不克如期收到

米——陝西華縣安徽宿縣之米價，自六月至八月略見上漲，因該兩處秋收前田地多被淹沒，以致農作物歉收。

小麥——自六月至八月除山西靜樂外，各地小麥價格，均形上漲，安徽宿縣八月份小麥價格為一九三○年以來之最高紀錄，由於田地水患所致。

大麥——自六月至八月除山西靜樂，陝西華縣外，各地大麥價格均呈上漲趨勢。

高粱——華北氣候適宜本家高糧豐收，故價格相當下降。

芝蔴
豌豆——黃豆豌豆及芝蔴之七八月份價格較之本年四，五，六各月報價出
黃豆　　入甚微。

第一表　　鄉鎮市場的白米批發價格
TABLE 1.—WHOLESALE PRICES OF WHITE RICE IN RURAL MARKET TOWNS

年 Year		廣西 富川 羊岩 Kwangsi Fuchwan Yangai	江西 泰和 沿溪渡 Kiangsi Taiho Yenkitu	浙江 桐廬 橫村 Chekiang Tunglu Hwen- chwen	江蘇 武進 馳家橋 Kiangsu Wuchin Li Chai	江蘇 南京 中華門 Kiangsu Nanking Chung Hwa Men	湖北 黃陂 張家店 Hupeh Hwangpe Chang- chaiten	安徽 宿縣 Anhwei Suhsien	陝西 華縣 赤水 Shensi Hwa- hsien Ch'shui
		每市石元數[1]							
		yuan per shih tan[1]							
	1930	—	—	—	13.91	—	—	15.50	—
	1931	—	—	—	9.75	—	—	10.79	—
	1932	—	—	—	9.46	—	—	11.76	—
	1933	—	—	—	6.76	—	—	9.07	—
	1934	—	—	—	8.69	—	—	8.10	—
	1935	—	—	—	10.53	—	—	10.26	—
	1936	7.05	5.18	—	9.56	—	7.90	10.52	—
十 月	Oct. 1935	—	5.41	—	10.14	—	—	8.65	—
一 月	Jan. 1937	8.09	5.60	10.26	10.43	9.50	7.87	11.28	15.08
二 月	Feb.	8.09	5.60	10.26	10.62	9.40	7.59	11.20	16.16
三 月	Mar.	8.20	5.70	9.36	10.43	8.75	7.59	11.15	15.62
四 月	Apr.	11.25	5.79	9.36	9.75	8.40	7.59	11.20	15.08
五 月	May	11.76	5.02	9.36	10.24	8.40	7.69	10.96	13.46
六 月	June		4.44	8.64	9.27	8.30	7.87	11.10	12.93
七 月	July		5.50		9.66		7.78	11.40	14.00
八 月	Aug.		4.64		9.66		7.50	12.80	14.00

1.—市石＝一公石　　　　1.　One shih tan = one hectolitre.

— 312 —

CROP PRICES

Due to the Sino-Japanese hostilities, price reports from some localities have not been received promptly.

Rice : From June to August, prices in Hwahsien, Shensi, and Suhsien, Anhwei, advanced slightly as a result of damage to local crops by flood.

Wheat: From June to August prices of wheat advanced in all localities, except Tsingloh, Shansi. In Suhsien, Anhwei, the August price was the highest recorded since 1930, reflecting flood conditions.

Barley: From June to August barley prices also advanced except in Tsingloh, Shansi, and Hwahsien, Shensi.

Kaoliang: Weather conditions in North China have been favorable for kaoliang and prices have declined considerably.

Soybeans, field peas and sesame: The prices for soybeans, field peas and sesame during July and August were not significantly different from prices in April, May and June.

第二表　　鄉鎮市塲之小麥批發價價格
TABLE 2.—WHOLESALE PRICES OF WHEAT IN RURAL MARKET TOWNS

年 Year	江西 泰和 沿溪渡 Kiangsi Taiho Yenkitu	江蘇 武進 禮家橋 Kiangsu Wuchin Li Chai	江蘇 南京 中華門 Kiangsu Nanking Chung Hwa Men	湖北 黄陂 張家店 Hupeh Hwang- pe Chang- chaiten	湖北 遠安 南關 Hupeh Yuanan South gate	安徽 宿縣 Anhwei Suhsien	陝西 華縣 赤水 Shansi Hwa- hsien Chihui	山西 靜樂 Shensi Tsing- loh
			每市担元數[2] *yuan per shih picul[2]*					
1930	—	4.42	4.96	—	—	3.77	—	7.48
1931	—	3.43	4.28	—	—	4.95	—	5.74
1932	—	3.32	3.54	—	—	4.32	—	5.12
1933	—	2.91	2.61	—	—	2.87	—	3.28
1934	—	3.08	2.80	—	—	2.56	—	2.68
1935	—	3.61	3.42	—	—	3.31	—	2.88
1936	4.03	4.87	4.38	5.09	4.15	4.51	—	4.58
十月 Oct. 1935	2.58	3.84	3.24	3.68	3.24	3.77	—	2.65
一月 Jan. 1937	7.22	6.17	5.83	6.15	6.09	5.76	9.43	7.68
二月 Feb.	5.84	6.05	5.68	5.83	5.71	5.73	9.77	7.12
三月 Mar.	6.70	5.93	5.87	5.83	5.33	5.73	9.77	7.33
四月 Apr.	4.04	5.99	5.20	3.81	4.19	5.60	9.77	6.07
五月 May	6.87	5.70	4.97	3.93	3.81	5.05	8.03	6.84
六月 June	5.15	4.89	4.62	4.12	2.89	5.30	6.98	6.98
七月 July	3.69	5.70		4.50	4.34	5.79	7.33	5.93
八月 Aug.	5.76	6.11		4.57	3.81	6.10	8.03	6.84

2.—一市担＝五十公斤　　2. One shih picul = 50 kilograms.

第三表　鄉鎮市塲之大麥批發價格
TABLE 3.—WHOLESALE PRICES OF BARLEY IN RURAL MARKET TOWNS

年 Year	江蘇 武進 戚家橋 Kiangsu Wuchin Li Chai	江蘇 南京 中華門 Kiangsu Nanking Chung Hwa Men	湖北 黃陂 張家店 Hupeh Hwangpe Chang- chaiten	湖北 遠安 南關 Hupeh Yuanan South gate	安徽 宿縣 Anhwei Suhsien	陝西 華縣 赤水 Shensi Hwa- hsien Chishui	山西 靜樂 Shansi Tsingloh
			每市担元敕 *yuan per shih picul*				
1930	6.03	3.48		—	2.28	—	4.22
1931	5.09	3.32		—	3.34	—	2.59
1932	4.74	2.63		—	2.96	—	2.90
1933	3.70	2.00		—	1.54	—	1.30
1934	3.97	1.75		—	1.37	—	1.05
1935	4.57	2.19		—	2.25	—	1.83
1936	5.42	3.10	3.12	3.03	2.99	—	3.58
十月 Oct. 1935	4.74	2.14	3.42	2.51	2.68	—	1.68
一月 Jan. 1937	5.43	4.29	3.25	3.93	3.71	5.87	4.65
二月 Feb.	5.52	4.43	3.25	3.67	3.67	6.29	4.84
三月 Mar	5.78	5.36	3.42	4.50	3.60	6.29	4.84
四月 Apr.	5.00	4.05	2.65	3.40	3.31	7.54	4.19
五月 May	4.48	3.61	2.23	1.83	2.97	7.54	4.28
六月 June	4.66	3.82	2.40	2.20	3.00	5.87	4.47
七月 July	5.78		2.40	2.36	3.41	6.29	3.17
八月 Aug.	5.52		2.65	2.09	3.11	5.03	3.26

第四表　鄉鎮市塲之高粱批發價格
TABLE 4.—WHOLESALE PRICES OF RED KAOLIANG IN RURAL MARKET TOWNS

年 Year	湖北 遠安 南關 Hupeh Yuanan South gate	安徽 宿縣 Anhwei Suhsien	河北 正定 傅家村 Hopen Chengting Fuchaichwen	陝西 華縣 赤水 Shensi Hwahsien Chishui	山西 靜樂 Shansi Tsingloh
		每市担元敕 *yuan per shih picul*			
1930	—	2.13	3.59	—	4.06
1931	—	3.63	3.52	—	2.51
1932	—	3.41	3.56	—	1.95
1933	—	1.61	2.52	—	0.83
1934	—	1.31	2.09	—	0.72
1935	—	2.24	3.09	—	1.20
1936	2.32	3.00	4.69	—	2.30
十月 Oct. 1935	2.51	2.41	3.49	—	1.31
一月 Jan. 1937	3.18	3.41	5.62	5.12	2.33
二月 Feb.	2.93	3.36	5.54	5.12	2.77
三月 Mar.	3.43	3.29	5.75	5.12	3.42
四月 Apr.	2.09	3.16	5.19	6.98	3.06
五月 May		2.77	4.97	9.30	2.99
六月 June		3.00		5.12	3.13
七月 July		3.14		5.12	2.77
八月 Aug.		2.39		4.65	2.84

第五表　鄉鎮市場之黃豆批發價格
TABLE 5.—WHOLESALE PRICES OF YELLOW SOYBEANS IN RURAL MARKET TOWNS

年 Year	江西 泰和 沿溪渡 Kiangsi Taiho Yenkitu	江蘇 武進 戚家橋 Kiangsu Wuchin Li Chai	江蘇 南京 中華門 Kiangsu Nanking Chung Hwa Men	湖北 黃陂 張家店 Hupeh Hwangpe Chang- chaiten	湖北 遠安 南關 Hupeh Yuanan South gate	安徽 宿縣 Anhwei Suhsien	陝西 華縣 赤水 Shensi Hwa- hsien Chishui	山西 靜樂 Shansi Tsingloh
			每市担元數 *yuan per shih picul*					
1930	—	5.51	5.51	—	—	3.86	—	5.00
1931	—	5.57	6.20	—	—	4.48	—	3.13
1932	—	4.31	5.43	—	—	4.81	—	2.54
1933	—	3.71	3.80	—	—	2.57	—	1.69
1934	—	3.17	3.16	—	—	1.99	—	1.19
1935	—	5.53	3.69	—	—	2.83	—	1.63
1936	5.56	4.91	5.16	5.02	3.58	4.52	—	3.19
十月 Oct. 1935	3.44	3.71	3.83	4.57	3.16	3.02	—	1.74
一月 Jan. 1937	6.01	5.33	6.59	4.57	4.57	4.96	5.80	3.89
二月 Feb.	6.70	5.33	6.45	5.20	5.71	4.97	6.12	3.62
三月 Mar.	5.41	5.45	6.09	5.58	5.52	4.88	5.80	4.56
四月 Apr.	5.33	5.57	6.51	5.33	5.71	5.00	5.16	3.89
五月 May	5.41	5.27	6.52	5.33	4.57	5.06	6.44	3.69
六月 June	4.47	5.15	6.73	5.26	3.88	4.79	5.48	3.89
七月 July	4.51	6.04		5.26	4.95	5.20	5.48	3.55
八月 Aug.	5.15	5.21		4.44	5.33	5.18	5.48	3.62

第六表　鄉鎮市場之豌豆批發價格
TABLE 6.—WHOLESALE PRICES OF FIELD PEAS IN RURAL MARKET TOWNS

年 Year	江蘇 南京 中華門 Kiangsu Nanking Chung Hwa Men	湖北 黃陂 張家店 Hupeh Hwangpe Chang chaiten	河北 正定 傅家村 Hopen Chengting Fuchaichwen	陝西 華縣 赤山 Shensi Hwa Hsien Chishui	山西 靜樂 Shansi Tsingloh
		每市担元數 *yuan per shih picul*			
1930	4.63	—	4.14	—	5.12
1931	4.77	—	4.31	—	3.08
1932	4.22	—	4.36	—	2.14
1933	3.25	—	2.98	—	1.14
1934	2.68	—	2.12	—	0.92
1935	3.15	—	3.23	—	1.81
1936	3.80	3.13	4.75	—	2.91
十月 Oct. 1935	2.89	4.16	3.18	—	1.74
一月 Jan. 1937	3.73	3.69	5.96	8.40	3.60
二月 Feb.	3.66	3.75	6.08	8.40	3.98
三月 Mar.	4.04	3.57	6.23	8.40	4.13
四月 Apr.	4.35	3.63	6.59	7.50	3.85
五月 May	4.35	3.69	6.23	6.60	3.23
六月 June	4.97	3.63		6.00	3.79
七月 July		3.63		6.00	3.11
八月 Aug.		3.75		6.00	3.17

第七表　　鄉鎮市場之芝蔴批發價格

TABLE 7.—WHOLESALE PRICES OF SESAME IN RURAL MARKET TOWNS

年 Year	江蘇 南京 中華門 Nanking Chung Hwa Men	安徽 宿縣 Anhwei Suhsien	河北正定 傳家村 Hopeh Chengting Fuchaichwen	陝西華縣 赤水 Shensi Hwahsien Chishui
	每市担元數			
	yuan per shih picul			
1930	8.22	4.86	6.97	—
1931	12.14	9.34	7.91	—
1932	12.31	10.28	7.63	—
1933	7.52	4.82	4.86	—
1934	5.24	3.40	4.49	—
1935	5.91	4.49	6.08	—
1936	9.01	6.96	7.76	—
十月 Oct. 1935	5.28	4.33	6.44	
一月 Jan. 1937	11.06	7.29	8.16	13.95
二月 Feb.	11.38	7.20	9.02	13.95
三月 Mar.	11.38	7.20	9.23	13.95
四月 Apr.	10.38	7.13	9.23	11.63
五月 May	10.08	7.23	9.02	13.95
六月 June	10.57	7.05		7.91
七月 July		7.26		8.37
八月 Aug.		7.35		9.30

楊 蔚　YANG WEI

盧盛懷　LU SHENG-HWAI

經 濟 統 計

ECONOMIC FACTS

南京金陵大學農學院農業經濟系出版
DEPARTMENT OF AGRICULTURAL ECONOMICS
COLLEGE OF AGRICULTURE AND FORESTRY
UNIVERSITY OF NANKING
NANKING, CHINA

第八期 No. 8 　　　　　　　　一九三八年一月 January, 1938

第一表　　米價格之季節變動指數

中國五省六個地區

TABLE 1.—INDEX NUMBERS OF SEASONAL VARIATION OF
PRICES OF RICE

6 localities, 5 provinces, China

月份 Month	冬麥高粱區 河 北 正 定 Winter Wheat-kaoliang Area: Hopeh, Chengting	揚 子 水 稻 小 麥 區 Yangtze Rice-wheat Area:			四川水稻區 四 川 涪 陵 Szechwan Rice Area: Szechwan, Fowling	水稻兩穫區 廣 西 容 縣 Double Cropping Rice Area: Kwangsi, Jung
		安 徽 六 安 Anhwei, Liuan	江 蘇 武 進 Kiangsu, Wuchin	江 蘇 上 海 Kiangsu, Shanghai		
		指數，　全年平均=一〇〇 Index, average for year = 100				
一月 Jan. ..	101.9	97.3	96.7	93.3	102.4	99.0
二月 Feb. ..	102.3	99.8	97.9	97.3	101.7	98.3
三月 March	102.9	102.1	98.7	97.7	100.9	100.6
四月 April .	103.1	101.8	98.1	97.1	99.6	102.9
五月 May ..	102.6	102.6	98.9	99.3	99.7	102.2
六月 June .	102.6	102.3	101.5	102.9	98.5	101.6
七月 July ..	102.1	102.0	105.9	107.9	97.8	100.9
八月 August	101.0	98.6	105.4	109.3	95.8	100.2
九月 Sept. .	94.6	98.3	104.8	107.6	97.4	99.6
十月 Oct. ..	94.0	97.9	98.7	100.4	100.6	98.9
十一月 Nov. .	95.4	98.8	96.1	93.9	102.5	98.2
十二月 Dec. ..	97.5	98.5	97.3	93.5	103.1	97.6
平均 Average	100.0	100.0	100.0	100.0	100.0	100.0
研究包括 Years 之年份 studied	1907– 1931	1914– 1932	1894– 1931	1896– 1930	1915– 1930	1909– 1931

農產物價格之季節變動及貯藏之獲利性

農民所得物價在收穫時輒較其他時期為低。收穫期間，農民因急於清償債務，不得不廉價脫售其產品以獲得必需之現金，且貯藏居奇，不獨損壞堪慮，且冒水火風險，又須佔用資金。故本季收穫時期至下季收穫時期中，價格之增加，必須高於此期內之貯藏成本，始為有利可圖。

本文之目的在計算農產物價之季節變動，以決定貯藏之利益，及收穫時即行割賣之損失[1]。

各種農作物價格之季節變動

物價季節變異指數均經分別計算。各指數為陽曆十二個月每月之平均物價，而以十二個月之平均數為一〇〇，因此如六月份之米價季節變異指數為一〇五，即謂六月份之價格高於全年百分之五。

因本文包括之研究期間一般物價之長期趨勢係向上，故年終數月之價格恒高於年初數月。在計算指數時，此種趨勢必須予以糾正，使指數所指為既無向上，亦無向下趨勢之長時期內之季節變動。

米：在本文所有資料中，米價之季節變動，以上海與武進兩地較其他市場為高（第三一七頁第一表）。上海批發市場八月之指數為一〇九·三，一月為九三·三（全年平均＝一〇〇）本地米之供給，夏季恒低，而十二月及每年一月恒高。洋米進口雖可調濟本地米之供求，但不足減滅價格之季節變異。夏季之高價足以抵償秋收至次夏之貯屯及運輸費用。每當夏季市場中洋米充斥，秋收成數復以氣候變異不定，不易估計，運米上海每有重大虧蝕之虞，故夏季米價較高，自九月至十一月價格驟跌，則因新穀登場，長江流域及浙江之米源源輸入也。

武進位於上海西北九二英里，為揚子水稻小麥區，其季節變動不若上海之大，此因農村貯屯費用較低之故。同時一部分稻產貯藏之目的不在牟利，而純為積穀防饑，或慮稻產脫售後現款將受幣值貶落之損失。

---

1 本文研究資料，除江蘇上海武進兩地外，餘皆蒐用卜凱教授調查之「中國土地利用」資料。又有一部份資料乃店商付與商販之價格，而非直接付與農民之價格。但除上海之批發市價外，其餘皆可視為農民所得物價，因是項資料均係直接自生產區域蒐集者。上海資料摘自一九三一年六月上海市政府食糧管理委員會出版之「食糧問題」第一四九——一五〇及一六二——一六三頁，且為上產粳米之價格。

一九三一年九月以後因一般物價水準漲落猛烈校正甚為不易，故此後之季節變異未加分析，近來季節變動與一九三一年以前未必有顯著之不同，蓋貯藏與運銷情形均無重要之改變也。季節變動指數乃以物爾生氏之中位總實法計算，而以數學校正之。

— 318 —

SEASONAL VARIATION OF PRICES FOR FARM PRODUCTS AND THE PROFITABILITY OF STORAGE

Prices paid to farmers are often lower at harvest time than later. At harvest, pressing debts have to be repaid and produce is forced on the market to obtain the necessary cash. Also, to store and sell later involves the likelihood of deterioration, risks of fire and flood, and the use of capital. The costs of storage must be met by a corresponding increase in prices from harvest time until harvest time again.

The purpose of this study is to measure the seasonal variation of prices so that the profitability of storage and the losses incurred by having to sell at harvest time can be determined.[1]

Seasonal variation of prices of individual crops

Index numbers of seasonal variation have been calculated. These index numbers are averages of prices in each of the twelve months of the solar calendar. The mean of the twelve monthly averages equals 100. Thus, if the index of seasonal variation of prices of rice is 105 in July, this signifies that, on the average, prices in July are 5 per cent higher than in the year as a whole.

Because the general long term trend of prices was upward during the period studied, prices during the last months of the year tended to be higher than during the first months. In calculating the index numbers, this tendency has been allowed for, so that it is the seasonal variation to be expected during a period when the long term trend of prices is neither upward nor downward that is shown by the index numbers.

Rice: The seasonal variation of prices for rice was greater in Shanghai and Wuchin than in other markets for which data were available (table 1, page 317). On the Shanghai wholesale market, the index was 109.3 in August and 93.3 in January (average for the year=100). Arrivals of domestic rice are usually low in summer and high in December and the first month of the year. Imports from abroad tend to compensate for this variation in domestic supplies but do not eliminate the seasonal variation of prices. The costs of holding and transporting stocks to meet the summer demands are paid for by the higher prices.

---

1 Excepting the series for Shanghai and Wuchin, Kiangsu, the data used for this study were collected for Dr. J. Lossing Buck's investigation of *Land Utilization in China*. In some cases they are prices paid by shopkeepers to dealers who purchased from farmers and not prices paid directly to farmers. But, excepting the series of wholesale market prices in Shanghai, all the series are considered as similar in behaviour to prices received by farmers because they were reported from localities directly in the producing areas. The data for Shanghai were taken from; "The Food Committee of the Municipal Government of Greater Shanghai; '*Food Problems*,' pp. 149-150, 162-163, June, 1931," and are prices of domestic late rice.

Price movements after September, 1931, have not been analyzed for seasonal variation because of the difficulty of adjusting for the rapid fall and rise of the general price level after that date. It is improbable that, in recent years, the variations arising from seasonal causes have differed significantly from such variations prior to 1931 because no important changes in storage or marketing have been brought about.

The indices of seasonal variation were obtained by Person's median link relative method, using arithmetic adjustment of the medians.

安徽六安亦位於揚子水稻小麥區，但所產水稻較少於武進，小麥則較多。其米價季節變動較小，最高指數在五月（一〇二‧六）適在小麥收穫之前。緊隨水稻收穫後之十月份指數即跌至九七‧九。

河北正定位於冬麥高粱區，產米甚少，季節變動指數以四月爲最高（一〇三‧一），時在小麥收穫以前，十月爲最低（九四‧〇），時值水稻收穫之後。

四川涪陵位於四川水稻區，最低價格在八月收穫期（九五‧八），而最高在十二月（一〇三‧一）。

廣西容縣米價季節變動較任何一地爲小，蓋容縣位於水稻兩穫區，全年收穫兩次，一在六月，一在十一月。季節變動指數以第二次收穫後之十二月爲最低（九七‧六），而以四月爲最高（一〇二‧九），時在第一次收穫之前。

小麥：　小麥價格之季節變動，以位於冬麥高粱區之河北正定爲最大，其四月份之指數爲一一〇‧一，時在收穫之前，而新麥登場後之五月份指數僅及八八‧八（第三二〇頁第二表）。此項節季變動爲本文各種作物中之最大者。河南汲縣亦位於冬麥高粱區，麥價亦以五月（九三‧八）爲最低，而以九月（一〇三‧四）爲最高。

第二表　　小麥價格之季節變動指數
中國六省七個地區

TABLE 2.—INDEX NUMBERS OF SEASONAL VARIATION OF PRICES OF WHEAT

7 localities, 6 provinces, China

月份 Month	冬麥小米區 山西 太谷 Winter Wheat- millet Area: Shansi, Taiku	冬麥高粱區 河南 汲縣 Winter Wheat- kaoliang Area: Honan, Chi	河北 正定 Hopeh, Chengting	揚子水稻小麥區 安徽 六安 Yangtze Rice-wheat Area: Anhwei, Liuan	江蘇 武進 Kiangsu, Wuchin	江蘇 上海 Kiangsu, Shanghai	四川水稻區 四川 涪陵 Szechwan Rice Area: Szechwan, Fowling
指數，　全年平均＝一〇〇 Index, average for year = 100							
一月 Jan. ..	99.3	101.7	106.2	101.1	104.8	102.4	101.7
二月 Feb. ..	99.6	101.9	106.7	106.7	104.3	104.5	100.6
三月 March	99.0	100.3	109.2	110.2	105.5	104.6	100.1
四月 April .	100.2	98.8	110.1	107.5	101.0	102.8	97.8
五月 May ..	101.8	93.8	88.8	107.5	98.8	98.5	95.5
六月 June ..	100.8	96.0	91.3	90.5	92.7	95.7	94.9
七月 July ..	99.2	101.6	94.6	90.4	92.9	94.8	96.6
八月 August	98.6	102.2	97.1	90.3	94.8	96.2	99.1
九月 Sept. ..	97.3	103.4	98.2	97.6	97.9	98.1	103.4
十月 Oct. ..	100.6	101.9	98.4	97.5	100.9	100.4	103.1
十一月 Nov.	101.1	100.0	98.5	99.2	102.6	100.5	103.2
十二月 Dec.	102.5	98.4	100.9	99.0	103.8	101.5	104.0
平均 Average	100.0	100.0	100.0	100.0	100.0	100.0	100.0
研究包括 Years 之年份　studied	1912– 1929	1921– 1931	1907– 1931	1916– 1931	1894– 1931	1898– 1930	1915– 1930

Higher prices in summer may also be due to the greater risks of shipping rice to Shanghai at a time when foreign shipments have more influence on the market and estimates of the new domestic crop are liable to change rapidly because of changes in the weather. Prices decline rapidly from September to November when shipments of the new crop from the Yangtze Valley and Chekiang are increasing.

In Wuchin (Wutsin) which is 92 miles northwest of Shanghai and in the Yangtze Rice-wheat Area, the seasonal variation was not quite so great as in Shanghai. This is because the costs of storage are smaller in rural districts. It may also be due to the fact that, as in other rural districts, some grain was stored not for profit but for fear of crop failures or a loss in the real value of savings kept in the form of money.

Liuan, Anhwei, is also in the Yangtze Rice-wheat Area, but less rice and more wheat is grown there than in Wuchin, Kiangsu. The seasonal variation of rice prices was smaller and the index was highest in May (102.6) just before the wheat harvest. The index sagged to 97.9 in October following the rice harvest.

第三表　小米價格之季節變動指數
中國山西河南及河北三省三個地區
TABLE 3.—INDEX NUMBERS OF SEASONAL VARIATION OF PRICES OF MILLET
3 localities, Shansi, Honan and Hopeh, China

月份 Month	冬麥小米區 山　西 太　谷 Winter Wheat- millet Area: Shansi, Taiku	冬麥高粱區 河　南 汲　縣 Winter Wheat-kaoliang Area: Honan, Chi	河　北 正　定 Hopeh. Chengting
指數，全年平均＝一〇〇 *Index, average for year = 100*			
一月 January	98.1	101.8	100.4
二月 February	97.8	102.0	100.6
三月 March	97.9	105.4	101.6
四月 April	99.3	105.6	101.8
五月 May	100.8	105.8	104.5
六月 June	102.8	106.0	104.7
七月 July	104.3	102.3	104.4
八月 August	100.3	96.1	93.3
九月 September	102.0	94.7	95.4
十月 October	99.3	94.9	96.5
十一月 November	98.9	92.6	98.3
十二月 December	98.5	92.8	98.5
平均 Average	100.0	100.0	100.0
研究包括之年份 Years studied	1912-1929	1921-1931	1907-1931

— 321 —

揚子水稻小麥區之麥價，均以三月爲最高。 六安之麥價自三月份之一
一〇‧二，下跌至六月份收穫期之九〇‧五。 武進新麥登場在五六月間，
麥價自三月份之一〇五‧五，跌至五月份之九八‧八， 更跌至六月份之九
二‧七。上海批發市價則自三月份之一〇四‧六， 跌至五月份之九八‧五
，再跌至六月份九五‧七， 上海與武進之麥價季節變動之適應不如米價之
關係爲切，因上海小麥輸入仰賴於蘇浙兩省者， 亦不如米之多也。

四川涪陵麥價以五六月（收穫時）爲最低，而以十二月爲最高（一〇四
‧〇）此点與稻相同。

小米： 河北正定位於冬麥高粱區， 小米價格以六月爲最高（一〇四
‧七）以八月（九三‧三）及九月（九五‧四）爲最低，該兩月爲小麥收穫
期（第三二一頁第三表）。

河南汲縣亦位於冬麥高粱區，價格變動較大。 六月份指數爲一〇六‧
〇，十一月爲九二‧六。山西太谷位於冬麥小米區， 價格之季節低点遲至
二月（九七‧八），其時脫售產品，大都爲陰曆年關還債之用。

第四表　　玉米價格之季節變動指數
中國山西河北及四川三省三個地區
TABLE 4.—INDEX NUMBERS OF SEASONAL VARIATION OF PRICES OF CORN
3 localities, Shansi, Hopeh and Szechwan, China

月 份 Month	冬麥小米區 山 西 太 谷 Winter Wheat- millet Area: Shansi, Taiku	冬麥高粱區 河 北 正 定 Winter Wheat- kaoliang Area: Hopeh, Chengting	四川水稻區 四 川 涪 陵 Szechwan, Rice Area: Szechwan, Fowling
	指數，全年平均＝一〇〇 Index, average for year = 100		
一月 January	96.7	101.8	103.0
二月 February	96.3	102.4	103.2
三月 March	99.6	103.7	101.4
四月 April	100.4	104.6	102.2
五月 May	102.1	104.6	100.5
六月 June	102.5	104.6	94.9
七月 July	102.1	94.1	94.9
八月 August	101.0	94.3	95.5
九月 September	102.0	97.2	96.1
十月 October	101.6	97.2	99.1
十一月 November	98.6	97.1	103.1
十二月 December	97.1	98.3	106.2
平均 Average	100.0	100.0	100.0
研究包括之年份 Years studied	1912-1929	1907-1931	1915-1930

Chengting, Hopeh, is in the Winter Wheat-kaoliang Area, where very little rice is grown. The index of seasonal variation was highest in April (103.1) before the wheat harvest, and lowest in October (94.0) after the rice harvest.

In Fowling, Szechwan, in the Szechwan Rice Area, the lowest prices were in August, the harvest month (95.8), and the highest were in December (103.1).

In Jung, Kwangsi, the seasonal variation was smaller than in any of the other localities. Jung is in the Double Cropping Rice Area and can depend on two harvest, one in June and the other in November. The index of seasonal variation was lowest in December (97.6) after the second crop, and highest in April (102.9) before the first.

Wheat: The seasonal variation of wheat prices was greater in Chengting, Hopeh, in the Winter Wheat-kaoliang Area, than elsewhere, the index being 110.1 in April just before harvest, and 88.8 in May when the new crop was entering the market (table 2, page 320). This seasonal variation was the largest recorded for any crop. In Chi, Honan, which is also in the Winter Wheat-kaoliang Area, wheat prices were also lowest in May (93.8) but highest in September (103.4).

In the Yangtze Rice-wheat Area, prices were highest in March, in Liuan. Prices declined from 110.2 in March to 90.5 in June, the harvest month, and in Wuchin, where the new crop enters the market in May and June, prices declined from 105.5 in March to 98.8 in May and 92.7 in June. On the Shanghai wholesale market, prices declined from 104.6 in March to 98.5 in May and 95.7 in June. Shanghai does not depend on Kiangsu and Chekiang as much for its wheat as for its rice so the correspondance of the seasonal movements in Shanghai and Wuchin was not so close for wheat as for rice.

In Fowling, Szechwan, prices were lowest in May and June, the harvest months, but, as for rice, were highest in December (104.0).

Millet: In Chengting, Hopeh, in the Winter Wheat-kaoliang Area, prices for millet were highest in June (104.7) and lowest in August (93.3) and September (95.4), the harvest months (table 3, page 321).

In Chi, Honan, which is also in the Winter Wheat-kaoliang Area, the variation was greater, the index being 106.0 in June and 92.6 in November. In Taiku, Shansi, in the Winter Wheat-millet Area, prices reached their seasonal low even later, in February (97.8) at the time when produce is sold to liquidate debts due at the Chinese New Year.

玉米： 太谷與正定玉米價格之季節變動與小米相似（第三二二頁第四表），四川水稻區涪陵之玉米價格以六七月收穫時為最低（九四·九），而與米麥相同，以十二月為最高。

高粱： 太谷與正定高粱價格之季節變動與小米及玉米相似，惟太谷之最高價格較早一個月為五月（一○三·一）（第三二四頁第五表）。

大麥： 江蘇武進大麥之季節變動甚廣，三月份之指數為一○五·八，至五月收穫時僅為八九·八（第三二五頁第六表）。

大豆： 大豆價格之季節變動，以揚子水稻小麥之安徽六安為最大。自八月新豆未登場時之一○五·一，跌至十月之九一·一（第三二六頁第七表）。最高價格在五六兩月（一○七·四，一○七·六）。 江蘇武進亦然，其五月份價格為一○三·七，六月份為一○三·四，至八月份則跌為九五·九。

冬麥高粱區之河北正定，大豆價格以七月為最高（一○四·四），而以八月為最低（九四·六）。

第五表　　高粱價格之季節變動指數
中國山西太谷及河北正定
TABLE 5.—INDEX NUMBERS OF SEASONAL VARIATION OF PRICES OF KAOLIANG
Taiku, Shansi, and Chengting, Hopeh, China

月　份 Month	冬麥小米區 山　西 太　谷 Winter Wheat-millet Area: Shansi, Taiku	冬麥高粱區 河　北 正　定 Winter Wheat-kaoliang Area: Hopeh, Chengting
	指數，　全年平均＝一○○ Index, average for year = 100	
一月 January	95.5	101.6
二月 February	95.2	103.3
三月 March	99.2	103.2
四月 April	102.4	103.2
五月 May	103.1	103.1
六月 June	102.8	103.3
七月 July	102.4	99.9
八月 August	102.1	93.2
九月 September	101.8	94.8
十月 October	100.0	96.7
十一月 November	99.6	98.5
十二月 December	95.9	99.2
平　均　Average	100.0	100.0
研究包括之年份 Years studied	1912-1929	1907-1931

Corn: In Taiku and Chengting, the seasonal movement of prices for corn was similar to that of prices for millet (table 4, page 322). In Fowling in the Szechwan Rice Area, prices for corn were lowest at harvest in June and July (94.9) and, as for rice and wheat, highest in December.

Kaoliang: In Taiku and Chengting the seasonal movement of prices for kaoliang was similar to that of prices for millet and corn, except that in Taiku the highest prices were one month earlier, in May, (103.1) (table 5, page 324).

Barley: The seasonal variation of barley prices in Wuchin, Kiangsu, was wide, the index being 105.8 in March, and only 89.8 at harvest time in May (table 6, page 325).

第六表　大麥價格之季節變動指數
中國江蘇武進　一九〇九年至一九三一年

TABLE 6.—INDEX NUMBERS OF SEASONAL VARIATION OF PRICES OF BARLEY.

Wuchin, Kiangsu, China, 1909-31

月 份 Month	指數，全年平均＝一〇〇 Index, average for year = 100
一月January	105.0
二月February	104.5
三月March	105.8
四月April	103.5
五月May	89.8
六月June	94.3
七月July	93.9
八月August	95.9
九月September	98.7
十月October	102.0
十一月November	103.5
十二月December	103.1
平均 Average	100.0

Soybeans: The seasonal variation of soybean prices was greatest in Liuan, Anhwei, in the Yangtze Rice-wheat Area, falling from 105.1 in August, before the new crop was ready, to 91.1 in October (table 7, page 326). The highest prices were paid in May and June (107.4, 107.6). This was true also in Wuchin, Kiangsu, where prices were 103.7 in May and 103.4 in June and declined to 95.9 in August.

In Chengting, Hopeh, in the Winter Wheat-kaoliang Area, prices were the highest in July (104.4) and lowest in August (94.6).

In Fowling in the Szechwan Rice Area, prices were lowest in July (97.8) and August (97.7), the harvest months, but highest in January (103.4). Rice and wheat prices in this locality were highest in December.

Field peas: Prices for field peas were at their lowest in Fowling in April (98.0) the harvest month, and highest in September (102.8) (table 8, page 327). In Chengting, the low harvest prices were in May (96.9) and June (96.7) and the highest prices in March (103.2).

四川水稻區涪陵之價格最低為七月（九七・八），與八月（九七・七）時為大豆收穫期，而以一月為最高（一○三・四）該地之米麥價格均以十二月為最高・

　　豌豆：　涪陵豌豆價格以四月收穫時為最低（九八・○），而以九月為最高（一○二・八）（第三二七頁第八表）。正定之最低價價格在五月（九六・九）與六月（九六・七），而最高價格在三月（一○三・二）。

　　芝蘇：　河北正定之芝蘇價格收穫時跌落甚速（第三二七頁第九表），其最高價格在六月（一○三・七）與七月（一○三・六），而最低價格則在八月（九五・六）與九月（九六・○）。

第七表　　大豆價格之季節變動指數
中國四省四個地區

TABLE 7.—INDEX NUMBERS OF SEASONAL VARIATION OF
PRICES OF SOYBEANS

4 localities, 4 provinces, China

月份 Month	冬麥高粱區 河北 正定 Winter Wheat-kaoliang Area: Hopeh, Chengting	揚子水稻小麥區 安徽 六安 Yangtze Rice-wheat Area: Anhwei, Liuan	江蘇 武進 Kiangsu, Wuchin	四川水稻區 四川 涪陵 Szechwan Rice Area: Szechwan, Fowling
指數，全年平均＝一○○ *Index, average for year = 100*				
一月 January	100.5	94.0	101.7	103.4
二月 February	100.9	103.1	100.8	102.8
三月 March	101.3	103.3	101.7	102.2
四月 April	103.1	103.5	102.5	102.0
五月 May	103.5	107.4	103.7	99.2
六月 June	104.0	107.6	103.4	98.4
七月 July	104.4	104.8	102.5	97.8
八月 August	94.6	105.1	95.9	97.7
九月 September	95.9	94.9	94.9	100.5
十月 October	96.3	91.1	96.5	99.3
十一月 November	96.9	91.4	97.3	97.9
十二月 December	98.6	93.8	99.1	98.7
平均 Average	100.0	100.0	100.0	100.0
研究包括之年份 Years studied	1907-1931	1916-1922	1909-1931	1915-1924

最低價格月以後之價格變動

　　為比較各地區之季節變動計，曾將最低指數月以後季節變動指數增高之百分率加以計算（第三二八頁至三三四頁第十至十八表）。此增高百分率表明商品價格經過多年無漲落趨勢之長期內最理想之平均增加。

中國河北正定及四川涪陵

TABLE 8.—INDEX NUMBERS OF SEASONAL VARIATION OF PRICES OF FIELD PEAS
Chengting, Hopeh, and Fowling, Szechwan, China

月 份 Month	冬麥高粱區 河 北 正 定 Winter Wheat-kaoliang Area: Hopeh, Chengting	四川水稻區 四 川 涪 陵 Szechwan Rice Area: Szechwan, Fowling
指數，全年平均＝一○○ Index, average for year = 100		
一月 January	101.2	100.4
二月 February	103.1	99.4
三月 March	103.2	98.9
四月 April	101.2	98.0
五月 May	96.9	98.6
六月 June	96.7	98.2
七月 July	98.3	99.6
八月 August	98.4	100.8
九月 September	99.8	102.8
十月 October	99.9	101.0
十一月 November	100.1	101.0
十二月 December	101.1	101.3
平均 Average	100.0	100.0
研究包括之年份 Years studied	1907-1931	1915-1930

第九表　芝蔴價格之季節變動指數

中國河北正定一九○七年至一九三一年

TABLE 9.—INDEX NUMBERS OF SEASONAL VARIATION OF PRICES OF SESAME.
Chengting, Hopeh, China, 1907-31

月 份 Month	指數，全年平均＝一○○ Index, average for year = 100
一月 January	98.6
二月 February	99.0
三月 March	100.4
四月 April	102.3
五月 May	103.3
六月 June	103.7
七月 July	103.6
八月 August	95.6
九月 September	96.0
十月 October	97.9
十一月 November	98.9
十二月 December	100.7
平均 Average	100.0

Sesame: In Chengting, Hopeh, prices for sesame declined rapidly at harvest (table 9, page 327). The highest prices were in June (103.7) and July (103.6) and the lowest in August (95.6) and September (96.0).

Price changes following month of lowest price

In order to facilitate comparison of the seasonal movements in different localities, the percentage increases in the index of seasonal variation following the months in which the index was lowest have been computed (tables 10—18, pages 328—334). These percentage increases show the average increase to be expected over a series of years when the long-term trend of commodity prices is neither upward nor downward.

計算季節變動指數最低月以後，價格上升，下降，或保持不變之年數時，該期間內，物價向上之長期趨勢不能取消[2]。以故季節變動指數最低月後價格上升之年數勢較長期趨勢水平時爲多。 然比較季節變動指數最低月以後價格上升，下降，及相等之年數，仍足表示月與月間變動歷年來之差異。

米： 上海價格自一月至七月上升者，三五年中有三三年，平均上升數爲百分之一五‧六(第三二八頁第十表)。 武進物價自十一月至次年七月上升者，三八年中佔二九年，平均上升數爲百分之九‧七。 除河北正定因十月之價格特低，以後月份上升之年數甚大外，其餘各地之最低價格月後之價格上升之年數均不如上海武進爲多。

第十表　米最低價之月以後之價格變動
中國五省六個地區

TABLE 10.—RICE—PRICE CHANGES FOLLOWING MONTH
OF LOWEST PRICES

6 localities, 5 provinces, China

		河北正定 Hopeh, Chengting	安徽六安 Anhwei, Liuan	江蘇武進 Kiangsu, Wuchin	江蘇上海 Kiangsu, Shanghai	四川涪陵 Szechwan, Fowling	廣西容縣 Kwangsi, Jung
研究所包括之年份	Years studied	1907–1931	1914–1932	1894–1931	1896–1930	1915–1930	1909–1931
年數	Number of years	25	19	38	35	16	23
最低中位價格之月	Month of lowest median price	十月 Oct.	一月 Jan.	士一月 Nov.	一月 Jan.	八月 Aug.	士二月 Dec.

以下月數以後之價格變動 Change in price after:

對最低中位價格月之中位價格百分比
per cent of median price in month of lowest median price

三個月後	3 months	8.4	4.6	1.9	4.1	7.0	3.1
六個月後	6 months	9.7	4.8	2.9	15.6	6.2	4.1
九個月後	9 months	8.6	0.6	9.7	7.6	4.1	2.0

各月份價格高於(十)低於(一)及等於(二)最低中位價之年數
Number of years when prices were higher (+), lower (−), and the same (=) after:

		+	−	=	+	−	=	+	−	=	+	−	=	+	−	=	+	−	=
三個月後	3 months	20	4	1	13	4	2	21	13	4	23	12	0	15	1	0	10	8	5
六個月後	6 months	22	3	0	15	4	0	22	14	2	33	2	0	14	1	1	13	6	4
九個月後	9 months	22	3	0	11	8	0	29	7	2	24	11	0	13	3	0	8	11	4

2. 自一八九四年至一九三一年一般物價水準每月之平均上升率爲複率百分之〇‧一九七。

In counting the number of years in which prices advanced, declined, or remained the same following the month in which the index of seasonal variation was lowest, the long-term upward trend of commodity prices during the period studied could not be allowed for.[2] The number of years in which prices advanced from the month when the index of seasonal variation was lowest was thus greater than it would have been in a period when there was no long term upward tendency. A comparison of the number of years in which prices advanced, declined, and remained the same following the month of lowest index does, however, indicate the variation between years with respect to the month to month movements.

Rice: In Shanghai, prices advanced from January to July in 33 out of 35 years, the average advance being 15.6 per cent (table 10, page 328). In Wuchin, prices advanced from November to July in 29 out of 38 years, the average advance being 9.7 per cent. Except in Chengting, Hopeh, where prices in October were especially low, advances following the month of lowest prices were not as great in other markets as in Shanghai and Wuchin.

第十一表　小麥最低價之月以後之價格變動
中國六省七個地區
TABLE 11.—WHEAT—PRICE CHANGES FOLLOWING MONTH OF LOWEST PRICES
7 localities, 6 provinces, China

	山西 太谷 Shansi, Taiku	河南 汲縣 Honan, Chi	河北 正定 Hopeh, Chengting	安徽 六安 Anhwei, Liuan	江蘇 武進 Kiangsu, Wuchin	江蘇 上海 Kiangsu, Shanghai	四川 涪陵 Szechwan, Fowling
研究所包 Years 括之年份 studied	1912–1929	1921–1931	1907–1931	1916–1931	1894–1931	1898–1930	1915–1930
年數 Number of years	18	11(a)	25	16	38	33	16
最低中位 Month of 價格之月 lowest median prices	九月 Sep.	五月 May	五月 May	八月 Aug.	六月 June	七月 July	六月 June

以下月數以後 Change in 之價格變動 price after:

對最低中位價格月之中位價格百分比
per cent of median price in month of lowest median price

三個月後 3 months	5.3	9.0	9.3	9.9	5.6	5.9	9.0
六個月後 6 months	1.7	6.6	10.9	18.2	12.0	8.1	9.6
九個月後 9 months	3.6	8.6	20.2	19.0	13.8	8.4	5.5

各月份價格高於(十)低於(一)及等於(二)最低中位價格月之年數
Number of years when prices were higher (+), lower (−), and the same (=) after:

	+	−	=	+	−	=	+	−	=	+	−	=	+	−	=	+	−	=	+	−	=
三個月後 3 months	13	4	1	7	2	1	23	1	1	12	3	1	28	8	2	27	6	0	16	0	0
六個月後 6 months	12	4	2	6	3	1	23	1	1	14	2	0	28	9	1	28	5	0	15	1	0
九個月後 9 months	10	8	0	7	3	0	23	1	1	14	2	0	34	2	2	29	4	0	11	3	2

(a) 十年六個月　Ten years 6 months.

2　From 1894 to 1931, the general level of commodity prices rose at an average compound rate of 0.1097 per cent per month.

小麥： 河北正定之麥價自五月至次年二月上升者，二五年中佔二三年，平均上升數爲百分之二〇‧二（第三二九頁第十一表）。

安徽六安麥價自八月至次年二月之平均上升數幾與前同（百分之一八‧二）。

江蘇武進麥價自六月至十二月之平均上升數爲百分之一二‧〇，自六月至次年三月者爲百分之一三‧八。山西太谷麥價之上升甚小。

小米： 河南汲縣價格十一月至次年六月平均上升數爲百分之一四‧三，惟各年季節變動之差異甚大（第三三〇頁第十二表）。上述各月價格實際下降者十年中有四年。

河北正定價格自八月至次年五月上升者二五年中有二二年，平均上升數爲百分之一二‧〇。

山西太谷價格之季節變動甚小。

玉米： 河北正定七月後玉米價格之上升與該地小米八月後價格之上升情形相似（第三三一頁第十三表）。

四川涪陵價格自六月至十二月上升者，一六年中佔一三年，平均上升數爲百分之一一‧九。

第十二表　　小米最低價之月以後之價格變動
中國山西河南及河北三省三個地區

TABLE 12.—MILLET—PRICE CHANGES FOLLOWING MONTH OF LOWEST PRICES

3 localities in Shansi, Honan and Hopeh, China

	山　西 太　谷 Shansi, Taiku	河　南 汲　縣 Honan, Chi	河　北 正　定 Hopeh, Chengting
研究所包括之年份 Years studied	1912-1929	1921-1931	1907-1931
年　數 Number of years	18	11(a)	25
最低中位價格之月 Month of lowest median price	二月 February	十一月 November	八月 August
以下月數以後 Change in price 之價格變動　　after:			

対最低中位價格月之中位價格百分比
per cent of median price in month of lowest median price

三個月後 3 months	3.1	10.2	5.4
六個月後 6 months	2.6	14.3	7.8
九個月後 9 months	1.1	3.8	12.0

各月份價格高於(十)低於(一)及等於(＝)最低中位價月之年數
Number of years when prices were higher (+), lower (—), and the same (＝) after:

	+ — ＝	+ — ＝	+ — ＝
三個月後 3 months	13 5 0	6 4 0	16 6 3
六個月後 6 months	8 8 2	5 4 1	20 5 0
九個月後 9 months	7 10 1	7 3 0	22 3 0

(a) 十年六個月 Ten years, 6 months.

Wheat: In Chengting, Hopeh, wheat prices advanced from May to February in 23 out of 25 years, the average advance being 20.2 per cent (table 11, page 329). In Liuan, Anhwei, the average advance from August to February was almost as great (18.2 per cent).

In Wuchin, Kiangsu, the advance averaged 12.0 per cent from June to December and 13.8 per cent from June to March. In Taiku, Shansi, the advance was small.

Millet: Prices at Chi, Honan, advanced by an average of 14.3 per cent from November to June but there was considerable variation between years in this seasonal movement (table 12, page 330). Prices actually declined between these months in 4 out of 10 years.

At Chengting, Hopeh, prices advanced from August to May in 22 out of 25 years, the average advance being 12.0 per cent. Seasonal movements at Taiku, Shansi, were small.

Corn: In Chengting, Hopeh, the advance of corn prices after July was similar to the advance of millet prices after August (table 13, page 331).

第十三表　　玉米最低價之月以後之價格變動

中國山西河北及四川三省三個地區

TABLE 13.—CORN—PRICE CHANGES FOLLOWING MONTH
OF LOWEST PRICES

3 localities, in Shansi, Hopeh and Szechwan, China

	山 西 太 谷 Shansi, Taiku	河 北 正 定 Hopeh, Chengting	四 川 涪 陵 Szechwan, Fowling
研究所包括之年份 Years studied	1912-1929	1907-1931	1915-1930
年　數 Number of years	18	25	16
最低中位價格之月 Month of lowest median price	二月 February	七月 July	六月 June
以下月數以後 Change in price 之價格變動　after:			
	對最低中位價格月之中位價格百分比 *per cent of median price in month of lowest median price*		
三個月後 3 months	6.0	3.3	1.3
六個月後 6 months	4.9	8.2	11.9
九個月後 9 months	2.4	11.2	6.8
各月份價格高於(十)低於(—)及等於(=)最低中位價之年數 Number of years when prices were higher (+), lower (—), and the same (=) after:			
	+ — =	+ — =	+ — =
三個月後 3 months	13 1 4	19 5 1	10 4 2
六個月後 6 months	11 3 4	20 4 1	13 1 2
九個月後 9 months	9 6 3	22 3 0	13 2 1

第十四表　高粱最低價之月以後之價格變動
中國山西太谷及河北正定
TABLE 14.—KAOLIANG—PRICE CHANGES FOLLOWING MONTH OF LOWEST PRICES
Taiku, Shansi, and Chengting, Hopeh, China

	山 西 太 谷 Shansi, Taiku	河 北 正 定 Hopeh, Chengting
研究所包括之年份 Years studied	1912-1929	1907-1931
年　數 Number of years	18	25
最低中位價格之月 Month of lowest median price	二 月 February	八 月 August
以下月數以後之價格變動 Change in price after:		

對最低中位價格月之中位價格百分比
per cent of median price in month of lowest median price

		太谷	正定
三個月後	3 months	8.3	5.7
六個月後	6 months	7.1	10.8
九個月後	9 months	4.6	10.6

各月份價格高於(十)低於(一)及等於(二)最低中位價格月之年數
Number of years when prices were higher (+), lower (—), and the same (=) after:

		+	—	=	+	—	=
三個月後	3 months	14	2	2	20	4	1
六個月後	6 months	10	4	4	23	2	0
九個月後	9 months	6	7	5	24	1	0

第十五表　大麥最低價之月以後價格變動
中國江蘇武進　一九〇九年至一九三一年
TABLE 15.—BARLEY — PRICE CHANGES FOLLOWING MONTH OF LOWEST PRICES
Wuchin, Kiangsu, China, 1909-31

年　數 Number of years		23
最低中位價格之月 Month of lowest median price		五月 May
以下月數以後 之價格變動 Change in price after:	對最低中位價格月之中位價格百分比 <i>per cent of median price in month of lowest median price</i>	
三個月後 3 months	6.8	
六個月後 6 months	15.3	
九個月後 9 months	16.4	

各月份價格高於(十)及低於(一)最低中位價月之年數
Number of years when prices were higher lower
after:

	higher	lower
三個月後 3 months	15	8
六個月後 6 months	17	6
九個月後 9 months	19	4

高粱：　正定八月後高粱價格之上升可與該地小米價格之上升相比擬(第三三二頁第十四表)。價格自八月至次年五月上升者，二五年中有二四年。

大豆：　安徽六安價格自十月至次年七月上升者，一七年中佔一六年，平均上升數爲百分之一五・〇(第三三三頁第十六表)。河北正定自八月至下年五月上升百分之九・四，而四川涪陵之豆價僅升百分之一・五。

In Fowling, Szechwan, prices advanced from June to December in 13 out of 16 years, the average advance being 11.9 per cent.

Kaoliang: In Chengting, the advance of kaoliang prices after August was comparable to that of millet prices (table 14, page 332). Prices advanced from August to May in 24 out of 25 years.

Soybeans: In Liuan, Anhwei, prices advanced from October to July in 16 out of 17 years, the average advance being 15.0 per cent (table 16, page 333). From August to May prices advanced by 9.4 per cent in Chengting, Hopeh, but by only 1.5 per cent in Fowling, Szechwan.

第十六表　　大豆最低價之月以後之價格變動

中國四省四個地區

TABLE 16.—SOYBEANS—PRICE CHANGES FOLLOWING MONTH OF LOWEST PRICES

4 localities, 4 provinces, China

	河 北 正 定 Hopeh, Chengting	安 徽 六 安 Anhwei, Liuan	江 蘇 武 進 Kiangsu, Wuchin	四 川 涪 陵 Szechwan, Fowling
研究所包括之年份 Years studied	1907-1931	1916-1932	1909-1931	1915-1924
年　數 Number o years	25	17	23	10
最低中位價格之月 Month of lowest median price	八　月 August	十　月 October	九　月 Sept.	八　月 August
以下月數以後之價格變動 Change in price after:				

對最低中位價格月之中位價格百分比
per cent of median price in month of lowest median price

三個月後 3 months	2.4	3.2	4.4	0.2
六個月後 6 months	6.7	13.6	7.2	5.2
九個月後 9 months	9.4	15.0	9.0	1.5

各月份價格高於(十)低於(一)及等於(＝)最低中位價月之年數
Number of years when prices were higher (+), lower (—), and the same (=) after:

	+ — =	+ — =	+ — =	+ — =
三個月後 3 months	19 4 2	10 6 1	17 5 1	6 4 0
六個月後 6 months	24 1 0	13 3 1	17 5 1	4 2 4
九個月後 9 months	25 0 0	16 1 0	18 3 2	4 5 1

第十七表　豌豆最低價之月以後之價格變動
中國河北正定及四川涪陵
TABLE 17.—FIELD PEAS—PRICE CHANGES FOLLOWING MONTH OF LOWEST PRICES
Chengting, Hopeh, and Fowling, Szechwan, China

	河北 正定 Hopeh. Chengting	四川 涪陵 Szechwan. Fowling
研究所包括之年份 Years studied	1907-1931	1915-1930
年　數 Number of years	25	16
最低中位價格之月 Month of lowest median price	六　月 June	四　月 April

以下月數以後之價格變動
Change in price after:

對最低中位價格月之中位價格百分比
per cent of median price in month of lowest median price

		河北	四川
三個月後	3 months	3.2	1.6
六個月後	6 months	4.6	3.1
九個月後	9 months	6.7	2.4

各月份價格高於(十)低於(一)及等於(二)最低中位價格月之年數
Number of years when prices were higher (+), lower (—), and the same (=) after:

		+	—	=	+	—	=
三個月後	3 months	17	8	0	11	3	2
六個月後	6 months	15	7	3	12	4	0
九個月後	9 months	23	2	0	10	5	1

第十八表　芝蔴最低價之月以後之價格變動
中國河北正定一九〇七年至一九三一年
TABLE 18.—SESAME — PRICE CHANGES FOLLOWING MONTH OF LOWEST PRICES.
Chengting, Hopeh, China, 1907-31.

年　數 Number of years	25
最低中位價格之月 Month of lowest median price	八月 August

以下月數以後
之價格變動
Change in price
after:　　對最低中位價格月
之中位價格百分比
*per cent of median
price in month of
lowest median price*

三個月後	3 months	3.5
六個月後	6 months	3.6
九個月後	9 months	8.1

各月份高於(十)及低於(一)最低中位價月之年數
Number of years when prices were higher lower after:

		higher	lower
三個月後	3 months 17		8
六個月後	6 months 19		6
九個月後	9 months 23		2

最低價格月之購買力與以後價格變異之關係

貯藏作物之獲利性，不僅取決於價格之季節變動，抑且受氣候統制之不規則之供給變異之影響。當米價低於一般物價水準時（即米之購買力低時），則米價上升之可能較再降之可能為大。此因本年天時順利，作物豐登，致價格下落，而下年未必繼續如此也。同樣當米價因歉收而較高時，不久必有跌落之可能，蓋次年之收成未可預卜也。故貯藏時產品價格之購買力實為預測日後價格變異之南針。

Relation of purchasing power in month of lowest price to price changes later

The profitability of storing crops is determined not only by seasonal movements but also by irregular changes in supplies caused chiefly by the weather. In years when the price of rice is low compared to the general level of commodity prices (i.e. the purchasing power of rice is low), an advance in price is more probable than a further decline. This is because the weather conditions that produced good crops and forced prices down will probably not continue during the succeeding year. Similarly, when the price of rice is comparatively high, because of poor crops, it will probably fall later because poor crops for a second year are improbable. The purchasing power at the time of storage is thus an indicator of changes in price to be expected later.

For some of the series, the purchasing power of prices in the months when the index of seasonal variation was lowest have been calculated. The years were then divided into three groups according to the purchasing powers in these months. The actual price changes, 3, 6, 9, and 12 months after the month when the index was lowest were then averaged. These changes are chiefly the result of seasonal and irregular movements in the supply of and demand for the respective commodities. To a slight extent they also reflect the continually rising level of commodity prices during the periods studied. From 1894 to 1931, this level rose at an average compound rate of 0.1097 per cent per month.

Rice: In Wuchin, Kiangsu, the index of seasonal variation was lowest in November. The purchasing power of the November price was less than 91, (1910-14 = 100) thirteen times during the years 1894-1931. On these occasions, there was an average increase in price of 11.8 per cent from November to May and of 10.9 per cent from November to the following November. Prices advanced from November to June in 9 out of the 13 years and from November to the following November in 8 out of the 13 (table 19, page 336).

The purchasing power of the November price was more than 110.5, twelve times during the years 1894—1931. On these occasions there was an average decrease in price of 1.1 per cent from November to May and of 0.2 per cent from November to the following November. Prices advanced from November to May in only 5 out of the 11 years and from November to November in 7 out of the 11.

關於季節變動指數最低月之價格購買力會將一部分材料加以計算。依購買力之大小將年數分為三組。然後求得最低指數月以後三，六，九及十二個月之實際平均價格變異。此種變異大都為各種物品供求之季節及不規則變異之結果。同時亦微受本文已括時期內一般物價向上之長期趨勢之影響。自一八九四年至一九三一年該水準每月之上升率為複率百分之○・○九七。

　　米：　江蘇武進之季節變動指數以十一月為最低，一八九四年至一九三一年間十一月份米價之購買力小於九一者（一九一○――一九一四年＝一○○）計十三次。在此情形下價格自十一月至次年五月平均上升百分之一一・八，十一月至次年同月平均上升百分之一○・九，價格自十一月至次年六月上升者一三年中占九年。自十一月至次年同月上升者一三年中占八年（第三三六頁第十九表）。

　　一八九四年至一九三一年之間十一月份價格購買力大於一一○・五者計有十二次。在此情形下，十一月至次年五月價格下降百分之一・一，十一月至次年同月下降百分之○・二。自十一月至次年五月價格上升者一一年中僅占五年，自十一月至次年同月上升者，一一年中僅有七年。

第十九表　米最低價格月（十一月）價格購買力對以下月份價格變動之關係
江蘇武進　一八九四年至一九三一年

TABLE 19.—RICE—RELATION OF PURCHASING POWER IN MONTH OF LOWEST PRICE (NOVEMBER) TO PRICE CHANGES DURING FOLLOWING MONTHS

Wuchin, Kiangsu, 1894 —1931

	十一月份之購買力 （一九一○年至一九一四年＝一○○） Purchasing power in November (1910-14 = 100)		
	小　於 Less than 91.0	91.0 — 110.5	大　於 More than 110.5
十一月份之購買力 Purchasing power in November	81	100	129
年　數 Number of years	13	13	12
以下月份之價格平均變動 Mean change in price to following:	十一月份平均價格之百分比 *per cent of mean price in November*		
二月　February	8.6	3.8	-7.0
五月　May	11.8	6.7	-1.1
八月　August	21.8	14.7	8.6
十一月　November	10.9	2.2	-0.2

各月份價格高於（十）低於（一）及等於（＝）最低中位價月之年數
Number of years when prices were higher (+), lower (—), and the same (=) after:

	＋ — ＝	＋ — ＝	＋ — ＝
三個月後 3 months	8　5　0	8　5　0	3　7　1
六個月後 6 months	9　2　2	9　3　1	5　6　0
九個月後 9 months	8　4　1	10　2　1	7　4　0
十二個月後 12 months	8　5　0	6　7　0	7　4　0

It was not profitable to store in years when the purchasing power was more than 110.5 in November but, if the costs of storage from November until just before the next harvest were, per month, less than 2 per cent of the November price, it would have been profitable in years when the purchasing power of the November price was less than 91.0.

Wheat: In Chengting, Hopeh, the index of seasonal variation was lowest for May. On the 9 occasions between 1909 and 1931 when the purchasing power of the May prices was less than 99 (1910-14 = 100), prices advanced by an average of 16.9 per cent from May to November and by 4.9 per cent from May to the following May (table 20, page 337). On the 8 occasions when the purchasing power of the May price was more than 115, prices advanced by an average of 4.2 per cent from May to November and declined by an average of 10.6 per cent from May to the following May. If the costs of storage were less than 2 per cent per month, it was profitable to store until before the next harvest in years when the purchasing power of the May price was less than 99.0. It was not profitable in years when the purchasing power was more than 115.0 in May.

第二十表　小麥最低價格月(五月)價格購買力對以下月份價格變動之關係
河北正定　一九〇七年至一九三一年
TABLE 20.—WHEAT—RELATION OF PURCHASING POWER IN MONTH OF LOWEST PRICE (MAY) TO PRICE CHANGES DURING FOLLOWING MONTHS
Chengting, Hopeh, 1907 — 1931

	五月份之購買率　(一九一〇年至一九一四年＝一〇〇) Purchasing power in May (1910-14 = 100)		
	小　於 Less than 99.0	99.0 — 115.0	大　於 More than 115.0
五月份之購買力 Purchasing power in May	93	105	131
年　數 Number of years	9	8	8
以下月數之價格之平均變動 Mean change in price to following:	五月份平均價格之百分比 per cent of mean price in May		
八月　August	12.9	14.1	3.6
十一月　November	16.9	19.7	4.2
二月　February	33.3	24.5	3.9
五月　May	4.9	10.0	-10.6

各月份價格高於(十)低於(一)及等於(＝)最低中位價月之年數
Number of years when prices were higher (+), lower (—), and the same (=) after:

		+ — =	+ — =	+ — =
三個月後	3 months	9 0 0	8 0 0	6 1 1
六個月後	6 months	9 0 0	8 0 0	6 1 1
九個月後	9 months	8 0 0	7 1 0	4 3 1
十二個月後	12 months	7 1 0	4 3 1	3 5 0

故十一月份之價格購買力大於一一〇・五之年份，貯藏不能獲利。但如十一月至次收穫前每月之貯藏費用小於十一月價格百分之二，則於十一月價格購買力小於九一・〇之年份內貯藏，容或有利可圖。

小麥：　河北正定季節變動指數最低者為五月。一九〇九年至一九三一年間五月份價格購買力小於九九者有九次（一九一〇——一九一四年＝一〇〇）。自五月至十一月麥價平均上升百分之一六・九，自五月至次年五月平均上升百分之四・九（第三三七頁第二〇表）。五月份價格購買力大於一一五者有八次，其中麥價自五月至十一月平均上升百分之四・二，自五月至次年五月下降者百分之一〇・六。如每月貯藏費用能小於百分之二，則凡五月份價格購買力小於九九・〇之年份內貯藏至次年收穫前脫售，有利可獲。惟在五月份價格購買力大於一一五之年份內貯藏，則不能獲利也。

江蘇武進之季節變動指數最低為六月，其理與上述者同（第三三八頁第二一表）。

第廿一表　小麥最低價格月（六月）價格購買力對以下月份價格變動之關係

江蘇武進　一八九四年至一九三一年

TABLE 21.—WHEAT—RELATION OF PURCHASING POWER IN MONTH
OF LOWEST PRICE (JUNE) TO PRICE CHANGES DURING
FOLLOWING MONTHS

Wuchin, Kiangsu, 1894 — 1931

	六月份之購買力 （一九一〇年至一九一四年＝一〇〇） Purchasing power in June (1910-14 = 100)		
	小　於 Less than 100.0	100.0 — 112.0	大　於 More than 112.0
六月份之購買力 Purchasing power in June	88	106	126
年　數 Number of years	13	13	12
以下月數之價格之平均變動 n change in price to following:	六月份平均價格之百分比 *per cent of mean price in June*		
九月　September	8.9	7.4	4.1
士二月　December	20.6	13.6	7.0
三月　March	27.8	17.8	5.1
六月　June	7.8	7.0	−8.2
各月份價格高於(十)低於(一)及等於(＝)最低中位個月之年數 Number of years when prices were higher (+), lower (—), and the same (=) after:	+ — =	+ — =	+ — =
三個月後　3 months	10　2　1	9　3　1	9　3　0
六個月後　6 months	13　0　0	9　3　1	6　6　0
九個月後　9 months	12　0　0	10　2　1	8　4　0
士二個月後　12 months	9　1　2	8　4　1	4　7　1

In Wuchin, Kiangsu, where the index of seasonal variation was lowest in June, the same principles held true (table 21, page 338).

Barley: If the costs of storage were less than 4 per cent per month, it was profitable to store barley in Wuchin, Kiangsu, from May until before the next harvest in years when the purchasing power of the May price was less than 93.5 (1910-14 = 100) (table 22, page 339).

Soybeans: In Chengting, Hopeh, the index of seasonal variation for soybean prices was lowest in August. For 9 occasions, between 1907 and 1931, when the purchasing power of the August price was less than 95, (1910-14 = 100) the average increase in price from August to February was 33.7 per cent and from August to the following August, 20.2 per cent (table 23, page 340). If the costs of storage were less than 4 per cent per month, it was profitable to store on these occasions. It was not profitable to store when the purchasing power of the August price was more than 114.

第廿二表　元麥最低價格月(五月)價格購買力對以下月份價格變動之關係

江蘇武進　一九〇九年至一九三一年

TABLE 22.—HULLESS BARLEY—RELATION OF PURCHASING POWER IN MONTH OF LOWEST PRICE (MAY) TO PRICE CHANGES DURING FOLLOWING MONTHS

Wuchin, Kiangsu, 1909 — 1931

	五月份之購買力　(一九一〇年至一九一四年=一〇〇) Purchasing power in May (1910-14 = 100)		
	小　於 Less than 93.5	93.5 — 110.0	大　於 More than 110.0
五月份之購買力 Purchasing power in May	86	99	119
年　數 Number of years	8	8	7
以下月數之價格之平均變動 Mean change in price to following:	五月份平均價格之百分比 per cent of mean price in May		
八月　August	12.3	10.4	−5.6
十月　November	22.5	20.8	−1.2
二月　February	36.3	12.7	−1.5
五月　May	11.8	0.8	−5.6

各月份價格高於(十)低於(一)及等於(=)最低中位價月之年數

Number of years when prices were higher (+), lower (−), and the same (=) after:

	+ − =	+ − =	+ − =
三個月後　3 months	6 2 0	8 0 0	1 6 0
六個月後　6 months	6 2 0	8 0 0	2 5 0
九個月後　9 months	7 1 0	6 1 0	2 4 1
吉個月後　12 months	6 2 0	3 3 1	2 5 0

大麥： 在江蘇武進如每月貯藏費用少於百份之四，則凡五月價格購買力小於九三‧五（一九一〇──一九一四年＝一〇〇）之年份貯藏大麥至次年收穫前脫售當可獲利（第三三九頁第二二表）。

大豆： 河北正定豆價季節變動指數最低者爲八月，一九〇七年至一九三一年有九年之八月豆價購買力小於九五（一九一〇──一九一四年＝一〇〇）此數年內價格自八月至次年二月之平均上漲百分之三三‧七，自八月至次年八月平均漲百分之二〇‧二（第三四〇頁第十三表）。如每月貯藏費用小於百分之四，在上述情形下貯藏當有利可圖，惟八月之購買力大於一一四之年份，則不能獲利。

在江蘇之武進設每月貯藏費用能小於百分之三，則凡九月價格購買力小於九五‧五之年份內貯藏至次年收穫前脫售，均有利可獲（第三四一頁第二四表）。

第廿三表 大豆最低價格月（八月）價格購買力對於以下月份價格變動關係

河北正定 一九〇七年至一九三一年

TABLE 23.—SOYBEANS—RELATION OF PURCHASING POWER IN MONTH OF LOWEST PRICE (AUGUST) TO PRICE CHANGES DURING FOLLOWING MONTHS

Chengting, Hopeh, 1907 — 1931

	八月份之購買力 （一九一〇年至一九一四年＝一〇〇） Purchasing power in August (1910-14 = 100)		
	小 於 Less than 95.0	95.0 — 114.0	大 於 More than 114.0
八月份之購買力 Purchasing power in August	86	103	125
年 數 Number of years	9	8	8
以下月份之價格之平均變動 Mean change in price to following :	八月份平均價格之百分比 per cent of mean price in August		
十一月 November	4.8	0.9	4.4
二月 February	33.7	3.3	2.9
五月 May	35.0	2.4	13.0
八月 August	20.2	−8.5	−4.1

各月份價格高於（十）低於（一）及等於（＝）最低中位個月之年數

Number of years when prices were higher (+). lower (—), and the same (=) after:

	+ — =	+ — =	+ — =
三個月後 3 months	8 1 0	5 2 1	6 1 1
六個月後 6 months	8 1 0	4 2 1	5 2 1
九個月後 9 months	8 1 0	4 3 0	7 1 0
十二個月後 12 months	6 3 0	3 4 0	1 6 1

第廿四表　大豆最低價格月(九月)價格購買力對於以下月份價格變動關係

汇蘇武進　一九〇九年至一九三一年

TABLE 24.—SOYBEANS—RELATION OF PURCHASING POWER IN MONTH OF LOWEST PRICE (SEPTEMBER) TO PRICE CHANGES DURING FOLLOWING MONTHS

Wuchin, Kiangsu, 1909 —1931

	九月份之購買力 (一九一〇年至一九一四年=一〇〇) Purchasing power in September (1910-14 = 100)		
	小　於 Less than 95.5	95.5 — 105.0	大　於 More than 105.0
九月份之購買力 Purchasing power in September	86	100.0	113.0
年　數 Number of years	8	8	7
以下月份之價格之平均變動 Mean change in price to following :	九月份平均價格之百分比 *per cent of mean price in September*		
士月　December	13.6	3.6	2.5
三月　March	18.2	11.9	4.5
六月　June	28.7	14.2	5.6
九月　September	10.5	−0.3	−1.8

各月份價格高於(十)低於(一)及等於(=)最低中位價月之年數

Number of years when prices were higher (+), lower (—), and the same (=) after:

	+	—	=	+	—	=	+	—	=
三個月後　3 months	8	0	0	5	2	1	4	2	1
六個月後　6 months	8	0	0	7	0	1	4	1	1
九個月後　9 months	8	0	0	8	0	0	5	0	1
士個月後　12 months	5	3	0	4	3	1	3	3	0

In Wuchin, Kiangsu, it was profitable to store from September until before the next harvest in years when the purchasing power of the September price was less than 95.5, provided the costs of storage were less than 3 per cent per month (table 24, page 341).

Sesame: In Chengting, Hopeh, it was profitable to store sesame from August until the following May in years when the purchasing power of the August price was less than 88 (1910-14=100), provided the cost of storage was less than 2.5 per cent per month (table 25, page 342).

John R. Raeburn
Hu Kwoh-hwa

河北正定　一九〇七年至一九三一年

TABLE 25.—SESAME—RELATION OF PURCHASING POWER IN MONTH
OF LOWEST PRICE (AUGUST) TO PRICE CHANGES DURING
FOLLOWING MONTHS

Chengting, Hopeh, 1907 — 1931

	八月份之購買力　（一九一〇年至一九一四年＝一〇〇） Purchasing power in August (1910-14 = 100)		
	小　於 Less than 88.0	88.0 — 107.5	大　於 More than 107.5
八月份之購買力 Purchasing power in August	83	95	116
年　數 Number of years	9 .	8	8
以下月數之價格之平均變動 Mean change in price to following :	八月份平均價格之百分比 *per cent of mean price in August*		
十一月　November	6.8	8.7	0.9
二月　February	17.8	7.8	− 8.3
五月　May	25.8	11.0	− 7.8
八月　August	12.0	3.0	−11.5

各月份價格高於(十)低於(一)及等於(＝)最低中位價月之年數

Number of years when prices were higher (+), lower (—), and the same (=) after:

	+ — =	+ — =	+ — =
三個月後　3 months	8 1 0	4 4 0	4 3 1
六個月後　6 months	8 0 1	4 6 0	1 7 0
九個月後　9 months	9 0 0	4 3 0	1 7 0
十二個月後　12 months	8 1 0	3 4 0	2 6 0

　　芝蔴：　在河北正定設每月貯藏成本小於百分之二・五，則凡八月價格購買力小於八八（一九一〇——一九一四年＝一〇〇）之年份，自八月貯藏至次年五月當有利可獲。（第三四二頁第二五表）

雷伯恩

胡國華

第一表　　中國進口總值一九〇六年至一九三六年
TABLE 1.—VALUE OF IMPORTS TO CHINA, 1906 — 1936

年 份 Year	1. 全國進口淨值 Net imports to all China	2. 滿洲各關進口總值 Imports to Manchurian ports	3. 僞滿對中國之輸出 Exports of "Manchukuo" to China	4. 中國本部進口淨值未包括走私 Net imports of China proper not including smuggling	5. 中國本部之進口淨值包括走私量 Net imports of China proper including smuggling
		國幣十萬元 100,000 Chinese yuan			
1906	6,673	94		6,579	
1907	6,685	265		6,420	
1908	6,381	503		5,878	
1909	6,700	556		6,144	
1910	7,425	728		6,697	
1911	7,518	842		6,676	
1912	7,371	932		6,439	
1913	8,883	1,005		7,878	
1914	8,869	1,069		7,800	
1915	7,081	896		6,185	
1916	8,046	1,264		6,782	
1917	8,562	1,589		6,973	
1918	8,645	1,577		7,068	
1919	10,080	2,231		7,849	
1920	11,876	1,904		9,972	
1921	14,117	1,791		12,326	
1922	14,724	1,889		12,835	
1923	14,387	1,881		12,506	
1924	15,864	1,971		13,893	
1925	14,768	2,346		12,422	
1926	17,515	2,783		14,732	
1927	15,781	2,797		12,984	
1928	18,633	3,330		15,303	
1929	19,721	3,296		16,425	17,016
1930	20,406	3,070		17,336	18,356
1931	22,334	2,190		20,144	21,931
1932	16,347	1,122	557	14,668	16,303
1933	13,456		552	12,904	14,249
1934	10,297		657	9,640	11,187
1935	9,192		653	8,539	10,837
1936	9,415		1,017	8,398	10,752

Sources:

Column 1. 1906-1911　from : Academia Sinica, **Statistics of China's Foreign Trade 1867-1928.** Total value in Haikwan taels multiplied by 1.558 to convert to yuan.

1912-1936　from: National Tariff Commission: **Prices and Price Indexes in Shanghai.**

Column 2. 1906-1928　from: Academia Sinica, **Statistics of China's. Foreign Trade 1867-1928.** The totals for Manchurian ports were summed and multiplied by 1.558 to convert from Haikwan taels to yuan.

1929-1932　from: **Customs returns of 'Manchukuo.'**

(Continued on page 345).

一九〇六年至一九三六年間中國之國際貿易

本文之目的在研究中國（東三省除外）國際貿易價值與數量之變遷。

一九三二年七月以前，中國國際貿易統計數字包括東三省。中國本部與東三省貿易統計之分割，不能完全精確，蓋因（一）東三省之淪亡，改變其一部分與中國本部之貿易路線，及（二）自一九三二年七月一日以後，中國對滿洲之貿易並未完全列爲國際貿易。欲將中國自一九〇六年以後之國際貿易估計，惟有將一九三二年以前，中國進出口總數值中減去東三省之進出口之數值，並將一九三二年事變後中國進出口貿易數字中減去對僞滿之進出口數值。

年來華北走私甚盛，欲求準確之進口數字，或在正常狀態下所應有之進口總值，均極困難[1]。故研究時，除官方發表之進口總數外，其包括估計走私數字之進口總數，亦應注意（第三四三頁第一表）。

進 出 口 之 價 值

自一九〇六年至一九三二年，中國進口總值，除走私外，計增百分之二〇六（第三四七頁第一圖）。以長期上升趨勢而論，在世界大戰時期（一九一四年至一九一九年）進口較低，但自一九一九年至一九二二年及自一九二七年至一九三一年則增加甚速。一九三一年至一九三六年，除走私未計外，以元計算之進口總值銳減百分之六八，而一九三六年總數幾低至與一九一九年相等。

其他關於中國國際貿易資料之應用困難，均係參攷雷滿著「中國國際貿易」一九二六年上海商務印書館出版，及李卓敏著「中國國際貿統易計之估價」南開社會經濟季刊第一至三十一頁一九三七年四月出版。

第一表　來源：

第一欄：一九〇六年 —— 一九一一年採自：中央研究院「六十五年來中國國際貿易統計」總值乘以一·五五八使由海關兩單位換算爲國幣單位。

一九一二年 —— 一九三六年：國定稅則委員會「上海物價月報」

第二欄：一九〇六年 —— 一九二八年採自：中央研究院「六十年來中國國際貿易統計」滿洲各關之總值之和乘以一·五五八使由海關兩單位換算爲國幣單位。

一九二九年 —— 一九三二年採自：僞滿之海關貿易報告册。

第三欄：一九三二年 —— 一九三六年採自：僞滿之海關貿易報告册。

第四欄：一九〇六年 —— 一九三一年：第一欄減第二欄

一九三二年：第一欄減第二欄及第三欄

一九三三年 —— 一九三六年：第一欄減第三欄

第五欄：第一欄加中國銀行所估計之走私數量

THE FOREIGN TRADE OF CHINA 1906 — 1936

The purpose of this study is to consider changes in the quantity and value of the foreign trade of China excluding the three Northeastern Provinces (Manchuria).

Until July 1932, the trade of Manchuria was included in official statistics with that for China. The separation of the statistics for Manchuria from those for China cannot be done with complete accuracy because (1) the loss of Manchuria altered the routing of part of her trade with China, and (2), since July 1, 1932, not all of China's trade with Manchuria has been tabulated in China's official statistics as " foreign trade." A comparatively reliable estimate of the foreign trade of China since 1906, can be obtained only by deducting the imports and exports of the three Northern Provinces from the imports and exports of all China before the change in 1932, and deducting the imports from and exports to " Manchukuo " from the imports and exports of China after the change.

A serious difficulty is that in recent years the smuggling of goods to North China has been so extensive that an accurate estimate either of the actual total imports or of the imports that would have been made under completely regulated conditions is impossible.[1] It is therefore necessary to consider both the officially published totals and totals which include the approximate amount of smuggling as estimated (table 1, page 343).

Value of imports and exports

From 1906 to 1931, the total yuan value of imports to China, excluding smuggling, increased by 206 per cent (figure 1, page 347). During the World War period 1914-1919 imports were, considering the long term upward tendency, comparatively low, but from 1919 to 1922 there was a rapid increase. There was also

---

1   For other difficulties connected with the use of data on China's foreign trade, reference is made to Remer: The Foreign Trade of China (Commercial Press, Ltd., Shanghai, China, 1926), and Mr. Choh Ming Li: China's International Trade Statistics: An Evaluation, Nankai Quarterly, pp. 1-31, April 1937, Tientsin.

Sources of table 1 continued:

Column 3. 1932-1936 from: Customs returns of ' Manchukuo.'

Column 4. 1906-1931 by deducting column 2 from column 1.
           1932   by deducting columns 2 and 3 from column 1.
           1933-1936 by deducting column 3 from column 1.

Column 5. By adding to column 4 the amount of smuggling as estimated by the Bank of China.

TABLE 2.—VALUE OF EXPORTS FROM CHINA, 1906 — 1936

年 份 Year	1. 全 國 出 口 淨 值 Net exports from all China	2. 滿洲各關 出口總值 Exports from Manchurian ports	3. 中國對僞 滿之輸出 Exports from China to 'Manchukuo'	4. 中國出口淨值 （滿洲除外） Net exports of China excluding Manchuria
	國 幣 十 萬 元 *100,000 Chinese yuan*			
1906	3,684	113		3,571
1907	4,119	164		3,955
1908	4,310	425		3,885
1909	5,281	888		4,393
1910	5,933	905		5,028
1911	5,879	1,059		4,820
1912	5,773	923		4,850
1913	6,283	1,053		5,230
1914	5,550	1,062		4,488
1915	6,526	1,066		5,460
1916	7,506	1,383		6,123
1917	7,212	1,511		5,701
1918	7,570	1,704		5,866
1919	9,828	2,435		7,393
1920	8,439	2,300		6,139
1921	9,368	2,392		6,976
1922	10,203	2,565		7,638
1923	11,730	3,054		8,676
1924	12,024	3,248		8,776
1925	12,096	3,333		8,763
1926	13,466	4,123		9,343
1927	14,312	4,508		9,804
1928	15,445	4,980		10,465
1929	15,824	4,257		11,567
1930	13,942	3,967		9,975
1931	14,170	4,639		9,531
1932	7,675	1,984	167	5,524
1933	6,118		798	5,320
1934	5,352		576	4,776
1935	5,758		320	5,438
1936	7,057		381	6,676

來源：

第一欄：一九〇六年 —— 一九一一年採自： 中央研究院「六十五年來中國國際貿易統計」總值
　　　　乘以一・五五八使單位由海關兩換算爲國幣。
　　　　一九一二年 —— 一九三六年採自： 國定稅則委員會「上海物價月報」。

第二欄：一九〇六年 —— 一九二八年採自： 中央研究院「六十五年來中國國際貿易統計」滿洲
　　　　各關之和乘以一・五五八使單位由海關兩換算爲國幣。
　　　　一九二九年 —— 一九三二年採自： 僞滿之海關貿易報告冊。

第三欄：一九三二年 —— 一九三六年採自： 僞滿之海關貿易報告冊。

第四欄：一九〇六年 —— 一九三一年：第一欄減第二欄
　　　　一九三二年：第一欄減第二欄及第三欄
　　　　一九三三年 —— 一九三六年：第一欄減第三欄

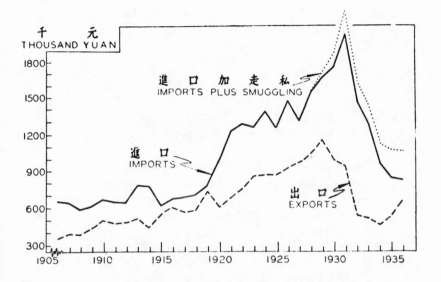

第一圖　中國進出口之淨值（滿洲除外）一九〇六年至一九三六年

　　一九二九年出口總值達最高峰，自一九二九年至一九三二年則迅速下跌，一九三二年後增加甚微。進口值最高峰在一九三一年，自一九三一年至一九三四年則銳減。

FIGURE 1.—NET IMPORTS AND EXPORTS OF CHINA, EXCLUDING MANCHURIA,
1906-1936

　　The total value of exports reached a peak in 1929, declined rapidly to 1932 and has since risen slightly. The total value of imports reached a peak in 1931 and declined rapidly to 1934.

Sources of Table 2:	
Column 1. 1906-1911	from: Academia Sinica, **Statistics of China's Foreign Trade 1867-1928.** Total value in Haikwan taels multiplied by 1.558 to convert to yuan.
1912-1936	from: National Tariff Commission: **Prices and Price Indexes in Shanghai.**
Column 2. 1906-1928	from: Academia Sinica, **Statistics of China's Foreign Trade, 1867-1928.** The totals for Manchurian ports were summed and multiplied by 1.558 to convert from Haikwan taels to yuan.
1929-1932	from: **Customs returns of 'Manchukuo.'**
Column 3. 1932-1936	from: **Customs returns of 'Manchukuo.'**
Column 4. 1906-1931	by deducting column 2 from column 1.
1932	by deducting columns 2 and 3 from column 1.
1933-1936	by deducting column 3 from column 1.

中國以元計算輸出值，自一九〇六年至一九二九年增百分之二二四。自一九二九年至一九三四年減百分之五九，自一九三四年至一九三六年復增百分之四〇。

進出口總值之指數（一九二二年至一九二八年＝一〇〇）圖示於第二圖第三四八頁。當歐戰期間，輸出指數較高，但自一九二九年後漸低。一九三一年輸入指數達其高峰。自一九三四年後輸入總值（包括走私量）鮮有變動。同時輸出指數上漲，而進出口值幾回復基年比率。然一九三六年貿易總量之低，並不亞於一九一九年及一九二〇年。

元之外滙價格與中國進出口總值之關係

元之美元價格對於進出口值，並無固定關係。歐戰期間元之美元價格達於最高峰，但進口數值反較低，而出口數量之趨勢亦顯未受影響。自一九二五年至一九三一年，元之美元價格跌百分之五八，而進口則增百分之七〇。自一九三一年至一九三五年，元之美元價格增百分之六五，而進口則減百分之六三。故元值低賤，固不能減少輸入，而元值昂貴，亦不能增多輸入。在一九三一年，當元之美元價格極低時，輸出量甚低。當一九三〇年元之美元價格極高時，輸出指數雖漸升，然仍屬甚低。

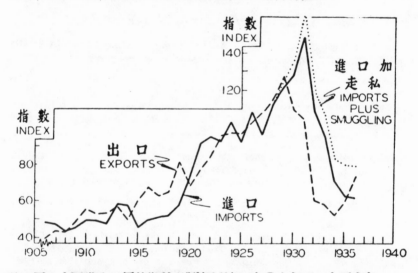

第二圖　中國進出口價值指數（滿洲除外）一九〇六年至一九三六年

一九二二年至一九二八年＝一〇〇

進口指數之高峰在一九三一年，出口者在一九二九年，近年來進出口貿易數字特低。

FIGURE 2.—INDEX NUMBERS OF THE VALUE OF IMPORTS TO AND EXPORTS FROM CHINA, EXCLUDING MANCHURIA, 1906-1936, (1922-1928=100)

Imports reached their peak in 1931, exports in 1929. The total value of trade has been exceptionally low in recent years.

a rapid increase from 1927 to 1931.   From 1931 to 1936, the yuan
value of imports excluding smuggling, declined by 68 per cent, the
amount for 1936 being almost as low as that for 1919.

The Yuan value of China's exports increased gradually from
1906 to 1929 by a total of 224 per cent.   From 1929 to 1934 it
declined by 59 per cent; from 1934 to 1936 it increased by 40
per cent.

Index numbers of the total value of imports and exports are
shown in   figure 2, page 348 (1922-1928 = 100).   Exports were
high relative to imports during the World War period but declined
after 1929.   Imports reached their peak in 1931.   Since 1934,
there has been little change in the total value of imports including
smuggled goods.   Exports have increased and the ratio of exports
to imports has returned to approximately its 1922-1928 value.
But, the total amount of trade was as low in 1936 as in 1919-1920.

*Relation of the foreign exchange value of the yuan to the total
value of China's imports and exports*

There has been no constant relationship between the U.S.
dollar value of the yuan and the total value of imports or exports
(figure 3, page 350).   During the World War period, the dollar
value of the yuan reached a peak but imports were comparatively
low and the trend of exports was, apparently, unaffected.   From
1925 to 1931, the dollar value of the yuan declined by 58 per cent
but imports increased by 70 per cent.   From 1931 to 1935, the
dollar value of the yuan increased by 65 per cent but imports
declined by 63 per cent.   A 'cheap' yuan did not reduce imports
nor did a 'dear' yuan increase them.   In 1931, when the yuan was
very 'cheap' in terms of U.S. dollars, exports were very low.   In
spite of the long term upward tendency, they were as low in 1919
when the yuan was especially ' dear.'

*Relation of the foreign exchange value of the yuan to China's trade
balance*

The relationship of the foreign exchange value of the yuan
to the balance between imports and exports has been exactly the
opposite of that commonly expected.   The exact difference
between the total value of China's imports and the total value of
her exports cannot be computed, but the differences between the
totals as obtained from table 1 and 2, pages 343, 346 give a
comparatively reliable measure of the general movements.   When
the U.S. dollar value of the yuan was at its highest, in 1919, the
excess of imports over exports was at its lowest (figure 4, page
351).   When the yuan was at its lowest, in 1931 and 1932, the

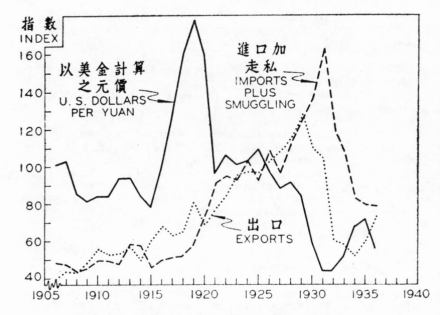

第三圖　國幣之美元價格指數及中國進出口價值指數（滿洲除外）一九〇六
　　　　年至一九三六年

一九二二年至一九二八年＝一〇〇

貴價之元並不鼓勵進口亦不能減少出口，廉價之元並不能減少進口亦不能增加出口。

FIGURE 3.—INDEX NUMBERS OF THE U.S. DOLLAR VALUE OF CHINESE YUAN AND
THE VALUE OF IMPORTS TO AND EXPORTS FROM CHINA, EXCLUDING
MANCHURIA, 1906 — 1936, (1922 — 1928 = 100)

A ' dear ' yuan did not increase imports and reduce exports nor did a ' cheap ' yuan
reduce imports and increase exports.

元之外滙價格與中國國際貿易差之關係

　　元之外滙價格與貿易差之關係，適與普通所期望者相反。中國入超或
出超之正確數字，雖無法統計，然依照第一表及第二表（第三四三頁及
三四六頁）計算所得之總數，可得一較爲可靠之材料。一九一九年元之美
元價格達其最高峰時，入超數值最低。當一九三一及一九三二年元之價值
極低時，入超則達其最高峰。故元值之貶低，並不增加輸出亦不減少輸入
。當一九三二年至一九三五年以美元計算之銀價上升，以美元計算之元價
亦漲，但輸入迅減而入超數值亦跌。

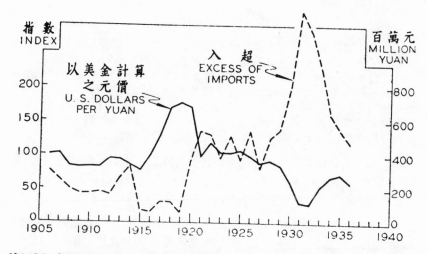

第四圖　國幣之美元價格指數及中國之入超（滿洲除外）一九〇六年至一九三六年

一九二二年至一九二八年＝一〇〇

國幣外滙價值之變動並不能左右進出口比率

FIGURE 4.—INDEX NUMBERS OF THE U.S. DOLLAR VALUE OF CHINESE YUAN AND THE EXCESS OF IMPORTS INTO CHINA, EXCLUDING MANCHURIA, 1906 -- 1936, (1922 —1928 = 100)

The foreign exchange value of the yuan has not determined the ratio of imports to exports.

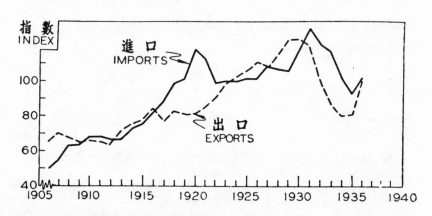

第五圖　中國之進出口物價指數（南開大學編製）一九〇六年至一九三六年

一九二二年至一九二八年＝一〇〇

FIGURE 5.—NANKAI INDEX NUMBERS OF PRICES OF IMPORTS AND EXPORTS, CHINA, 1906 — 1936, (1922 — 1928 = 100)

進出口之數量

以進出口物價之變動，故其歷年總值之變遷，不能正確計算實際貿易數量之消漲。南開大學經濟研究所編製之進出口物價指數圖示於第五圖第三五一頁。自一九〇六年至一九三一年，物價上漲，乃因銀值下跌所致。自一九三一年至一九三五年，物價下跌，則因銀值上漲所致。一九三五年後，物價復行回漲。歐戰期間，輸入物價甚高，按進口貨多為金屬與製成品，故大受戰事影響。一九三一年後，輸出物價較輸入物價下跌尤速，蓋出口貨以原料品居多，在世界市場之跌落常較製造品為劇也。

進出口數量之計算亦可以進出口物價指數除進出口總值指數而得（第三五二頁第六圖），此法雖不若以進出口數量直接計算其指數為準確，然計算方法則較簡易，以之觀察進出口之大概趨勢亦為適用。

一九三一年以前，輸入量之增加不若輸入價值迅速。在歐戰時期輸入特少，自一九二〇年至一九二二年則增加迅速，而一九二二年至一九三一年則增加較緩。一九三一年後，輸入銳減，輸出指數於一九二七年至一九二九年，達其最高峰，而自一九二九年至一九三二年迅速下跌。自一九三一年後，則復增加。

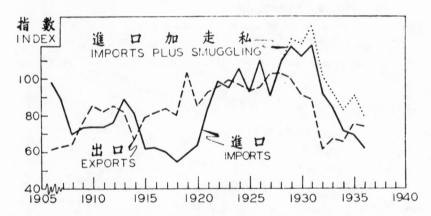

第六圖　中國進出口數量之指數（滿洲除外）一九〇六年至一九三六年

一九二二年至一九二八年＝一〇〇

歐戰期間輸入減少，自一九三一年中國經濟恐慌開始後更形銳減，輸出量最高在一九二九年自是以後由於歐西各國不景氣之影響輸出數量亦減。

FIGURE 6.—INDEX NUMBERS OF THE QUANTITY OF IMPORTS TO AND EXPORTS FROM CHINA, EXCLUDING MANCHURIA, 1906 — 1936, (1922 — 1928 =100)

Imports were low during the World War period and were greatly reduced after 1931 when deflation began in China. Exports reached their peak in 1929, after which they declined because of deflation abroad.

excess of imports was at its highest. A 'cheap' yuan did not result in increased exports and reduced imports. When the U.S. dollar price of silver rose from 1932 to 1935, the value of the yuan increased in terms of dollars but imports were rapidly reduced and the excess of imports over exports also declined.

The quantity of imports and exports

Because of changes in the prices of imports and exports, year to year changes in the total value do not accurately measure changes in the physical volume of trade. The index numbers of prices of import and export commodities, calculated by the Nankai Institute of Economics, are shown in figure 5, page 351. From 1906 to 1931, prices advanced because of the declining value of silver. From 1931 to 1935, they declined because of the rising value of silver. Since 1935, there has been reflation. In the World War period, prices of imports were high. Imports are chiefly metals and manufactured goods and these were greatly affected by the War. After 1931, prices of exports declined more rapidly than prices of imports because exports are chiefly raw materials and, on world markets, these declined more than manufactured goods.

By dividing the index numbers of the total value of imports and of exports by the index numbers of prices, measures of the quantity of imports and of exports are obtained (figure 6, page 352). These are not as accurate as could be obtained by the much more difficult method of computing index numbers of quantity directly from the quantity figures themselves, but they are sufficiently reliable in showing the general movements.

The quantity of imports did not increase as rapidly as the total value prior to 1931. Imports were particularly small in the War years, increased rapidly from 1920 to 1922 and less rapidly from 1922 to 1931. After 1931 they were greatly reduced. Exports reached their peak in 1927-1929 and declined rapidly from 1929-1932. There has been some revival since 1932.

Relation of the foreign exchange value of the yuan to the quantity of imports and exports

The U.S. dollar value of the yuan is compared to the quantity of imports in figure 7, page 354. The foreign exchange ratio of the yuan does not appear to have directly determined imports. The same principle holds true for exports (figure 8, page 355). Nor is there evidence that during periods when the foreign exchange was comparatively steady, 1908-1915 and 1921-1929, the volume of trade was especially good.

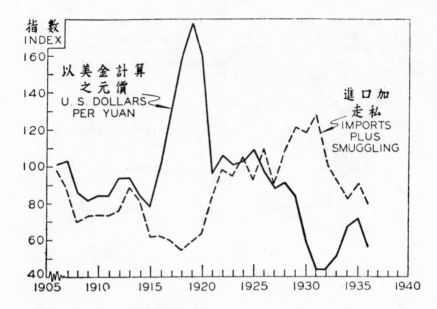

第七圖　國幣之美元價格與中國之進口數量指數（滿洲除外）一九○六年至
一九三六年

一九二二年至一九二八年＝一○○

元之外滙價值並不能影響進口數量。

FIGURE 7.—INDEX NUMBERS OF THE U.S. DOLLAR VALUE OF CHINESE YUAN AND
THE QUANTITY OF IMPORTS TO CHINA, EXCLUDING MANCHURIA, 1906 — 1936,
1922 — 1928 = 100

The foreign exchange value of the yuan has not determined imports.

元之外滙價格與進出口數量之關係

　　進口數量與元之美元價格比較，圖示於 第三五四頁第七圖。元之外滙
率顯然未能直接影響進口量，而出口數量亦不受其支配，（第三五五頁第
八圖）。 此外當外滙穩定時， 如一九○八年至一九一五年，一九二一年至
一九二九年貿易數量亦不見特別增多。

影響進出口數量之各種因子

　　中國進口貨輸入之多寡，全視其經濟之枯榮而定。世界大戰時， 進口
貨物價格高漲，輸入因以減少，然其大部份則由於一九三一年後， 國內物
價慘跌所致，蓋當時以物品計算之銀價開始上漲也。 大體言之一九三一年

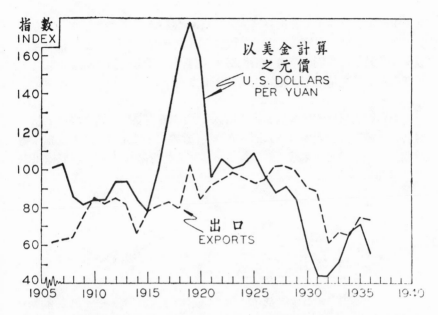

以美金計算
之元價
U. S. DOLLARS
PER YUAN

出　口
EXPORTS

第八圖　國幣之美元價格與中國之出口數量指數（滿洲除外）一九○六年至
　　　　一九三六年

一九二二年至一九二八年＝一○○

元之外滙價值並不能影響出口數量。

FIGURE 8.—INDEX NUMBERS OF THE U.S. DOLLAR VALUE OF CHINESE YUAN AND
THE QUANTITY OF EXPORTS FROM CHINA, EXCLUDING MANCHURIA, 1906 — 1936,
1922 — 1928 = 100

The foreign exchange value of the yuan has not determined exports.

Factors affecting the quantity of imports and exports

The quantity of goods imported by China depends chiefly on
China's own prosperity.　During the World War, the high prices
of imports reduced their volume, but a greater reduction was
caused by domestic deflation after 1931, when the commodity
value of the silver yuan began to rise.　China's import trade did
not, on the whole, suffer from world trade conditions, until after
1931.　China's own demand was more than fully sustained for
two years after serious deflation in gold standard countries began
in 1929.　Reflation in China following the currency reform of
November 1935, has corrected many of the domestic maladjustments which deflation brought about so that, under peaceful
conditions, a large increase of imports might be expected.

前，中國進口貿易並未受世界商業之影響。 當一九二九年世界金本位國家物價開始慘跌時，中國之需求曾能維持不受波及者在二年以上。 自一九三五年十一月實行幣制改革後物價囘漲， 使前此所受之失調現象漸告恢復，故在內外昇平之情形下，輸入之增加應為意料中事。

　　中國輸出量以國外市場需要為增減， 而國外需要則以國外經濟之枯榮為轉移。輸出減少非始自一九三一年， 實肇於一九二九年各金本位國家物價開始下跌之時。一九三二年以後，世界經濟情形漸趨轉好， 我國輸出亦漸見增加。

雷　伯　恩
胡　國　華

中國中部迤東各處農具之研究

　　本研究所謂『用具』包括 (1) 鋤，鏟等具， (2) 犂，耙，風車等器，及 (3) 扁担，晒籃，船隻等設備。 本研究企圖調查關於每一農民所有或所用之一切用具。

　　欲謀農具未來之改良，則必須詳知目前農具使用之情形。 本研究具有下列目的：(1) 收集農具現況之可靠材料；(2) 研究農具使用之效率；(3) 研究目前農民使用農具遭遇之問題及 (4) 設立一區研究農具之方法， 以便推廣他區。

　　本農具研究，係採用調查方法。本調查設實地調查員十四人， 收集浙，蘇，皖，贛，鄂五省，一一處，一，四二六農家之農具材料。 此一一處，均位於揚子平原。

　　揚子平原已耕種之土地，約有百分之七一。全區人口密度甚高， 每方英里平均有八九七人。所調查之各田場， 作物面積平均為三一‧二畝[1]；其中水稻佔一四‧六，小麥佔九‧二，及其他作物七‧四畝。 作物面積之利用，非常集約。作物複種指數為一八七，易言之， 平均每一○○畝作物

---

[1]　六畝＝1英畝

The quantity of China's exports depends chiefly on foreign demand and this, in turn, on prosperity abroad. Exports declined not after 1931, but after 1929 when deflation in the 'gold standard' world began. Since 1932. exports have slowly increased because of a general improvement in economic conditions abroad.

There is good reason to expect a continuation, occasionally interrupted, of this revival.

John R. Raeburn

Hu Kwoh-hwa

FARM IMPLEMENTS IN EAST CENTRAL CHINA

The term " implement " as used in this study includes: (1) implements such as hoes and shovels; (2) machines such as plows, harrows, fan mills; and (3) equipment such as carrying poles, drying baskets and boats. An attempt was made to obtain information in regard to all implements owned or used by each farmer interviewed.

It was considered that a detailed knowledge of the present use of farm implements was needed as a basis for study of possible future improvements. The present study was undertaken with the following purposes: (1) To obtain reliable information in regard to existing conditions; (2) to study efficiency in use of farm implements; (3) to study the problems with which farmers are confronted in the use of implements; and (4) to establish a method of study of farm implements in one region of China which might be repeated in other regions.

The farm implement study was carried out by the survey method. Fourteen field workers collected farm implement records for 1426 farms in 11 localities of 5 provinces—Chekiang, Kiangsu, Anhwei, Kiangsi, and Hupeh. All localities are in the Yangtze Plain region.

About 71 per cent of the land area of the Yangtze Plain is cultivated. The entire region is densely populated, having an average of 897 people per square mile. Farms for which information was obtained had an average of 31.2 mow [1] of crops made up as follows: rice 14.6, wheat 9.2, and other crops 7.4 mow. Crop land is used very intensively. The index of double cropping was 187, or an average of 187 mow of crops were grown each year on 100 mow of crop land. The soil is deep and fertile and has been used for rice production for many centuries. The

---

1   6 mow = 1 acre.

地，每年生長作物一八七畝。土壤深而肥，且用以栽種水稻，已數百年於茲。氣候冬寒而夏濕熱，全年降雨量爲四四英吋，其中百分之四六降於六，七，八三個月。本區實行無圍籬耕種制。農舍均集合於小村，農民由此出發，各至其小塊田地耕作。每一農民平均有五·二塊，且每塊又得分成數坵耕種之。農民之飼養役畜者，僅佔半數。其中飼養水牛者，約有百分之七五，養黃牛者祇百分之二五。

製造成本及投資

農具製造地点，亦由調查而得。各種農具，有百分之八四係在本地附近市鎮或村莊所製造，百分之九係由塲主本人或家人所製造，百分之七係在中國大城市所製造。

每一田塲農具之平均價值爲四七·九元 [2]，其現值爲二七·七元，或原值百分之五八。

如比較田塲農具投資，即知揚子平原農具價值，約抵田地價值百分之之三·三，而美國則爲百分之九·四。揚子平原，每一英畝作物面積之農具價值爲美金三·三元，而美國則爲七·九九元。中國生產農產品，其農具勞力，及土地三者之最有利益之組合，爲其所用勞力較美國多，而其所用農具較美國少。

下列兩者，亦視爲農具成本變動之一部分原因：(1) 種類與品質，及(2)某區或某店之製造量。平均言之，某地如有百分之二七農民購置某種農具，則其價格每較另一地有百分之八〇農民購置該種農具高出百分之四五。各種農具既有百分之九三在農家或本地附近市鎮或村莊所製造，則大量農具必在多數農民購置之地製造。農具集中一處，大量製造，似較爲經濟，且其品質亦較爲優美。

資本爲中國農業生產之一大費用。每農家全年使用之成本爲一一·三九元；其中約百分之五〇爲投資利息，百分之三〇爲使用費用，及百分之二〇爲折舊。若干主要農具全年之使用費用，表述於第一表第三六〇頁。

每田塲所有作物面積平均在六·七畝者，其農具現值爲九元，而平均在一三三·四畝者，其農具現值則爲九九元。足見農具投資之增加，較田塲面積之增加爲小。

---

2. 一九三五年間平均一元等於〇·三六美元

climate is cold in the winter but hot and humid in the summer. The annual rainfall is about 44 inches with 46 per cent falling in June, July, and August. The open field (unfenced) system of cultivation is practiced. Farmers' homes are grouped together in small villages from which the farmers go out to work their small non-adjoining fields. Farmers have an average of 5.2 parcels, and each parcel may be divided into two or more fields for cultivation. Only about one-half of the farmers own work animals. Of those farmers owning work animals about 75 per cent own water buffalo and about 25 per cent own oxen.

Manufacture, cost and investment

The place of manufacture of farm implements was obtained from farmers. It was found that 84 per cent of all implements were made locally at a nearby town or village, 9 per cent were made at home by the farmer or members of his family, and 7 per cent were made in a large Chinese city.

The average cost of implements per farm was 47.90 yuan[2] and the present value was 27.70 yuan or 58 per cent of the cost.

When comparing the farm investment which is in implements, it will be found that, for the Yangtze Plain, the value of implements amounts to 3.3 per cent of the value of farm land, but, for the United States, 9.4 per cent. The value of implements per acre of crop land is U.S. $3.30 for the Yangtze Plain, and U.S. $7.99 for the United States. The most profitable combination of implements, labor, and land for the production of agricultural products in China includes a smaller proportion of implements and a larger proportion of labor than in the United States.

Two factors accounting for part of the variation in cost of implements are (1) kind and quality, and (2) volume made in a given locality or shop. On the average, individual implements cost 45 per cent more in localities where an average of only 27 per cent of the farmers own such implements than in localities where an average of 80 per cent of the farmers own such implements. Since 93 per cent of all implements are made at home or locally in a nearby town or village, it is believed that a larger volume of implements is manufactured in one plant in localities where a larger proportion of farmers own such implements. It appears that a substantial saving can be made by the manufacture of implements in larger volume in one plant. It is believed that higher quality implements would also result from larger volume of manufacture in one plant.

---

2 During 1935, 1 yuan was on the average, equivalent to U.S. $0.36.

第一表　中國中部逼東——處一四二六田塲農具全年之使用成本

TABLE 1.—ANNUAL COSTS OF OPERATION FOR FARM IMPLEMENTS
1426 farms, 11 localities, East Central China

農 具 名 稱 Implement	投資利息 Interest on investment	使用費用 Operating expense	折　舊 Depreciation	總 成 本 Total cost
	元 yuan	元 yuan	元 yuan	元 yuan
耕犂 Plow	0.580	0.510	0.240	1.33
牛車 Animal wooden chain pump	3.860	1.310	1.130	6.30
脚車 Foot wooden chain pump	2.160	1.220	0.690	4.07
手車 Hand wooden chain pump	1.210	0.470	0.390	2.07
耕耙 Harrow	0.460	0.280	0.210	0.95
釘耙 Digging hook	0.085	0.150	0.066	0.30
禾耙 Scuffle hoe	0.042	0.012	0.045	0.10
連枷 Flail	0.023	0.002	0.029	0.05
鐮刀 Sickle	0.026	0.012	0.037	0.08
糞桶 Night soil bucket	0.130	0.130	0.063	0.32
扁担 Carrying pole	0.044	0.001	0.029	0.05
糞杓 Wooden ladle	0.024	0.012	0.035	0.07

　　每畝作物農具之現值，乃爲測量農具投資效率之最善方法。田塲作物面積平均在六‧七畝者，其農具現值爲一‧三四元，但若田塲面積增至四三‧八畝，則其現值減至○‧七八元。如田塲面積再增，則每畝作物農具之投資，無顯著之增減。

農具效率　大坵田地之工作，恒較小坵者爲速。有三五田塲其田坵大小平均在一畝以下，每日十小時可犂地二‧九畝。有一五三田塲，其田坵大小，平均在九畝或九畝以上，每日可犂地四‧七畝，或較田塲在一畝以下者，多犂地百分之六二。蓋以小坵田塊囘轉工作，費時甚多，而耕犂與役畜移運於各小塊田坵之間，亦頗費時。

　　中國農民，普通居於小村，而耕種其附近之散塊田地。每一農民所耕種之田地，每多零星分散於其村莊各方，且距離遠近，各有不同。農民往返時間，爲由農舍至田間或往來於田坵間所費時間之數量。往返時間之多寡，直接與農舍至田間之平均距離有關（第三六二頁第二表）。每畝水稻栽種，往來所費時間，每因由農舍至田間距離之增加，而由一‧六小時增至九小時，但此無須注意，因往來所費時間僅佔生產水稻所費總時間百分之四‧一。

Capital is an expensive factor in agricultural production in China. The total annual cost per farm for using implements is 11.39 yuan. Of this amount, about 50 per cent is interest on investment, 30 per cent is operating expense, and 20 per cent is depreciation. The annual cost of using some of the more important individual implements is shown in table 1, page 360.

The present value of implements per farm is 9 yuan on farms having an average of 6.7 mow of crops and 99 yuan on farms having an average of 133.4 mow of crops. The increase of the investment in implements is less than proportional to the increase in size of farm.

Efficiency of investment in farm implements may best be measured by the present value of implements per mow of crops. This is 1.34 yuan for farms averaging 6.7 mow but decreases to 0.78 yuan as the size of farm increases to an average of 43.8 mow of crops. With further increases in size of farm the investment in implements per mow of crops shows no distinct upward or downward trend.

Efficiency

Work can be performed at a more rapid rate in large than in small fields. On 35 farms where the average size of fields was less than 1 mow, plowing was done at the rate of 2.9 mow per ten-hour day. On 153 farms where the average size of fields was 9 mow or more, the rate of plowing was 4.7 mow per day or 62 per cent more than on farms where fields averaged less than 1 mow in size. For small fields, much time is spent in turning at the end of the field or at corners and in transferring the plow and work animals from one small field to another.

Chinese farmers usually live in small villages and cultivate non-adjoining fields near their village. Fields cultivated by one farmer may be located in different directions and at different distances from the village. Travel time is the amount of time farmers spend traveling from their homes to fields and traveling between fields. Travel time varies directly with variations in the average distance to fields (table 2, page 362). The fact that travel time per mow of rice increase from 1.6 hours to 9.0 hours with an increase in average distance from farmstead to fields should not be given too much consideration because travel time makes up only 4.1 per cent of the total time required in rice production.

第二表　中國中部迤東一一處一三九一田場之田間距離與往來時間之關係

TABLE 2.—RELATION BETWEEN DISTANCE TO
FIELDS AND TRAVEL TIME

1391 farms, 11 localities, East Central China

農舍至田間平均距離 Average distance, farmstead to fields	田　場 Farms	每次所費時間 Travel time for one trip	每畝水稻往來所費時間 Travel time for 1 mow of rice
里 (a) li (a)	數　目 number	分　數 minutes	小　時 hours
Less than 1	863	3.7	1.6
1	476	10.3	5.4
2	46	17.5	7.0
3	6	26.3	9.0
總計　All farms.	1,391	6.6	3.2

(a)　三華里等於一英里　　(a) Three li equal one mile.

　　農民耕種之田坵，其間距離之變異，較農舍距離田坵之變異為甚。此乃由於農民所耕種之田坵，多位於其村各方。如最遠田坵之距離增加，則每田場水稻畝之距離增加，每畝往來時間增加，惟每畝水稻生產所需之總人工則減。如欲謀生產水稻效率之增高，則應注意於最遠田坵間之距離，與農舍至田坵間之距離及其影響往來時間之關係。但須注意者，乃生產水稻，往來所費時間僅佔所需總人工之小部分，他如田坵大小土壤性質，土地投資，及每田場水稻面積等因素，須更加以考慮。

　　農具之工作效率，租用者較自有者為高，而借用者較自有者為低。由一，○五六具耕犁材料之表示，租用之犁，每日十小時耕地四・○畝；自有之犁，耕地三・一畝；借用者僅耕地二・二畝。此乃因農民租用時議定，須按時或按日付費，故使用租用之農具較速也。借用之犁，在相同之時間內，較自有之犁少耕地百分之二九。借用農具，需取用及歸還，此乃工作遲緩原因之一也。

　　工作效率，常受所用役畜之影響。黃牛耕地，每日耕地三・六六畝，如用水牛，則每日可耕地四・一一畝，較黃牛多耕百分之一二。且水牛所耕之地或較黃牛為佳。

The distance between fields cultivated by farmers varies more than distance from farmstead to fields. This is true because fields cultivated by some farmers are located in two or more directions from their farmstead. With an increase in distance between furthest fields, there is an increase in mow of rice per farm, an increase in travel time per mow, and a decrease in total man labor required per mow in the production of rice. In planning for greater efficiency in the production of rice, some consideration should be given to distance between furthest fields and distance from farmstead to fields, and the influence of these on travel time. It should be kept in mind, however, that travel time makes up a relatively small proportion of the total man labor required to produce rice, and that other factors such as size of field, quality of soil, investment in land, and amount of rice per farm are more important considerations.

The rate of work is higher with hired implements than with owned implements and lower with borrowed implements than with owned implements. Information for 1056 plows shows that a hired plow is made to cover 4.0 mow in a ten-hour day; an owned plow, only 3.1 mow; a borrowed plow, only 2.2 mow. Since farmers sometimes pay for hired implements at an agreed rate per hour or per day, they use hired implements at a more rapid rate. Borrowed plows cover 29 per cent less within a given period of time than do owned plows. Extra time in getting and returning borrowed implements partly accounts for the lower rate of work.

Rate of work is influenced by type of work animal used. The rate of plowing with an ox is 3.66 mow per day, while with a water buffalo it is 4.11 mow per day, 12 per cent more. Also the quality of plowing done with a buffalo may be better than that done with an ox.

Improvement of implements

In determining whether one type of implement is an improvement over another type, consideration should be given to the following: (1) annual cost of using, (2) convenience in using, (3) rate of work, (4) quality of work, (5) ease of performing work.

農 具 之 改 進

欲決定某種農具較優於另一種農具時，則應考慮下列各点：（1）全年使用費用，（2）使用利便，（3）工作效率，（4）工作優劣，（5）工作時之利便。

任何改進農具計劃，首應考慮變更及改進，確與農民有益，並此項計劃，須使農民能組織及耕種其土地，而能獲較高及較有效之生產。關於農具應考慮於下列諸点：——（1）原價，（2）全年使用費用，（3）是否在農忙時使用，（4）每年使用時間，（5）其他交替方法及其費用之比較，（6）本農具在多數田場是否重要。

下列農具之改進，對於中國農民似覺有莫大之利益：（1）水車，（2）耕犁，（3）鐮刀，（4）推車，及（5）船隻。

輸入國外製造農具之希望不大，因其售賣價格較本地製造者為高。中國之借貸費用又高，故農民多無鉅資投於農具。

與中國農具有關之一大問題，乃為善用其資本。合作共用農具，似可解決此種問題。凡農具之使用，與田場工作之與季節及氣候情形無關者，且無須在短期內使用者，則其合作使用，或可成功，由二家以上農民共用。農具之使用與此種工作有關者，如打落，磨粒，軋花，及運輸產品售賣，均屬此類。農具之使用與季節性有關者，如插秧，灌溉，鋤草及收穫等，其合作共用之機會極小。

如農民之田場面積過小，不足購置農具與役畜，以進行其季節工作時，則可用一交替方法，即僱用鄰人或其他農工，以進行此種工作。投資利息實為每年使用農具及役畜費用中最大之一項目。有時小田場農民，僱用人工進行數種田場工作，較本人購置此種工作所需要之農具及役畜為經濟。

金 克 敦

潘 鴻 聲

In any program designed to improve farm implements, consideration should first be given to those changes and implements which will be of greatest benefit to farmers in making it possible for them to organize and operate their farms for higher and more efficient production. Consideration should be given to the following points in regard to implements: (1) initial cost, (2) annual cost of using, (3) whether used during busy season, (4) length of time used annually, (5) alternative methods and cost of doing work, and (6) whether the implement is important on most farms.

It appears that improvments in the following implements might be of greatest benefit to Chinese farmers: (1) irrigation pumps, (2) plow, (3) sickle, (4) wheelbarrow, and (5) boat.

The chance of success in importing foreign-made implements is not great since the price for which they would have to be sold is much higher than the cost of making implements locally. The cost of credit is high in China and farmers cannot afford to have large sums invested in farm implements.

One of the big problems in connection with farm implements in China is to conserve the use of capital. Cooperative ownership of implements helps to solve this problem in some cases. Implements used in connection with farm operations that do not need to be performed within a short time according to season and weather conditions offer possibilities of successful cooperative ownership and use by two or more farmers. Implements used in connection with such operations as threshing grain, grinding grain, ginning cotton, and transporting produce to be sold, are of this class. Implements used in connection with seasonal operations such as setting rice, irrigating, cultivating, and harvesting grain offer little possibility for successful cooperative ownership.

If the size of farm is too small for the farmer to own implements and work animals to perform seasonal operations, one alternative is to hire a neighbor or other worker to perform such operations. Interest on investment is a very expensive item in the annual cost of using work animals and farm implements. It is sometimes more economical for farmers on small farms to hire some farm operations done than to own the implements and work animals necessary for them.

T. O. King
Pan Hong-shen.

南京物價之研究

金陵大學農業經濟系，對於南京中華門及北門橋兩市場之物價，曾有多年之調查與記載。并將該項物價編成指數以表示物價普通之動向。

中 華 門 市 場

中華門附近之農民，其在半徑二十二里（七·三英里）周圍內者，均在此出售產物並購買各種必需品。此市場內之各種現象，均可與其他純粹鄉村市場互相比較。

農民在中華門市場出售之物品以稻米為大宗，其總值約佔各種出售品總值百分之五十。小麥佔百分之十二；大麥佔百分之五；蛋類則佔百分之六。

農民在此所購之物則以麵粉，掛麵，豬肉，棉花，棉布及煤油為主，約佔農民購進物品總值百分之七十。豆油，蘇油，鹽，及煙等物亦復重要，約佔購進物品總值百分之十二。

農民所得及所付物價指數乃依照各種物品之重要性，加以相當權數計算之。（第三六八頁及第三六九頁第一表及第二表）農民所得物價指數之組合因子，與所付物價不同。農民所得物價指數變動甚鉅，因其大半取決于稻麥之價格，而稻麥之價格又多視作物收成狀況，如氣候之影響為轉移。農民所付物價指數變動較小，半因該指數之編製乃由較多數物品之價格，計算而來（第三七〇頁第一圖）。

此項材料所代表之時期內，二指數均受國幣價值變更之影響。自一九三一年九月至一九三五年十月國幣價值高漲。上海原料品之批發物價，跌落百分之三十三。自一九三五年十月至一九三七年六月，國幣價值下跌。上海原料品之批發物價上漲百分之四十三。

農民所付物價指數之漲落，恆以上海批發物價為轉移。（第三七一頁第二圖）自一九三一年九月至一九三五年十月，此指數下落百分之二十七。自一九三五年十月至一九三七年六月，復上漲百分之二十八。一九三五年十一月，我國幣制改革後，此類物品價格之上漲，不若上海原料品價格之速。一九三七年六月至十月，指數上升百分之十六。小麥價格上漲百分之十六；鹽漲百分之十三；煤油漲百分之二十四；香煙漲百分之七十八；糖漲百分之八十一。

際通貨緊縮時期，中華門農民所得物價之跌落，遠較其所付物價及上海原料品批發物價為甚。一九三四年六月，農民所得物價指數，曾降低至五十五，（一九三一年＝一〇〇）。一九三四年六月之價格若與一九三一年

PRICES IN NANKING

Prices in the Chung Hwa Men and Peh Men Chiao markets in Nanking have been recorded for a number of years by the Department of Agricultural Economics, Nanking University. Index numbers have been computed from these prices in order to show the general movements.

Chung Hwa Men Market

Farmers from within a radius of about 22 li (7.3 miles) sell their produce and buy many of their various requirements in the Chung Hwa Men market. The functions of this market are comparable to those of a market town serving an entirely rural area.

Of the commodities sold by farmers at Chung Hwa Men, rice is by far the most important, making up about 50 per cent of the total value of sales. Wheat makes up 12 per cent; barley, 5 per cent; and eggs, 6 per cent.

The farmers' chief purchases are wheat flour and spaghetti, pork, cotton and cotton cloth and kerosene, which together make up about 70 per cent of the total purchases. Soybean and sesame oils, salt, and tobacco are also important. Together they make up about 12 per cent of the total purchases.

Index numbers of prices received for produce sold and of prices paid for purchases have been calculated so as to give to the various commodities " weights " in accordance with their relative importances (table 1, 2; pages 368, 369). The composition of the index for prices received is different from that for prices paid. The index of prices received is variable, chiefly because it is determined largely by prices for rice and wheat and these fluctuate according to crop conditions, as affected by the weather. The index of prices paid is less variable partly because it is computed from prices for a larger group of commodities. (figure 1, page 370).

During the period for which data are available, both indices were affected by changes in the commodity value of the National currency. From September 1931 until October 1935, the yuan rose in value. Wholesale prices of raw materials in Shanghai declined by 33 per cent. From October 1935 to June 1937 the yuan fell in value. Wholesale prices of raw materials in Shanghai advanced by 43 per cent.

The index of prices paid by farmers followed the course of wholesale prices in Shanghai (figure 2, page 371). From September 1931 to October 1935, this index fell 27 per cent and from

平均物價相較，則農民必須多售百分之八十二之產品，始可得同量之現金。一九三三年之作物收成較一九三一年爲佳，但決不能補償物價下跌損失之鉅。各種捐稅及債務之支付，因而發生困難矣。

一九三四年晚春及夏季，旱魃爲災。夏季作物收成大減。因此農民所得物價，於六月後猛漲。農民所得與所付物價雖難分軒輊，但農民因歇收關係僅有少量出售。一九三四年作物收成雖較一九三一年猶差，但價格仍低，蓋因國幣價值增高，一般物價水準降跌之故也。

自一九三五年十月我國幣制改革後，此等現象始獲有較佳之調整，蓋因國幣對黃金之價值貶低，而黃金本身以各種物品計算之價值，復同時降落也。于是中國物價水準上昇極速，倘此次一般物價之高漲，未曾發生，則中華門之一九三六年及一九三七年農產物價必將低于一九三四年及一九三五年也。除一九三六至一九三七年之冬小麥外，一九三六年及一九三七年之收成實較一九三四至一九三五年者爲豐。但價格反高。即國幣貶值，一般物價水準高漲之影響也。

第一表　南京中華門農民所得物價加權綜合指數一九三一年至一九三七年
一九三一年＝一〇〇　(a)

TABLE 1.—WEIGHTED AGGREGATIVE INDEX NUMBERS OF PRICES RECEIVED BY FARMERS, CHUNG HWA MEN, NANKING, 1931 — 1937, (1931 == 100) (a)

年 Year	一月 Jan.	二月 Feb.	三月 Mar.	四月 Apr.	五月 May	六月 June	七月 July	八月 Aug.	九月 Sep.	十月 Oct.	十一月 Nov.	十二月 Dec.	年平均 Year
1931	88	91	91	90	89	90	112	116	113	109	111	—	100
1932	98	110	109	109	90	95	86	74	70	65	64	65	94
1933	69	70	67	68	66	56	49	47	55	58	57	56	58
1934	56	58	50	50	54	55	71	71	80	72	77	84	71
1935	78	84	82	84	79	80	77	69	71	71	73	72	84
1936	76	79	88	88	92	81	84	74	68	74	82	92	89
1937	96	96	94	86	82	82	101	96	85	80			

(a) 下列爲指數所包含之物品及其權數(量衡單位均爲一九三一年一月所通用者)：

(a) The commodities included and their respective weights were as follows (the units of weight and measure were those in use in January 1931):—

農產品 Grains:

黃稻 Rice, yellow unhulled .... 12.0 tan 石
小麥 Wheat, red .... 2.0 tan 石
大麥 Barley, hulless ...... 1.0 tan 石
玉米 Corn .... 0.3 tan 石
蠶豆 Broad beans .... 0.2 tan 石
豌豆 Field peas .... 0.3 tan 石
黃豆 Soybeans, yellow . 0.2 tan 石
青豆 Soybeans, green .. 0.1 tan 石
料豆 Soybeans, grey ... 0.3 tan 石

紅豆 Red beans .... 0.1 tan 石
綠豆 Green beans .... 0.1 tan 石
飯豆 Cow peas .... 0.2 tan 石
芝蔴 Sesame .... 0.05 tan 石

園產品 Vegetables:
青菜 Cabbage .... 1.0 picul 斤
青蘿蔔 Turnips .... 1.0 picul 斤
黃豆牙 Soybean sprouts .. 1.0 picul 斤

畜產品 Animal Products:
雞蛋 Eggs, hen .... 200 個
鴨蛋 Eggs, duck .... 50 個

October 1935 to June 1937 it rose 28 per cent. The advance following the currency reform of November 1935 was not as rapid for this group of commodities as for the group of raw materials in Shanghai. From June to October 1937, the index rose by 16 per cent. Wheat prices rose by 16 per cent; salt, 13; kerosene 24; cigarettes, 78; and sugar, 81 per cent.

During the deflation period, prices received by farmers for their own produce declined much more than the prices they paid for purchases in Chung Hwa Men or prices of raw materials in Shanghai. By June 1934, the index of prices received had fallen to 55, (1931 = 100). In order to obtain the same amount of cash, farmers would have had to have sold 82 per cent more produce at June 1934 prices than at the average prices of 1931. Crops were better in 1933 than in 1931 but not sufficiently better to make up for much of the decline of prices. Debts and taxes were therefore difficult to pay.

第二表　南京中華門農民所付物價加權綜合指數 一九三一年至一九三七年
一九三一年＝一〇〇 (a)

TABLE 2.—WEIGHTED AGGREGATIVE INDEX NUMBERS OF PRICES PAID BY FARMERS, CHUNG HWA MEN, NANKING, 1931 — 1937, (1931 = 100) (a)

年 Year	一月 Jan.	二月 Feb.	三月 Mar.	四月 Apr.	五月 May	六月 June	七月 July	八月 Aug.	九月 Sep.	十月 Oct.	土月 Nov.	吉月 Dec.	年平均 Year
1931	95	98	90	90	103	103	108	104	102	103	103	—	100
1932	103	98	94	93	90	93	93	92	92	95	95	95	94
1933	99	94	89	88	82	80	81	80	80	80	82	86	85
1934	88	83	76	78	78	75	73	74	76	75	73	77	77
1935	74	77	81	81	75	80	74	73	77	74	79	82	77
1936	96	89	92	95	88	86	84	83	81	82	91	96	89
1937	99	97	98	96	95	95	94	93	105	110			

(a) 下列為指數所包含之物品及其權數(量衡單位均為一九三一年一月所通用者)：

(a) The commodities included and their respective weights were as follows (units of weight and measure were those in use in January 1931) :—

食料 Foodstuffs:

麵　粉	Wheat flour	100 catties 斤
切　麵	Spaghetti	80 catties 斤
萬字糕	Cake, Swastika	10 pack 包
猪　肉	Pork	8 catties 斤
豆　油	Soybean oil	20 catties 斤
蔴　油	Sesame oil	10 catties 斤
醬　油	Soybean sauce	30 catties 斤
細　鹽	Salt, refined	60 catties 斤
白　糖	Sugar, refined	10 catties 斤
燒　酒	Liquor, barley	10 catties 斤
青　菜	Cabbage	50 catties 斤
紅　棗	Dates, dried	5 catties 斤
瓜　子	Melon seeds	4 catties 斤

衣料 Clothing:

棉　花	Cotton, raw	10 catties 斤

Cotton cloth, white

白土布	" coarse	50 feet 尺
白洋布	" fine	80 feet 尺
布綫洋	Twills	30 feet 尺
紗　襪	Stockings	30 pairs 雙

燃料 Light:

煤　油	Kerosene	200 catties 斤
火　柴	Matches	30 pkts. 斤

雜項 Miscellaneous:

紙　烟	Cigarettes	100 pkts. 包
絲　烟	Tobacco	10 liang 兩
茶	Tea	50 liang 兩
生髮油	Hair oil	0.2 catties 斤
草　紙	Paper, grass	20 tao 刀
手　巾	Towel	10 pieces 條
桐　油	Wood oil	5 catties 斤
苧　蔴	Ramie	20 liang 兩

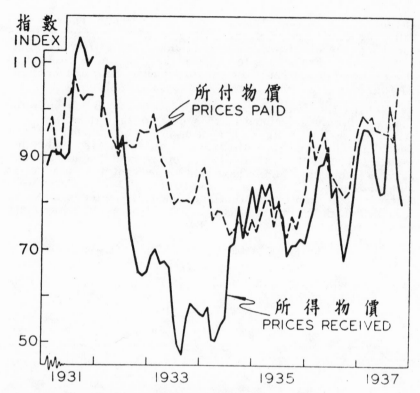

第一圖　南京中華門農民所得及所付物價之加權綜合指數，一九三一年一月至一九三七年十月。

一九三一年＝一〇〇

作物收成之差異影響農民所得物價指數較所付物價指數為甚。二者對於一九三一年至一九三五年之通貨緊縮及一九三五年後之回漲均受影響。

FIGURE 1.—WEIGHTED AGGREGATIVE INDEX NUMBERS OF PRICES RECEIVED AND PAID BY FARMERS IN THE CHUNG HWA MEN MARKET, NANKING, JAN. 1931 — OCT. 1937

1931 = 100

Variations in crop production have affected the index of prices received more than the index of prices paid. Both indices were affected by the general deflation from 1931 to 1935 and the reflation thereafter.

　　設以一般原料品之物價水準未動因而國幣之物品價值，自一九三一年至現在始終保持平穩狀態，則一九三一年及一九三四年因歉收關係，農民所得物價必高，而一九三三，一九三六及一九三七等年因作物豐收，農民所得物價必低。農人出售農產品數量之變異，恆為物價變動而糾正其一部。因一九三一年國幣價值之低，一九三一及一九三五年之上漲，及一九三五年後之下跌，農民所得物價於一九三一年過高，而於一九三三與一九三四年則又過低也。

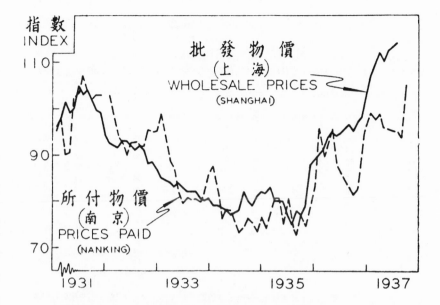

指數
INDEX

批發物價
(上海)
WHOLESALE PRICES
(SHANGHAI)

所付物價
(南京)
PRICES PAID
(NANKING)

第二圖　南京中華門農民所付物價指數及上海原料品物價指數，一九三一
年一月至一九三七年十月。

一九三一年＝一〇〇

南京農民所付物價較上海原料品批發物價之暴漲爲緩。

FIGURE 2.—INDEX NUMBERS OF PRICES PAID BY FARMERS IN CHUNG HWA MEN
MARKET, NANKING, AND PRICES OF RAW MATERIALS IN SHANGHAI, JAN.
1931 — OCT. 1937 (1931 = 100)

Prices paid by farmers in Nanking have lagged behind the rapid advance of wholesale
prices of raw materials in Shanghai.

In 1934, a severe drought in the late spring and summer
reduced the summer crops and prices received by farmers
advanced rapidly after June. The gap between prices received
and prices paid disappeared but farmers had little to sell because
crops were small. The crops of 1934 were smaller than those of
1931, but prices were lower because the general level of commodity
prices had declined—the yuan had risen in value.

Better adjustment returned only after the currency reform
of November 1935, when the yuan was reduced in value in terms
of gold which was itself declining in terms of commodities. The
general level of prices in China rose rapidly. If this advance had
not been brought about, prices of farm produce at Chung Hwa Men
would have been lower in 1936 and 1937 than in 1934 and 1935.

第三表　　南京北門橋零售物價之加權綜合指數一九二四年至一九三七年。
一九三一年＝一〇〇　(a)

TABLE 3.—WEIGHTED AGGREGATIVE INDEX NUMBERS OF RETAIL PRICES IN PEH MEN CHIAO, NANKING, 1924 — 1937, (1931 = 100) *(a)*

年 Year	一月 Jan.	二月 Feb.	三月 Mar.	四月 Apr.	五月 May	六月 June	七月 July	八月 Aug.	九月 Sep.	十月 Oct.	十一月 Nov.	十二月 Dec.	年平均 Year
1924	73	74	71	72	69	67	70	68	65	64	61	62	68
1925	65	66	66	68	69	73	73	72	69	72	71	74	70
1926	75	81	81	79	79	83	82	80	81	80	80	81	80
1927	85	86	97	95	93	92	97	98	92	89	85	86	91
1928	91	91	92	94	94	90	88	87	85	86	90	92	90
1929	94	97	96	—	—	—	—	—	99	103	103	103	99
1930	107	108	108	106	107	108	115	107	99	95	90	91	103
1931	94	100	98	95	100	96	102	110	104	103	99	99	100
1932	99	94	94	90	89	94	94	93	82	78	77	79	89
1933	80	82	77	74	74	73	73	74	68	71	71	70	74
1934	70	71	67	69	70	70	75	77	80	78	80	80	74
1935	79	78	76	76	74	77	79	73	73	75	81	80	77
1936	83	84	85	84	84	84	86	87	84	81	82	91	85
1937	96	97	96	93	92	92	93	101	95	95			

(a) 下列為指數所包含之物品及其權數(量衡單位均為一九二四年至一九三一年四月所通用者)：

(a) The commodities included and their respective weights were as follows (the units of weight and measure were those in use from 1924 to April 1931) :—

五穀類 **Grains:**

秈　米	Rice, early	11.00 tan 石
糯　米	Rice, glutinous .	0.10 tan 石
蠶　豆	Broad beans	0.03 tan 石
豌　豆	Field peas	0.01 tan 石
綠　豆	Green beans	0.10 tan 石
紅　豆	Red beans	0.01 tan 石
江　豆	Cow peas...........	0.01 tan 石
黃　豆	Soybeans	0.02 tan 石
芝　蔴	Sesame	0.01 tan 石
玉蜀黍	Corn	0.04 tan 石
稻　子	Rice, unhulled ...	0.20 tan 石

蔬菜類 **Vegetables:**

馬鈴薯	Potatoes, Irish .	10 catties 斤
青蘿蔔	Turnips, green .	5 catties 斤
山　藥	Yam	2 catties 斤
蒜　苗	Garlic	6 catties 斤
蘿蔔頭	Radish, winter .	50 catties 斤
生　薑	Ginger	2 catties 斤
洋　葱	Onions	1 catty 斤
藕	Lotus roots	200 catties 斤
青　菜	Cabbage, green .	200 catties 斤
白　菜	Cabbage, white .	50 catties 斤
菠　菜	Spinach	40 catties 斤
芹　菜	Celery	20 catties 斤
青韮菜	Leeks, green	20 catties 斤
白韮菜	Leeks, shoots.....	5 catties 斤

大　葱	Onions, Welsh ...	2 catties 斤
豆芽菜	Bean sprouts......	40 catties 斤
蠶豆米	Broad beans	5 catties 斤
豌豆葉	Field pea leaves .	6 catties 斤
雪裏紅	Si li hong	6 catties 斤
竹　筍	Bamboo shoots...	20 catties 斤
大　蒜	Garlic, green......	1 catty 斤
苞　菜	Cabbage, rolling	20 catties 斤

肉類 **Animal products:**

牛　肉	Beef	45 catties 斤
猪　肉	Pork	100 catties 斤
雞　肉	Chicken	50 catties 斤
鴨　肉	Duck	30 catties 斤

魚類 **Fish:**

鯉　魚	Carp, common ...	4 catties 斤
青　魚	Carp, common, black	30 catties 斤
鯤子魚	Carp, black, small	3 catties 斤
白連魚	Carp, silver	15 catties 斤
黃連魚	Carp, yellow	15 catties 斤
鯿　魚	Bream, fresh water	11 catties 斤
白　魚	Pai yü	22 catties 斤
鯽　魚	Carp, golden......	50 catties 斤
鱠　魚	Mandarin	5 catties 斤
蝦　子	Shrimps	10 catties 斤

(Continued on next page).

Excepting the 1936-37 winter wheat crop, 1936 and 1937 crops were bigger than 1934-1935 crops, but prices were higher because of the rise of the general price level brought about by depreciation of the yuan.

If the commodity value of the yuan as measured by the general level of prices for raw materials had been kept steady from 1931 to the present time, prices received by farmers would have been high in 1931 and 1934 because of poor crops and low in 1933, 1936 and 1937 because of good crops. Variations in the amount of produce available for sale would have been partly corrected by price changes. Because the yuan was low in value in 1931, increased in value from 1931 to 1935 and fell in value thereafter, prices received were too high in 1931, and much too low both in 1933 and 1934.

Peh Men Chiao Market

The Peh Men Chiao market serves retail buyers in north central Nanking. All kinds of food and clothing, household goods, and fuel are retailed, the commonest buyers being from middle class families.

(a) (Continued from Preceding Page).

水菜類 **Fruits:**

香 蕉	Banana	10 catties 斤
橄 欖	Olives	0.2 catties 斤
美國苹果	Apples, American	1 catty 斤
啞叭梨	Pears	10 catties 斤
荸 薺	Waterchestnuts ..	10 catties 斤
美 橘	Oranges, American	5 catties 斤

其他食品 **Miscellaneous foods:**

栗 子	Chestnuts	4 catties 斤
白 果	Ginkgo nuts	0.1 catties 斤
核 桃	Walnuts	0.2 catties 斤
桂 圓	Lungngans	0.5 catties 斤
蜜 棗	Honey dates	2 catties 斤
灰 棗	Dates, grey	3 catties 斤
紅 棗	Dates, red..........	1 catty 斤
豆 油	Soybean oil	75 catties 斤
蔴 油	Sesamum oil	25 catties 斤
猪 油	Lard	30 catties 斤
醬 油	Soy sauce	120 catties 斤
醋	Vinegar	15 catties 斤

衣料類 **Clothing and fibers:**

洋 布	Cotton cloth, fine	50 feet 尺
本 布	" " coarse	60 feet 尺

燃料類 **Fuels:**

稻 草	Rice straw	3 piculs 批

蘆 柴	Reeds	10 piculs 批
劈 柴	Firewood	5 piculs 批
枝子柴	Dried stems	1 picul 批
板 炭	Charcoal, chestnut	5 piculs 批
	Charcoal, black...	4 piculs 批
煤	Coal	1 ton 噸

雜項類 **Miscellaneous:**

高梁酒	Kaoliang wine ...	10 catties 斤
燒 酒	Liquor, barley ...	4 catties 斤
紹興酒	Shao-sin wine ...	20 catties 斤
紅玫瑰酒	Red rose wine ...	4 catties 斤
白 糖	Sugar, white	25 catties 斤
鹽	Salt	50 catties 斤
乾 麵	Wheat flour	60 catties 斤
切 麵	Spaghetti	50 catties 斤
西瓜子	Melon seeds	5 catties 斤
花生仁	Peanuts, shelled	10 catties 斤
梳頭油	Hair oil	1 catty 斤
毛 巾	Towel	50 pieces 條
皮 絲	Tobacco	5 liang 兩
茶	Tea No. 1 (Yin Tsing)	60 liang 兩
	No. 2 (Chu Lang)	60 liang 兩
	No. 3 (Chien Tiou)	1 liang 兩
	No. 4 (Po Kuh)	1 liang 兩

北門橋市塲

　　北門橋市塲爲南京中北部零購顧客荟集之所。各種食品，衣料，家用品及燃料等均屬零星發售，大多數之顧主均爲中等階級。

　　該處物價于一九二四年即由卜凱博士首先記錄，以後每週均有調查報告，迄今未斷。此指數之計算，曾加以相當權數，其估計係根據十五個中等家庭每年購買數量爲準（第三七二頁第三表）。米估購買總值百分之二十七；豬肉估百分之七；魚類估百分之八；豆油估百分之四；柴炭估百分之七；煤炭估百分之五。米之地位估絕對重要，因其價格之變動，指數亦逐爲之漲落。此指數可視爲南京中等家庭所需之食物，衣着，燃料及瑣碎用品等生活費變動之準繩。但房租，捐稅，及電水等費，則未計入。

　　北門橋零售物價指數較上海原料品批發物價指數變動爲劇，因其受作物收成情況之影響也（第三七六頁第三圖）。一九三〇年，作物收成荒歉，北門橋指數較高；一九三六年及一九三七年，因作物收成良好，北門橋指數故較低。但一九三一年前中國物價水準之高漲，一九三一年至一九三五年十月之下跌，及一九三五年十月後之飛漲，其影響於北門橋物價之漲落者，較之作物生產，尤爲重大。自一九二四年至一九三一年，該指數昇高至百分之四十七。一九三一年至一九三五年十月則下跌百分之二十四。一九三五年十月至一九三七年十月復又上漲百分之二十五。

　　工資與薪金之購買力，乃受食物，衣着及燃料等零售物價之變動所支配。南京以薪金工資爲生者，多爲政府職工，其薪金及工資，較爲固定。自一九三一年至一九三四年因物價低落，工資薪金之購買力遂上漲。一九三四年大旱使物價稍漲，但物價回漲之主要因子，則爲以物品計算之國幣價值之跌落也 1。物價之回漲，復使固定工資薪金之購買力減低。設非一九三六及一九三七兩年，作物收成特別良好，則工資薪金購買力之減低，將尤甚焉。

雷　伯　恩
胡　國　華
戈　福　鼎

1　關於影響中國一般物價水準諸因子之詳論請參看經濟統計第五期第一九七至二一一頁，一九三七年五月出版。

Prices were first recorded in 1924 by Dr. J. Lossing Buck and weekly reports have been obtained up to the present time. The index computed from these retail prices has been " weighted " on the basis of estimates of the yearly purchases obtained for 15 middle class households (table 3, page 372). Of the total value of purchases, rice makes up about 27 per cent; pork, 7; various kinds of fish, 8; soybean oil, 4; charcoal, 7; coal, 5. Rice is by far the most important commodity and changes in the price of rice are usually reflected by a change in the index. The index can be considered as a measure of changes in the cost to middle class families in Nanking, of food, clothing, fuel, and miscellaneous supplies. It does not measure changes in rent, taxes or the cost of electricity and water.

The index is more variable than the index for raw material prices in Shanghai because it is influenced more by crop conditions (figure 3, page 376). In 1930, the index for Peh Men Chiao was relatively high because of poor crops, whereas, in 1936 and 1937, it was relatively low because of good crops. But the rise of China's general price level prior to 1931, the fall from 1931 to October 1935 and the rapid rise thereafter affected prices in Peh Men Chiao even more than did variations in crop production. The index advanced by 47 per cent from 1924 to 1931, fell by 24 per cent from 1931 to October 1935, and rose by 25 per cent from October, 1935 to October, 1937.

Changes in the retail prices of food, clothing and fuel determine the purchasing power of wages. Many of the wage earners of Nanking were government employees with comparatively fixed wages. From 1931 to 1934 the decline of prices increased the purchasing power of these wages. The drought of 1934 raised prices slightly but the major part of the reflation has been brought about by those factors affecting the value of the yuan in terms of all commodities.[1] The reflation of prices has again reduced the purchasing power of fixed wages. The reduction would have been greater if the yield of crops in 1936 and 1937 had not been especially good.

John R. Raeburn
Hu Kwoh-hwa
Ko Fuh-ting

---

1 For a fuller discussion of factors affecting the general level of prices in China, see *Economic Facts* No. 5, pp. 197-211; May, 1937.

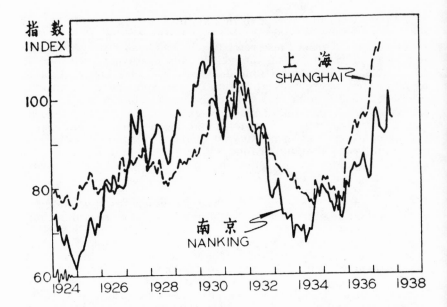

第三圖　南京北門橋零售物價之加權綜合指數及上海原料品批發物價之
　　　『沙爾白克司答的司脫』指數，一九二四年一月至一九三七年十
　　　月。

一九三一年＝一〇〇

　　南京食物，衣着，燃料及雜項物品零售物價之指數恆隨上海原料品批發物價指數而變動，但
亦受作物來源，尤其是稻米來源之影響。一九三六及一九三七兩年，南京零售物價曾經相當低落
，其原因乃以夏季作物收成良好之故也。

FIGURE 3.—WEIGHTED AGGREGATIVE INDEX NUMBERS OF RETAIL PRICES IN PEH
MEN CHIAO, NANKING, AND SAUERBECK-STATIST INDEX OF WHOLESALE PRICES
OF RAW MATERIALS IN SHANGHAI, JAN. 1924 — OCT. 1937
1931 = 100

　　The index of retail prices of food, clothing, fuel and miscellaneous supplies in Nanking
has followed the course of wholesale prices of raw materials in Shanghai but has also been
determined by crop supplies, particularly the supply of rice. During 1936 and 1937, the index
of retail prices in Nanking was relatively low because the yields of summer crops were large.

經 濟 統 計
ECONOMIC FACTS
南京金陵大學農學院農業經濟系出版
DEPARTMENT OF AGRICULTURAL ECONOMICS
COLLEGE OF AGRICULTURE AND FORESTRY
UNIVERSITY OF NANKING
NANKING, CHINA

第九期 No. 9　　　　　　　一九三八年四月 April, 1938

第 一 圖　　重慶之批發物價
FIGURE 1.—WHOLESALE PRICES IN CHUNGKING.

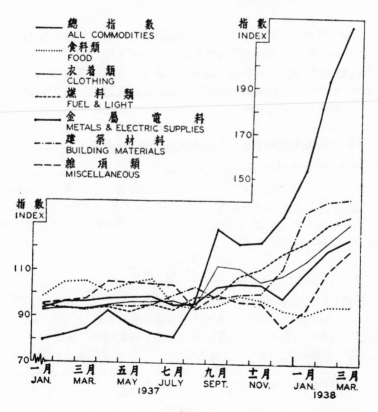

近兩年來中國鄉鎮物價之變遷

物價高低，因地域而不同，於是各地農產之種類，亦因此而互異。農產價格，時有漲落，農民商人，亦不能不依此以爲其經營事業之準繩。一地物價之變動，必由兩種因素以造成之：（一）因幣制關係所促成之物價水準之升降，（二）當地當時之特殊經濟環境。研究地方物價變動之個別差異時，此種經濟環境之分析甚屬重要。

過去之研究物價者，証明如中國與他國之貨幣本位相同，或中國與各國之物價，能以同一貨幣表示之，則兩者之變動，極爲類似[1]。但一國有一國之特殊情形，一地有一地之個別狀況，此種特殊情形與個別狀況，每爲一般統計學者所忽視。因而凡遇各地物價之漲落，不能相互脗合時，即以統計技術不精，或物價報告之失確而解釋之。實則各地物價之漲落，絕難期其完全脗合，因有特殊背景故也。故統計學者對地方情形，亦須予以深切之注意。

金陵大學農業經濟系爲研究目前中國農村物價之漲落計，爰於兩年前開始調查各地物價之工作。前後成立報告中心者，已三十餘所。第因經費及報告員之訓練所限，迄今按期塡報，資料滿意者，祇有十五處。其中四處因記錄年限過短，現無統計價值。另兩處因接近都市，不應以之代表鄉村。本文材料，係根據九處之報告而成，華中爲江西泰和之沿溪渡，湖北遠安之南關，江蘇武進之禮家橋與湖北黃陂之張家店；華北則爲山西之靜樂，安徽之宿縣，陝西華縣之赤水，陝西橫山之波羅堡，及河北正定之傅家村。（第三八〇頁第一圖）

自民國二十四年九月至民國二十六年九月之兩年內，吾國曾經歷兩大空前事件，其影響於國計民生者甚鉅。其一即民國二十四年十一月之宣佈放棄銀本位制，其二即民國二十六年七月暴發之中日戰爭。此二者均爲研究物價者所不可忽視者也。

物價之普遍上漲

吾國自民國二十四年十一月四日，正式放棄銀本位，而穩定法幣對英磅或美元之滙價後，其物價水準，已漸與英美等國，趨於一致。概言之：自民國二十四年九月起，吾國農民所付之物價與其所得之物價，均見上漲（第三八二頁第一表第三八一頁第二圖）。

1 　經濟統計第二三九頁及二七四頁

PRICE CHANGES IN CHINESE RURAL MARKET TOWNS
September, 1935 to October, 1937

Geographical price differentials explain part of the differences in the types of farm enterprise. Chronological changes in agricultural prices control the activities of farmers and business men. Price fluctuations in any locality are determined by two forces, *(a)* the movement of the general price level which is, in general, affected by monetary factors, and *(b)* the local economic situation prevailing at the particular moment to which due consideration must be given to explain the discrepancies in price movement between individual localities. Studies have been made which showed that the price movement in China is usually similar to price movements in other countries if the monetary standards are the same or converted into the same terms.[1] Frequently the peculiarities of different localities are over-looked by statisticians and the discrepancies in price changes are usually attributed either to the crudeness of the statistical method or the inaccuracy of the price reporting service.

Price reports have been started during the last two years by the Department of Agricultural Economics of the University of Nanking, for the purpose of ascertaining current price changes in rural China. Due to limitations of funds and trained personnel, only fifteen localities have sent in reports regularly. Four localities are not included in the present analysis because their reports covered too short a period, and two other localities have had to be omitted because of their urban rather than rural status. The nine remaining localities include the following: Taiho, Kiangsi; Yuanan, Hupeh; Wuchin, Kiangsu and Hwangpe, Hupeh in Central China and Tsingloh, Shansi; Suhsien, Anhwei; Hwahsien, Shensi; Hwenshan, Shensi and Chengting, Hopeh, in North China (figure 1, page 380).

During the two years from September, 1935, to September, 1937, China experienced two unprecedented events which seriously affected the economic life of the nation. The first was the formal abandonment of the silver standard in November, 1935, and the second was the outbreak of hostilities between Japan and China in July, 1937. Any study of price changes must take these two happenings into consideration.

General upward trend of prices

After China officially went off the silver standard on November fourth, 1935 and pegged her currency to the pound Sterling or the United States dollar, her price level became analagous to those in other gold-using countries such as the United States and England. Generally speaking, the trend of prices, both received and paid by farmers in China since September, 1935, has been upward (table 1, page 382 and figure 2, page 381).

---

1 *Economic Facts,* pp. 239, 274.

如以民國二十五年爲基期，則農民所得之物價指數，自民國二十四年九月之最低數七五而漲至民國二十六年十月之一一二・五，兩年間之最高指數爲二十六年三月之一二一・四。如與最低之七五相較，則上漲達百分之六十二也。至農民所付物價之指數其上漲趨勢，亦與所得物價同，兩年間之最低点亦爲民國二十四年之九月，其指數爲八八・七，自是逐漸高漲，至民國二十六年十月，該指數竟達一二七・八，爲該期內之最高記錄。

農民所得物價之長期趨勢，可以方程式 Y＝80.208＋1.680X 代表之，二十六個月來每月上漲之量，爲民國二十五年平均之百分之一・六八。至農民所付物價之長期趨勢，其方程式則爲 Y＝87.13＋1.333X 因之每月高漲之量，爲二十五年平均之百分之一・三三三，因之農民所付物價之上漲，不若所得物價爲急劇。(第三八一頁第二圖)

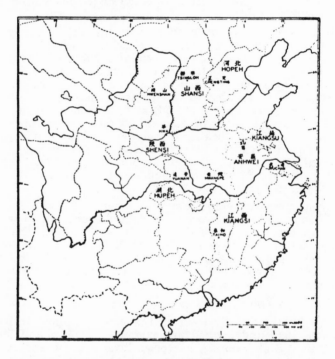

第 一 圖　報 告 物 價 各 鎮 市 之 位 置

FIGURE 1.—LOCATION OF TOWNS SENDING PRICE REPORTS.

The index numbers of prices received by farmers advanced from 75 in September, 1935, the lowest point in the period, to 112.5 in October, 1937, if the average of 1936 is considered to be 100. The peak occurred in March, 1937, representing an advance of 62 per cent from the beginning or lowest point in the period.

Likewise, the index numbers of prices paid by farmers disclosed the same general trend with a few exceptions which will be discussed later. The lowest point, 88.7, also occurred at the beginning of the period. Prices paid by farmers advanced steadily until October, 1937, when the index number reached 127.8, the highest point in the period (table 2, page 383).

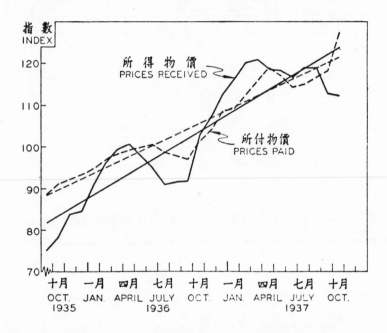

第二圖　中國鄉鎮市場農民所得與所付物價之指數民國廿四年九月至廿六年十月

民國二十五年＝一〇〇

農民所得物價之變動，較所付物價為劇，然其趨勢則皆步漲。

FIGURE 2.—INDEX NUMBERS OF PRICES RECEIVED AND PAID BY FARMERS, IN CHINA, SEPTEMBER 1935 TO OCTOBER 1937.

1936 = 100

Price trends were upward, prices received by farmers fluctuated more violently than prices paid.

第一表　中國九鎮市農民所得物價之指數，民國廿四年九月至廿六年十月

民國二十五年＝一〇〇

TABLE 1.—INDEX NUMBERS OF PRICES RECEIVED BY FARMERS IN 9 RURAL CHINESE MARKET TOWNS SEPTEMBER 1935 — OCTOBER 1937

1936 = 100

地　區 Localities	華中 Central China					華北 North China						各地平均
	江西泰和 Taiho, Kiangsi	湖北遠安 Yuanan, Hupeh	江蘇武進 Wuchin, Kiangsu	湖北黄陂 Hwangpe, Hupeh	平均數 Average	山西靜樂 Tsingloh, Shansi	陝西華縣(a) Hwa Hsien (a) Shensi	安徽宿縣 Hsien, Anhwei	陝西橫山 Hwen-Shan, Shensi	河北正定 Chengting, Hopeh	平(b)均數 Average (b)	平均數 Average of all localities
調査物品數目 Number of commodities	17	18	8	17	—	15	22	38	18	37	—	—
1935												
九月 Sept.	75.8	94.0	84.7	—	84.8	53.5	86.3	47.4	67.8	—	65.2	75.0
十月 Oct.	76.7	99.4	91.8	—	89.3	52.0	90.4	80.1	68.9	—	67.0	78.2
十一月 Nov.	79.9	98.9	104.4	—	94.4	58.7	94.7	87.9	73.1	—	73.2	83.8
十二月 Dec.	81.0	98.4	98.2	—	92.5	64.8	94.8	87.7	78.3	—	76.9	84.7
1936												
一月 Jan.	84.0	98.7	95.0	112.5	97.6	74.1	95.4	88.4	83.8	—	82.1	90.9
二月 Feb.	95.3	102.8	96.4	111.5	101.5	84.8	97.3	93.1	88.7	—	88.9	96.1
三月 Mar.	102.0	102.4	101.2	114.4	104.4	83.0	98.1	101.3	93.0	—	92.4	99.3
四月 Apr.	99.7	103.1	103.6	113.9	105.1	82.0	100.1	104.7	97.2	—	94.6	100.6
五月 May	105.5	103.2	102.7	98.2	102.4	81.8	99.3	96.9	100.0	94.3	93.2	97.8
六月 June	97.0	91.7	99.0	105.8	98.4	79.8	97.1	90.0	100.8	95.6	91.6	95.0
七月 July	86.7	90.6	96.2	89.1	90.6	80.8	101.6	96.4	97.5	91.4	91.5	91.1
八月 Aug.	86.0	93.8	95.7	84.3	90.0	84.2	103.4	101.1	98.3	89.0	93.2	91.6
九月 Sept.	98.8	87.5	95.0	85.5	91.7	82.2	106.5	95.9	97.7	91.5	91.8	91.8
十月 Oct.	122.0	100.6	99.2	100.6	105.6	130.9	151.8	101.5	95.8	100.7	100.5	103.0
十一月 Nov.	112.6	109.9	103.2	95.5	105.3	108.4	157.1	111.1	114.5	103.8	109.4	107.4
十二月 Dec.	114.0	118.5	112.5	90.6	108.9	105.5	182.1	119.6	137.7	103.4	116.6	112.7
1937												
一月 Jan.	122.2	120.1	115.0	102.1	114.8	112.1	183.1	117.2	135.8	106.2	117.8	116.3
二月 Feb.	129.4	124.8	113.8	102.9	117.7	115.7	171.2	117.0	151.6	109.1	123.4	120.5
三月 Mar.	124.2	121.4	111.2	107.1	116.0	128.3	167.3	118.6	150.4	109.8	126.8	121.4
四月 Apr.	120.7	113.7	106.4	112.4	113.3	110.7	155.3	116.8	150.8	118.6	124.2	118.8
五月 May	125.7	103.5	110.1	115.4	113.7	105.5	143.8	110.8	147.7	129.0	123.2	118.5
六月 June	126.3	108.8	104.6	114.1	113.3	113.2	136.5	113.6	138.4	—	121.7	116.9
七月 July	127.4	116.7	111.5	114.2	117.4	103.5	131.7	121.0	139.2	—	121.2	119.1
八月 Aug.	134.7	105.9	112.7	112.0	116.3	106.3	125.4	124.3	138.0	—	122.9	119.1
九月 Sept.	142.7	101.2	106.2	112.2	115.6	98.5	108.9	116.8	—	—	107.6	113.0
十月 Oct.	139.5	95.6	—	107.8	114.3	—	—	107.2	—	—	107.2	112.5

(a) 計算平均數時華縣除外，因該處受西安事變之影響致物價變動與其他各地差別太大。

Hwa hsien was excluded when average were computed, because price movement there was conspicuously different as compared with those in other localities due to the Sian incident.

(b) 平均數包括下列四處：靜樂，宿縣，橫山及正定。

Averages were computed by including four localities; Tsingloh, Su hsien, Hwenshan and Chengting.

第二表　中國九鎮市農民所付物價之指數，民國廿四年九月至廿六年十月

民國二十五年＝一〇〇

TABLE 2.—INDEX NUMBERS OF PRICES PAID BY FARMERS IN 9 RURAL CHINESE MARKET TOWNS SEPTEMBER 1035 — OCTOBER 1937

1936 = 100

地　區 Localities	華　中 Central China					華　北 North China						各地平均
	江西泰和 Taiho, Kiangsi	湖北遠安 Yuanan, Hupeh	江蘇武進 Wuchin, Kiangsu	湖北黃陂 Hwangpe, Hupeh	平均數 Average	山西靜樂 Tsingloh, Shansi	陝西華縣(a) Hwa Hsien (a) Shensi	安徽宿縣 Hsien, Anhwei	陝西橫山 Hwen-Shan, Shensi	河北正定 Chengting, Hopeh	平均數(b) Average (b)	Average of all localities
調查物品數目 Number of commodities	45	41	51	53	—	34	46	73	41	52	—	—
1935												
九月 Sept.	97.3	84.3	86.9	—	89.5	--	95.9	85.1	90.1	—	87.6	88.7
十月 Oct.	97.3	94.5	90.1	—	94.0	—	95.6	82.8	91.2	—	87.0	91.2
十一月 Nov.	97.4	90.0	93.3	—	93.6	—	95.1	87.5	93.9	—	90.7	92.4
士月 Dec.	95.8	91.6	93.0	—	93.5	—	97.1	90.2	96.9	—	93.6	93.5
1936												
一月 Jan.	93.7	96.2	93.1	98.3	95.3	—	96.7	90.5	98.3	—	94.4	95.0
二月 Feb.	96.2	101.1	93.7	100.2	97.8	—·	97.1	90.4	101.2	—	95.8	97.1
三月 Mar.	97.8	101.8	99.5	100.0	99.8	—	95.9	92.6	99.5	—	96.0	98.5
四月 Apr.	100.0	99.2	101.4	103.3	101.0	—	98.1	92.6	99.3	—	96.0	99.3
五月 May	101.8	101.4	100.8	98.8	100.7	—	98.3	95.6	101.8	99.5	99.0	100.0
六月 June	99.0	98.9	98.9	106.1	100.7	—	98.3	101.0	99.2	101.3	100.5	100.6
七月 July	92.8	99.3	100.5	101.4	98.5	—	102.6	100.6	97.1	99.7	99.1	98.8
八月 Aug.	94.1	97.5	100.8	97.3	97.4	—	107.0	108.6	89.2	87.9	98.6	97.9
九月 Sept.	102.4	94.4	98.7	92.9	97.1	88.0	105.2	108.2	97.6	94.7	97.1	97.1
十月 Oct.	110.9	100.4	101.7	101.0	103.5	96.9	94.1	106.0	96.7	97.3	99.7	101.6
十一月 Nov.	105.8	105.3	102.0	100.4	103.4	108.4	104.5	105.1	105.3	101.4	105.0	104.2
士月 Dec.	105.2	117.5	108.9	101.3	108.2	107.1	118.0	106.0	116.1	106.3	108.9	108.6
1937												
一月 Jan.	106.0	110.7	107.2	121.2	111.3	102.7	126.2	107.6	111.8	106.9	107.2	109.3
二月 Feb.	106.1	116.0	110.7	130.3	115.8	102.5	123.6	108.6	117.7	109.5	109.6	112.7
三月 Mar.	105.1	115.4	109.9	133.0	115.8	117.4	124.1	112.6	126.3	107.0	115.8	115.8
四月 Apr.	102.8	117.1	108.6	134.1	115.6	111.1	120.2	110.3	127.9	141.3	122.6	119.2
五月 May	104.9	115.6	110.2	127.1	114.4	114.0	121.9	113.0	118.5	135.3	120.2	117.3
六月 June	101.4	114.1	103.6	132.5	112.9	119.9	116.1	112.7	118.1	—	116.9	114.6
七月 July	107.0	114.4	108.1	128.6	114.5	115.7	120.4	113.3	120.0	—	116.4	115.3
八月 Aug.	107.2	118.1	106.7	130.5	115.6	120.2	119.6	118.8	117.0	—	118.7	116.9
九月 Sept.	112.9	113.8	109.3	140.4	119.1	123.6	119.7	119.0	—	—	121.3	119.8
十月 Oct.	117.5	120.3	—	152.7	130.2	—	—	120.8	—	—	120.8	127.8

(a) 計算平均數時華縣除外，因該處受西安事變之影響致物價變動與其他各地差別太大。

Hwa hsien was excluded when average were computed, because price movement there was conspicuously different as compared with those in other localities due to the Sian incident.

(b) 平均數包括下列四處：靜樂，宿縣，橫山及正定。

Averages were computed by including four localities; Tsingloh, Su hsien, Hwenshan and Chengting.

第三表　　中國鄉鎮農產品購買力指數

民國二十五年＝一○○

TABLE 3.—PURCHASING POWER OF AGRICULTURAL PRODUCTS IN CHINA.

1936 = 100

日　期 Date	華　中 Central China	華　北 North China	平　均 Average
1935			
九月 September	94.7	74.4	84.6
十月 October	95.0	77.0	85.7
十一月 November	100.9	80.7	90.7
十二月 December	98.9	82.2	90.6
1936			
一月 January	102.4	87.0	95.7
二月 February	103.8	92.8	99.0
三月 March	104.6	94.3	100.8
四月 April	104.1	98.5	101.3
五月 May	101.7	94.1	97.8
六月 June	97.7	91.1	94.4
七月 July	92.0	92.3	92.2
八月 August	92.4	94.5	93.6
九月 September	94.4	94.5	94.5
十月 October	102.0	100.8	101.4
十一月 November	101.8	104.2	103.1
十二月 December	100.6	107.1	103.8
1937			
一月 January	103.1	109.9	106.4
二月 February	101.6	112.6	106.9
三月 March	100.2	109.5	104.8
四月 April	98.0	101.3	99.7
五月 May	99.4	102.5	101.0
六月 June	100.4	104.1	102.0
七月 July	102.5	104.1	103.3
八月 August	100.6	103.5	101.9
九月 September	97.1	88.7	94.3
十月 October	87.8	88.7	88.0

農民所得物價之變動較所付物價為劇

當物價上漲時，農民所得物價之上升，較所付物價為速。反之，如物價下跌時，亦以所付物價之跌落較慢。自民國二十四年九月至民國二十五年四月，農民所得物價指數，自七五漲至一○○・六，共漲二五・六点。而農民所付物價之指數，則僅自八八・七漲至九九・三，不過一○・六点而已。又自民國二十五年九月至民國二十六年三月所得物價上升二九・六点；而農民所付物價之指數祇漲一八・七点，此種差異，可以兩種理由解釋之：(一)農民出售之農產品與其所購買之必需品性質互異。(二)農民以田場價格銷售而以零售價格購買。易言之，即零售價格之變動，遠遜於田場價格也。

— 384 —

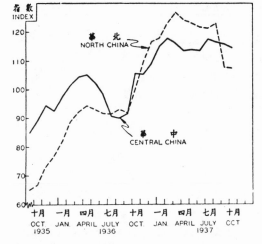

第三圖 華中與華北農民所得物價之指數，民國廿四年九月至廿六年十月

農民所得物價之變動，華北較華中為劇，夏季數月中其指數皆低。

民國二十五年＝一〇〇

FIGURE 3.—INDEX NUMBERS OF PRICES RECEIVED BY FARMERS IN CENTRAL CHINA AND NORTH CHINA, SEPTEMBER 1935 TO OCTOBER 1937.

1936 = 100

Prices received by farmers were low in the summer months. They fluctuated more violently in North China than in Central China.

Statistically speaking, the upward trend of prices received by farmers in the last 26 months may be expressed by a straight line: $Y = 80.208 + 1.680X$, which indicates that, on the average, the monthly increase of prices received was 1.68 per cent of the average price in 1936. Similarly, the trend of prices paid by farmers may be summarized by the equation, $Y = 87.13 + 1.333X$. Hence, the monthly increase was 1.333 per cent. The rate of increase in prices received was, consequently, greater than that of prices paid (figure 2, page 381).

More violent fluctuation in prices received than in prices paid

In a period of rising prices, prices received by farmers, rise faster than prices paid, and in a period of falling prices, prices received fall faster than prices paid. Prices received rose from 75 in September, 1935, to 100.6 in April, 1936, an increase of 25.6 points while prices paid rose from 88.7 to 99.3, an increase of only 10.6 points during the same period. Again, the index of prices received by farmers advanced another 29.6 points from September, 1936, to March, 1937, while the index of prices paid advanced only 18.7 points. This difference may be attributed to two factors, *(a)* the kinds of products produced by farmers and the kinds of products bought are different, and *(b)* farmers sell at farm prices and buy at retail prices. In other words, retail prices fluctuated less than farm prices.

— 385 —

民國二十六年八月以後所得物價與所付物價之變動趨向相反

中日戰事始於二十六年七月，其對於農村物價之影響，最初並不顯著。迨至八月，農民所付物價指數，於兩月之中，條漲一〇点；而其所得價格，幾跌七点。其主要原因，係交通阻隔，運輸停滯，致農產品之輸出與消費品之輸入，均感不便，而且運費增加，輸出品之價遂跌，輸入品之價遂漲。此種現象或將繼續相當時日。但如戰事持久，而生產減少，則農產品之價格終必因供給缺乏而上漲。

民國二十五年與二十六年夏季價格之下跌

民國二十五年與二十六年之農產，就大體言之，均係豐收，因之該兩年內五月及六月之農產價格，跌落頗鉅，二十五年八九月間之價格仍低，而二十六年同期之價格，則因各地水災與戰禍之影響，價格畧見上漲。

兩夏農民所付物價，亦見跌落，蓋因一部農民出售之產品，復爲其他農民所購買。致農民所得物價與所付物價，發生類似之變動。

華 北 物 價 之 漲 落 較 甚 於 華 中

華北農民所付物價與所得物價之漲落，遠甚於華中各地（第三八五頁第三圖及第三八八頁第四圖），而以所得價格，尤爲明顯。運輸及分配費用，旣感穩定，因之各地物價之等量漲落，其比率若用指數表示時，益不能相等，華北多數之鄉鎮，與市場間之交通，遠不及華中爲便利。同一等級之出口牧品，華中之價格，必較華北爲高，緣其運輸成本較低也，故華中物價漲落之指數，其變動恒遜於華北。

農民所付物價之變動較小，故華北農民所付物價，與華中比較，其漲落之差異，亦遠不若農民所得物價之顯著也。

農 產 物 之 購 買 力 暴 跌

農產品購買力指數者，代表定量之農產物在不同之時期所能交換其他物品之相對數量也。農產品購買力指數與農民購買力指數畧有不同。蓋因農民出售農產之數量，非月月盡同，如農產品之購買力大，而農民所能出售之農產品數量太少時，則農民之購買力反小。反之，即農產品購買力低，然因農民有大量之產品出售，其購買力亦可增高。但在一極短之時期內，農產品之購買力忽然暴跌，則農民所受之經濟壓迫，固可不言而喻。

Tendency of prices received and prices paid to fluctuate in opposite directions since August, 1937

The Sino-Japanese hostilities began in July, 1937. No effect could be observed until August, when the index number of prices paid by farmers suddenly jumped ten points within two months, while the index number of prices received dropped almost seven points. This was chiefly the effect of the stoppage of transportation which made the export of agricultural products and the import of consumers' goods exceedingly difficult and costly. The same trend may continue for some time, but it is probable that eventually prices received by farmers will go up, due to the gradual depletion of the supply of farm products in rural districts because of war conditions.

Low prices in the summers of 1936 and 1937

Crop conditions in both 1936 and 1937 were, in general, very favorable, hence prices of agricultural products dwindled rapidly in May and June in both years. In August and September, 1936, prices were still low while in the same period in 1937 prices were fairly high due to the flood and war conditions in various parts of the country.

Prices paid by farmers also fell during these two summers because in some cases products sold by some farmers were bought by other farmers. Hence the same changes occurred in prices received and prices paid by farmers.

Price situation in North China – more fluctuation than in Central China

Prices received and paid by farmers in North China fluctuated more violently than those in Central China (figure 3, page 385, and figure 4, page 388). However, the contrast was not so marked in prices paid as in prices received. Inasmuch as the costs of transportation and distribution remained comparatively stable, an equal rise or fall of prices in various localities resulted in an unequal ratio of rise or fall of prices as expressed by index numbers. Rural towns in Central China are more accessible to the market than those in North China, therefore, with lower costs of distribution and higher prices for the same grade of export commodity, the advance or decline of prices on a percentage basis are less than in North China. Prices paid by farmers varied less than prices received. In fact, the differences were insignificant in comparison with differences in prices received by farmers in North and Central China.

The Slump of the Purchasing Power of Agricultural Products

Index numbers of the purchasing power of agricultural products represent the relative amount of other commodities exchanged for a definite amount of agricultural products in different periods. They may not express the purchasing power of

屆夏季，農民所得物價恒低，故農產品之購買力，於二十五年及二十六年夏，均係下跌，而尤以二十六年夏之跌落爲劇。除農產品價格因受季節之關係而下降外，暴日侵華，交通阻梗，致農民所得之價格狂跌，農民所付之價格猛漲，實爲農產品購買力暴跌之主要原因。此次農產品購買力之慘落，實揭示吾國農民所受災難與窘迫之一斑。

平穩之物價水準，固爲吾人理想中之需要，但一種物價之升降，隨之以他種物價之上漲或下落，雖能紊亂物價機構並予農民以痛苦，然其影響之巨，遠不若一種物價之升降，繼之以他種物價相反之變動也，今日吾國農民，除直接之戰禍外，其間接閱歷之經濟厄運，亦爲前者所未有。苟能便利交通，扶植貿易，俾農民所得與所付物價，得以調整，則其於國民生計，農民生活，造福匪淺也。

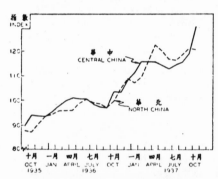

第四圖　華中與華北農民所付物
價之指數，民國廿四年九月至
廿六年十月

民國二十五年＝一〇〇

農民所付物價，華北與華中皆逐漸上漲，惟因戰事影響，於最後兩月內，華中之指數突然上漲。

FIGURE 4.—INDEX NUMBERS OF PRICES PAID BY FARMERS IN CENTRAL CHINA AND NORTH CHINA, SEPTEMBER 1935 TO OCTOBER 1937.

1936 = 100

Prices paid by farmers rose steadily in both North and Central China. The sudden upward curve for Central China at the end of the period was caused by the war.

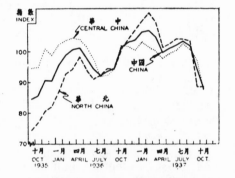

第五圖　華中與華北農產品購買力
民國廿四年九月至廿六年十月

民國二十五年＝一〇〇

華北農產品之購買力之漲落較華中爲劇烈。

FIGURE 5.—THE PURCHASING POWER OF AGRICULTURAL PRODUCTS IN CENTRAL AND NORTH CHINA, SEPTEMBER 1935 TO OCTOBER 1937.

1936 = 100

The purchasing power of agricultural products in North China was more vacillating than in South China.

farmers accurately, because farmers may have very little to sell when the purchasing power of agricultural products is high and very much to market when it is low. The slump of the purchasing power of agricultural products, however, gives us, at least, some idea about the misfortune of farmers. Prices received by farmers were usually low in summers. The purchasing power of agricultural products was consequently very low in the summers of both 1936 and 1937. Its decline in 1937 was, however, still more speedy and intense, because of the rapid advance of prices paid by farmers and the momentous fall of prices received due to their seasonal characteristics, and because of transportation difficulties caused by the Japanese invasion. The slump of the purchasing power of agricultural products discloses the distress and calamity of farmers. It is very desirable to have a stable price level. A fall or rise in one group of commodities followed by other groups may cause some trouble, due to the chaos of price structure, but worst of all is the rise or fall in certain groups of commodities followed by an opposite rise or fall in some other groups. Farmers in China are now experiencing a monstrous economic catastrophe in addition to other distresses caused by the Japanese invasion. Any measure to bring the prices of agricultural products up and to keep other prices down would benefit farmers immensely.

At the end of 1935 and the early part of 1936, the purchasing power of agricultural products in North China was much lower than that in Central China (table 3, page 384 and figure 5, page 388), because the prices received by farmers in North China then were very low (figure 3, page 385). Since July, 1936, the former surpassed the latter. The purchasing power of agricultural products in North China was therefore more vacillating than in Central China.

Fluctuations of purchasing power of agricultural products over-shadowed by the fluctuation of prices received by farmers

Theoretically, a rise in the farm price of agricultural products may not result in a rise of their purchasing power, because prices of other commodities bought by farmers may also rise proportionately. As a matter of fact, the fluctuation of prices paid by farmers was not so violent as that of prices received, but the purchasing power of agricultural products was affected to a much larger extent by the latter than the former, even though their purchasing power was calculated by including both factors. The gross correlation coefficient between prices received and purchasing power was $+0.78$, while the one between prices paid and purchasing power was only $+0.48$. Therefore 61 per cent of the variation of the purchasing power of agricultural products was determined by the variation of prices received and other associated factors, and only 23 per cent by the variation of prices paid and other factors. As a consequence, any measure to control the fluctuations of prices received would yield more effect upon the welfare of farmers.

— 389 —

民國二十四年終與二十五年年初，華北農產品之購買力較低，而華中則較高（第三八四頁第三表及第三八八頁第五圖）。蓋因當時華北農產品之價格過低所致也（第三八五頁第三圖）。自二十五年七月起華北指數，即逐漸向上，超過華中之指數，可見華北農產品購買力之變動較華中為大也。

農民所得物價之升降為農產品購買力高低之主要原因

按理，農產品價格之升漲，不一定必能提高農產品之購買力，因其他物品之價格，或亦有同樣之上漲也。但証之事實，農民所付物價之變動遠不若所得物價。故農產品購買力之高低，實以其本身之價格為轉移。農產品購買力與農民所得物價之相關係數為 +0.78 而與農民所付物價之相關係

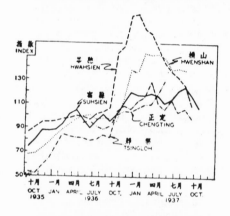

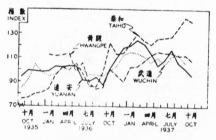

第六圖　華北各鄉鎮農民所得物
　　價之指數，民國廿四年九月
　　至廿六年十月

民國二十五年＝一〇〇

民國二十五年冬，因大軍雲集，繼以西安事變，華縣及橫山之物價指數，遂高於其他各地。

FIGURE 6.—INDEX NUMBERS OF PRICES RECEIVED BY FARMERS IN RURAL MARKET TOWNS IN NORTH CHINA, SEPTEMBER 1935 TO OCTOBER 1937.

1936 = 100

Military expeditions and the Sian incident raised prices in Hwahsien and Hwenshan, Shensi to a much higher level in the winter of 1936.

第七圖　華中各鄉鎮農民所得物
　　價之指數，民國廿四年九月
　　至廿六年十月

民國二十五年＝一〇〇

泰和農民所得之物價，於民國二十六年春夏，因大水為災，致較他處為高。

FIGURE 7.—INDEX NUMBERS OF PRICES RECEIVED BY FARMERS IN RURAL MARKET TOWNS IN CENTRAL CHINA, SEPTEMBER 1935 TO OCTOBER 1937.

1936 = 100

Prices received by farmers in Taiho remained at a higher level in the spring of 1937 due to the flood.

— 390 —

The fact that a positive correlation coefficient existed between prices paid and the purchasing power, needs, undoubtedly, some explanation. When prices went up, prices received by farmers went up more quickly than prices paid, and when prices fell, the former fell more quickly than the latter. Thus a high purchasing power of agricultural products was usually associated with both high prices received and high prices paid. When the effect of the variation of prices received was eliminated, the partial correlation coefficient between the purchasing power of agricultural products and prices paid by farmers was −0.83, therefore a very high negative relationship.

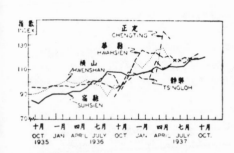

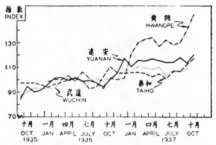

第八圖　華北各鄉鎮農民所付物價之指數，民國廿四年九月至廿六年十月

民國二十五年＝一〇〇

因推行美棉致肥料農具等之需求增加，故民國廿六年四月，正定農民所付之物價猛烈上漲。

FIGURE 8.—INDEX NUMBERS OF PRICES PAID BY FARMERS IN RURAL MARKET TOWNS IN NORTH CHINA, SEPTEMBER 1935 TO OCTOBER 1937.

1936 = 100

Prices paid by farmers in Chengting rose abruptly owing to the urgent need for fertilizers, farm implements, etc. in April 1937 caused by the rapid spread of American cotton.

第九圖　華中各鄉鎮農民所付物價之指數，民國廿四年九月至廿六年十月

民國二十五年＝一〇〇

黃陂因賦稅增加，農民所付之物價，自二十六年一月起較他處升高。

FIGURE 9.—INDEX NUMBERS OF PRICES PAID BY FARMERS IN RURAL MARKET TOWNS IN CENTRAL CHINA, SEPTEMBER 1935 TO OCTOBER 1937.

1936 = 100

Prices paid by farmers in Hwangpe shifted to a higher level since January 1937 owing to the newly imposed surtaxes.

僅爲數＋0.48，故農產品購買力之變動，受農民所得物價及其相聯因素之影響者，佔百分之六十一，而受農民所付物價及其相聯因素之影響者，僅佔百分之二十三。因之欲支配農產品之購買力而俾益農民，則對於農民所得物價，尤應特別注意。

最可異者，爲農產品購買力與農民所付物價間之正相關也。然一經探究，則其理亦頗明顯。當物價上升時，農民所得物價之升漲率較所付物價爲速。反之，物價下降時，前者亦較後者之下降率爲大。故購買力高時，所得物價與所付物價同高，購買力低時，兩種價格亦同低。若將農民所得物價之影響剔除，則購買力與所付物價之純相關係數爲－0•83其關係不但相反，而相反之程度亦極大。

鄉鎮物價因受當地特殊情形之影響其變動頗不一致

華北華中各地之物價，雖均係上漲，然其升降狀態，頗不一致（第三八二頁第一表及第三八三頁第二表第三九〇及三九一頁第六圖至第九圖）。其所以不能盡同之故，除報告失確與統計不精外，當然以各地情形之懸殊爲其主要原因。

民國二十五年秋，陝西大軍雲集，繼以十二月之西安事變，因之華縣及橫山之物價指數，逐月暴漲，嗣後華縣農民所得物價跌落，而橫山農民所得物價，則仍堅挺未墜，蓋因荒旱之故也。

民國二十六年四月，正定農民所得物價，因天乾而上漲，其地農民所付物價，則忽然狂漲。蓋因農具及肥料等，農民多於春季購置之，且當時因推廣美棉故，肥料之需要激增，其價格遂亦陡漲。

湖北之黃陂於民國二十六年一月，因貨物之稅捐增加，水路之交通阻滯，農民所付之價格遂漲，此後漲落，雖與他處相似，然其價格水準，則已較他處爲高矣。

結　論

戰事果延長也，則農民所得物價之下跌，與其所付物價之上漲，殆將縱賾一時，生產充裕之地，農產輸出將愈感困難，而生產不足之處，農民所付購進物品之價格，亦必因供給之減少而更高，其終也供給日漸告竭，加以戰時難以避免之通貨膨脹，於是一切物價，均將步漲矣。

楊　　蔚

盧　盛　懷

Prices in rural towns affected by local conditions

Prices in different localities fluctuated dissimilarly along the general upward trend. The uniformity in the oscillation of the prices paid by farmers in both Central and North China was, however, very striking (tables 1 and 2, pages 382 and 383; figures 6-9, pages 390 and 391). These discrepancies of the price fluctuations in different localities can only be attributed to the dissimilarity of local conditions besides the crudeness of statistical methods and the inaccuracy of the reports.

Military expeditions and the subsequent Sian incident in December, 1936, raised the price level in Hwa Hsien and Hwenshan, Shensi, suddenly. Prices in these two places were abnormally high as compared with other localities. After the incident was over, prices received in Hwahsien dropped very quickly, while they remained at a very high level in Hwenshan due to drought.

Prices received by farmers in Chengting advanced impetuously in April, 1937, because of the drought. Prices paid by farmers there spurted still more rapidly due to the rise in the prices of farm implements, fertilizers, etc., which were needed and bought by the farmers in the spring. The rapid spread of American cotton in Chengting stimulated the use of fertilizers, hence, enhanced their prices.

Newly imposed surtaxes on consumption goods, and the trouble of water transportation in Hwangpe since January, 1937, lifted prices paid by farmers there to a high level. The price index advanced from 101 in December, 1936, to 121 in January, 1937. After that the price movement there became similar to other places.

Conclusion

Should the present war continue, the rising trend of prices paid by farmers and the falling trend of prices received by farmers would continue for some time. Farmers in surplus areas would find difficulty in securing outlets for their products, while farmers in deficient areas would have to pay still higher prices for their purchases. Eventually all prices would rise because of depleted supply and unavoidable inflation caused by war.

W. Y. Yang

Lu Sheng-hwai

中國物價之柔性

柔活物價爲緊縮時期跌落甚速之物價，反之非柔活物價則係跌落較爲遲緩者，在物價挺漲期內，柔活物價之增加速率較非柔活物價爲猛。

歐西各國不柔活物價甚多。債券、工資，捐稅及運輸費用，在一般物價跌落時，均不能迅速削減。因此製造品零售價格之跌落不若基本物品批發價格爲速。且許多公司恒多統制其商品價格，使於一般物價水準開始下落數月後，其出品價格仍保持高價不變。維持價格一舉，不論其削減銷售量至若何程度，通常皆認爲良好之營業政策。製造品價格之不柔性每易引起物價關係之嚴重失調現象。緊縮時期後基本物品之價格較製造品之價格過於低廉，致基本物品生產者無力購買。於是以基本物價算計之生產者借款利息，工資，捐稅，運輸及銷售等費用，均感非常繁重。

中國經濟機構不若歐西複雜，本文之目的，即在決定中國物價之柔性，並研究其受物價膨漲及緊縮影響之關係。

鄉鎮與都市批發物價　將上海與其西二七六華里（九一英里）之江蘇武進之批發物價作一比較。武進物價雖表顯長期之漲勢，然其柔性並不較上海爲大（第三九六頁第一圖）[1]。若中國之運銷成本能如美國一般固定則在緊縮時期，其物價之跌落必較上海物價爲速，而在回漲時期其上漲亦較速也。

天津食糧批發物價與其西四五〇華里（一五〇英里）之河北正定農民所得物價亦能作一比較。天津物價之柔活幾與正定物價相同（第三九七頁第二圖）[2]。

都市之批發與零售物價　天津市場之批發與零售物價均經分別編爲指數，一九二六年至一九三六年之歷年平均可供吾人參考[3]。當一般物價水

1　物價指數爲下列數種物品價比之簡單平均。

　　武進——粳稻，蠶豆，糯米，小麥，蠶繭，黃豆

　　上海——蘇同機粳米，漢口蠶豆，常熟機粳米，漢口小麥，無錫乾繭。

2　物價指數爲下列數種物品價比之簡單平均。

　　正定——小麥，芝蔴，小米，玉米，黃豆，白豆，綠豆。

　　天津——紅小麥，芝蔴，黃小米，白玉米，黃豆，白豆，綠豆。

3　物價指數爲下列數種物品價比之簡單平均。

　　批發物價——麵粉，黃玉米，白小米，小吉豆，黃豆，香油，鹽，豬肉，羊肉，牛肉，煤，煤油，棉紗（十六支），棉紗（十支），棉花。

　　零售物價——麵粉，玉米粉(河北)，小米，綠豆，黃豆芽，蔴油，鹽，豬肉，羊肉，牛肉，煤油，白市布，色市布，花條布。

THE FLEXIBILITY OF PRICES IN CHINA

'Flexible' prices are those that, during a deflation period, decline promptly. 'Inflexible' prices decline later or more slowly. During a period of advancing prices, 'flexible' prices increase more rapidly than 'inflexible' prices.

In Western countries many prices are inflexible. Debts, wages, taxes, transportation and marketing costs cannot be scaled down rapidly when the general price level declines. Retail prices of manufactured goods thus decline less rapidly than wholesale prices of basic commodities. Also, many corporations 'administer' the prices of their products, often maintaining them constant at a high level for many months after the general decline begins. To maintain prices is quite commonly regarded as a good business policy no matter how much it may curtail the volume of sales. The inflexibility of the prices of manufactured goods leads to serious maladjustments of price relationships. After deflation, basic commodities are too cheap in terms of manufactured goods. Basic producers cannot buy. Producers' costs for credit, wages, taxes, transportation and marketing are very expensive in terms of basic commodities.

China's economic structure is less complicated than that of the West. This study was made in order to determine the flexibility of prices in China and to consider this in relation to the effects of inflation and deflation.

Rural and urban wholesale prices

A comparison can be made of wholesale prices in Shanghai and in the market town of Wuchin (Wutsin), Kiangsu, which is 275 li (91.7 miles) to the west. Prices in Wuchin were no more flexible than prices in Shanghai, although they showed a long term tendency to rise relative to Shanghai prices (figure 1, page 396).[1] If transportation and marketing costs had been relatively inflexible, as in the United States, prices in Wuchin would have declined more rapidly than prices in Shanghai during the deflation period, and would have risen more rapidly during reflation.

A comparison can also be made of wholesale prices of food in Tientsin and prices paid to farmers in the market town of Chengting, Hopei, which is 450 li (150 miles) to the west. Prices in Tientsin were almost as flexible as prices in Chengting (figure 2, page 397).[2]

---

[1] The index numbers of prices are simple means of relatives for the following commodities:
Wuchin: Rice, unhulled; Broad beans; Rice, glutinous; Wheat; Coccoons; Soybeans.
Shanghai: Rice, Soochow; Broad beans, Hankow; Rice, Changshu; Wheat, Hankow; Cocoons, Wusih.

[2] The index numbers of prices are simple means of relatives for the following commodities:
Chenating: Wheat, sesame, millet, corn, yellow soybeans, white soybeans, green beans.
Tientsin: Red wheat, sesame, yellow millet, white corn, yellow soybeans, white soybeans, green beans.

準漲落時零售物價之柔活與批發物價相同（第三九七頁第三圖）。自一九三〇年至一九三四年，批發物價下跌百分之三二，零售物價下跌百分之三〇，自一九三四至一九三六年批發物價上漲百分之四二，零售物價上漲百分之四一。

南京中華門農民所得之批發物價，亦可與南京北門橋消費者所付之零售物價作一比較。零售物價與批發物價之曲線，極為密接，（第三九八頁第四圖）[4]。南京之運銷成本，亦如天津一般，甚為柔活。

運 輸 及 銷 售 費 用 之 柔 性

中國運輸費用勞力之成分，較歐西各國為多，而資本成分較少。中國勞工缺乏相當組織，而純為個人化，且競爭至烈，勞工協會與運費委員會等組織在中國向不佔若何重要之地位。勞工之開支大部為食物，因此較歐西各國之柔性為大，蓋歐西勞工之生活費用，大部份為衣着，租金，捐稅，教育及衞生等費用。是故當中國物價下降之際，其輸運費用下落亦甚迅速。

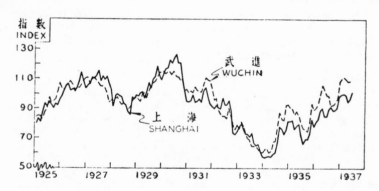

第一圖　江蘇武進農民所得物價及上海批發物價指數，一九二五年一月至一九三七年六月

一九二五年至一九二八年＝一〇〇

上海批發物價之柔活，一若武進農民所得物價，蓋中國運銷成本之柔活性甚大也。

FIGURE 1.–INDEX NUMBERS OF PRICES RECEIVED BY FARMERS IN WUCHIN, KIANGSU, AND WHOLESALE PRICES IN SHANGHAI, JAN. 1925-JUNE 1937

1925 – 1928 = 100

Wholesale prices in Shanghai were as flexible as prices received by farmers in Wuchin, Transportation and marketing costs are comparatively flexible in China.

4　零售與批發物價指數，均為下列數種物品價比之簡單平均，米，小麥，玉米，蠶豆，豌豆，黃豆，青豆，綠豆，紅豆，豇豆，料豆，芝麻，青菜。黃豆芽。

City wholesale and retail prices

Index numbers of prices have been constructed for both wholesale and retail markets in Tientsin and a comparison can be made of yearly averages for the years 1926 to 1936.[3] Retail prices were as flexible as wholesale prices during both advances and declines of the general level (figure 3, page 397). From 1930 to 1934 wholesale prices declined by 32 per cent; retail prices, by 30 per cent. From 1934 to 1936, wholesale prices advanced by 42 per cent; retail, by 41 per cent.

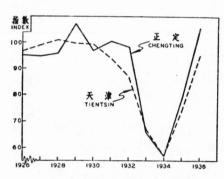

第二圖　河北正定農民所得物價及天津批發物價指數自一九二六年至一九三六年

一九二八年至一九三○年＝一○○

天津物價之柔性幾與正定農民所得物價同

FIGURE 2.—INDEX NUMBERS OF PRICES RECEIVED BY FARMERS IN CHENGTING, HOPEI, AND WHOLESALE PRICES IN TIENTSIN, 1926-1936

1928 - 1930 = 100

Prices in Tientsin were almost as flexible as prices received by farmers in Chengting.

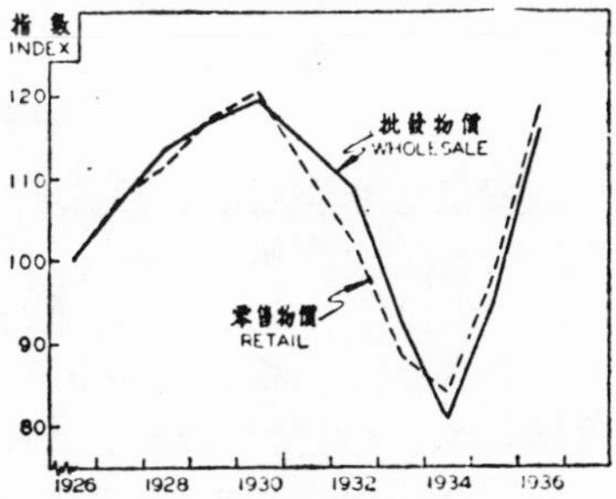

第三圖　天津批發與零售物價指數一九二六年至一九三六年

一九二六年＝一○○

零售物價之柔活與批發物價同，因分配成本柔活之故也。

FIGURE 3.—INDEX NUMBERS OF WHOLESALE AND RETAIL PRICES IN TIENTSIN, 1926 - 1936.

1926 = 100

Retail prices were as flexible as wholesale prices because the cost of distribution was flexible.

3　The index numbers are simple means of relatives for:—

Wholesale prices: wheat flour, yellow corn, white millet, green small beans, yellow soybeans, sesamum oil, salt, pork, mutton, bee, coal, kerosene, cotton yarn (16 count), cotton yarn (10 count), raw cotton.

Retail prices: wheat flour, Peiho corn flour, millet, green beans, soybean sprouts, sesamum oil, salt, pork, mutton, beef, coal balls, kerosene, white native shirting, colored native shirting, drills.

除運輸外，在中國其他各種銷售費用之柔性亦大。都市批發物價與零售物價之邊際利益，大部充作店員之工資及利潤。普通零售商店實行之酬償制度，實為造成費用强大柔性之主要原因，蓋店中大部份工作，皆由家人或學徒担任，店方僅須供給膳宿而已。至於普通店員之固定工資，僅佔一小部，其餘大部為年終紅利，其分配額之多寡，視該年利潤之厚薄而定。零售商店間雖亦有價格協定，但普通競爭甚烈。

除運輸與銷售成本較為柔活外，因營業手續之簡當與牌號及廣告推銷類貨品價格管理之缺乏，遂致都市零售物價變動之趨勢不論於物價膨漲或緊縮時期，皆緊隨批發物價。

生活費用之柔性

中國食物之零售物價變動既緊隨批發物價，且食物一項佔生活費用之最大部份，故整個物價機構之柔性，遠較歐西經濟制度下之物價柔性為大。上海及天津生活費用指數之柔性，與其批發物價水準相同，惟特受農作物價變動之影響，（第三九九頁第五，六圖）。歐西各國生活費之柔性小於批發物價水準，其受作物產量變異之影響，亦較中國者為小。

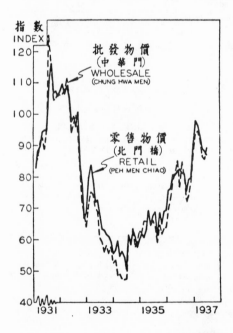

第四圖　南京批發物價與零售物價指數，自一九三一年一月至一九三七年六月

一九三一年＝一〇〇

零售物價緊隨批發物價之曲線，蓋南京與天津同，分配成本甚為柔活也。

FIGURE 4.—INDEX NUMBERS OF WHOLESALE AND RETAIL PRICES, NANKING, JAN. 1931–JUNE 1937

1931 = 100

Retail prices followed the course of wholesale prices very closely. As in Tientsin, costs of distribution were very flexible.

In Nanking, wholesale prices received by farmers at the Chung Hwa Men market can be compared to retail prices paid by consumers at the Peh Men Chiao market. Retail prices followed the course of wholesale prices very closely (figure 4, page 398).[4] In Nanking, as in Tientsin, costs of distribution were very flexible.

第五圖： 上海生活費與農作物及基本物品價格之指數，自一九二六年一月至一九三七年六月

一九三一年＝一〇〇

生活費之柔性與基本物品批發價格相同，惟時受農作物之影響。

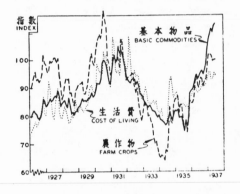

FIGURE 5.—INDEX NUMBERS OF THE COST OF LIVING AND WHOLESALE PRICES OF FARM CROPS AND BASIC COMMODITIES, SHANGHAI, JAN. 1926–JUNE 1937

1931 = 100

The cost of living has been as flexible as wholesale prices of basic commodities but has been especially influenced by prices of farm crops.

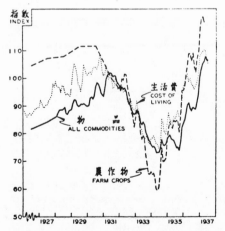

第六圖： 天津生活費指數及一般物品與農作物批發物價指數一九二六年一月至一九三七年六月

一九三一＝一〇〇

生活費之柔性與一般物價水準同，惟時受農作物價格之影響。

FIGURE 6.—INDEX NUMBERS OF THE COST OF LIVING AND WHOLESALE PRICES OF FARM CROPS AND 'ALL' COMMODITIES, TIENTSIN, JAN. 1926–JUNE 1937

1931 = 100

The cost of living has been as flexible as the general price level but has been especially influenced by prices of farm crops.

4 The index numbers of both retail and wholesale prices are simple means of relatives for the following commodities:—

Rice, wheat, corn, broad beans, field peas, soybeans, green soybeans, green beans, red beans, cow peas, grey soybeans, sesame, cabbage, soybean sprouts.

原料品與製造品之價格

　　當一九三一至一九三五年緊縮時期內，上海與天津棉織品價格跌落之迅速與棉花價格同（第四〇〇頁第七，八圖）。上海絲經繡緞跌落之迅速亦與乾繭同（第四〇二頁第九圖）。故製造商邊際利益之跌落，勢必與運銷商之邊際利益同其速度。然當此時期，上海天津新法製造之實際成本之跌落並未能如此迅速。一九三一至一九三四年，上海工業工資僅跌落百分之二（第四〇二頁第十圖），然製成成品價格之跌落甚速，因（一）新式紗廠與繅絲廠之間，競爭甚烈(二)機製品與內地家庭土布發生競爭，(三)如欲維持價格與一般物價水準之上，則不能暢銷之存貨勢必因之蘊積。物價跌落，運銷商之邊際利益隨之減少，致一般紗廠除非犧牲血本外，無法經營。若干廠家遂以此停業倒閉，工業利潤自因物價上漲所造成之一九三一年之高水準，慘跌至一九三五年之低水準，公司股票價格亦反映此種跌落（第四〇三頁第十一圖）[5]。

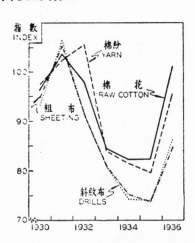

第七圖：上海棉花及棉製品之批發
　　　物價，一九三〇至一九三六年

一九三〇年＝一〇〇

棉製品價格之柔性與棉花價格同。

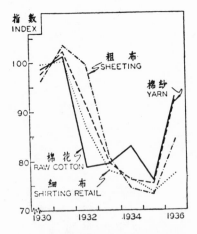

第八圖：天津棉花，棉紗及粗布之
　　　批發價格與細布之零售價格，
　　　一九三〇至一九三六年

一九三〇年至一九三一年＝一〇〇

棉製品價格之柔性幾與棉花價格同。

5　普通股票格價指數為下列公司股票價比之簡單平均：—
　　英商怡和紗廠有限公司，普通股；上海紡織株式會社；英商業廣有限公司；英商中國公共
　．汽車有限公司；中國工程礦業公司。

The flexibility of transportation and marketing charges

Transportation costs in China involve more labor and less capital than in Western countries. The labor is not organised but highly individualistic and competitive. Workers unions and freight rate committees play no significant part. Laborers' expenses are chiefly for food and are thus more flexible than in the West, where clothing, rent, taxes, education and health expenses make up a larger proportion of the cost of living. During a period of declining prices, transportation costs therefore decline comparatively promptly.

Marketing costs other than transportation are also flexible in China. The margin between city wholesale and retail prices goes chiefly for the wages and profits of storekeepers. The system of payment generally practised in retail stores ensures a very significant flexibility. Much of the work is done by members of the same family or by apprentices receiving only food and lodging. For ordinary clerks, only a small part of the total costs are fixed wages, the remainder being in the form of 'bonuses' which vary directly with the profits for the year. Price agreements among retail merchants are not unknown but generally there is complete competition.

In addition to the comparative flexibility of transportation and marketing costs, the absence of complicated processing and administratively set prices for branded and advertised goods allows city retail prices to follow more closely the trend of wholesale prices both during deflation and inflation.

The flexibility of the cost of living

Because, in China, retail prices of food follow wholesale prices closely and food is by far the largest item in the cost of living, there is much greater flexibility in the whole price structure than is possible under Western economic systems. Index numbers of the cost of living in Shanghai and Tientsin have been as flexible as the general level of wholesale prices but have been especially influenced by the movement of prices of farm crops (figure 5, 6; page 399). In Western countries, the cost of living is less flexible than the general level of wholesale prices and variations in crop production have less influence than in China.

Prices of raw materials and manufactured goods

During the deflation period from 1931 to 1935 prices of manufactured cotton goods in Shanghai and Tientsin declined as rapidly as prices of raw cotton (figures 7, 8; page 400). In Shanghai, steam filatured silk and silk crepe declined almost as rapidly as dried cocoons (figure 9, page 402). Manufacturers' margins must therefore have declined as rapidly as did distributors' margins. The actual costs of manufacturing by modern methods in Tientsin and Shanghai could not have declined as rapidly during this period. Industrial wages in Shanghai declined by only 2 per cent from 1931 to 1934 (figure 10, page 402). Prices of manufactured goods were, however, rapidly reduced because, first, there was complete competition between modern mills and

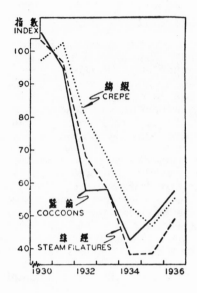

第九圖： 上海乾繭，絲經，縐緞之批發物價，一九三〇至一九三六年

一九三〇年至一九三一年＝一〇〇

一九三一年至一九三四年之絲價跌落一半，縐緞價之柔性幾與乾繭及絲經同。

FIGURE 9.—WHOLESALE PRICES OF SILK COCOONS, STEAM FILATURES AND CREPE, SHANGHAI, 1930–1936

1930–1931 = 100

Between 1931 and 1934 prices of silk were halved. Prices of crepe were almost as flexible as prices of cocoons and filatures.

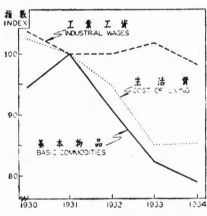

第十圖： 上海基本物品批發物價，工業工資與生活費之指數，一九三〇至一九三四年

一九三一年＝一〇〇

自一九三一年至一九三四年，物價及生活費跌落甚速，而工業工資則比較穩定。

FIGURE 10.—INDEX NUMBERS OF WHOLESALE PRICES OF BASIC COMMODITIES, INDUSTRIAL WAGES AND THE COST OF LIVING, SHANGHAI, 1930–1934

1931 = 100

From 1931 to 1934, prices and the cost of living declined rapidly but industrial wages remained comparatively unchanged.

結　論

　　中國物價水準之下降對於社會福利之影響，不能歸咎於農產物價與批發物價之下跌速於零售物價及生活費。中國物價機構遠較經濟制度複雜之歐西各國為柔活。

　　中國物價緊縮之主要影響由於債務，捐稅，租金及農工業工資之固定而乏柔和性。當物價下落時，債務及利息不能相當減低，甚至在農村中，利率反見增加，蓋田塲收入減少時，借欵需要必更迫急[6]。我國農民

6　見經濟統計第七期第二八三至二八五頁，一九三七年十月出版。

第十一圖： 上海普通股票價格與基本物品批發物價之指數一九二八年一月至一九三七年六月

一九二八年＝一〇〇

在一九三一年前物價上升利益激增，股票價格之上漲較物價尤速。當物價下降之際，利益減低，股票價格遂迅下跌，迄一九三七年六月股票價格尚未完全回復。

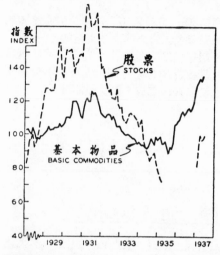

FIGURE 11.—INDEX NUMBERS OF PRICES OF COMMON STOCKS AND WHOLESALE PRICES OF BASIC COMMODITIES, SHANGHAI, JAN. 1928–JUNE 1937

1928 = 100

During the advance of commodity prices prior to 1931, profits increased rapidly and stock prices rose more rapidly than commodity prices. When commodity prices declined profits were reduced and stock prices fell rapidly. Stock prices have not yet recovered fully from this deflation.

filatures; second, there was competition in the interior with native cloths produced by family labor; and third, large unsold stocks would have accumulated if prices had been maintained higher than the general price level. The reduction of distributors' margins as prices declined made it impossible for some mills to operate except at a loss. Some were closed. Industrial profits declined rapidly from the high level of 1931, which was due to a period of rising prices, to a very low level in 1935. Prices of corporation stocks reflected this decline (figure 11, page 403).[5]

Conclusions

In China, the effects on general prosperity of a decline of the price level cannot be attributed to the fact that farm and wholesale prices decline more rapidly than retail prices and the cost of living. China's price structure is much more flexible than that of Western countries which have a much more complicated economic system.

The major effects of deflation in China are rather due to the comparative inflexibility of debt charges, taxes, rents, and farm and industrial wages. When prices decline, debts and interest rates are not correspondingly scaled down. In rural districts interest rates may even increase since the demand for credit is greater when farm incomes are reduced.[6] The burden of debts,

---

5   The index numbers of prices of common stocks are simple means of relatives for: Ewo Cotton Mills, Ordinary, Shanghai Cotton Manufacturing, Shanghai Land Investment, China General Omnibus, China Engineering and Mining.

6   See *Economic Facts* No. 7 pp. 291-295, October 1937.

負債平時已甚繁重，當物價下跌時必益爲增加，致農村威受破產之威脅，農民之捐稅及工資並不隨物價迅速下跌，故其購買力遂無形削減，即製造品價格與農產價格同樣下跌，農民亦無力購買大量製造品。製造公司既不能隨物價之下落而削減其成本，銷售數量則又大減，遂不得不遭受相當之損失。

自一九三五年十月後中國之物價猛漲，農村及工業區域情形亦逐驟然好轉，此大都因物價與債務，捐稅，租金及工資之關係恢復常態。一九三一年至一九三四年緊縮時期之所以引起種種嚴重問題者，即以上述各項僅能緩緩下跌耳。中國零售物價雖較歐西各國爲柔活，然一九三一年至一九三五年十月間，因國幣以物品計算之價值飛漲之故，仍受損匪淺。

雷伯恩
胡國華

河南開封農場大小與土地利用之關係

利用土地，所以滿足人類生活之所需，如衣，食，住，娛樂，及文化之發展。土地利用之精密與否，不獨因自然因素而異，如氣候，土壤及地勢，且受人爲之影響，如種族，習慣，風俗，宗敎及生活方法等。

於河南開封，曾舉行一百農場之土地利用調查。此一百農場中，計有佃農四，半自耕農七，餘爲自耕農。皆位於平坦之丁等土地分類區內[1]，多爲壤砂及粉砂粘壤性之土壤。

本調查之目的，爲確知農場土地利用之現狀，及決定其精良及適當利用與農場大小之關係。

開封每年之平均雨量，爲五六六公分[2]，以七八兩月之雨量爲最高。冬日嚴寒。作物之生長季約爲二三六日。春季狂風，常爲害於農作物。

農場面積平均爲三二‧四畝[3]。作物面積爲二九‧七畝。作物畝爲四一‧九。成年男子單位爲五‧六。

---

1 豫鄂皖贛四省三十四縣土地分類之研究　金陵大學農學院農業經濟系出版
2 頁博明著：中國氣候區域論　金陵大學農學院農業經濟系出版
3 一畝地畝 = 1.1024 市畝 = 0.0735 公頃

large enough in 'normal' times, becomes so increased as to threaten widespread rural bankruptcy. The purchasing power of the farming population is reduced also because taxes and wages remain comparatively high. They cannot buy as large a volume of manufactured goods even though the prices paid decline as much as prices of farm produce. Manufacturing companies suffer because they cannot cut their costs as rapidly as prices decline and the volume of sales is reduced.

The rapid advance of prices in China since November, 1935, resulted in a very rapid improvement of conditions both in rural and industrial districts. This was chiefly because a more normal relationship between commodity prices and debts, taxes, rents, and wages was restored. Deflation from 1931 to 1934 had had serious consequences because these items could be only slowly reduced. Even though retail prices were much more flexible than in Western countries, China suffered greatly from an increase in the commodity value of the yuan from September, 1931, to October, 1935.

John R. Raeburn
Hu Kwoh-hwa

RELATION OF SIZE OF FARM TO UTILIZATION OF FARM LAND IN KAIFENG, HONAN

The land is utilized to supply man with food, clothing, shelter, recreation and culture. The intensity of land use is not only dependent upon natural factors such as climate, soil and topography, but also upon human factors such as, race, habit, custom, religion, and mode of living.

Utilization of farm land was studied in Kaifeng Hsien, Honan, North China, upon one hundred farms. Most farms are operated by owners. Out of the one hundred farms, four are operated by tenants and seven by part owners. All are located in class II land area[1] on level land with loamy sand and silty clay loam soils.

The purpose of this study is to outline the present use of farm land and determine its best and most efficient use in relation to size of farm.

The average annual rainfall is 566 cm.[2] The months of highest rainfall are July and August. The winter is severely cold, and the length of growing season about 236 days. Violent winds in the spring constantly do harm to crops.

The average farm area per farm is 32.4 mow,[3] crop area 29.7 mow and crop mow area 41.9 mow. The number of persons per farm family is 5.6 adult male units.

1 Land classification of 84 Hsien in Anhwei, Honan, Hupeh and Kiangsi. Department of Agricultural Economics, University of Nanking.
2 B.B. Chapman, the Climates and Regions of China, Department of Agricultural Economics, University of Nanking.
3 One local mow = 1.1024 shih mow = 0.0735 hectares.

農塲面積之利用

農塲面積之利用計分爲普通作物，菜園，果園，墳塋，道路河流及壩堤等，池塘，農舍及晒塲等八項。普通作物所佔之面積最大，佔總面積百分之八九（第四○八頁第一表）。農舍面積及道路河流壩堤等面積次之，各佔百分之三·三。其他如果園佔百分之二·一，晒塲佔百分之一，墳塋佔千分之六，菜園佔千分之五，池塘僅佔千分之二。

小農塲內，農舍面積佔農塲總面積百分之五·二；中農塲內者佔百分之三·六；大農塲內者佔百分之二·六。是以農塲面積之大者，則其農舍面積利用之效率更高也。

小農塲內，河流壩堤道路等面積，所佔之百分數，亦較中大兩種農塲爲大。至墳塋面積，則在大中小三種農塲內，其所佔之面積百分率均同，爲百分之○·六。自土地利用之精密及適當方面觀之，則增加農塲面積或爲一補救之方策。

作物面積之季別利用

作物面積內，生長各季別之作物。夏季作物，乃種於冬季作物之後者，是以夏季作物面積百分數，與冬季作物之面積百分數有關，但較低耳。

作物複種指數以中農塲較高，爲一五四·七；大農塲次之爲一三七·六；小農塲僅爲一二七·九（第四○八頁第二表）。中農塲作物複種指數之所以較高，係因土地優良所致，觀其每畝地價之爲二八·○元（第四○九頁第三表）及作物指數之爲一一○·二，皆較大小兩種農塲爲高。作物面積之精密及適當利用，與農塲大小並無關係。但與田地價格及其生產力之關係極爲密切。

中小農塲之農夫，爲消費及儲藏便利起見，多種食糧及不易腐爛之作物。故菜園面積僅佔作物面積百分之一·二及一·三；而大農塲內者，竟達百分之三·一（第四○八頁第二表）。

小麥爲主要之冬季作物，中等農塲內小麥作物面積之百分數，較高於大農塲及小農塲者（第四○九頁第四表）；因中農塲之田地較優，冬季常不休閒，故其複種指數亦較高也。

小米，高粱，花生及紅薯等，皆爲主要之春季作物。小農塲內小米作物面積之百分數爲三·六（第四一○頁第五表），中農塲者爲百分之四，大農塲者爲百分之七·二。農塲之大者其小米面積之百分數亦大。小米稭乃工畜之主要飼料。大農塲內工畜數目多，小米稭之需要量高，故其作物面積之百分數亦高。

Use of Farm Land

Farm land is classified into eight groups: field crops, vegetable gardens, fruit orchards, grave yards, rivers and dykes, ponds, farmsteads and threshing floors. Field crops represent the largest item in these eight groups, which on the average, amount to 89 per cent of farm area (table 1, page 408). Farmsteads and rivers, dykes, and roads, rank next, representing 3.3 per cent each. Fruit orchards occupy 2.1 per cent of the farm area, threshing floors 1.0 per cent, grave yards, 0.6 per cent, vegetables, 0.5 per cent and ponds, 0.2 per cent.

The farmstead area is 5.2 per cent of the farm area for small sized farms as compared with 3.6 per cent for medium sized ones, and 2.6 per cent for large farms. It is evident that the larger the size of farm, the more efficiently is the farmstead area used.

The percentage of farm area in rivers, dykes, roads etc. is also greater for the group of small sized farms, than for both the medium and large sized farms. Grave yards occupy 0.6 per cent of the farm area in all three groups. From the standpoint of the more efficient use of land, the enlargement of the size of farms is probably one of the few possible remedies.

Seasonal use of crop land

Crop area is devoted to growing various crops at different seasons. Summer crops are grown after winter crops, so that the percentage of summer crops in the total crop area is definitely related to the percentage of winter crops. In most cases, the crop area in summer crops is less than that in winter crops.

The index of double cropping for the group of medium sized farms, 154.7, is higher than for the group of large sized farms, 137.6, and for the group of small sized farms, 127.9 (table 2, page 408). The most important reason for this higher index may be attributed to the better grade of land on the medium sized farms, as the average land value of 28.0 yuan per mow (table 3, page 409) and crop index of 110.2, for these farms are much higher than for the other two groups. The efficient use of crop area has no relationship to size of farm, but it has a close relationship to land value and the productivity of land.

The percentage of crop area in fruit crops is higher in the group of large sized farms, 3.1 per cent, (table 2 page 408), than 1.2 and 1.3 per cent for the groups of medium and small sized farms, because farmers in the group of small and medium sized farms are eager to have more food and non-perishable crops for consumption and storage.

Wheat is a very important winter crop. The percentage of crop area in wheat in the group of medium sized farms is higher than in either the small sized or large sized groups (table 4, page 409). In the group with better land, less land would be allowed in the winter. Therefore there is a larger area of winter crops and a higher index of double cropping.

Foxtail millet, kaoliang, peanuts and sweet potatoes are important spring crops. The percentage of crop area in foxtail millet in the group of small sized farms is 3.6 (table 5, page 410)

第一表　河南開封一百農家農塲大小與土地利用之關係
TABLE 1.—RELATION OF SIZE OF FARM TO THE USE OF LAND
100 farms, Kaifeng, Honan, 1937

作物畝 Crop mow	組距 Range	二四・五以下 Less than 24.5		二四・五 至四九・〇 24.5-49.0		四九・〇以上 More than 49.0		平均 Average	
	平均 Average	17.9		34.9		75.6			
農家數目 Number of farms		33		36		31		100	
		畝 百分數 mow percent		畝 百分數 mow percent		畝 百分數 mow percent		畝 百分數 mow percent	
普通作物面積 Area of field crops		13.68	87.4	22.16	90.2	52.77	89.0	28.85	89.0
菜園 Vegetable gardens		.08	.5	.06	.2	.35	.6	.16	.5
菓園 Fruit orchards		.19	1.2	.28	1.1	1.65	2.8	.67	2.1
坟塋 Grave yards		.09	.6	.18	.7	.33	.6	.19	.6
河流堤壩道路等 River, dykes, roads, etc.		.68	4.3	.70	2.9	1.86	3.1	1.06	3.3
池塘 Ponds		.00	.0	.00	.0	.20	.3	.06	.2
農舍 Farmsteads		.82	5.2	.88	3.6	1.55	2.6	1.07	3.3
晒塲 Thres..ing floors		.12	.8	.31	1.3	.60	1.0	.34	1.0
總農塲面積 Total farm area		15.66	100.0	24.57	100.0	59.31	100.0	32.40	100.0

第二表　河南開封一百農家農塲大小與各季別作物面積之關係
TABLE 2.—RELATION OF SIZE OF FARM TO PERCENTAGE OF CROP
AREA DEVOTED TO VARIOUS CROPS IN DIFFERENT SEASONS
100 farms, Kaifeng, Honan, 1936

作物畝 Crop mow	組距 Range	二四・九以下 Less than 24.9	二四・九至 四九・〇 24.9-49.0	四九・〇以上 More than 49.0	平均 Average
	平均 Average	17.9	34.9	75.6	41.9
農家數目 Number of farms		33	36	31	100
		百分數 per cent	百分數 per cent	百分數 per cent	百分數 per cent
多年生作物 Perennial crops (fruits)		1.3	1.2	3.1	2.3
冬季作物 Winter crops		33.3	56.1	40.5	43.7
春季作物 Spring crops		65.4	42.7	56.4	54.0
夏季作物 Summer crops		27.9	54.7	37.6	40.8
總計（複種指數） Total (index of double cropping)		127.9	154.7	137.6	140.8

as compared with 4.0 per cent for medium sized farms and 7.2 per cent for large sized farms. The larger the size of farm the higher is the percentage of crop area in foxtail millet. The straw of foxtail millet is a valuable feed for labor animals. The large sized farm has a large number of labor animals, the demand for foxtail millet straw for feed is high, therefore the percentage of crop area in this crop is also high.

The percentage of crop area in kaoliang and peanuts is higher on small sized farms than on medium and large sized farms. Kaoliang is a very important food crop. Its stalks are commonly used as fuel and material for the construction of houses. Peanuts are a cash and non-perishable crop and have a high labor requirement. The abundance of human labor and the urgent need of food and fuel crops on small sized farms determine the growing of these crops in a large percentage of the crop area.

第三表　河南開封一百農家農塲大小與田地價格及作物指數之關係

TABLE 3.—RELATION OF SIZE OF FARMS TO LAND
VALUE AND CROP INDEX

100 farms, Kaifeng, Honan, 1936

組距 Range	作物畝 Crop mow		農家數目 Number of farms	作物指數 Crop index	每畝田地價格 Land value per mow
		平均 Average			
畝 mow		畝 mow	數目 number	百分數 per cent	元 yuan
二四‧九以下　Less than 24.9		17.9	33	98.3	19.9
二四‧九至四九 24.9－49		34.9	36	110.2	28.0
四九以上　More than 49		75.6	31	94.0	20.1
平均 Average		41.9	100	101.3	22.2

第四表　河南開封一百農家農塲大小與冬季作物面積百分數之關係

TABLE 4.—RELATION OF SIZE OF FARMS TO PERCENTAGE
OF CROP AREA IN WINTER CROPS

100 farms, Kaifeng, Honan, 1936

作物畝 Crop mow	組距 Range	二四‧九以下 Less than 24.9	二四‧九五 四九‧〇 24.9－49.0	四九‧〇以上 More than 49.0	平均 Average
	平均 Average	17.9	34.9	75.6	41.9
農家數目 Number of farms		33	36	31	100
		百分數 per cent	百分數 per cent	百分數 per cent	百分數 per cent
大麥 Barley		4.7	1.5	1.6	2.1
小麥 Wheat		28.6	54.6	38.9	41.6

TABLE 5.—RELATION OF SIZE OF FARMS TO PERCENTAGE
OF CROP AREA IN SPRING CROPS
100 farms, Kaifeng, Honan, 1936

作物畝 Crop mow	組距 Range	二四・九以下 Less than 24.9	二四・九至 四九・〇 24.9–49.0	四九・〇以上 More than 49.0	平均 Average
	平均 Average	17.9	34.9	75.6	41.9
農家數目 Number of farms		33	36	31	100
		百分數 per cent	百分數 per cent	百分數 per cent	百分數 per cent
棉花 Cotton		.6	0.0	0.1	0.2
小米 Foxtail millet		3.6	4.0	7.2	5.8
綠豆 Green bean		1.5	0.7	0.9	0.9
高粱 Kaoliang		20.4	15.8	18.5	18.0
花生 Peanuts		31.8	19.9	23.9	24.0
黍子 Proso-millet (glutinous)		0.0	0.0	0.5	0.3
稷子 Proso-millet (non-glutinous)		0.6	0.0	1.4	0.9
紅薯 Sweet potato		4.3	0.9	1.9	2.0
黃豆 Soybean, yellow		0.9	0.4	0.5	0.5
青菜及蘿蔔 Vegetables and carrots		1.7	1.0	1.5	1.4

　　小農塲內高粱及花生面積之百分數，皆較中大農塲為高。高粱乃重要之食粮作物，其稭稈又可用為燒柴及建築房舍之材料。花生所需要之人工量較多，且為不易膲爛而易於出售之農作物。小農塲內因有多量之人工，並因食粮燃料之急需，故其種植高粱及花生作物之面積百分數亦大。

　　中農塲各種夏季作物面積之百分數，皆高於大小兩種農塲(第四一一頁第六表)，蓋因其所種之冬季作物較多故也。綠豆在夏季作物中甚為重要，其面積之百分數，與農塲之大小適成正比例。

摘　要

　　非生產面積之百分數，為填塞，河流堤壩，道路，農舍及晒塲等，皆以小農塲較高，故大農塲內田地之利用，較為精良且適當也。

　　作物面積利用之精密限度，與農塲大小無關，但與作物指數及田地價格成一正比。即作物指數及田地價格高者，其複種指數亦較高。小農塲擁有多量之人工，故需用人工工作量較多之花生，其種植面積，反較中大農塲者為多。

崔毓俊

TABLE 6.—RELATION OF SIZE OF FARMS TO PERCENTAGE
OF CROP AREA IN SUMMER CROPS

100 farms, Kaifeng, Honan, 1936

作 物 畝 Crop mow	組 距 Range	二四‧九以下 Less than 24.9	二四‧九至 四九‧〇 24.9–49.0	四九‧〇以上 More than 49.0	不均 Average
	不 均 Average	17.9	34.9	75.6	41.9
農家數目 Number of farms		33	36	31	100
		百分數 per cent	百分數 per cent	百分數 per cent	百分數 per cent
黑豆 Black bean		0.0	0.0	2.2	1.3
豇豆 Cow pea		1.6	0.5	0.7	0.8
小米 Foxtail millet		3.3	4.7	1.9	2.9
綠豆 Green bean		11.1	11.8	12.6	12.2
黍子 Proso-millet (glutinous)		2.5	17.3	5.5	8.2
稷子 Proso-millet (non-glutinous)		2.2	5.9	2.0	3.6
紅薯 Sweet potato		1.6	3.1	3.5	3.1
青豆 Soybean, green		0.0	0.2	0.8	0.5
黃豆 Soybean, yellow		5.6	11.2	7.4	8.2

Most of the summer crops occupy a higher percentage of crop
area on the medium sized farms than on the small and large sized
farms (table 6, page 411). This is the result of the high percentage of the crop area in winter crops. The green bean is the most
important summer crop. The percentage of crop area in green
beans shows a direct relationship to size of farm.

Summary The percentages for non productive uses, such
as grave yards, rivers and dykes, roads, farmsteads and threshing
floors are higher in the small sized farms than the large ones.
That is, the larger the size of farm, the more efficient is the use
of the farm area.

The intensity of the use of crop area has no relationship to
the size of farm, but has a direct relationship to the crop index
and land value, that is, the higher the crop index and land value,
the higher is the index of double cropping. Because of the
abundance of human labor on the small sized farms, peanuts
which have a high labor requirement, are grown in a larger area
than on medium and large sized farms.

Tsui Ruh-tsuin

四川之農產物價 (宣統二年至民國二十三年)

資 料 來 源

本編之材料係由四川中心農事試驗場蒐集，委託本系統計分析之。所包括為四川省肥沃之區域內十五縣二十五年之材料（自宣統二年至民國二十三年）。

編 製 方 法

該項資料包括農產品價格，及農民購買之商品價格，第因年代過長不免時有中斷之憾。統計時其遺漏時期少於三個月者皆用插入法補接之。農民收付價格兩者之總指數之計算皆係採用簡單幾何平均法。每一種物品之價格指數為各地各該項物品價格指數之總平均。其材料豐富之數縣則另編有個別之指數。

第一圖 四川農民出售之農產品價格與所付之商品價格指數，宣統二年至民國二十三年

民國十三年至十七年＝一○○

農民所付物價之變動，較農民所得物價為規則，漲跌亦較遲緩。在世界大戰期間，兩種物價之變動，呈相反之趨勢。

FIGURE 1.—INDEX NUMBERS OF PRICES OF AGRICULTURAL PRODUCTS SOLD AND OF PRICES OF COMMODITIES PAID BY FARMERS IN SZECHWAN, 1910-1934

1924 - 1928 = 100

Prices received by farmers were more erratic and rose and fell more rapidly than prices paid by farmers. During the world war their movements were in opposite directions.

FARM PRICES IN SZECHWAN 1910 — 1934

Sources of data

Data on farm prices in 15 hsien in Szechwan have been collected by the Szechwan Central Agricultural Experimental Station and sent to this Department for statistical analysis. This study covers a very fertile part of Szechwan. Data are available for a period of 25 years, from 1910 — 1934.

Method of compilation

Data of prices of agricultural products sold by farmers and prices of commodities purchased by farmers are available. Unfortunately the data are very scanty and they are sometimes not available for quite a long period. They are only interpolated when less than three months are missing. The general indices of both prices received and paid by farmers are simple geometric averages of prices of available commodities. The price index of each commodity is the average index of price indices of all localities, where such prices are available. Individual indices have been compiled for several localities, where sufficient commodity prices are available.

Prices of agricultural products sold by farmers

Prices in Szechwan had a rapid rising trend during 1910 — 1931 (figure 1, page 412). The main cause was the falling value of silver, because Szechwan was also on the silver standard, like the other parts of China.

Compared with prices in Wuchin, Kiangsu, Szechwan prices rose more rapidly than Wuchin prices (figure 2, page 416). The prices during 1910 — 1918 were especially low. The chief reason for this was apparently the devaluation of Szechwan currency.

Since the prices were quoted in Szechwan silver dollars, the changing value of the dollar would greatly affect the prices. Before 1911, the silver content of the Szechwan dollar was Kuping ₮0.72, which decreased to Kuping ₮0.71 in 1911 and to ₮0.70 in 1914. After 1918 a large quantity of 50 cents silver dollars, of depreciated content, had been coined. In 1926 there were 40 mints established by different military authorities and nearly 70 kinds of depreciated yuan were circulated. It was not until 1928 that the currency was unified. This unsteady period is unfortunately the base period of our indices. All these caused the prices from 1910 to 1918 to be relatively low.

In addition to this, Szechwan had an unfavorable balance of trade as a result of the decreasing value of the Szechwan dollar in terms of Shanghai currency. The exchange rate between Szechwan and Shanghai was especially low during 1910 — 1911, ranging from Szechwan ₮880 to ₮950 in exchange for 1,000

農 民 出 售 之 農 產 品 價 格

自宣統二年至民國二十年間四川物價有上漲之趨勢（第四一二頁第一圖）。其主要原因爲銀價之下跌，蓋四川亦如中國其他各地以銀爲本位也。

試以四川物價與江蘇武進物價相較，前者上漲較後者爲速（第四一六頁第二圖）。自宣統二年至民國七年之間該省物價特低，其主要原因顯爲川幣之貶值。

四川物價既以川幣計算，則銀元價值之變遷，影響物價自鉅。宣統三年以前每一四川銀元含銀庫平〇‧七二兩，宣統三年減爲〇‧七一兩，民國三年再減至〇‧七〇兩。自民國七年後更有大批之輕質半元銀幣鑄出。民十五年，川省各地方軍事當局競設造幣廠，達四十處之多，而市上輕質銀元亦幾近七十種。迨至民國十七年，川省幣制始告統一。本物價指數之基期，不幸適在此不安定時期內，宣統二年至民國七年物價之所以較低職是故也。

此外由於川幣申滙之滙率下降之故，川省對外貿易遂呈逆差之現象，自宣統二年至三年，川滬間之滙率特低，每千兩申銀兌換川銀八八〇兩至九五〇兩，民國元年以後數年因禁銀出境之結果，使川申滙率日漸增高。易言之即川幣日益貶值也。至民國五年十月，省當局更進而宣佈白銀不得自重慶運往內地。重慶之銀價遂較內地低十分之一。凡此幣值之變遷，皆爲宣統二年至三年間之物價低落，民國二年後物價上漲以及民國四年後物價下跌之主要原因。

再者農產品之供給情形，亦爲影響農產物價之一因素，在該時期之初，禁種鴉片之法令執行頗厲。大部份土地皆得復用以耕種農作物，致供給增加。此項禁令雖不久廢弛，但其結果已足解釋宣統二年至民國七年農產物價低落之原因。

宣統三年農作豐收，農產物價因之特低。民國四年患旱，而民六至民七年間，收穫復豐。此亦足解明宣統二年至民國七年之物價變動。

民國二十年，四川物價繼續上漲，而武進物價則陡跌。此大都由於十九年之旱災，及是年各地之水災。1

民國二十年以後銀價之上漲，使四川物價陡然下跌，然不若武進之急速耳。此種現象仍係受幣值變動之影響。民國二十年之下半季滙率陡漲。爲制止白銀之流出起見，省當局乃實行禁運白銀出境，川省幣制不復以白銀爲本位。四川物價遂較上海爲高。

---

1 聚興誠銀行之報告

Shanghai taels. From April, 1912, the silver embargo was in force for several years, and the exchange rate became higher and higher. That is, the Szechwan dollar was growing cheaper. Beginning from October, 1916, another new currency measure was introduced. Silver was not allowed to be transported from Chungking to the interior. The difference between Chungking currency and that of the interior was one tenth. These monetary changes largely explain the low prices during 1910 — 1911, and the rising prices since 1913 and falling prices after 1915.

Furthermore, the supply of agricultural products was also partly responsible. In the beginning of this period, the law of anti-opium cultivation was strictly enforced. A large part of land was therefore available for the cultivation of agricultural products, which caused the supply to increase. But later, the anti-opium law was practically abandoned. This also explains why the prices of agricultural products during 1910 — 1918 were low.

In the year 1911, crops were good. Prices were therefore especially low. In 1915 there was a drought. During 1917 — 1918 the harvest was again a good one. These conditions help to explain the price movement during 1910 — 1918.

Szechwan prices kept on rising in 1931, while prices in Wuchin fell precipitously. This was mostly due to the drought in 1930 and the fatal inundation[1] in different parts of Szechwan in the same year.

After 1931, prices in Szechwan also fell precipitously, due to the rising value of silver, but not so rapidly as the prices in Wuchin. This was again chiefly due to the currency changes. Since the latter part of 1931 the exchange rate had risen sharply. In order to check the out-flow of silver, the silver embargo was enforced. Szechwan currency was no longer on the silver standard. This caused the prices in Szechwan to become higher than those in Shanghai.

Prices began again to rise in the latter part of 1933. Then the Communists invaded Szechwan in 1933 and crossed the Wu river in January 1934. People were very excited and capital flew out of Szechwan, amounting approximately to 30 million dollars. The Szechwan dollar was still more devaluated in terms of Shanghai currency. The year 1934 was also one of drought and prices rose in consequence.

The price indices in different localities in Szechwan are shown in figure 3 (page 417). It might be supposed at first that Szechwan was divided into many political units. Taxes were not uniform, transportation was difficult, the ban on the export of agricultural

---

1   Private report of Young Brothers Banking Corporation.

民國二十二年之下半季，物價復行上漲。其時共黨侵入四川，翌年一月越過烏江，川民擾然，杌隉不安。資金外流約達三千萬元之鉅，四川銀幣之申滙率亦高，加之二十三年之乾旱，物價遂復上漲。

　　四川各地物價指數圖示於第四一七頁第三圖。其時四川軍人各自為政，形成分割局勢。各地捐稅，名目繁多，殊不一致。交通阻梗，運輸困難，農產輸出時受阻礙，各地物價變動，似應完全不同。然第三圖顯示四川各地物價之趨勢，除短期之紛亂外大體相同，此復可証明貨幣價值為決定一般物價水準之主要因素。

　　本篇蒐集之川申滙率僅自民國十六年始，如將四川物價根據川申滙率（民國十七年＝一〇〇）以申幣計算之如（第二圖所示），則四川與武進之物價除民國二十年外各年大都近似。

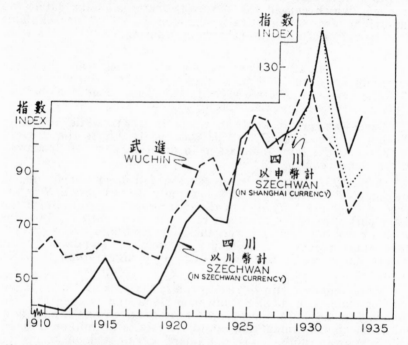

第二圖　四川與江蘇武進農產物價指數，宣統二年至民國二十三年

民國十三年至十七年＝一〇〇

　　四川與武進物價變動之趨勢相同，因兩處物價皆係以白銀計算之，宣統二年至民國七年，四川物價比較其低，當民國二十年武進物價突跌之際，彼則繼續上漲，如四川物價以申幣計算之，（根據民國十七年＝一〇〇之川申滙率）則與武進之物價指數可更為接近。

FIGURE 2.—INDEX NUMBERS OF PRICES OF AGRICULTURAL PRODUCTS IN SZECHWAN AND IN WUCHIN, KIANGSU, 1910 – 1934

1924 – 1928 = 100

　　They had the same trend in rising and falling, because their prices were both in silver. Szechwan prices were relatively low during 1910 – 1918 and continued to rise in 1931, while Wuchin prices fell precipitously. If Szechwan prices were calculated in terms of Shanghai currency, with 1928 as 100, the price relationship between Wuchin and Szechwan would be closer in most years.

products was frequently in force. Thus entirely different price movements might have been expected, but figure 3 shows that prices in different localities in Szechwan have shown nearly the same trend, although not without temporary disturbances. It is proved once more, that the value of money is the main factor in determining the average price level.

The exchange rate between Szechwan and Shanghai has been available since 1927. If the prices in Szechwan were calculated in terms of Shanghai currency, with the exchange rate of 1927 as 100, as shown in figure 2, the price relationship between Szechwan and Wuchin was, for most years, closer than the relationship between the different currencies, except during 1931.

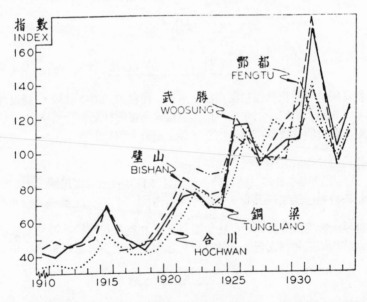

第三圖　四川武勝(七種物品)酆都(五種物品)璧山(五種物品)合川(六種物品)銅梁(五種物品)農產物價指數，宣統二年至民國二十三年。

民國十三年至十七年＝一〇〇

宣統二年至民國十三年，川省之政治經濟雖極紊亂，然各地物價變動之趨勢大致相同。

FIGURE 3.—INDEX NUMBERS OF PRICES OF AGRICULTURAL PRODUCTS IN WOOSUNG (7 COMMODITIES), FENGTU (5 COMMODITIES), BISHAN (5 COMMODITIES), HOCHWAN (6 COMMODITIES) AND TUNGLIANG (5 COMMODITIES) IN SZECHWAN. 1910 - 1934

1924 - 1928 = 100

Although Szechwan was divided into many political and economic units during this period, the average price indices had, in the long run, the same trend, although not without temporary disturbances.

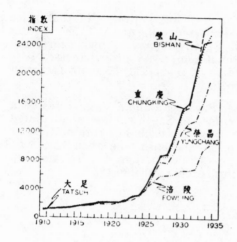

第四圖　四川各地之銅元價格

民國十四年以前四川各地之銅元價格一致徐徐上漲，其後則分歧甚遠。

FIGURE 4.—PRICES OF COPPER COINS IN DIFFERENT LOCALITIES IN SZECHWAN 1910 — 1914.

The prices of copper coins in different localities in Szechwan had the same slow rising trend until 1925, then were wide apart from each other.

農民所付之商品價格

農民所付物價指數僅包括商品十一種。而白布之價格材料，最早爲民國四年，煤油爲民國十二年故以此指數代表農民所付之平均價格，不無遺憾之處，農民所付與所得物價指數變動之趨勢大致相同。

農民所付物價之變動較農民所得物價爲規則，蓋所付者均爲零售價格也。又其漲跌亦不若農民所得物價爲迅速，自宣統三年至民國二十年所得物價指數自四〇漲至一三九，而所付物價指數僅自四二漲至一三〇。

世界大戰期間，農民所付物價繼續上漲，而農民所得物價則繼續下跌，此兩種物價之相背而行，且爲時如是之久，實屬例外之現象。

銅元之跌價

宣統三年至民國十四年間，川省銀元換銅元之兌換率，雖畧上漲，然大致尚稱穩定（第四--八頁第四圖）。各地銅元價值幾盡相同。但其後因造幣廠鑄造劣質銅元過多，遂使銅元價值開始迅速下跌。各地銅元價值亦屬不同，其原因大槪由於各種銅元之重量不同，以及銅元之流動時受限制。四川物價大多以銅元計，即在今日亦然。由於各地物價受銅元價值變動之影響有先後大小之分。因之各地以銀元計算之物價變動，趨勢亦難盡同。此亦本研究末期四川各地農產物價變動迥異之原因也。

王　廉

Prices of commodities paid by farmers

The index numbers of prices of commodities paid by farmers included only 11 commodities. The price of white cloth was only available from 1915 and that of kerosene from 1923. This index is therefore not so representative as a measure of average prices paid by farmers. The index number of prices paid by farmers had the same trend as that of prices received by farmers.

The index numbers of prices paid by farmers were less erratic than those of prices received by farmers, because they were retail prices, which rise or fall less rapidly than prices received by farmers. During 1910 — 1931 prices received rose from an index of 40 to 139, while prices paid rose from 42 to 130.

During the world war, prices paid by farmers continued to rise, while prices received by farmers fell. This is the only exception of significant duration of prices received and prices paid moving in opposite directions.

Depreciation of copper coins

The ratio between silver and copper coins was relatively stable, although it was not without a slight rising trend during 1910 — 1925 (figure 4, page 418). The value of copper coins was nearly the same in all localities, but due to the over production of depreciated copper coins by different mints, under the auspices of various military authorities, the copper coins began to depreciate by leaps and bounds. The value of copper coins was different in different localities. This was probably because the various coins were different in weight and their movement was restricted. Most of the prices in Szechwan, even until recently, were quoted in coppers. The prices did not respond to the changing value of coppers as uniformly and as quickly in different localities, therefore, the prices converted in terms of silver had not exactly the same trend in different localities. This is also one of the reasons why the farm prices in Szechwan show different movements in different localities in the latter part of our study.

Wang Lien

重慶之批發物價

自日軍侵華，津滬淪陷後，重慶在吾國商業經濟上之地位日見重要。國內之銀行，工廠，商店及游資等漸有集中重慶之趨勢，於是重慶商業動態之科學研究，在此抗戰之際，已成刻不容緩之要舉。四川省政府建設廳駐渝辦事處，前以曾有批發物價指數之編製，惟因限於人力財力舛誤自所難免，且發表較慢，難供實用，本系原擬在重慶編製可靠之物價指數與商業動態指數，茲經與建設廳商妥，合作進行，以免重複並由雙方各增人財，期臻完善。以下爲建設廳駐渝辦事處文先俊君與本系駐渝代表李德賢君之報告，惜因運輸困難，渝市輸入貨物中，因來源斷絕，以致無市者頗不乏例，有時並無代以其他商品。故近數月來，僅包括物品九十一種或九十種（第三七七頁第一圖），幸閱者注意。

楊　蔚

民國二十七年一月份物價漲落情形

重慶市薑售物價之指數，在本年度之一月份發生鉅大之變動，其總指數較前月份昇上達百分之一一，（第四二二頁第一表）開戰後之最高紀錄，本月份所調查之物價項目除夏布無成交外，共計九十一項，其中有五十項貨物之價格指數高過前月，廿六項較低下，餘十五項則無變動，茲將其結果分列於第四二三頁第二表中。

按渝地居民日常所用之必需物品，除極少數係本地土產外，大多數皆爲進口之機製品，由上海方面輸入者則佔大多數。因此重慶進口貨物之價格，向視下江供給量之多寡爲轉移，然自戰事暴發長江封鎖以後，巨額之來源，忽告漸絕，而各地移居川地者，反見增多，需求亦即上昇，以有限之存貨應付巨額之需要，本廳困難，況開封長江，與夫進口貨之來源，皆爲目下無從預測之事實，故而進口貨之價格，日趨向榮，反之依賴下江市場之川產土貨，則因航運中斷，銷途停滯，價格方面，遭受罕有之慘跌，而此巨大之漲風跌勢，遂成爲産生本月份重慶市物價巨浪之主要原因矣。

總計六大類物價指數中，變動最大者，以類別言當推建築材料及五金電料各漲起百分之二四‧二及二〇‧二，實際上凡進口貨物之價格，多少無不上漲。建築材料共分九種，價格上昇者計有八種，其中以大市瓦，楠板，及石灰三項，漲勢最厲，皆在百分之五十以上，良以渝地人口加增，需屋特多，土木大興所致也，此類指數之平均漲額，居全體之首席。五金電料全係進口貨物，故價格皆上漲，最大爲皮錢漲百分之三二‧七，最

— 420 —

WHOLESALE PRICES IN CHUNGKING

The importance of th. Chungking market has been accentuated since the paralysis of the Eastern ports. This is evidenced by the floating in of outside capital, firms, factories and banking institutions. Hence the demand for a business barometer of a scientific nature becomes increasingly urgent. Wholesale prices were collected and index numbers were compiled by the Chungking office of the Bureau of Reconstruction of the Szechwan Provincial Government since January, 1937. Owing to the limitations of personnel and funds, errors of different types were absolutely unavoidable and the dissemination of this information was usually delayed. It was the intention of this Department to compile a reliable price index and to publish it as promptly as possible. Arrangements were made for this Department to work in cooperation with the Bureau. Past figures were checked. The following is the first monthly report for January, February, and March, 1938, which was compiled by Mr. H. T. Wen, of the Chungking office of the Bureau of Reconstruction, and Mr. T. H. Lee of this Department.

Owing to the difficulties of transportation, many imported articles have disappeared from the Chungking market recently. Sometimes it is even impossible to find a substitute for the making of our index numbers. In this report for January, February, and March, 1938, only 90 or 91 commodities are included instead of 92 as was prescribed in the beginning. Figure 1, page 377, shows the general trend of wholesale prices in Chungking since January, 1937.

W. Y. Yang

Explanatory Notes for January, 1938

The general index of Chungking wholesale prices in January advanced 11 points as compared with the previous month (table 1, page 422). Fifty out of 91 commodities went up, 26 went down and 15 remained unchanged (table 2, page 423).

Excepting the small amount of goods produced locally, the main supply of goods for consumption comes from other ports, mostly from Shanghai. Their prices are, therefore, determined considerably by the supply conditions outside Szechwan. Since the outbreak of the Sino-Japanese war, the stoppage of transportation along the lower Yangtze and the rapid increase of population in this province have raised the prices of imported goods enormously and depressed those of exported goods correspondingly.

Out of these six groups, building materials and metals and electric supplies advanced the most. Building materials showed an increase of 24.2 points and metals and electric supplies 20.2 points. Eight out of nine kinds of building materials went up.

小爲聞鉄漲百分之六•二，全體平均漲額在各類中之上漲佔次位者。雜項類之指數較上月份漲百分之七•四，計有七種貨價上漲，三種下落，其餘二種價格與上月相同，漲價貨中，紙類之漲額最高，新聞紙與毛邊紙各漲百分之二九以上，其餘如琴棋牌及小大英香煙，亦以供少求多，漲價百分之一九以上。跌價最大之貨物爲當歸，跌百分之一一•一，次爲猪鬃，百分之五•〇及桐油百分之四•八。衣料類價格指數，平均而論，上落有限，計漲百分之六•一，然而細分其內容，則漲勢實足嚇人，全類共有十七種貨物，上漲者雖則有六種，且幾皆爲毛呢，嗶嘰等，然以產地全在京滬一帶，今來源已絕，供給中斷，故有三種羊毛織品，皆較上月昇上百分之四五以上。燃料類各種貨物中除虎牌火柴之漲額最鉅外，計百分之三八•八，其餘各物之漲落額尚算平穩。

本月份各類之平均指數較上月爲低者，惟食料一類，計跌落百分之一•八。分析言之，則以下江市場爲銷貨尾閭之榨菜下降最慘，計跌百分之三一•五，高粱亦跌百分之一三•二，或因農民經濟困難及壯丁訓練而減

第一表　重慶躉售物價指數

(簡單幾何平均)

民國二十六年＝一〇〇

TABLE 1.—INDEX NUMBERS OF WHOLESALE PRICES IN CHUNGKING

(Simple Geometric Average)

1937 = 100

類別 Groups	總指數 All commodities.	食料類 Food	衣料類 Clothing	燃料類 Fuel and light	金屬及電料類 Metals & electric supplies	建築材料類 Building materials	雜項類 Miscellaneous
項數 No. of commodities	92	32	18	10	11	9	12
1937							
一月 January	93.5	98.5	92.8	94.6	79.8	92.5	95.3
二月 February	96.2	104.8	93.5	93.5	82.0	93.8	96.5
三月 March	96.7	105.3	93.4	93.5	84.7	92.9	97.6
四月 April	97.9	100.8	95.1	94.0	92.6	94.9	105.2
五月 May	98.3	104.5	96.4	92.2	86.5	94.5	104.8
六月 June	98.8	106.4	96.6	95.3	83.0	95.2	104.2
七月 July	95.1	95.4	97.0	93.3	81.5	99.5	103.8
八月 August	95.7	93.8	94.5	98.6	97.1	103.0	93.7
九月 September ...	103.1	95.0	112.1	99.1	127.9	98.2	99.7
十月 October	104.4	98.5	111.2	107.7	121.6	99.9	96.9
十一月 November ...	104.0	97.5	105.4	110.9	122.3	100.4	96.3
十二月 December	98.3	93.2	108.1	117.6	133.6	111.4	86.0
1938							
一月 January	109.3	91.4	114.2	122.3	153.8	135.6	93.4
二月 February	119.2	95.1	122.7	130.1	193.7	140.3	109.9
三月 March	124.0	95.1	130.4	133.6	216.8	141.4	118.9

Tiles, board and lime recorded the greatest gain. Their increases from December, 1937, were all above 50 points, due to the strong demand for new buildings as caused by the sudden increase in the city population.

In the group of metals and electric supplies, insulated wire advanced by 32.7 points and round iron by 6.2 points. The index of the miscellaneous group advanced by 7.4 points. Seven out of 12 commodities went up, three went down, two remained unchanged. Among those which went up from the previous month, paper rose most remarkably. Both newsprinting paper and Moa Bien paper advanced by more than 29 points. Others, such as Chin Chee cigarettes and Ruby Queen cigarettes, advanced more than 19 points on account of shortage of supply. Those that dropped severely were Dan Kwei (Ligusticum acutilobum, S. ct. L.) by 11.1 points, bristles by 5 points and wood oil by 4. 8 points.

Clothing showed an increase of only 6.1 points from December, 1937. Only 6 out of 17 commodities went up, but the magnitude of the increase of these few commodities is astonishing. Imported clothing materials as serges and tweeds advanced enormously. Three kinds of woolen cloths advanced by more than 45 points. There was not much change in the prices of fuels except Tiger Brand matches which rose 38.8 points. The food group was the only one which declined. The average index dropped by 1.8 points. Salted turnip, which had been dependent upon the markets along the lower Yangtze, fell by 31.5 points. Kaoliang dropped by 13.2 points. The low demand for kaoliang wine was probably the reason for this drop. Broad beans were the only product in this group that advanced as much as 18.2 points. Fluctuations in the prices of other foodstuffs were comparatively small (table 3, page 424).

第二表　民國廿七年一月與廿六年十二月各種物品價格升降之比率

TABLE 2.—NUMBER AND PERCENTAGE OF COMMODITIES FOR WHICH PRICES WERE HIGHER, LOWER OR UNCHANGED IN JANUARY 1938 THAN DECEMBER 1937

類　　別 Groups	總　計 Total		漲 Higher		落 Lower		平 Unchanged	
	項數 No.	百分比 %	項數 No.	百分比 %	項數 No.	百分比 %	項數 No.	百分比 %
總　指　數 General Index	91	100	50	54.9	26	28.6	15	16.5
食　料　類 Food	52	100	13	40.6	13	40.6	6	18.8
衣　料　類 Clothing	17	100	6	35.3	7	41.2	4	23.5
燃　料　類 Fuel and light	10	100	5	50.0	3	30.0	2	20.0
金屬及電料類 Metals and electric supplies	11	100	11	100.0	0	0.0	0	0.0
建築材料類 Buidling materials	9	100	8	88.9	0	0.0	1	11.1
雜　項　類 Miscellaneous	12	100	7	58.3	3	25.0	2	16.7

— 423 —

少製酒量，致高粱之需要額減低也。 漲價物品惟葫豆一項最高計漲上百分之一八・二，在粮荒貴時斯物向為川地貧民之粮米代替品， 此次漲價原因恐亦在此，其餘食品漲落互見惟皆不大耳， 本月份之物價指數與去年同月之比較列於第四二四頁第三表以備參攷。

馬牌洋灰，三角鐵，十六支汽球棉紗，廿支採蓮及卅二支好做棉紗等五項物品因來源漸絕存底亦少，恐日後缺貨，故自去年一月份始另代以其他牌名之貨物，即川牌水泥，洋鋼，十六支荆州，廿支老司球及卅二支四平蓮棉紗等特附誌之。

民國二十七年二月份物價漲落情形

二月份重慶躉售物價指數升爲一一九・二較上月增九・九， 九十一項物價中有六十九項上漲，十三項下落，九項未有變動，茲將詳細結果表列於第四二四頁第四表。

二月份米粮價格除綠豆，葫豆，兩項畧跌外， 其餘米麥等十五項均向上漲，菜油，猪油，燒酒，大糖酒等項銷塲不旺則向下跌， 猪肉醬油醋等價格未有變動，花鹽巴鹽等又形漲價，食料類指數， 由上月之九一・四升爲九五・一。衣料品中毛織品，因時令已過價格未漲， 冲直貢呢價格微跌，其他棉布棉紗棉花及川綢等無不騰漲，蓋以來源絕少，存貨供銷有日漸不濟之勢，衣料類指數遂由上月之一一四・二突增爲一二二・七，燃料類中白炭因冬令寒季已過，銷路頓滯，價格遂落，末炭價亦跌落，其他燃料價均上漲，尤以煤油洋燭，漲勢最凶，燃料指數昇達一三〇・一，金屬電料類中無有不漲價者，而上漲程度高於各類之上， 就中尤以圓鐵竹節鋼爲

第三表　民國廿七年一月與二十六年一月各種物價升降之比較

TABLE 3.—COMPARISON OF PRICE INDEXES IN JANUARY 1938
WITH THOSE OF THE CORRESPONDING MONTH OF 1937

類　別 Group	指　數 Index		較二十六年 (＋)或減(—) Increase (＋) or decrease (—) as compared with January 1937
	二十七年一月 Jan. 1938	去年同月 Jan. 1937	
總　指　數 General index	109.3	93.5	(Points) ＋15.8
食　料　類 Foodstuff	91.4	98.5	— 7.1
衣　料　類 Clothing	114.2	92.8	＋21.4
燃　料　類 Fuel and light	122.3	94.6	＋27.7
金屬及電料類 Metals & electric supplies	153.8	79.8	＋74.0
建築材料類 Building Materials	135.6	92.5	＋43.1
雜　項　類 Miscellaneous	93.4	95.3	— 1.9

Explanatory Notes for February, 1938

The general index of Chungking wholesale prices in February, 1938, rose to 119.2, an increase of 9.9 points from January (table 1, page 422). Sixty-nine out of 91 commodities went up, 13 went down and nine remained unchanged (table 4, page 425).

In the food group, green beans and broad beans declined slightly; prices of fifteen other foodstuffs such as rice, wheat, etc. went up; prices of rapeseed oil, kaoliang wine, and lard dropped on account of the dull market. Salts went up; pork, soy sauce and vinegar remained unchanged. The general index for food-stuffs advanced from 91.4 in January to 95.1 in February. Within the clothing group, woolen cloths remained unchanged due to warmer weather; venetians declined slightly; other materials like cotton cloths, cotton yarn, cotton and silk, Szechwan Brand, all went up as a result of shortage of supply. Hence, the average index for clothing, went up from 114.2 in January to 122.7. The index for fuel and light was 130.1 in February. As the weather became warmer, the demand for anthracite was reduced and the prices of these commodities sagged accordingly. Other fuels like kerosene oil and imported candles rose violently.

All articles in the group of metals and electric supplies rose in February. The average index for the group went up to 193.7. Round iron and bamboo steel advanced the most owing to the increasing demand for air defence buildings caused by frequent Japanese air raids. The index of building materials went up to 140.3. Lime and stones dropped; soft wood and cement, Szechwan Brand, remained unchanged; all others went up. The miscellaneous group went up from 93.4 in the previous month to 109.9. Cigarettes and newsprinting paper rose most violently. Mao Bien paper went down; soap remained unchanged.

第四表　二月份各種物品價格之升降比率

TABLE 4.—NUMBER AND PERCENTAGE OF COMMODITIES FOR WHICH PRICES WERE HIGHER, LOWER OR UNCHANGED IN FEBRUARY THAN JANUARY, 1938

類　　別 Groups	總　計 Total		漲 Higher		落 Lower		平 Unchanged	
	項數 No.	百分率 %	項數 No.	百分率 %	項數 No.	百分率 %	項數 No.	百分率 %
總　指　數 General index	91	100	69	75.8	13	14.3	9	9.9
食　料　類 Foodstuff	32	100	22	68.7	7	21.9	3	9.4
衣　料　類 Clothing	17	100	13	76.5	1	5.9	3	17.0
燃　料　類 Fuel and light	10	110	8	80.0	2	20.0	0	—
五金電料類 Metals & electric supplies ...	11	100	11	100.0	0	—	0	—
建築材料類 Building materials	9	100	5	55.6	2	22.2	2	22.2
雜　項　類 Miscellaneous	12	100	10	83.4	1	8.3	1	8.3

最，此因本月內頻來空襲警報，建築防空地下室者需要甚多， 此種物品遂自然居奇矣。金屬電料類指數遽昇至一九三‧七， 建築材料類中石灰及條石價格下跌，杉木條與川牌水泥，未有變動， 其他各項則向上漲，指數昇為一四〇‧三。雜項類中僅毛邊紙一項價格下跌，肥皂一項價未變動，其他各項無不上漲，而紙烟新聞紙漲勢最猛， 雜項類指數遂由上月之九三‧四增至一〇九‧九。

二月份指數與上年同期之比較見第四二八頁第五表。

民國二十七年三月份物價漲落情形

三月份之重慶市躉售物價總指數，大體尚稱平穩，較二月份高出百分之四八，惟與去年同月之物價總指數相比較，則上昇之高度，又開戰後之新紀錄，本月份所調查之物價項目， 除夏布因未及時令尚無交易及亞浦耳則形燈泡缺貨外，共有九十項，其中物價上漲者佔半數以上， 計有五十二項，落下者二十項，其餘十八項之價格並無變動，茲將其結果列表於第四二八頁第六表中。

漲勢最烈之貨物，仍屬金屬電料類，指數較前月昇上達百之二十三‧一，良以來源缺乏需求不減所致也。 此類中各貨之價格除洋釘跌落百分之一三外，餘皆上漲，而以亞浦耳長形燈泡為尤甚， 較上月高出百分之九八‧五，較去年同月突昇百分之一五二‧二，皮綫則雖高百分之三九‧一，綫及新燃較去年同月高百分之一八二‧六，漲勢之厲， 可算登峯造極矣。他如花鉛絲等電料漲勢亦兇， 計各昇上百分之四八‧七及二三‧一，漲勢佔次位之貨物為雜類指數，較上月高出百分之九‧〇， 此類貨物共有十二之六‧四種，除小車牌肥皂價格照舊外，其餘各貨之價格無不上漲， 計新聞紙百分，毛邊紙一二‧八，本省土產現有外銷之希望，故價格漸向上游，計當歸較上月高出百分之一六‧九，川芎八‧三及桐油七‧三，本月份之衣料類物價指數漲百分之七‧七，各貨價格無不上昇，三峽布與三峽呢則因各界添製制服需用特多，故漲勢最烈， 計各昇上百分之三三‧七及二〇‧七，單衣料亦因時令關係互趨漲勢。 燃料類之物價指數，雖昇上百分之三‧五然各物之上漲者多限於進口貨如虎牌火柴漲百分之二九‧一，僧帽牌洋燭二七‧三及煤油九‧二，土產燃料，末炭漲百分之一一‧五，白炭三‧九，但輪炭與連礄炭反各跌百分之三〇‧〇及六‧三，蓋經濟部擬將川產礦煤運供武漢工廠，故對於價格，已限制其自由漲落矣。 建築材料類各貨之價格變動尚算平穩，故價格指數只高出百分之一‧一，其中惟三種貨價漲勢畧高，計栳板昇上百分之七‧四，大市瓦五‧九， 及小連二條

Explanatory notes for March, 1938

The general index of Chungking wholesale prices in March was comparatively stable. Compared with that of the previous month it only advanced 4.8 points, but it was enormously higher compared with the same period for last year (table 1, page 422). Fifty-two out of 90 commodities went up in March, 20 went down and 18 remained unchanged (table 6, page 428).

Metals and electric supplies is still the group which advanced the most. Owing to the increasing demand and short supply, the index was 23.1 points higher than for last month. Within this group, only nails fell 13 points, the others all rose, especially the Oppel long bulb, which advanced 98.5 points as compared with February, and was 152.2 points above the index for March, 1937. Insulated wire rose only 39.1 points, but was 182.6 points higher than for the same period last year. Flexible cord and lead wire each advanced 48.7 and 23.1 points, respectively.

The miscellaneous group rose 9.0 points, and with the exception of soap, which remained unchanged, all commodities were higher than last month. Among these, newsprinting paper advanced 6.4 points; Mao Bien paper 12.8; Dan Kwei (Ligusticum acutilobum S. et L.) 16.9; Conioselinumn univitatum Turez 8.3 and wood oil 7.3 points.

The clothing group advanced 7.7 points. Sang-shia tweed and Sang-shia cloth advanced 33.7 and 20.7 points on account of a strong demand for uniform materials and thinner clothing as the weather became warmer.

The index for fuel and light rose 3.5 points, mostly caused by the rising prices of imported goods. Matches, Tiger brand, rose 29.1; candle-crown 27.3 and kerosene 9.2 points. The National Ministry of Economics is planning to transport Szechwan coal products to Hankow for use in factories, thus price fluctuations were somewhat limited. Building materials fluctuated slightly this month, rising only 1.1 points. The three commodities which rose somewhat higher were wooden boards, 7.4 points; tiles 5.9; and stones, 4.8 points.

The general index for the food group remained unchanged, only slight fluctuations occurring for different commodities. The fall in the price of cereals this month was partly due to the weak demand caused by the gradual outflow of population, but the main reason was probably the Government's abandonment of the business tax since April 1st. The rising price of kaoliang wine caused the price of kaoliang to rise proportionately. The price of white sugar rose owing to a strong demand, while Yunnan brick tea advanced on account of a shortage of supply.

Lee Teh-hsien
Wen Hsien-tsuin

石四・八，玻璃與二四磚跌落百分之九・一及二・九。食料類價格指數與前月相同，各種貨物之價格則漲落互見，惟不甚鉅耳。粮價本月份一致下瀉，自百分之三・四至九・九不等，恐因居民疏散後，需要減低所致，惟主要原因實係自四月份起免徵米業稅（即營業稅），故而價格看跌至於高粱價格之畧漲，則因燒酒價漲之故也。白糖因外銷胃濃，洋茶則存貨缺乏，故各漲上百分之一八・五及一六・三。

本月份各類之價格指數與去年同月之比較列於第四二九頁第七表中，以供參攷。

第五表　民國二十七年二月與二十六年同月各種物價升降之比較
TAELE 5.—COMPARISON OF PRICE INDEXES IN FEBRUARY 1938 WITH THE CORRESPONDING MONTH OF 1937

類 別 Group	指　數 Index		較二十六年份 (＋)或減(—) Increase (＋) or decrease (—) as compared with February 1937
	二十七年二月 Feb. 1938	二十六年二月 Feb. 1937	
總　指　數 General index	119.2	96.2	(Points) ＋ 23.0
食　料　類 Foodstuff	95.1	104.8	— 9.7
衣　料　類 Clothing	122.7	93.5	＋ 29.2
燃　料　類 Fuel and light	130.1	93.5	＋ 36.6
金屬及電料類 Metals & electric supplies	193.7	82.0	＋111.7
建築材料類 Building Materials	140.3	93.8	＋ 46.5
雜　項　類 Miscellaneous	109.9	96.5	＋ 13.4

第六表　三月份各種物品價格之升降比率
TABLE 6.—NUMBER AND PERCENTAGE OF COMMODITIES FOR WHICH PRICES WERE HIGHER, LOWER OR UNCHANGED IN MARCH THAN FEBRUARY, 1938

類 別 Group	總 計 Total		漲 Higher		落 Lower		平 Unchanged	
	項數 No.	百分率 %	項數 No.	百分率 %	項數 No.	百分率 %	項數 No.	百分率 %
總　指　數 General index	90	100	52	57.8	20	22.2	18	20.0
食　料　類 Food	32	100	11	34.4	14	43.7	7	21.9
衣　料　類 Clothing	17	100	15	88.2	1	5.9	1	5.9
燃　料　類 Fuel and light	10	100	6	60.0	2	20.0	2	20.0
金屬及電料類 Metals and electric supplies	10	100	6	60.0	1	10.0	3	30.0
建築材料類 Building materials	9	100	3	33.3	2	22.0	4	44.5
雜　項　類 Miscellaneous	12	100	11	91.7	0	0.0	1	8.3

第七表　民國二十七年三月份與二十六年同月各種物價升降之比較

TABLE 7.—COMPARISON OF THE PRICE INDEX IN MARCH 1938
WITH THAT OF THE CORRESPONDING MONTH OF 1937

類別 Group	指數 Index		較二十六年增 (十)或減(—) Increase (+) or decrease (—) as compared with March 1937
	二十七年三月 March 1937	去年同月 March 1938	
總　指　數 General index	124.0	96.7	(Points) + 27.3
食　料　類 Foodstuff	95.1	105.3	— 10.2
衣　料　類 Clothing	130.4	93.4	+ 37.0
燃　料　類 Fuel and light	133.6	93.5	+ 40.1
金屬及電料類 Metals & electric supplies	216.8	84.7	+132.1
建築材料類 Building Materials	141.4	92.9	+ 48.5
雜　項　類 Miscellaneous	118.9	97.6	+ 21.3

李　德　賢

文　先　俊

— 429 —